D1403520

Bridging the Pacific

Toward Free Trade and Investment between China and the United States

C. Fred Bergsten
Gary Clyde Hufbauer
Sean Miner
Assisted by Tyler Moran

PETERSON INSTITUTE FOR INTERNATIONAL ECONOMICS

WASHINGTON, DC
OCTOBER 2014

MIX
From responsible sources
FSC
www.fsc.org
FSC® C010236

C. Fred Bergsten, senior fellow and director emeritus, was the founding director of the Peterson Institute for International Economics from 1981 through 2012. He is a member of the President's Advisory Committee on Trade Policy and Negotiations and received the 2013 World Trade Award from the National Foreign Trade Council. He was assistant secretary of the Treasury for international affairs (1977–81) and assistant for international economic affairs to the National Security Council (1969–71). He has authored 41 previous books on a wide range of international economic policy issues, including *The Long-Term International Economic Position of the United States* (2009, designated a "must read" by the *Washington Post*), *China's Rise: Challenges and Opportunities* (2008), *China, The Balance Sheet: What the World Needs to Know Now About The Emerging Superpower* (2006), and *The United States and the World Economy: Foreign Economic Policy for the Next Decade* (2005).

Gary Clyde Hufbauer, Reginald Jones Senior Fellow at the Peterson Institute for International Economics since 1992, was the Maurice Greenberg Chair and Director of Studies at the Council on Foreign Relations (1996–98), the Marcus Wallenberg Professor of International Finance Diplomacy at Georgetown University (1985–92), senior fellow at the Institute (1981–85), deputy director of the International Law Institute at Georgetown University (1979–81), deputy assistant secretary for international trade and investment policy of the US Treasury (1977–79), and director of the international tax staff at the Treasury (1974–76). Among his numerous coauthored books are *Economic Normalization with Cuba: A Roadmap for US Policymakers* (2014), *Local Content Requirements: A Global Problem* (2013), *The United States Should Establish Permanent Normal Trade Relations with Russia* (2012), *Figuring Out the Doha Round* (2010), *Economic Sanctions Reconsidered*, 3rd edition (2007), and *US-China Trade Disputes: Rising Tide, Rising Stakes* (2006).

Sean Miner has been a research analyst at the Peterson Institute since June 2013. He spent nearly three years in Beijing, where he studied Chinese, worked at a small consulting firm in the energy industry, and studied for a semester at the China Studies Institute based in Peking University. While earning his MBA from George Washington University, he was a graduate intern at the US and Foreign Commercial Service, East Asia Pacific Office, where he supported the National Export Initiative and wrote extensively on Myanmar's economic and political situation. He also worked at the US Trade and Development Agency, East Asia Office, in support of US companies exporting to China. Before going to China he graduated from the University of Texas with a bachelor's degree in government. He speaks conversational Chinese and Spanish.

Tyler Moran has been a research analyst at the Peterson Institute since June 2013. He graduated with honors from the College of William and Mary in May 2013, where he majored in mathematics and economics. His prior research experience includes higher education issues in economics, as well as various topics in linear algebra.

PETERSON INSTITUTE FOR INTERNATIONAL ECONOMICS
1750 Massachusetts Avenue, NW
Washington, DC 20036-1903
(202) 328-9000   FAX: (202) 659-3225
www.piie.com

Adam S. Posen, *President*
Steven R. Weisman, *Vice President for Publications and Communications*

Graphics typeset by Kevin A. Wilson, Upper Case Textual Services, Lawrence, Massachusetts
Cover Design by Richard Fletcher Design
Printing by UBP

Printed in the United States of America
16   15   14   5   4   3   2   1

Library of Congress Cataloging-in-Publication Data
Bergsten, C. Fred, 1941– author.
 Bridging the Pacific : toward free trade and investment between China and the United States / C. Fred Bergsten, Gary Clyde Hufbauer and Sean Miner; assisted by Tyler Moran.
  pages cm
 ISBN 978-0-88132-691-8
 1. China—Foreign economic relations—United States. 2. United States—Foreign economic relations—China. I. Hufbauer, Gary Clyde, author. II. Miner, Sean, author. III. Title.
 HF1456.5.C6B47 2014
 337.51073—dc23

                                      2013050420

This publication has been subjected to a prepublication peer review intended to ensure analytical quality. The views expressed are those of the authors. This publication is part of the overall program of the Peterson Institute for International Economics, as endorsed by its Board of Directors, but it does not necessarily reflect the views of individual members of the Board or of the Institute's staff or management.

The Peterson Institute for International Economics is a private, nonprofit institution for the rigorous, intellectually open, and honest study and discussion of international economic policy. Its purpose is to identify and analyze important issues to making globalization beneficial and sustainable for the people of the United States and the world and then to develop and communicate practical new approaches for dealing with them. The Institute is completely nonpartisan. The Institute's work is funded by a highly diverse group of philanthropic foundations, private corporations, and interested individuals, as well as income on its capital fund. About 35 percent of Institute resources in our latest fiscal year were provided by contributors from outside the United States.

A list of all our financial supporters for the preceding year is posted at http://piie.com/supporters.cfm.

Contents

Preface

The United States and China are the two largest, and most important, economies in the world. Their economic performance and policies will go far to determine the prosperity and stability of the global economy. They are, respectively, the traditional leader of the international system and the emerging superpower. The relationship between them, and their ability to work together, will play a vital role in determining both the short-term and longer run prospects for the world economy.

The Peterson Institute for International Economics has therefore committed itself to analyzing the Chinese economy and its interactions with the United States (and the rest of the world), and to making proposals for constructive integration of China with the global economy. Nicholas Lardy, our Anthony M. Solomon Senior Fellow, has analyzed the evolution and rebalancing of the Chinese economy in a series of Institute studies from his *China in the World Economy* in 1994 to *Markets over Mao: The Rise of Private Business in China*, which we published in September 2014. Arvind Subramanian, our Dennis Weatherstone Senior Fellow, described the rise of China and its global implications in *Eclipse: Living in the Shadow of China's Economic Dominance* in 2011. Lardy and C. Fred Bergsten, the Institute's Director Emeritus, coauthored (with colleagues from CSIS) two volumes aimed at explaining the US–China relationship to a broader public, *China: The Balance Sheet*, in 2006 and 2008. Lardy and Senior Fellow Morris Goldstein focused on the dollar-renminbi exchange rate in several publications over the past decade. We have published eight policy briefs and working papers on China-related issues in the last two years, drawing on the next generation of experts on China's economy, created a dedicated blog "China Economic Watch" on the Institute's website, and now publish a regular metric of China Rebalancing.

Still, we needed to tackle China's behavior, current and potential, in the trade arena. Trade and investment issues have played a central role in the US–China economic relationship at all three levels of international interaction: global, regional and bilateral. We have carefully assessed the course of China's own trade policies and their impact on the United States, starting with *Managing the Costs of Protection in China* by three Chinese scholars in 1998 through *US-China Trade Disputes: Rising Tide, Rising Stakes* by our Reginald Jones Senior Fellow, Gary Clyde Hufbauer, with Yee Wong and Ketki Sheth in 2006. Ongoing Institute studies on the World Trade Organization, on the Asia-Pacific Economic Cooperation forum and especially recent work by Jeffrey J. Schott and colleagues on the Trans-Pacific Partnership, have paid close attention to the role and posture of China in determining trade flows and negotiation outcomes.

This new analysis by Bergsten, Hufbauer, and Sean Miner considers the potential gains from and feasible means toward, freer trade and investment between China and the United States. This study crucially and realistically considers how such deeper China–US economic integration could come about bilaterally or through their joint participation in regional agreements such as the Trans-Pacific Partnership or a Free Trade Area of the Asia Pacific—as well as the terms needed to assure such integration would be beneficial for the majority of people in both countries. To do so, this volume draws on the extensive record of Institute studies of potential free trade agreements (FTAs) and how to achieve them between the United States and other countries. The Institute has conducted more than a dozen such analyses over the years, some of which were seen as aspirational fantasies at the time, but which later became reality—notably the NAFTA and the Korea–United States FTA, which were heavily influenced by prior Institute proposals in practice. Whether or not an FTA between China and the United States will occur, we certainly believe that this new effort will contribute significantly and practically to improved economic relations between China and the United States—not least by showing how great the mutual benefits would be.

We are grateful to those beyond the lead authors who contributed to this book. Chapter 2, which presents a comprehensive analysis of the macroeconomic and sectoral effects of both a China-United States FTA and the several regional initiatives, was prepared by Peter A. Petri, Michael G. Plummer, and Fan Zhai. Chapter 3, which offers an in-depth perspective on the adjustment requirements for US workers under such an FTA, was written by our nonresident senior fellow Robert Z. Lawrence. Chapter 12, which addresses the US export control regime and its possible effects on China, was authored by Asha Sundaram, a professor at the University of Cape Town. Sherry Stephenson, a senior fellow at the International Centre for Trade and Sustainable Development, contributed to chapter 7 on service barriers.

The Peterson Institute for International Economics is a private, nonprofit institution for rigorous, intellectually open, and honest study and discussion of international economic policy. Its purpose is to identify and analyze important issues to making globalization beneficial and sustainable for the people of the United States and the world and then to develop and communicate practical new approaches for dealing with them. The Institute is completely nonpartisan.

The Institute's work is funded by a highly diverse group of philanthropic foundations, private corporations, and interested individuals, as well as income on its capital fund. About 35 percent of Institute resources in our latest fiscal year were provided by contributors from outside the United States. This study was made possible by the generous support of the China-US Exchange Foundation, the US Chamber of Commerce, and the C.V. Starr Foundation. Partial funding was also provided by Qualcomm, Inc. A list of financial supporters of the Institute for the preceding year is posted at http://piie.com/supporters.cfm.

The Executive Committee of the Institute's Board of Directors bears overall responsibility for the Institute's direction, gives general guidance and approval to its research program, and evaluates its performance in pursuit of its mission. The Institute's President is responsible for the identification of topics that are likely to become important over the medium term (one to three years) that should be addressed by Institute scholars. This rolling agenda is set in close consultation with the Institute's research staff, Board of Directors, and other stakeholders.

The President makes the final decision to publish any individual Institute study, following independent internal and external review of the work. Interested readers may access the data and computations underlying Institute publications for research and replication by searching titles at www.piie.com.

The Institute hopes that its research and other activities will contribute to building a stronger foundation for international economic policy around the world. We invite readers of these publications to let us know how they think we can best accomplish this objective.

ADAM S. POSEN
President
September 2014

I

THE CONTEXT

Toward Free Trade and Investment between China and the United States

Summary

China and the United States are the two largest economies in the world, and their sizable two-way trade and investment ties are growing rapidly. They increasingly seek to cooperate on a wide range of international economic, monetary, financial, trade, and environmental issues. They have created an extensive network of consultative arrangements, with over 60 working groups that meet annually on a wide array of topics. They provided joint leadership of the global recovery from the financial crisis of 2008–09.

But they collide on a large and growing number of topics as well, with each expressing concerns about policies of the other. They frequently take each other to the World Trade Organization (WTO) over trade disputes and occasionally retaliate against each other's barriers. Mistrust pervades their economic and security relationship. Their large external surpluses (China) and deficits (United States) constitute a big part of the global imbalances that the G-20 has repeatedly sought to correct to support stability in the world economy.

It is thus both natural and necessary to consider how to improve the future economic relationship between China and the United States. One way to do so is by negotiating a comprehensive China–US trade and investment agreement (CHUSTIA). Such an agreement would be historic, joining the world's two largest economies and a pair of geopolitical rivals with an overall relationship that is crucial for regional and global stability.

Economically, annual exports for each country under a CHUSTIA could increase by as much as $500 billion. US exports to China, which now fall far short of what normal economic relationships would suggest (Baily and Bosworth 2014), could almost double. National income could grow by about 2 percent in

China and 0.6 percent in the United States. The level of productivity could rise by almost 2 percent in China and almost 1 percent in the United States. These would be substantial economic spurs for both countries.

In contrast, China will lose as much as $100 billion of annual income and exports from a Trans-Pacific Partnership (TPP) in which it does not participate. It will also lose considerably from a preferential Transatlantic Trade and Investment Partnership (TTIP) between the United States and the European Union, its two major export markets. The United States will experience marginal losses from China's own less ambitious preferential trade agreements. A CHUSTIA would enable both countries, especially China, to recoup much of these losses.

A US–China agreement could also help each country achieve its internal rebalancing goals, China toward greater consumption and services and the United States toward larger investment and exports—two highly complementary and mutually reinforcing goals. A critical determinant of the feasibility of a CHUSTIA will be China's ability to accomplish its reform program and whether, like some previous Chinese governments, it sees trade liberalization as a helpful and even decisive support for that process. Taken together, a CHUSTIA and macroeconomic rebalancing could contribute significantly to reducing the global current account imbalances of the two economies and the bilateral imbalance between them. This would create a substantial number of new jobs in the United States. The United States should condition its participation on a Chinese commitment to achieve accelerated rebalancing.

The distributional effects would be mildly positive for US services and agriculture and for Chinese manufacturing, and mildly negative for US manufacturing. The gross and especially net employment effects would be very modest compared to ongoing changes in the giant US economy. About 50 million jobs turn over annually in the United States, of which about 20 million represent involuntary separations. Our estimates suggest that new jobs would be created in export industries that sell more to China—170,000 additional jobs annually, for a cumulative total of 1.7 million over a 10-year phase-in period.

The adverse adjustment effect from a CHUSTIA might range between 100,000 and 170,000 US workers involuntarily separated per year who could not quickly find reemployment, and this effect could last for a phase-in period of 10 years. While the absolute figure is large, it is between 0.5 and 1.0 percent of annual involuntary separations and the cumulative 10-year total of 1.0 to 1.7 million represents at most a little over 1 percent of the total US labor force of 155 million. In many cases, the adjustment would simply reduce, by a small amount, the growth of output and employment in affected sectors. The total estimated permanent US income gains are at least $1.25 million for each involuntary job separation that results from larger US imports from China on account of freer trade under a CHUSTIA.

Nevertheless, the adjustment burdens counsel extended phase-in periods for some aspects of liberalization. Additional support measures from the US government may be needed, particularly for US manufacturing industries that face increased competition from Chinese imports. The United States should adopt a stronger trade adjustment assistance program, or a consolidation of worker training programs as President Obama has proposed, in conjunction with a CHUSTIA or earlier if politically possible.

Beyond the economic gains for both countries, a CHUSTIA should reduce the risk of economic conflict between the countries, limit the discrimination against each other inherent in their current and pending preferential trade deals, and strengthen their overall relationship by reducing the mistrust that now pervades it. A CHUSTIA could provide a major public good for the world by fostering deeper ties between its two largest economies and thus limiting the risk of spillovers from disputes between them.

This book is not arguing for any single path toward greater economic integration. China and the United States could achieve freer trade through either a conventional bilateral agreement or Chinese accession, along with other Asian countries, to the TPP. The TPP could be fused with the Regional Comprehensive Economic Partnership (RCEP) in Asia, if it were concluded in the near future. As chair of the Asia Pacific Economic Cooperation (APEC) forum in 2014, China has proposed a feasibility study of a comprehensive Free Trade Area of the Asia Pacific (FTAAP), which could either subsume TPP and RCEP or stand alongside one or both of them. In any of these cases, China–US side agreements would probably be necessary to address bilateral issues outside the regional framework, such as macroeconomic rebalancing. Similar side agreements were reached when Japan recently joined the TPP talks.

Between themselves, the two countries could approach free trade through either a single comprehensive agreement on all key topics or a step-by-step series of compacts on individual issues, starting with the current bilateral investment treaty (BIT) talks. The latter approach could include, and agree to count, several plurilateral negotiations that are already under way—some with, some without China—and in which China–US agreement will be pivotal for overall success: the Trade in Services Agreement (TiSA), the agreement to eliminate tariffs on the Environmental Goods Agreement (EGA), the second International Technology Agreement (ITA2), and Chinese accession to the Government Procurement Agreement (GPA) in the World Trade Organization (WTO). Stand-alone agreements beyond investment might also be reached on tariffs, agriculture, and government procurement. These could provide building blocks for an eventual comprehensive agreement.

The major US request should be for China to liberalize its rapidly growing services sector, since this could foster a large expansion of US exports and employment opportunities. Services liberalization also would promote major Chinese rebalancing objectives and rapid development of the country's domestic services industry as well so the subject might be another candidate for a self-balancing stand-alone agreement, either bilaterally or through the TiSA talks.

Other priority issues for negotiations would include intellectual property rights (IPR) protection and the investment cluster, comprising state-owned enterprises (SOEs) and competition policy as well as foreign direct investment

(FDI) beyond the BIT, as well as a dispute settlement mechanism to ensure effective implementation of the CHUSTIA. As an FTA partner, China could obtain preferred access to US supplies of natural gas. Broader export control issues, beyond agriculture and energy and especially including high-technology products, are also of high priority to China and must be addressed.

At least two essential issues—cyberespionage and currency—could best be handled through parallel, perhaps multilateral, negotiations rather than a bilateral or regional trade agreement. It would be desirable to address labor and the environment, especially climate change, in a similar manner. Failing such alternatives, all of these would have to be included in a CHUSTIA in light of their high priority in the United States.

Based on the analysis in this study, we recommend that China and the United States pursue the broadest and deepest possible reduction of barriers between their economies through the earliest possible accession of China—along with several other Asian countries—to the TPP. They should seek to negotiate a bilateral CHUSTIA if the regional approach cannot be worked out in a reasonable period of time.

China and the United States are unlikely to embark on a CHUSTIA-like agenda in the near future in light of their current trade negotiations with other countries and the acute sensitivity of many of the issues involved. They should begin paving the way, however, through quiet consultations, perhaps sectoral agreements through ongoing plurilateral negotiations, and new initiatives to clear the decks of big parallel issues. These preliminary steps should help the two countries launch a trade initiative at the earliest possible date.

The Negotiating Background

In 1993–94, China and the United States articulated a vision to achieve free trade and investment between them. They did so when they joined the rest of the APEC forum at its initial summit held in Seattle in 1993, in declaring their objective of "free and open trade and investment in the Asia Pacific region." The following year, APEC leaders gathered in Bogor, Indonesia, and announced the Bogor Goals, an ambitious mandate to achieve free trade and investment for APEC's industrialized nations by 2010, and for developing economies by 2020. Since China was then and remains today a developing country, the year 2020 should be regarded as its relevant target for freeing trade. APEC, with its goal of supporting sustainable economic growth and prosperity throughout the Asia Pacific region, has committed to these Bogor Goals at every one of its annual summits over the past two decades.

Over the past 20 years, there has been considerable progress in reaching this goal. China adopted a number of unilateral trade liberalization programs through the late 1990s and early 2000s, often announcing them with much fanfare at APEC summits. The signal development was China's entry into the WTO, which occurred in 2001 after 15 years of negotiation, and the simultaneous US acceptance of permanent normal trade relations (PNTR) with China.

China slashed many of its tariffs and adopted wide-ranging commitments for additional liberalization as a result.

During this same period, however, China and the United States entered into preferential trade agreements with a number of other countries—14 for China, 20 for the United States—and hence the two countries increasingly discriminated against each other while they continued reducing their trade barriers selectively. Most of the US FTAs were with smaller countries, and China's agreements were relatively shallow in their coverage, so the adverse trade diversion effects on the other superpower were modest. The main, though still mild, exceptions were the US agreements with Canada and Mexico to form the North American Free Trade Agreement (NAFTA) in 1994 and its agreements with Australia in 2007 and Korea in 2012.

The potential for negative developments in China–US trade ties rose dramatically when both decided to launch new preferential megaregional agreements in recent years. The United States reengaged in talks for the TPP, which now includes a dozen APEC members following the addition of Japan in 2013. Successful TPP implementation would cost China about $35 billion to $45 billion in annual income and exports by 2025, given the current group of 12 participants (see chapter 2). Chinese costs could grow to $110 billion per year with plausible early additions to TPP membership, including Korea and Indonesia. The TTIP between the United States and the European Union—China's two largest export markets—adds a further threat of major trade diversion.

For its part, China is actively negotiating its two most important bilateral agreements to date, with Korea and Australia, and has begun talks for a trilateral Northeast Asia compact with Korea and Japan. China is also participating in negotiations with the Association of Southeast Asian Nations (ASEAN) plus six—Australia, India, Japan, Korea, and New Zealand, as well as China—for the RCEP, which would amount to an East Asia Free Trade Area. Any such arrangement is likely to encompass liberalization that is much shallower and less rules-based than the TPP, and will probably take considerably longer to complete. But China's Asia track is clearly counterpoised to the US-led Pacific track, presaging a potentially divisive economic profile for the broader region and for China and the United States in particular (Petri, Plummer, and Zhai 2012). In April 2014 President Xi Jinping also proposed that China and the European Union "actively explore the possibility of a free trade area" and the EU cautiously indicated its "willingness to envisage" such an agreement "once the conditions are right."[1]

At least partly in response to this situation, China and the United States have recently begun a subtle but potentially historic process of pursuing free, or at least freer, trade and investment with each other. They energized talks to

---

1. Shawn Donnan and Andrew Byrne, "China Courts EU on Bilateral Trade Agreement," *Financial Times*, April 1, 2014.

conclude a BIT in June 2013 at a summit between Obama and Xi; these negotiations completed an 11th round in January 2014. China petitioned to join the plurilateral TiSA, championed by the United States, in late 2013 and participated in a new initiative in early 2014 to reduce tariffs on trade in EGA. Both countries were already involved in efforts to strengthen the GPA and the ITA2, though China's recalcitrance had stalled progress on both as of this writing (mid-2014) and is sending mixed signals on whether Beijing really wants to pursue international economic liberalization in support of its domestic development objectives.

China and the United States are nevertheless already engaged in significant efforts to liberalize trade and investment between them and with other countries on a series of issues that would likely form a major share of any arrangement that they might pursue: investment, trade in services, government procurement, and tariffs on information technology and the Environmental Goods Agreement. In 2013 China began to show considerable interest in associating with the TPP after previously dismissing the pact as a US geopolitical plot designed to "encircle China" (Li 2013). China apparently recognized that it would suffer the major trade diversion noted above and perhaps the disruption of its supply chains if it stayed outside, especially with Japan's entry to the agreement. Chinese authorities also wondered why they could not meet the "21st century standards" of the pact if active participant Vietnam could do so. At APEC meetings in early 2014, China also proposed a feasibility study of moving directly to an FTAAP. China and the United States should build on these evolving developments to seek free trade and investment between them, whether through a bilateral CHUSTIA or China's accession to the TPP. Such an agreement would be the most significant economic compact ever negotiated.

Domestic developments in both countries will be decisive to the feasibility of such a far-reaching idea. In China, the Xi government is actively implementing a wide-ranging program of economic reform that would seem to support, and perhaps benefit from, a new burst of trade and especially investment liberalization. China adopted such a strategy in the late 1990s to reinforce and spur the reforms that President Jiang Zemin and Premier Zhu Rongji were sponsoring at the time, and a number of other countries, most recently Japan under Prime Minister Shinzo Abe, have done so as well. There is potent resistance to some of those reforms, and hence to reductions of trade barriers, by key actors, including some SOEs. And as just noted, there are mixed signals in China's policies governing the variety of trade initiatives now being conducted around the region and the world.

The US situation is complex and somewhat contradictory as well. On the one hand, the Obama administration is pursuing the most aggressive US trade negotiating agenda in at least a generation with the TPP, TTIP, TiSA, and others cited above. The administration views all these steps as important contributions to restoring, and subsequently sustaining, economic growth and job creation in the United States. On the other hand, domestic support for these initiatives is shaky. In early 2014 Congress rejected the administration's request to consider granting new trade promotion authority that would provide a legislative framework for ongoing negotiations. Polls suggest that the public no longer favors trade liberalization, or perhaps even globalization more broadly, and has particular doubts about new trade agreements. NAFTA is still widely viewed as a job-costing mistake that colors attitudes about future deals.[2] The United States is not about to turn protectionist; the absence of broad protectionist reactions was a notable dog that did not bark during the recent Great Recession. But the appetite of the US public and political process for new trade-liberalizing compacts, especially with China, is highly uncertain.

International political and security concerns will also have a major bearing on the prospects for any new China–US economic accord. China's rapid ascension to power challenges US hegemony in Asia and potentially more broadly. The two countries are not adversaries, but they are not allies either, as partner countries in most previous FTAs have been. A CHUSTIA might help allay the bilateral tensions between the two countries, including on issues that range well beyond economics, but China and the United States would have to overcome their suspicions and mistrust sufficiently to launch such an enterprise in the first place, and then carry it through the lengthy and contentious process that is characteristic of any major trade negotiation.

Though we use the term *free trade area* throughout this study, we fully recognize that a move to completely free trade between China and the United States is unrealistic. Very few if any of the world's current free trade areas approximate anything like truly free trade. Thus we will frequently refer to the more accurate concepts of freer trade and investment, or liberalization of current barriers. The broader terms *free trade area* and *free trade agreement* are so common in the discourse on these topics that we nevertheless use them ourselves—though clearly the prospects of negotiations we are investigating, as ambitious as they are, would not in reality go quite that far.

China and the United States are the world's two largest economies and together account for about one-third of world output. They are the two largest trading nations and the two largest recipients of FDI. China is the world's largest exporter and largest or second-largest (to Germany) surplus country. The United States is the world's largest importer and deficit country. A trade agreement between them would be a very big deal for the world economy, with profound effects on both countries. It would open new export opportunities that would accelerate each country's economic growth. It would create new sources of import competition that would strengthen the productivity and competitiveness of each. Like any dynamic economic change, it would require internal adjustment among companies and especially workers. It would reinforce the rebalancing that both the US and Chinese economies need and have been pursuing. However, it would likely require substantial policy changes in

---

2. For an effective refutation of those criticisms, see Hufbauer, Cimino, and Moran (2014).

both China and the United States, especially coming on top of the other major trade compacts that both China and the United States have been negotiating.

Globalization has contributed, to some degree, to less equal income distribution in the United States, China, and virtually all other countries. There are heated disputes over the extent to which globalization is responsible for greater inequality in the United States, but no doubt about its sign. Major new trade agreements, especially with China, could extend that pattern. Hence additional policy steps will be needed to cope with the distributional implications of any agreement.

But the effect on overall relations between the two countries could be profound. There has never been a comprehensive trade agreement between countries with such different economic systems—one fully marketized and the other still far short of completing its transition from command economy to marketization. There has never been such an agreement between a full-blown democracy and an authoritarian state, or between rivals for global geopolitical leadership, especially an incumbent hegemon and a rising power that has not yet become fully engaged in the global leadership process. Negotiating and then implementing such an agreement would lead to a significant and historic strengthening of ties between China and the United States, despite the bumps in the road that will occur along the way.

The Case for a CHUSTIA

There are six reasons to consider engaging in such a historic venture even though it is a very challenging proposition and is unlikely to eventuate in the near future.

First are the substantial economic gains both countries could reap (see above). The sharp increases in exports would enable both countries to do more of what they do best, expanding their scale of production and jobs in sectors where they have demonstrable comparative advantages. As these sectors pay substantially higher wages than the national average, though income inequality might increase, the composition of employment would shift in desirable directions. Both countries would also see more attractive imports. Consumers would gain from a cheaper and more diversified array of goods and services. Producers could obtain lower-cost inputs for their final products, strengthening supply chains. These cost reductions, plus the enhanced competition from increased trade, would stimulate productivity gains that would strengthen both economies. The level of productivity in the United States would increase permanently by almost 1 percent, a major improvement.

Investment is also important. Sales by US firms in China were estimated at $450 billion in 2013 (US Chamber of Commerce 2013), only about one-third of which derive from exports from the United States. The stock of Chinese direct investment in the United States is also abnormally low and China places very high priority on expanding it. Including investment in a CHUSTIA would be of cardinal importance to both countries, and the current BIT negotiation will be a precursor of what might become possible more broadly.

The second reason to engage in a historic CHUSTIA venture is that the trade and investment liberalization achieved under the agreement would promote and enhance economic reform in both countries. This would add substantially to its direct payoff, as described above, and reinforce some of the top policy priorities of each country's leadership, notably the rebalancing of their economies: China in the direction of more consumption and services, the United States toward more investment and exports. It would follow the pattern of many countries that have pursued trade liberalization to promote reform, including Mexico through NAFTA, Korea through its US FTA, China through its entry to the WTO, and Japan prospectively through its participation in the TPP. This internal rebalancing would contribute to the international rebalancing of the two countries, promoting further reductions of the large Chinese global surplus and the large US global deficit, which take place largely with each other. The microeconomic effects of a CHUSTIA would thus reinforce the macroeconomic dimensions of the rebalancing process, including changes in exchange rates, which have been under way for some time but remain far from complete and must continue.

The third reason is that a CHUSTIA should reduce the risk of conflict between the economic superpowers. The sheer size and rapid growth of China–US trade and investment, along with their two very different economic and political systems, virtually guarantee that there will be frequent disputes between them, as there are now and have been for the past two decades. The current case-by-case method of addressing these problems is not working well, and overall economic relations seem to be deteriorating.[3] China seems unwilling or unable to meet US demands concerning commercial cyberespionage, IPR, SOEs, and exchange rates. The United States resists Chinese entreaties on US policies toward Chinese direct investment in the United States and US export controls. CHUSTIA negotiations could help resolve these contentious issues by providing a coherent and hopefully comprehensive framework within which to address specific problems, and by setting up a dispute settlement mechanism to handle most future disagreements. There now exist numerous consultative mechanisms between the two countries, such as the Strategic and Economic Dialogue and the Joint Commission on Commerce and Trade, but they operate without any agreed substantive context and possess no enforcement mechanisms.

---

3. Jeremie Waterman from the US Chamber of Commerce, speaking for the US business community, cited several areas of "noteworthy deterioration" in 2013: "antitrust policy implementation, access for express delivery service providers, further restrictions on China's largely closed telecommunication services market and even more stringent restrictions on foreign networks seeking to provide electronic payment services as well as anti-corruption targeted disproportionately on foreign companies." See Jeremie Waterman, Hearing on China's Implementation of and Compliance with Its Commitments to the WTO, statement before the Office of the US Trade Representative, November 8, 2013.

The WTO offers a useful framework of agreed principles and procedures, and both countries have used its dispute settlement mechanism to defuse tensions over some issues. But the WTO rules do not address a large and growing number of the topics of disagreement between China and the United States. A CHUSTIA could provide a supplementary and more promising approach by covering these issues and embedding them in a broader policy context, especially if initiated and consistently nurtured by the top political leadership of each country. There would still be contentious disagreements at all stages of the process, but the record of trade agreements is that they strengthen relations between the participants—sometimes dramatically.

Fourth, a new and improved framework for economic relations between the two countries could provide a bulwark against the very real possibility that security relations will remain conflicted or become even more so in the future. Economic cooperation fosters greatly expanded person-to-person contacts, ranging from corporate investors to tourists. Launching trade negotiations would be a major political act by the two leaderships, forcing each country to view the other as a partner as well as a rival, and to characterize each other in that way publicly, which could have a salutary effect on the overall relationship.

Fifth, a free trade agreement between China and the United States could anchor a healthy new economic architecture in East Asia and the Pacific by providing a practical method for achieving convergence between the two current tracks of economic integration in the region. The Asia-only track is already under way, as noted above, with the China–ASEAN agreement and a number of other bilateral FTAs. It may become generalized in RCEP negotiations. The Pacific track also includes several bilateral FTAs, notably the Korea-US FTA, and would be greatly expanded under a successful TPP.

The main risk of the two-track process, in economic and security terms, is that the two tracks could diverge and become competing blocs. Even though there is likely to be considerable overlap in the membership of the two tracks, their substantive templates will be quite different, with the TPP including more exacting disciplines and rigorous implementation. The APEC goal of forging new institutional linkages across the Pacific, for security even more than economic reasons, could be threatened and even shattered. Another risk from a permanent Asia-Pacific fissure would be the creation of a three-bloc world: the TPP, the RCEP, and the European Union. Such tripartite systems are dynamically unstable because each participant constantly jockeys for the support of one of the others against the third (Krugman 1993). APEC sought to overcome this problem by creating a cohesive Asia-Pacific construct as a single counterweight to the European Union.

It would be highly desirable for the two Asia-Pacific tracks to converge, to reap major economic benefits for all participants and avoid significant new difficulties. Negotiation of an FTAAP, which would essentially mesh the TPP and RCEP, represents one route to convergence. Chapter 2 of our study, however, shows that the economic payoff from adding a CHUSTIA to TPP and

RCEP, for the world economy as a whole and for China and the United States themselves, would be virtually as great as from concluding a comprehensive FTAAP. Moreover, an FTAAP might prove more difficult to negotiate, as it would require more than 25 countries involved in the constituent agreements to adopt another new set of rules and institutional arrangements, largely to satisfy China and the United States, after they had just spent considerable effort working out the RCEP and TPP and winning support for them in their national political processes. It might also prove difficult to fuse the more rigorous standards of the TPP and the presumably looser arrangements of the RCEP.

Another route to convergence between the two current tracks would be for more members of one to join the other. Japan, Malaysia, Singapore, Vietnam, Brunei, Australia, New Zealand, and prospectively Korea are involved in the negotiations for both the TPP and RCEP. As noted, China has begun to show an interest in joining the TPP and other Asian countries would surely follow China, if they do not join on their own anyway. Chinese membership in the TPP would be a plausible alternative to a CHUSTIA for China to achieve free trade and investment with the United States.

Finally, by resolving many of the trade frictions between China and the United States and providing mechanisms for addressing future disputes between them, a CHUSTIA would add to confidence around the world in the prospective stability of the global economy. Conflict between China and the United States is probably the greatest potential threat to the sustainability of international trade, investment, and even monetary arrangements. Henry Kissinger (2013) put it succinctly: "The key to an emerging world order is the relationship between China and the United States. China and the United States cannot solve the problems by themselves but the problems cannot be solved without cooperation between China and the United States ... so that cooperation is the great opportunity of our age." A CHUSTIA would be by far the most decisive and credible way to pursue such cooperation and reduce risks. It would represent a global public good of great significance.

The Hurdles

A number of significant hurdles would have to be overcome before China and the United States could seriously contemplate a CHUSTIA. Seven stand out.

First, both countries would face adjustment challenges under an agreement that achieved anything approaching free trade. Our analyses in chapters 2 and 3 show that, in light of the expected economic growth of the two economies, output would continue to expand in virtually all sectors. In the United States, however, baseline employment in manufacturing will continue to decline—albeit at a much slower pace than over the past decade—and a CHUSTIA would modestly accelerate that decline. Based on past experience (Autor, Dorn, and Hanson 2013), wage rates for US workers employed in industries that face competition from China might fall marginally.

As mentioned above, about 20 million Americans are involuntarily separated from their jobs in a typical year, and as many as 170,000 workers would have to change jobs per year as a result of a CHUSTIA during its implementation period, depending on how much liberalization the agreement encompasses. While 170,000 is a large number, some of these changes would be voluntary, and not more than 1 in 100 involuntary employment changes in the United States would result from CHUSTIA implementation. As chapter 3 shows, about one-third of the adjustments could occur through voluntary separation without requiring layoffs. For China, modest dislocations would occur in agriculture and a few services sectors, although China's continued rapid growth, especially in services as that sector sharply increases its share of the total economy, means that total production and employment will continue to rise in virtually all sectors.

There will nevertheless be concerns about adjustment burdens because of the absolute numbers of workers involved. The two governments can address these in the CHUSTIA negotiations by adopting extended phase-in periods for liberalization of particularly sensitive items and industries. A CHUSTIA will also require new domestic policy measures in the United States to improve the overall competitiveness of the US economy and especially to respond to the needs of trade-affected workers. The United States will need to strengthen trade adjustment assistance or put in place a comprehensive new program of worker training, as President Obama has proposed (see chapter 3). Overall US income gains from a CHUSTIA are estimated to total $1.25 million for each job shifted; hence, programs focused on strengthening US competitiveness and particularly helping laid-off workers could be readily financed by drawing on the large aggregate national income gains from the agreement itself.

However, perceptions are at least as important as reality in the politics of trade policy. Widespread views that NAFTA hurt employment in the United States have poisoned its trade politics ever since, most clearly in the cliffhanger vote on the Central American Free Trade Agreement (CAFTA) a decade later and even with respect to the later FTAs with Peru, Colombia, and Panama. Perceptions of the effects of the TPP, especially on jobs and adjustment requirements, will affect US thinking about a CHUSTIA, since the TPP will almost certainly be concluded before any bilateral or regional approach with China.

Second, the economic relationship between the two countries is very unbalanced. The United States is the world's largest deficit and debtor country, and by far the greatest portion of its imbalance is with China. China has been the world's largest or second-largest surplus country in recent years and most of this is with the United States. Its foreign exchange reserves at $4 trillion are almost four times as large as those of any other nation. The two countries have repeatedly pledged to rebalance their economies, both internally and externally, and their current account imbalances and currency misalignments have come down substantially: China's from 10 percent of its GDP in 2007–08 to less than 3 percent in 2012–13, and the United States' from more than 6 percent at its peak in 2009 to under 3 percent currently. However, the imbalances are still quite large and appear to be increasing again. In 2013 China's trade surplus rose to its highest level since 2008, its reserves rose by a record amount of over $500 billion, and its intervention in the currency markets soared once again, continuing to do so in the early part of 2014, when intervention propelled a renewed renminbi weakening that reversed, at least for a time, the steady appreciation since 2010. The International Monetary Fund (IMF) projects that, at current exchange rates, the Chinese and US current account imbalances will increase substantially in the medium term and that China's surplus will nearly double in size as a share of global GDP in five years. The politically salient bilateral imbalance, even when calculated in value-added terms rather than gross exports and imports,[4] has continued to climb steadily and still exceeds $200 billion annually.

The imbalances, and the currency and other policy distortions that underlie them, add to US reluctance to liberalize trade with China. The imbalances thus will prompt calls for a CHUSTIA to address them directly. Bipartisan congressional majorities in both the Senate and House of Representatives are insisting that "the TPP and all future US trade agreements include strong and enforceable foreign currency manipulation disciplines" to counter the practices that helped produce the US current account deficit and prevent future prolonged misalignments. Recent developments in Japan have generated much of that concern. But Congress would almost certainly insist that a CHUSTIA include an effective currency chapter unless international monetary arrangements can be reformed sufficiently in the near future to deal much more decisively with imbalances. The exchange rate is only part of the overall rebalancing process, albeit an integral part, so the United States should insist that any CHUSTIA or a separate side agreement commit China to substantial further imbalance adjustments and specify metrics against which to judge progress.

We noted above that the internal rebalancing of the two economies that a CHUSTIA would promote would accelerate the needed external rebalancing. Continued renminbi appreciation at its pace of 2010–13, or preferably 2005–08, would be encouraged by the structural changes stemming from a CHUSTIA and would eliminate most or all of China's global surplus over the next few years (Hufbauer and DeRosa 2013), although its sizable bilateral surplus with the United States would almost surely persist. The macroeconomic (rebalancing) and microeconomic (trade policy) dimensions of the relationship could and should proceed in tandem over the coming years.

Third, China and the United States have very different income levels. Parts of China, especially in the major metropolitan centers on its eastern coast, enjoy standards of living that reach middle-income levels. Per capita income in the country as a whole, however, is only about one-eighth that of the United

---

4. The Organization for Economic Cooperation and Development (OECD) has estimated that China's surplus with the United States would be 25 percent lower if measured in value-added terms.

States and only nearing one-fifth on purchasing power parity (PPP) terms. It will still be only one-quarter as large whenever China's total GDP comes to exceed that of the United States. The maximum previous gap in a major trade agreement was the roughly 5:1 ratio between the United States and Mexico before NAFTA, which sparked considerable resistance to the agreement in both countries.

The income disparity is a major reason why the aggregate benefits of the agreement would be so large, reflecting the countries' complementarity in economic structure and production costs. The disparity also underlines the sectoral restructuring that would be required, however, and thus the opposition in some sectors to the whole idea.

China sometimes argues that the disparity in levels of development justifies its rejection of the 21st century standards on which the United States insists in all its trade negotiations. The United States acknowledges that China would have difficulty adopting and implementing some of these standards at this stage of its development. However, the United States argues that China should continually strive to do so and that adhering to a high-standards agreement would accelerate China's development and promote many of the reforms espoused by its leadership. Vietnam's likely ability to accept TPP standards would suggest that China could do so as well. Many of the standards that China faced in joining the WTO 15 years ago were viewed as quite high at the time; China accepted them, some with substantial transition periods, to strengthen its own economy—though its difficulty in fully implementing some of them, regarding IPR protection and SOEs, raises a cautionary note concerning future agreements. China's current negotiations for FTAs with Australia and Korea, both of which already have high-standard FTAs with the United States, already pull China in this direction. Still, central issues for any China–US trade negotiation would be China's willingness, in pursuing its own national interests, to accept the standards the United States has endorsed, and US willingness, in the interest of reaching agreement with China, to moderate some of its requests.

The fourth hurdle is that China and the United States continue to operate very different economic systems. Prices clearly play a less pervasive role in the Chinese economy than in the United States. There is convergence toward a market system (Lardy 2014), but the absence of reliable price signals can distort economic analysis, such as our own, as well as the economy itself. State capitalism remains a major feature of the Chinese economy and observers fear that trends may be reverting back toward it. Some of the thorniest problems that a CHUSTIA would have to address—support for SOEs, failure to protect IPR, ongoing exchange rate manipulation, and cyberespionage against foreign firms—derive from central features of the Chinese economy. A CHUSTIA could help accelerate marketization in China and spur needed policy reforms in the United States. A key dynamic will be whether the economic reforms of the Xi Jinping government embrace external liberalization with that purpose in mind and whether the US government will recognize and pursue the essential complementary policies at home, such as infrastructure renovation.

Related to economic differences, the different political systems of the two countries constitute a fifth hurdle. This affects direct interactions between the governments in both negotiating and implementing any such agreement, as "authoritarian systems are intrinsically less transparent" (Lieberthal and Wang 2012, ix). Many top Chinese officials also apparently see the world in zero-sum terms (Lieberthal and Wang 2012, 29 and 31) while most Americans view international cooperation as a positive-sum game. In modern times, there has never been an FTA on anything like the scale of a possible China–US agreement between an authoritarian regime and a democracy.[5] The political differences between them could greatly complicate efforts to negotiate a mutually beneficial agreement.

A sixth difficulty is that a CHUSTIA would bring together, also for the first time to anything like this degree, major geopolitical rivals. One has to go back to the 19th century to find a rough parallel: The Cobden-Chevalier Treaty significantly reduced tariffs between the United Kingdom and France in 1860 when war between them was a real possibility. Germany and the United Kingdom were major trading partners in the run-up to World War I but never had a trade agreement.

The current situation is even more complicated because it brings together an incumbent global hegemon and a rising, credible candidate for world leadership that has already become an economic superpower. We know from history that integrating new powers into global leadership structures—whether political, economic, or related to security—is one of the most difficult and important challenges to international governance (Gilpin 1981). The failure to incorporate Wilhelmine Germany and to some extent the protectionist United States into the late 19th century global system contributed to the breakdown of the first era of globalization and subsequent massive conflict. Similar failures after World War I gave rise to Nazi Germany and Imperial Japan. The postwar experience with the European Union and democratic Japan, in which trade and economic agreements played an important part, has clearly been far better.

China and the United States negotiating an FTA in light of historical precedents would be a novel approach. As the incumbent power, the United States has written most of the current rules of the game. As an ascending power, China often feels aggrieved by being asked to play by those rules when it has no authorship of and perhaps not even much familiarity with them. A CHUSTIA would accurately reflect the centrality of economics in both the China–US relationship and today's globalized world, and offer a unique opportunity for the two economic superpowers to write new rules together, forging agreement where none existed previously, such as cybersecurity and climate change.

---

5. The United States has negotiated FTAs with "soft" authoritarian regimes, such as Morocco, Singapore, and arguably Mexico, when NAFTA was signed.

The final and most powerful hurdle, however, may be the pervasive lack of trust between the two countries (Lieberthal and Wang 2012). Many Chinese, including important elites and leadership groups, continue to believe that the United States seeks to limit their national rise and to surround them with its alliances. Many Americans believe that China is purposefully pursuing global domination at US expense or at least wants to eliminate the United States as a power in Asia. Both perceptions are all the more powerful by virtue of having some basis in reality.

The distrust permeates the economic relationship as well. Many Chinese see US unwillingness to sell them high-technology products, or to permit them to invest in sensitive US industries, as evidence of a strategy of containment reminiscent of the Cold War. Many Americans see China's support of SOEs and continued rejection of key market-oriented reforms as indicators of a mercantilist mindset more preoccupied with national military and economic strength than the welfare of the population. The problem extends to each party's doubts about the other party's sincerity in faithfully implementing commitments. China doubts that the United States will really liberalize its export controls or investment policies despite repeated US declarations of an intent to do so. Americans often charge that China has not fulfilled obligations that it accepted over a decade ago when joining the WTO and are skeptical that its repeated declarations to rebalance its economy, and stop relying on trade surpluses and an undervalued currency, will ever be realized. Some Americans believe that China cynically tries to get the best of both worlds, taking full advantage of the openness of the global economy to spur its growth and development but cheating on the rules of that system when it can get away with doing so, as on currency and IPR protection.

The mistrust between China and the United States has taken a sharp leap upward in both countries. In 2012, Kenneth Lieberthal and Wang Jisi had already concluded that "strategic distrust will inevitably impose very high costs on all concerned if it continues to grow at its current rapid pace" and that "it is possible that growth in strategic distrust cannot be avoided" (Lieberthal and Wang 2012, 39). Even more recently, the increasing prevalence of cyber-attacks from China, especially for commercial spying, has elicited a wave of US hostility against espionage in an area widely regarded as beyond acceptable boundaries. Revelations of global snooping by the US National Security Agency (NSA) have added to the sense in China and around the world of unbridled US interventionism, power, and hypocrisy.

As a concept, mistrust is as elusive to analyze as it is pernicious to a relationship and difficult to overcome. But it "can produce, over time, a self-fulfilling prophecy of antagonistic relations that are basically zero sum on all sides" (Lieberthal and Wang 2012, 39). The clear presence of bilateral mistrust suggests a need for confidence-building measures wherever possible, as in the relatively modest steps that the two countries are now undertaking in BIT and green goods negotiations. They must keep this underlying reality in mind when deciding whether and, if so, how to pursue the ambitious designs this study addresses.

In addition to the above hurdles to a CHUSTIA, there are important intellectual hurdles to the type of analysis in this book. Most of the underlying data are relatively solid, although there are questions about both the accuracy and objectivity of some of the Chinese numbers. Our economic models, however, while state-of-the art in a technical sense, necessarily rest on assumptions that do not always reflect the real world. The standard model used to estimate trade, growth, and job effects assumes for methodological reasons that trade agreements are long-term propositions that produce no net changes in trade balances or national employment levels. We respect those constraints but temper them with obvious realities that can change the results, such as the possibility that a CHUSTIA would be accompanied by rebalancing measures to reduce US trade deficits and Chinese trade surpluses (see chapters 2 and 17).

The results derived from economic models are only as good as the numbers plugged into them. In our case, it is very difficult to quantify the degree of restrictiveness of many nontariff barriers, especially for services trade, an important component of China–US trade. Hence we candidly characterize some of our results as rough guesses to alert readers to the high degree of imprecision in those findings. Chapter 2 reports sensitivity tests of several analyses, concluding that they could be as much as one-third off in either direction. There are many things we do not know about the underlying economies, including some of the factors that limit trade and especially investment, that may affect the variables we address. There are, in sum, significant shortcomings in our—and everybody else's—analyses of these issues, and they should not be interpreted as precise point estimates of likely outcomes. However, we believe that both the directions and orders of magnitude that we derive throughout this study are correct. They are consistent with both economic theory and intuition, and most are supported by previous analyses of the relevant data.

Another methodological issue bears mentioning. We have attempted to present the CHUSTIA issue in a balanced manner, taking full account of both the Chinese and US perspectives in addressing it. To that end, we have consulted actively with a large number of Chinese officials and experts on the numerous topics involved. However, we understand US viewpoints much more thoroughly and our presentations undoubtedly reflect that bias. We hope that this study will induce some of our Chinese counterparts to prepare parallel analyses, correcting where we may err in depicting Chinese points of view and otherwise lending their sense of equilibrium to the discussion.

The Economic Context

The contest between considerations for and against a CHUSTIA will play out against a very rich and robust, if also contentious and often tendentious, economic situation. China and the United States are the two largest economies in the world and are likely to remain in those positions for the indefinite future. Excluding the European Union as a group, they are the largest global traders. Trade between China and the United States already totals over $600 billion per year and reasonable projections suggest that, largely because of continued rapid growth in China, it will almost triple over the coming decade even without any new liberalization agreements. What China and the United States do together, or in conflict with each other, thus will have substantial worldwide ramifications. They already decisively determine the outcomes of most global trade and other economic negotiations, as well as the fate of international economic institutions; it is difficult to imagine the effective resolution of any global economic issue without US and Chinese concurrence.[6]

But the world economy affects China and the United States at least as much as they affect the world economy. China is one of the most open economies in the world, in terms of the share of trade in a country's GDP. It courageously embraced globalization as a central element of its development strategy, reducing its tariffs and other trade barriers well below those in any other large developing economy. Chinese authorities, led by President Jiang Zemin and Premier Zhu Rongji, deliberately used trade liberalization to promote domestic economic reform in the late 1990s and early 2000s, imposing the new international rules on provincial and party leaders around the country. They made concessions greater than those of any other developing country when joining the WTO. Inward direct investment became a key driver of technology transfer, export prowess, and job creation. China's embrace of the world economy was hugely successful, though it overdid globalization in one sense by relying so heavily on large and growing trade surpluses to sustain its growth rate over much of the past decade.

A key question today involves the interaction between the reforms President Xi has promised and China's international position. Those reforms, and especially their focus on boosting consumption and the services sector, should permit and encourage external liberalization. As in earlier periods, further increases in integration with the world economy would promote the leadership's reform agenda by supporting this rebalancing of the domestic economy and consequently its external economic position. Recent indications of increased Chinese engagement in international trade activities, such as its interest in the TPP and green goods initiative, meaningful talks with the United States on a BIT, and launching the Shanghai Pilot Free Trade Zone, suggest some coincidence between internal and external reform—though China's reluctant stance in the ITA2, GPA, and perhaps the TiSA talks suggests hesitation as well.

---

6. This is the essential case for creating an informal but very active G-2 between China and the United States (as initially proposed in Bergsten 2005). Such a relationship seems to be developing in process terms: President Obama has met with his Chinese counterparts on an average of every quarter since he took office over five years ago, and there are more than 60 regular bilateral dialogues between the two countries every year. Meetings of the mind on substantive issues have obviously progressed much less rapidly.

We suspect that the interaction will go far to determine China's attitude toward negotiating closer economic ties with the United States. If the leadership decides to push for structural reform, and that external liberalization can be an important driver thereof, then initiatives previously thought to be highly unlikely may become quite realistic. Domestic interests always determine international stances on such issues, and a CHUSTIA is no exception.

For its part, the United States has globalized faster than any high-income country in modern times. Including investment income, the share of trade in its economy quadrupled from 1960 to 2010 to a level of about 40 percent, considerably higher than for the European Union or Japan—though still less than China's level, which is well above 60 percent. About one-fifth of all US manufactured output is exported, generating millions of jobs in that key sector, and the potential for adding jobs in the service sector through increased sales abroad is enormous (Jensen 2011).

A Peterson Institute for International Economics team calculated in 2005 that the US economy was $1 trillion per year richer (in 2004 dollars) as a result of its integration with the world trading system over that same 50-year period, adding almost $10,000 or 10 percent to average household incomes (Bradford, Grieco, and Hufbauer 2005). That team also calculated that annual gains of another $500 billion were available from eliminating remaining trade barriers. This study suggests that as much as one-third of that total could be obtained from the posited liberalization with China.

The United States is in great need of rebalancing and further trade expansion to boost its tepid growth rate and help reduce unemployment, which remains stubbornly high. Fiscal policy will remain restrictive for at least several years, to restore a sustainable profile to the national debt, and will not have much scope for stimulus over the longer run due to the budgetary costs of an aging population. Monetary policy is very near its zero bound, and quantitative easing is already being phased down, so interest rates are likely to rise when the world economy strengthens. Meanwhile, the US external deficit of about $400 billion per year continues to drain about 2 million jobs from the economy. Trade appears to offer one of the few avenues for accelerating US growth and creating good jobs.

President Obama set a goal of doubling US exports over the five-year period to 2014. That target will be badly missed despite being based on a year (2009) when the Great Recession temporarily depressed foreign sales. The administration is now seeking to promote exports through its major trade negotiations, the TPP and TTIP. A CHUSTIA would be very much in the spirit of that strategy and, as chapter 2 shows, would generate considerably larger export expansion for the United States than even a TPP that included the 16 countries that seem likely to join the agreement after a second round of negotiations. As described above, a CHUSTIA accompanied by rebalancing of the two economies would be even better.

Both China and the United States could derive major benefits from increased trade and investment. There are several paths forward: multilateral liberalization in the WTO through a revived Doha Round or some wholly new initiative; plurilateral sectoral deals such as TiSA and ITA2; regional arrangements such as RCEP, the TPP, or possibly an FTAAP and TTIP; bilateral negotiations with each other or other countries; or unilateral action, as China has done on numerous occasions in the past. These paths are mutually reinforcing, with successful "competitive liberalization" initiatives often proceeding simultaneously (Bergsten 1996). There can even be direct linkages among the paths: partners in a bilateral negotiation could agree to work together in broader regional and multilateral forums to advance some of their bilateral goals. The United States often has insisted that its partners in bilateral talks support its initiatives in broader groupings. This study addresses primarily the bilateral CHUSTIA alternative but also looks at alternative mechanisms through which the functional equivalent might be achieved, such as through Chinese accession to the TPP, fusion between the TPP and RCEP, or perhaps an FTAAP. It embeds the analysis in the broader trade architecture that now exists and is being built in so many directions, to ask what a CHUSTIA could add and what economic and political difficulties it will face.

What Might a CHUSTIA Contain?

If Chinese and US authorities decide to pursue an FTA, two major sets of questions arise. First, what might be the substantive content of such an agreement? Second, what negotiating modalities might the countries pursue, accounting for the other trade agreements in which they are involved and the broader political context in which they would be operating? We offer a range of options to help promote thoughtful discussion in both countries and to provide possible points of departure when the time comes to make decisions.

We are also fully aware of the gravity, and political sensitivity in both countries, of any decision to launch a CHUSTIA initiative. We therefore want to offer alternatives for proceeding incrementally, perhaps starting the process through separate agreements on one or two of the fifteen topics that we address as possible elements of an eventually comprehensive FTA. We structure our discussion of some of the issues as pointing toward either a single chapter of an overall compact or, more modestly and perhaps more immediately, a stand-alone arrangement that would be largely self-balancing and thus make sense on its own whether or not it is integrated into something broader over time. China and the United States might pursue some issues within the framework of a broader plurilateral agreement, such as the GPA in the WTO. The basic concept is to think of these individual topics, and efforts to reach accommodation on them, as possible stepping stones or building blocks toward something larger, but also as items worth addressing in and of themselves even if nothing more extensive eventuates. Successful negotiations on individual topics could generate positive momentum toward a broader compact and help overcome the mistrust that threatens the relationship between the two countries.

The current China–US BIT negotiation is a case in point. Our analysis suggests that FDI in both directions, especially from China into the United States, could expand rapidly in the coming years. The potential gains from a sizable expansion of such activity could add significantly to the economic payoff from a CHUSTIA. The countries have agreed that investment between them is a priority topic and now seek to negotiate a BIT that would improve the investment climate in both nations. Chapter 13 in this study suggests several possible areas of agreement that range beyond what is currently contemplated for the BIT.

As for the substance of a possible CHUSTIA, we analyze fifteen discrete topics that could be considered for inclusion. Our list draws on the record of previous FTAs by both countries plus, in three cases, issues about which China, the United States, or both have expressed strong concerns: export controls, currency and rebalancing, and cyberespionage. An initial phase of the process would undoubtedly determine which items from this list could be placed on the agenda for negotiations, whether comprehensive or issue by issue. We offer our own suggestions in the concluding chapter of this study after assessing each topic in the chapters that follow.

Each chapter summarizes General Agreement on Tariffs and Trade (GATT) and WTO provisions that address the topic in question, even if tangentially. We then search for further guidance in existing US and Chinese FTAs, which will presumably be augmented when the TPP, the pending China–Korea FTA and China–Australia FTA, and eventually the RCEP are concluded. The individual chapters emphasize differences between the US and Chinese positions. At this early juncture, it is useful to illuminate potential sticking points to provide a realistic view of the landscape ahead.

It would be more feasible politically, and perhaps more desirable substantively, to pursue an incremental approach in sectors that offer opportunities for a high degree of reciprocity within their individual confines. This is the theory behind the BIT negotiations, in which each country has a keen interest in enhancing access and strengthening protections for its investments in the other. Another possibility might be government procurement, in which each country seeks increased ability to participate in the large infrastructure projects of the other—including at the subfederal level through the states of the United States and the provinces in China. We first discuss the issues that might be susceptible to stand-alone agreements.

Some of the sectors under consideration are unbalanced in the direction of requests by one of the potential partner countries. The US desire to tighten China's IPR enforcement far outweighs any reciprocal Chinese interest in such US enforcement. China's hope to achieve access to energy supplies from the United States has no US parallel. Significant liberalization in these areas would presumably have to be part of a broader deal encompassing tradeoffs across topics. We address this cluster of topics together.

In essence, we distinguish between sectors that are potentially susceptible to intrasectoral reciprocity or only to intersectoral reciprocity. Liberalization could presumably proceed on a stand-alone basis more easily on intrasectoral topics. Intersectoral candidates would probably need to be part of a broader package. We are mindful of this criterion in assessing the prospects for each sector and where it might fit into the overall picture for a trade agreement between China and the United States.

A third group of issues may be better addressed through parallel agreements, perhaps in a broader multilateral context, rather than inclusion in a CHUSTIA or even in separate bilateral accords. The most obvious candidates are cyberespionage and currency. We discuss these in a separate cluster while acknowledging that they may have to be included in a CHUSTIA if alternative arrangements cannot be agreed on a timely basis.

How Might a CHUSTIA Proceed?

We envisage that China–US economic talks, whether aiming for a comprehensive FTA, a selective sector-by-sector approach, or something in between, could proceed under either of two broad mandates from their governments. The more ambitious would be for Chinese and US leaders, after going through the appropriate domestic procedures, to publicly set a goal of achieving a comprehensive FTA and direct their negotiators to pursue that goal. They could also set a firm deadline, as the United States has done de facto in the past through the expiration dates of the Trade Promotion Authority granted by Congress,[7] or leave that issue open to see how the talks proceed, as with all current negotiations. The more incremental strategy would be for the leaders to direct their teams to start negotiating on specific issues: one or more, specified from the outset or left to be determined later, explicitly viewed as one-off agreements, linked to the future evolution of something broader, or with that critical decision simply left open.

There are three basic options on the international side. The most straightforward is a bilateral negotiation like those that the two countries have already conducted with numerous trade partners. This would have the virtues of simplicity and familiarity. It might be the most appropriate technique for the two largest economies in the world in pursuing such a historic and potentially pathbreaking arrangement. As a bilateral initiative, it would potentially have the most far-reaching effects on relations between the two countries.

An alternative is to embed a China–US FTA in a broader compact that includes a number of other countries in the region. China could join the TPP, in which it has shown increasing interest. As the current negotiations for the RCEP and TPP essentially represent a two-track process toward liberalizing trade in Asia and the Pacific, the two agreements could merge at a later stage. As China will be a charter member of the RCEP and the United States a charter member of the TPP, any such integration would represent at least a step toward

---

7. The Korea–US FTA, for example, was agreed literally within ten minutes of the expiration of US fast track authority (TPA) in 2007.

freer trade—defined by whatever hybrid emerged from an RCEP-TPP negotiation—between those two countries. A third possibility, which China mentioned in APEC meetings in early 2014, is to move directly toward an FTAAP with the TPP and its presumably higher standards (and perhaps RCEP) remaining intact in addition.

Achieving free trade or significant liberalization between two major economies indirectly has at least two precedents. About one-half of the economic effect of the TPP will be freer trade between the United States and Japan (chapter 2, table 2.12). In a much earlier period, the two-track liberalization of trade in postwar Europe by the original Common Market (led by France and Germany) and the European Free Trade Association (led by the United Kingdom) essentially merged into the European Community and then the European Union.

The choice between methods[8] will presumably turn on Chinese and US assessments of the economics and politics of the issues at the time. The criticism in the United States of achieving freer trade with Japan through the TPP has been very modest compared with the extensive Japan-bashing and fear of Japanese dominance in the 1980s. There might be less risk of failure for a China–US initiative—which would have major negative repercussions on their overall relationship—from pursuing an indirect route rather than the direct bilateral path. In addition, the effects of the two different paths would be quite different for a number of other countries in the region. Non-TPP members, such as Indonesia and Thailand, would not obtain increased access to the United States after a CHUSTIA unless they negotiated their own FTAs with the United States or joined a TPP without China's doing so. Non-RCEP members, such as Canada and Mexico, would have to negotiate their own FTAs with China to get increased access to its market. These countries will presumably try to influence the decisions of the two superpowers in the direction of merging the TPP and RCEP into an FTAAP rather than pursuing their own bilateral agreement.

Interim Steps

Whether and how China and the United States decide to pursue intensified economic cooperation, their decisions on the matter are presumably some time away. In the interim, and before they are in a position to set a firm course of action, they might initiate informal consultations through which they could share views on their current regional negotiations and trade policies

---

8. Another possibility is of course multilateral liberalization in the WTO, whether through a renamed Doha Round or a wholly new initiative. All previous WTO or GATT rounds have only pursued modest reductions in trade impediments, however, so this approach would be highly unlikely to produce free trade between China and the United States. We nevertheless consider several multilateral—or at least plurilateral—possibilities, such as the TiSA for services and ITA2 for high-technology products, where the ambition of the participants appears to be sufficiently high to posit the possibility of substantial liberalization.

more broadly, getting a better sense of what the potential partner is thinking. Kissinger (2013, 180) suggests that the two countries begin any of their cooperative efforts "with a common analysis of where we think the international system is going and should go."

Such conversations could proceed bilaterally, perhaps through the Strategic and Economic Dialogue. If that would raise concerns about the reactions of other countries, or domestic anxieties within either country, they could proceed in a regional forum such as APEC, which has been sponsoring discussions of existing bilateral FTAs and their implications for its long-term Bogor Goal of achieving "free and open trade and investment in the Asia-Pacific region."[9] Unofficial conversations can be carried out through the variety of track II dialogues between the two countries. The US–China CEO and Former Senior Officials' Dialogue, conducted by the US Chamber of Commerce and the China Center for International Economic Exchange, have addressed these issues most directly and positively to date.

Another timing issue could prove to be important. Both countries currently have very active negotiating agendas, the United States with the TPP and TTIP, and China with Korea, Australia, and the RCEP. Some observers believe the two countries would be hard pressed to take on major new trade initiatives in the near future. Yet the demonstrated dynamic of competitive liberalization suggests that excluded partners may be eager to close incipient gaps in their trade patterns sooner rather than later, or even head them off, implying that it might be better to strike while the iron is hot. No definitive judgment is possible at this point, but these timing considerations should be kept in mind in considering a strategy for how to proceed.

This volume turns now to detailed analyses of each of the key issues that will be central to any decision to launch a new trade initiative between China and the United States. In chapter 2, Peter A. Petri, Michael G. Plummer, and Fan Zhai assess the prospects in the coming decade for overall trade between the two countries and their global trade positions, both on their current policies and whether they significantly liberalize trade between them. They examine the economic effects of an FTA on other major parts of the region and the world as well as on China and the United States themselves, with substantial sectoral disaggregation to show how an agreement might work in practice. They assess the interaction between a possible CHUSTIA and the macroeconomic rebalancing processes that are currently under way and will presumably continue. Finally, the chapter provides a systematic comparison of alternative routes to China–US free trade and a cumulative assessment of the potential interactions among a CHUSTIA, the TPP, the RCEP, and an FTAAP.

Chapter 3, by Robert Z. Lawrence, addresses the adjustment challenges that a CHUSTIA would pose for the United States. It reviews several prominent analyses of the effects over the past two decades of China–US trade, especially on employment and manufacturing wages, and the relevance of those studies

---

9. Bogor Declaration in 1994, www.apec.org (accessed on July 17, 2014).

to the prospects of a move to relatively free trade and investment between the two countries. It then offers several proposals for US policy responses to those adjustment challenges.

The remainder of the chapters except the last address each of the specific topics that might be covered in a comprehensive negotiation, in parallel compacts, or as stand-alone components that could become building blocks for a broader agreement. The final chapter then draws together all these elements to reach conclusions on the merits of the idea and how the two governments might proceed.

Before turning to these topics, however, we briefly detour to a recent case of extensive trade liberalization between the United States and another major Asian country. We do so because we believe it is relevant for considering the prospects for a CHUSTIA and because it offers a more optimistic perspective for viewing the possibility of a pathbreaking agreement than can be found in either country at this time.

Postscript: The Path to a Korea–US FTA (KORUS)

In 2000 Han Duk-soo, then Korea's minister of trade, later to become prime minister and ambassador to the United States, asked the Institute for International Economics (as PIIE was then called) to prepare an initial study of a possible FTA between his country and the United States. Minister Han readily acknowledged that there was no active discussion of the issue in Korea, which was the case in the United States as well. He further noted that, to the extent the idea had been considered at all, there was great hostility to it in the Korean agricultural community and widespread opposition from business.

Minister Han had a vision, however, that a KORUS, as it came to be called later, was an idea whose time might come. He believed that the way to start a discussion was to conduct a thorough analysis to see whether the concept made sense and what the main hurdles might be to pursuing it. If the results were positive, others might be stimulated to address the issue and it might enter the policy discourse in both countries.

The Institute regarded such a topic as an ideal addition to its research agenda as it offered an opportunity for precisely the kind of thought leadership that a think tank should provide. This was especially true on the proposed topic, as Institute researchers had previously done some of the pioneering studies of earlier US FTAs, with Canada and then with Mexico through NAFTA. The Institute expert on trade negotiations, senior fellow Jeffrey J. Schott, immediately agreed to take on the project and persuaded Inbom Choi, a trade economist with experience in Korean think tanks and a former high government official, to join the research team to provide an equal Korean perspective.

The authors completed their study with all deliberate speed and the Institute released the results in April 2001 (Choi and Schott 2001). It soon became the subject of seminars and conferences in both countries, including some at the Institute, and began to enter the policy discussion. At one of these events in 2003, most of the Korean participants continued to express skepticism as to whether their government could ever overcome domestic political opposition to the idea, especially from agriculture, but others asked whether the payoff from an FTA with the United States might be great enough to permit a breakthrough. At another Institute event in 2004, US Trade Representative Robert Zoellick indicated, for the first time in public, that he could contemplate adding Korea to the growing list of countries with which he was negotiating FTAs whenever Korea indicated that it was ready to seriously include agriculture in such talks. Meanwhile Trade Minister Kim Hyun-chong in Korea was exercising remarkable leadership in forging a brilliant strategy of multiple FTAs for his country and launching complementary domestic policies, especially regarding agriculture, that enabled them to eventually command the necessary support in Korea's national assembly.

Informal prenegotiations for KORUS took place in 2004 and 2005 and formal negotiations began in 2006. Final agreement was reached in 2007, literally at the very hour that the existing Trade Promotion Authority for the US government—which has yet to be renewed—was expiring. The outgoing Bush administration could not submit the new agreement, or similar agreements with Colombia and Panama, for congressional approval because the new Democratic majority in the House of Representatives was unreceptive. But the Obama administration was finally able to do so, after a substantial delay and minor modifications of the agreement, and won ratification of KORUS in 2011.

KORUS entered into force in March 2012 and now stands as the most important FTA that the United States has ever negotiated in Asia, perhaps anywhere. For Korea, it is clearly the most important FTA it has signed, along with its agreement with the European Union. It took 12 years for Minister Han Duk-soo's idea to become reality. It began with a study that the Institute undertook at a time when there was literally no interest in, and even considerable opposition toward, the entire concept. Patience was needed, but was finally rewarded, and the wait was well worth it.

A similar evolution could conceivably occur regarding the idea of a China–US FTA. Such a pact would clearly be the most important in which either party has ever participated. There is now very little discussion of the idea in either country, and to the extent that there is, at least in the United States, the majority of opinion is negative; there is reluctance to contemplate Chinese membership in the TPP let alone a bilateral pact with the United States. Strong leadership would be needed in both countries to convert this skepticism into support.

At least one far-sighted and highly influential person in each country, however, has had a vision of a China–US FTA as a way to deal with the countries' ongoing trade frictions and place their overall relationship on a stronger footing. Maurice R. ("Hank") Greenberg—former chairman of American International Group, now chairman and CEO of C.V. Starr and Company, and one of the most experienced and highly respected US business leaders regarding China—originated the discussion in 2009 while noting that the idea "would take ten years to work out." It was later picked up by the China–US Exchange Foundation and its chairman, C. H. Tung, the first chief executive of Hong Kong and now vice chairman of the Standing Committee of the Chinese People's Political Consultative Conference. The foundation's report, *US–China Economic Relations in the Next Ten Years: Towards Deeper Engagement and Mutual Benefit*, in early 2013 called for serious think tank study of the idea over the coming year and for the two governments to institute a process toward negotiations on it if the study produced positive conclusions. The US Chamber of Commerce and the China Center on International Economic Exchange then promoted the project; in 2011 they together instituted a track II US-China CEO and Former Senior Officials' Dialogue to discuss economic relations between the two countries.

This study attempts to fulfill the first part of the mandate from the 2013 report with the hope that, as in the case of KORUS, it will lead to serious consideration of the idea of a China–US FTA in both countries and perhaps eventual policy initiatives. A CHUSTIA would be even more significant than KORUS, in both partner countries and the world as a whole, with stakes that are enormous and a payoff that could be far greater. The analysis that follows, and the conclusions and recommendations that are offered at the end, seek to spark active debate on an idea whose time might be coming.

References

Autor, David H., David Dorn, and Gordon H. Hanson. 2013. The China Syndrome: Local Labor Market Effects of Import Competition in the United States. *American Economic Review* 103, no. 6: 2121–68.

Baily, Martin Neil, and Barry P. Bosworth. US Manufacturing: Understanding Its Past and Its Potential Future. *Journal of Economic Perspectives* 28, no. 1 (2014): 3–26.

Bergsten, C. Fred. 1996. *Competitive Liberalization and Global Free Trade: A Vision for the Early 21st Century*. Working Paper 96-15. Washington: Peterson Institute for International Economics.

Bergsten, C. Fred. 2005. *The United States and the World Economy: Foreign Economic Policy for the Next Decade*. Washington: Peterson Institute for International Economics.

Bradford, Scott C., Paul L. E. Grieco, and Gary Clyde Hufbauer. 2005. The Payoff to America from Global Integration. In *The United States and the World Economy: Foreign Economic Policy for the Next Decade*, ed. C. Fred Bergsten. Washington: Peterson Institute for International Economics.

Choi, Inbom, and Jeffrey J. Schott. 2001. *Free Trade Between Korea and the United States?* Policy Analyses in International Economics 62. Washington: Peterson Institute for International Economics.

Dobson, Wendy. 2013. *Partners and Rivals: The Uneasy Future of China's Relationship with the United States*. Toronto: University of Toronto.

Gilpin, Robert. 1981. *War and Change in World Politics*. Cambridge, UK: Cambridge University Press.

Hufbauer, Gary Clyde, Cathleen Cimino, and Tyler Moran. 2014. *NAFTA at 20: Misleading Charges and Positive Achievements*. Policy Brief 14-13. Washington: Peterson Institute for International Economics.

Hufbauer, Gary Clyde, and Dean DeRosa. 2013. The Long-Term Outlook for US–China Trade. In *US–China 2022: US–China Economic Relations in the Next Ten Years*. Washington: China–US Focus.

Jensen, J. Bradford. 2011. *Global Trade in Services: Fear, Facts, and Offshoring*. Washington: Peterson Institute for International Economics.

Kissinger, Henry A. 2013. United States–China Relationship. In *Finance, Development, and Reform*, ed. Andrew Sheng. Beijing: China Citic Press.

Krugman, Paul R. 1993. Regionalism versus Multilateralism: Analytical Notes. In *New Dimensions in Regional Integration*, ed. Jaime de Melo and Arvind Panagariya. Cambridge, UK: Cambridge University Press.

Lardy, Nicholas R. 2014. *Markets over Mao: The Rise of Private Business in China*. Washington: Peterson Institute for International Economics.

Li Xiangyang. 2013. TPP: A Major Challenge to China in the Process of Its Rise. In *China and the World: Balance, Imbalance, and Rebalance*, ed. Shao Binhong. Leiden: Koninklijke Brill NV.

Lieberthal, Kenneth, and Wang Jisi. 2012. *Addressing US–China Strategic Distrust*. Washington: Brookings Institution.

Petri, Peter A., Michael G. Plummer, and Fan Zhai. 2012. *The Trans-Pacific Partnership and Asia-Pacific Integration: A Quantitative Assessment*. Policy Analyses in International Economics 98. Washington: Peterson Institute for International Economics.

US Chamber of Commerce. 2013. *From International to Interstates: Assessing the Opportunity for Chinese Participation in U.S. Infrastructure*. Washington.

The Effects of a China–US Free Trade and Investment Agreement

PETER A. PETRI, MICHAEL G. PLUMMER, AND FAN ZHAI

The terrain of the world trading system is shifting, with meganegotiations now under way among 12 countries in the Asia-Pacific for the Trans-Pacific Partnership (TPP), 16 countries in Asia for the Regional Comprehensive Economic Partnership (RCEP), between the European Union and the United States for the Transatlantic Trade and Investment Partnership (TTIP), and between the European Union and Japan. Economies producing nearly 80 percent of world GDP are engaged in one or more of these initiatives.

None of the negotiations, however, includes both China and the United States, the world's two largest economies. Any such negotiation would be challenging: the two countries are close trade partners, but also competitors, and they differ in many ways. For now, China and the United States are pursuing separate negotiating tracks—China in the RCEP and bilateral efforts, and the United States in the TPP and with Europe. These efforts can be seen as a contest of templates, designed to define rules that are ultimately expected to cover wider trade (Petri 2012). Each partnership hopes to entrench a system that liberalizes trade and investment, but also favors its leading industries, economic model, and strategic interests.

Direct cooperation between China and the United States would be enormously productive in this context, not least because it would mitigate frictions

Peter A. Petri is the Carl J. Shapiro professor of international finance at Brandeis International Business School, a senior fellow at the East-West Center, and a visiting fellow at the Peterson Institute for International Economics. Michael G. Plummer is Eni professor of economics at the School of Advanced International Studies (SAIS), Johns Hopkins University, and a senior fellow at the East-West Center. Fan Zhai is managing director of the China Investment Corporation. The views expressed are the authors' and do not necessarily reflect those of the institutions with which they are affiliated. The authors are grateful for comments on an earlier draft by C. Fred Bergsten, Wendy Dobson, David Dollar, Gary Hufbauer, and Sean Miner.

that might otherwise arise. China–US cooperation could begin with issues where early agreements are possible—such as the investment treaty negotiations under way—and with mechanisms for dealing with others in the future. The vision of a comprehensive China–US trade and investment agreement (CHUSTIA) provides a compelling framework for these efforts.

We estimate that a CHUSTIA would generate global income gains of $403 billion per year in 2025, compared to a projected world GDP of $103 trillion (these and other results cited in this chapter are expressed in 2007 US dollars).[1] It would generate greater gains for China than the RCEP agreement, and greater gains for the United States than a TPP without China. The results suggest that the agreement would be especially valuable for China because it has larger initial distortions, but it would increase trade, investment, and productivity in both countries. Productivity gains are also important in recent trade models and in the results reported in this study (see, e.g., Melitz and Redding 2014).

We also estimate that a CHUSTIA would involve significant adjustments. In the United States, some 1.7 million jobs in import-competing and related industries would have to shift over time to export-producing and related industries. Up to 1 million of these transitions, or 104,000 jobs per year, assuming a decade-long adjustment period, could result in involuntary job losses. These numbers represent a small percentage of typical annual job separations in the United States, and the economy would gain $1.25 million or more for each involuntary separation associated with CHUSTIA. Nevertheless, the results suggest that careful attention will have to be paid to policies that mitigate losses for affected workers (see chapter 3).

The China–US economic relationship is developing in a difficult macroeconomic context. The current account positions of the two countries have been sharply imbalanced in recent years, and surpluses in China and deficits in the United States remain contentious in the wake of the global financial crisis. The imbalances are narrowing, but slowly and unevenly, particularly in the United States. This study thus also examines the possibilities for accelerated rebalancing. Combining rebalancing policies with a CHUSTIA would have many advantages, whether or not a formal agreement explicitly links these two areas of policy.

Finally, if a CHUSTIA were concluded alongside the TPP and RCEP, the total benefits would approach those of a Free Trade Area of the Asia-Pacific (FTAAP), a long-envisioned objective of the Asia-Pacific Economic Cooperation (APEC) process. The three agreements represent a long step toward APEC's Bogor Goals of free trade and investment throughout the Asia-Pacific. They might offer a relatively manageable path toward these benefits and to reenergizing the global integration process.

---

1. The model has been developed as part of our ongoing study of Asia-Pacific trade relationships. It is described most fully in Petri, Plummer, and Zhai (2012b). Results, data, and publications are posted at asiapacifictrade.org (accessed on June 29, 2014).

Estimating the Trade Effects of a Free Trade Agreement

We explore the effects of a CHUSTIA and other policy alternatives with an advanced computable general equilibrium (CGE) model. Such models have become the standard tool for analyzing complex, prospective policy changes. Though far from perfect, they are the most effective of available alternatives.[2] Ex post empirical validation of CGE models is difficult (Dixon and Rimmer 2009) but a salient finding is that past models have significantly underestimated the effects of large agreements such as the North American Free Trade Agreement (NAFTA) (Kehoe 2005). However, datasets have improved in recent years, due largely to the contributions of the GTAP consortium,[3] and the present model also incorporates significant theoretical and empirical innovations. It includes mechanisms to recognize the role of firm heterogeneity in international trade and special features to simulate multilateral agreements. It also draws on a new dataset on trade agreement templates for projecting a potential China–US accord (see boxes 2.1 and 2.2).

None of the above improvements, however, should be interpreted as eliminating the fundamental uncertainties involved in this exercise. A CHUSTIA would be a large and complicated project and this first effort to assess its benefits is bound to be speculative. Previous studies have tested our model,[4] but its structure, parameters, and assumptions are subject to errors of measurement and judgment. Modeling detailed global production and trade patterns requires extensive data representing input and output, trade, demand, taxes, and many other relationships within and among 18 sectors in 24 economies. These data are assembled from many sources and must be further adjusted to achieve accounting consistency requirements that primary information does not usually meet.

The study's consistent, comprehensive dataset imposes a cutoff date for new information to permit adjustments for consistency. The core data were collected by the GTAP consortium for 2007 and were adjusted and released

---

2. The United States government does not publish modeling results while negotiations are under way, but the evaluation that the US International Trade Commission (USITC) prepares for Congress once agreements are concluded is typically based on a CGE model (see, e.g., USITC 2007). Aside from CGE models, econometric gravity models have also been used to study agreements (see, e.g., Felbermayr et al. 2013), but they are valid only to the extent that past agreements and circumstances can be considered equivalent to those of proposed new agreements. Also, gravity models provide much less structural information for analyzing country and sectoral effects.

3. Global Trade Analysis Project, www.gtap.agecon.purdue.edu (accessed on June 29, 2014).

4. These include analyses of the Association of Southeast Asian Nations (ASEAN) Economic Community (Petri, Plummer, and Zhai 2012a; Petri and Plummer 2013), the Trans-Pacific Partnership (Petri, Plummer, and Zhai 2012b), the economic prospects of ASEAN, China, and India (Petri and Zhai 2013), and Korea's trade policy options (Petri 2013).

Box 2.1 The computable general equilibrium model

Computable general equilibrium (CGE) analysis accounts for interactions among firms, households, and governments in multiple product markets in several countries and regions of the world economy. Firms are assumed to maximize profits and consumers to maximize utility. After transfers among firms, households, and governments, incomes are spent on goods and services, or are saved and invested, both at home and abroad. To compute an equilibrium solution, the model adjusts prices to make supply equal demand for each product and factor of production (labor, capital, and land) in every region. The effects of FTAs are simulated by changing tariffs and other parameters that affect trade, and the model then adjusts prices, output, trade, income, and demand levels to reach a new equilibrium.

The mathematical structure of a CGE model reflects assumptions about market structure, trade patterns, consumer preferences, production technology, market equilibrium conditions, factor supplies, taxes, and many other economic relationships. These assumptions are represented by input-output tables and elasticities and other parameters, such as how consumption demand responds to income. The structure is built up from multiple data sources and the model is calibrated to yield an initial solution that matches data for a benchmark year. Simulations then provide quantitative predictions for the evolution of economies over time and for the effects of policy interventions. They show, for example, how an FTA causes trade creation (the more efficient division of labor within a trade zone) and trade diversion (inefficiencies from discrimination against outsiders). Because CGE models usually assume normal unemployment, their solutions are appropriate mainly for medium-term analysis.

This study uses an 18-sector, 24-region CGE model, based on an innovative specification by Zhai (2008). The model recognizes that firms differ in productivity even within narrowly defined sectors. Thus, FTAs affect not only intersectoral specialization but also the distribution of firms within industries. Liberalization causes more productive firms to export and less productive firms to shrink, and raises each sector's average productivity. This specification predicts greater benefits than conventional approaches based on intersectoral specialization effects alone.

Retrospective studies have shown that estimates developed with conventional CGE models, such as NAFTA and several European agreements, have substantially underpredicted actual results (Kehoe 2005). The likely reason is that traditional models predicted trade increases for producers that already export (the intensive margin of trade), but had no mechanisms for anticipating new exporting activities (the extensive margin of trade). Recent research confirms the importance of the latter and thus our model is likely to produce more accurate estimates.

In previous applications, the model has been used to study the development of the ASEAN Economic Community, the long-term growth of ASEAN, China, and India, and the effects of the TPP, RCEP, and other regional trade agreements. Most of these applications also report the results of a side model to estimate effects on foreign direct investment, but those linkages are not used in this study. The model is described in detail in Petri, Plummer, and Zhai (2012b).

To assess how the provisions of economic partnership agreements (EPAs) affect nontariff barriers, we collected data on past Asia-Pacific trade agreements and assigned a score to each provision in each agreement. The scores were based on the issue coverage of the provision and related WTO data (see Petri, Plummer, and Zhai 2012b, appendix D). These scores were normalized so that the best 10 percent of agreements negotiated in the past received a score of 100. We then assumed that best-practice trade policies would eliminate two-thirds of the share of barriers—the actionable share. This ratio is roughly consistent with the little empirical evidence available, but is nevertheless somewhat arbitrary.

We found large and systematic differences across agreements in these scores. As figure 2.B1 shows, recent US agreements had higher scores than ASEAN agreements on average, especially in provisions related to competition,

Figure 2.B1   Scores of EPA provisions

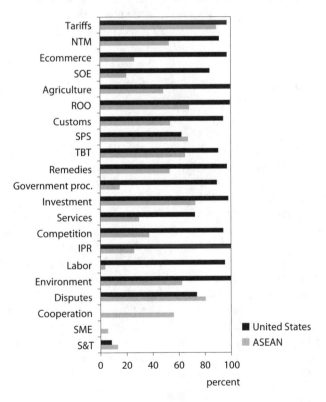

ASEAN = Association of Southeast Asian Nations; IPR = intellectual property rights; NTM = nontariff measures; ROO = rules of origin; SME = small and medium enterprises; SOE = state-owned enterprises; SPS = sanitary and phytosanitary measures; S&T = science and technology; TBT = technical barriers to trade

Source: Model calculations.

(continues on next page)

Box 2.2   Trade agreement templates and nontariff barriers
(continued)

intellectual property rights, government procurement, state-owned enterprises, and labor. ASEAN agreements had higher scores than US agreements in only a few areas, including dispute resolution and cooperation (typically provisions on capacity building). Evidently US templates are deeper with more emphasis on legal provisions across a wider range of policy issues.

What might explain the differences? Asian templates are negotiated by mainly emerging-market economies with comparative advantages in manufacturing—hence the focus on market access for goods. The templates the United States has negotiated reflect the typical interests of advanced economies in services, investment, intellectual property, and sometimes agriculture. They also emphasize rules-based approaches that are common in a developed-country institutional setting. Both templates include measures to attract domestic political support, but those too reflect their political setting: Asian agreements focus on cooperation and technology and US agreements on labor and the environment.

---

in final form in March 2012.[5] Thus our 2010 base year solution is in part a projection based on 2007 parameters together with estimates of productivity growth and other time-varying factors, constrained to match some actual 2010 national accounts and employment aggregates. Therefore the results for 2010 are internally consistent, but do not agree in all details with other later information available for specific variables and countries.

We address modeling uncertainties in two ways. First, we run simulations to examine the effects of changes in data and assumptions. This makes it possible to quantify how specific parameters, and hence possible errors in them, affect outcomes. Second, we make our estimating methodology fully transparent and invite readers to compare assumptions to their own evidence or judgment. Extensive documentation is provided on sources of information—which typically point to additional layers of documentation as well as the sources of proprietary data and software used in the analysis—and on the structure of model parameters and assumptions. These efforts go well beyond this chapter to related technical publications (Petri et al. 2012b) and a website dedicated to the model.[6] Our strategies are designed to enable readers to understand difficult modeling choices. Future versions of the model will reduce potential error through additional research and analysis, but it would

---

5. We first estimated the model using the beta version of the current GTAP 8 dataset that became available in mid-2011. That is also when most parameters on trade barriers and trade agreements were collected. A 2011-based GTAP 9 dataset is currently in preparation and is scheduled to be available in late 2014.

6. See www.asiapacifictrade.org (accessed on June 29, 2014).

be naïve to expect that they will eliminate the uncertainty inherent in assessing policy change. As noted elsewhere (Petri et al. 2012b), the aggregate results could be easily one-third higher or lower than those projected. Yet many estimated effects are so large that even sizable adjustments would leave key qualitative conclusions unchanged.

Two features of the model—so-called closure rules—are especially important for understanding its results. Both are widely used in medium-term CGE modeling but may appear counterintuitive to some readers. First, global trade balances are exogenously specified; in most scenarios they are held constant at 2010 levels in dollar terms. This means that China's global trade surplus is projected to decline to 1.4 percent of GDP by 2025, while the US trade deficit is projected to decline to 3.1 percent of GDP.[7] A CHUSTIA also would be constrained to this trade balance path. The reason for this approach is that, in the short to medium run, current account balances are dominated by capital flows that CGE models cannot adequately predict. While trade balances are exogenously set, they can be changed, and we will examine the effects of faster reductions in them.

Second, the policy simulations assume that employment levels in both countries return to and then remain at full employment. Thus, the simulations describe changes in the patterns, but not levels, of employment. The rationale is that CGE models cannot predict the labor market environment in the distant future. Thus, average, full employment conditions are assumed to hold in medium- and long-term projections. Under this assumption, policies that change the demand for labor result in changing real wages rather than employment. The model thus projects the gains from trade in terms of income gains rather than jobs created.[8]

The assessment of policy changes is conceptually straightforward. Because trade agreements are implemented gradually over time, we first construct a year-by-year baseline growth path for 2010 to 2025. This path incorporates expected rates of change in productivity, demand, and many other parameters,[9] as well as the implementation of free trade agreements (FTAs) that have been agreed but are not yet fully in place, such as the Korea–US FTA.

---

7. Like other magnitudes generated by the model, these projections are based mainly on 2007 data. Both China and the United States have in fact made somewhat faster progress than projected by 2013, but short-term projections suggest that imbalances will grow again in the near future.

8. If we instead predicted chronic future unemployment, then the model could be specified so that policies increasing the demand for labor drove up employment instead of real wages. Analysis in chapter 1 suggests that, under such circumstances, a CHUSTIA combined with accelerated Chinese rebalancing could boost US employment by over 1 million jobs over the course of a decade.

9. Overall growth assumptions are based on comprehensive global projections developed by CEPII (Fouré, Bénassy-Quéré, and Fontagné 2010). Since these estimates were published, the outlook for Asian growth has become less optimistic. For example, the 2011 CEPII projections envision 8.8 percent annual growth for China, perhaps two percentage points above more recent estimates. With a more conservative baseline, some results reported in dollar terms would be 20 percent lower in 2025, but would not change significantly when reported as percentages of GDP or trade.

The policy changes associated with a CHUSTIA and other trade policy alternatives are then superimposed on the baseline. In the case of a CHUSTIA, we assume implementation over the 2015–19 period, a schedule that is too ambitious politically but permits policy analysis in a compact time frame. It would make little difference to results for the future years we study (e.g., 2025) if the implementation were shifted to, say, 2016–20.

Unlike most other studies, our work bases the trade policy shocks used to represent potential agreements not on simple parametric assumptions but on the structure of past agreements. The template of a CHUSTIA is anticipated to be an average of recent Asian and US templates. As recent Asian FTAs ultimately eliminated 90 percent of most favored nation (MFN) tariffs and recent US agreements eliminated 96 percent (Petri, Plummer, and Zhai 2012b), we anticipate a China–US template to reduce tariffs by 93 percent. We apply a similar approach to nontariff barriers (NTBs; see box 2.2), first assigning scores to 21 provisions of past agreements and then mapping them into shocks to various NTBs. For example, if 10 of 21 possible FTA provisions affect services, and CHUSTIA scores on these provisions average 60 percent, then actionable service barriers—say, two-thirds of total barriers—would be reduced by two-thirds of 60 percent, or 40 percent.

The Value of a CHUSTIA

The scale of the China–US relationship and the barriers that restrain it lead us to expect significant benefits from liberalization. In 2010, China and the United States accounted for about one-third of world GDP, one-quarter of world exports, and one-fifth of world outward foreign direct investment (FDI). All of these shares are likely to rise over our projection period. By 2025, the two economies will be roughly similar in size. The bilateral economic relationship is therefore likely to become more consequential over time; it will appear to be perhaps twice as significant to US policymakers as it does now, and equally significant, at a high level, from a Chinese perspective.

Impediments to Trade and Investment

Table 2.1 summarizes current trade barriers in China–US trade and those that we assume would be left after a China–US agreement. Table 2.2 then shows how different agreements would affect the protection parameters used to represent different barriers in the model. It indicates that we ultimately reduce NTBs under a CHUSTIA by 45 percent in goods and 40 percent in services. We also reduce NTBs in investment by 40 percent. We do not assume that barriers will be fully eliminated. Some political compromises are inevitable and impediments in part reflect conditions that will not yield to policy changes. Even full scheduled cuts do not reduce tariffs, as evidence tells us that tariff preferences are seldom fully used. The reduction rates used to represent different agreements depend on their detailed text, using mapping techniques described in

Table 2.1 Barriers to China–US trade and investment

	Barriers, circa 2010		After CHUSTIA	
	China	United States	China	United States
Tariffs (percent)				
Agriculture	3.2	1.5	1.2	0.6
Nonagriculture	4.6	3.0	1.7	1.1
Duty-free (percent lines)				
Agriculture	0.9	40.4	not estimated	
Nonagriculture	46.9	50.3		
NTBs (percent AVE)				
Agriculture	33.4	11.0	18.4	6.1
Nonagriculture	16.7	3.7	9.2	2.0
Services	76.5	3.9	45.8	2.3

AVE = ad valorem equivalent; CHUSTIA = China–US trade and investment agreement; NTB = nontariff barrier

Sources: Tariffs are aggregations based on the Global Trade Analysis Project database, www.gtap. agecon.purdue.edu (accessed on July 3, 2014); duty-free lines are from the World Trade Organiza-tion, stat.wto.org (accessed on July 3, 2014); NTB barriers are from the simulation model, based on data sources referenced in Petri, Plummer, and Zhai (2012b); after-CHUSTIA reductions are explained in table 2.2.

Petri, Plummer, and Zhai (2012b). As already noted, the templates of future agreements are based on those of existing agreements—in the CHUSTIA's case, on an average of Asian and US templates. As table 2.2 shows, a CHUSTIA is assumed to be more rigorous than the RCEP, but less rigorous than the TPP.

Tariff reductions will not be the main focus of China–US liberalization efforts because tariffs are already low in both countries, for multiple reasons.[10] China tends to impose low tariffs on US-sourced inputs, such as raw mate-rials and advanced machinery, and reserves its high tariffs for products such as textiles and apparel, which the United States does not export heavily. In addi-tion, an extensive processing trade system permits imports to enter duty-free in Chinese export industries. Nevertheless, as chapter 4 notes, tariff peaks exist in both countries, on apparel in both countries and on processed foods and chemicals in China.

NTBs, however, are considerably higher than tariffs, especially in China. They are usually quantified as tariff equivalents and are derived either by comparing prices in domestic markets to those charged by leading global suppliers, or by estimating the tariff that would have caused imports to miss

---

10. Other things being equal, more protected sectors will have lower trade weights than less protected ones, so trade-weighted averages, such as those in table 2.2, are biased downward. Simple average MFN rates, as published by the World Trade Organization, are approximately three times as high as weighted averages. See stat.wto.org (accessed on July 1, 2014).

Table 2.2   Assumptions used to simulate China–US and other agreements

			Reductions under CHUSTIA		
FTA	Members	Template	Tariffs × utilization	Goods NTBs	Services NTBs
CHUSTIA	China, United States	Average of TPP and RCEP templates	0.93 × 0.67	0.45	0.40
TPP-16	Australia, Brunei, Canada, Chile, Indonesia, Japan, Korea, Malaysia, Mexico, New Zealand, Peru, Philippines, Singapore, Thailand, United States, Vietnam	Recent US template (such as Korea–US agreement)	0.96 × 0.58	0.53	0.52
RCEP	Australia, Brunei, Cambodia, China, India, Indonesia, Japan, Korea, Laos, Malaysia, Myanmar, New Zealand, Philippines, Singapore, Thailand, Vietnam	Recent ASEAN template (such as China–ASEAN)	0.9 × 0.60	0.36	0.28
FTAAPX	Combined membership of TPP-16 and RCEP groupings	Average of TPP and RCEP templates	0.93 × 0.67	0.45	0.40

ASEAN = Association of Southeast Asian Nations; CHUSTIA = China–US trade and investment agreement; FTAAPX = Expanded Free Trade Area of the Asia-Pacific; NTB = nontariff barrier; RCEP = Regional Comprehensive Economic Partnership; TPP = Trans-Pacific Partnership

Note: The first value in the tariff column represents tariff reductions; the second value represents the estimated rate of utilization of tariff preferences.

Source: Authors' calculations. Detailed data sources are explained in Petri, Plummer, and Zhai (2012b).

the levels expected in a country, given its economic characteristics, by as much as is observed in the data. NTBs include excessive or opaque standards and regulatory requirements, complex approval processes, and outright prohibitions on the sale of products, services, and investments. Significant US NTBs include regulations that impede trade with China in high-technology products that have both military and commercial applications.

The protective effects of NTBs in service sectors are especially uncertain, but are important to this study because services are an area of strong US comparative advantage. The US Trade Representative (USTR 2013) identified numerous policies that restrict US cross-border exports and the commercial presence of service firms abroad, including limits on equity ownership, difficult approval processes for operations such as branch banking, restrictions on products marketed, and burdensome capital and other regulatory requirements.

NTBs are ideally quantified by translating regulatory impediments into numerical restrictiveness indexes, and then extracting tariff equivalents from econometric studies of how these indexes affect trade flows. The World Bank has recently published comprehensive Services Trade Restrictiveness Indexes (STRIs; see table 2.3) and a parallel effort is under way at the Organization for Economic Cooperation and Development (OECD). However, neither set of results has been mapped into tariff equivalents so far. The service NTB equivalents listed in table 2.1 rely instead on Hufbauer, Schott, and Wong (2010), who estimate average tariff equivalents at 77 percent for China and 4 percent for the United States.[11]

How accurate are our NTB estimates, particularly for service barriers? Alternative estimates are scarce (see chapter 7, appendix A, for available calculations). Estimating the tariff equivalents of NTBs is difficult and uncertain, and especially so for trade in services. The most important recent study completed since the model's cutoff date suggests very similar service tariff equivalents to those used here for China (70 percent), albeit considerably higher ones for the United States (51 percent).[12] Still other estimates range from 30 to 121 percent for China and from 9 to 77 percent for the United States.[13] These are wide ranges, suggesting serious gaps in knowledge. Within those ranges, our service tariff equivalents are near estimated medians. Nevertheless, given the uncertainty about these numbers, our alternative scenario (CHUSTIA-LSL, or less service liberalization) assumes only one-half of the service liberalization reported in table 2.1 and used in central CHUSTIA solutions. The results of this scenario are reported where they make a difference, mainly in sectoral tables for trade, output, and employment. Recent studies provide evidence for setting US service barriers higher, but these changes would not significantly affect CHUSTIA results because the model projects services to be only 1 percent of Chinese exports to the United States even in 2025.

Income Gains

As the barriers facing China–US trade are still extensive, the benefits from reducing them turn out to be large. As figure 2.1 shows, significant gains would begin to appear in 2015, the assumed starting date of implementation. By 2025 China's income gains would reach $330 billion per year (1.9 percent

---

11. These and other estimates are examined in detail in chapter 7 and its appendix. The Peterson Institute estimates and those reported in table 2.1 differ slightly due to a different method of aggregating the underlying results.

12. The study was conducted at the Centre d'Etudes Prospectives et d'Informations Internationales (CEPII) research institute by Fontagné, Guillin, and Mitaritonna (2011). The figures in the text are unweighted averages of the CEPII results. The details suggest especially high rates of protection in China for traded services such as finance (93 percent), communications (85 percent), and business services (98 percent).

13. Estimates by Joseph Francois, quoted by Brown and Stern (2000) and Walsh (2006), define the lower and upper ends of these ranges for both countries. Francois does not cover the entire service sector and the average includes only those subsectors for which he reports estimates. By late 2014 more information should be available based on the new World Bank and OECD restrictiveness indexes.

Table 2.3   STRIs (percent)

Service	Code	China	United States	ASEAN/E[a]	BRIS[b]
Overall		36.6	17.7	43.8	37.1
Financial	1000	34.8	21.4	34.9	37.6
Banking	1010	32.5	21.3	36.9	40
Lending by banks	1012	28.8	21.3	35.7	40
Acceptance of deposits by banks	1013	36.3	21.3	38.2	40
Insurance	1020	38.3	21.7	31.7	33.8
Automobile insurance	1021	55	32.5	33.3	34.4
Life insurance	1022	55	27.5	31.7	34.4
Reinsurance	1023	5	5	30	32.5
Telecommunications	2000	50	0	37.5	31.3
Fixed-line telecommunications	2010	50	0	37.5	31.3
Mobile telecommunications	2020	50	0	37.5	31.3
Retail	3000	25	0	33.3	25
Transportation	4000	19.3	7.9	47.9	31.7
Air passenger international	4020	67.5	22.5	30.6	52.2
Maritime shipping international	4060	15	25	37.1	21.3
Maritime auxiliary services	4070	25	0	50	25
Road freight domestic	4080	0	0	54.2	31.3
Rail freight domestic	4090	0	0	62.5	31.3
Professional	5000	66	54	65.8	59.9
Accounting and auditing	5010	45	52.5	61.7	47.5
Accounting	5011	40	50	58.3	47.5
Auditing	5012	50	55	65	47.5
Legal	5020	80	55	68.5	68.1
Legal advice foreign law	5021	40	40	45	45
Legal advice domestic law	5022	100	62.5	75	78.1
Legal representation in court	5023	100	62.5	85.4	81.3

ASEAN = Association of Southeast Asian Nations; BRIS = Brazil, Russia, India, and South Africa; STRI = Services Trade Restrictiveness Index

a. ASEAN/E is the simple average of ASEAN's emerging economies: Cambodia, Indonesia, Malaysia, the Philippines, Thailand, and Vietnam.
b. BRIS is a simple average of the BRIS countries.

Source: World Bank STRI database, iresearch.worldbank.org (accessed on July 5, 2014).

of GDP), and US gains would approach $130 billion per year (0.6 percent of GDP). These trade-related gains increase if we count the effects of liberalizing FDI by roughly 25 percent based on an average of estimates we report in other studies. Sharply cutting service barrier liberalization—modeled in CHUSTIA-LSL—would in turn reduce gains for China to $230 billion (1.3 percent of GDP) and for the United States to $109 billion (0.5 percent of GDP). Relatively large gains for China are not surprising because China's higher initial barriers imply a larger potential for improving domestic productivity by reducing distortions. In addition, both countries would benefit from lowering barriers on each other's products. Finally, China's preferential access to US markets would enable it to capture US imports now coming from other countries.

As figure 2.1 shows, non-CHUSTIA countries would lose $57 billion per year. Figure 2.2 further dissects the third-country effects of a CHUSTIA. A few countries—Brunei, Chile, New Zealand, and Australia—are complementary to the Chinese and US economies, mainly as raw material exporters, and would benefit. However, others would be negatively affected, especially exporters competitive with China (Taiwan, Malaysia, Thailand, and Vietnam) and those with prior FTAs with the United States (Canada, Mexico, Korea, and Singapore). But these third-party losses are not large in relative terms; they account for only 12 percent of China–US benefits, so ample resources should be available for mitigating such side effects. The adverse effects on third economies are partly due to trade diversion, the new bilateral discrimination introduced by a CHUSTIA, and partly to preference erosion, the elimination of prior discrimination that excluded economies enjoyed under existing agreements. These have different economic consequences. Trade diversion worsens the terms of trade of FTA members and thereby erodes global efficiency, but preference erosion improves the terms of trade of FTA members and enhances global efficiency.[14]

Modest adverse effects on third parties may seem surprising given the emphasis in the traditional literature on the beggar-thy-neighbor motivation of bilateral or regional trade agreements (Viner 1950; Lipsey 1960). However, the results are consistent with more recent empirical work that focuses on the trade-creating and productivity-improving effects of FTAs (see Petri et al. 2012b for a survey). On average, tariff barriers have fallen considerably across the Asia-Pacific region, reducing the potential for transfers of government revenue in the tariff-imposing country to firms abroad. Also, modern trade theory recognizes that liberalization can improve productivity in partner economies, and so tends to generate benefits well in excess of transfer gains. Gravity model results reported by Hufbauer and Schott (2009) found little trade diversion from an array of potential trade agreements in the Asia-Pacific region.

---

14. The terms of trade for a country are defined as the average price of its exports divided by the average price of its imports.

Figure 2.1 Benefits generated by a CHUSTIA, 2010–25

billions of 2007 dollars

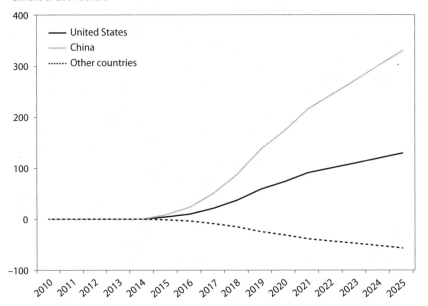

CHUSTIA = China–US trade and investment agreement
Source: Model simulations.

Moreover, the adverse effects of trade agreements on employment in partner countries are commonly exaggerated, while the gains are often underappreciated, as shown by recent analysis of NAFTA (Hufbauer, Cimino, and Moran 2014). Chapter 3 reports a similar analysis of potential US employment effects and income gains from closer US trade relations with China.

Sources of Gains

What explains the income gains from the China–US agreement? The major sources of benefits included in the modeling methodology are productivity growth due to shifts in production from less to more productive sectors and from less to more productive firms; changes in the relationship between the prices of exports and imports (terms of trade); the increased availability of product varieties in consumption and intermediate production; and faster capital accumulation due to higher incomes.

Productivity increases explain most of the overall trade-related income gains. China and the United States gain 1.9 percent and 0.7 percent, respectively, from permanent productivity improvements. A second source of effects involves terms of trade changes, which show how expensive it is to obtain a given quantity of imports for exports. Terms of trade effects favor China,

Figure 2.2   Income gains from a CHUSTIA, 2025 (percent of GDP)

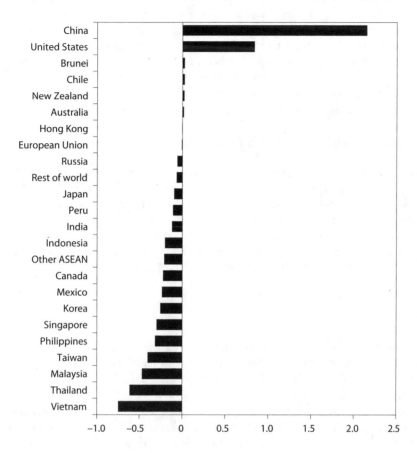

ASEAN = Association of Southeast Asian Nations; CHUSTIA = China–US trade and investment agreement
Source: Model calculations.

because its real exchange rate would appreciate and make imports cheaper, but reduce US benefits a little. A third source of effects—typically gains from greater trade—involves the availability of more varieties of products in both countries, making it possible to deliver higher utility per dollar of expenditure. In particular, a CHUSTIA would make new, more varied US services available in China, and more specialized machinery and manufactured products available in the United States.

Our relatively large estimated benefits are well within the range of results obtained elsewhere. More standard CGE modeling shows smaller effects (Ma and Shi 2013), but econometric studies often project larger ones. Felbermayr and colleagues (2013) estimate that FTAs have increased trade by an average of 67 percent in the past, generating high single-digit or low double-digit percentage gains in GDP. On theoretical grounds, Yasuyuki Todo also argues for large effects, noting that increased competition and interdependence across the innovative sectors of different countries would increase not only productivity levels, but also the rate of technical progress. Even a small increment in that rate—Todo suggests 0.5 percent—would lead to large benefits over time.[15] There is much anecdotal evidence that, in the long run, periods of global trade advances are correlated with strong economic performance. However, all of these effects are quite speculative and have therefore been omitted from this study.

Sectoral Implications of a CHUSTIA

While economic analysis generally emphasizes economywide benefits, political debates typically focus on narrower effects. Individual workers and investors are less concerned with aggregate results than with trade, production, and employment in their sectors and industries. Even if attractive opportunities open in other sectors, taking advantage of them involves uncertainty and costs, including adjustment and investment. We turn to sectoral results with the qualification that more detailed results are inevitably associated with larger potential error bands.

Trade

Liberalization allows sectors and firms with comparative advantages, including the most productive firms in every sector, to grow relative to others, and generates expansion in trade. Table 2.4 shows that a CHUSTIA would increase Chinese and US global exports by 10 and 13 percent relative to the baseline, respectively, while the two countries would have similar percentage increases in imports. Table 2.4 also shows that bilateral trade changes would be much larger, with Chinese exports to the United States rising by 41 percent relative to the baseline and US exports to China rising by 109 percent relative to the baseline. Recall that these results assume that the global trade balances of both countries remain fixed. While two-way trade between China and the United States would grow sharply, the US bilateral trade deficit with China would change less, and even this change would be offset by changes in US deficits and Chinese surpluses in third countries.

Tables 2.5A and 2.5B report the composition of trade changes. These results are driven by greater intersectoral trade, as well as additional two-way trade in every sector. Intersectoral changes reflect broad comparative advantage at work, increasing China's exports in manufacturing and US exports in various types of raw materials and services. Intrasectoral changes, in turn, reflect the expansion of productive firms throughout the economy. This leads

---

15. Yasuyuki Todo, "Estimating the TPP's Expected Growth Effects," Research Institute of Economy, Trade, and Industry, Report no. 153, April 2013.

Table 2.4   Projected effects of a CHUSTIA on trade, 2025

	China		United States	
	Baseline (billions of US dollars)	**Change** (percent)	**Baseline** (billions of US dollars)	**Change** (percent)
Global exports	4,597	10.3	2,813	13.3
Global imports	4,253	10.9	3,577	10.8
Bilateral exports	1,121	41.2	447	108.9

CHUSTIA = China–US trade and investment agreement

Note: Values in 2007 US dollars, free-on-board prices.

Source: Model simulations.

to additional two-way trade in all industries, especially manufacturing. The two-way trade flows are likely to reinforce the cross-border supply chains connecting the two countries. The international input-output tables of a GTAP-based CGE model track international transactions in global supply chains much the same way as do the input-output tables of the trade in value added datasets recently developed by the World Trade Organization (WTO) and the OECD.

Table 2.5A shows that Chinese exports would expand vigorously in machinery, metals, and other manufacturing subsectors. Increases are also projected for Chinese exports of apparel and footwear, due to reductions in relatively high US tariffs, giving China a competitive edge against other countries. Chinese exports would be largely unchanged in services, but these sectors would grow rapidly due to domestic demand under baseline assumptions. Table 2.5B shows that US exports would expand in food and beverage products, advanced manufacturing subsectors such as electrical equipment and metals, and in some subsectors that participate in global supply chains, such as textiles. US exports would rise substantially in services, such as construction; trade, transport, and communications; and private services. The last of these subsectors is the largest in the input-output industry classification, with projected US exports in 2025 of $489 billion and a 14 percent increase under a CHUSTIA.

Comparing the CHUSTIA-LSL and central scenarios shows significant differences, particularly in the composition of trade, but in the end does not lead to different conclusions. With low service liberalization, trade would increase less than under the central scenario. Chinese exports would rise by 9 percent rather than 10 percent, and US exports by 12 percent rather than 13 percent. The composition of trade would also shift less toward services. The expansion in US service exports would be 6 percent rather than 18 percent, partly offset by larger increases in primary product exports (14 percent rather than 13 percent) and manufactured goods exports (15 percent rather than 11 percent). But curtailing service liberalization would still leave benefits largely

Table 2.5A Projected trade effects for China, 2025

	Exports			Imports		
	Baseline (billions of US dollars)	CHUSTIA central (percent)	CHUSTIA-LSL (percent)	Baseline (billions of US dollars)	CHUSTIA central (percent)	CHUSTIA-LSL (percent)
Primary products	3	–2.1	–1.4	1,169	4.3	4.1
Rice	0	0.8	1.7	1	1.3	1.8
Wheat	0	8.8	9.5	1	12.3	12.6
Other agriculture	1	–0.4	0.9	461	6.3	6.4
Mining	2	–3.3	–3.0	705	3.0	2.5
Manufactures	4,451	10.5	9.3	2,372	8.9	11.1
Food, beverages	9	0.7	1.0	216	5.6	6.8
Textiles	111	10.3	10.0	134	6.4	7.3
Apparel, footwear	200	16.3	15.7	100	6.9	8.8
Chemicals	388	13.4	11.8	585	7.7	9.5
Metals	492	10.5	9.1	331	10.2	12.9
Electrical equipment	1,164	4.2	3.8	416	4.5	6.2
Machinery	1,322	11.0	9.4	373	9.8	12.9
Transport equipment	289	11.8	9.5	102	26.0	31.0
Other manufactures	476	19.7	17.7	115	19.5	22.9

(continues on next page)

Table 2.5A Projected trade effects for China, 2025 (continued)

	Exports			Imports		
	Baseline (billions of US dollars)	CHUSTIA central (percent)	CHUSTIA-LSL (percent)	Baseline (billions of US dollars)	CHUSTIA central (percent)	CHUSTIA-LSL (percent)
Services	143	2.1	–1.0	713	28.6	13.0
Utilities	0	–0.6	–1.3	3	9.5	5.3
Construction	11	1.1	–0.8	16	20.4	9.9
Trade, transport, communications	88	2.2	–1.1	331	19.4	9.7
Private services	42	2.1	–1.0	261	46.1	19.4
Public services	1	–0.7	–1.4	102	15.5	8.4
Total	4,597	10.3	9.0	4,253	10.9	9.5

CHUSTIA = China–US trade and investment agreement; LSL = low service liberalization

Note: Values in 2007 dollars, free-on-board prices.

Source: Model simulations.

Table 2.5B Projected trade effects for the United States, 2025

	Exports			Imports		
	Baseline (billions of US dollars)	CHUSTIA central (percent)	CHUSTIA-LSL (percent)	Baseline (billions of US dollars)	CHUSTIA central (percent)	CHUSTIA-LSL (percent)
Primary products	222.4	12.7	13.9	243.6	1.2	2.9
Rice	2.0	–4.2	–3.2	0.6	4.6	5.0
Wheat	10.1	–14.9	–14.1	0.9	15.8	16.6
Other agriculture	156.7	16.9	17.8	49.7	7.6	8.3
Mining	53.7	6.5	8.4	192.5	–0.5	1.5
Manufactures	1,662.4	10.8	15.1	3,010.7	11.8	10.7
Food, beverages	126.1	10.0	12.9	81.1	4.7	4.0
Textiles	33.7	18.0	22.2	82.6	9.6	9.3
Apparel, footwear	15.5	45.6	51.5	142.9	12.1	11.4
Chemicals	381.4	9.4	13.0	433.6	11.0	9.9
Metals	149.7	16.5	21.7	320.3	13.0	12.2
Electrical equipment	142.1	22.4	27.3	417.0	6.5	6.8
Machinery	326.0	8.1	13.4	679.2	14.1	12.8
Transport equipment	345.6	6.3	10.1	484.8	5.5	4.4
Other manufactures	142.4	9.5	14.1	369.2	23.5	21.1

(continues on next page)

Table 2.5B Projected trade effects for the United States, 2025 *(continued)*

	Exports			Imports		
	Baseline (billions of US dollars)	CHUSTIA central (percent)	CHUSTIA-LSL (percent)	Baseline (billions of US dollars)	CHUSTIA central (percent)	CHUSTIA-LSL (percent)
Services	928.4	17.8	5.9	322.3	8.6	5.0
Utilities	5.4	3.2	1.3	3.1	2.3	2.0
Construction	12.8	18.7	6.3	3.5	11.0	5.5
Trade, transport, communications	210.9	25.5	7.9	144.1	9.5	5.5
Private services	489.3	18.4	5.7	123.4	9.9	5.7
Public services	210.1	8.9	4.4	48.3	2.5	2.0
Total	2,813.2	13.3	12.0	3,576.6	10.8	9.7

CHUSTIA = China–US trade and investment agreement; LSL = low service liberalization

Note: Values in 2007 dollars, free-on-board prices.

Source: Model simulations.

intact. We estimate that it would reduce China's gains from a CHUSTIA by 30 percent and US gains by 16 percent.

Output

Tables 2.6A and 2.6B report output projections, measured in value-added terms.[16] These results reflect domestic and international drivers. In both countries, the marginal propensity to consume services is relatively high and so, over time, manufacturing grows less rapidly than services.[17] Table 2.6A shows that China's manufacturing sector will expand by 192 percent between 2010 and 2025, compared to 256 percent for value added as a whole, despite China's strong position in global manufacturing markets. Table 2.6B also shows that US manufacturing will expand less rapidly than the US economy, although the margin of difference will be smaller.

A CHUSTIA would increase total value added in both countries and change its composition. In keeping with results for trade, Chinese value added would rise mostly in manufacturing, while US increases would focus on primary products and services. However, some segments of all sectors would expand with the growth of two-way exports. Because tables 2.6A and 2.6B show changes relative to expanding baselines, even a negative result from a CHUSTIA does not necessarily mean an absolute decline over time. The baseline shows increases in the output of every sector in both countries. Accounting for the trade effects under a CHUSTIA, only the US electrical equipment sector would register a small absolute decline over time. A comparison of the CHUSTIA central and LSL scenarios shows, predictably, smaller output shifts between services and manufacturing. These effects are similar to those computed for employment and will be discussed below.

Employment

As noted above, we do not project changes in the level of employment under different trade agreements. Trade-induced shifts in the composition of jobs could improve the quality of employment: Trade increases the employment share of exporting firms, and research shows that these firms are unusually productive and offer relatively high wages. However, trade policy leads to systematic changes in the composition of employment that could generate significant adjustment burdens. This is especially likely if the changes occur quickly, in inflexible labor markets, in a period of pervasive unemployment, or without sufficient resources for adjustment.

---

16. The model generates sectoral value added at factor cost, but to avoid discrepancies between these measures and GDP at market prices, sectoral value added results are reported scaled up to market prices.

17. For a more detailed discussion of the US case, see Kehoe, Ruhl, and Steinberg (2013).

Table 2.6A Output (value-added) effects for China, 2010–25

	2010 (billions of US dollars)	Baseline 2025 (billions of US dollars)	Change (percent)	CHUSTIA Central (percent)	CHUSTIA LSL (percent)
Primary products	560	1,948	247.6	1.9	0.8
Rice	36	130	258.3	1.9	1.3
Wheat	8	24	221.4	1.6	0.7
Other agriculture	378	1,407	271.9	1.7	0.8
Mining	138	386	179.7	2.8	0.7
Manufactures	1,805	5,269	191.9	3.8	2.4
Food, beverages	139	405	190.6	1.0	0.9
Textiles	60	102	68.4	3.8	2.4
Apparel, footwear	73	207	183.9	4.8	3.8
Chemicals	257	640	148.6	2.8	1.1
Metals	487	1,346	176.4	3.5	2.1
Electrical equipment	142	462	225.3	3.9	2.1
Machinery	299	1,054	252.6	5.0	3.3
Transport equipment	119	420	253.8	2.4	1.1
Other manufactures	228	633	177.3	6.2	4.6

(continues on next page)

Table 2.6A Output (value-added) effects for China, 2010–25 *(continued)*

| | Baseline | | | CHUSTIA | |
	2010 (billions of US dollars)	2025 (billions of US dollars)	Change (percent)	Central (percent)	LSL (percent)
Services	2,484	10,032	303.8	0.8	1.2
Utilities	61	182	197.0	2.7	1.9
Construction	333	1,288	286.4	2.7	2.3
Trade, transport, communications	561	1,619	188.8	-0.1	0.7
Private services	753	2,575	242.0	-1.0	0.5
Public services	776	4,367	462.8	1.6	1.5
Total	4,850	17,249	255.7	1.9	1.5

CHUSTIA = China–US trade and investment agreement; LSL = low service liberalization

Note: Values in 2007 dollars.

Source: Model simulations.

Table 2.6B   Output (value-added) effects for the United States, 2010–25

| | Baseline | | | CHUSTIA | |
	2010 (billions of US dollars)	2025 (billions of US dollars)	Change (percent)	Central (percent)	LSL (percent)
Primary products	275	447	62.3	5.0	6.3
Rice	2	3	35.5	3.5	4.0
Wheat	7	9	25.8	–6.6	–6.0
Other agriculture	144	236	64.4	10.8	11.4
Mining	122	198	62.5	–1.3	0.8
Manufactures	2,163	2,803	29.6	–4.3	–2.2
Food, beverages	295	430	45.9	1.9	1.8
Textiles	50	64	27.7	–4.3	–1.7
Apparel, footwear	28	36	29.1	–8.0	–5.7
Chemicals	364	468	28.4	–1.6	0.3
Metals	296	364	23.0	–5.4	–2.3
Electrical equipment	57	58	2.3	–5.2	–1.6
Machinery	452	532	17.6	–9.0	–5.6
Transport equipment	252	356	41.6	0.6	2.5
Other manufactures	370	495	33.8	–9.4	–7.4

(continues on next page)

55

Table 2.6B Output (value-added) effects for the United States, 2010–25 *(continued)*

| | Baseline | | | CHUSTIA | |
	2010 (billions of US dollars)	2025 (billions of US dollars)	Change (percent)	Central (percent)	LSL (percent)
Services	11,612	17,024	46.6	1.6	0.8
Utilities	241	315	30.5	0.3	0.2
Construction	846	1,458	72.3	1.9	1.3
Trade, transport, communications	2,319	3,377	45.6	1.5	0.8
Private services	4,721	6,712	42.2	1.8	0.8
Public services	3,484	5,162	48.2	1.2	0.7
Total	14,050	20,273	44.3	0.8	0.5

CHUSTIA = China–US trade and investment agreement; LSL = low service liberalization

Note: Values in 2007 dollars.

Source: Model simulations.

Tables 2.7A and 2.7B report employment results.[18] Total employment levels are determined outside the model, based on trends in the working-age population and labor force participation. Along the baseline, Chinese employment peaks in 2015 and then declines slowly thereafter; in the United States, excess unemployment in 2010 is assumed to be eliminated gradually, and employment is then assumed to grow in proportion to the labor force.[19] Sectoral employment levels, however, are determined by the model, and show significant compositional changes even on the baseline. These changes reflect trends in demand, international competition, and especially labor productivity. In China, large declines in employment—at least 5 million workers each—are projected in agriculture, mining, food and beverages, and trade, transport, and communications, all sectors with high expected productivity gains. Large increases in employment—again, at least 5 million workers each—are in turn projected in public services, machinery, and construction, all areas with rising domestic or international demand. In the United States, the projections show more muted effects, as employment is already heavily concentrated in services. Gains would be concentrated in primary products, where international demand will be strong, and services, driven by both domestic and international demand. Manufacturing employment would decline, due partly to the relatively slow growth of demand and partly to rising productivity.

A CHUSTIA would intensify the US shift from manufacturing employment toward services, as the central scenario projects service exports that respond to substantial service liberalization in China. Approximately 500,000 US workers (4.7 percent of manufacturing employment) would shift from manufacturing to services over 15 years under this scenario.[20] As table 2.7B also shows, these

---

18. The GTAP database measures employment in efficiency units—essentially workers that would be employed by a sector if it paid average wages. These numbers are higher than actual employment in high-wage industries and lower in low-wage industries. For the United States, actual initial employment levels are also available, so the tables in this section report more realistic employment measures by applying model-projected rates of increase to actual initial employment data; see Bureau of Economic Analysis, estimates of state employment data, www.bea.gov (accessed on July 8, 2014).

19. Projections of employment are especially difficult in the United States at present, due to the unexpected decline in labor force participation rates. While the baseline itself is sensitive to these assumptions, moderate adjustments in the baseline estimates would not significantly affect the employment effects of trade agreements.

20. As chapter 3 will show, the econometric results in Autor, Dorn, and Hanson (2013) for historical periods are similar to those of input-output models, such as those on which the present CGE estimates are based. Autor, Dorn, and Hanson also find that manufacturing job losses can spill over into unemployment and other adverse effects on localities affected by import competition, or at least did so in the context of the heavy manufacturing job losses of the 2000s. The 500,000 figure is different from the 1 million or so involuntary job loss figure mentioned earlier. The 1 million figure represents cumulative short-term unemployment due to rising imports. The job losses may originate in manufacturing, but then spread to upstream and downstream sectors. The 500,000 figure describes the long-term shift from manufacturing to service employment over a period of 15 years. CHUSTIA would also have an offsetting effect on the US labor market, since increased

Table 2.7A Employment effects for China, 2010–25

	Baseline			CHUSTIA	
	2010 (millions of jobs)	2025 (millions of jobs)	Change (percent)	Central (percent)	LSL (percent)
Primary products	164.5	146.4	−11.0	−0.5	−0.8
Rice	10.8	9.6	−11.1	−0.4	−0.3
Wheat	2.5	2.0	−20.0	−0.7	−0.9
Other agriculture	130.1	120.3	−7.5	−0.6	−0.8
Mining	21.1	14.4	−31.5	0.5	−0.9
Manufactures	160.7	149.2	−7.2	2.1	1.2
Food, beverages	22.6	15.7	−30.5	−1.1	−0.7
Textiles	4.5	2.5	−45.6	2.1	1.3
Apparel, footwear	8.8	8.1	−8.0	3.0	2.5
Chemicals	18.7	15.0	−19.4	1.2	0
Metals	40.2	36.0	−10.5	1.8	0.9
Electrical equipment	9.2	11.0	18.7	2.6	1.2
Machinery	24.6	29.4	19.5	3.4	2.1
Transport equipment	10.0	12.5	25.3	1.0	0
Other manufactures	22.0	18.9	−13.9	4.3	3.2

(continues on next page)

Table 2.7A   Employment effects for China, 2010–25 *(continued)*

| | Baseline | | | CHUSTIA | |
	2010 (millions of jobs)	2025 (millions of jobs)	Change (percent)	Central (percent)	LSL (percent)
Services	426.6	467.6	9.6	−0.5	−0.1
Utilities	8.8	5.9	−33.0	0.7	0.3
Construction	40.7	54.8	34.9	1.1	1.0
Trade, transport, communications	58.3	51.4	−11.9	−1.8	−0.8
Private services	68.2	68.1	−0.2	−2.5	−0.9
Public services	250.6	287.4	14.7	−0.2	−0.1
Total	751.8	763.1	1.5	0	0

CHUSTIA = China–US trade and investment agreement; LSL = low service liberalization

Notes: The model measures and projects employment in "efficiency units" used in the underlying Global Trade Analysis Project data. Model projections, in percentage changes, are then applied to 2010 actual employment data to generate meaningful reports. For China, a 2010 actual employment total is used and allocated to industries using model results. For the United States, 2010 data by industry are from Bureau of Economic Analysis full-time-equivalent employment statistics, retrieved from www.bea.gov/iTable/iTable.cfm?reqid=51&step=51&isuri=1&5102=44 (accessed on February 6, 2014).

Sources: Model simulations; Bureau of Economic Analysis data, www.bea.gov (accessed on July 5, 2014).

Table 2.7B Employment effects for the United States, 2010–25

	Baseline			CHUSTIA	
	2010 (millions of jobs)	2025 (millions of jobs)	Change (percent)	Central (percent)	LSL (percent)
Primary products	1.74	2.06	18.2	3.6	5.3
Rice	0.02	0.02	–1.6	1.7	2.4
Wheat	0.05	0.05	–9.8	–8.3	–7.8
Other agriculture	1.03	1.22	18.8	8.0	9.2
Mining	0.64	0.77	20.1	–2.5	0
Manufactures	11.23	10.83	–3.6	–4.7	–2.4
Food, beverages	1.56	1.66	6.1	0.7	1.1
Textiles	0.23	0.22	–5.3	–4.7	–2.0
Apparel, footwear	0.18	0.18	–2.0	–7.9	–5.6
Chemicals	1.86	1.76	–5.1	–2.1	0
Metals	1.60	1.46	–9.0	–5.6	–2.5
Electrical equipment	0.35	0.30	–13.5	–3.3	0.2
Machinery	2.06	1.79	–13.1	–9.1	–5.7
Transport equipment	1.32	1.42	7.9	0	2.2
Other manufactures	2.08	2.05	–1.4	–9.7	–7.6

(continues on next page)

Table 2.7B Employment effects for the United States, 2010–25 *(continued)*

	2010 (millions of jobs)	Baseline 2025 (millions of jobs)	Change (percent)	CHUSTIA Central (percent)	LSL (percent)
Services	107.62	115.46	7.3	0.4	0.1
Utilities	0.55	0.52	–4.8	–0.6	–0.3
Construction	5.42	6.86	26.5	0.5	0.6
Trade, transport, communications	21.69	23.06	6.3	0.5	0.2
Private services	41.67	43.57	4.6	0.7	0.2
Public services	38.30	41.45	8.2	0	0
Total	120.60	128.36	6.4	0	0

CHUSTIA = China–US trade and investment agreement; LSL = low service liberalization

Notes: The model measures and projects employment in "efficiency units" used in the underlying Global Trade Analysis Project data. Model projections, in percentage changes, are then applied to 2010 actual employment data to generate meaningful reports. For China, a 2010 actual employment total is used and allocated to industries using model results. For the United States, 2010 data by industry are from Bureau of Economic Analysis full-time-equivalent employment statistics, retrieved from www.bea.gov/iTable/itable.cfm?reqid=51&step=51#reqid=51&step=51&isuri=1&5102=44 (accessed on February 6, 2014).

Sources: Model simulations; Bureau of Economic Analysis data, www.bea.gov (accessed on July 5, 2014).

shifts would be cut roughly in half under a CHUSTIA-LSL. Service employment losses in China and gains in the United States would be similarly moderated. In other words, low service liberalization, whether due to lower initial barriers or less ambitious agreements, would mean more modest adjustments in the labor markets of both countries, but also lower overall benefits.

Manufacturing employment is of particular concern in the United States given that 5.6 million manufacturing jobs were lost between 2000 and 2010 (Henderson 2012), and approximately one-quarter of the losses during 2000–2007 have been attributed to trade with China (Autor, Dorn, and Hanson 2013). Since the depth of the recession in 2010, manufacturing employment has recovered somewhat, but most projections still envision declines in the longer term (Kehoe, Ruhl, and Steinberg 2013). The baseline shows approximately 400,000 fewer manufacturing jobs in 2025 than in 2010[21] due to technology and international competition. Total manufacturing job declines rise to roughly 900,000 jobs under central CHUSTIA assumptions and to 660,000 jobs under CHUSTIA-LSL assumptions. These losses amount to only 11 percent and 8 percent of the annualized rate of manufacturing job losses experienced from 2000 to 2010, but nevertheless argue for closer analysis and mitigating policies.

Large manufacturing job losses in the 2000s did not lead to overall unemployment; US unemployment rates fell to a low of 4.6 percent during the decade. However, an apparent reduction in the quality of jobs—sometimes portrayed as a shift from manufacturing to fast food restaurants—may have contributed to disappointing wage trends. To understand this connection, it is important to recognize that the 2000s were unusual from a macroeconomic perspective, in that the United States dramatically increased its trade deficits during this period. In effect the United States shifted jobs from import-competing sectors not to export jobs but to jobs in services to meet domestic demand. As average wages in service industries are lower than those in manufacturing, these compositional changes most likely contributed to wage stagnation. There is no reason to expect such results, however, from a balanced expansion of exports and imports, as would likely occur with a new trade agreement. Export industries, especially exported service industries, pay substantially higher wages than other sectors of the economy. A shift from import-competing jobs to export-based jobs should therefore have wage-boosting effects.

A CHUSTIA would increase the role of trade in both economies, raising exports by 10 percent in China and 13 percent in the United States. This should increase the availability of good jobs in both countries. As table 2.8 estimates,

---

demand for US service exports would support American jobs. As spelled out in chapter 3, for each $1 billion increase in service exports, around 4,500 US jobs will be supported.

21. This projection is consistent with those of the Bureau of Labor Statistics.

Table 2.8   Employment generated by exports, 2025

Indicator	China	United States
Labor force (millions of jobs)	763.1	128.4
Direct employment in exports (millions of jobs)	30.0	7.7
Direct and indirect employment/direct employment (millions of jobs)	2.78	1.67
Direct and indirect employment due to exports (millions of jobs)	83.4	12.8
Additional exports under CHUSTIA (percent)	10.3	13.3
Additional export-related employment under CHUSTIA (millions of jobs)	8.6	1.7

CHUSTIA = China–US trade and investment agreement

Sources: Model simulations; OECD Trade in Value Added database, stats.oecd.org (accessed on July 5, 2014).

these changes would result in 8.6 million new export-related jobs in China and 1.7 million more export-related jobs in the United States. Andrew B. Bernard and colleagues (2007) show that US exporting firms are 11 percent more skill-intensive than other firms and, even holding skill levels constant, pay 6 percent higher wages. These differences appear to be larger for service exports. J. Bradford Jensen (2011, table 3.3) reports that US jobs in tradable business services pay on average $66,454 per year compared to $42,226 in nontradable business services and $49,952 in tradable manufacturing. In other words, compensation in traded services is one-third higher than in the manufacturing jobs that might be eliminated. These studies did not analyze the characteristics of firms that succumb to import competition, but contrasts with those are probably still greater.

However, a CHUSTIA would also increase imports and consequently the possibility of unemployment or difficult job transitions for some workers. Many of the workers displaced from low-wage, import-competing manufacturing jobs will not be able to obtain the new higher-wage jobs created. David Autor, David Dorn, and Gordon Hanson (2013) show that transitions in the past decade, in the context of much greater manufacturing job losses, have been costly for workers, federal subsidy programs, and the communities where unemployed workers live. Chapter 3 estimates that, at the upper bound, higher Chinese imports under the central CHUSTIA scenario could increase the number of dislocated workers by 1.04 million between 2015 and 2025, or 104,000 workers per year during the implementation period. Combining our $130 billion estimate of trade gains under CHUSTIA with the estimate of 104,000 annual job dislocations, chapter 3 estimates that $1.25 million of benefits would be generated per adversely affected worker, representing approximately 12.5 times their estimated lifetime costs. Since this result uses an upper-bound estimate of labor dislocation, the benefits per worker may be larger, and adding investment-related gains would further increase the margin. Moreover, the gains from the agreement would continue indefinitely and grow over time, while adjustments would mostly end with the implementation period. Yet no matter how high the ratio of gains to potential costs, compensation may be politically and practically difficult to deliver to the right people and communities. Chapter 3 addresses these challenges in detail; sharing the benefits of trade agreements broadly is essential if their economic promise is to be fully realized.[22]

Macroeconomic Rebalancing and a CHUSTIA

So far this study has addressed the microeconomics of the China–US relationship, even though recent discussions have emphasized macroeconomic issues. For over a decade, both countries have had unusually large macroeconomic imbalances. However, significant progress has been made—China's current account surplus has declined from 10 percent in 2007 to under 3 percent in 2012, with preliminary data indicating China's 2013 surplus will be even lower, while the US current account deficit has declined from 5 percent in 2007 to 2.3 percent in 2013.[23] Both countries are taking steps to reduce the imbalances that remain. China has tightened credit and permitted wages to rise and, until recently, allowed steady appreciation in the exchange value of the renminbi. The United States has started fiscal consolidation and is gradually curtailing quantitative easing. But these policy initiatives are working slowly; rebalancing is politically difficult and still has a long way to go in both countries.

Could concerted Chinese–US policies help? US officials have asked for faster renminbi appreciation, while China has argued for an early end to US quantitative easing and more fiscal restraint. Some believe that introducing currency provisions into trade agreements could intensify macroeconomic cooperation. The proposed Bipartisan Congressional Trade Priorities Act of 2014—an early attempt at new fast-track legislation to permit the president to negotiate FTAs subject to an up-or-down vote by Congress—directs negotiators to include provisions to ensure "that trade partners avoid manipulating exchange rates, such as through cooperative mechanisms, enforceable rules, reporting, monitoring, transparency, or other means, as appropriate."[24]

The congressional proposal does not explain what exchange rate provisions would be required and past agreements have not included such terms (see chapter 17). While we cannot estimate how such provisions might affect

---

22. The benefits of trade liberalization become Pareto-optimal—benefiting everyone—if trade policy is accompanied through distributive policies that transfer a part of the gains from trade to those adversely affected. The theory does not suggest any automatic mechanism to ensure Pareto optimality.

23. Based on data from the International Monetary Fund, External Balance Assessment, www.imf.org (accessed on July 8, 2014); US Bureau of Economic Analysis, balance of payments, www.bea.gov (accessed on July 8, 2014); China's State Administration of Foreign Exchange, balance of payments, www.safe.gov.cn (accessed on July 8, 2014).

24. Staff of the Senate Finance Committee and Ways and Means Committee, "Overview of the Bipartisan Congressional Trade Priorities Act of 2014," www.finance.senate.gov (accessed on July 2, 2014).

a CHUSTIA, we can examine policies that would accelerate macroeconomic rebalancing, policies that both China and the United States are pursuing in any case. Under current macroeconomic conditions, trade liberalization and rebalancing policies appear to reinforce each other. Because Chinese trade barriers are higher than US barriers, trade liberalization by both countries would add more net demand for imports in China than in the United States. Similarly, the rebalancing policies now contemplated would add net demand in China (in part satisfied through net imports) and reduce net demand in the United States (meaning more net exports).

Accelerated rebalancing would mean an increase in Chinese demand and reduction in US demand, so to keep trade balances constant the renminbi would have to appreciate. In contrast, mutual liberalization through a CHUSTIA would require the renminbi to depreciate, as its initial effect would be a relatively large increase in Chinese demand for foreign products. Thus, if the two policies were implemented together, they would require smaller exchange rate changes than either alone. They also would impose smaller dislocations on many sectors, making the politics of cooperation more attractive. The policy combination echoes a standard recommendation to countries considering liberalization in the context of a trade surplus: They should act quickly on trade liberalization and capture the associated gains, rather than allow appreciation alone to reduce surpluses.

The fortuitous coincidence of macro- and microeconomic goals holds under present macroeconomic circumstances. But macroeconomic goals tend to have shorter time frames than microeconomic ones. For example, the macroeconomic goal of lowering the US unemployment rate has a horizon of three years of less, while the microeconomic goal of raising US productivity performance is at least a five-year project. Moreover, macroeconomic conditions often change; the present sluggish conditions will not necessarily persist. Cooperation on both macro- and microeconomic policies is important, but our results do not provide a case for linking them permanently in a trade agreement.

The Macroeconomics of the Baseline

The macroeconomic assumptions built into the baseline scenario are simple and conservative. As already noted, trade balances are set at 2010 levels in real dollar terms, meaning that they will fall relative to GDP over time. The resulting ratios of trade balance to GDP are plotted in figure 2.3 (left scale). Also, China and the United States are assumed to converge to and then maintain full employment. In effect, the baseline already includes some rebalancing—demand shifts toward sustainable combinations of domestic and international demand in both countries. Under present circumstances, this implies more consumption and a lower rate of international savings in China, and less consumption (by government or the private sector) and a higher rate

Figure 2.3   Baseline trade imbalances (left scale) and real renminbi/dollar exchange rate (right scale), 2010–25

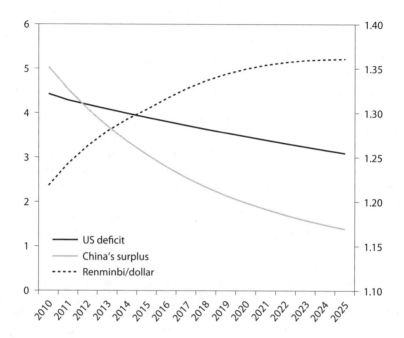

Source: Model calculations.

of international savings (or more precisely, lower dissavings) in the United States.

Rebalancing cannot be accomplished, however, through demand changes alone; it also requires exchange rate changes to switch expenditures to the right combination of domestic and international products. The baseline model projects that the gradual rebalancing built into the baseline—the reduction in China's trade surplus and the US trade deficit relative to GDP—will require the real value of the renminbi to rise from an index value of 100 in 2007 to 1.36 in 2025 (see figure 2.3, right scale).[25] The projection shows that this 36 percent real renminbi appreciation, relative to its 2007 level, would proceed more rapidly in the beginning of the simulation period (around 2 percent per year) than in its later stages (under 1 percent per year).

---

25. The year 2007 corresponds to the year used to assemble the GTAP database, which contains many of the technical parameters used in our simulation model. The base year—the start of our simulations—is 2010, and some key macroeconomic variables were updated with actual data for that year.

Can the above results be interpreted as exchange rate projections? The CGE model is designed to track the long-term structural effects of trade policy changes and not exchange rate movements. It does not include explanations of how short-term capital flows might change, and those changes often dominate exchange rate movements in the short and medium terms.[26] Rather, the model assumes a constant trade balance, or no changes in capital movements beyond the reinvestment of foreign income. It thus provides information about the real exchange rate only to the extent that the capital flow assumptions are correct.

The projections of the model for years that are now behind us correspond reasonably well to observed trends (figure 2.3). The nominal exchange rate of the renminbi to the dollar was 7.61:1 in 2007 and 6.31:1 in 2012, so in this interval, the nominal renminbi appreciated by 21 percent relative to the dollar. However, real renminbi appreciation against the dollar during this period was 28 percent, counting the more rapid rise of the CPI in China than in the United States. Thus in 2012 the actual real exchange rate index stood at 1.28, close to the model-projected value of 1.27 for that year. The model generated these results using exogenous values for capital flows and the trade balance—actual values up to 2010, held constant thereafter. The accuracy of subsequent projections will likewise depend on whether the model's capital flow assumptions are valid in future years.

An Accelerated Rebalancing Scenario

Although much rebalancing has already occurred, policymakers in both countries would welcome further progress. We therefore examine an accelerated rebalancing scenario by reducing Chinese and US international imbalances more quickly than in the baseline solution. Specifically, the scenario assumes that China's domestic demand will be increased to drive its net international savings to zero, while US demand will be reduced—and its net international savings increased—by an equal amount, requiring no adjustments in net spending in other economies.

The accelerated rebalancing initiative is assumed to take effect over five years starting in 2015, similar to the CHUSTIA. By 2020 it would drive China's global trade surplus to zero, compared to a baseline value of 2 percent of GDP. This amounts to a reduction in China's trade balance of $286 billion. We assume that the US global trade balance would increase by the same amount, while trade balances in other countries would be unaffected.[27] Various events or policies could bring about these effects—cyclical developments, tax policy

---

26. Unanticipated economic shocks, usually transmitted through variations in the demand for and supply of capital assets, typically generate smaller quantity adjustments in production and correspondingly lead to larger price adjustments, including in exchange rates and sometimes overshooting eventual equilibrium prices. See Obstfeld and Rogoff (2005).

27. Beyond 2020, absolute current account levels are again kept constant.

changes to raise consumption in China and reduce it in the United States, corresponding government expenditure changes, or combinations of these. What matters is the size and, to a lesser extent, the composition of net expenditure changes. As the effects of accelerated rebalancing are most evident just when the scenario is fully implemented in 2020, this section reports results up to 2020 rather than 2025.

Table 2.9 summarizes rebalancing alternatives. The first two columns show the already substantial rebalancing incorporated in the baseline between 2010 and 2020. In China, 8 percent of GDP is projected to shift to consumption from investment and net exports, while in the United States, 3 percent of GDP is expected to shift from consumption to investment and net exports. Significant parts of this change have already taken place. The accelerated rebalancing scenario would increase shifts from net exports to household and government consumption by a further 2 percent of GDP in China, and from consumption to net exports by an additional 1.6 percent of GDP in the United States. But these opposite changes in Chinese and US domestic demand would not, by themselves, yield a new trade equilibrium. Real exchange rates would also have to adjust, as explained in the famous discussion of the transfer problem in Keynes (1929). Because domestic demand is biased toward purchases of home-produced goods, additional Chinese demand tends to raise demand for Chinese-produced goods, while falling US demand tends to reduce demand for US-produced goods. Therefore, the prices of Chinese-produced goods have to rise relative to US-produced goods to achieve full employment in both countries. Such market pressures on prices and exchange rates will lift the real value of the renminbi.

The simulations show that 2.3 percent additional real appreciation of the renminbi-dollar exchange rate (table 2.9, fifth column) would be required for accelerated rebalancing, that is, to effect a $286 billion decrease in the Chinese trade balance and an equal increase in the US trade balance. Rebalancing and real exchange rate changes are two sides of a coin. Without real exchange rate changes, demand rebalancing cannot be completed, and without demand changes real exchange rate changes cannot be sustained. Faster rebalancing would accelerate renminbi appreciation compared with the baseline scenario. As a result, Chinese exports would fall by 1.4 percent of GDP and US exports would rise by 1 percent of GDP, with imports moving in the opposite direction. There would be equal and opposite changes in the global trade balances of China and the United States, but the change in their bilateral trade balance would not be as large.[28] In 2020 China's bilateral exports to the United States would be 7 percent lower, and US exports to China would be 11 percent higher, reducing China's bilateral surplus against the United States from $553 billion to $460 billion. Thus, about one-third of the $286 billion shift in the global

---

28. Bilateral trade balances depend on microeconomic factors and, despite media interest, are not significant in most economic analyses. This paper focuses mainly on how the two countries' global trade might be affected.

Table 2.9 Macroeconomic effects of policy alternatives, 2010–20

| | Baseline | | | Accelerated rebalancing | | CHUSTIA | | Both | |
	2010	2020	Change 2010–20	2020	Change from baseline	2020	Change from baseline	2020	Change from baseline
Real exchange rate index									
Dollar value of renminbi (2007=100)	121.8	134.9	10.8	137.7	2.3	133.8	–0.4	136.1	1.7
Chinese demand (percent GDP)									
Consumption	35.0	43.4	8.4	45.3	1.9	43.4	0.1	45.3	2.0
Investment	44.0	38.6	–5.4	38.6	0	38.7	0.1	38.7	0.1
Government	16.0	16.0	0	16.1	0.1	15.9	–0.1	16.0	–0.1
Exports	29.8	24.1	–5.8	22.7	–1.4	26.1	2.0	24.8	0.8
Imports	24.8	22.1	–2.7	22.7	0.6	24.2	2.1	24.8	2.8
Trade balance	5.0	2.0	–3.1	0	–2.0	2.0	0	0	–2.0
US demand (percent GDP)									
Consumption	72.6	69.6	–3.0	68.0	–1.6	69.6	0	68.0	–1.6
Investment	16.0	18.0	2.0	18.0	0	18.0	0	18.0	0
Government	15.9	15.9	0	15.9	0	15.9	0	15.9	0
Exports	11.4	13.7	2.3	14.8	1.0	15.1	1.4	16.2	2.5
Imports	15.8	17.2	1.4	16.6	–0.6	18.6	1.4	18.1	0.9
Trade balance	–4.4	–3.5	1.0	–1.9	1.6	–3.4	0	–1.9	1.6

CHUSTIA = China–US trade and investment agreement

Note: Values in 2007 dollars, projected relative prices.

Source: Model simulations.

trade balances of the two countries would involve their bilateral balances, with the rest coming from lower Chinese and higher US net exports to the rest of the world.

Accelerated Rebalancing and a CHUSTIA

The rebalancing scenario and a CHUSTIA could be pursued in parallel, making an attractive policy combination. When the two policies have the same-signed effects—US exports rise under both a CHUSTIA and rebalancing—the increase is greater than under either policy alone. When the two policies have opposite-signed effects, their combination yields a small net effect. In many cases, the combination results in moderate changes and lower adjustment costs.

Accelerated rebalancing and a CHUSTIA would affect exchange rates in opposite ways. Under accelerated rebalancing, the renminbi would appreciate faster than in the baseline scenario to help drive demand from Chinese to US products. Under a CHUSTIA, the renminbi would appreciate more slowly than in the baseline, as liberalization in both countries would generate relatively strong demand for US products by taking a bigger bite out of China's higher barriers. The net effect would be moderate renminbi appreciation, an attractive outcome for policymakers interested in keeping the currency stable. Rebalancing would draw additional imports from the United States without requiring larger renminbi changes. Because it would bring some Chinese production back home, it would also dampen dislocations in US labor markets. Thus, both policies would have more moderate effects than either alone for trade expansion and the exchange rate. Chinese exports would grow 0.8 percent (in contrast to –1.4 percent with rebalancing and 2.0 percent with a CHUSTIA), and US imports would grow 0.9 percent (in contrast to –0.6 percent with rebalancing and 1.4 percent with a CHUSTIA).

Figure 2.4 shows that accelerated rebalancing would result in earlier renminbi appreciation, but that the gap relative to the baseline would later shrink, because the baseline itself projects additional rebalancing over time. In contrast, a CHUSTIA would slow renminbi appreciation, because liberalization provides an alternative and economically more productive way to make US goods more competitive in the Chinese market. The two policies together would yield results similar to the baseline.

Sectoral Implications of Rebalancing

The moderating effect of combining the two policies is especially evident in the sectoral results reported in tables 2.10A and 2.10B. This is because accelerated rebalancing and a CHUSTIA would have opposite effects on structural trends in the two economies. Accelerated rebalancing would speed up long-term structural change in China and slow it in the United States. China is becoming more consumer-friendly and service-oriented as it develops,

Figure 2.4 Real renminbi/dollar rate in alternative simulations (2007=1), 2010–25

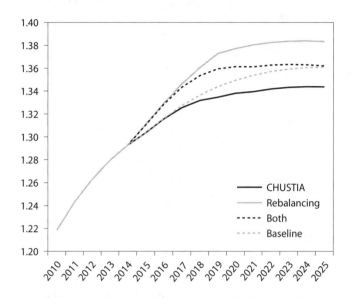

CHUSTIA = China–US trade and investment agreement
Source: Model calculations.

and as rebalancing would contribute to this shift, it would reduce manufacturing employment in China by –2 percent compared to the baseline. While the United States is also becoming more service-oriented over time, it got ahead of long-term trends through international borrowing in the 2000s. Therefore rebalancing would slow the trend and increase US manufacturing employment by 4.1 percent.

A CHUSTIA, in contrast, would increase manufacturing employment in China by 1.8 percent and reduce it in the United States by –3.2 percent. Since accelerated rebalancing and a CHUSTIA have largely opposite effects, implementing both policies together could dampen sectoral dislocations in both countries. (One exception is in primary industries in the United States, where the policies have similar positive effects.) In most sectors, the combined policies produce smaller net results. With both policies US manufacturing employment would increase by 0.5 percent—not a decline, as under a CHUSTIA, but also not as much growth as under rebalancing. Modest transitions, in turn, give businesses and individuals more time to adjust to change.

The TPP, RCEP, and CHUSTIA

A CHUSTIA would potentially join and complement an extensive negotiating agenda in the Asia-Pacific. In this section, we compare five possible trade policy

Table 2.10A   Output (value-added) effects for China, 2010–25

| | Baseline | | | Policy scenarios, 2025 | | |
	2010	2025	Change (percent)	Rebalance (percent)	CHUSTIA (percent)	Both (percent)
	Value added (billions of dollars)					
Primary products	560	1,948	247.6	−0.8	1.1	0.2
Manufacturing	1,805	5,269	191.9	−3.1	3.0	−0.2
Services	2,484	10,032	303.8	0	0.5	0.3
Total	4,850	17,249	255.7	−1.1	1.4	0.1
	Employment (millions of jobs)					
Primary products	164	146	−11.0	0.6	−0.6	0
Manufacturing	161	149	−7.2	−2.0	1.8	−0.1
Services	427	468	9.6	0.5	−0.4	0
Total	752	763	1.5	0	0	0

CHUSTIA = China–US trade and investment agreement
Note: Values in 2007 dollars.
Source: Model simulations.

Table 2.10B   Output (value-added) effects for the United States, 2010–25

| | Baseline | | | Policy scenarios, 2025 | | |
	2010	2025	Change (percent)	Rebalance (percent)	CHUSTIA (percent)	Both (percent)
	Value added (billions of dollars)					
Primary products	275	447	62.3	3.8	3.9	7.7
Manufacturing	2,163	2,803	29.6	4.2	−3.0	1.2
Services	11,612	17,024	46.6	−0.5	1.0	0.6
Total	14,050	20,273	44.3	0.2	0.5	0.9
	Employment (millions of jobs)					
Primary products	2	2	18.2	3.5	2.9	6.2
Manufacturing	11	11	−3.6	4.1	−3.2	0.5
Services	108	115	7.3	−0.5	0.3	−0.2
Total	121	128	6.4	0	0	0

CHUSTIA = China–US trade and investment agreement
Note: Values in 2007 dollars.
Source: Model simulations.

scenarios: the TPP, RCEP, CHUSTIA, parallel implementation of all three, and an expansive agreement encompassing the Asia-Pacific region, called FTAAPX, as explained below.

The TPP negotiations—based on a 2005 agreement among Brunei, Chile, New Zealand, and Singapore—have now expanded to 12 countries, and Korea, the Philippines, Thailand, Laos, and Indonesia have indicated an interest in membership. While negotiators are committed to concluding an agreement in the near future, they are said to envision a living agreement that makes subsequent expansions possible. China has recently expressed support for regional agreements and is said to be studying the TPP.[29]

The RCEP negotiations are at an early stage and there is much uncertainty about their ambition and progress. FTAs are already in place among the 10 ASEAN countries, between them and all other RCEP partners, and among many pairs of these partners. However, there are no agreements among the region's largest economies: China, India, Japan, and Korea. China, Japan, and Korea signed an investment treaty in 2013 and a trade negotiation is also under way, but political frictions make an early agreement unlikely. China–Korea negotiations are more advanced and are likely to succeed. Still, questions persist about what RCEP can accomplish beyond providing an umbrella for existing agreements.

Most optimistically, the trans-Pacific and Asian tracks would converge into a broad regional agreement that would include most economies on both tracks plus other APEC members such as Russia and Taiwan. This is the endpoint to APEC's Yokohama Vision (APEC 2010), which outlines a huge trading area including both China and the United States under a single set of rules. We find that significant progress toward freer trade in the Asia-Pacific could be achieved through parallel TPP, RCEP, and CHUSTIA agreements. This path would not lead to a single set of rules right away, but it might be achieved more quickly than other options.

Two questions arise. First, to what extent could the three parallel agreements deliver the benefits associated with a single, regionwide agreement? In other words, would completing the missing China–US link make a dent in closing the gap between the TPP and RCEP agreements and regional free trade? Second, would three parallel agreements mitigate the adverse effects of a CHUSTIA on third countries?

Comparative Results

To address these issues, we compare a CHUSTIA to potential TPP and RCEP agreements, as well as two broader regional trade policy scenarios. The TPP scenario included in this comparison is a 16-country configuration of the agreement, consisting of the current 12 negotiating countries[30] plus Indonesia, Korea, the Philippines, and Thailand. In addition, we examine a scenario that

---

29. B. Spegele and T. Catan, "China Suggests Shift on US-Led Trade Pact," *Wall Street Journal*, May 31, 2013.

30. Simulations based on other configurations of TPP membership, including the current 12 negotiating parties, are reported in Petri et al. (2012b) and on the website asiapacifictrade.org.

assumes the parallel implementation of CHUSTIA, TPP, and RCEP, without an overarching agreement to connect the three. Finally, we explore a regional free trade area that includes all economies in the TPP and RCEP, even if they are not APEC members. This requires adding India and smaller ASEAN economies (Cambodia, Laos, and Myanmar) to the 21-country APEC grouping and thus represents an extended version of the Free Trade Area of the Asia-Pacific proposed by APEC, which we call FTAAPX.

Figure 2.5 summarizes how these agreements cover the economic links of the Asia-Pacific region, defined as all economies that are members of the TPP-16, RCEP, or APEC. Dark grey cells indicate a rigorous, TPP-style template. Light grey cells are covered by RCEP, and those of an intermediate grey are covered by the CHUSTIA. Blank cells would be addressed only by a broad FTAAP.[31]

Table 2.11 shows that the TPP, RCEP, and CHUSTIA would all deliver significant and roughly similar global income gains by 2025. Among them, the RCEP would generate the largest benefits ($545 billion), followed by the CHUSTIA ($403 billion) and then the TPP-16 ($334 billion). An important difference among these alternatives is that the CHUSTIA would channel benefits mainly to China and the United States, so for these two countries it would be preferable to the other two agreements. The three agreements together, however, would generate far higher gains of $1.186 trillion. The FTAAPX would lead to the best outcome with benefits of $1.869 trillion. These results show that the three smaller agreements are complementary, and also that the broadest agreements generate the greatest benefits. If the three smaller agreements were substitutes—covering mostly overlapping trade flows—they would yield little more value together than individually. Yet their joint benefits are only slightly lower than the sum of their individual benefits ($1.281 trillion). Thus, overlaps between agreements—for example, Malaysia–Japan trade would be covered by both the TPP and RCEP—are not nearly as significant as differences.

Table 2.12 reports export comparisons. This table shows some significant trade diversion and preference erosion effects for countries not included in agreements. China's exports would decline by $108 billion under the TPP-16, and Europe's by $158 billion if all three smaller agreements were implemented. These results indicate the pressures that are likely to argue for expansion if the megaregional initiatives are realized. The TPP, RCEP, and CHUSTIA taken together would generate export gains that are nearly as large as the sum of their independent effects, again confirming their complementarity.[32]

---

31. Some of these links are covered by bilateral agreements not shown in the chart.

32. Comparing income gains in table 2.11 with export increases in table 2.12 indicates that income gains are approximately half as large as export gains, and around one-quarter as large as two-way trade increases, assuming import effects comparable to export effects. Hufbauer, Schott, and Wong (2010) report a value of around 0.4 for a comparable ratio.

Figure 2.5 Schematic network of Asia-Pacific trade agreements

	CN	CL	MX	PE	US	BD	CH	HK	IN	ID	JP	KR	ML	PH	SG	TW	TH	VN	OA	AU	NZ	RU
Canada **CN**		T	T	T	T	T			T	T	T	T	T	T	T	T	T	T		T	T	
Chile **CL**	T		T	T	T	T			T	T	T	T	T	T	T	T	T	T		T	T	
Mexico **MX**	T	T		T	T	T			T	T	T	T	T	T	T	T	T	T		T	T	
Peru **PE**	T	T	T		T	T			T	T	T	T	T	T	T	T	T	T		T	T	
United States **US**	T	T	T	T		T	C			C	T	T	T	T	T	T	T	T		T	T	
Brunei **BD**	T	T	T	T	T		R		R	TR	TR	TR	TR	TR	TR	TR	TR	TR	R	TR	TR	
China **CH**					C	R			R	R	R	R	R	R	R	R	R	R	R	R	R	
Hong Kong **HK**																						
India **IN**						R	R			R	R	R	R	R	R	R	R	R	R	R	R	
Indonesia **ID**	T	T	T	T	T	TR	R		R		TR	TR	TR	TR	TR	TR	TR	TR	R	TR	TR	
Japan **JP**	T	T	T	T	T	TR	R		R	TR		TR	TR	TR	TR	TR	TR	TR	R	TR	TR	
Korea **KR**	T	T	T	T	T	TR	R		R	TR	TR		TR	TR	TR	TR	TR	TR	R	TR	TR	
Malaysia **ML**	T	T	T	T	T	TR	R		R	TR	TR	TR		TR	TR	TR	TR	TR	R	TR	TR	
Philippines **PH**	T	T	T	T	T	TR	R		R	TR	TR	TR	TR		TR	TR	TR	TR	R	TR	TR	
Singapore **SG**	T	T	T	T	T	TR	R		R	TR	TR	TR	TR	TR		TR	TR	TR	R	TR	TR	
Taiwan **TW**																						
Thailand **TH**	T	T	T	T	T	TR	R		R	TR	TR	TR	TR	TR	TR			TR	R	TR	TR	
Vietnam **VN**	T	T	T	T	T	TR	R		R	TR	TR	TR	TR	TR	TR		TR		R	TR	TR	
Other ASEAN **OA**									R	R	R	R	R	R	R		R	R		R	R	
Australia **AU**	T	T	T	T	T	TR	R		R	TR	TR	TR	TR	TR	TR		TR	TR	R		TR	
New Zealand **NZ**	T	T	T	T	T	TR	R		R	TR	TR	TR	TR	TR	TR		TR	TR	R	TR		
Russia **RU**																						

CHUSTIA = China–US trade and investment agreement; R = Regional Comprehensive Economic Partnership; T = Trans-Pacific Partnership-16

Notes: Multiple letters represent flows covered by more than one agreement. Grays indicate the quality of the template (darker means more rigorous). Table does not include other partnership agreements.

Source: Authors' compilation.

Table 2.11 Income gains under alternative FTAs, 2025

Economy	GDP 2025 (billions of 2007 US dollars)	Income gains (billions of 2007 US dollars)					Change from baseline (percent)				
		TPP-16	RCEP	CHUSTIA	All three	FTAAPX	TPP-16	RCEP	CHUSTIA	All three	FTAAPX
Americas	24,867	117.0	2.5	120.1	228.7	309.8	0.5	0	0.5	0.9	1.2
Canada	1,978	9.3	-0.1	-4.4	4.0	21.6	0.5	0	-0.2	0.2	1.1
Chile	292	3.1	0	0.1	3.0	6.7	1.1	0	0	1.0	2.3
Mexico	2,004	30.9	2.8	-4.8	26.1	73.1	1.5	0.1	-0.2	1.3	3.6
Peru	320	5.2	0	-0.3	4.4	6.0	1.6	0	-0.1	1.4	1.9
United States	20,273	68.4	-0.1	129.6	191.2	202.4	0.3	0	0.6	0.9	1.0
Asia	34,901	230.3	530.2	296.5	970.1	1,374.0	0.7	1.5	0.8	2.8	3.9
Brunei	20	0.4	1.0	0	1.1	1.1	1.8	4.7	0	5.6	5.5
China	17,249	-82.4	210.8	330.3	454.3	581.9	-0.5	1.2	1.9	2.6	3.4
Hong Kong	406	-1.3	30.0	0	28.9	53.8	-0.3	7.4	0	7.1	13.3
India	5,233	-6.9	86.5	-6.3	72.6	213.6	-0.1	1.7	-0.1	1.4	4.1
Indonesia	1,549	54.2	16.8	-3.1	50.4	36.8	3.5	1.1	-0.2	3.3	2.4
Japan	5,338	83.6	76.3	-5.1	136.5	157.0	1.6	1.1	-0.2	2.6	2.9
Korea	2,117	43.4	70.7	-5.4	91.0	112.8	2.0	3.3	-0.3	4.3	5.3
Malaysia	431	28.4	12.9	-2.0	35.4	40.5	6.6	3.0	-0.5	8.2	9.4
Philippines	322	20.5	7.0	-1.0	22.2	15.6	6.4	2.2	-0.3	6.9	4.9
Singapore	415	7.7	1.0	-1.2	6.5	9.2	1.9	0.2	-0.3	1.6	2.2
Taiwan	840	-6.4	-16.1	-3.4	-22.7	46.5	-0.8	-1.9	-0.4	-2.7	5.5

(continues on next page)

Table 2.11 Income gains under alternative FTAs, 2025 *(continued)*

Economy	GDP 2025 (billions of 2007 US dollars)	Income gains (billions of 2007 US dollars)					Change from baseline (percent)				
		TPP-16	RCEP	CHUSTIA	All three	FTAAPX	TPP-16	RCEP	CHUSTIA	All three	FTAAPX
Asia											
Thailand	558	42.2	14.7	-3.4	40.6	28.1	7.6	2.6	-0.6	7.3	5.0
Vietnam	340	47.5	17.1	-2.5	52.6	73.8	14.0	5.0	-0.7	15.5	21.7
Other ASEAN	83	-0.5	1.5	-0.2	0.7	3.3	-0.6	1.8	-0.2	0.8	3.9
Oceania	1,634	10.7	18.6	0.3	26.2	29.2	0.7	1.1	0	1.6	1.8
Australia	1,433	7.4	16.8	0.2	22.0	24.3	0.5	1.2	0	1.5	1.7
New Zealand	201	3.3	1.8	0	4.2	4.9	1.7	0.9	0	2.1	2.4
Others	41,820	-24.2	-6.8	-14.0	-39.4	156.3	-0.1	0	0	-0.1	0.4
Europe	22,714	-4.9	5.1	-1.5	-0.4	-36.4	0	0	0	0	-0.2
Russia	2,865	-3.0	-5.3	-1.7	-9.2	271.7	-0.1	-0.2	-0.1	-0.3	9.5
Rest of world	16,241	-16.3	-6.6	-10.8	-29.8	-79.0	-0.1	0	-0.1	-0.2	-0.5
World	103,223	333.8	544.6	402.9	1,185.6	1,869.3	0.3	0.5	0.4	1.1	1.8
Memorandum											
TPP-16	38,016	455.5	238.6	96.5	691.3	813.9	1.2	0.6	0.3	1.8	2.2
RCEP	36,535	248.7	534.9	300.2	990.1	1,302.9	0.7	1.5	0.9	2.8	3.7
APEC	58,951	16.9	458.1	421.7	1,142.5	1,767.8	0.6	0.8	0.7	1.9	3.0

APEC = Asia-Pacific Economic Cooperation; ASEAN = Association of Southeast Asian Nations; CHUSTIA = China–US trade and investment agreement; FTA = free trade agreement; FTAAPX = Expanded Free Trade Area of the Asia-Pacific; RCEP = Regional Comprehensive Economic Partnership; TPP = Trans-Pacific Partnership

Source: Model simulations.

Table 2.12   Export increases under alternative FTAs, 2025

Economy	Exports 2025 (billions of 2007 US dollars)	Export increases (billions of 2007 US dollars)					Change from baseline (percent)				
		TPP-16	RCEP	CHUSTIA	All three	FTAAPX	TPP-16	RCEP	CHUSTIA	All three	FTAAPX
Americas	4,163	260.2	-8.1	342.1	551.0	781.9	6.3	-0.2	8.2	13.2	18.8
Canada	597	17.7	-2.4	-13.7	1.7	34.0	3.0	-0.4	-2.3	0.3	5.7
Chile	151	4.5	-1.3	-1.3	2.1	9.2	3.0	-0.8	-0.9	1.4	6.1
Mexico	507	40.1	-0.5	-15.0	22.3	102.3	7.9	-0.1	-3.0	4.4	20.2
Peru	95	7.4	-0.2	-1.0	5.8	10.6	7.8	-0.3	-1.1	6.1	11.1
United States	2,813	190.5	-3.7	373.2	519.1	625.9	6.8	-0.1	13.3	18.5	22.3
Asia	10,403	517.8	1,420.0	371.6	2,101.5	3,434.5	5.0	13.7	3.6	20.2	33.0
Brunei	9	0.3	0.9	-0.1	1.1	1.2	3.8	10.5	-0.6	12.4	13.3
China	4,597	-107.8	638.3	472.2	982.2	1,590.1	-2.3	13.9	10.3	21.4	34.6
Hong Kong	235	-3.6	39.9	-2.6	34.0	73.9	-1.5	17.0	-1.1	14.5	31.5
India	869	-13.2	237.9	-11.9	211.0	536.1	-1.5	27.4	-1.4	24.3	61.7
Indonesia	501	98.3	52.6	-7.3	112.4	119.3	19.6	10.5	-1.4	22.5	23.8
Japan	1,252	202.5	225.1	-15.8	357.3	419.0	16.2	18.0	-1.3	28.5	33.5
Korea	718	94.5	173.6	-16.7	205.7	244.2	13.2	24.2	-2.3	28.6	34.0
Malaysia	336	44.2	20.2	-6.9	50.4	56.1	13.2	6.0	-2.0	15.0	16.7
Philippines	163	33.5	10.8	-3.5	31.3	27.5	20.6	6.6	-2.2	19.2	16.8
Singapore	263	13.3	-5.7	-7.7	-1.5	-5.0	5.1	-2.2	-2.9	-0.6	-1.9
Taiwan	712	-17.5	-40.3	-11.3	-60.2	150.8	-2.5	-5.7	-1.6	-8.5	21.2

(continues on next page)

Table 2.12 Export increases under alternative FTAs, 2025 *(continued)*

Economy	Exports 2025 (billions of 2007 US dollars)	Export increases (billions of 2007 US dollars)					Change from baseline (percent)				
		TPP-16	RCEP	CHUSTIA	All three	FTAAPX	TPP-16	RCEP	CHUSTIA	All three	FTAAPX
Asia											
Thailand	476	82.7	34.7	–9.7	83.1	74.6	17.4	7.3	–2.0	17.5	15.7
Vietnam	239	92.1	29.9	–6.3	94.6	139.3	38.6	12.5	–2.6	39.6	58.3
Other ASEAN	34	–1.6	2.1	–0.8	0	7.3	–4.6	6.2	–2.3	–0.1	21.6
Oceania	392	20.4	45.5	–2.4	53.5	65.5	5.2	11.6	–0.6	13.7	16.7
Australia	332	15.7	42.8	–1.9	47.9	59.0	4.7	12.9	–0.6	14.4	17.8
New Zealand	60	4.7	2.7	–0.5	5.6	6.5	7.8	4.4	–0.9	9.3	10.8
Others	13,457	–143.7	–73.7	–121.4	–292.8	–233.9	–1.1	–0.5	–0.9	–2.2	–1.7
Europe	7,431	–75.6	–41.6	–65.6	–157.8	–328.9	–1.0	–0.6	–0.9	–2.1	–4.4
Russia	1,071	–9.3	–6.2	–8.0	–20.4	334.8	–0.9	–0.6	–0.7	–1.9	31.3
Rest of world	4,955	–58.8	–25.9	–47.8	–114.6	–239.7	–1.2	–0.5	–1.0	–2.3	–4.8
World	28,415	654.7	1,383.7	589.9	2,413.2	4,048.0	2.3	4.9	2.1	8.5	14.2
Memorandum											
TPP-16	8,512	942.0	579.4	265.8	1,539.0	1,923.6	11.1	6.8	3.1	18.1	22.6
RCEP	10,795	538.2	1,465.5	369.2	2,155.0	3,500.0	5.0	13.6	3.4	20.0	32.4
APEC	15,126	803.8	1,211.2	716.1	2,474.6	4,073.2	5.3	8.0	4.7	16.4	26.9

APEC = Asia-Pacific Economic Cooperation; ASEAN = Association of Southeast Asian Nations; CHUSTIA = China–US trade and investment agreement; FTA = free trade agreement; FTAAPX = Expanded Free Trade Area of the Asia-Pacific; RCEP = Regional Comprehensive Economic Partnership; TPP = Trans-Pacific Partnership

Source: Authors' simulations.

Finally, tables 2.11 and 2.12 also permit comparisons of the smaller agreements with broad, regional free trade. The FTAAPX, an agreement that would cover two-thirds of the world economy by 2025, would generate global income benefits of $1.9 trillion and export gains of $4 trillion. The FTAAPX would generate additional benefits compared to its component agreements by implementing more rigorous rules for many regional links that would otherwise be covered by weaker rules, by establishing broader cumulation of rules of origin across the region and by covering the blank cells of figure 2.5 including trade among Hong Kong, Taiwan, Russia, and other Asia-Pacific economies; between the United States and India; and among China and several countries in the Americas. Hong Kong, Taiwan, and Russia would especially benefit from an FTAAPX, as they would gain access that they do not have under the other agreements. India and the United States would also see benefits, as they do not jointly participate in other agreements. However, a few countries—Indonesia, Thailand, and Philippines—would be negatively affected, since they would face keener competition from China and others in some export markets.

From a global perspective, a broad regional agreement would generate enormous benefits. However, for countries that already participate in one or more of the smaller agreements, the changes would be modest, and sometimes even negative. Because the main incremental gains would accrue to newcomers, the incentives of TPP, RCEP, and CHUSTIA members to pursue an FTAAPX would be limited once the three smaller agreements were in place, even if the group's attraction were to rise dramatically for still-excluded economies.

Dynamics of Regional Alternatives

Successful negotiating tracks develop momentum over time. The TPP negotiations have already drawn in new partners and may attract others. The TPP and RCEP have also stimulated each other's development and contributed to the launch of new negotiations between the European Union and Japan and the United States. This synergy is constructive—with key economies involved, regional agreements can capture much of the gains only global agreements once promised. And if large regional agreements unify rules of origin, which many currently intend to do, they can begin to knit together the smaller accords. Finally, agreements negotiated in parallel by overlapping partners seem likely to adopt similar rules—often borrowed from each other—thus reducing the variability of international rules.

Yet concluding the three new regional agreements could reduce incentives for regional consolidation. Asia-Pacific economies that join both the TPP and RCEP would have preferential access to most Asia-Pacific markets and would gain little from further regional integration. Japan and Korea could achieve 87 and 81 percent, respectively, of the benefits from FTAAPX by participating in the smaller agreements. Similarly, a CHUSTIA would reduce the incentives for China and the United States to reach a regional accord. There may be additional cost savings from truly regional rules not yet included in our simulations, but the economic case for FTAAPX will weaken once the smaller (but still very large) accords are completed.

In the end, successes on all three agreements should make it easier to take the additional steps toward a regional agreement. With a full matrix of agreements among the largest economies in place, the costs of consolidating rules will diminish. If the benefits from increased market access are modest, the costs of adjustment will be as well. Meanwhile, consolidated rules would make the trading system more predictable and its management simpler for businesses and governments. And the rules might be further extended to economies across the world that would be undoubtedly attracted to this large trading zone. Considering these opposing factors, it is not easy to say whether the three agreements will make it more or less likely that regional or even wider agreements will be reached.

The politics of regional integration are equally difficult to predict, but could favor a three-agreement strategy. One insight into the politics of trade is that groups adversely affected by policy changes feel them with disproportional intensity and unite to oppose new agreements (Baldwin 1989; Haggard and Webb 1993). Adversely affected groups in every country tend to believe—and unfortunately, there is little experience to prove them wrong—that they will not be compensated from total gains, no matter how large. Accordingly, agreements involving many countries face opposition from multiple opponents who are motivated to defeat them. Smaller agreements with like-minded partners, such as the three analyzed here, might be more easily fine-tuned to prevent the development of large antitrade coalitions.

Conclusions

The results of this study support Chinese and US interest in a CHUSTIA. China is estimated to gain $330 billion from the agreement alone and $454 billion from the TPP, RCEP, and CHUSTIA together. The United States would gain $130 billion from the CHUSTIA alone and $191 billion from all three. A CHUSTIA offers greater benefits for China than the RCEP, and greater benefits for the United States than the TPP. The three agreements are largely complementary, and their benefits approach those of regional free trade in the Asia-Pacific.

The gains would be driven by export increases of 10 percent for China and 13 percent for the United States, and somewhat smaller investment effects. The gains would result mainly from increased productivity and would generate more sectoral specialization as well as greater two-way trade between China and the United States. Export increases are projected in nearly all sectors of the US economy. Nevertheless, the effects would include structural changes, especially in the United States, favoring additional employment shifts from manufacturing to service industries. These shifts, however, could be much more gradual than in the past—or could be made so—and would be modest in relation to normal labor force turnover. They are also much more likely to be wage increasing than similar shifts were in the past. These considerations notwithstanding, all shifts could impose hardship on some workers and suggest that part of a CHUSTIA's large benefits should be used to mitigate adverse adjustment effects.

Faster macroeconomic rebalancing—more rapid reductions in China's current account surplus and the US current account deficit—would complement a CHUSTIA and make it easier to accommodate its trade-enhancing effects. Higher domestic demand in China would provide markets for additional Chinese imports that CHUSTIA generates. At the same time, a shift in Chinese production toward domestic demand would ease the pressure on import-competing producers in the United States. If policies to accelerate rebalancing and a CHUSTIA were adopted together, smaller exchange rate adjustments would be required and producers would have more time to adjust to the deeper integration of the Chinese and US economies.

The broad effects estimated for a CHUSTIA are relatively robust, but the sectoral results are much more sensitive to detailed modeling assumptions. In one set of simulations we examined the implications of cutting service liberalization in half, either because barriers are overestimated or because agreements would result in more modest liberalization than projected. This alternative solution shows that global benefits would fall by 27 percent, that there would be fewer new Chinese exports of manufactures in exchange for US primary goods and services, and that fewer workers would have to shift among industries, lowering adjustments costs.

A CHUSTIA would negatively affect some Asia-Pacific countries, especially trade-oriented ASEAN economies. These effects could be mitigated if China and the United States also concluded the TPP and RCEP negotiations. The effects of the three agreements would be nearly additive, suggesting that they are largely complementary. The most optimistic outcome would be convergence of the trans-Pacific and Asian tracks into a regional agreement that includes all economies from both tracks. Given reasonably compatible subregional agreements, this consolidated solution might be easier to reach. At the same time, countries participating in smaller agreements will have diminishing incentives to pursue regional integration. But even without that ideal endpoint, much progress can be made toward freer trade in the Asia-Pacific through parallel TPP, RCEP, and China–US efforts.

As emphasized throughout this study, the estimates represent a first effort to address an exceptionally ambitious initiative. They are subject to substantial uncertainties about some model parameters and the agreements themselves. Sensitivity experiments reported in our other studies suggest errors of one-third in either direction; the potential errors in the complex China–US setting are likely to be larger.[33] Nevertheless, the bottom line is that a China–US trade agreement would deliver large benefits. This conclusion is broadly supported by the results, even if adjusted for possible errors, and would be reinforced by

---

33. Further detail on results and data is provided at asiapacifictrade.org.

indirect consequences of effective China–US cooperation, such as improved investor and consumer confidence, more competition, and accelerating innovation. China–US cooperation could also help to ensure the stable political and security relationships that are the ultimate foundations of prosperity in both countries.

References

APEC (Asia-Pacific Economic Cooperation). 2010. *The Yokohama Vision–Bogor and Beyond*. Singapore.

Autor, David H., David Dorn, and Gordon H. Hanson. 2013. The China Syndrome: Local Labor Market Effects of Import Competition in the United States. *American Economic Review* 103, no. 6 (October): 2121–68.

Baldwin, Robert E. 1989. The Political Economy of Trade Policy. *Journal of Economic Perspectives* 3, no. 4: 119–35.

Bernard, Andrew B., J. Bradford Jensen, Stephen J. Redding, and Peter K. Schott. 2007. Firms in International Trade. *Journal of Economic Perspectives* 21, no. 3: 105–30.

Brown, Drusilla K., and Robert M. Stern. 2000. *Measurement and Modeling of the Economic Effects of Trade and Investment Barriers in Services*. Discussion Paper 453. Ann Arbor: School of Public Policy, University of Michigan.

Dixon, Peter B., and Maureen T. Rimmer. 2009. *Validating a Detailed, Dynamic CGE Model of the US*. Centre of Policy Studies, Monash University, Melbourne (June 25).

Felbermayr, Gabriel J., Mario Larch, Lisandra Flach, Erdal Yalcin, and Sebastian Benz. 2013. *Dimensions and Effects of a Transatlantic Free Trade Agreement Between the EU and US*. Study commissioned by German Federal Ministry of Economics and Technology, Munich (February).

Fontagné, Lionel, Amélie Guillin, and Cristina Mitaritonna. 2011. *Estimations of Tariff Equivalents for the Services Sector*. Paper 2011-24. Paris: Centre d'Etudes Prospectives et d'Informations Internationales.

Fouré, Jean, Agnès Bénassy-Quéré, and Lionel Fontagné. 2010. *The World Economy in 2050: A Tentative Picture*. Paris: Centre d'Etudes Prospectives et d'Informations Internationales.

Haggard, Stephan, and Steven B. Webb. 1993. What Do We Know about the Political Economy of Economic Policy Reform? *World Bank Research Observer* 8, no. 2: 143–68.

Henderson, Richard. 2012. Industry Employment and Output Projections to 2020. *Monthly Labor Review* (January): 65–83.

Hufbauer, Gary Clyde, and Jeffrey J. Schott. 2009. *Fitting Asia-Pacific Agreements into the WTO System*. Chapter 12 from *Multilateralizing Regionalism: Challenges for the Global Trading System*. Cambridge, UK: Cambridge University Press.

Hufbauer, Gary Clyde, Jeffrey J. Schott, and Woan Foong Wong. 2010. *Figuring Out the Doha Round*. Washington: Peterson Institute for International Economics.

Hufbauer, Gary Clyde, Cathleen Cimino, and Tyler Moran. 2014. *NAFTA at 20: Misleading Charges and Positive Achievements*. Policy Brief 14-13. Washington: Peterson Institute for International Economics.

Jensen, J. Bradford. 2011. *Global Trade in Services: Fear, Facts, and Offshoring*. Washington: Peterson Institute for International Economics.

Kehoe, Timothy J. 2005. An Evaluation of the Performance of Applied General Equilibrium Models on the Impact of NAFTA. In *Frontiers in Applied General Equilibrium Modeling: In Honor of Herbert Scarf*, ed. Timothy J. Kehoe, Thirukodikaval Nilakanta (T. N.) Srinivasan, John Whalley. Cambridge, UK: Cambridge University.

Kehoe, Timothy J., Kim J. Ruhl, and Joseph B. Steinberg. 2013. *Global Imbalances and Structural Change in the United States.* Staff Report 489. Minneapolis: Federal Reserve Bank.

Keynes, John Maynard. 1929. The German Transfer Problem. *Economic Journal* 39, no. 153 (March): 1–7.

Lipsey, Richard. 1960. The Theory of Customs Unions: A General Survey. *Economic Journal* 70, no. 279: 496–513.

Ma, Jun, and Audrey Shi. 2013. Economic Benefits of TPP Entry for China. *Emerging Markets Monthly: Finding Pre-Tapering Leftovers* (Deutsche Bank) (November 7): 13–18.

Melitz, Marc J., and Stephen J. Redding. 2014. *Missing Gains from Trade?* Discussion Paper 1254. London: Centre for Economic Performance.

Obstfeld, Maurice, and Kenneth S. Rogoff. 2005. Global Current Account Imbalances and Exchange Rate Adjustments. *Brookings Papers on Economic Activity* 36, no. 1: 67–146.

Petri, Peter A. 2012. Competing Templates in Asia-Pacific Economic Integration. In *Asia at a Tipping Point: Korea, the Rise of China, and the Impact of Leadership*, ed. Gilbert Rozman. Washington: Korea Economic Institute.

Petri, Peter A. 2013. The New Landscape of Trade Policy and Korea's Choices. *Journal of East Asian Economic Integration* 17, no. 4: 333–59.

Petri, Peter A., and Michael G. Plummer. 2013. *ASEAN Centrality and the ASEAN–US Economic Relationship.* Honolulu: East-West Center.

Petri, Peter A., Michael G. Plummer, and Fan Zhai. 2012a. ASEAN Economic Community: A General Equilibrium Analysis. *Asian Economic Journal* 26, no. 2: 93–118.

Petri, Peter A., Michael G. Plummer, and Fan Zhai. 2012b. *The Trans-Pacific Partnership and Asia-Pacific Integration: A Quantitative Assessment.* Policy Analyses in International Economics 98. Washington: Peterson Institute for International Economics.

Petri, Peter, and Fan Zhai. 2013. *Navigating a Changing World Economy: ASEAN, the People's Republic of China, and India.* Working Paper 404. Tokyo: Asian Development Bank Institute.

USITC (United States International Trade Commission). 2007. *US-Korea Free Trade Agreement: Potential Economy-Wide and Selected Sectoral Effects.* Washington.

USTR (United States Trade Representative). 2013. *2013 National Trade Estimate Report on Foreign Trade Barriers.* Washington.

Viner, Jacob. 1950. *The Customs Union Issue.* New York: Carnegie Endowment for International Peace.

Walsh, Keith. 2006. *Trade in Services: Does Gravity Hold? A Gravity Model Approach to Estimating Barriers to Service Trade.* Discussion Paper 183. Dublin: Institute for International Integration Studies, Trinity College.

Zhai, Fan. 2008. Armington Meets Melitz: Introducing Firm Heterogeneity in a Global CGE Model of Trade. *Journal of Economic Integration* 23, no. 3: 575–604.

Adjustment Challenges for US Workers

ROBERT Z. LAWRENCE

Modern trade agreements, such as the China–US trade and investment agreement (CHUSTIA) proposed here, cover far more than tariff barriers. This means that they provide an opportunity not only to stimulate trade and investment but also to anchor domestic economic reforms and assist countries to adopt policies they ought to be adopting in any case.[1] Current US policies to aid dislocated workers and communities are woefully inadequate. A CHUSTIA could remove some of the political obstacles to implementing more effective and equitable policies; it could provide an ideal opportunity to improve policies that could aid all US dislocated workers and communities, regardless of the reasons for their displacement.

Over the past decade, the expansion of trade with China has had both benefits and costs. By providing consumers with lower prices and greater choice and by inducing improvements in productivity, manufactured imports from China in 2008 are estimated to have raised US living standards by 0.6 percent of US GDP, or $250 per person (Edwards and Lawrence 2013, 150). But while it may have benefitted the economy as a whole, for some workers, firms, and regions, the expansion of Chinese trade has also meant costly and painful adjustment,[2] particularly because it has occurred in an unforgiving

Robert Z. Lawrence is a nonresident senior fellow at the Peterson Institute for International Economics and the Albert L. Williams Professor of Trade and Investment at the John F. Kennedy School of Government at Harvard University. The author is extremely grateful to Lawrence Edwards, Gary Hufbauer, Steve Hipple, and Sean Miner for their comments and assistance.

1. See, e.g., Galal and Lawrence (2005).

2. See, e.g., Autor et al. (2013); Autor, Dorn, and Hanson (2013a; 2013b); and Pierce and Schott (2012).

environment: The economy has had two recessions since the late 1990s, almost no aggregate employment growth, a decline in manufacturing employment of almost six million jobs, and stagnant real wages.

In chapter 2 Peter A. Petri, Michael G. Plummer, and Fan Zhai (PPZ) simulated the effect of a China–US free trade agreement (FTA) using a computable general equilibrium model. They conclude that a US–China FTA could generate additional benefits amounting to 0.6 percent of US GDP by 2025—$130 billion in 2007 dollars. Their simulation also indicates that to reap these benefits the US economy will have to undergo structural adjustment. Between 2015 and 2025 the share of manufacturing employment in the economy would have to decline by an additional 0.5 percentage points, while US exports and imports would increase by an additional 13 and 11 percent, respectively.

The PPZ simulations provide useful information about the eventual structure of the economy, but they assume—as is appropriate for a long-run analysis—that employment and nominal current account balances are unchanged. As a result they offer no data on the actual dislocation and adjustment challenges that an agreement is likely to present for individual US workers and communities. Yet an understanding of these challenges is required, for both a full appreciation of the effect of an agreement and consideration of policies that could mitigate the adjustment costs. To do this, it is necessary to move beyond the estimates of net employment effects of the FTA on industries and sectors and to consider effects at the worker level.

The recent experience with Chinese imports is helpful because the volume of additional import growth that PPZ predict would be induced by a CHUSTIA is quite similar to the growth that has occurred over the past decade. The first section of this chapter draws on recent experience to develop a three-step methodology to estimate involuntary displacement, in manufacturing and in the economy overall. I obtain upper-bound estimates of job displacement by calculating the US employment equivalence of Chinese import growth since 2000, using input-output tables. Second, I use the work of David Autor, David Dorn, and Gordon Hanson (2013a) to extract the share of Chinese import growth that was due to increased US demand and thus would not have reduced actual US employment. Third, using data on the share of job separations from manufacturing that are typically voluntary, I make an additional correction to come up with a final estimate of the number of workers that Chinese imports might have involuntarily displaced.

The estimates suggest that involuntary displacement due to Chinese trade has been significant, on the order of 97,000 manufacturing workers per year between 2000 and 2007. However, using the biennial Displaced Workers Surveys produced by the Bureau of Labor Statistics (BLS) as a benchmark, these job losses probably accounted for less than one-fifth of involuntary job losses in US manufacturing and less than 5 percent of involuntary displacement in the economy overall over the same period.[3] While extensive, and painful and

---

3. Bureau of Labor Statistics, "Displaced Workers Summary," August 24, 2012, www.bls.gov (accessed on July 8, 2014).

costly for the workers involved, the losses due to the adjustment to increased Chinese imports are outweighed by the dislocation that routinely occurs in the US labor market even when the overall unemployment rate is low. This suggests that while the adjustment challenges posed by trade are important, the far more significant effects of adjustment due to other sources should not be ignored.

The next section of this chapter reviews the evidence on wage effects and the costs of dislocation. The literature does not provide much evidence that trade with developing countries has been a major driver of recent aggregate US income inequality. While it reports some adverse effects on the wages of workers employed in occupations, firms, and regions that compete with China, it indicates that the workers who are actually displaced bear the highest costs. Workers displaced from long-tenured jobs could experience lifetime losses equal to two years of their earnings at the time of displacement. If these workers are displaced during recessions, their losses could be even greater.

In the third section of this chapter I apply the results from the previous sections to the PPZ simulations to estimate the amount of involuntary worker displacement that could occur as a result of the agreement, as well as the net social benefits and costs. The results, shown in table 3.1, suggest that an upper bound of 1.04 million workers could be dislocated over the ten years that the FTA is implemented—an average of 104,000 per year. The estimated annual aggregate benefit of 0.6 percent of GDP predicted by PPZ implies benefits of $1.25 million in 2007 dollars per displaced worker—$130 billion divided by 104,000—in 2025. The two-year loss of worker lifetime incomes in 2025 is likely to be about $100,000 in 2007 dollars. This implies social benefits about 12 times greater than the costs to displaced workers during the final year of adjustment, with only benefits remaining thereafter.

The fourth section discusses appropriate policy responses in light of the evidence. Current US policies distinguish unemployed workers according to the reasons for their displacement. Only the small proportion of workers who can make the case that they were laid off due to increased trade receive the more generous trade adjustment assistance (TAA) that provides training and some health benefits, as well as wage-loss insurance, for older workers. Most US workers that have been laid off receive only modest unemployment benefits, which were temporarily extended in response to the Great Recession but normally expire after six months. Some workers, on a first-come, first-served basis, also participate in programs for dislocated workers, but these programs provide far fewer benefits than TAA.

A TAA program with a more generous wage-loss insurance program should be part of the legislation implementing a CHUSTIA. It would be even more desirable to extend and improve these benefits in a consolidated worker adjustment program that aids all displaced workers, regardless of the reasons for their displacement. While training and other forms of search and relocation assistance should be provided, the centerpiece of this new

Table 3.1 Effect of additional CHUSTIA import growth on worker displacement, 2015–25 (millions of jobs)

	Manufacturing	Total
Employment content of imports	1.55	2.03
Adjusted for demand	1.16	1.52
Adjusted for voluntary separations	0.80	1.04
Benefit per displaced worker in 2025		$1.25 million

CHUSTIA = China–US trade and investment agreement

Sources: Authors' calculations based on Bureau of Labor Statistics Employment Projections, Inter-Industry Relationships, www.bls.gov (accessed on July 5, 2014) and chapter 2 of this volume.

program should be wage-loss insurance. These additional benefits could be financed through a reform of the system for collecting unemployment taxes that would make the system more progressive while increasing the overall amount of revenue raised. Finally, to deal with unforeseen shocks and the possibility of recession, the trade agreement should include a special safeguards provision that would moderate the pace of implementation to reflect extensive industry dislocation.

Effects of Chinese Imports on US Jobs

Americans often talk about the effects of trade on jobs, but what precisely they have in mind is not always clear. When considering such effects on workers, it is important to distinguish between the use of the term *jobs* as a synonym for total positions or employment opportunities and the use of *jobs* as a synonym for the individual employment (or unemployment) experiences of workers. Over any time period, while the total number of employment positions in the economy might not change (a net concept) the number of individual workers that are hired for and lose these positions could be large (a gross concept).[4] It is more difficult to find employment when unemployment is high; in net terms, the general availability of employment opportunities will affect the costs associated with job changes. But these costs will also depend on the magnitude and nature of gross flows, particularly whether job changes occur through voluntary—because people quit to change jobs or retire—or involuntary displacement through layoffs and discharges.

---

4. Macroeconomic monetary and fiscal policies are generally the appropriate instruments to ensure an adequate number of employment positions in the economy. But if individual workers are required to change jobs, even when overall employment is unchanged, microeconomic policies, such as unemployment insurance, training, and search and relocation assistance, may be required to aid adjustment.

Figure 3.1   Gross and net changes in US employment, 2001–13 (number of jobs)

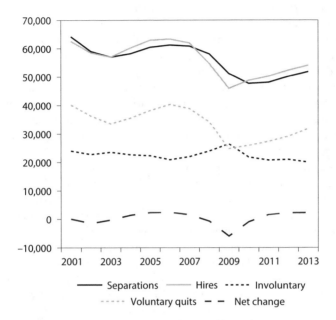

Source: Bureau of Labor Statistics, JOLTS data, www.bls.gov/jlt.

Derived from establishment surveys, in its Job Opening and Labor Turnover Survey (JOLTS) the BLS estimates the number of US workers involved in hires and separations.[5] Figure 3.1 illustrates these concepts, showing how changes in annual aggregate US employment, net jobs (the bottom line) reflect the small difference between much larger numbers of hires and separations (the gross changes).

Trade models and most studies estimate net employment effects at the industry level. But even if increased exports at the industry level offset increased imports, the demand for the services of particular workers or firms may not be left unchanged. In principle, a complete account of the effects of a CHUSTIA on US workers would not only project net employment but also explicitly estimate the effects on hires and both voluntary and involuntary separations.

---

5. Bureau of Labor Statistics, JOLTS databases, 2013, www.bls.gov (accessed on July 8, 2014).

Upper-Bound Estimates

In practice, it is not easy to translate estimates of the trade effects of an FTA into estimates of the effects on the adjustment costs imposed on individual workers. Nonetheless, I can obtain an extreme estimate of displacement by assuming, first, that every dollar Americans spend on Chinese imports substitutes for a dollar they were spending on similar products made in the United States, and second, that the labor that was producing that US output was actually laid off. Such an approach would provide an upper-bound estimate of worker displacement by ignoring the possibilities that adjustment could occur through voluntary attrition and that import growth could occur because of additional demand for imports, rather than the displacement of a given level of spending on domestic products.

One way to obtain an upper-bound estimate is to use an input-output table indicating the employment required from every US industry for each dollar of final demand. As most Chinese imports are manufactured products and the US manufacturing sector has been a focus of particular concern, I start by considering US manufacturing employment. As table 3.2 shows, using the input-output tables for total employment requirements provided by the BLS, in 2000 replacing manufactured imports from China would have required 695,000 US manufacturing jobs. For 2007 a similar calculation indicates that replacement of manufactured imports would have required 2.02 million US manufactured jobs.[6] This suggests that between 2000 and 2007 the US manufacturing labor content equivalence of the growth of Chinese imports averaged an increase of 188,000 manufacturing jobs per year.[7] Since 2007, US manufactured goods imports from China have continued to increase, rising from $315 billion in 2007 to $356 billion in 2010 and $450 billion in 2012. But the growth in output per worker in the United States implied that, despite the 43 percent rise in imports from China between 2007 and 2012, the manufacturing employment content of these imports was only 90,000 higher in 2012 than in 2007. This is a good example of the powerful role that increased productivity growth has played in reducing employment growth in US manufacturing.

---

6. Between 2000 and 2007 value added per full-time employee in US manufacturing increased from $81,600 to $122,300. Although the value of imports from China tripled, the employment equivalence increased by only 109 percent.

7. Using a similar analysis, Robert Scott (2010) obtains somewhat larger job content estimates. Our approach assumes that, had domestic products been more expensive, Americans would have purchased a smaller volume of them—that is, unitary demand elasticity. Scott's approach implicitly assumes a zero demand elasticity. He estimates that between 2000 and 2010 the average increase in Chinese manufacturing jobs content was 200,000 per year: "Between 2001 and 2011, the trade deficit with China eliminated or displaced more than 2.7 million US jobs, over 2.1 million of which (76.9 percent) were in manufacturing" (Scott 2010, 1).

Table 3.2 US employment equivalence of US manufacturing imports from China, 2000–2012

	2000	2007	2010	2012	Annual change 2000–2007	Annual change 2007–12
Manufacturing imports from China (billions of US dollars)	97.09	315.13	356.08	450.03		
US employment equivalence (millions of jobs)[a]						
Manufacturing jobs	0.70	2.02	2.01	2.10	0.189	0.018
Total jobs	1.29	3.03	2.90	3.35	0.249	0.090

a. Estimated using input-output tables.

Sources: USITC DataWeb, http://dataweb.usitc.gov (accessed on July 5, 2014); Bureau of Labor Statistics, www.bls.gov (accessed on July 5, 2014).

Demand vs. Supply

The use of ex post data to infer effects on actual changes in US employment is problematic, because it estimates the job content of all import growth and fails to distinguish the reason imports have increased, in particular whether demand or supply has shifted. When Americans increase their spending, sales of both domestic and imported products increase, and there might be no actual decline in US employment—imports and domestic employment might both increase. On the other hand, if imports increase because the foreign supply curve shifts outward, and import growth reflects an increase in the foreign share of a given amount of domestic spending, domestic employment opportunities will be lost. If US demand expands, job opportunities might be reduced in the hypothetical sense that Americans might have bought more domestic products had imports not existed. But if the concern relates to actual dislocation, it is preferable to undertake estimates in which causation is explicitly accounted for and supply and demand shocks are explicitly distinguished.

In this regard, the work of Autor, Dorn, and Hanson (2013a) (ADH) on Chinese imports is especially helpful. The authors invest considerable effort to isolate the employment effects that can be ascribed to supply rather than demand shifts, using Chinese exports to third countries to capture import growth that reflects Chinese productivity growth rather than an increase in US demand. They find that imports from China that reflect such supply-driven changes led to "a net reduction in U.S. manufacturing employment of 548 thousand workers between 1990 and 2000 and a further reduction of 982 thousand workers between 2000 and 2007" (ADH 2013a, 2140). This implies that since 2000 there was an annual average reduction of manufacturing employment of 140,000 per year—as would be expected, a number lower than the

188,000 obtained from input-output analysis that assumes all imports lead to a decline in domestic employment.[8]

Justin R. Pierce and Peter K. Schott (2012) offer additional insight into the possible role of the suppression of new hires in the adjustment process using differences between the Smoot-Hawley and most favored nation (MFN) tariff rates to estimate the manufacturing employment effects of granting China permanent normal trade relations (PNTR) in 2000. They estimate that reductions in manufacturing employment of 29.6 percent were attributable to PNTR and decompose their estimated effects into those that occur due to actual displacement of jobs in existing firms and those that occur due to the suppression of the addition of new jobs and the entry of new firms. They estimate that 13.0 of the predicted 29.6 percentage points—44 percent—was due to the suppression of the job creation margins of plant expansion and plant births.

Voluntary and Involuntary Separations

In this context, the distinction between employment opportunities and the actual experience of job loss is important. The ADH estimates do not tell precisely how many workers may have experienced involuntary unemployment. Some of the reductions in employment positions in manufacturing could be accomplished through voluntary attrition and some through the suppression of additional hiring or new plant births that might otherwise have taken place.

As figure 3.1 indicates, based on data from the quarterly JOLTS, in the overall economy, voluntary separations—including quits, retirements, and deaths—typically account for a high share of job separations, even when the manufacturing sector has been under duress. Between 2001 and 2007 the average annual number of separations from manufacturing jobs was 5 million, of which 2.8 million were (voluntary) quits and retirements and 2.2 million were (involuntary) discharges or layoffs. Thus about 55.5 percent of separations from US manufacturing were voluntary in this period. However, the averages may conceal important differences in behavior at the firm level and are likely to overstate the opportunities for painless downsizing available to US firms experiencing extreme competitive pressures. For such firms it is likely that involuntary displacements account for much more of the job loss than is typical of manufacturing under normal conditions. The estimates are also sensitive to demand conditions. Voluntary separations accounted for 48 and 31 percent of manufacturing separations in the recession years of 2001 and 2009, respectively, while they were much larger—some 61 percent of separations—during the expansion years of 2005 and 2006. A conservative parameter for the share of

---

8. Their estimate of a reduction in manufacturing employment of 548,000 over the 1990s is also similar to but less than the input-output estimates of the manufacturing employment content of Chinese imports in 2000 of 695,000. This could reflect that the input-output estimates of the US manufacturing job equivalence of all Chinese imports include the job content of Chinese imports before 1990.

separations that might be voluntary would be the lowest annual average for manufacturing over the past decade, namely 31 percent.

In sum, the ADH analysis places the loss of manufacturing employment opportunities due to Chinese imports between 2000 and 2007 at 140,000 per year. While this estimate eliminates the employment content of imports due to increased US demand, it represents an upper bound of the layoffs and discharges caused by the rise in Chinese imports, as voluntary departures could account for some of the separations. It would be reasonable to use the 31 percent of all separations from manufacturing that occurred voluntarily in the recession year of 2009 to provide a conservative adjustment factor to account for this possibility. That adjustment would leave a figure of about 97,000 workers—69 percent of 140,000—as an adjusted ADH estimate of involuntary annual separations owing to Chinese imports between 2000 and 2007.

China's Share

What share of overall displacement did Chinese trade account for? One benchmark to answer this question is the Displaced Workers Survey,[9] compiled by the BLS using US household data. This survey focuses on workers who lose permanent jobs for reasons beyond their control, such as plant closings and insufficient demand. As might be expected given its narrower scope, it obtains significantly lower estimates than the JOLTS numbers for involuntary discharges because it excludes seasonal and temporary workers as well as workers who have been discharged for cause rather than inadequate demand. In addition the survey is taken only every two years and thus does not count workers involved in more than one separation in the two-year period more than once.[10]

Between 2001 and 2007, on average, the Displaced Workers Surveys report that 688,000 workers were displaced annually from manufacturing, roughly one-fifth of all workers displaced over those years. The ADH estimates of the manufacturing losses of 140,000 per year over the same period would imply that Chinese trade was responsible for about 20 percent of worker displacement from manufacturing. However, this would be an upper bound, as it would include voluntary separations. Assuming that an additional 30 percent of the adjustment could be achieved through voluntary separations would reduce

---

9. Bureau of Labor Statistics, "Displaced Workers Summary."

10. The Displaced Workers Survey question is: "During the last 3 calendar years, that is, January 2007 through December 2009, did (you/name) lose a job or leave one because: (your/his/her) plant or company closed or moved, (your/his/her) position or shift was abolished, insufficient work, or another similar reason?" The layoffs and discharges count in the JOLTS is composed of several elements: involuntary separations initiated by the employer, including layoffs with no intent to rehire; formal layoffs lasting or expected to last more than seven days; discharges resulting from mergers, downsizing, or closings; firings or other discharges for cause; terminations of permanent or short-term employees; and terminations of seasonal employees.

the share of manufacturing workers actually displaced by Chinese imports to around 97,000 workers annually, about 14 percent of total displacements.

Beyond Manufacturing

While much of the discussion about displaced workers has concentrated on manufacturing, this ignores the substantial displacement that occurs outside the manufacturing sector. Between 2001 and 2007, the average annual number of displaced workers was 2.87 million. The input-output estimates in table 3.2 indicate that the overall US employment equivalence of the increase in Chinese imports between 2000 and 2007 of 249,000 per year was 31 percent larger than the equivalence of the increase of 189,000 per year in in manufacturing employment alone. This would imply that Chinese trade displaced 127,000 US workers annually, or 4.4 percent of total annual displacements. Clearly, while 4.4 percent is a significant number, an overwhelming share of displacement in the US economy is not due to Chinese trade (see table 3.3).

Effects of Chinese Imports on Wages

When considering the wage effects of Chinese trade it is important to distinguish between the part of wages that reflect general returns—that is, payments for attributes that are valued regardless of the job (e.g., a college versus a high-school education)—and the part of wages that represents payments for specific skills that can be realized only in particular jobs or occupations (e.g., butchers, airplane mechanics). If workers at various skill levels and capital were homogeneous and fully mobile, trade with China could affect wages at different skill levels and the returns to capital with general attributes regardless of the industry or location of employment. Increased trade with China could, in principle, depress the relative wages of unskilled workers relative to skilled workers across the US economy and the returns to labor relative to those of capital in all industries. On the other hand, if wages mainly reflect returns that are specific to particular jobs, firms, and occupations, most of the effects would be felt by workers directly affected by Chinese competition.[11] In addition, if workers are fully mobile and their skill sets are entirely general, displaced workers will obtain new jobs at the same wages as they were previously earning and the costs of job loss will be incurred only during unemployment. But if earnings are the result of specific returns, in addition to costs incurred as a result of unemployment, workers could experience substantial and more permanent reductions in earnings even after finding new jobs.

Trade economists have applied models emphasizing either general or specific returns to factors of production. Much of the early work on the effects of trade on wages in the 1980s and 1990s examined the role of trade in changing

---

11. This intuition was first developed in classic papers such as Jones (1965), Mussa (1974), and Neary (1978).

Table 3.3 Annual average displaced US workers, 2001–10 (thousands of jobs)

	Total	Manufacturing	Share of total (percent)
2001–02	3,474	966	28
2003–04	2,402	584	24
2005–06	2,240	485	22
2007–08	4,028	739	18
2009–10	4,312	754	17
Average	3,291	706	21

Note: Data are for total displaced workers with no tenure rights on the lost job.

Source: Bureau of Labor Statistics, unpublished Displaced Workers Survey data, www.bls.gov (accessed on July 5, 2014).

the returns to skilled and unskilled workers throughout the US economy—in other words, the effects on wage inequality. Such studies used models assuming that workers were perfectly substitutable and mobile. In the 1980s and 1990s, studies based on these approaches suggested that some of the blame for wage inequality (between 10 and 20 percent) could be placed on trade (Cline 1997).

More recently, however, studies applying the methodologies to data since 2000 do not find large effects on economywide skill differentials attributable to either imports in general or Chinese imports in particular (Edwards and Lawrence 2013). Over the past decade, all workers have fared poorly. But wages at the low end of the wage distribution have not fared especially poorly relative to those in the middle; instead, income inequality has risen because of stronger earnings growth at the very top of the income distribution and an increased share in income going to profits.[12]

Recent studies have also considered the effect of trade on specific wages at the level of firms, occupations, regions, and industries (see Harrison, McLaren, and McMillan 2010). All told, while there is mixed evidence of a wage-loss effect on other workers, especially those who are unskilled and share an occupation, industry, or location with workers who are displaced by imports, the studies find that the workers who are actually displaced mostly bear the significant losses. Avraham Ebenstein and colleagues (2009) find no effect of import competition at the level of industry wages, but do find a depressing effect on occupational wages, especially among displaced workers forced to find jobs outside manufacturing. Autor, Dorn, and Hanson (2013a) similarly find that Chinese manufacturing imports did not reduce local wages in the manufacturing firms that were exposed to Chinese competition, but did depress local

---

12. According to Elsby, Hobjin, and Sahin (2013), the offshoring of imports in manufacturing has not raised the profit rate but has concentrated US manufacturing in more capital-intensive production activities, thereby raising the share of profits in income.

wages more generally.[13] John McLaren and Shushanik Hakobyan (2012), an exception, find no effect on local wages from NAFTA but do find downward pressure on industrywide wages.

The research on the effects of trade confirms that human capital is partly specific to industries and occupations (see Jacobson, LaLonde, and Sullivan 1993 and Kambourov and Manovskii 2009). This implies that the industry and occupation switching that import competition induces will destroy human capital. Workers displaced by such developments often experience permanent losses; some never return to the labor force while others are forced to take new jobs at lower wages. Henry S. Farber (2005) examines displacement from manufacturing in general and import-competing industries in particular and reports that about two-thirds of displaced workers find new full-time jobs, but at an average wage loss of 13 percent—17 percent if one accounts for forgone wage growth during the unemployment transition. This average disguises a range of experiences: 36 percent gained reemployment at or above previous earnings, whereas 25 percent suffered earnings losses of 30 percent or more.

Workers who endure mass layoffs appear to experience especially large wage losses. Studying effects on workers displaced from their jobs to similar nondisplaced workers, Kenneth A. Couch and Dana W. Placzek (2010) find large immediate losses in annual earnings of around 30 percent. Six years later, earnings losses still range from 13 to 15 percent. Till von Wachter, Jae Song, and Joyce Manchester (2009) find that job displacements during the early 1980s led to large and persistent earnings losses that lasted over 20 years. Recent research also suggests that the general state of the labor market can amplify the costs of displacement. As Steven J. Davis and von Wachter (2011, 1) conclude,

> In present-value terms, men lose an average of 1.4 years of predisplacement earnings if displaced in mass-layoff events that occur when the national unemployment rate is below 6 percent. They lose a staggering 2.8 years of predisplacement earnings if displaced when the unemployment rate exceeds 8 percent. These results reflect discounting at a 5 percent annual rate over 20 years after displacement.

Effects of an FTA

If a CHUSTIA is implemented in whole or in part, past experience may be prologue. The PPZ CHUSTIA simulations imply that the additional adjustment challenges that an FTA would present for US manufacturing would resemble those presented by Chinese import growth over the past decade. They also imply that the national benefits from the agreement are likely to far outweigh the costs imposed on the workers who are dislocated.

PPZ estimate that an FTA would increase US exports and imports by 13.3 and 10.8 percent respectively, with most of the increase in US imports

---

13. They estimate a decline of 0.76 log points in mean weekly earnings over 17 years for each $1,000 increase in Chinese import exposure per worker. See ADH (2013a, 2146).

occurring in manufactured goods, which would grow by an additional 11.8 percent, or $355 billion (in 2007 dollars). In 2010 the input-output analysis used in table 3.2 indicates that the manufacturing employment content of US manufactured goods imports from China was 2.012 million workers. By 2025, in PPZ's baseline projection, US imports from China increase to $1.121 trillion (2007 dollars), an increase of 227 percent over imports in 2010 ($342 billion in 2007 dollars). Between 2010 and 2025, the PPZ projections also assume that productivity in US manufacturing increases by 34 percent.[14] This suggests that, in the baseline case, the US manufacturing employment equivalence of Chinese imports in 2025 would be 4.7 million jobs.

PPZ then estimate that an FTA would increase US imports by an additional $355 billion. In 2025 this gain would represent an increase in net US imports equal to 31.7 percent of baseline imports from China and an additional 1.55 million US manufacturing employment equivalence. In table 3.1 the US manufacturing employment equivalence represented by the growth in Chinese imports between 2000 and 2010 is of a similar order of magnitude, namely 1.32 million workers. As indicated above, this defines an upper bound of the dislocation that would take place through actual worker displacement over the decade, because it includes growth in US demand that increased Chinese supplies might fill, as well as reductions in employment that could occur through voluntary attrition.

The ADH estimates of job losses of 140,000 annually between 2000 and 2007 were 75 percent of the annual estimate of 189,000 US employment equivalence manufacturing jobs relating to Chinese imports, reported in table 3.2 using the input-output tables. Applying the 75 percent parameter to allow for import growth due to demand reduces the projected loss of employment positions to 1.16 million over the first decade of CHUSTIA implementation (0.75 × 1.55 million = 1.16 million). Voluntary quits typically make up over half of all separations. Conservatively, using the 31 percent share that, according to the JOLTS data, represented the share of voluntary quits in total separations during the recession year of 2009 as an adjustment factor, I estimate that actual displacement would be about 800,000 over the decade (1.16 million × 69 percent), or about 80,000 manufacturing jobs per year.

Such a number is very speculative because the degree to which the adjustment can be achieved through attrition will depend crucially on the overall environment in which it takes place. Workers are more likely to separate from their existing jobs when there are lots of alternative employment opportunities available. Adjustment is less painful in an economy with strong overall growth.

---

14. In the PPZ projection, manufacturing output per US worker rises from $116,300 to $156,600 between 2010 and 2025, that is, by 34.6 percent (PPZ tables 2.8 and 2.9). These estimates imply an annual growth in labor productivity of 2 percent per year, considerably lower than the 2.7 percent annual increase projected by the Bureau of Labor Statistics through 2020. Using the lower PPZ estimate of productivity growth reduces the US manufacturing employment content of US manufactured imports from China in 2025 by about 10 percent. See Bureau of Labor Statistics, Employment and Productivity Data, www.bls.gov (accessed on July 8, 2014).

Other things being equal, rapid import growth on account of supply shocks is likely to be especially disruptive. The more gradually the agreement is phased in, the greater would be the possibilities of adjustment through the suppression of new hires and through new firm births, rather than through the actual displacement of existing workers.

Total Displacement Due to the FTA

Manufactured goods contain inputs from other sectors. The input-output analysis in table 3.2 indicates that, between 2000 and 2007, the total employment content of the rise in US imports from China was 31.8 percent larger than the manufacturing content. Applying this ratio to 1.55 million—the projected loss of manufacturing jobs between 2015 and 2025—yields estimates of the employment equivalence of additional Chinese imports due to a CHUSTIA of 2.03 million between 2015 and 2025 (1.55 million × 1.33). This is in line with the 2 million additional jobs PPZ estimate for exports. This estimate should be adjusted to take account of demand growth and voluntary attrition. Following the procedure presented earlier yields an estimate of 1.04 million workers from all sectors of the economy that might actually be discharged as a result of the agreement—an average of 104,000 per year.

Jobs Gained under a CHUSTIA

Substantial upsides in the jobs picture should not be forgotten. PPZ forecast that the United States will gain 1.7 million US export-related jobs from a CHUSTIA over 10 years, averaging 170,000 per year, 64 percent higher than the estimate of total workers displaced. They also forecast a 13.3 percent increase in annual US exports in 2025 resulting from a CHUSTIA, which translates into extra US exports of $374 billion (at 2007 prices). The implied jobs coefficient in 2025 is 4,500 jobs supported per billion dollars of increased exports (1.7 million jobs divided by $374 billion). This figure aligns with recent calculations by the United States Trade Representative (USTR), which found that, in 2013, for every $1 billion increase in exports, the manufacturing sector gains 5,400 jobs and the services sector gains 5,900 jobs. US productivity will be higher in 2025 than in 2013, which explains the lower jobs coefficient in the PPZ analysis.[15] Thus the employment that the FTA would add would far exceed the number of workers that it displaced. PPZ assume that under an accelerated rebalancing scenario, the Chinese trade surplus would be reduced to zero by 2020, implying a reduction of $286 billion over 5 years. They also assume an equal increase in the US trade balance, reflecting an increase in the US savings rate and a decrease in the Chinese savings rate. If the trade deficit were to be reduced, as in the PPZ rebalancing scenario, import growth would be smaller,

---

15. The USTR figure calculates only direct jobs, but the PPZ forecast includes indirect as well as direct jobs. See USTR (2014).

and the degree to which additional job creation would outweigh actual job loss would be even greater. If the $286 billion scenario works out, it would represent 1.6 percent of US GDP in 2020.

Cost-Benefit Ratio

According to PPZ, by 2025, the annual US gains from an FTA with China are $130 billion per year. Annual displacement of 104,000 implies benefits of $1.25 million per displaced worker in the final year of adjustment.[16] Davis and von Wachter (2011, 25) estimate that men between the ages of 21 and 50, with 3 or more years of job tenure, would experience a present-value lifetime earnings loss after a mass-layoff event equal to twice their annual earnings.[17] The median wage of workers in the 2012 Displaced Workers Survey that covers those who lost jobs in 2010 and 2011 was $39,000 in current dollars and $36,000 in 2007 dollars.[18] Assuming real wage growth of 2 percent per year between 2010 and 2025, the wage measured in 2025 would be $48,300 in 2007 dollars. The lifetime cost in earnings displacement in 2025 would therefore be $96,600— twice that figure. Accounting for these losses suggests that the benefits of a CHUSTIA could be 12 times the losses to displaced workers in 2025. The total displacement of 1.04 million workers due to the agreement over the entire period of adjustment would represent 0.8 percent of US employment in 2025, while the benefits from the agreement would represent 0.6 percent of GDP. Since the gains can be reaped every year after the agreement has been implemented, while adjustment costs are incurred only once, the large net benefits of an agreement are clear.

Conclusions

The evidence on employment and wages paints a consistent picture. Actual displacement due to Chinese competition has been substantial, although it probably accounted for less than one-fifth of such displacement from US manufacturing in recent years and less than 5 percent of overall displacement in the economy at large. In general, job loss is painful and costly for the workers who experience it. Imports induced by increases in foreign supplies can also have adverse effects on general wages in specific locations, occupations, and industries. But the negative effects of import competition on the wages of manufacturing workers who do not lose their jobs appear modest.

---

16. In the relatively normal year of 2007, the median wages of displaced workers were $34,684 and median reemployment wages were $34,268. Moreover 64.3 percent were reemployed, 7 percent worked part time, 7 percent were self-employed, 9 percent were unemployed, and 12 percent were not in the labor force.

17. The loss would be 1.7 times earnings if layoffs occur during an expansion and 4 times earnings during a recession year.

18. Unpublished BLS data.

The simulations imply that a US–China FTA could lead to the involuntary displacement, over a 10-year period, of 1.04 million workers, about 800,000 of whom would be laid off from manufacturing jobs. The costs for some of these workers could be large, but all told are likely to be less than one-twelfth of the benefits from the agreement during the years of adjustment. Moreover, the economy will enjoy the full value of the estimated annual benefits once the adjustment has been made.

Toward a Comprehensive Adjustment Program

According to the BLS, a significant share of displaced workers—typically around half of those who are reemployed—can find another job reasonably rapidly without a substantial reduction in wages.[19] Many find better-paying jobs. These workers generally have relatively high levels of education and capabilities, such as marketing and managerial talents that can be applied to a variety of activities. Workers with these attributes tend to quit their jobs before dislocation (see Autor et al. 2013; Ebenstein et al. 2009). But other workers are less fortunate. Some experience long spells of unemployment because their skills and experience are less portable and eventually they are forced to accept jobs at lower wages. Others, especially older workers, respond by permanently withdrawing from the labor force. The overall context of the displacement episode also matters. A weak national or local economy can materially raise the costs of adjustment. This suggests that policy responses to these concerns should focus on assisting displaced workers, providing benefits regardless of the reasons they have been displaced. It also suggests that new trade policies should take the overall macroeconomic situation into consideration. This section first describes the programs currently available for displaced workers, and then provides recommendations for their enhancement.

Programs for Displaced Workers

In addition to unemployment insurance, along with job placement and recruiting assistance given to workers and firms at job centers, the federal government operates a number of programs under the Workforce Investment Act designed to assist US workers in need. Several programs focus on workers who are either disadvantaged, low skilled, or young. For our purposes the most relevant program is the Dislocated Worker Program, which assists laid-off workers with services such as job search and placement, individual counseling, and training. The federal budget allocated about $1.4 billion dollars to the Dislocated Worker Program between 2008 and 2010 and about $1.2 billion annually in 2011 and 2012 respectively.

Only a small proportion of all displaced workers actually benefit from the Dislocated Worker Program and those that receive benefits find that they are

---

19. Bureau of Labor Statistics, "Displaced Workers Summary."

not especially valuable. According to the Displaced Workers Survey, in 2007 and 2008 about 8 million US workers were displaced, of which 3.6 million had held their jobs for at least three years. In 2009 and 2010 the total number of displaced workers was 8.6 million, of which 4.3 million were long tenured. In 2011, 4.2 million were displaced. Thus, on average in these years, more than 4 million workers were displaced annually. By contrast, the number of workers that participated in the Dislocated Worker Program annually averaged 486,000. The figure suggests that only 12 percent of displaced workers received any benefits from the program. Given appropriations of $1.4 billion, the spending works out to around $2,500 per beneficiary in these years. In 2012, as 1 million workers participated in program spending, their benefits averaged only about $1,000 per participant.

In addition to the Dislocated Worker Program, the more generous TAA operates to assist workers dislocated through trade expansion. TAA provides extended unemployment insurance, training benefits, subsidies for healthcare, relocation benefits and assistance, and a wage-loss insurance program for workers over 50. Workers can obtain these benefits only after they successfully petition the Department of Labor and can prove that international competition was responsible for their job loss.

Table 3.4 reports the number of workers certified and participating in TAA. Compared with the typical annual average rates of displacement for workers in manufacturing and workers in the overall economy from 2010 to 2011 of 0.8 million and 4.3 million workers, respectively, the share of all displaced workers certified as eligible for the TAA is, again, very small. Even in the more generous TAA program, the costs per participant are relatively low.

The TAA program has been justified as a way to redistribute some of the gains from trade agreements to those who lose. It has also often been an essential part of the political bargain necessary for trade agreements to pass in Congress. But the focus on job losses due to trade is problematic. While international trade has been an important reason for dislocation in the US economy, as the discussion in the previous section has shown, trade is only one of many factors leading workers to lose their jobs through no fault of their own. Changes in demand, new corporate strategies, the adoption of new technologies and production methods, and decisions to relocate production to other plants all contribute to the volatility of an economy already affected by business cycle fluctuations, shocks owing to plant closures, crop failures, and other localized sources of distress.

Dislocation due to international trade can impose costs, but the same is true for shocks arising from other causes. Thus while there is a political rationale for isolating trade as a source of job loss, on broad social equity grounds, the case for the distinctive treatment of trade-affected workers is weak. Workers who lose their jobs for other reasons are likely to experience similar costs and difficulties as workers with the same attributes who lose their jobs solely due to trade. Yet workers dislocated for reasons other than trade have access only to far less generous and comprehensive programs than the TAA.

Table 3.4 Number of workers certified and participating in TAA program, 2010–12

TAA	Certified	Participation	Budget (millions of dollars)	Cost per participant (dollars)
2010	287,061	227,882	975	4,280
2011	196,030	104,743	702	3,582
2012	131,011	81,510	855	6,524

TAA = Trade Adjustment Assistance

Source: Department of Labor, annual reports on TAA to the Committee on Finance of the Senate and Committee on Ways and Means of the House of Representatives.

Originally, the TAA's distinctive feature was that, compared with other workers, the program provided TAA-eligible workers with unemployment insurance for longer periods of time. While this was a meaningful benefit, it would have been more appropriately termed *nonadjustment assistance* because workers could receive benefits only by not working.[20] In later years the program was modified to condition the receipt of unemployment insurance extensions and other benefits on workers' participation in training programs. This requirement was justified on the grounds that training aids workers in obtaining new jobs. But while training might be an appropriate path for some workers, it is not necessarily appropriate for all.

While some workers were granted waivers from participation in training, those that have taken training have not been particularly successful. Many workers who complete petitions and are actually certified as eligible for the program chose not to participate. This suggests that they believe their time is better spent in searching for a job on their own rather than undertaking training. This is not so surprising, since the amount spent on training per worker suggests that the value of the training benefit is not especially high. Some workers may view participation in training programs not as a way to upgrade their skills, but as the price they must pay to receive extended unemployment benefits.

A recent cost-benefit study by Mathematica (2012) suggests that eligible workers who do not participate in training might have made the right choice.[21] The study compared workers that had received training under TAA with a

---

20. There was some evidence that high-paying firms, such as auto companies, took advantage of the program to lay off their workers ("park them") during periods of slack so that they could be recalled when demand picked up.

21. "Without considering the benefits of TAA stemming from the possibility that it promotes free trade, the *net benefit to society* of the TAA program as it operated under the 2002 amendments was negative $53,802 per participant. The main reason for the negative net benefits was that participants had lower earnings than comparison group members ... The *net benefit to TAA participants* under the 2002 program was negative $26,837, roughly 50 percent of the net benefit to society" (Mathematica 2012, i).

reference group of workers with similar attributes that had not received training.[22] The authors concluded that the costs of the training outweighed the benefits, not only from a social viewpoint that took account of potential savings in other benefits workers might have received (e.g, less unemployment insurance). Even more troubling, the costs outweighed the benefits for the workers themselves: They earned less than the control group for the four years under study. These findings suggest that, when it comes to adjustment assistance, one size does not fit all. Workers will benefit from training to differing degrees. Some might obtain the new skills required for more remunerative jobs, but others might not find new jobs requiring the skills for which they were trained. For others, training programs are expensive holding pens. Problems also stem from the additional confusion, time-consuming application and certification processes, and duplicative administrative costs that result from operating one set of programs for the TAA and another for other displaced workers. Eligibility criteria for the program have been frequently altered, creating both confusion, and at times, high rejection rates for TAA petitions.[23]

Improved Programs for Displaced Workers

The weak foundations for a TAA program that distinguishes trade-displaced and other workers, as well as preconditions benefits on the receipt of training, suggest that the time has come for substantial reforms. Some have argued that, because of the flaws in the TAA, the program should be eliminated. Others have acknowledged its imperfections but defended the program as better than nothing. Neither of these responses is adequate for US workers experiencing displacement. The two sets of programs should be consolidated and enhanced as part of a new grand bargain, in which the adoption of a CHUSTIA would be accompanied by a new comprehensive worker adjustment program that would assist all dislocated US workers, regardless of the reasons for their displacement.

In its budget proposals for fiscal year 2014, the Obama administration proposed just such a change in the form of a Universal Displaced Worker (UDW) Program that would integrate the TAA and Dislocated Worker programs into an expanded whole, delivered through the nationwide American Job Center network. This revamped program would aid all workers regardless of the reason for their displacement. The budget called for spending $4 billion on this program in 2014: $1.16 billion for income support, $1.255 billion

---

22. See Marcal (2001). Compared to unemployment insurance exhaustees and TAA nontrainees, the newly acquired skills help in finding jobs but not in raising wages. Reynolds and Palatucci (2008) reach similar conclusions.

23. Autor, Dorn, and Hanson (2013c) find that workers displaced by imports are substantially more likely to rely on Social Security Disability Insurance than on TAA. In a recent overview, Autor and Hanson (2014) survey this and other labor market impacts of increased trade between the United States and low-wage countries (principally China) over the last two decades.

for training, $727 million for reemployment services, and $686 million for wage loss insurance. While the budget proposals seem sensible for providing workers on training programs with additional income support, as well as assistance in job search and relocation, the wage-loss insurance program should be larger than what the administration has proposed.

Why Wage-Loss Insurance?

Diversification is a common strategy when economic risks are high, either at work or in investments. But most workers have one job at a time, so diversification is not easily achieved. Public unemployment insurance is one mechanism to partly insure against the risk of job loss, but its coverage is incomplete because it does not deal with the erosion in specific human capital that leads to lower wages in the future—a loss that is especially severe for workers with low educational levels. Public investment in training can, in principle, allow workers to develop new skills and increase their earning opportunities. But as already noted, training is not appropriate for all. As an additional mechanism, wage-loss insurance could compensate workers for reduced pay as a result of the erosion in their specific human capital.

In a volatile economy workers face risks that they have great difficulty insuring against. An important risk is the erosion of the value of their human capital during times of unemployment and employment at less suited jobs. A wage-loss program would not only provide insurance benefits but also speed up adjustment and save on unemployment benefits, by encouraging workers to accept jobs earlier and at lower wages than they might otherwise. It could offset some of the disincentives unemployment insurance creates.

All forms of insurance can give rise to moral hazard and other undesirable incentive effects, and thus need to be designed with some care. Unemployment insurance can reduce the incentive to find new work. Partly to deal with this effect, income replacement rates are partial, well below 100 percent, and provided for only a limited period of time. Wage loss insurance might similarly reduce the incentive to continue searching for a new job at higher pay, especially if the insurance fully compensates workers for lower wages in their new jobs. Again, however, by making compensation only partial and temporary, workers retain skin in the game, and continue to face incentives to search for jobs with higher wages and better long-run earnings potential.

The costs of such a program will depend on the ages of the workers to be covered, the job tenure required for eligibility, the proportion of wages to replace, and the duration of the benefit period. There have been several estimates of such costs. The Worker Empowerment Act of 2007, introduced by Senator Charles Schumer (D-NY) and Representative Jim McDermott (D-WA), proposed one such comprehensive wage insurance program that would replace 50 percent of a worker's lost wages for up to two years, with a cap of $10,000 per year, provided that the workers meet certain requirements, such as having held the previous job for at least two years. If limited to workers above age 50, this program was estimated to cost around $4 billion annually.[24] While such a program would be desirable, one that included workers above the age of 45 would be well worth the additional costs, on the order of $2 billion annually.

A New Funding Mechanism

In 2012, US unemployment insurance programs received $51 billion through an extremely regressive system of taxation that operates through payroll taxes—a tax averaging 3.7 percent on the first $13,046 each worker earned. While the ceiling applied to contributions to the fund is low, benefits are tied to previous earnings up to a higher ceiling. The result is that taxes on low-wage workers implicitly pay for the benefits middle-income workers receive. A worker earning $13,000 a year would contribute exactly the same amount as a worker earning $50,000 a year. But if both were unemployed for six months and received benefits with a 50 percent replacement rate, the worker earning $13,000 would receive a total of $3,250 while the worker earning $50,000 would receive $12,500.

The taxes collected by both federal and state governments have such regressive properties. The federal government collects an unemployment tax that is typically 0.6 percent of earnings up to $7,000. This implies that contributions for most workers are $42. States raise most of the revenues; on average in 2012, contributions were $361 per worker, less than 0.8 percent of total wages paid, with a tax rate of 3.5 percent up to the state ceiling. But unemployment insurance typically replaces about half of a worker's previous earnings up to a maximum benefit level. In 2012 the maximum benefit ranged from $235 per week in Mississippi to $653 per week ($979 with dependents) in Massachusetts. Because benefits are capped, unemployment insurance benefits replace a smaller share of wages for higher-wage workers, with the average replacement rate typically close to 50 percent. Unemployment insurance revenues—federal plus state—were equal to just 1 percent, about $51 billion out of the $5 trillion in total wages earned by workers on whom unemployment taxes were paid in 2012. However, it represented 3.7 percent of taxable wages, which were $1.35 trillion. By completely eliminating the ceiling, a tax of only 1 percent would raise a similar amount of money and cut taxes on most workers' wages. An additional tax rate of 0.1 percent would raise $5 billion annually, enough to fund a wage-loss insurance program for workers over 45. It would be a simple matter, in the context of such an adjustment, to raise the additional revenues required for a more generous wage-loss insurance program and for extended coverage of younger workers. Ideally, this would be implemented

---

24. Brainard, Litan, and Warren (2005) estimated that a wage insurance program that replaces 50 percent of earnings losses for workers over 45 (up to a maximum of $10,000 a year) for up to two years would cost roughly $3.5 billion annually and require an insurance premium of roughly $25 per worker a year.

only when states repaid the money to restore their positions in the Federal Unemployment Tax Act (FUTA).

Safeguards

The terms for the implementation of a CHUSTIA should reflect the differences in sector sensitivities by providing the most vulnerable sectors with longer adjustment periods. In addition, however, the broader economic context in which that adjustment is required is likely to strongly influence the costs of adjustment for individual workers. Implementing a CHUSTIA in an economy with high unemployment and large numbers of discouraged workers not even looking for work is likely to be far more costly than implementing an agreement in an economy with very high utilization rates, very low unemployment rates, and a shortage of workers.

The current safeguards provisions in the World Trade Organization (WTO) are quite difficult to implement in practice. They require that injury be due to unforeseen circumstances and deal only with injury due to imports. However, if a sector is depressed, economywide implementation of a CHUSTIA—or any trade agreement—could foster additional harm. Given the magnitude of a CHUSTIA's adjustment challenges, it would be desirable to include a special safeguard provision that would allow the pace of implementation to be slowed in the face of serious difficulties, but would not permit additional protection. Conventional safeguard provisions, in the face of substantial injury caused by Chinese imports, could also be invoked.

Conclusion

The need for improved US labor market adjustment policies is clear. Even under normal circumstances, when unemployment is low, the US economy generates considerable dislocation through involuntary layoffs. Under current circumstances, with a high overall unemployment rate and an extraordinarily high share of long-term unemployed workers, the case for improved measures to get workers back to work is strong. But while the demand for vocational training job search assistance and wage-loss compensation is high, political deadlock has hampered the government's ability to supply such services.

In the current budget context, it is no surprise that the Obama administration's proposals for a universal displaced worker program have not made much headway. As a result, the immediate focus has been on renewing the TAA program. Senators Max Baucus (D-MT) and Susan Collins (R-ME) proposed the passage of bipartisan renewal legislation in mid-2013. The renewal and continuation of this program would be an essential complement to a China–US FTA. Together with a CHUSTIA that generates significant benefits to Americans overall, however, it would be even more desirable for the Congress to implement the proposals for improved adjustment assistance put forward in this chapter.

References

Autor, David H., David Dorn, and Gordon H. Hanson. 2013a. The China Syndrome: Local Labor Market Effects of Import Competition in the United States. *American Economic Review* 103, no. 6 (October): 2121–68.

Autor, David H., David Dorn, and Gordon H. Hanson. 2013b. The Geography of Trade and Technology Shocks in the United States. *American Economic Review* 103, no. 3: 220–25.

Autor, David H., David Dorn, and Gordon H. Hanson. 2013c. *Untangling Trade and Technology: Evidence from Local Labor Markets.* Working Paper 18938. Cambridge, MA: National Bureau of Economic Research.

Autor, David H., David Dorn, Gordon H. Hanson, and Jae Song. 2013. *Trade Adjustment: Worker-Level Evidence.* Working Paper 19226. Cambridge, MA: National Bureau of Economic Research.

Autor, David H., and Gordon H. Hanson. 2014. Labor Market Adjustment to International Trade. *NBER Reporter 2014* no. 2. Cambridge, MA: National Bureau of Economic Research.

Brainard, Lael, Robert E. Litan, and Nicholas Warren. 2005. *Insuring America's Workers in the New Era of Off-Shoring.* Policy Brief 143. Washington: Brookings Institution.

Cline, William R. 1997. *Trade and Income Distribution.* Washington: Peterson Institute for International Economics.

Couch, Kenneth A., and Dana W. Placzek. 2010. Earnings Losses of Displaced Workers Revisited. *American Economic Review* 100, no. 1: 572–89.

Davis, Steven J., and Till von Wachter. 2011. Recessions and the Costs of Job Loss. *Brookings Papers on Economic Activity* 43, no. 2 (fall): 1–72.

Edwards, Lawrence, and Robert Z. Lawrence. 2013. *Rising Tide: Is Growth in Emerging Economies Good for the United States?* Washington: Peterson Institute for International Economics.

Elsby, Michael, Bart Hobjin, and Aysegul Sahin. 2013. The Decline of the US Labor Share. *Brookings Papers on Economic Activity* (fall): 1–64.

Ebenstein, Avraham, Ann Harrison, Margaret McMillan, and Shannon Phillips. 2009. *Estimating the Impact of Trade and Offshoring on American Workers Using the Current Population Surveys.* Working Paper 15107. Cambridge, MA: National Bureau of Economic Research.

Farber, Henry S. 2005. *What Do We Know about Job Loss in the United States? Evidence from the Displaced Workers Survey, 1984–2004.* Industrial Relations Section Working Paper 498. Princeton, NJ: Princeton University.

Galal, Ahmed, and Robert Z. Lawrence. 2005. *Anchoring Reform with a US-Egypt Free Trade Agreement.* Washington: Peterson Institute for International Economics.

Harrison, Anne E., John McLaren, and Margaret S. McMillan. 2010. *Recent Findings on Trade and Inequality.* Working Paper 16425. Cambridge, MA: National Bureau of Economic Research.

Jacobson, Louis S., Robert J. LaLonde, and Daniel G. Sullivan. 1993. Earnings Losses of Displaced Workers. *American Economic Review* 83, no. 4: 685–709.

Jones, Ron. 1965. The Structure of Simple General Equilibrium Models. *Journal of Political Economy* 73: 57–72.

Kambourov, Gueorgui, and Iourii Manovskii. 2009. Occupational Mobility and Wage Inequality. *Review of Economic Studies* 76, no. 2: 731–59.

Mathematica Policy Research and Social Policy Research. 2012. *Estimated Impacts for Participants in the Trade Adjustment Assistance (TAA) Program Under the 2002 Amendments.* Final Report Prepared as Part of the Evaluation of the Trade Adjustment Assistance Program (August). Washington.

Marcal, Leah H. 2001. Does Trade Adjustment Assistance Help Trade-Displaced Workers? *Contemporary Economic Policy* 19, no. 1: 59–72.

McLaren, John, and Shushanik Hakobyan. 2012. *Looking for Local Labor Market Effects of NAFTA*. NBER Working Paper 16535. Cambridge, MA: National Bureau of Economic Research.

Mussa, Michael. 1974. Tariffs and the Distribution of Income: The Importance of Factor Specificity, Substitutability, and Intensity in the Short and Long Run. *Journal of Political Economy* 82, no. 6 (November/December): 1191–203.

Neary, Peter J. 1978. Short-Run Capital Specificity and the Pure Theory of International Trade. *Economic Journal* 88, no. 351: 488–510.

Pierce, Justin R., and Peter K. Schott. 2012. *The Surprisingly Swift Decline of US Manufacturing Employment*. Working Paper 18655. Cambridge, MA: National Bureau of Economic Research.

Reynolds, Kara M., and John S. Palatucci. 2008. *Does Trade Adjustment Assistance Make a Difference?* Economics Working Paper (August). Washington: American University.

Scott, Robert E. 2010. *Rising China Trade Deficit Will Cost One-Half Million U.S. Jobs in 2010*. Issue Brief 283. Washington: Economic Policy Institute.

von Wachter, Till, Jae Song, and Joyce Manchester. 2009. Long-Term Earnings Losses Due to Mass Layoffs During the 1982 Recession: An Analysis Using US Administrative Data from 1974 to 2004. New York: Columbia University. Photocopy.

USTR (US Trade Representative). 2014. *2014 Trade Policy Agenda and 2013 Annual Report*. Washington.

II

POTENTIAL SELF-BALANCING STAND-ALONE AGREEMENTS

4

Merchandise Tariffs

With this chapter, we start delving into the nuts and bolts of trade and investment issues between the United States and China, and we continue digging for the next 14 chapters. Nearly all the issues explored would be fair game in talks over a China–US trade and investment agreement (CHUSTIA) and would certainly trigger lively debate between US and Chinese negotiators. But many of them, including the subject of this chapter, will scarcely interest the broader US or Chinese publics if some variant of CHUSTIA gets off the ground. So why do we dig into subjects such as tariff schedules, agricultural quotas, and many others? First, we want to illuminate the difficult terrain that a serious trade and investment agreement between China and the United States must traverse. CHUSTIA and its variants cannot be a feel-good diplomatic initiative. Hard differences must be reconciled for a pact to make sense. Second, trade associations and members of Congress will want to know what effects such a pact portends for their industries and constituencies, respectively.

To link this chapter to chapter 2, table 4.1 lists weighted averages of applied tariffs at the two-digit harmonized system (HS) code level, both from the World Bank's World Integrated Trade Solution (WITS) and the Global Trade Analysis Project (GTAP) Tariff Analytical and Simulation Tool for Economists (TASTE). Recall that the GTAP dataset underlies the computable general equilibrium (CGE) model that was used in chapter 2 to calculate the trade effects of CHUSTIA liberalization.[1]

---

1. The CGE model in chapter 2 employed 2007 trade weights, while the TASTE database reports averages weighted by 2004 trade data.

Table 4.1 Tariff chapters and average applied rates (percent, rounded)

2-digit HS code	Product name	China[a] WITS	China[a] GTAP	United States[b] WITS	United States[b] GTAP
	Weighted average[c]	5.5	6.4	2.7	2.5
1	Live animals	5	5	0	0
2	Meat and edible meat offal	12	14	3	3
3	Fish and crustaceans, molluscs, and other aquatic invertebrates	11	12	0	0
4	Dairy produce; birds' eggs; natural honey; edible	5	8	1	3
5	Products of animal origin, not elsewhere specified	15	16	0	0
6	Live trees and other plants; bulbs, roots, and the like	6	7	3	0
7	Edible vegetables and certain roots, and tubers	7	11	8	5
8	Edible fruit and nuts; peel of citrus fruit or melons	12	18	4	1
9	Coffee, tea, maté, and spices	15	17	1	0
10	Cereals[d]	65	0	6	10
11	Products of the milling industry; malt; starches; inulin; wheat gluten	18	17	4	0
12	Oil seeds and oleaginous fruits; miscellaneous grains, seeds, and fruit	2	7	0	1
13	Lac; gums, resins, and other vegetable saps and extracts	13	14	1	0
14	Vegetable plaiting materials; vegetable products not elsewhere specified or included	4	5	0	0
15	Animal or vegetable fats and oils and their cleavage products; prepared edible fats; animal or vegetable waxes	10	10	3	2
16	Preparations of meat, of fish, or of crustaceans, molluscs, and other aquatic invertebrates	12	12	4	1
17	Sugars and sugar confectionery	11	21	8	22
18	Cocoa and cocoa preparations	10	10	4	4
19	Preparations of cereals, flour, starch, or milk; pastry cooks' products	12	19	4	5
20	Preparations of vegetables, fruit, nuts, or other parts of plants	16	16	6	9
21	Miscellaneous edible preparations	18	18	7	17

(continues on next page)

Table 4.1   Tariff chapters and average applied rates (percent, rounded)
(continued)

2-digit HS code	Product name	China[a] WITS	China[a] GTAP	United States[b] WITS	United States[b] GTAP
22	Beverages, spirits, and vinegar	14	27	7	2
23	Residues and waste from the food industries; prepared animal feed	5	5	1	31
24	Tobacco and manufactured tobacco substitutes	10	23	77	21
25	Salt, sulphur, earths, stone, plastering materials, lime, and cement	2	3	0	0
26	Ores, slag, and ash	0	0	0	0
27	Mineral fuels, mineral oils, and products of their distillation; bituminous substances; mineral waxes	2	6	0	0
28	Inorganic chemicals; organic or inorganic compounds of precious metals, of rare-earth metals, of radioactive elements, or of isotopes	4	6	2	1
29	Organic chemicals	5	6	2	1
30	Pharmaceutical products	3	5	0	0
31	Fertilizers	4	49	0	0
32	Tanning or dyeing extracts; tannins and their derivatives; dyes, pigments, and other coloring matter; paints and varnishes; putty and other mastics; inks	8	8	4	4
33	Essential oils and resinoids; perfumery, cosmetic, or toilet preparations	12	20	1	1
34	Soap, organic surface-active agents, washing preparations, lubricating preparations, artificial waxes, prepared waxes, polishing, or scouring preparations, candles and similar articles, modeling pastes, "dental waxes" and dental preparations with a basis of plaster	9	10	1	0
35	Albuminoidal substances; modified starches; glues; enzymes	9	10	2	0
36	Explosives; pyrotechnic products; matches; pyrophoric alloys; certain combustible preparations	9	9	4	0
37	Photographic or cinematographic goods	13	39	3	0
38	Miscellaneous chemical products	6	5	2	1
39	Plastics and articles thereof	7	10	4	2
40	Rubber and articles thereof	9	9	3	1

(continues on next page)

Table 4.1 Tariff chapters and average applied rates (percent, rounded) *(continued)*

2-digit HS code	Product name	China[a]		United States[b]	
		WITS	**GTAP**	**WITS**	**GTAP**
41	Raw hides and skins (other than fur skins) and leather	6	5	3	0
42	Articles of leather; saddlery and harness; travel goods, handbags, and similar containers; articles of animal gut (other than silkworm gut)	13	16	9	9
43	Fur skins and artificial fur; manufactures thereof	16	19	3	0
44	Wood and articles of wood; wood charcoal	0	1	3	0
45	Cork and articles of cork	5	4	0	0
46	Manufactures of straw, of esparto, or of other plaiting materials; basketware and wickerwork	9	9	4	0
47	Pulp of wood or of other fibrous cellulosic material; recovered (waste and scrap) paper, or paperboard	0	0	0	0
48	Paper and paperboard; articles of paper pulp, of paper, or of paperboard	6	8	0	0
49	Printed books, newspapers, pictures, and other products of the printing industry; manuscripts, typescripts, and plans	2	2	0	0
50	Silk	10	13	0	0
51	Wool, fine, or coarse animal hair; horsehair yarn and woven fabric	28	28	13	1
52	Cotton	5	10	9	10
53	Other vegetable textile fibers; paper yarn and woven fabrics of paper yarn	9	9	3	1
54	Manmade filaments	5	10	10	10
55	Manmade staple fibers	4	6	7	7
56	Wadding, felt, and nonwovens; special yarns; twine, cordage, ropes, and cables and articles thereof	10	15	2	4
57	Carpets and other textile floor coverings	10	18	2	6
58	Special woven fabrics; tufted textile fabrics; lace; tapestries; trimmings; embroidery	10	16	7	8
59	Impregnated, coated, covered, or laminated textile fabrics; textile articles of a kind suitable for industrial use	9	11	4	1
60	Knitted or crocheted fabrics	11	16	12	10

(continues on next page)

Table 4.1   Tariff chapters and average applied rates (percent, rounded) *(continued)*

2-digit HS code	Product name	China[a]		United States[b]	
		WITS	GTAP	WITS	GTAP
61	Articles of apparel and clothing accessories, knitted or crocheted	16	19	14	11
62	Articles of apparel and clothing accessories, not knitted or crocheted	16	20	10	11
63	Other made up textile articles; sets; worn clothing and worn textile articles; rags	13	17	7	7
64	Footwear, gaiters, and the like; parts of such articles	15	17	13	17
65	Headgear and parts thereof	13	16	5	8
66	Umbrellas, sun umbrellas, walking sticks, seat sticks, whips, riding crops, and parts thereof	12	13	5	6
67	Prepared feathers and down and articles made of feathers or of down; artificial flowers; articles of human hair	19	22	3	5
68	Articles of stone, plaster, cement, asbestos, mica, or similar materials	13	12	2	1
69	Ceramic products	9	12	6	4
70	Glass and glassware	14	13	5	6
71	Natural or cultured pearls, precious or semiprecious stones, precious metals, metals clad with precious metal, and articles thereof; imitation jewelry; coin	4	6	5	8
72	Iron and steel	1	2	0	0
73	Articles of iron or steel	8	9	1	0
74	Copper and articles thereof	1	2	2	0
75	Nickel and articles thereof	6	5	1	0
76	Aluminum and articles thereof	2	4	3	1
78	Lead and articles thereof	6	2	2	0
79	Zinc and articles thereof	2	2	2	0
80	Tin and articles thereof	8	6	2	0
81	Other base metals; cermets; articles thereof	7	6	4	4
82	Tools, implements, cutlery, spoons, and forks, of base metal; parts thereof of base metal	9	10	4	5

(continues on next page)

Table 4.1   Tariff chapters and average applied rates (percent, rounded) *(continued)*

2-digit HS code	Product name	China[a] WITS	China[a] GTAP	United States[b] WITS	United States[b] GTAP
83	Miscellaneous articles of base metal	10	11	2	0
84	Nuclear reactors, boilers, machinery, and mechanical appliances; parts thereof	4	5	0	0
85	Electrical machinery and equipment and parts thereof; sound recorders and reproducers, television image and sound recorders and reproducers, and parts and accessories of such articles	2	3	1	0
86	Railway or tramway locomotives, rolling stock and parts thereof; railway or tramway track fixtures and fittings and parts thereof; mechanical (including electromechanical) traffic signaling equipment of all kinds	4	4	1	0
87	Vehicles other than railway or tramway rolling stock, and parts and accessories thereof	23	20	2	2
88	Aircraft, spacecraft, and parts thereof	3	3	0	0
89	Ships, boats, and floating structures	8	7	1	0
90	Optical, photographic, cinematographic, measuring, checking, precision, medical, or surgical instruments and apparatus; parts and accessories thereof	4	4	1	1
91	Clocks and watches and parts thereof	14	15	2	1
92	Musical instruments; parts and accessories of such articles	18	21	4	5
93	Arms and ammunition; parts and accessories thereof	13	13	2	1
94	Furniture; bedding, mattresses, mattress supports, cushions, and similar stuffed furnishings; lamps and lighting fittings, not elsewhere specified or included; illuminated signs, illuminated nameplates, and the like; prefabricated buildings	5	11	2	2
95	Toys, games, and sports requisites; parts and accessories thereof	10	12	1	0

(continues on next page)

Table 4.1   Tariff chapters and average applied rates (percent, rounded)
(continued)

2-digit HS code	Product name	China[a]		United States[b]	
		WITS	GTAP	WITS	GTAP
96	Miscellaneous manufactured articles	16	19	3	6
97	Works of art, collectors' pieces, and antiques	6	4	0	0

GTAP = Global Trade Analysis Project; HS = harmonized system; WITS = World Integrated Trade Solution

a. WITS data are weighted at the 6-digit level using US export values for 2011. GTAP data are from the MAcMaps-HS6 database, which reports 2004 data.
b. Weighted at the 6-digit level using Chinese export values for 2012. GTAP data are from the MAcMapsHS6 database, which reports 2004 data.
c. Chinese tariffs are weighted by 2011 imports from the United States while US tariffs are weighted using 2012 imports from China.
d. There appears to be a discrepancy in the Tariff Analytical and Simulation Tool for Economists (TASTE) database in cereals. World Trade Organization tariff data show that China levied substantial duties on cereal imports in 2004, whereas the TASTE database reports a zero percent tariff.

Sources: World Bank, World Integrated Trade Solution (WITS) database (2013), http://wits.worldbank.org; GTAP, www.gtap.agecon.purdue.edu.

While the two-digit tariff averages in WITS and GTAP are similar for most product categories, there are a few notable differences,[2] which largely reflect that the two datasets are based on trade volumes for different years: WITS reports data based on 2012 trade volumes for the United States and 2011 trade volumes for China, while GTAP tariffs are based on 2004 trade volumes for both countries. In product categories that have relatively little trade, the average applied two-digit tariff rate can shift significantly—with no change in the tariff schedule—if the composition of trade within the two-digit HS chapter changes sharply. However, the overall picture is much the same for the two databases. For bilateral trade, WITS reports a 5.5 percent average tariff for China and a 2.7 percent average for the United States, while TASTE reports a 6.4 percent average tariff for China and a 2.5 percent average for the United States. For the United States, tariff rates from the two sources have a Pearson correlation coefficient of 0.52, indicating a strong positive correlation. For China, the coefficient is 0.32, indicating a weaker correlation. This is largely due to the discrepancy for HS chapter 10 (cereals): the GTAP data appear to be erroneous, and if chapter 10 is excluded, the coefficient rises to a substantially stronger 0.68.

Meanwhile, again revisiting chapter 2, table 4.2 lists the ad valorem equivalents (AVEs) of nontariff barriers (NTBs) incorporated in the GTAP dataset. As can be seen, the AVEs are specified for very broad product groups.[3] For

---

2. One particularly notable difference is HS 10 (cereals), where TASTE reports duty-free status. This clearly conflicts with data from both Comtrade and the WTO.

3. NTBs on agricultural products—mainly quotas—are examined in chapter 6. While identifiable NTBs on manufactured goods, such as cumbersome customs procedures, will certainly be a

Table 4.2 US and Chinese nontariff barrier AVEs

	China	United States
Rice	33.4	11.0
Wheat	33.4	11.0
Other agriculture	33.4	11.0
Natural resources	8.4	1.9
Textiles	16.7	3.7
Chemicals	16.7	3.7
Metals	16.7	3.7
Electrical equipment	16.7	3.7
Machinery	16.7	3.7
Other manufactures	16.7	3.7

AVE = ad valorem equivalent

Source: GTAP, www.gtap.agecon.purdue.edu (accessed on July 3, 2014).

China, the GTAP database puts the AVE figure at 17 percent, and for the United States, 4 percent.

Trade negotiators haggle over tariffs and NTBs at a very fine level, often six-digit HS tariff lines. In this chapter we do not delve into the highly detailed tariff line items that make trade negotiations all-night affairs. But we do try to illuminate individual products at the four-digit HS level that will likely attract attention because they have generous tariff protection.

China's Accession to the WTO

Turning to tariff issues in prior negotiations, when China joined the World Trade Organization (WTO) in 2001, US hopes were high that exports to China would increase dramatically. China sharply lowered its import tariffs, while the United States, like other WTO members, maintained the tariff schedule agreed in the Uruguay Round. Between 2001 and 2011 US exports to China rose five-fold. But the big winner from liberalization was China itself, as the eastern coastal provinces became the hub of factory Asia, importing components from the region and exporting finished manufactures to Europe, North America, and the world. As one consequence, China's merchandise trade surplus with the United States has been running around $300 billion annually in recent

---

subject of continuing discussion between the United States and China, we do not explore NTBs on manufactures in this chapter; however, they are included in the CGE model in chapter 2, through tariff equivalent coefficients in the GTAP model.

years. Lower Chinese tariffs were crucial to China's industrial triumph over the past decade, but import tariffs and export taxes remain well above zero.[4]

Some commentators express the hope that new arrangements between China and the United States will reduce the huge imbalance in manufactured goods trade (Casey 2012).[5] It's hard to say whether these hopes will be realized. Chapter 2 predicts that even if Chinese tariffs are reduced dramatically, China's manufactured exports will increase more than US manufactured exports in dollar terms. However, US manufactured exports will increase more in percentage terms, 13 percent versus 10 percent for the Chinese side. Moreover, in the accelerated rebalancing-plus-CHUSTIA scenario over the period 2015 to 2025, described in chapter 2, the US current account would improve by $324 billion in 2020, compared to the baseline scenario. In turn, this would imply a substantial improvement in the US manufactures trade balance.

Tariff Objectives in Free Trade Agreements

The foundation of every free trade agreement (FTA) is the near elimination of import tariffs and export taxes between the parties. That is the objective, no matter what the parties' starting merchandise trade balance is, what the likely change in that balance will be as a consequence of the FTA, or how the parties' respective average heights of tariff walls differ. In the past, countries seeking to conclude an FTA have assumed that external exchange rate adjustments and internal price adjustments, over the period of implementation, will offset changes in trade balances resulting from the FTA itself. Based on these precedents an FTA between China and the United States will almost certainly seek the ultimate objective of zero tariffs and zero export taxes, even though the zero rates may be phased in over a decade or longer. Any rebalancing of Chinese trade surpluses and US trade deficits would very likely be the subject of a separate agreement (as discussed in chapters 1 and 2), and not become a pretext for indefinite maintenance of tariff barriers.

This chapter reviews US and Chinese current and past tariff rates, concentrating on manufactures[6] and paying special attention to peaks in the US and Chinese tariff schedules. In a reciprocal FTA, the political obstacles to phasing out tariffs below 5 percent ad valorem are usually modest;[7] the hardest negotiations generally center on tariffs above 15 percent. High import tariffs may

---

4. This chapter covers normal export taxes. Export controls for national security purposes are covered in chapter 12.

5. See also Ernest Preeg, "US Trade in Manufactures Flat While Chinese Trade Soars," Manufacturers Alliance for Productivity and Innovation (MAPI), May 16, 2013, www.mapi.net (accessed on May 19, 2014).

6. Agricultural barriers are discussed in chapter 6.

7. However, the unilateral MFN reduction of tariffs below 5 percent can be quite difficult, as the experience of Chile and Mexico demonstrates.

enable uncompetitive firms to sell their products in domestic markets, but these are exactly the industries in which the partner country often sees the greatest opportunities. The political economy question is whether the partner country is willing to pay enough, in market access terms, for the high-tariff country to overcome its own domestic political opposition by harnessing local export interests to the cause of liberalization. Since high export taxes play a similar role in guarding uncompetitive firms—in this context, firms that use raw materials—our review examines both high import tariffs and high export taxes that will likely be at the center of FTA talks.

Penalty Duties

The discussion so far excludes penalty duties and similar measures imposed as remedies to compensate for imports that may be considered unfair or injurious— namely antidumping duties; countervailing duties; safeguard duties, including market disruption cases against Chinese imports; and US Tariff Act Section 337 exclusion orders against pirated and counterfeit goods. Antidumping duties target foreign firms that allegedly engage in predatory pricing. These duties are meant to prevent foreign firms from flooding the domestic market with cheap goods and driving domestic producers out of business. Countervailing duties target foreign firms that allegedly gain an unfair advantage due to subsidies received from the home government. Safeguard duties are designed to enable a domestic industry to regain its footing in the face of fairly traded but highly competitive foreign competition. Section 337, when invoked, simply closes the US market to foreign goods that infringe on US patents, copyrights, or trademarks.

In their FTAs, neither China nor the United States has waived the possible imposition of antidumping or countervailing duties. Neither has eliminated safeguard duties. And, if anything, the FTAs reinforce Section 337 exclusion orders for pirated or counterfeit products. Based on this record, the prospects for curtailing unfair and injurious trade remedies in the CHUSTIA are slight.

Penalty Provisions in Other FTAs

In contrast to the United States and China, the European Union has abolished antidumping, countervailing, and safeguard duties among its members, as have Australia and New Zealand in their Closer Economic Relations agreement. The Canada-Chile FTA took antidumping measures off the table, while both parties committed to "consult with a view to defining subsidy disciplines further and eliminating the need for domestic countervailing duty measures on trade between them."[8] We question whether these examples could serve as precedents for a China–US FTA because each country fears the possibility of

---

8. From chapter M, article M-05 of the Canada–Chile Free Trade Agreement, www.sice.oas.org (accessed on June 23, 2014).

unfair or injurious imports from the other (Hufbauer and Woollacott 2010). We can, however, see a faint possibility for procedural changes in statutes that would give affected domestic users legal standing to object to the imposition of duties in administrative hearings. Such changes would give voice to domestic households and industries that purchase the imported goods in question.

Market Economy Status

US antidumping duties can bite hard when levied against China, since the United States has labeled China a nonmarket economy (NME). When levying duties against a foreign firm from a country regarded as a market economy, the duties are calibrated based on the costs in the firm's home country. However, if the firm's home country is an NME, then it is assumed that home country costs are artificial and do not reliably reflect true costs. So instead, duties are based on costs in a similar market economy country. This assumes that true costs would be the same in the NME country and its chosen proxy if the NME were a market economy. The assumption is almost certainly false in the case of China, since Chinese industry is particularly efficient relative to other emerging countries that might serve as proxies.[9]

Under its Protocol of Accession to the WTO, China will automatically be granted de facto market economy status in 2016.[10] Many countries have granted China market economy status ahead of schedule. Japan, the United States, and the European Union are not among them. Australia, however, granted market economy status to China at the start of bilateral FTA negotiations in 2005.[11] China might request a similar concession from the United States from the start. China is by far the most frequent target of US antidumping duties, accounting for 94 of the 297 antidumping orders currently in place.[12] Granting market economy status would affect all future antidumping cases and might require recalculation of penalty rates in existing antidumping cases. While the overall economic effect of reducing antidumping duties would be relatively

---

9. For example, Thailand was used as a proxy in a US antidumping case against China of solar panels; Thai costs were used as a substitute to calculate manufacturing costs in China. A 31 percent tariff was put on US imports of Chinese solar panels. See Keith Bradsher and Diane Cardwell, "US Slaps High Tariffs on Chinese Solar Panels," *New York Times*, May 17, 2012.

10. The Protocol of Accession does not confer market economy status to China in 2016, but it does require the use of Chinese costs and prices in antidumping cases, which amounts to the same thing in practice. See the discussion below. It is an open question whether China would make concessions to obtain market economy status from the United States.

11. Mendaka Abeysekera, "Australia Grants Full Market Economy Status to China," Asian Tribune, April 20, 2005, www.asiantribune.com (accessed on May 19, 2014). As Australia's FTA negotiations with China are still under way eight years later, it appears that the concession did not speed up the talks.

12. US International Trade Commission, antidumping and countervailing duty orders as of May 29, 2013, www.usitc.gov (accessed on July 8, 2014).

slight, the political cost of recognizing China as a market economy could be substantial in the next year or two. However, this political cost should diminish sharply once the NME methodology for calculating antidumping duties is discontinued in 2016.

One commentator, Bernard O'Connor, wrote in 2011 that China's market economy status is not automatic according to the legal text of the WTO.[13] Indeed, the text in the WTO does not clearly state that China will automatically get market economy status at a certain date.[14] Article 15 (d) states that "the provisions of subparagraph (a)(ii) shall expire 15 years after the date of accession," which was December 11, 2001. Article 15 (a)(ii) states that "the importing WTO Member may use a methodology that is not based on a strict comparison with domestic prices or costs in China if the producers under investigation cannot clearly show that market economy conditions prevail in the industry producing the like product with regard to manufacture, production and sale of that product." Whether or not China is awarded a "market economy" label, what seems certain is that the methodology the United States currently uses in antidumping cases—namely, drawing on data from a proxy market economy to value Chinese prices and costs—will expire in December 2016. After that date, Chinese prices and costs must be used in making antidumping determinations.

Tariffs in the WTO

In the 19th century, before the institution of the income tax, public revenue was an important function of tariffs, and that is still true in a few small countries. But the overriding purpose of tariff legislation since World War I has been to protect selected branches of industry and agriculture. In response, bilateral trade treaties in the early 20th century were designed to limit, on a reciprocal basis, the protective effect of national tariff schedules. This goal was the driving force behind the General Agreement on Tariffs and Trade (GATT) signed in 1947. Today predictable access to foreign markets remains a core objective of the WTO rulebook.

The three types of tariffs are ad valorem, specific, and mixed. After World War II, specific tariffs—so much duty levied per unit, weight, or volume—were common, but today ad valorem tariffs dominate. These tariffs, expressed as a percentage of customs value,[15] have the advantage of transparency in protective effect, are easily compared across countries, and facilitate reciprocal bargaining. Largely owing to nine rounds of multilateral trade negotiations since

---

13. Bernard O'Connor, "Market-Economy Status for China Is Not Automatic," VoxEU, November 27, 2011, www.voxeu.org (accessed on May 19, 2014).

14. See Article 15, World Trade Organization, Accession of the People's Republic of China, WT/L/432, November 23, 2001, www.worldtradelaw.net (accessed on May 19, 2014).

15. Methods of determining customs value are agreed in the World Customs Organization, based in Brussels.

the GATT was formed, average tariffs on industrial products for advanced countries are now below 4 percent ad valorem.[16]

Plurilateral Agreements in the WTO

Currently three plurilateral agreements are being negotiated in the WTO to lower tariffs. The Trade in Services Agreement (TiSA) focuses on lowering barriers to services trade (see chapter 7). An update to the Information Technology Agreement (ITA2) focuses on lowering tariffs for a longer list of information technology products. The third agreement seeks to eliminate tariffs on environmental goods (EGA).

The first ITA was negotiated at the Singapore Ministerial in December 1996 and comprised 29 members. A slew of new IT products have entered the market since then, and now 70 countries are looking to update the deal. China joined the ITA in 2003 and has benefited greatly from it, purchasing technology inputs tariff-free and using them to make finished goods for the export market. Many observers regard this updated plurilateral agreement as a litmus test of Chinese intentions. In November 2013, China for the second time refused to eliminate tariffs on a substantial number of IT tariff lines. Criticism came from all sides. US Trade Representative Michael Froman publicly challenged China's stance, as did EU Trade Commissioner Karel De Gucht. Japan, South Korea, Canada, Norway, Taiwan, Australia, Costa Rica, and others also made critical comments.[17] ITA talks were suspended, awaiting a change of position in Beijing. Nothing happened at the ninth WTO Ministerial meeting, held in Bali, Indonesia, in December 2013, and there was no breakthrough as of mid-2014.

Structure of Tariff Schedules

Modern tariff schedules enumerate thousands of products in great detail. Under the auspices of the World Customs Organization, 175 countries have adopted the harmonized system (HS) of customs classification, which has become the international standard for reporting import and export values to customs and other government agencies. The first 6 digits of the HS are used universally. Each country may then add to the original 6 digits to suit its own protective and statistical needs, creating 8- or even 10-digit codes. The United States has 1,100 lines in the 4-digit code and over 18,000 lines in the 10-digit code, implying an average of just over 16 10-digit lines in every 4-digit HS code.

---

16. See World Trade Organization, "Tariffs: More Bindings and Closer to Zero," www.wto.org (accessed on May 19, 2014). Unilateral tariff reductions have been important in many Latin American and Asian countries.

17. Inside US Trade, "ITA Expansion Talks Suspended Again; No Timeline for Resumption Set," *World Trade Online*, November 22, 2013, insidetrade.com (accessed on May 19, 2014).

Table 4.3　Level of detail in the US tariff schedule

HS code type	Approximate number of lines
2-digit	97
4-digit	1,100
6-digit	4,300
8-digit	9,500
10-digit	18,000

HS = harmonized system

Sources: Harmonized Tariff Schedule of the United States Annotated, www.usitc.gov; US Census Bureau, www.census.gov.

Table 4.3 gives the approximate number of lines at each level of the system for the US tariff schedule.

Agreed tariff schedules, listing thousands of items from the 6- to 10-digit level, are bound in the GATT and put a ceiling on duties that can be collected on imports from other WTO members. However, countries often apply tariffs at lower rates than the GATT-bound schedules because they see the advantage to their national economies of unilaterally reducing protection. As a general rule, applied tariffs, whether at the bound rate or below, must be imposed at the same rate on imports from all WTO members, in a central application of the famous most favored nation (MFN) principle. However, the WTO permits partners in a free trade area or customs union to apply lower tariffs, on a preferential basis, to one another, which is a central goal of most FTAs. Because China and the United States are not FTA partners, they apply their GATT-bound MFN tariff schedules, or slightly lower applied rates, to bilateral trade.

Chinese and US MFN Applied Tariff Rates

The WITS columns in table 4.1 show MFN applied average rates for the 97 HS codes at the two-digit level. The Chinese tariff on nearly every two-digit product substantially exceeds the US tariff. The weighted average Chinese tariff on US merchandise exports was 5.5 percent in 2011, while the weighted average US tariff on all Chinese exports was 2.7 percent.

Nicholas Lardy (2002) presents a somewhat different view of China's tariffs. China introduced high import tariffs in the early 1980s; the average statutory tariff was 56 percent in 1982. During the 1990s China made many adjustments in the run-up to joining the WTO so that by 2001 the average statutory rate was 15 percent. However, China applies low or zero tariffs on large imports of raw materials and capital goods and exempts certain intermediate goods from the bound tariff rates. As major categories, China exempts from import tariffs raw materials, capital goods used in joint ventures and wholly foreign owned enterprises, and parts and components used to assemble products for the export market.[18] These practices have had a large and favorable effect on Chinese firms and were a major factor in China's manufacturing expansion.

The exemptions permit duty-free imports, which enable producers to operate at international prices when selling in foreign markets. The exemptions lowered the share of goods subject to import tariffs to less than 40 percent in the first half of 2000. Tariff revenue calculated as a percentage of total import value was very low. In 1986 tariff revenue was 16 percent of total imports. This figure dropped to 2.8 percent in 2000 and 2.4 percent in 2012, painting a different picture than the weighted average of MFN applied rates. Lardy attributes the fall in tariff revenue as a percentage of import value to several factors. The share of duty-free imports rose as foreign direct investment (FDI) increased and export processing became more important. Meanwhile China collected zero or near-zero tariffs on fuel and mineral imports. In 2011 China's total imports were $1.7 trillion, with fuel and minerals accounting for nearly 30 percent of that, at around $515 billion—$275 billion for fuel and $240 billion for minerals.[19]

The low tariff revenue calculations, however, do not portray the effects of protective tariff barriers on imports of manufactured or agricultural products destined for consumption within China. So far as is known, those imports bear the full burden of China's MFN bound tariff schedule. That is the Chinese tariff protection that foreign partners, including the United States, are eager to dismantle.

China's duty exemption provision on intermediate goods provides very slight relief to US exporters, since few of their shipments to China are parts and components used to manufacture Chinese exports. The US Harmonized Tariff Schedule (HTS) has a four-digit line, HTS 9802, for imported products, which partly embody US exports.[20] The US tariff on these items applies only to the value added abroad, not the value of US parts and components. In 2012 the total value of such imports from China was only $52 million, a trivial fraction of total US imports from China. Of course some US exports to China are assembled into products sold to third countries and thus are eligible for Chinese duty exemption, and some Chinese exporters to the United States may not take advantage of HTS 9802, but based on the minuscule amount of HTS 9802 imports, these other avenues for potential duty exemption on US manufactured exports are probably quite small. For these reasons, the CGE model estimates reported in chapter 2 assume that US exports to China, and Chinese

---

18. The exemption of intermediate goods conforms to the duty drawback provisions of the WTO Agreement on Subsidies and Countervailing Measures (ASCM).

19. See World Trade Organization, "Merchandise Trade," International Trade Statistics 2012, www.wto.org (accessed on May 19, 2014).

20. HTS 9802 is a lineal descendant of Sections 806.30 and 807.00 in the old US tariff schedule, provisions that were intensely used for turnaround imports from Mexico before the North American Free Trade Agreement was enacted.

exports to the United States, are entirely final goods or intermediates used for processing and sale to the domestic market, not the export market. Hence the applied MFN tariff rates of both countries represent the appropriate tariff walls for calculating the benefits of liberalization.

To summarize, the CHUSTIA would sharply narrow the difference in scheduled tariffs—not overnight, but over a period of 5 to 10 years—as China lowers its tariff walls and as both countries approach zero tariff rates on bilateral merchandise trade.

Exceptionally High and High Tariffs

Table 4.4 identifies the large number of four-digit HS lines in the Chinese tariff schedule that have either exceptionally high ad valorem rates (50 percent and above) or high rates (15 to 49 percent). These items presumably would be the focus of US demands in FTA negotiations. Likewise, table 4.4 identifies the much smaller number of four-digit HS lines in the US tariff schedule with exceptionally high and high tariffs (only the tobacco tariff is exceptionally high). Several of these will be the focus of Chinese demands.

Tariffs in FTAs

Hundreds of FTAs have been concluded in the past 25 years, and for nearly all of them a central motivation was to slash tariffs on trade between the partners, getting rates as close to zero as domestic politics would permit. FTAs cut tariffs to levels far below GATT-bound rates, but on a preferential basis between the partners.

In bilateral FTAs, because the lower (or zero) tariffs are intended to apply only to imports from FTA partners, rules of origin are needed, in principle, to deter trade deflection in line items for which the MFN applied tariffs of the FTA partners differ significantly (e.g., 2 percent ad valorem or more). Trade deflection happens when imports from a third country, not a member of the FTA, are imported into one of the partners—the one with the lower tariff on that line item—and then reexported to the other partner at a low or zero tariff. Avoiding trade deflection sounds reasonable, but in practice, rules of origin are written into FTAs not only to deter trade deflection but also to protect certain supplying industries (e.g., textiles or auto parts) in partner countries. Thus, as in the WTO, in an FTA the hard bargaining usually centers on line items with peak tariffs. The rules of origin are intensely debated on these line items, partly to deter trade deflection, but also to prolong the protection of industries that have historically been shielded from international competition.

Table 4.4 High Chinese tariffs: treatment under China–Chile FTA, 2006

Exceptionally high MFN applied tariffs

4-digit HS code	Product name	MFN applied percent[a]	China–Chile zero-duty year
2205	Vermouth and other wine, flavored	65	Year 10
1001	Wheat and meslin	65	Exempt
1005	Maize (corn)	65	Exempt
1006	Rice	65	Exempt
1101	Wheat or meslin flour	65	Exempt
2403	Other manufactured tobacco and substitutes	57	Year 10
1701	Cane or beet sugar and chemically pure sucrose	50	Exempt

High MFN applied tariffs in the China–Chile FTA

4-digit HS code	Product name	MFN applied[b] percent	China–Chile zero-duty year
2206	Other fermented beverages	40	Year 5
5203	Cotton, carded or combed	40	Exempt
1102	Cereal flours other than of wheat or meslin	40	Exempt
5101	Wool, not carded or combed	38	Exempt
7114	Articles of goldsmiths' or silversmiths' wares	35	Year 5
7116	Articles of natural or cultured pearls	35	Year 10
3102	Mineral or chemical fertilizers, nitrogenous	34	Partly exempt
2202	Waters, including mineral waters	32	Year 10
2101	Extracts, essences, and concentrates, of coffee, tea, etc.	31	Year 10
8711	Motorcycles and cycles fitted with an auxiliary motor	30	Year 2
0811	Fruit and nuts, uncooked or cooked by steaming or boiling	30	Year 10
0812	Fruit and nuts, provisionally preserved	30	Year 10
2006	Vegetables, fruit, nuts, preserved by sugar	30	Year 10
9207	Musical instruments, electrically amplified	30	Year 5
7113	Articles of jewelry and parts containing precious metals	29	Year 10
0804	Dates, figs, pineapples, avocados, etc., fresh or dried	28	Year 10
1517	Margarine, other edible animal fats and oils	27	Year 10
6809	Articles of plaster or of compositions based on plaster	26	Year 10

(continues on next page)

Table 4.4 High Chinese tariffs: treatment under China–Chile FTA, 2006
(continued)

	High MFN applied tariffs in the China–Chile FTA		
4-digit HS code	Product name	MFN applied[b] percent	China–Chile zero-duty year
1904	Prepared foods obtained by the swelling or roasting of cereals	25	Year 10
1103	Cereal groats, meal, and pellets	25	Partly exempt
8703	Motor cars and other motor vehicles, transport of persons	25	Year 2
9614	Smoking pipes and cigar or cigarette holders	25	Year 5
0210	Meat and edible meat offal, salted, in brine, dried or smoked; edible flours and meals of meat or meat offal	25	Year 10
0814	Peel of citrus fruit or melons (including watermelons), fresh, frozen, dried, or provisionally preserved in brine, in sulphur water, or in other preservative solutions	25	Year 10
2001	Vegetables, fruit, nuts, and other edible parts of plants, prepared or preserved by vinegar or acetic acid	25	Year 10
2003	Mushrooms and truffles, prepared or preserved but not by vinegar or acetic acid	25	Year 10
2102	Yeasts (active or inactive); other single-cell microorganisms, dead (but not including vaccines of heading 3002); prepared baking powders	25	Year 10
2402	Cigars, cheroots, cigarillos, and cigarettes, of tobacco or of tobacco substitutes	25	Year 10
9613	Cigarette lighters and other lighters, whether or not mechanical or electrical, and parts thereof other than flints or wicks	25	Year 10
8702	Motor vehicles for the transport of ten or more persons, including the driver	25	Year 2
0813	Fruit, dried, other than that of headings 08.01 to 08.06	25	Year 10
6401	Waterproof footwear with outer soles and uppers of rubber or plastics that are fixed together by bonding or similar processes	24	Year 2
6404	Footwear with outer soles of rubber, plastics, leather, or composition leather and uppers of textile material	24	Year 2
6507	Headbands, linings, covers, hat foundations, hat frames, peaks (visors), and chin straps for headgear	24	Year 2

(continues on next page)

Table 4.4   High Chinese tariffs: treatment under China–Chile FTA, 2006
(continued)

	High MFN applied tariffs in the China–Chile FTA		
4-digit HS code	**Product name**	**MFN applied[b] percent**	**China–Chile zero-duty year**
5103	Waste of wool or of fine or coarse animal hair, including yarn waste but excluding garnetted stock	24	Partly exempt
6402	Other footwear with outer soles and uppers of rubber or plastics, nesoi	23	Year 2
1603	Extracts and juices of meat, fish or crustaceans, molluscs or other aquatic invertebrates	23	Year 5
1516	Animal or vegetable fats and oils and their fractions, partly or wholly hydrogenated, etc., whether or not refined, but not further prepared	23	Year 10
6405	Other footwear	22	Year 2
1804	Cocoa butter, fat, and oil	22	Year 5
9208	Musical boxes, fairground organs, mechanical singing birds, other musical instruments, nesoi; decoy calls; whistles; other mouth-blown signal devices	22	Year 5
9617	Vacuum flasks and other vacuum vessels, complete with cases; parts thereof other than glass inners	22	Year 5
6102	Women's or girls' overcoats, car coats, capes, cloaks, anoraks (including ski jackets), and similar articles, knitted or crocheted, nesoi	21	Year 2
8522	Parts and accessories suitable for use solely or principally with the apparatus of 8519 to 8521	21	Year 5
7016	Paving blocks, etc., for building purposes; glass cubes, etc., for decorative purposes; leaded glass articles; foam glass in blocks, panels, etc.	21	Year 5
7101	Pearls, natural or cultured, not strung, mounted, or set; pearls, natural or cultured, temporarily strung for convenience of transport	21	Year 5
9604	Hand sieves and hand riddles	21	Year 5
9607	Slide fasteners and parts thereof	21	Year 5
9618	Tailors' dummies and other mannequins; automatons and other animated displays for shop window dressing	21	Year 5
7612	Aluminum casks, drums, cans, and similar containers, nesoi, of a capacity of not over 300 liters (79.3 gal.)	21	Year 10
9507	Fishing rods, line fishing tackle; nets (fish landing, butterfly, etc.); hunting decoy birds, etc.; parts and accessories thereof	21	Year 10

(continues on next page)

		High MFN applied tariffs in the China–Chile FTA	
4-digit HS code	Product name	MFN applied[b] percent	China–Chile zero-duty year
9611	Date, sealing, or numbering stamps, etc. (including devices for printing, etc., labels) for hand use; hand-operated composing sticks and printing sets	21	Year 10
1212	Locust beans, seaweeds, etc., sugar beet and sugar cane; fruit stones and kernels and other vegetable products used for human consumption, nesoi	21	Year 5
6505	Hats and other headgear, knitted or crocheted, or made up from lace, felt, or other textile fabric, in the piece (no strips); hairnets of any material	21	Year 10
4303	Articles of apparel, clothing accessories, and other articles of fur skin	20	Year 10
8521	Video recording or reproducing apparatus, whether or not incorporating a video tuner	20	Year 10
7322	Radiators, air heaters, and hot air distributors having a motor-driven fan or blower, not electrically heated, and parts thereof, of iron or steel	20	Year 10
9103	Clocks with watch movements, excluding instrument panel and similar clocks for vehicles, aircraft, spacecraft, or vessels	20	Year 5
6702	Artificial flowers, foliage, and fruit and parts thereof; articles made of artificial flowers, foliage, or fruit	20	Year 2
6504	Hats and other headgear, plaited or made by assembling strips of any material, whether or not lined or trimmed	20	Year 2
6701	Skins and other parts of birds with their feathers	20	Year 2
6703	Human hair, dressed or otherwise worked; wool or other animal hair or other textile materials, prepared for use in making wigs or the like	20	Year 2
6803	Worked slate and articles of slate or of agglomerated slate	20	Year 2
8715	Baby carriages and parts thereof	20	Year 2
0904	Pepper of the genus Piper; fruits of the genus Capsicum (peppers) or of the genus Pimenta, dried, crushed, or ground	20	Year 5
4001	Natural rubber, balata, gutta-percha, guayule, chicle, and similar natural gums, in primary forms or in plates, sheets, or strips	20	Year 5

(continues on next page)

4-digit HS code	Product name	High MFN applied tariffs in the China–Chile FTA	
		MFN applied[b] percent	China–Chile zero-duty year
4201	Saddlery and harness for any animal (including traces, leads, knee pads, muzzles, saddle cloths, saddle bags, dog coats, and the like), of any material	20	Year 5
0209	Pig fat free of lean meat and poultry fat (not rendered or otherwise extracted), fresh, chilled, frozen, salted, in brine, dried, or smoked	20	Year 10
0408	Birds' eggs, not in shell and egg yolks, fresh, dried, cooked by steam, etc., molded, frozen, or otherwise preserved, sweetened or not	20	Year 10
1106	Flour and meal of dried leguminous vegetables (hd. 0713), of sago or roots, etc. (hd. 0714); flour, meal, and powder of fruit and nuts, etc. (ch. 8)	20	Year 10
2209	Vinegar and substitutes for vinegar obtained from acetic acid	20	Year 10
9601	Worked ivory, bone, tortoiseshell, horn, coral, and other animal carving material and articles thereof (including articles obtained by molding)	20	Year 10
1104	Cereal grains, otherwise worked (hulled, rolled, etc.), except rice (heading 1006); germ of cereals, whole, rolled, flaked, or ground	20	Partly exempt
1521	Vegetable waxes (other than triglycerides), beeswax, other insect waxes, and spermaceti, whether or not refined or colored	20	Exempt
4414	Wooden frames for paintings, photographs, mirrors, or similar objects	20	Exempt
9608	Ballpoint pens; soft-tipped pens, and markers; fountain pens and other pens; duplicating stylos; mechanical pencils; pen holders, etc.; parts thereof	20	Year 10
2103	Sauces and preparations thereof; mixed condiments and mixed seasonings; mustard flour and meal and prepared mustard	20	Year 10
7011	Glass envelopes (including bulbs and tubes), open, and glass parts thereof, without fittings, for electric lamps, cathode ray tubes, or the like	20	Year 5
7117	Imitation jewelry	20	Year 10
1108	Starches; inulin	20	Year 5
2002	Tomatoes prepared or preserved otherwise than by vinegar or acetic acid	19	Year 10

(continues on next page)

Table 4.4   High Chinese tariffs: treatment under China–Chile FTA, 2006 *(continued)*

4-digit HS code	Product name	MFN applied[b] percent	China–Chile zero-duty year
	High MFN applied tariffs in the China–Chile FTA		
3301	Essential oils, concretes, and absolutes; resinoid; extracted oleoresins; concen. of essen. oils and terpenic by prods.; aqueous solutions, etc., of essen. oil	19	Year 10
9606	Buttons, press fasteners, snap fasteners and press studs, button molds, and other parts of these articles; button blanks	19	Year 5
0410	Edible products of animal origin, nesoi	19	Year 5
0504	Animal guts, bladders, and stomachs (other than fish), whole and pieces thereof, fresh, chilled, frozen, salted, in brine, dried, or smoked	19	Year 10
2008	Fruit, nuts, and other edible parts of plants, otherwise prepared or preserved, whether or not containing added sweetening or spirit, nesoi	19	Year 10
3701	Photographic plates and film, flat, sensitized, unexposed, not of paper, paperboard, or textiles; instant print film, flat, sensitized, unexposed	19	Year 10
2105	Ice cream and other edible ice, whether or not containing cocoa	19	Year 10
2005	Vegetables, other than tomatoes, mushrooms, and truffles, prepared or preserved otherwise than by vinegar or acetic acid, not frozen exc. prdcts. of 2006	19	Year 10
1905	Bread, pastry, cakes, biscuits, and other bakers' wares; communion wafers, empty capsules for medicine, etc., sealing wafers, rice paper, etc.	19	Year 10
3703	Photographic paper, paperboard, and textiles, sensitized, unexposed	18	Year 10
4304	Artificial fur and articles thereof	18	Year 5
8310	Sign plates, name plates, address plates, and similar plates, numbers, letters, and other symbols (not illuminated), and parts thereof, of base metal	18	Year 5
8210	Hand-operated mechanical appliances, weighing not over 10 kg, for preparing, conditioning, or serving food or drink, and base metal parts thereof	18	Year 10
9615	Combs, hair slides, and the like; hairpins, curling pins, curling grips, hair curlers, and the like (excluding electrically operated), and parts thereof	18	Year 10
9616	Scent and similar toilet sprayers, and mounts and heads thereof; powder puffs and pads for the application of cosmetics or toilet preparations	18	Year 10

(continues on next page)

Table 4.4   High Chinese tariffs: treatment under China–Chile FTA, 2006
(continued)

4-digit HS code	Product name	MFN applied[b] percent	China–Chile zero-duty year
	High MFN applied tariffs in the China–Chile FTA		
9205	Wind musical instruments, nesoi, including clarinets, trumpets, and bagpipes	18	Year 10
8519	Sound recording or reproducing apparatus	18	Year 5
9602	Worked vegetable or mineral carving materials, etc.; molded or carved articles of wax, stearin, gum, resin, etc., nesoi; unhardened gelatin and articles	18	Year 5
2104	Soups and broths and preparations thereof; homogenized composite food preparations	18	Year 10
6802	Worked monumental or building stone and articles thereof, nesoi; mosaic cubes and the like and colored granules, chippings, and powder, of natural stone	18	Year 10
6101	Men's or boys' overcoats, car coats, capes, cloaks, anoraks (including ski jackets), and similar articles, knitted or crocheted, nesoi	18	Year 2
2106	Food preparations, nesoi	18	Year 10
0407	Birds' eggs, in shell, fresh, preserved, or cooked	18	Year 2
9206	Percussion musical instruments (for example, drums, xylophones, cymbals, castanets, maracas)	18	Year 2
7004	Drawn glass and blown glass, in sheets, whether or not having an absorbent, reflecting, or nonreflecting layer, but not otherwise worked	18	Year 5
9201	Pianos, harpsichords, and other keyboard stringed instruments	18	Year 5
9202	String musical instruments, nesoi, including guitars, violins, and harps	18	Year 5
0301	Live fish	18	Year 10
7003	Cast glass and rolled glass, in sheets or profiles, whether or not having an absorbent, reflecting, or nonreflecting layer, but not otherwise worked	17	Year 5
6211	Track suits, ski suits, and swimwear, not knitted or crocheted	17	Year 2
6112	Track suits, ski suits, and swimwear, knitted or crocheted	17	Year 2
6114	Other garments, knitted or crocheted	17	Year 2
6201	Men's or boys' overcoats, raincoats, cloaks, anoraks (including ski jackets), and similar articles, not knitted or crocheted, nesoi	17	Year 2

(continues on next page)

Table 4.4   High Chinese tariffs: treatment under China–Chile FTA, 2006 *(continued)*

		High MFN applied tariffs in the China–Chile FTA	
4-digit HS code	**Product name**	**MFN applied[b] percent**	**China–Chile zero-duty year**
4015	Articles of apparel and clothing accessories (including gloves, mittens, and mitts), for all purposes, of unhardened vulcanized rubber	17	Year 5
6202	Women's or girls' overcoats, raincoats, cloaks, anoraks (including ski jackets), and similar articles, not knitted or crocheted, nesoi	17	Year 2
6815	Articles of stone or other mineral substances (including carbon fibers, articles of carbon fibers, and articles of peat), nesoi	17	Year 5
6103	Men's or boys' suits, ensembles, suit-type jackets, blazers, trousers, bib and brace overalls, breeches and shorts (no swimwear), knitted or crocheted	17	Year 2
8714	Parts and accessories for motorcycles, bicycles, and other cycles, including parts and accessories for delivery tricycles and invalid carriages	17	Year 2
6206	Women's or girls' blouses, shirts, and shirt blouses, not knitted or crocheted	17	Year 2
6704	Wigs, false beards, eyebrows, and eyelashes, switches and similar articles, of human or animal hair or textile materials; articles of human hair, nesoi	17	Year 2
8506	Primary cells and primary batteries	17	Year 10
6106	Women's or girls' blouses and shirts, knitted or crocheted	17	Year 2
9405	Lamps and lighting fittings and parts thereof, nesoi; illuminated signs, etc., with a fixed light source and parts thereof, nesoi	16	Year 10
6301	Blankets and traveling rugs	16	Year 2
6203	Men's or boys' suits, ensembles, suit-type jackets, blazers, trousers, bib and brace overalls, breeches, etc. (no swimwear), not knitted or crocheted	16	Year 2
8513	Portable electric lamps designed to function on own energy source (dry batteries, storage batteries, magnetos), except for motor vehicles, etc.; parts	16	Year 10
6105	Men's or boys' shirts, knitted or crocheted	16	Year 2
2009	Fruit juices not fortified with vitamins or minerals (including grape must) and vegetable juices, unfermented and not containing additional spirits, whether or not containing added sweetening	16	Year 10

(continues on next page)

Table 4.4 High Chinese tariffs: treatment under China–Chile FTA, 2006 *(continued)*

		High MFN applied tariffs in the China–Chile FTA	
4-digit HS code	**Product name**	**MFN applied[b] percent**	**China–Chile zero-duty year**
1515	Fixed vegetable fats and oils (including jojoba oil) and their fractions, whether or not refined, but not chemically modified	16	Year 10
6104	Women's or girls' suits, ensembles, suit-type jackets, blazers, dresses, skirts, divided skirts, trousers, etc. (no swimwear), knitted or crocheted	16	Year 2
6210	Garments, made up of fabrics of felt or nonwovens and garments of textile fabrics (not knit, etc.) rubberized or impregnated, coated, etc., with plastics	16	Year 2
6204	Women's or girls' suits, ensembles, suit-type jackets, dresses, skirts, divided skirts, trousers, etc. (no swimwear), not knitted or crocheted	16	Year 2
6113	Garments, impregnated, coated, covered, or laminated with plastics, rubber, or other materials, knitted or crocheted	16	Year 2
6205	Men's or boys' shirts	16	Year 2
9109	Clock movements, complete and assembled	16	Year 5
9110	Complete watch or clock movements, unassembled or partly assembled; incomplete watch or clock movements, assembled; rough watch or clock movements	16	Year 5
9106	Time of day recording apparatus and apparatus for measuring, recording, or indicating intervals of time, with clock, etc., movement or synchronous motor	16	Year 10
4416	Casks, barrels, vats, tubs, and other coopers' products and parts thereof, of wood, including staves	16	Exempt
4417	Tools, tool bodies, tool handles, broom, or brush bodies and handles, of wood; boot or shoe lasts and trees of wood	16	Exempt
4301	Raw fur skins, nesoi (other than raw hides and skins usually used for leather), including heads, tails, and pieces or cuttings suitable for furriers' use	16	Year 5
6305	Sacks and bags, of textile materials, used for the packing of goods	16	Year 2
9209	Parts and accessories of musical instruments; metronomes, tuning forks, and pitch pipes	16	Year 5
6108	Women's or girls' slips, petticoats, briefs, panties, nightdresses, pajamas, negligees, bathrobes, and similar articles, knitted or crocheted	15	Year 2

(continues on next page)

Table 4.4   High Chinese tariffs: treatment under China–Chile FTA, 2006 (continued)

	High MFN applied tariffs in the China–Chile FTA		
4-digit HS code	**Product name**	**MFN applied[b] percent**	**China–Chile zero-duty year**
6115	Pantyhose, tights, stockings, socks, and other hosiery, including stockings for varicose veins and footwear without applied soles, knitted or crocheted	15	Year 2
9609	Pencils (with encased lead), nesoi, crayons, pencil leads, pastels, drawing charcoals, writing or drawing chalks and tailors' chalks	15	Year 10
4014	Hygienic or pharmaceutical articles, of unhardened vulcanized rubber, with or without fittings of hardened rubber	15	Year 5
1211	Plants and parts of plants (including seeds and fruits), used in perfumery, pharmacy, or for insecticidal or similar purposes, fresh or dried	15	Year 5
7310	Tanks, casks, vats, and similar containers, nesoi, of a capacity of not over 300 liters (79.25 gal.), of iron or steel	15	Year 10
6116	Gloves, mittens, and mitts, knitted or crocheted	15	Year 2
6303	Curtains (including drapes) and interior blinds; curtain or bed valances	15	Year 2
1902	Pasta, whether or not cooked or stuffed or otherwise prepared, including spaghetti, lasagna, noodles, etc.; couscous, whether or not prepared	15	Year 10
8528	Television receivers, including video monitors and video projectors	15	Year 10
6212	Brassieres, girdles, corsets, braces, suspenders, garters, and similar articles and parts thereof, whether or not knitted or crocheted	15	Year 2
6406	Parts of footwear; removable insoles, heel cushions and similar articles; gaiters, leggings, and similar articles, and parts thereof	15	Year 2
0902	Tea, whether or not flavored	15	Year 5
0905	Vanilla	15	Year 5
0909	Seeds of anise, badian, fennel, coriander, cumin, or caraway; juniper berries	15	Year 5
0910	Ginger, saffron, tumeric (curcuma), thyme, bay leaves, curry, and other spices	15	Year 5
1202	Peanuts (groundnuts), not roasted or otherwise cooked, whether or not shelled or broken	15	Year 5
1203	Copra	15	Year 5
1204	Linseed, whether or not broken	15	Year 5

(continues on next page)

Table 4.4   High Chinese tariffs: treatment under China–Chile FTA, 2006 *(continued)*

	High MFN applied tariffs in the China–Chile FTA		
4-digit HS code	Product name	MFN applied[b] percent	China–Chile zero-duty year
1903	Tapioca and substitutes thereof prepared from starch, in the form of flakes, grains, pearls, siftings, or similar forms	15	Year 5
6904	Ceramic building bricks, flooring blocks, support or filler tiles and similar products	15	Year 5
6905	Roofing tiles, chimney pots, cowls, chimney liners, architectural ornaments, and other ceramic constructional goods	15	Year 5
7006	Glass (cast, rolled, drawn, blown or float, surface ground, etc.) bent, edge-worked, engraved, enameled, or otherwise worked, not framed or fitted	15	Year 5
9605	Travel sets for personal toilet, sewing, or shoe or clothes cleaning (other than specified manicure and pedicure sets)	15	Year 5
9610	Slates and boards, with writing or drawing surfaces, whether or not framed	15	Year 5
0401	Milk and cream, not concentrated nor containing added sweetening	15	Year 10
0409	Natural honey	15	Year 10
1105	Flour, meal flakes, granules, and pellets of potatoes	15	Year 10
1601	Sausages and similar products, of meat, meat offal, or blood; food preparations based on these products	15	Year 10
1602	Prepared or preserved meat, meat offal, or blood, nesoi	15	Year 10
1805	Cocoa powder, not containing added sugar or other sweetening matter	15	Year 10
6913	Statuettes and other ornamental ceramic articles	15	Year 10
7005	Float glass and surface ground or polished glass, in sheets, whether or not having an absorbent, reflecting/nonreflecting layer, but not otherwise worked	15	Year 10
9508	Merry-go-rounds, boat swings, shooting galleries, and other fairground amusements; traveling circuses, theaters, etc.; parts and accessories thereof	15	Year 10

FTA = free trade agreement; HS = harmonized system; MFN = most favored nation; nesoi = not elsewhere specified or included

a. Weighted using Chinese export values at the 6-digit level.

b. Chinese MFN applied rates at the 6-digit level within each 4-digit heading are weighted with US export values for 2011.

Sources: China–Chile FTA, annex 1, section 2; World Bank, World Integrated Trade Solution (WITS) database (2013), http://wits.worldbank.org.

Chinese Import Tariffs

Tariffs in China are set by the Customs Tariff Commission of the State Council. The council—China's senior political body and effectively its cabinet—must approve the tariff rates that the commission recommends, and MFN rates are rarely higher than China's GATT-bound rates.[21] Bound rates limit the tariff level for virtually all items enumerated in China's tariff schedule.

Official statistics show that China's MFN applied rates are slightly lower than its GATT-bound tariffs. In 2011 the simple average for bound tariffs on imports of agricultural products was 15.7 percent, while the simple average for applied MFN rates was 15.6 percent. The simple average for bound tariffs on nonagricultural products was 9.2 percent, and the simple average for applied MFN rates was 8.7 percent. In table 4.1, the Chinese averages for the two-digit codes are calculated based on dollar amounts of US exports to China (in 2011) for lines at the six-digit level. Likewise the US averages are calculated based on dollar amounts of Chinese exports to the United States (in 2012) at the six-digit level. As mentioned, China's applied rates are higher than US applied rates for almost all the two-digit codes.

China's applied tariff schedule has changed little since the last WTO review in 2009. China has low tariffs for imports used in its export industries, products such as machines and components. In 2010 and 2011, over 600 items specified in China's 8-digit HS tariff lines were subject to especially low interim applied tariffs. In 2012, the exceptional coverage was extended to 730 lines, and the average ad valorem rate for these items was 4.4 percent, only half the normal applied MFN rate.[22] The changes in 2012 reduced a few tariffs on energy products, consumer goods, and components used by strategic emerging industries.

China's four-digit MFN applied tariff schedule reveals the details of high protection. Table 4.4 identifies products that face high or exceptionally high import duties. At the end of 2011, wine, wheat, and rice all faced exceptionally high tariffs of 65 percent.[23] However, in 2012 China reduced its wine tariff to 14 percent ad valorem, leading to a surge of wine imports.[24] Cotton, wool, corn, and cereals are all at or above 38 percent, certainly a high level. A few nonagricultural products are represented in the high tariff list, such as motorcycles and automobiles, with tariffs of 41 percent and 25 percent, respectively.[25] In

---

21. A few lines in China's tariff schedule appear to have MFN applied rates that slightly exceed the WTO bound rates. Evidently no WTO member has felt it worthwhile to challenge these excessive rates.

22. According to WTO tariff data, tariffdata.wto.org (accessed on July 8, 2014).

23. China's rice tariff exceeds the GATT-bound rate of 51 percent.

24. In addition to the tariff, China levies a value-added tax at the rate of 17 percent and consumption tax at the rate of 10 percent on wine. See Duty Calculator, www.dutycalculator.com (accessed on May 19, 2014).

25. Baizhu Chen, "Tear Down This Wall—The Chinese Tariff Wall," *Forbes*, July 12, 2012, www.forbes.com (accessed on May 19, 2014).

2010, the total value of Chinese imports with tariffs of 15 percent or higher exceeded $150 billion.[26] Chinese tariff lines also change constantly; in August 2013 China raised its import tariff on narrow-body aircraft weighing between 25 and 45 tons. The applied tariff rose from 1 percent to 5 percent—the WTO bound rate—resulting in millions of dollars' difference in the landed price of imported aircraft. The tariff on imported aircraft over 45 tons was left at the 1 percent rate. The new tariff schedule may especially affect US aircraft manufacturers, as their products tend to be in the lighter 25- to 45-ton range.[27]

Table 4.4 shows, for 4-digit high tariff lines, the zero-duty year for China's preferential tariffs in its FTA with Chile, signed in 2006. Six exceptionally high tariff products are found at the 4-digit HS level (tariffs above 50 percent), and only two of those tariffs expire by year 10 (wine and tobacco). The other four are simply exempt from any tariff reduction (wheat, corn, rice, and sugar). For the high tariffs in the range of 15 to 49 percent, of which there are 177 lines, 71 of those tariffs expire in year 10, 52 expire in year 5, and 43 expire in year 2. Seven of the lines are exempt from tariff reduction, including cotton, cereal, and wool, while 4 others are partly exempt.

US Import Tariffs

US tariff rates are comparatively low and virtually all are bound in the GATT. In 2011 the simple average MFN applied tariff for agricultural imports was 5.0 percent. For nonagricultural products, the simple average MFN applied tariff was 3.3 percent.

However, like other countries the United States has peak tariffs in its schedule. For high tariff items, table 4.5 shows the 2012 US rates on its imports from Mexico under the North American Free Trade Agreement (NAFTA) and the scheduled zero-duty years in its FTA with Korea. In the exceptionally high category are tobacco products, with a tariff rate of 350 percent.[28] At the 4-digit HS code level, about 24 product categories face high applied MFN tariffs, in the range of 15 percent to 50 percent, including trucks for the purpose of transporting goods,[29] onions, track suits, ice cream, several

---

26. World Trade Organization, "Tariff Download Facility," tariffdata.wto.org (accessed on May 19, 2014).

27. Inside US Trade, "USTR Flags China's Anti-Monopoly Enforcement in Trade Barriers Report," NewsStand, April 4, 2014.

28. Paper clip imports—a 10-digit line principally imported from China—face a tariff of over 100 percent, which Congress renewed in 2011 for 5 more years to protect two US companies. Alex Brokaw, "10 Everyday Items That Cost You Way More Thanks to U.S. Import Taxes," Daily Finance, July 26, 2012, www.dailyfinance.com (accessed on May 19, 2014).

29. US duties of 25 percent on delivery and light trucks are a relic of the so-called chicken war between the United States and Europe in 1963. Today, from the perspective of the US auto industry, the high tariff serves to ensure that virtually all delivery and light trucks sold in the US market are made in the United States or its NAFTA partners.

Table 4.5 High US tariffs: treatment under NAFTA and Korea–US FTA
(percent or zero-duty year)

4-digit HS code	Product name	MFN applied[a] percent	Mexico (2012)[b] percent	Zero-duty year in Korea–US FTA
2403	Tobacco and tobacco substitute manufactures, nesoi; homogenized or reconstituted tobacco; tobacco extracts and essences	350	0	Year 10
2401	Unmanufactured tobacco; tobacco refuse	70	0	Year 10
0804	Dates, figs, pineapples, avocados, guavas, mangoes, and mangosteens, fresh or dried	30	0	Year 5
6112	Track suits, ski suits and swimwear, knitted or crocheted	25	0	Year 1
6106	Women's or girls' blouses and shirts, knitted or crocheted	21	0	Year 10
6105	Men's or boys' shirts, knitted or crocheted	20	0	Year 10
0704	Cabbages, cauliflower, kohlrabi, kale, and similar edible brassicas, fresh or chilled	20	0	Year 8
0703	Onions, shallots, garlic, leeks, and other alliaceous vegetables, fresh or chilled	20	0	Year 10
6402	Footwear, with outer soles and uppers of rubber or plastics, nesoi	20	0	Year 12
6114	Other garments, knitted or crocheted	20	0	Year 12
2105	Ice cream and other edible ice, whether or not containing cocoa	19	6	Year 10
5112	Woven fabrics of combed wool or combed fine animal hair	19	0	Year 1
6103	Men's or boys' suits, ensembles, suit-type jackets, blazers, trousers, bib and brace overalls, breeches and shorts (no swimwear), knitted or crocheted	18	0	Year 1
6401	Waterproof footwear with outer soles and uppers of rubber or plastics which are fixed together by bonding or similar processes	18	0	Year 12
6404	Footwear, with outer soles of rubber, plastics, leather, or composition leather and uppers of textile materials	18	0	Year 12
2202	Waters, including mineral waters and aerated waters, containing added sweetening or flavored, and other nonalcoholic beverages, nesoi	17	1	Year 10
6001	Pile fabrics, including long pile fabrics and terry fabrics, knitted or crocheted	17	0	Year 5

(continues on next page)

Table 4.5   High US tariffs: treatment under NAFTA and Korea–US FTA
(percent or zero-duty year) *(continued)*

4-digit HS code	Product name	MFN applied[a] percent	Mexico (2012)[b] percent	Zero-duty year in Korea–US FTA
6102	Women's or girls' overcoats, car coats, capes, cloaks, anoraks (including ski jackets), and similar articles, knitted or crocheted, nesoi	16	0	Year 1
6111	Babies' garments and clothing accessories, knitted or crocheted	16	0	Year 1
6101	Men's or boys' overcoats, car coats, capes, cloaks, anoraks (including ski jackets), and similar articles, knitted or crocheted, nesoi	16	0	Year 1
6109	T-shirts, singlets, and other vests, knitted or crocheted	16	0	Year 10
6115	Pantyhose, tights, stockings, socks, and other hosiery, including stockings for varicose veins and footwear without applied soles, knitted or crocheted	15	0	Year 5
6209	Babies' garments and clothing accessories	15	0	Year 1
5809	Woven fabrics of metal thread and woven fabrics of metallized yarn (heading 5605), of a kind used in apparel, as furnishing fabrics, etc., nesoi	15	0	Year 1

FTA = free trade agreement; HS = harmonized system; MFN = most favored nation; NAFTA = North American Free Trade Agreement; nesoi = not elsewhere specified or included

a. Weighted using Chinese export values at the 6-digit level.
b. Tariffs on US imports from Mexico under NAFTA weighted using Mexican export values at the 6-digit level.

Sources: Korea–US FTA, annex 2-B; World Bank, World Integrated Trade Solution (WITS) database (2013), http://wits.worldbank.org.

items of clothing, and a significant specific duty on midvalue sports shoes.[30] Nearly all these tariffs have been phased out under NAFTA for Mexican imports. In the Korea–US agreement, tariffs on 4 of these items expire within 12 years, 7 within 10 years, and most of the rest within 5 years or even 1 year. As mentioned earlier, the list of high tariff items excludes penalty duties on imports considered unfair and, as a point of information, the United States has several antidumping and countervailing duty orders outstanding against Chinese imports (and vice versa).

---

30. The US tariff, around $5 per midvalue pair, is designed to protect the US company New Balance and around 4,000 US jobs from Chinese competition. See Timothy Aeppel, "New Balance Sweats Push to End US Shoe Tariffs," *Wall Street Journal*, February 27, 2013.

Conclusions

China's average applied MFN tariff rate for goods imported from the United States is twice as high as the average US tariff on imports from China (5.5 percent versus 2.7 percent). Correspondingly, from the standpoint of duty-free market access, the United States has more to gain than China. Yet despite a sharper reduction in manufactures tariffs by China than the United States, according to the CGE model reported in chapter 2, a CHUSTIA will deliver China a bigger manufactures export gain in absolute dollar terms (over the baseline level) than the United States. However US gains will be somewhat larger in percentage terms. Finally, in the accelerated rebalancing-plus-CHUSTIA scenario, the US manufactures trade balance would improve considerably, compared to the baseline scenario.

Previous Chinese FTAs with countries outside of Asia show that China is willing to slash its nonagricultural tariffs, but reluctant to reduce tariffs on sensitive agricultural imports. In the Chile–China FTA, wheat, corn, rice, sugar, cotton, cereal, and wool were totally exempt from tariff reductions. Chinese tariffs on over 70 lines in the 4-digit HS code require fully 10 years to be zeroed out. In an FTA with the United States, China would likely do its best to delay liberalization of these same lines and couple tariff reductions with tariff rate quota limitations.

For its part, in past FTAs, the United States has been willing to slash tariffs on a large majority of items, but with long-term phaseout periods or outright exclusions for highly sensitive agricultural products (e.g., sugar, dairy, tobacco). Eventually, however, nearly 100 percent of products imported from FTA partners enter the United States duty free. Would the United States agree to zero out nearly all tariffs (allowing for phaseout periods) in a CHUSTIA? This seems likely, and is the goal we would recommend, as the United States has nearly achieved this outcome with Australia and Korea as well as in NAFTA.

References

Casey, Joseph. 2012. *Patterns in US–China Trade Since China's Accession to the World Trade Organization.* Washington: US–China Economic and Security Review Commission.

Hufbauer, Gary Clyde, and Jared C. Woollacott. 2010. *Trade Disputes between China and the United States: Growing Pains so Far, Worse Ahead?* Working Paper 10-17. Washington: Peterson Institute for International Economics.

Lardy, Nicholas R. 2002. *Integrating China into the Global Economy.* Washington: Brookings Institution.

5

Government Procurement

Government procurement of goods and services represents a large share of economic activity in modern economies, typically about 15 percent of GDP. Table 5.1 presents illustrative figures for the United States, China, and a few other large countries. China's Ministry of Finance estimated that government procurement in 2011 was $179 billion, and that it had grown 25 percent annually over the previous seven years.[1] Government efficiency requires low-cost and high-quality procurement of goods and services from the private sector—everything from highway construction to medical services to data processing. For supplies to the military and intelligence services, justifiable national security arguments can be made that private contractors should be national firms. For the majority of government procurement, national security is not an issue. Yet government procurement has historically been off-limits to international competition, as a means of ensuring that domestic firms, with their strong political connections, are the only bidders. Reflecting this reality, Article III(8a) of the General Agreement on Tariffs and Trade (GATT), drafted in 1947, excluded government procurement from its national treatment obligation.

The World Bank and regional development banks—the InterAmerican Development Bank, the Asian Development Bank, and others—pioneered requirements for open procurement and international competition in loans and grants for sponsored projects. But only in the past 40 years has government procurement been liberalized in the world trading system, first in the GATT

---

1. Office of the US Trade Representative, "Fact Sheet: 23rd US–China Joint Commission on Commerce and Trade," December 19, 2012.

Table 5.1   Government procurement levels, 2008

Country	Procurement (percent of GDP)
United States	11.4
Canada	12.3
Germany	16.8
France	17.5
United Kingdom	18.9
China	20.0

Sources: OECD (2011); European Union Chamber of Commerce in China (2011).

and the World Trade Organization (WTO), and more recently in free trade agreements (FTAs).

GATT and WTO Agreements

Tokyo Round GPA

One of several plurilateral codes agreed in the Tokyo Round (1974–79) of GATT negotiations was the Agreement on Government Procurement (GPA), signed in 1979 and entering into force in 1981.[2] It was the first such agreement under GATT auspices and was quite limited in scope, applying only to goods contracts valued at SDR (special drawing rights) 150,000 or more procured by the central governments of signatory governments. Only 12 advanced countries—counting the 15 members of the European Common Market as one member—signed the agreement; only the contracts of agencies the signatories inscribed were covered; signatories could ask for offsetting concessions from potential foreign bidders; and tariff concessions were not part of the code (Trebilock, Howse, and Eliason 1995).

The agreement made market access to the procurement of each member's public agencies available only to other GPA members. All WTO members were free to join the GPA, and the WTO extended benefits to nonmembers on a conditional most favored nation (MFN) basis, though they had to accept the responsibilities of the GPA and open their own procurement markets to gain access to members' procurement markets. Even between GPA members, the MFN principle did not always operate; in several instances, members partially denied access to other members on the argument of insufficient reciprocity.

2. See "Agreement on Government Procurement: Tokyo Round Government Procurement Code," www.worldtradelaw.net (accessed on May 20, 2014).

The GPA was amended in 1987, with the amendments entering into force in 1988. The most significant provisions in the Protocol of Amendments lowered the threshold value of contracts to SDR 130,000, covered leasing contracts, and made bidding procedures more transparent.[3]

Uruguay Round GPA

Further liberalization was achieved in the Uruguay Round (1986–94) Agreement on Government Procurement, signed in 1994 and entering into force in 1996 (Macrory, Appleton, and Plummer 2005). The number of signatories increased from 12 to 15—again counting the 27 members of the European Union as one signatory. Coverage included services as well as goods for scheduled entities. Nondiscrimination provisions were bolstered to ensure equal treatment between signatories. Offsetting requirements were generally prohibited, except that developing countries could negotiate permissible offsets upon their accession to the GPA. The general value threshold was kept at SDR 130,000, but for covered construction services, a threshold of SDR 5,000,000 was set for some signatories. Importantly, procurement by subcentral governments was covered to the extent inscribed in member country schedules.[4] The conditional MFN character of the GPA remained and bilateral reciprocity persisted under the larger GPA umbrella.

The US trade representative (USTR) took an interesting legal position regarding the coverage of state governments in the GPA, a position that it continues to hold in FTA negotiations. Notwithstanding the Commerce Clause (Article I, section 8, clause 3 of the US Constitution), which assigns Congress authority over interstate and foreign commerce, and notwithstanding the Supremacy Clause (Article VI, clause 2), which gives federal laws supremacy over state laws, the USTR has taken the position that while states can be invited to voluntarily schedule their procurement in the GPA, they cannot be compelled to do so.[5] The USTR takes the same position for the government procurement chapters in US FTAs. This is politically expedient, as it serves the interests of many state legislatures and governors, but it limits the USTR's ability to seek the coverage of subcentral procurement abroad.

---

3. See "Agreement on Government Procurement: Revised Text," General Agreement on Tariffs and Trade, 1998, www.wto.org (accessed on May 20, 2014).

4. See World Trade Organization, "Overview of the Agreement on Government Procurement," www.wto.org (accessed on May 20, 2014).

5. Inside US Trade, "Key Areas of TPP Talks at Different Stages after 30 Months of Effort," World Trade Online, insidetrade.com (accessed on May 20, 2014).

China's Accession to the GPA

While the Doha Round, which began in 2001, seems stalled, progress has been made on a separate track to amend and improve the Uruguay Round GPA.[6] In December 2011, signatories to the GPA launched negotiations to expand its coverage to a range of $80 to $100 billion per year—though this is still a small fraction of global government procurement. China and eight other WTO members are expected to join the amended GPA. Most interesting for our purposes are potential terms for Chinese accession to the GPA.

US actions in the past few years limiting foreign firms' access to its public procurement markets have largely taken the form of Buy American bills and resolutions. The most important was the Buy American provision in the American Reinvestment and Recovery Act of 2009 (the $789 billion stimulus bill); subsequently, many follow-on bills have been proposed and a few have been enacted, in both state and federal legislatures.[7]

When China joined the WTO in 2001, it agreed to join the GPA "as soon as possible,"[8] according to its WTO accession documents. During the past decade, however, China has pursued a two-track approach to government procurement (USTR 2012). At home, in several ways, China has raised the barriers to foreign firms' participation. Abroad, in Geneva, China has gradually and modestly improved its offers to other GPA members. In 2002, China passed its Government Procurement Law, which in many respects follows the UN Model Law on Procurement of Goods.[9] However, the Chinese law directed central and subcentral public procurement agencies to prioritize local goods in their procurement decisions. The law covers about half of China's public works; the rest are subject to the Tendering and Bidding Law of 2000, which likewise favors domestic products. Draft implementing rules apparently gave a strong preference to software developed in China—potentially a large market for US information technology firms. In 2005 China suspended work on these draft rules, but it is hard to tell whether informal guidance has had the same effect. In 2007 China issued two administrative measures that strongly favor "indigenous innovation products" for public procurement, though according to the US–China Business Council, these measures

---

6. See World Trade Organization, "The Re-Negotiation of the Agreement on Government Procurement (GPA)," www.wto.org (accessed on May 20, 2014).

7. See the "Buy American/Buy America" chapter in Hufbauer and Schott (2013). In 2013 Senator Charles Schumer (D-NY) attempted to persuade the New York Metropolitan Transport Authority to cancel the purchase of Chinese steel for repairs to the Verrazano Bridge; see "NY Senator Calls on MTA to Avoid Chinese Steel," Associated Press, July 12, 2013.

8. WTO, *Report of the Working Party on the Accession of China*, WT/MIN(01) 3, November 10, 2001.

9. The Government Procurement Law of the People's Republic of China was passed on June 29, 2002, and went into effect on January 1, 2003. The law can be found at english.gov.cn (accessed on June 23, 2014).

have largely been rescinded.[10] In 2009 China's Ministry of Industry and Information Technology issued a circular applying to its own procurement and the procurement of subsidiary agencies, strongly prioritizing domestic goods and services. Other branches of the central government have issued similar Buy China directives.

Meanwhile, in the GPA negotiations, the United States and other members have asked China to take several steps toward liberalization: not requiring intellectual property to be first registered in China and owned by a local Chinese firm to qualify as indigenous innovation for the purposes of public procurement contracts; not prioritizing local firms or domestic products in procurement decisions; covering to some extent the procurement of state-owned enterprises; and implementing GPA provisions more quickly than China's proposal of a 15-year phase-in period.

Recent developments in the GPA have shown China inching toward accession to the agreement. China submitted its most recent offer to join the GPA in December 2013, when it made important concessions but still fell short of expectations. The United States and the European Union have both expressed dissatisfaction with the offer; as a USTR spokesman put it, "China made progress in areas consistent with its 2013 Strategic & Economic Dialogue commitment, including by lowering thresholds and increasing sub-central and other coverage, but remains short of the finish line."[11] The disappointment came from China's continued insistence on three big exceptions contained in its previous offer. One allows China to depart from the national treatment standard in important cases; the second allows China to require technology transfer and domestic content in certain cases; and the third limits central government coverage to its Beijing offices only, and would not include central government offices located in other parts of the country. Additionally, the United States has asked that coverage of the service sectors be scheduled in two-digit Central Product Classification (CPC) code. China's offer instead schedules covered services—such as online information and database retrieval, sewage services, and maintenance and repair of motor vehicles—in the more narrow four-digit CPC code, and consultancy service related to computer installation in the three-digit CPC code.[12] The offer does cover six additional provinces—Chongqing, Liaoning, Hubei, Henan, Hebei, and Henan—some of which are very large. But four of these would be subject to additional implementation delays, pushing their opening to six years after the deal is agreed. Moreover, there are still issues with the value threshold China has suggested for covered procurement, including SDR 20 million—over $30 million as of January 2014—for construction services tendered by subcentral agencies, a very

---

10. US-China Business Council, *China's Innovation and Government Procurement Policies*, May 1, 2013, www.uschina.org (accessed on June 23, 2014)

11. "U.S. Says China's Newest GPA Offer Falls Short of the Finish Line," China Trade Extra, china-tradeextra.com (accessed on January 23, 2014).

12. Ibid.

high figure considering that the United States and many other countries set their thresholds at SDR 5 million.[13] China's next offer is anticipated in 2014, and modest improvements are expected.

US Coverage in the GPA and FTAs

US coverage of government procurement in the GPA is scheduled in five annexes to the agreement, together with qualifying general notes.[14] The US schedules, like those of other GPA members, are positive lists, meaning that federal and state agencies are not covered unless specifically named. Generally, for covered agencies, the schedules include procurement of goods and services for contracts with a value of SDR 130,000 and more. Construction is also covered, but with a threshold of SDR 5 million or more. Procurement is defined to include leases as well as outright purchases.

In several instances the schedules name an agency and then note exceptions. The Department of Transportation is on the US positive list, but the Federal Aviation Administration, an agency of the department, is excluded. In practice, this means that airport construction is excluded from foreign competition. Several federal power agencies, such as the Tennessee Valley Authority and the Bonneville Power Administration, are scheduled, but not all are. Annex 2, which lists the coverage of state agencies, is rather sparse, reflecting the voluntary nature of state coverage.

The North American Free Trade Agreement entailed considerably greater coverage of state agencies than the GPA did, because the possibility of doing business with public agencies in Canada or Mexico attracted firms in several US states. The government procurement chapters in other US FTAs have not enlarged much on the WTO GPA. In chapter 17 of the Korea–US FTA, both parties reaffirm their commitment to the GPA's procedures and scheduled obligations.[15] Both parties have modestly extended their GPA lists of covered central government agencies, but did not add to the coverage of subcentral agencies. Additional procedures are specified, such as electronic bids. The FTA also establishes a Government Procurement Working Group for joint consultations.

Prospects for the CHUSTIA

Based on the negotiating record, the biggest step is for China to join the WTO GPA and constructively address the issues listed above. The CHUSTIA chapter

---

13. Inside US Trade, "New China GPA Offer Adds Six Provinces, But Still Falls Short of Demands," World Trade Online, insidetrade.com (accessed on May 20, 2014).

14. See World Trade Organization, "Appendices and Annexes to the GPA," www.wto.org (accessed on May 20, 2014).

15. See free trade agreement between the United States and Korea (KORUS), chapter 17, Government Procurement, www.ustr.gov (accessed on May 20, 2014).

on government procurement might spell out additional procedural safeguards. If the United States can increase the coverage of state agencies and provide some coverage of airport construction, China should be more forthcoming on provincial and SOE coverage. However, the WTO GPA will likely remain the center stage of government procurement liberalization for both countries.

There are enormous opportunities for both countries in an enlarged GPA. A recent report commissioned by the US Chamber of Commerce (2013) on investment opportunities for China in US infrastructure projects sizes up the prospects. The report predicts that the United States will need over $8 trillion worth of infrastructure investment through 2030. China has ample financial capacity and construction management skills to participate in many of these projects, especially in areas such as energy, transportation, and water. Chinese firms, with extensive experience building airports, subways, highways, and rail lines, could become highly competitive suppliers. But procurement by US government agencies is generally limited to participants in the WTO GPA. Until China fully accedes to the GPA and becomes a designated country on that list, its ability to participate in US infrastructure projects will remain limited.

References

European Union Chamber of Commerce in China. 2011. *Public Procurement in China: European Business Experiences Competing for Public Contracts in China.* Beijing.

Hufbauer, Gary Clyde, and Jeffrey J. Schott. 2013. *Local Content Requirements: A Global Problem.* Policy Analyses in International Economics 102. Washington: Peterson Institute for International Economics.

Macrory, Patrick, Arthur Appleton, and Michael Plummer, ed. 2005. *The World Trade Organization: Legal, Economic and Political Analysis.* New York: Springer.

OECD (Organization for Economic Cooperation and Development). 2011. *Government at a Glance 2011.* Paris.

Trebilock, Michael, Robert Howse, and Antonia Eliason. 1995. *The Regulation of International Trade.* London: Routledge.

US Chamber of Commerce. 2013. *From International to Interstates: Assessing the Opportunity for Chinese Participation in US Infrastructure.* Washington.

USTR (United States Trade Representative). 2012. *Report to Congress on China's WTO Compliance.* Washington.

6

Agriculture

For centuries, Chinese dynasties controlled the output and distribution of food supplies as a sure way of ensuring social order. Following World War II, after Mao Zedong vanquished Chiang Kai-shek and restored peace across China, food production and sale again became a central tool of public policy. At that time agriculture was produced in collective units, with local leaders deciding which crops would be grown and to whom they would be sold. A large share was sold to the central government at fixed (low) prices. Even as Deng Xiaoping and his successors relaxed detailed production quotas on industrial goods and allowed greater sway for market forces, agricultural quotas remained a mainstay of successive five-year plans. Food self-sufficiency remains a state priority to this day, and to that end the Ministry of Agriculture controls domestic prices and international trade in basic foodstuffs, cotton, and other products. While visiting farmers in July 2013 President Xi Jinping stated that "we must rely on ourselves for grain security," showing just how important Chinese leaders consider the issue.[1] As recently as January 2014 a senior official at the Ministry of Agriculture stated that China seeks self-reliance in the production of staples, asserting that 97 percent of some key grains, including rice and wheat, come from domestic production.[2] But this policy seems to be evolving, as the State Council issued guidelines the following month stating that China would focus more on domestic production of food grains (rice and wheat) rather than feed grains (soybeans and corn), emphasizing quality over quantity. The guidelines also stipulated more production of meat, vegetables, and fruit, which require

---

1. "Daily Bread," *Economist*, October 26, 2013.

2. "China Focus: China Vows Self-Sufficiency in Grain Production," news.xinhuanet.com, January 22, 2014 (accessed on May 27, 2014).

less land per million dollars of output than feed grains. A side benefit is that imports of feed grains will lower prices for livestock farmers, especially poultry producers.[3] Within these contradictory declarations, there may be room for a massive realignment of China's self-sufficiency doctrine, especially if climate change severely reduces arable land.

China may be something of an outlier in the scope of its interventionist agricultural policies, but it has plenty of company. Historically agriculture has been the most highly protected sector of merchandise trade, reflecting the essential role of food and, equally important, the political voice of farmers. In many countries, including China, government assumes responsibility for stabilizing the prices of key food and feed grains (rice, wheat, corn, soybeans), to protect both cities from high prices and farmers from low prices. Prices are stabilized through a combination of extensive domestic price and production controls and, on the international side, quotas, tariffs, and a public agency that controls trade and holds buffer stocks. In nearly all countries, government is responsible for ensuring the safety of food supplies; for this purpose, sanitary and phytosanitary (SPS) standards are the key. Facing this array of public concerns and policy instruments, liberalizing agricultural trade has been a long and slow struggle.

Chapter 4 examines Chinese and US agricultural tariffs; as explained there, these tariffs are generally high in China, and exceptionally high on selected products in both countries. This chapter takes a qualitative look at US and Chinese quotas on agricultural imports, as well as Chinese public agencies that control agricultural trade. In terms of quantitative assessments, the best we have are the Global Trade Analysis Project (GTAP) data.[4] For China, paddy rice, wheat, and other agricultural products are all assigned ad valorem equivalents (AVEs) of 33 percent for their nontariff barriers. For the United States the AVEs for the same products are all 11 percent. The other focus of this chapter is SPS standards, particularly differences between World Trade Organization (WTO) and free trade agreement (FTA) approaches for ensuring that SPS standards do not discriminate against imports.

Table 6.1 summarizes two-way agricultural trade in 2012, as well as each country's agricultural exports to the world. The United States runs a large export surplus in this sector with China, around $15 billion in 2012. Soybeans are dominant, accounting for almost 60 percent of US agricultural exports to China. Cotton is another large item, accounting for 13 percent. But US exports of cereals, such as wheat and corn, as well as fruits such as apples, oranges, and pears, would be much larger in the absence of Chinese trade barriers. In China–US trade and investment agreement (CHUSTIA) talks, the United States would

---

3. Lucy Hornby, "China Scythes Grain Self-Sufficiency Policy," *Financial Times*, February 11, 2011.

4. See G. Badri Narayanan and Terrie L. Walmsley, eds., Global Trade, Assistance, and Production: The GTAP 7 Data Base, Center for Global Trade Analysis, Purdue University, 2008, www.gtap.agecon.purdue.edu (accessed on July 9, 2014).

Table 6.1   US and China international agricultural trade, 2012 (millions of US dollars)

Product	United States			China		
	Global exports	Global imports	Exports to China	Global exports	Global imports	Exports to the United States
Live animals	1,200	2,600	72	580	500	17
Meat, etc.	16,000	5,800	1,000	980	4,100	4
Fish	4,700	13,000	1,100	11,000	5,500	1,700
Dairy, eggs	4,200	2,200	270	530	3,300	12
Other animal products	870	920	150	2,100	440	280
Live trees	380	1,900	4	260	140	19
Vegetables	3,400	7,900	24	6,900	2,400	480
Fruit	12,000	11,000	530	3,800	3,800	150
Coffee, tea, etc.	1,000	8,400	20	1,900	310	180
Cereals	21,000	3,300	1,500	440	4,800	1
Milling products	940	1,400	11	600	580	25
Oil seeds, etc.	29,000	2,400	15,000	2,600	39,000	210
Lac; gums, resins	680	4,400	48	990	200	190
Plaiting materials	48	87	19	91	190	10
Animal, vegetable fats	4,400	6,200	350	570	13,000	85
Prepared meat, fish	1,900	4,700	80	9,000	180	1,200
Sugars	2,500	4,600	130	1,300	2,500	160
Cocoa	1,500	4,200	49	330	620	9
Prepared cereal, flour	3,800	5,400	76	1,500	1,900	140
Prepared fruit, vegetables	4,500	7,200	190	7,600	620	1,400
Prepared food (other)	7,000	4,200	150	2,200	950	240
Beverages, spirits	6,400	21,000	92	1,400	3,100	41
Food residue, waste	9,700	2,700	940	2,900	3,000	620
Tobacco, substitutes	1,600	1,900	120	1,300	1,300	9
Albuminoidal substances	2,900	2,800	210	2,200	2,600	230
Raw hides, skins	3,200	7,000	140	450	700	22
Fur skins, artificial fur	600	890	140	3,100	380	47
Wool	65	3,500	13	2,600	330	35
Cotton	8,200	17,000	3,530	15,000	1,200	290
Total	153,684	158,597	25,958	84,221	97,640	7,806

Sources: World Trade Organization, International Trade Statistics (2013); World Bank, World Integrated Trade Solution (WITS) database (2013), http://wits.worldbank.org.

largely play the role of offense regarding agricultural tariff and nontariff barriers, while for the most part China would play defense.

WTO Rulebook

Quantitative Restrictions

Article XI of the 1947 General Agreement on Tariffs and Trade (GATT), incorporated into the GATT in 1994, calls for the general elimination of import and export quotas and licensing restrictions that have a similar effect. To a very large extent, WTO members have brought their trade regimes into compliance with Article XI. However, Article XI(2c) permits quantitative restrictions on agricultural imports that are imposed in conjunction with limits on domestic production of the same commodity. GATT members agreed on this exception in 1955, at the insistence of the Dwight D. Eisenhower administration, to insulate the US dairy market from foreign competition. Other countries have used the same exception to buttress their domestic agricultural programs. In successive GATT rounds and FTAs, countries are gradually phasing out these quantitative controls on agricultural imports.

Article XI(2a) allows temporary export controls to alleviate critical shortages of foodstuffs and other raw materials. In 1973, during the Richard Nixon administration, the United States imposed export controls on soybeans and other feed grains to quell a run-up in US domestic prices. Japan was the main target and this episode is still recalled, very unfavorably, by Japanese leaders today, four decades after the event. At the time, however, neither Japan nor any other country challenged the United States in the GATT. Quite recently, China invoked Article XI(2a) and other GATT provisions in its defense of export controls on a range of minerals. China lost the panel and appellate body decisions, respectively, in 2011 and 2012.[5] The tenor of the appellate body decision sharply narrows future resort to Article XI(2a) unless the export controls are truly temporary. However, WTO members can still impose export taxes, unless they have agreed not to do so in their GATT schedules.

Public Trade Bodies

Article XVII of the GATT deals with state trading enterprises (STEs), a term including public agencies that control agricultural imports and exports.[6] This

---

5. For the WTO summary of the case, see World Trade Organization, "China—Measures Related to the Exportation of Various Raw Materials," Dispute DS394, www.wto.org (accessed on May 27, 2014).

6. On July 30, 1999, the WTO Working Party on State Trading Enterprises adopted an "Illustrative List of Relationships between Governments and State Trading Enterprises and the Kinds of Activities Engaged in by these Enterprises." The key features of an STE are a government or nongovernment body or marketing board that enjoys exclusive or special rights or privileges,

article addresses apprehensions after World War II that some government-sanctioned monopolies might play fast and loose, manipulating agriculture and other markets. In subsequent decades, STEs have distorted world trade in important and not-so-important commodities, from oil (e.g., the Organization of the Petroleum Exporting Countries and its offshoots at the national level) to cocoa, coffee, tin, and a few other commodities. However, article XVII has rarely been invoked in GATT or WTO disputes.

In the absence of more extensive judicial interpretation, Article XVII[7] as written is too general to bite against STE trading practices. Article XVII(1b) declares that STEs shall

> make any such purchases or sales solely in accordance with commercial considerations, including price, quality, availability, marketability, transportation and other conditions of purchase or sale, and shall afford the enterprises of the other contracting parties adequate opportunity, in accordance with customary business practice, to compete for participation in such purchases and sales.

A note on commercial considerations in the clause reads:

> The charging by a state enterprise of different prices for its sales of a product in different markets is not precluded by the provisions of this Article, provided that such different prices are charged for commercial reasons, to meet conditions of supply and demand in export markets.

The appellate body decided the only WTO case centering on article XVII in 2004. In the case, the United States asserted that the Canadian Wheat Board did not conduct transactions in accordance with commercial considerations. The panel rejected the US allegations for lack of sufficient evidence. One commentator (Smith 2006) observed that the term *commercial considerations* is rather fuzzy, particularly in light of the note reproduced above, making it hard to bring a successful case in the WTO.

Sanitary and Phytosanitary Agreement

Among the Tokyo Round (1974–79) codes was the Agreement on Technical Barriers to Trade (TBT). The TBT Agreement had provisions on SPS measures, but during the Uruguay Round (1986–94) negotiations it was recognized that national SPS measures could go beyond the legitimate purpose of protecting human, animal, and plant health and veer into economic protection of domestic agricultural interests. The SPS Agreement, which entered into force in

---

which result in influencing the level or direction of imports or exports. WTO online database, document G/STR/4.

7. GATT text can be found at www.wto.org (accessed on July 9, 2014).

January 1995, requires WTO members to base their SPS standards on sound science. The key provision in paragraph 2 of Article 5 reads:[8]

> Members shall ensure that any sanitary or phytosanitary measure is applied only to the extent necessary to protect human, animal or plant life or health, is based on scientific principles and is not maintained without sufficient scientific evidence, except as provided for in paragraph 7 of Article 5 [allowing provisional measures while scientific evidence is sought].

To achieve this broad objective, the SPS Agreement enunciates several supporting provisions: standards must be transparent; countries must maintain a point of inquiry to answer technical questions; standards must not discriminate among WTO members; countries are strongly encouraged, but not compelled, to adopt international SPS standards; and importing countries shall accept SPS standards equivalent to those demonstrated by an exporting country.

Several WTO dispute settlement cases have invoked the SPS Agreement and many ministerial decisions have added interpretive guidance.[9] Based on the record since 1995, discriminatory practices and economic protection through the misuse of SPS measures are major concerns of agricultural exporters. In its FTAs, the United States has supplemented, to a modest extent, the provisions of the SPS Agreement.

Negotiations for a CHUSTIA would give serious attention to nontariff barriers, including the use of SPS measures. Other countries often view China's nontariff barriers as both vague and restrictive. US International Trade Commission analysis indicates that nontariff barriers exert a greater adverse effect on US agriculture exports to China than applied tariffs; by implication, the tariff equivalent of China's NTBs on agriculture exceeds 15 percent ad valorem (as mentioned, the GTAP model uses a 33 percent figure for China's NTBs on agricultural products). China's zero tolerance for ractapamine and continued restrictions on US pork because of H1N1 severely limit US exports. Chinese restrictions to avert bovine spongiform encephalopathy (BSE), or mad cow disease, stopped US beef exports in 2003 and continue today. The risk of avian influenza supposedly justifies bans on poultry from certain states. All these restrictions are contrary to reports from the World Organization for Animal Health (OIE), which has cleared US animals.

---

8. For the text of the SPS Agreement, see World Trade Organization, "The WTO Agreement on the Application of Sanitary and Phytosanitary Measures," www.wto.org (accessed on May 27, 2014).

9. For a WTO summary of decisions and reference documents (not up to date) see WTO, Sanitary and Phytosanitary Measures: Committee, "Major Decisions and Reference Documents," www.wto.org (accessed on May 27, 2014).

Agriculture in US FTAs

To illustrate the treatment of agriculture in US FTAs we examine just two: the FTA with Australia (AUSFTA), a world-class agricultural exporter, and the FTA with Korea (KORUS), a country with poor growing conditions and a major agricultural importer. As the previous chapter has already explored the difference between GATT-bound most favored nation (MFN) tariffs and FTA tariffs on sensitive agricultural imports, here we focus qualitatively on quotas and SPS measures.

Australia–US FTA (2004)

In AUSFTA, Australia played offense in agriculture and the United States played defense. With very few exceptions, Australia immediately opened its agricultural markets to imports from the United States. AUSFTA's chapter 3 on agriculture illustrates the maximum extent of US agricultural liberalization in an FTA with a strong agricultural country.

Broadly speaking, while the United States conceded additional market access to Australian farmers and ranchers, it did so at a measured pace. The agreement calls for the eventual elimination of nearly all US agricultural tariffs, but replaces many of them with duty-free quotas that gradually expand over time. Meanwhile, above-quota imports from Australia are subject to tariff rate quotas (TRQs), meaning high tariffs on imports in excess of the duty-free quantity. Quotas on the most sensitive agricultural imports are not phased out—that is, enlarged or eliminated—until the 18th year; quotas on less sensitive imports are phased out sooner. In the highly sensitive category are beef and dairy imports (big Australian exports), as well as tobacco, peanuts, cotton, and avocados (lesser Australian exports). For these highly sensitive products the quotas and TRQs are not eliminated until the 18th year. Sugar was so sensitive in domestic US political terms that the United States denied any liberalization.[10] Conceivably, with more at stake in the multilateral Trans-Pacific Partnership (TPP), the United States might offer some sugar liberalization, perhaps capped by a TRQ, especially if Japan does likewise.

To illustrate US liberalization of highly sensitive products, the tariff of US 4.4c/kg of beef—about 1 percent on a tariff equivalent basis—imported within the quota limit, initially 378,000 tons annually, was immediately eliminated; however, a much higher over-quota tariff of 26.4 percent will remain in place for 8 years, and then be phased out and eliminated by year 18. The quota was

---

10. The absence of sugar liberalization, given Australia's military alliance with the United States dating from World War I, was surprising. This episode speaks to the generosity of the US sugar industry in campaign finance, and to the crucial role of Florida in presidential races. To some extent, the United States liberalized sugar trade with Mexico under the North American Free Trade Agreement (NAFTA), but those provisions have been the subject of almost continuous dispute, in both NAFTA and the WTO.

increased in year 2 by 15,000 tons annually. Every 2 years, it rises by an additional 5,000 tons until it is eliminated in year 19.

In contrast, in-quota tariffs for dairy were eliminated in the first year, and while out-of-quota tariffs are not scheduled to be reduced, there will be annual increases in the quota amount. The quota for milk, cream, and ice cream was 7.5 million liters in the first year, with an increase of 6 percent annually starting in the second year. The protection for sugar is far stronger, as the agreement did not provide any reduction in the highly protective tariff.

Korea–US FTA (2011)

In KORUS, Korea played defense in agriculture and the United States played offense. In future trade with Korea, the United States will apply TRQs on a few sensitive products, such as dairy, but all agricultural quotas and tariffs are scheduled for elimination within 10 years. China is a much stronger agricultural producer than Korea. However, KORUS's chapter 3 dealing with agriculture illustrates what a country with strong defensive interests might have to concede in an agreement with the United States and other agricultural exporters such as Australia, Chile, and New Zealand.

Korea eliminated two-thirds of its tariffs on agricultural lines and used TRQs for most of the rest, with out-of-quota tariffs scheduled for elimination over 18 years. Rice was the most sensitive import for Korea, with rice and rice products excluded from any tariff reductions, although the agreement requires that Korea abide by its WTO commitments to increase the quota for rice imports. That commitment was 4 percent of Korean consumption as of full implementation in 2004, a figure that amounted to 205,228 tons of rice imports in 2004. Beef and dairy were also highly sensitive agricultural imports for Korea; for these, full elimination of quotas and tariffs takes place over a period of 15 years. Other sensitive products include potatoes and honey; for these, TRQs were implemented, with the quota increasing a few percent annually in perpetuity. Starches, barley, and soybeans are also subject to TRQs, with gradual liberalization.

To illustrate, beef has an initial TRQ of 270,000 tons, increasing 2 percent per year for 15 years, with the elimination of the quota after year 15. The duty-free quota for cheese started at 7,000 tons, growing 3 percent annually, with elimination after 15 years. Milk powder has an initial TRQ of 5,000 tons, growing 3 percent annually in perpetuity. Potatoes begin at 3,000 tons, which also increases 3 percent annually in perpetuity. Similar schedules apply to honey and barley.

SPS Chapters

Chapter 8 in the Korea–US FTA on SPS measures affirms the WTO SPS Agreement but makes one important advance—that is, establishing a committee on SPS matters composed of American and Korean experts charged with close cooperation bilaterally, in the WTO, and in other international councils. In the language of Article 8.3(3):[11]

> Recognizing that the resolution of sanitary and phytosanitary matters must rely on science and risk-based assessment and is best achieved through bilateral technical cooperation and consultation, the Committee shall seek to enhance any present or future relationships between the Parties' agencies with responsibility for sanitary and phytosanitary matters. For these purposes, the Committee shall:
>
> (a) recognize that scientific risk analysis shall be conducted and evaluated by the relevant regulatory agencies of each Party; enhance mutual understanding of each Party's sanitary and phytosanitary measures and the regulatory processes that relate to those measures;
>
> (b) consult on matters related to the development or application of sanitary and phytosanitary measures that affect, or may affect, trade between the Parties;
>
> (c) consult on issues, positions, and agendas for meetings of the WTO Committee on Sanitary and Phytosanitary Measures established under the SPS Agreement, the Codex Alimentarius Commission, the World Organization for Animal Health (OIE), the relevant international and regional organizations operating within the framework of the International Plant Protection Convention, and other international and regional fora on food safety and on human, animal, or plant life or health;
>
> (d) promote coordination of technical cooperation activities in relation to development, implementation, and application of sanitary and phytosanitary measures;
>
> (e) improve bilateral understanding related to specific implementation issues concerning the SPS Agreement, including clarification of each Party's regulatory frameworks and rulemaking procedures; and
>
> (f) review progress on addressing sanitary and phytosanitary matters that may arise between the Parties' agencies with responsibility for such matters, including progress on annual animal health, plant health, and meat, poultry, and processed egg products technical meetings.

KORUS chapter 8 concludes with the declaration that "neither Party may have recourse to dispute settlement under this Agreement for any matter arising under this Chapter." In other words, disputes between the United States and Korea on SPS matters will be handled solely in the WTO. AUSFTA's chapter 7 is practically the same, with the same committee structure and responsibilities as well as exclusion of dispute settlement under the FTA. It appears that both parties were wary of conflicting jurisprudence between WTO and FTA panels, and for this reason chose to give exclusive SPS jurisdiction to the WTO.[12]

---

11. KORUS text can be found at www.ustr.gov/trade-agreements/free-trade-agreements/korus-fta/final-text.

12. The SPS provisions in chapter 7 of NAFTA arguably could be the subject of dispute resolution under chapter 20 of NAFTA, but that seems unlikely. The NAFTA text was concluded before the

Agriculture in Chinese FTAs

China has concluded FTAs with several Asian countries as well as with Chile and New Zealand, two major agricultural exporters. These illuminate China's willingness to liberalize its agricultural quotas and enlarge its obligations under the WTO SPS Agreement.

ASEAN–China Free Trade Agreement (ACFTA) (2004)

In 2000, Chinese Premier Zhu Rongji proposed that the Association of Southeast Asian Nations (ASEAN) and China enter into an FTA. By the end of 2004 China and ASEAN had signed an accord to establish a free trade area by 2010, linking China with Brunei, Indonesia, Malaysia, the Philippines, Singapore, and Thailand. Trade between ASEAN and China has more than doubled, from $192 billion in 2008 to $400 billion in 2012.[13] In 2015 Cambodia, Laos, Myanmar, and Vietnam will also join the new pact. The trade in goods framework agreement was signed in 2004 by all parties and implemented in 2005. Reduction or elimination of tariffs is to happen under five different schedules. The first is the early harvest program, followed by the normal tracks I and II (products that are not so sensitive), and finally sensitive and highly sensitive lists.

The early harvest program was to begin the reduction of tariffs before 2010, and to reduce tariffs on certain products over three years, starting in 2004. This included all items under chapters 1 through 8 in the harmonized system (HS) code, unless excluded in the FTA's annex. The early harvest program covered animals, forestry products, fruits, and vegetables. Among exclusions, states listed products such as vegetable oils, coffee, and grains that would have until 2012 for their tariffs to be removed.

The sensitive list allowed 400 items at the HS 6-digit level to maintain tariffs up to 20 percent after 2012 for China. Roughly 40 percent of the items on the highly sensitive list could keep tariffs up to 50 percent after 2012, but these were mainly wood products. Thus tariffs on most of China's agricultural products that the early harvest program did not cover were eliminated for ASEAN exporters by 2012.

China–Chile FTA (2005)

In the 2005 FTA with Chile, China initially kept many of its high MFN tariffs on agricultural products, with liberalization over long phaseout periods. Both countries have greatly benefited from the FTA, with two-way trade expanding from $9 billion in 2006 to nearly $30 billion in 2011. Commentators in the

---

Marrakesh Agreement that sealed the SPS provisions in the WTO, and dispute settlement in the WTO is more expeditious than in NAFTA.

13. Liz Gooch, "Asia Free-Trade Zone Raises Hopes, and Some Fears About China," *New York Times*, December 31, 2009; Xinhua, "Backgrounder: ASEAN–China Free Trade Area," *China Daily*, www.chinadaily.com.cn (accessed on June 23, 2014).

official press have called for increased agricultural cooperation and for the doubling of two-way trade by 2015, to $60 billion.[14]

Copper and other minerals were granted immediate duty-free access, but most agricultural products faced initial high tariffs. Nearly 300 products at the HS 8-digit level, many of them agriculture products, started the FTA with tariffs of 20 percent or more, with a 10-year phaseout period. Wine and tobacco products had initial tariffs of over 50 percent, while specialty products such as salmon, grapes, and apples had lower tariffs. All these products were subject to the 10-year phaseout and, since the FTA was signed, agricultural exports from Chile to China have soared. Phaseout schedules reflect the number of years in the phaseout period. A 10-year phaseout would decrease the tariff rate by 10 percent from the base tariff per year and a 2-year phaseout would decrease the tariff rate by 50 percent of the base per year. Wool, maize, forestry, cotton, sugar, grains, and some cooking oils were all exempt from the phaseout schedules, so their tariffs remain unchanged.

China–New Zealand FTA (2008)

After China and New Zealand signed an FTA in 2008, New Zealand's exports to China quadrupled, largely due to the lowering of agricultural tariffs on the Chinese side. Two-way trade rose 235 percent from 2008 to 2013. New Zealand's dairy industry enjoyed an export surge thanks to lower Chinese tariffs, and exports will increase further as tariffs are phased out completely. But China was careful to retain protection on some agricultural products: many grains (such as maize), wool, forestry, sugar, cotton, and several vegetable oils. Tariffs on these items will remain at their MFN rates. Among these, the wool and forestry exemptions most seriously reduce New Zealand's exports.

Before the FTA, China's average tariff on agricultural imports from New Zealand was 15 percent. In the agreement, China will phase out many of its tariffs. Liquid milk, butter, and cheese are subject to a 10-year tariff phaseout period, while powdered milk is subject to a 12-year phaseout period. However, all these dairy products are subject to quota restrictions that will continue to limit the quantity of imports for 5 years past the tariff expiration dates.

China lists TRQs in its GATT-bound schedules on agricultural products such as vegetable oil, wheat, rice, maize, sugar, and wool. The only product from New Zealand affected is wool, and a country-specific tariff rate quota (CTRQ) was created for this. The initial quota was 25,000 tons of wool and 450 tons of wool tops, growing 5 percent annually for 5 years. The quotas then will remain at 5th-year levels unless the parties decide otherwise. New Zealand was

---

14. Qin Jize and Cheng Guangjin, "China, Chile Expected to Double Trade," *People's Daily Online*, June 28, 2012, english.peopledaily.com.cn (accessed on May 27, 2014).

accorded tariff relief for a majority of forestry products, but products such as processed wood and paper had no tariff liberalization.[15]

Like Chile, New Zealand is a relatively small exporter of agricultural products to China. Chile accounts for less than 1 percent of China's agricultural imports and New Zealand accounts for a little more than 3 percent. Skeptics might question whether, in light of these small shares, China's liberalization in the two FTAs could serve as a precedent for liberalization in a China–US FTA. Our view is that the two FTAs establish a benchmark, and that China will be placed in a weak defensive position if it tries to backtrack.

Australia–China FTA (AUCFTA)

China and Australia have been negotiating an FTA since 2005.[16] Negotiations have stalled several times, but in March 2014, Chinese Premier Li Keqiang stated in his opening remarks of the National People's Congress that China will "accelerate" negotiations with Australia.[17] China's reluctance to open its agricultural sector to Australian products has been a contentious issue. China's strong defensive positions, especially advocated by the Ministry of Agriculture (MOA), stem from three major considerations. First, the ministry doubts that liberalization will significantly increase the productivity of Chinese agriculture, as the sector's competitiveness has barely improved since WTO accession in 2002. Second, some of the hundreds of millions of Chinese farmers could lose part of their income, causing social instability. Chinese farmers are among the poorest citizens and many are unskilled in other lines of work. A potential fall in agricultural income is worrisome as unrest among peasants and ethnic minorities has been rising in recent years. Third, China historically has been concerned about food security and in the past has advocated a policy of 95 percent self-sufficiency for food staples. Australia has a competitive advantage in the production of wheat, barley, rice, cotton, and sugar—all products regulated in China by the National Development and Reform Commission (NDRC). SOEs control trade of these staples within China and they are reluctant to give up control. In theory Australia could help China ensure food security, but if a distinction can be made, China focuses more on self-sufficiency than food security. However, with China's growing population, limited farm land, and water shortages, the country may be forced to import more food in the coming years—a practical reality that could open the door for meaningful agricultural agreements with countries including Australia and the United States.

---

15. The document "Key Outcomes: New Zealand-China Free Trade Agreement," www.chinafta. govt.nz (accessed on May 27, 2014) summarizes the FTA.

16. This section draws from Jiang (2013).

17. Philip Wen, "China to Accelerate Australia Free Trade Agreement," *Sydney Morning Herald*, March 5, 2014.

Conclusion

The United States has serious complaints about Chinese farm subsidies and other market access barriers. A good example is the wheat industry. The United States is a major contributor to world wheat trade, accounting for 20 percent of global exports. US Wheat Associates, a lobbying organization for US wheat exporters, claims that China's domestic support for its wheat farmers has exceeded its WTO-agreed de minimis entitlement spending of 8.5 percent of the value of production.[18] Domestic subsidies that stimulate Chinese production displace wheat imports. Market access barriers have further depressed US wheat exports to China. Wheat imports under the Chinese tariff rate quota system have not fully used the available quota due to administrative obstacles. Regulations such as import licenses and TRQ applications burden US exporters. Further, the out-of-quota tariff rate of 65 percent, together with a 13 percent value-added tax (VAT) that may not be imposed on domestic wheat sales, serve to reduce Chinese wheat imports even more.

With two-way agriculture trade at $34 billion in 2012, both sides can gain from trade concessions that increase market access for farmers (Meador and Bugang 2013). US exports of agricultural products to China account for 17 percent of total US agriculture exports and 27 percent of total Chinese agricultural imports (table 6.1). While soybeans account for approximately 60 percent of US agricultural exports to China, all products have shown significant gains over the past decade (table 6.2).[19] US agricultural exports to China have increased by a factor of 12 since 2002, rising from $2.2 billion to $26.0 billion. Chinese agricultural exports to the United States have quadrupled since 2002, from $1.8 billion to $7.7 billion, and China has shown particular strength in exports of fish, prepared meats, and prepared fruits and vegetables. These specialty exports could see significant growth to the US market with a CHUSTIA in place.

Past FTAs by both countries indicate a limited willingness to open their agriculture sectors, but many sticking points will be contested. China's tariff schedule has a simple average applied MFN rate of 15.6 percent on agriculture, much higher than the US average of 4.9 percent. A China–US FTA would presumably schedule much lower average applied rates on the Chinese side, perhaps phased in over 5 to 10 years, and lower protection of sensitive products on the US side.

The treatment of tobacco and tobacco products could be a very sensitive issue for the United States. Unmanufactured tobacco probably faces the highest tariff in the US tariff schedule and has been a point of contention in recent trade talks. In the ongoing TPP negotiations, there are already signs of

---

18. See US Wheat Associates, "2014 National Trade Estimate Report: Foreign Trade Barriers: China," October 18, 2013, www.regulations.gov (accessed on May 27, 2014).

19. Data from David Miller, director of research and commodity services, testimony to the US Chamber of Commerce, April 2013.

Table 6.2 US and Chinese bilateral agricultural trade by year, 2002–12 (millions of US dollars)

	Chinese exports to the United States	US exports to China
2002	1,800	2,200
2003	2,300	5,200
2004	2,600	5,900
2005	3,200	5,700
2006	4,200	7,400
2007	4,900	9,100
2008	5,600	13,000
2009	5,100	14,000
2010	6,300	19,000
2011	7,300	20,000
2012	7,700	26,000

Source: World Bank, World Integrated Trade Solution (WITS) database (2013), http://wits.worldbank.org.

controversy over the US Trade Representative's proposal on tobacco,[20] which reduces the influence of public health officials in determining whether or not a smoking measure is discriminatory. The proposal has drawn the ire of both business and antismoking groups, and there is little doubt that those groups will have something to say about a US-China FTA, since China is a major player in the tobacco industry. In 2009 China produced 3 million tons of tobacco leaf—43 percent of global production—making it by far the largest producer of tobacco.[21] China is also a major exporter of tobacco, although US exports to China greatly exceed Chinese exports to the United States.[22] Much of China's tobacco production goes toward domestic consumption, as China is the world's largest consumer of cigarettes. With that in mind, the US tobacco lobby will likely be conflicted in its stance, wary of competing with the world's largest producer, but elated to gain better access to the world's largest market.

Both countries would benefit from a joint SPS committee, similar to the one established in KORUS, to enhance cooperation and closely examine

20. Simon Lester, "Trade, Tobacco, and the TPP," *Huffington Post*, September 3, 2013, www. huffingtonpost.com (accessed on June 24, 2014).

21. Michael Eriksen, Judith Mackay, Hana Ross, *The Tobacco Atlas*, 4th ed., tobaccoatlas.org (accessed on June 23, 2014).

22. Data are from the United Nations Comtrade Database, comtrade.un.org (accessed on June 23, 2014).

measures that restrict agriculture imports. In light of Chinese SPS barriers that are contrary to reports from the World Organization for Animal Health, the United States might well insist on a provision that accords weight to the pronouncements of that organization.

Premier Li Keqiang recently stated that agriculture production was the foundation of China's economy and serves as insurance to stabilize growth, control inflation, and mitigate risks.[23] Recent events such as floods in the northeast, drought in the west, and disease in pig and chicken farms underscore China's long-term dependence on agricultural imports and the crucial role of trade agreements with agricultural exporters such as the United States and Australia. In a CHUSTIA, China would probably ask for language guarding against discriminatory or lengthy export controls of agricultural products, but in the present framework of China's self-sufficiency policy. If the framework evolves significantly, assurances against export controls could become more important.

Subsidized farming is an issue that concerns both countries. Historically the United States has argued that domestic agricultural subsidies can be addressed only in the WTO, not in FTAs, because the effects of subsidies are global with respect to imports and exports. This doctrine could be modified in the two megaregional agreements under negotiation, the TPP and the Transatlantic Trade and Investment Partnership (TTIP). If either agreement addresses domestic agricultural subsidies or domestic price controls, very likely the United States will press the same issue in a CHUSTIA.

Two larger questions remain, however. The first is whether China will soon be willing to depart from its centuries-old policies of self-sufficiency and central control of agricultural production and distribution. Any departure could be as revolutionary as the industrial implications of Deng Xiaoping's famous quote: "It doesn't matter whether the cat is black or white, as long as it catches mice." In our judgment, China's transition from total control of agriculture to partial liberalization will be slow and measured, much as is happening in Korea and Japan. However, difficult growing conditions in the northern and western provinces, exacerbated by periodic droughts, coupled with a shift in the Chinese diet toward more meat, should make larger imports of feed grains, pork, and beef politically much more acceptable. The second question is whether a US trade and investment agreement with China could enlist sufficient congressional support without significant liberalization of Chinese controls. Again this is a guess, but we do not believe that wholesale removal of barriers within 5 years is necessary; instead a 10- or 20-year path of gradual liberalization might suffice for this key component of a larger agreement. Additionally, the United States could give China an exception for liberalizing rice, much as Korea received in KORUS, and probably as Japan will receive in the TPP.

---

23. Xinhua, "China Underlines Stable Agricultural Production," *China Daily*, www.chinadaily.com (accessed on May 27, 2014).

References

Jiang, Yang. 2013. *China's Policymaking for Regional Economic Cooperation.* London: Palgrave Macmillan.

Meador, M. Melinda, and Wu Bugang. 2013. China Agricultural Trade Report in 2012 (February 25). Washington: USDA Foreign Agricultural Service.

Smith, Vincent H. 2006. *Regulating State Trading Enterprises in the GATT: An Urgent Need for Change? Evidence from the 2003–2004 U.S.-Canada Grain Dispute.* Agricultural Marketing Policy Paper 12 (February). Bozeman, MT: Montana State University.

III

POTENTIAL COMPONENTS OF A COMPREHENSIVE AGREEMENT

7

Service Barriers

Approximately 14 percent of Americans are employed in tradable business service firms; manufacturing firms, by comparison, employ only 10 percent of the total US workforce (Jensen 2011).[1] In 2007 business service sector jobs paid an average salary of $56,000, some $10,000 more than the average salary in manufacturing. But largely because of high nontariff barriers (NTBs), only 5 percent of US business service firms engage in exporting, compared to 25 percent of US manufacturing plants (Jensen 2011). US manufacturing firms export approximately 20 percent of their annual output, but US business service firms export only 4 percent. That said, in 2013, US service exports amounted to $681 billion, and the US service trade surplus was approximately $229 billion.[2] In short, the United States has a latent, but strong, comparative advantage in exporting business services.[3]

---

1. Sherry M. Stephenson made a major contribution to this chapter. Stephenson is a senior fellow at the International Centre for Trade and Sustainable Development (ICTSD) in Geneva and a senior advisor for services trade at the Organization of American States (OAS) in Washington.

2. Moreover, official statistics often undercount the direct service exports that they purport to measure, such as McKinsey consulting services for foreign clients. Official statistics can be found at US Bureau of Economic Statistics. See US Department of Commerce, Bureau of Economic Analysis, "International Economic Accounts," www.bea.gov (accessed on May 29, 2014).

3. Of course many services—haircuts, taxi rides, restaurant meals—remain nontradable, in the sense of cross-border supply, because consumption and production must be performed at the same place and at the same time. Such services may, however, be delivered abroad through direct investment, discussed in chapter 13. Ernest Preeg (2014) of the Manufacturers Alliance argues that the US surplus in services has peaked, mainly because royalties and licenses represent around one-third of the surplus in business services, and those receipts have been roughly flat at $82 to

Official statistics do not measure indirect services embodied in manufactured exports, such as software services purchased from Oracle,[4] nor do they count the sale value of services delivered by American establishments operating abroad, such as retailing by Wal-Mart and McDonalds, or financial services by JPMorgan Chase and Citigroup. However, earnings by American establishments operating abroad do show up in the current account. Box 7.1 surveys these indirect exports. That they loom large in the overall picture underscores US comparative advantage in the services sectors. Yet high foreign barriers clearly limit US direct cross-border exports of services.

Jobs supported by merchandise exports are highly visible, and for a long time were considered the hallmark of a strong economy. Goods shipped from a manufacturing plant and containers stacked at ports tell their own story. Airplanes, tractors, and CAT scan equipment sold abroad are easy to visualize. In contrast, managerial or technical services jobs supported by service exports are not always obvious. But solid positions are at stake. When foreign visitors rent US cars or stay in US hotels, those service exports support US jobs. The same is true in higher education, when foreign students study in a US classroom or purchase distance learning delivered over the internet. Commercial presence in a foreign country, as when the law firm White & Case sets up an office in Paris, also creates US service exports, made possible by direct investment abroad.

Fees paid to an architectural firm for designing a building abroad count as an export, as do fees paid to Bechtel when it designs and builds a bridge or a power plant in another country. American project managers who supervise construction jobs abroad are US exporters. Research and development conducted by a foreign firm in the United States likewise counts as an export. When the Boston Consulting Group provides managerial advice to foreign firms it is exporting, as it is when Young & Rubicam rolls out an advertising portfolio for a foreign client. Any doctor in the United States who operates on a foreigner is providing services that count as exports. Computer programmers who design ATM software used abroad are exporting their services. So are accountants who audit the books of foreign firms. An engineering firm that cleans water sources abroad is exporting a service. Express delivery firms such as FedEx and UPS are major service exporters when they deliver documents and goods around the world.

Movies and music loom large in US service exports. Feature-length films and TV shows screened and broadcast abroad, as well as US music sold to foreign customers, generate huge revenue streams for the US entertainment industry. Similarly, software producers, ranging from large corporations such as Microsoft to small developers of smartphone apps, are significant US exporters.

$85 billion over the past three years. However, Preeg's forecast does not contemplate dramatic liberalization of barriers to cross-border trade in business services.

4. See OECD, "OECD-WTO Database on Trade in Value-Added," fact sheet, May 2013, www.oecd.org (accessed on May 29, 2014).

Box 7.1 Indirect exports of services

Although recorded direct cross-border services exports account for less than 30 percent of US exports of goods and services—some $632 billion in 2012—service firms make an indirect contribution not reflected by that statistic. This was revealed by a joint OECD-WTO report measuring domestic value added as a proportion of export value and examining the sources of that value added.[1] The domestic value-added share was calculated by subtracting imported inputs from export values. In 2009 the US share of domestic value added was the highest among OECD countries, at 89 percent.

The OECD-WTO report further found that US service sectors—such as finance, engineering, and transportation—contribute 26 percent of the value added in US exports of manufactures. Likewise, service sectors contribute 29 percent to the value-added in agricultural exports. US efficiencies in services production are a major source of competitive advantage in US exports of manufactured and agricultural goods.

Based on the available data, in 2012 the indirect service contribution to gross US exports amounted to about $340 billion. Thus, when indirect service exports are added to direct exports, the service sectors accounts for 44 percent of the value added embodied in US gross exports. The combined figure for US direct and indirect exports of services in 2012 was about $970 billion.

The service story does not stop there. US direct investment abroad is concentrated in the service industries, accounting for 73 percent of the outward FDI stock in 2012 ($3.3 trillion out of $4.5 trillion). The foreign affiliates of US-based multinational corporations in the service sectors realized sales of $2.6 trillion in 2011—in other words, a larger figure than the combined US direct and indirect service sector exports.

As well, at the global level services contribute a larger share of export value added than they do of gross exports. Table 7.1 gives basic statistics on merchandise and services trade for the years 1980, 1995, and 2008. Direct and indirect export value added by the service sectors, expressed as a share of total exports, expanded from 29 percent to 43 percent between 1980 and 2008. Unsurprisingly, given China's heavy involvement in manufacturing, its service sectors contribute a smaller share of value added to manufacturing exports than the US service sectors. Moreover, the value added by foreign services outweighs the contribution of domestic services in some Chinese industries. In the electrical equipment industry, Chinese services contributed about 13 percent of value while foreign services contributed 15 percent of value added. Foreign services also marginally outweighed domestic service contributions in the wood and paper industry, as well as the chemicals industry. Overall, services account for 30 percent of Chinese export value added. However, roughly one-third of that is value added by foreign services. Chinese service sectors account for less than 20 percent of value added in exports, less than half the comparable US figure.

---

1. OECD, International Trade and Balance of Payments, OECD-WTO Trade in Value Added (May 2013), stats.oecd.org (accessed on July 4, 2014).

Table 7.1   Global tradability of goods and services, 1980–2008
          (percent)

		Share of world exports			Tradability[a]		
		1980	**1995**	**2008**	**1980**	**1995**	**2008**
Gross trade	Merchandise	83	80	80	43	53	85
	Services	17	20	20	7	7	10
Value added	Merchandise	71	62	57	30	33	47
	Services	29	38	43	10	11	16

a. Tradability is the property of a good or service that can be sold in another location distant from where it was produced.

Source: Subramanian and Kessler (2013).

Even though they are not officially counted as service exports, license and royalty fees collected from foreign users support thousands of US jobs.

The US finance industry is another major exporter, through fees paid to, say, Wilmington Trust for its wealth management services, or to the Vanguard Group for its mutual funds. Foreign companies that purchase casualty insurance from Chubb are importing US services. Financial services are so important, and so tightly linked with direct investment abroad, that we examine them separately in chapter 8.

Opportunities abound for the direct export of US services, as rising incomes in China and other fast-growing emerging markets increase the proportion of service expenditures in their GNPs. But high barriers to service imports have so far stifled the potential growth of US exports. Huge improvements to communications technology enable medical, legal, educational, engineering, and financial services to be delivered remotely and thus traded internationally. Based on the results presented in chapter 2, table 7.2 offers a very rough guess of the gains US services industries might make under a China–US trade and investment agreement (CHUSTIA) through direct exports. The guesses start with the baseline projected profile of US service exports in 2025 in the absence of a CHUSTIA (the baseline comes from chapter 2).[5] Each service industry's predicted share of the gains from a CHUSTIA equals its share of US services exports to the world. These are of course rough guesses and other methodologies could produce very different results.

Quantitative Estimates of Barriers

Expressing barriers to service imports as ad valorem equivalents (AVEs) is an art, not a science. The core reason is that nearly all the barriers are NTBs and

---

5. Projected service exports in chapter 2 are for total services. The division in table 7.2 between service industries conforms to the same proportions as 2012 actual service exports to China.

Table 7.2   Projected gains in US services exports to China

	US exports to China (billions of US dollars)		
	Baseline (2025)	Projected increase from CHUSTIA	Projected total (2025)
Total	126.0	218.0	344.0
Banking	10.4	27.5	37.9
Insurance	0.4	5.7	6.1
Transportation	11.5	29.6	41.1
Communications	0.5	4.7	5.2
Computer/information services	1.8	4.8	6.6
Royalties/licenses	20.2	44.9	65.1
Professional business services	5.4	49.9	55.4
Education	24.0	8.4	32.5
Travel	51.8	42.4	94.2

CHUSTIA = China–US trade and investment agreement

Source: Authors' calculations.

thus regulatory in nature. Many regulations create entry costs: The foreign supplier is not permitted to sell locally at all or is limited in the amount it can sell. FedEx and UPS are not permitted to deliver express packages between cities in China. Other regulations create an ongoing hassle by subjecting foreign suppliers to cumbersome paperwork as they try to expand. This is the situation with foreign banks that want to expand their branch networks in China. Such barriers are not easily expressed as a percentage of sales because, as the barrier is relaxed and sales increase, the AVE per sales unit drops.

Yet AVEs are an essential building block for quantitative calculations of the effects of liberalization, such as the computable general equilibrium (CGE) results presented in chapter 2. Moreover, AVEs provide convenient shorthand figures for comparing service trade barriers with merchandise trade barriers. For both reasons, scholars have expended a lot of effort attempting to translate domestic regulations, trade commitments, and observed trade patterns into AVEs. Early attempts led to quantitative estimates in the form of index values rather than AVEs. More recent work, based largely on observed trade patterns, has generated AVEs.

In the first phase, pioneered by Bernard Hoekman (1996), commitments that individual World Trade Organization (WTO) members made in the General Agreement on Trade in Services (GATS) were benchmarked against the most liberal extant provisions then known for a range of services and modes of delivery. The gap between commitments and benchmarks was assigned a numerical value between 100 and 0. Hoekman's numerical values are best interpreted as indexes. Lionel Fontagné, Amélie Guillin, and Cristina Mitaritonna (2011) summarize the publications of other scholars who have followed Hoekman's lead. The World Bank's Services Trade Restrictiveness Index (STRI) represents one of the better methods for measuring service barriers. A more recent study, now at the forefront of indexes for measuring service barriers, was released in May 2014 by the Organization for Economic Cooperation and Development (OECD). The OECD's index (also called STRI) shows that China's barriers in 18 service sectors were generally more restrictive than the average scores for 40 other developed and developing economies. China was in the top 5 of the most restricted services sectors in 14 of the 18 categories: broadcasting, road freight transport services, commercial banking, couriers, computers, construction, distribution, insurance, legal, maritime transport, motion pictures, rail freight transport, sound recording, and telecoms.[6] Table 7A.2 shows the OECD scores for the United States and China. Appendix 7A to this chapter describes both the World Bank and OECD indexes further.

In the second phase of research, pioneered by the Australian Productivity Commission (Warren 2000), indexes of commitments and regulatory barriers were compared with price-to-cost margins in selected sectors to generate AVEs. Fontagné, Guillin, and Mitaritonna (2011) also summarize additional studies in this phase, and appendix 7A presents selected results using the price-to-cost margin approach for US and Chinese AVEs.

The third phase of research, pioneered by Joseph Francois (1993) two decades ago but neglected until the mid-2000s, uses residuals from gravity model equations of trade patterns to infer AVEs on services trade. Numerous assumptions and complicated mathematics are required for this approach and needless to say, scholars differ as to the appropriate assumptions and mathematics. Fontagné, Guillin, and Mitaritonna (2011) once again summarize the literature and present their own estimates for nine service sectors in 65 countries. Appendix 7A presents selected results using the gravity model approach for US and Chinese AVEs.

There is an important difference between most of the index value estimates of service trade barriers and the gravity model estimates. Some of the index values combine barriers to cross-border trade with barriers to foreign direct investment (FDI) and barriers to the movement of natural persons. The gravity model AVE estimates, in contrast, reflect only barriers to cross-border services trade. Such cross-border AVE estimates are most appropriate for trade effect calculations.

Appendix table 7A.2 reports Chinese and US AVE values based on gravity model estimates used for the CGE analysis of trade effects reported in chapter 2.[7] Those AVE estimates, based on research done five years ago, are embedded

---

6. China Trade Daily, "OECD Service Barrier Index Shows China with Above Average Score in All Covered Sectors," May 16, 2014.

7. The AVE values used in the CGE analysis are those reported by Hufbauer, Schott, and Wong (2010).

in thousands of CGE equations and will be revised only if the model is updated generally. However, research done in recent years has generated better AVE estimates, and appendix table 7A.2 reports the Chinese and US AVE values that we think are the best currently available: those that Fontagné, Guillin, and Mitaritonna (2011) calculated for China and those that Koen Berden and colleagues (2009) calculated for the United States. These newer estimates do not differ much from the older AVE estimates for China and the United States embedded in the CGE model.

As said at the beginning, however, AVE calculations of barriers to services trade remain an art, not a science. For that reason, chapter 2 reports trade effect estimates using AVE reductions that are only 40 percent of the estimated barriers shown in appendix table 7A.2. Additionally, chapter 2 estimates the effect for half of the original estimate for liberalization in services, called less services liberalization (LSL). Service barriers come in many flavors, are deeply embedded in regulatory practices, and are not eliminated nearly as easily as tariffs. Thus the assumed reduction in service barriers, under a CHUSTIA, is much smaller than the AVE values currently reported. We turn now to review the liberalization commitments previously scheduled in the WTO GATS and in US and Chinese free trade agreements (FTAs).

WTO Rulebook

The GATS

The GATS—a key feature of the Marrakesh Agreement signed in 1994 and one of the pillars of the World Trade Organization—classified all services trade into four modes. Mode 1 trade is similar to trade in goods: The consumer and producer remain in their respective home countries and services are delivered across the border by telecommunications or post rather than ships. Medical advice and distance learning received over the internet fall under mode 1. In mode 2, the purchaser travels to use a service supplied in another country. Tourism and study abroad are familiar examples. Less well known mode 2 service activities include ship and aircraft repairs when the craft is in a foreign port. In mode 3, a company establishes a subsidiary or branch abroad to sell into a foreign market, requiring FDI in a service activity. Citibank operating in Singapore is an example. Last, under mode 4, an individual leaves his home country for temporary employment abroad.

The GATS agreement in the WTO seeks to apply core merchandise trade principles of the GATT to trade in services. GATS signatories agreed to extend the most favored nation (MFN) and national treatment principles to services trade, but allowed ample room for one-time exceptions to the MFN principle. Moreover, national treatment is guaranteed only under the conditions scheduled for the sector and mode of supply in a country's commitments (the so-called positive list approach). When the Uruguay Round was concluded and the Marrakesh Agreement signed, WTO members generally did not expand liberalization using the national treatment principle or other means of new market access in their schedules to the GATS. The main exceptions, where fresh liberalization was subsequently negotiated, were in telecoms and financial services.[8] Similarly, lengthy negotiations in the Doha Round have not produced further liberalization. The GATS attempted to provide rules to govern services trade, but the limited scope of new commitments on market access in services trade over the past two decades reveals that GATS has not been very successful as a negotiating forum.

As with the GATT, the GATS does not preclude members from entering into a preferential agreement with other members, nor does it prevent members from granting one another mutual recognition of their regulatory standards and certification requirements. Accordingly, the limited amount of negotiated liberalization of services trade over the past two decades has largely taken place in bilateral FTAs. We examine this record in a later section.

Trade Facilitation

The most significant achievement of the ninth WTO ministerial conference, held in Bali, Indonesia, in December 2013, was the Trade Facilitation (TF) Agreement. Improved TF services could foster major increases in trade between China and the United States. A 2010 study found that, on a global basis, China–US two-way trade could expand by about $200 billion from broadly defined trade facilitation.[9] Sea freight and air cargo delivery can still be cumbersome between the United States and China. The United States needs major infrastructure improvements, including port and road upgrades. In China, customs clearance bottlenecks are common at ports; foreign transportation companies are hampered from efficient distribution inside China by overly strict regulations; and air cargo firms have little flexibility to adapt to changing patterns of demand. Adopting the World Customs Organization's standardized practices would significantly improve efficiency at Chinese ports. These standards reflect global best practice, and along with better rail and road connections, they would enable small firms and individuals to import goods on their own.

The General Administration of Customs (GAC), China's agency in charge of collecting customs duties, also protects China from illegal imports. Recent regulations to deter illegal imports have raised the general level of barriers to legal imports. All importers and exporters must register with the customs administration to obtain a customs registration code.[10] Additionally, the previous

---

8. The telecom and the financial services negotiations both concluded in 1997 and were incorporated into the GATS through Protocols IV and V.

9. Hufbauer, Schott, and Wong (2010), based on Wilson, Mann, and Otsuki (2005). See also Hufbauer and Wong (2011). The broad definition of trade facilitation includes the estimated gains from services infrastructure, port efficiency, customs environment, and regulatory environment.

10. For GAC Order 197, see ETCN, "Decree no. 97 of the General Administration of Customs of the P.R. China," November 25, 2010, www.e-to-china.com (accessed on May 29, 2014).

exemption of de minimis duty exemptions was reduced from 400RMB ($65) to 50RMB ($6), creating an unnecessary burden for small shipments.[11] By comparison, the US de minimis figure is $200, and legislation under consideration would raise that level to $800.[12] As China implements the TF agreement over the next five years, these and other improvements should improve the trade landscape, for both goods and services.

The Trade in Services Agreement

The Trade in Services Agreement (TiSA) is a plurilateral pact launched by the Really Good Friends (RGF), a group of WTO members that opened negotiations in 2012. The group includes the world's largest advanced nations, accounting for more than two-thirds of global trade in services (Hufbauer et al. 2012). Motivated by the longstanding stalemate in the WTO's Doha Development Agenda (DDA) and primarily pressured by the business community, which is fully aware of the importance of services in modern economies, the RGF group seeks an agreement that will reduce barriers to services trade among TiSA members. The negotiation is not a part of the Doha Round, but it is a plurilateral effort designed to meet the conditions laid out in GATS Article V. An agreement under Article V is required to have "substantial sectoral coverage" with respect to the volume of services trade, number of sectors, and modes of supply, and to eliminate "substantially all discrimination" among members.

TiSA's effects on US–China relations remain to be seen. China expressed interest in joining TiSA negotiations in September 2013, and the United States and other TiSA members are considering their response.[13] While China's interest could be driven by a fresh appreciation that services imports support manufacturing and improve the quality of life, it might also reflect China's rising competitiveness in some services industries. Higher educational attainment and improved labor productivity will foster greater competitiveness in the Chinese tradable service sectors. According to China's National Board of Statistics, production of services exceeded industrial output as a share of GDP in 2013, a remarkable milestone.[14] These circumstances should give Chinese service firms an export interest in lowering barriers worldwide.

---

11. For GAC Order 33, see FedEx, "Notice of New Regulation: Import and Export of Samples and Advertising Materials," July 2, 2010, www.fedex.com (accessed on May 29, 2014).

12. The Customs Modernization Act of 1993 Section 321 set the rate at $200. See HR 1020 for the proposal to increase the level to $800: Library of Congress, "Bill Text, 113th Congress (2013–2014), HR 1020 IH," thomas.loc.gov (accessed on May 29, 2014).

13. Shawn Donnan, "China in Push to Join US-led $4tn Services Trade Talks," *Financial Times*, September 23, 2013.

14. S.C., "Doing Stuff, Not Making Stuff," *Economist*, January 20, 2014.

China has been increasingly active on the international construction scene, including in the United States. China Construction America, a subsidiary of China State Construction Engineering, has recently undertaken public works contracts at the state and local levels. In 2011 the company won a contract to renovate New York City's Alexander Hamilton Bridge.[15] What TiSA or a CHUSTIA will mean for Chinese construction companies is unclear, as Chinese construction firms are more likely to pursue state and local projects. Generally, the states are bound by US FTAs only to the extent they agree. Customarily they resist new obligations in US FTAs, but for reasons of state self-interest such resistance could weaken.

Before China's recent change of heart, all five BRICS—Brazil, Russia, India, China, and South Africa—had shown little interest in a plurilateral agreement on services trade.[16] At the moment, the other BRICS remain skeptical. These countries account for a large portion of the one-third of international services trade that current RGF members do not cover. As figure 7.1 shows, the BRICS tend to have relatively high barriers to services imports, whether measured by AVEs or by mode 1 index values in the Services Trade Restrictiveness Index (STRI). Bringing the BRICS into TiSA could lead to substantial gains. With that in mind, the RGF negotiators are drawing on many features of the GATS to make TiSA as familiar as possible to developing members of the WTO.

TiSA negotiations are still at an early stage, so exactly what form the agreement will take is not clear. However, some features are emerging. While GATS applied a positive list approach to schedule commitments for services trade, TiSA is moving toward a hybrid approach.[17] Members will still schedule market access commitments under the positive list approach, but national treatment obligations will be handled under a negative list approach, in which members commit to national treatment in all sectors except those where an exception is scheduled.

As mentioned earlier, US manufacturing firms export around 20 percent of their output, compared to 4 percent for services firms (through direct exports). If TiSA liberalization is sufficiently ambitious over a period of 5 to 10 years, the export-sales ratio in services might rise to 10 percent—half the figure for manufactures. At that ratio, service export gains would be substantial. OECD countries might see an estimated $720 billion in increased exports; of this amount, US exports would increase by nearly $300 billion. Exports of this magnitude would support approximately 1.5 million new jobs in the United States (Hufbauer, Jensen, and Stephenson 2012).

---

15. Kirk Semple, "Bridge Repairs by a Company Tied to Beijing," *New York Times*, August 10, 2011.

16. However, China signed a services agreement with Taiwan on June 21, 2013. See Cindy Wang, "China Signs Pact with Taiwan to Open Services Trade Sectors," *Bloomberg*, June 21, 2013.

17. Inside U.S. Trade, "U.S. Proposes Alterations To TISA Text, Delaying Market Access Offers," July 3, 2013.

Figure 7.1 AVE tariff levels and World Bank STRI

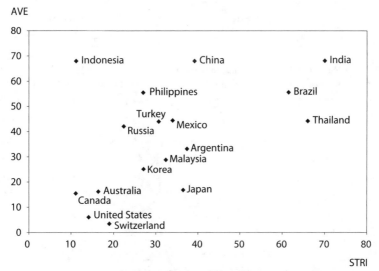

AVE = ad valorem equivalent; STRI = Services Trade Restrictiveness Index
Sources: World Bank STRI database, iresearch.worldbank.org (accessed on July 4, 2014);
Fontagné, Guillin, and Mitaritonna (2011).

US and Chinese FTA Commitments

On the basis of information put together by the WTO Secretariat, all major
countries that have negotiated regional or preferential trade agreements over
the last 20 years have gone beyond their GATS services commitments agreed in
1994, in many cases very significantly (Roy 2011). This is also the case for the
United States and China, which have subjected several new subsectors to new
or improved commitments in their FTAs (see tables 7.3 and 7.4). Aside from its
FTA commitments, the United States made extensive commitments in telecom
and financial services agreements in 1997. China made several commitments
in its WTO accession protocol in December 2001. The difference between the
GATS and the new bilateral agreements is most striking for China in mode 3
(FDI), where Chinese FTAs have scheduled greater opening for direct investment.

New US negotiating initiatives that encompass services include the TiSA
effort in the margins of the WTO, the Trans-Pacific Partnership (TPP) with
countries in Asia and the Pacific, and the Transatlantic Trade and Investment
Partnership (TTIP) with the European Union. Nearly all the negotiating proposals remain confidential, but some information has been leaked to specialized
trade reports. China is not yet participating in any of the three megaregional
negotiating initiatives, but has expressed interest in joining TiSA talks. China
is participating in the Regional Comprehensive Economic Partnership (RCEP)

Table 7.3 Services commitments in US FTAs (percent subsectors covered)

	United States GATS+[a]			Partner GATS+[a]		
Partner	Market access	National treatment	Full liberalization[b] (FTA total)	Market access	National treatment	Full liberalization[b] (FTA total)
Australia	50.8	52.9	63.2	57.9	55.4	62.3
Bahrain	51.0	53.7	65.0	69.2	80.0	48.2
Chile	49.7	51.4	62.1	44.8	69.7	27.4
Jordan	4.7	4.5	30.3	30.5	30.2	33.5
Morocco	51.1	50.8	61.9	87.9	87.1	63.1
Oman	49.4	51.1	62.3	42.4	68.9	64.0
Peru	48.2	50.9	60.2	87.6	85.3	59.7
Singapore	50.7	50.2	62.1	76.9	74.4	53.2
Average	44.5	45.7	58.4	62.2	68.9	51.4

FTA = free trade agreement; GATS = General Agreement on Trade in Services

a. GATS+ refers to the percent of subsectors in which a party made commitments beyond its GATS obligations in market access or national treatment.
b. Full liberalization refers to the percent of subsectors in which there were no market access or national treatment restrictions in the FTA.

Source: Miroudot, Sauvage, and Sudreau (2010).

Table 7.4 Services commitments in Chinese FTAs by partner (percent)

	China GATS+[a]			Partner GATS+[a]		
Partner	Market access	National treatment	Full[b] (FTA total)	Market access	National treatment	Full[b] (FTA total)
Hong Kong	16.9	5.0	20.5	n.a.	n.a.	n.a.
Macau	16.6	4.8	20.5	n.a.	n.a.	n.a.
New Zealand	17.6	17.1	18.5	18.7	18.7	24.8
Singapore	19.7	19.2	18.2	17.4	20.8	37.4
Average	17.7	11.5	19.4	18.1	19.8	31.1

FTA = free trade agreement; GATS = General Agreement on Trade in Services; n.a. = not applicable

a. GATS+ refers to the percent of subsectors in which a party made commitments beyond its GATS obligations in market access or national treatment.
b. Full refers to the percent of subsectors in which there were no market access or national treatment restrictions in the FTA.

Source: Miroudot, Sauvage, and Sudreau (2010).

in the Asia-Pacific region, a compact between the Association of Southeast Asian Nations (ASEAN) and six major Asian economies. However, RCEP is not as advanced as the TPP or TiSA and no agreement has yet been reached on the negotiating modality for services.

Because TiSA and the megaregional texts remain confidential, we draw on the FTAs that the United States and China have concluded to survey their respective barriers.

Overview of US Services Restrictions

There has been very little variation in the level of services commitments that the United States has offered and bound in its various FTAs. Figure 7.2 illustrates the level of services commitments between the United States and three of its FTA partners: Chile (2004), Singapore (2004), and Australia (2005). US commitments are nearly the same in all 3 agreements and quite similar in all 12 of its FTAs, with the exception of the US–Jordan FTA (see table 7.3). This suggests that the United States would most likely offer a similar level of services commitments in a possible FTA with China.

The best way to obtain an overview of services restrictions in the US economy is by examining the information in US commitments in the FTA negotiated with Korea in March 2012. The United States has negotiated the services components of its FTAs under a negative list format, so that the restrictions listed in the annexes of nonconforming measures reflect restrictions that are applied in practice. References to actual laws and regulations accompanying the description of each measure support the listed restrictions. Four annexes in US FTAs, including the FTA with Korea (KORUS), correspond to restrictions on services and investment. These cover different types of measures and encompass several restrictions.

Annex I, on standstill measures, involves existing measures that violate one or more of the core disciplines of the given FTA: the principles of national treatment, market access, and most favored nation (MFN) status. The annex also addresses measures that violate rules against local presence requirements and performance requirements, as well as rules that prevent senior managers and directors from entering a country along with FDI. These measures are subject to a ratchet; if unilaterally liberalized, the liberalization should not be subsequently withdrawn. Annex II, on optional restrictions and exclusions, deals with measures or sectors for which the signatory may retain existing restrictions and impose future new restrictions, and even permanently exclude these measures or sectors from the FTA in question. Annexes III A and III B, on financial services standstill measures and optional restrictions and exclusions, respectively, follow annexes I and II for financial services, including ratchet provisions.

The annexes of nonconforming measures for the United States in the KORUS FTA, which can be taken as a proxy for other recent US FTAs, indicate that restrictive measures in annexes I, II, and III A and B are few in number.

Figure 7.2 GATS+ commitments in US FTAs (percent of subsector)

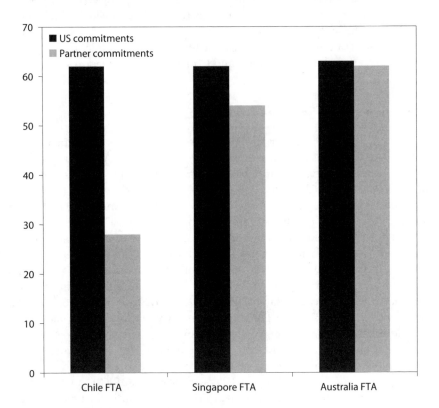

FTA = free trade agreement; GATS = General Agreement on Trade in Services
Source: Miroudot, Sauvage, and Sudreau (2010).

At face value, this would seem to indicate that restrictions on services in the US economy are not that great, given that fairly few sectors and measures are actually listed. However, judging the services panorama by the number of entries alone does not give an accurate picture of how much the US economy may be protected in the services area. To evaluate protection, it is necessary to qualitatively assess the degree of potential restrictiveness of the respective measures.

Annex I: Standstill Measures for Services Trade and Investment

There are only 12 US entries in annex I. Nine of these are related to sectors and most are linked to some type of strategic or security concern. The latter include measures covering atomic energy; mining and pipeline transportation, including oil and gas pipelines; air transport, as domestic air space is restricted to operations by US carriers only, and the same applies to specialty air services and customs brokers for air transport; communications, restricting radio licenses for foreigners; and professional services, restricting practice before the US Patent and Trademark Office to US citizens or lawful aliens for which there is a reciprocity requirement.

However, 3 of the 12 measures listed in the US annex are of a different nature, covering all sectors in the US economy rather than specific sectors. These measures refer to cross-border trade and investment. Cross-border trade and investment in services covers all existing measures maintained at the state and local level. In other words, existing state and local measures are exempt from FTA disciplines for services and investment. In investment, foreign firms cannot use small business registration forms and thus cannot qualify for small business benefit programs. Foreign firms also cannot take advantage of Overseas Private Investment Corporation (OPIC) insurance and loan guarantees.

The above three horizontal reservations affect the entire operation of the FTA for services and investment. States are bound to the current level of openness in their laws and regulations, and a ratchet applies to new liberalization that they may implement. But because the FTA does not require states to dismantle existing measures, as a practical matter the scope of new FTA disciplines is limited to the federal level. As many professional services, as well as education and health services, are certified and accredited at the state level, this creates a huge gap in the coverage of disciplines in the United States.

Annex II: Optional Restrictions and Exclusions for Services Trade and Investment

In annex II the United States has listed only six measures. This would seem to indicate that it has excluded very few services from FTA disciplines. Two of the measures in question cover areas typically reserved for governments in services agreements, namely social services and minority affairs. Two of the measures cover sectors that either could be considered sensitive and related to national security or have become subject to entrenched protectionism, depending upon one's perspective: communications (e.g., sharing of radio spectrum, satellite, and digital audio services) and maritime transport (e.g., reservation of internal US waterways, which includes coastal shipping, to US vessels under the Jones Act).

However, the remaining two measures apply to all sectors. One exemption relates to the MFN obligation. It effectively exempts all trade agreements signed before the KORUS from MFN treatment with respect to Korea, but it exempts trade agreements signed after the KORUS from the MFN obligation in only three areas: aviation, fisheries, and maritime matters. The second exemption is very broad, applying to all cross-border services trade. As it states: "The US reserves the right to adopt or maintain any measure that is not inconsistent with US' obligations under Article XVI of the GATS."[18] This would

---

18. See annex II of the KORUS agreement, www.ustr.gov (accessed on June 24, 2014).

appear to give the United States a blanket exemption to undertake new restrictions in the area of market access for any measure not identified in the GATS. However, since the United States took on significant market access obligations in the GATS, in what way this exemption will actually be used remains to be seen.

Annex III A: Financial Services Standstill Measures

Annex III A contains 16 entries, of which 13 apply to banking services and three to insurance services. The restrictions on banking affect primarily market access and national treatment and define several banking activities that are controlled or unavailable to foreign banks, including interstate banking. Two restrictions affect the operations of foreign insurance companies for activities in the US market. Additionally, two horizontal measures are included in the annex, and these affect all core disciplines for all banking and insurance activities and exempt "all existing non-conforming measures of all states, DC and Puerto Rico." Thus, in a similar manner to the measures exempted in annex I, all existing state and local measures are exempt from the scope of the trade agreement, but they cannot be made more restrictive and if subsequently liberalized, the ratchet applies.

Annex III B: Optional Restrictions or Exclusions for Financial Services

In annex III B the United States has included only one measure relating to market access for insurance firms, which states "the US reserves the right to adopt or maintain any measure that is not inconsistent with the US' obligations under Article XVI of the GATS." As in annex II, this would appear to give the United States a blanket exemption to undertake new restrictions in the area of market access on insurance for all measures not identified in the GATS. However, again, because the United States took on significant market access obligations in the GATS, in what way this broad exemption will actually be used remains to be seen.

Summarizing the US Annexes

The qualitative examinations of the most recent US FTAs for their commitments on services and investment suggests that US service sectors are generally open to modes 1 and 3, exactly as the World Bank's STRI database and most AVE calculations indicate (see appendix 7A). The two services sectors that remain highly protected are the transport sector (both maritime and air) and the professional services sector (mode 4). The practice of exempting existing measures at the state and local level from the disciplines of trade agreements implies little liberalization of professional services. Financial services also show more restrictions than other sectors and further liberalization may be difficult in the near term, given the continued fallout of the 2008–09 financial crisis. However, compared to other countries, the US financial service sector has many foreign players.

Perhaps the highest federal barriers to Chinese services in the United States are represented in the actions against the Chinese firms Huawei and ZTE Corporation. In October 2012 the US House Intelligence Committee issued a report in which US firms were "strongly encouraged to consider the long-term security risks associated with doing business with either ZTE or Huawei for equipment or services."[19] An article in Xinhua called the report "far from convincing" and both companies fought back, saying they had been unfairly targeted.[20] US companies are not expressly forbidden from purchasing equipment or services from Huawei and ZTE, although several departments in the US government are.[21]

Overview of Chinese Services Restrictions

The best way to obtain an overview of services restrictions in the Chinese economy is by examining its schedule of commitments in recent high-quality trade agreements. For China, these are the FTAs negotiated with Chile (2006) and Costa Rica (2011). The normative text and nearly all the content of China's services schedules are similar in these two agreements. The FTAs that China has negotiated with partners in Asia, particularly ASEAN, have been less ambitious and contain less comprehensive sectoral coverage.

China has preferred to negotiate the services component of its FTAs under the positive list format. Under this approach, restrictions that could (and usually do) affect services and investment are set out differently than under a negative list approach. Measures affecting the entire economy are listed under the horizontal limitations section, while measures affecting individual service sectors are listed according to the 12 main sectors and 157 subsectors that the WTO has defined in Classification List W/120.[22] MFN limitations are listed at the end of the schedule. As the positive listing does not require comprehensive sectoral coverage for services, it is impossible to know if the entries in China's schedules cover all its existing services restrictions. Most

---

19. Simon Montlake, "U.S. Congress Flags China's Huawei, ZTE as Security Threats," *Forbes*, October 8, 2012, www.forbes.com (accessed on May 29, 2014).

20. Cao Kai, "US Congress Report on Huawei, ZTE Is Far from Convincing," news.xinhuanet.com, October 15, 2012 (accessed on May 29, 2014).

21. Section 516 of the Consolidated and Further Continuing Appropriations Act of 2013 bars NASA, the National Science Foundation, and the Departments of Justice and Commerce from purchasing systems made by companies with any connection to the Chinese government from March to September 2012. See www.govtrack.us/congress/bills/113/hr933/text (accessed on June 24, 2014).

22. The Services Sectoral Classification List is WTO document MTN.GNS/W/120, i-tip.wto.org/services (accessed on June 24, 2014).

likely this is not the case, although the ambitious FTAs mentioned have built on China's GATS schedule, which was considered to be quite comprehensive at the time of China's accession to the WTO (2002), particularly for infrastructure services (telecoms, financial services, distribution, and transport). Thus an examination of the content of China's schedule of commitments in the Chile and Costa Rica FTAs provides a reasonably robust picture of existing restrictions.[23]

Horizontal Measures Affecting Services Trade and Investment

Horizontal commitments indicate what treatment China gives to service sectors across the board. China has maintained the same horizontal commitments in its FTAs that it set out in its GATS services schedule of 2002. Limitations in this section apply to two areas: FDI (mode 3) and labor movement (mode 4). In FDI, China imposes a minimum equity of 25 percent for joint ventures and no horizontal equity ceiling, though ceilings are specified for individual sectors. There is no guarantee that foreign firms can establish branches in China unless indicated for specific sectors. As land is state-owned in China, foreign firms cannot purchase land but must lease, and leases have specific term lengths: 70 years for residential use, 50 years for industrial, and only 30 years for commercial, tourist, and recreational purposes. This last factor might deter certain types of investment that require long amortization periods.

Foreign firms in several enumerated sectors—among them, audiovisual, aviation, and medical—and in new service sectors cannot obtain subsidies. China offers only limited possibility for labor movement (mode 4) under its GATS and FTA schedules, defining only three categories of natural persons eligible for movement: intracorporate transferees, senior employees of foreign firms, and salespersons. The maximum stay in each category is three years.

Sectoral Measures Affecting Services Trade and Investment

With respect to commitments by sector, China has offered nearly identical schedules in its FTAs with Chile and Costa Rica. Most of the restrictions by sector are found on mode 3 (commercial presence, usually FDI). Investment restrictions affecting several services activities could be worrisome to US services firms. In legal advisory services, foreign law firms can provide legal services only in the form of representative offices and can give advice only on the legislation of their own country or international conventions. Joint ventures are required for professionals in the areas of taxation, medical and dental services, market research activities, photographic services, convention

---

23. While this is true for most sectors, the area of financial services has been omitted from China's FTAs with Chile and Costa Rica, and the area of telecommunications has been omitted from the China-Chile FTA. Nonetheless WTO commitments continue to apply in these sectors.

services, environmental services, business services (i.e., those incidental to agriculture, forestry, hunting, fishing, and mining), and oil and gas exploration. In the construction sector, China imposes a restriction on the types of construction activities that foreign investors can undertake, limiting these essentially to those funded by foreign sources or those in which Chinese expertise is limited. Regarding distribution, in the area of retail sales, China imposes restrictions on the number of retail outlets (less than 30). Additionally, no wholly foreign-owned retailers are permitted for chain stores. An education requirement calls for the establishment of joint schools. The areas of telecoms, transport, and financial services (securities only) operate under limits on FDI (see discussion below).

In addition to the above mode 3 restrictions, there are gaps in China's services schedule where mode 1 (cross-border trade) is left unbound (meaning no commitment) or is restricted. In education, there is no commitment on cross-border or online education services by foreign educational establishments. The advertising sector faces restrictions on foreigners providing cross-border advertising services. In air transport, there are restrictions on computer services for online reservation services, flight schedules, and other operations.

Despite the requirement that China imposes on investors to establish a joint venture in many service sectors, there is nonetheless no equity limit for many of these activities and 100 percent equity participation is often possible. Wholly foreign-owned enterprises are permitted for most professional services. Relatively few equity ceilings remain in China's FTA schedules on service activities. Wholly foreign-owned subsidiaries are also permitted in the tourism and travel sector for hotels, restaurants, and tour operators, other than those dealing with trips to Hong Kong, Macao, and Chinese Taipei. There are no restrictions on recreational, cultural, and sporting services activities for cross-border trade or FDI.

Besides the restrictions listed above, the situation in China deserves mention for four infrastructure sectors of particular importance: telecoms, transport, financial services, and digital services, though express delivery, legal services, and journalism are also significant.

Telecom Services

The Chinese Ministry of Industry and Information Technology (MIIT) regulates information and communications technology (ICT) firms and companies must generally get approval from it in order to operate. Under China's WTO commitments, it should not impede market access to foreign suppliers of computers and related services. But in 2013 MIIT released an updated catalogue of telecommunication services, subjecting four new categories to licensing requirements: long-term evolution (LTE) 4G, wire access infrastructure services, satellite-based fixed communication services, and mobile resale. In addition, a catch-all category with general wording might apply to a much broader area.[24] Foreign firms doing business in these categories will need a license from MIIT to operate in the named subsectors, and must use a joint venture with no more than 50 percent foreign ownership. The ministry has approved only four joint ventures since 2003.[25]

In software licensing, there has been progress in persuading the central government to require companies to purchase rather than simply copy software products, but progress has proven more elusive in provincial and local governments. China has agreed that state-owned enterprises (SOEs) will purchase legal software from companies such as Microsoft and Adobe, but these companies say that sales in China remain steady, so it is difficult to verify whether the new edicts have had much effect.

Telecommunication services are highly restricted, with a complete ban on foreign companies. China Mobile, China Unicom, and China Telecom—all SOEs—dominate the industry. Many other ICT services must be evaluated under the Multi-Level Protection Scheme (MLPS), a system that rates services in terms of their effects on national security, among other features. The rating runs from one to five, five needing the most protection, but any item scoring a three, four, or five is required to be secured by domestic IT security products. Loosening these restrictions would benefit both China and the United States, as newer areas such as cloud computing can bring significant efficiency advantages to users. However, recent disclosures about extensive US National Security Agency (NSA) surveillance make Chinese liberalization a remote proposition.

China's services schedule for telecoms in its FTA with Costa Rica is considerably simpler than its WTO GATS schedule of a decade earlier. Many telecom activities included in the earlier W/120 classification list[26] have changed with rapid technological advances in the ICT sector; hence a simplified schedule that encompasses all telecom activities is a useful innovation. China imposes limits on FDI in telecoms of no more than 50 percent, 49 percent, or 25 percent equity, depending on the activity. Joint ventures are required for mobile voice and data services. Domestic services are subject to geographical restrictions that will be lifted over time. Cross-border provision of telecom services is linked to FDI. For audiovisual technology (cinemas), FDI is limited to 49 percent equity. FDI limitations in telecoms and audiovisual technology will certainly be the subject of negotiation in any future FTA with the United States.

---

24. A summary of the changes can be found in Gordon Milner, Paul D. McKenzie, Sherry Yin, and Jing Bu, "China's MIIT Releases Long-Awaited Draft Amended Telecoms Catalogue for Public Comment," Morrison/Foerster client alert, June 13, 2013, www.mofo.com (accessed on May 29, 2014).

25. James Seng, "Making Sense of MIIT's Category of Telecommunications Services," CircleID, July 31, 2013, www.circleid.com (accessed on May 29, 2014).

26. See WTO, Services Sectoral Classification List.

Transport Services

In the area of transport services, China's FTAs exclude passenger transport (as do US FTAs). There are no restrictions on rail or road transport in China's schedule and wholly owned foreign subsidiaries are permitted, though maritime transport and air transport are restricted. Less than 49 percent equity participation in FDI is allowed in maritime shipping as well as in auxiliary services for maritime, and ships are able to operate only under China's national flag. Shipping on inland waterways by foreign vessels is not permitted, a restriction that mirrors the US Jones Act.

The United States and China signed their latest air transport agreement (ATA) on July 9, 2007. It modestly expanded an earlier agreement covering routes for passenger and cargo flights between the countries.[27] Since then, a few additional routes have been agreed, but a full open-skies agreement has proved elusive.[28] The absence of coordination between China's Civil Aviation Administration (CAAC) and the GAC has unnecessarily restricted access to select areas of China. The CAAC also restricts changes of airplane size, the switching of planes on a single flight number, and the right to serve two points on the same flight. None of these restrictions are consistent with the ATA.

Foreign companies are only allowed minority equity shares in aircraft repair. Computer reservation activities for air transport can only be carried out cross-border, in cooperation with Chinese aviation agents. Direct access and use of foreign reservation systems need approval from the CAAC. For freight forwarding agencies across all forms of transport, joint ventures are required and are subject to an operating term of 20 years.

Financial Services in China

China did not include updated financial services commitments in its FTAs with Chile and Costa Rica. The baseline accordingly reflects China's WTO schedule of commitments, in effect since 2002. Several areas of China's financial services sector seem relatively open according to its WTO commitments. There are no equity limits, geographical limitations, or clientele limitations on FDI in insurance lines—with the overriding exception of life insurance. While licenses must be obtained for nearly all financial activities, they are issued without quantitative restrictions, but they require compliance with prudential standards, which Chinese (and US) authorities flexibly interpret. That said,

---

27. The updated agreement can be found at US Department of State, "U.S.-China Air Transport Agreement of July 9, 2007," www.state.gov (accessed on May 29, 2014).

28. The United States has concluded open skies agreements with over 100 countries. These give airlines far greater control over decisions about routes, capacity, and pricing, enabling more competitive and efficient passenger and cargo transport. Details about these agreements can be found at the US State Department website, www.state.gov.

US financial firms are seriously concerned about multiple aspects of Chinese financial regulation. These issues are examined in chapter 8.

Digital Services in China

In the decade since China's WTO accession, the role of the internet has greatly expanded. China had 23 million internet users in 2000, or under 2 percent of the total population. By 2012 that number had grown to 538 million, or over 40 percent of China's population, giving China the world's largest number of web users.[29] The United States has seen major growth as well, with internet use growing from 33 percent to nearly 80 percent of the population over the same time period. Globally, over a third of people were classified as internet users in 2012. With rapid growth in the world's population of internet users, restrictions on digital commerce have become increasingly important, for both domestic and international networks.

Unconstrained data flows are responsible for tremendous economic gains. The McKinsey Global Institute calculated that open data could generate as much as $3 trillion more in global income annually, in just seven sectors of the world economy (Manyika et al. 2013). Open data are available without restrictions; are fundamental to new business models, from analysis of big data to cloud computing; and drive innovation, especially in small businesses.

The rules governing cross-border data flows are incomplete and therefore bilateral and regional agreements present an opportunity to create a framework for open data and to push for constructive policies. A National Foreign Trade Council (NFTC) report, which many US information technology firms endorsed, listed data flow priorities for the business community.[30] Three of these are among the report's key objectives. First is to expressly prohibit restrictions on legitimate cross-border information flow. Blocking access to information services and websites such as Twitter, Facebook, YouTube, and WordPress, as well as document sharing sites such as Dropbox and Google Drive, seriously impedes the conduct of business. Second is to prohibit local infrastructure or investment mandates. In pursuit of promoting local businesses, China has enacted policies that link market access to indigenous innovation policies. Quite often such policies seek the localization of servers and other IT equipment. Third is to promote international standards, dialogues, and best practices. Regulations that favor local providers of data services, or national standards that differ from international norms, contradict the goals of free and fair trade.

---

29. Miniwatts Marketing Group, "Top 20 Countries with the Highest Number of Internet Users, 2012," June 30, 2012.

30. See National Foreign Trade Council, "Promoting Cross-Border Data Flows: Priorities for the Business Community," www.nftc.org (accessed on May 29, 2014).

The NFTC's objectives are targeted at several practices found in emerging economies. Common restrictions include localization requirements, by which a country explicitly or implicitly requires a company to use local digital products and services when doing online business in the domestic market; thus credit and debit card data processing must take place within China (USTR 2012). More broadly, Chinese banks are not permitted to use any offshore data processing services for domestic noncorporate customer data (USITC 2013). China also requires data to be stored locally in some cases and directly supports Chinese cloud computing firms.

China's aforementioned MLPS covers banking, energy, telecommunications, education, and transit, placing heavy restrictions on certain industries. On its scale of one to five in terms of importance to national security, systems that receive a rank of three or higher must be provided by "a Chinese company, owned by Chinese citizens, and use core technology based on Chinese intellectual property" (USITC 2013). Ranks of three or higher are not uncommon, so this system creates a meaningful barrier to digital and physical commerce.

In the United States, legislation to protect open data is on the congressional agenda. The proposed Digital Trade Act of 2013 seeks to advance most of the NFTC's goals in future trade agreements and requires the president to prioritize digital trade. But the United States is not helping itself with some of its current policies. The continuing resolution to fund the government (HR 933), signed by the president on March 26, 2013, states that the Departments of Commerce and Justice, as well as the National Aeronautics and Space Administration (NASA), are barred from procuring IT systems that were produced, manufactured, or assembled by an entity that is owned, directed, or subsidized by China, unless federal law enforcement agencies give their approval.[31] Such legislation clearly lends itself to retaliation and invites restrictions on open data.

Express Delivery

China's Express Delivery Service (EDS) is one of the largest in the world, with estimated sales of around $5 billion in 2010.[32] But foreign companies are stifled by GAC rules that prevent them from connecting some cities in China to their major hubs in other regions. The GAC also requires that foreign carriers use domestic service contractors for localized services, limiting their ability to operate and expand. Moreover, the requirement that 100 percent of EDS packages be opened for inspection significantly slows imports of small packages. Relaxing some of these regulations and adopting global practices would permit more rapid and cheaper delivery within China.

---

31. The language is found in section 516 of the Commerce, Justice, Science, and Related Agencies Appropriations Act of the continuing resolution.

32. US Department of Commerce, "2nd U.S.-China Joint Commission on Commerce and Trade Fact Sheet," November 21, 2011, www.commerce.gov (accessed on May 29, 2014).

Legal Services

Advisory services face an array of restrictions when trying to operate in China. This is counter to the principle of reciprocity, as Chinese advisory firms are allowed to set up offices and export services to other trading partners, although with broad limits.[33] International law firms face strict regulations when trying to establish a representative office and the process can be unpredictable and lengthy. Moreover, after establishing its first representative office, the firm must wait an additional three years before opening another office. China restricts foreign lawyers from attending meetings between their clients and government agencies; this restriction conflicts with China's commitments under the WTO. International law firms are also subject to higher taxes than their domestic counterparts, ranging from an additional tax of 10 percent on repatriated profits to 45 percent on income paid to partners.

Journalism

From time to time, China blocks the English or Chinese versions of the *Wall Street Journal,* the *New York Times,* and Bloomberg. In December 2013, it became known that China was holding up the visas of journalists representing the *New York Times,* Bloomberg, and other publications. In November 2013, security officials visited Bloomberg offices in Shanghai and Beijing for unannounced inspections.[34] As James McGregor, former chief executive of Dow Jones in China, lamented, "it's getting to the point where these media companies and their ability to do business in China has been curtailed."[35] Chinese actions seem designed to make the foreign media more compliant in their reporting. But these actions also reduce ad revenue, making the Chinese measures a trade issue as well. US Vice President Joseph Biden, while in Beijing in December 2013, declared that the United States and China had "profound disagreements" on the role of journalism.[36] If US media firms cannot keep their reporters in China, if the firms are hassled by inspections, or if their English or Chinese websites are blocked, then obviously journalism faces high barriers in the Chinese market.

---

33. Around 10 Chinese law firms have established branches in the United States, and currently practice domestic US law. See AmCham China (2013).

34. Peter Elkind and Scott Cendrowski, "Chinese Authorities Conduct Unannounced Inspections of Bloomberg News," *CNN,* December 2, 2013, finance.fortune.cnn.com (accessed on May 29, 2014).

35. Kathy Chu and William Launder, "U.S. Media Firms Stymied in China," *Wall Street Journal,* December 6, 2013.

36. Margaret Talev, "Biden Prods Beijing on Journalists' Treatment as China Trip Ends," *Bloomberg,* December 5, 2013, www.bloomberg.com (accessed on May 29, 2014).

Summarizing China's Openness

China has not yet negotiated a services agreement on a negative list basis, so it is impossible to closely compare its restrictions with those of the United States. But China has excluded certain modes of supply from bound commitments in its recent FTAs, particularly cross-border trade (mode 1), and this would prove much more difficult under a negative list approach.

Some examples of China's nonbinding or effective exclusion from disciplines of cross-border services trade are in the areas of educational services, environmental services, distribution services, and incidental services related to mining. These represent gaps in China's commitments. Though mode 1 is not yet as important commercially as mode 3, it is fast gaining ground, and it would be important for China to bind mode 1 supply in future FTAs for sectors that have significant commercial promise (e.g., digital services).

Most restrictions in China's services schedules in its FTAs with Chile and Costa Rica are found on market access for FDI (mode 3, commercial presence). The most severe restrictions overall for foreign service suppliers in China are in the areas of foreign legal advisory services, telecoms, financial services, transport, distribution (retail chain stores), and construction (in the types of activities that can be undertaken).

Unbound entries appear in China's GATS schedule for national treatment. This means that China is not committing to any standard of treatment for foreign service suppliers; China could give better or worse treatment, and most foreign firms will fear worse. A few economic needs test (ENT) entries appear in China's schedule, with no criteria to illuminate how they might be applied.

Unlike the United States, China does not have blanket measures that exempt existing subfederal governments from coverage. On the contrary, the disciplines of the WTO GATS extend across the land. The obligation is repeated in China's FTAs with Costa Rica and Chile (Article 91.2 in both agreements on scope and coverage), which specify the following:

> For purposes of this Section, measures adopted or maintained by a Party means measures adopted or maintained by:
> (a) central, regional or local governments and authorities; and
> (b) non-governmental bodies in the exercise of powers delegated by central, regional or local governments or authorities.

From this perspective, China's commitments on services, even with the incompleteness and gaps in the positive listing, go further than those of the United States in that they apply to all levels of its entire economy.

The Australia–China FTA and the Shanghai Free Trade Zone

Services liberalization has proved divisive in negotiations between China and Australia, which began in 2005 but have gone through 19 rounds without resolution.[37] Since its WTO accession, China has been reluctant to liberalize its services sector any further. This frustrated Australia, which sees services, along with agriculture, as major areas where it stands to gain from an FTA with China. But China's service sector is immature compared to Australia's, and China is worried that Australian service firms will outcompete Chinese companies. The benefits of liberalization have not been persuasive to Chinese leaders and they prefer to take a slower approach. That is one reason for the new Shanghai Free Trade Zone (FTZ): to experiment with liberalization to determine how much is appropriate for China.

On September 29, 2013, China unveiled a new FTZ spanning some 29 square kilometers in Shanghai's commercial area. The goal of the zone is to transform the role of government in the market and economy. Many commentators see it as a testing area for further reforms that will be implemented across the nation, particularly in services. The State Council officially approved the FTZ in August 2013; the framework plan for the zone targets its implementation, mission, and measures. The administrative affairs and the pilot reforms are the responsibility of the Management Committee, an agency of the People's Government of Shanghai Municipality. One of the FTZ's core purposes is to improve administrative systems, focusing on the administration of trade, investment, finance, and supervision.

The FTZ will affect finance, insurance, shipping and transportation, and legal and professional services. Officials have stated that market access restrictions—such as requirements concerning the qualification of investors, limitations on foreign participation, and restrictions on business scope (except banks and ICT)—will be suspended or cancelled. Freer flows of capital in and out of the zone will facilitate outward- and inward-bound investment, and hopefully allow the market to play a decisive role in the economy.

China's first draft of a negative list scheduled over 190 business sectors that would be controlled in the zone, and foreign commentators viewed this as discouraging.[38] But in March 2014, Zhou Zhenhua, director of the Development Research Center of the Shanghai Municipal Government, stated that the negative list may be pared by as much as 40 percent, which would amount to very significant liberalization.[39] While several departments of the central government must approve the decision first, it shows a determination among Shanghai officials to open their service sector. The new regulations allow foreign investment in areas such as call centers, business communication services, and internet access providers. The regulations also allow up to 55 percent foreign ownership of virtual private networks and data and transaction processing firms. The State Council document also permits foreign enterprises to engage

---

37. This section draws from Jiang (2013).

38. James Areddy, "Name Game in Shanghai Trade Zone," *Wall Street Journal*, November 11, 2013.

39. Yiyao Wu, "Shanghai FTZ 'Negative List' May Be Cut by 40% to Boost More Interest," *China Daily*, March 25, 2014, usa.chinadaily.com.cn (accessed on May 29, 2014).

in the production and sale of electronic gaming equipment and assigns regulation of this topic to the Ministry of Culture.

Conclusions

The United States enjoys a significant comparative advantage in tradable services while estimates of the tariff equivalents of Chinese barriers consistently show high protection in this sector. With that in mind, it is not surprising that modeling exercises tend to show big gains for US exports if Chinese barriers were to be relaxed. Our computable general equilibrium (CGE) model (chapter 2) projects that US exports to China would expand by nearly $165 billion by 2025 under a CHUSTIA, or $55 billion under a less service liberalization model.

With such large prospective gains at stake, as well as China's relatively high barriers, one can certainly expect a strong offense from US negotiators. But China's willingness to compromise might be greater than one might expect. Chinese construction companies have accumulated an incredible amount of experience over the past decade and now regularly win contract bids in foreign countries. However, even as Chinese construction firms have become prominent in the United States, access to large federal US contracts has proved elusive for construction firms with ties to China, leading to the suspicion that some degree of discrimination is involved.[40] Some US observers would say that restricting investment by Chinese SOEs in the United States is justified, on the argument that SOEs receive unfair advantages in financing and regulation through their ties to the Chinese government. A service chapter in a CHUSTIA that limits discrimination against SOEs, coupled with agreeable operating rules for SOEs, could assuage both concerns.

There also seems to be increasing recognition in China that imported services can contribute to the economy in and of themselves. The FTZ experiment in Shanghai could encourage Chinese officials to expand liberalization to other areas if the Shanghai FTZ produces positive results. Both Chinese and foreign firms are anxious to learn the details and see the implementation of the Shanghai FTZ. Limited liberalization through the US–China Strategic and Economic Dialogue—particularly those discussed in the next chapter—could give further evidence that China is shifting away from a mercantilist view with respect to the services trade.

A future CHUSTIA would likely see a major focus on the services sector, given its tremendous importance for both trading partners, right now and in terms of future potential growth. The United States will probably insist on a negative list approach in the agreement. Liberalization of service barriers will depend much more on China than the United States, because Chinese barriers are much higher, services liberalization is more important for Chinese growth than US growth, and the remaining US barriers are highly resistant to

---

40. Michelle Caruso-Cabrera, "Proudly Built in the USA—by the Chinese," CNBC, May 22, 2013, www.cnbc.com (accessed on May 29, 2014).

liberalization. Thus it will be up to China to see that unequal liberalization serves its own economic interests. China should view a future FTA with the United States in the services area as a vehicle for achieving its own important objectives. Several factors suggest that this is a plausible scenario.

- *China's shift to domestic demand-led growth.* China has recognized the limitations of export-led manufacturing growth and has been reorienting its economy for the past two years toward an internal shift to domestic-led demand growth. This shift will favor a higher level of consumption of services, as well as a demand for better quality services in China.
- *Acknowledgment of new economic priorities.* In a major policy address on services by Chinese Premier Li Keqiang at the Global Services Forum Beijing Summit in June 2013, the premier recognized that the services sector in China is still weak in its contribution to value added (44.6 percent of China's GDP) and outlined the need for China's services industry to expand, reform, and liberalize. In the premier's words:[41]

> The Chinese service industry has ample room for growth. Vigorous development of the service industry is very important for promoting the strategic restructuring of the economy, pressing ahead with reform and opening up, and expanding international cooperation. Not only is the service sector increasingly becoming an accelerator of global economy recovery, ushering in new driving forces and new directions in development, it is also a new engine, a new motive force for long-term sustainable and healthy development, optimization and upgrading in the Chinese economy.

As part of the policy prescriptions to further develop China's trade in services and further open up its service sector to the outside world, the Chinese premier stated that China would focus on services:

> We will focus on expanding trade in services ... actively in fields such as information, logistics, finance, travel and tourism ... encourage businesses to take on more outsourcing work and welcome foreign companies that wish to engage in service outsourcing in China ... energetically promote investment in the service sector ... create an environment of fair competition for trade in services ... promote international liberalization and facilitation of trade in services ... oppose protectionism of every kind, eliminate trade barriers.... The development of the Chinese service sector has huge potential and a promising future, affording unlimited business opportunities.

This strong statement by the second–highest ranking official in China at a major international forum clearly signals a change in Chinese policy orientation, and foreshadows a willingness to further open the country's service

---

41. From Li Kequiang, keynote address at the Global Services Forum Beijing Summit and 2nd China Beijing International Fair for Trade in Services, June 2013, UNCTAD/DITC/TNCD/MISC/2013/17.

sector as part of a future growth strategy. This bodes well for key infrastructure service sectors in China, such as financial services, telecoms, and retail distribution. The Chinese authorities also recently expressed their interest in joining TiSA, alongside other major WTO service providers.[42]

■ *Rising wage levels in China.* Rapidly rising wage levels in China will push the economy and labor force into service sectors as manufacturing FDI goes elsewhere in Asia. Partly as a result of China's tremendous economic success, wages have been climbing and demands for a more skilled workforce have been increasing. Wages are rising for three reasons: a shortage of skilled workers in eastern China, where the majority of FDI-driven manufacturing still takes place; increasing experience and educational levels in the workforce; and government legal and regulatory measures to increase wage rates, embodied, for instance, in the Labor Contract Law of 2008. In essence, a combination of rising education and FDI has increased Chinese worker productivity. Together with a public policy of supporting higher incomes, these effects have translated into rising wages. In turn, higher wages will modestly discourage further FDI in the manufacturing sector and push Chinese firms to move up the value-added chain to increasingly skilled and technology-oriented production—activities that are primarily in the service sector.

References

AmCham China (American Chamber of Commerce in the People's Republic of China). 2013. *American Business in China: 2013 White Paper*. Beijing.

Berden, Koen G., Joseph Francois, Saara Tamminen, Martin Thelle, and Paul Wymenga. 2009. *Non-Tariff Measures in EU–US Trade and Investment: An Economic Analysis*. Rotterdam: Ecorys.

Fontagné, Lionel, Amélie Guillin, and Cristina Mitaritonna. 2011. *Estimations of Tariff Equivalents for the Services Sector*. Paper 2011-24. Paris: Centre d'Etudes Prospectives et d'Informations Internationales.

Francois, Joseph. 1993. Explaining the Pattern of Trade in Producer Services. *International Economic Journal* 7 (3) 23–31.

Hoekman, Bernard. 1996. An Assessment of the General Agreement on Trade in Services. In *The Uruguay Round and the Developing Economies*, ed. Will Martin and L. Alan Winters. Cambridge, UK: Cambridge University Press.

Hufbauer, Gary Clyde, J. Bradford Jensen, and Sherry Stephenson, assisted by Julia Muir and Martin Vieiro. 2012. *Framework for the International Services Agreement*. Policy Brief 12-10. Washington: Peterson Institute for International Economics.

Hufbauer, Gary Clyde, Jeffrey J. Schott, and Woan Foong Wong. 2010. *Figuring Out the Doha Round*. Policy Analyses in International Economics 91. Washington: Peterson Institute for International Economics.

Hufbauer, Gary Clyde, and Yee Wong. 2011. *Logistics Reform for Low-Value Shipments*. Policy Brief 11-7. Washington: Peterson Institute for International Economics.

---

42. See Donnan, "China in Push."

Jensen, J. Bradford. 2011. *Global Trade in Services: Fear, Facts, and Offshoring.* Washington: Peterson Institute for International Economics.

Jiang, Yang. 2013. *China's Policymaking for Regional Economic Cooperation.* London: Palgrave Macmillan.

Manyika, James, Michael Chui, Peter Groves, Diana Farrell, Steve Van Kuiken, and Elizabeth Almasi Doshi. 2013. *Open Data: Unlocking Innovation and Performance with Liquid Information.* London: McKinsey Global Institute.

Miroudot, Sébastien, Jehan Sauvage, and Marie Sudreau. 2010. *Multilateralizing Regionalism: How Preferential Are Services Commitments in Regional Trade Agreements?* Trade Policy Working Paper 106. Paris: Organization for Economic Cooperation and Development.

Preeg, Ernest H. 2014. *U.S. Trade Surplus in Business Services Peaks Out.* Washington: Manufacturers Alliance for Productivity and Innovation.

Roy, Martin. 2011. *Services Commitments in Preferential Trade Agreements.* Staff Working Paper ERSD-2011-18. Geneva: World Trade Organization.

Subramanian, Arvind, and Martin Kessler. 2013. *The Hyperglobalization of Trade and Its Future.* Working Paper 13-6. Washington: Peterson Institute for International Economics.

USITC (United States International Trade Commission). 2013. *Digital Trade in the US and Global Economies, Part 1.* Investigation no. 332-531. Washington.

USTR (United States Trade Representative). 2012. *Report to Congress on China's WTO Compliance.* Washington.

Warren, Tony. 2000. The Impact on Output of Impediments to Trade and Investment in Telecommunications Services. In Impediments to Trade in Services: Measurement and Policy Implications, ed. Christopher Findlay and Tony Warren. London: Routledge.

Wilson, John S., Catherine Mann, and Tsunehiro Otsuki. 2005. Assessing the Benefits of Trade Facilitation: A Global Perspective. *World Economy* 28, no. 6: 841–71.

Appendix 7A
Quantitative Estimates of Barriers to Services Trade and Investment

World Bank Services Trade Restrictiveness Index

Table 7A.1 shows the Services Trade Restrictiveness Index (STRI) values for the United States and China, distinguishing between mode 1 (cross-border) and mode 3 (commercial presence, mainly foreign direct investment, FDI). The index awards each industry a score between 0 and 100, with 0 being essentially open and 100 essentially closed. The specific numbers are derived from a survey, looking at individual industry-mode combinations (note that not all modes are examined for each industry, and mode 2 is not examined at all). There are four modes for the services trade total: mode 1 (cross-border supply), mode 2 (consumption abroad), mode 3 (commercial presence, mainly FDI), and mode 4 (movement of natural persons). In the World Bank score for each relevant industry-mode combination, a country receives points based on what its laws permit or prohibit.

To obtain an overall score for each industry (not shown in table 7A.1), the World Bank weights the individual industry-mode scores based on the estimated importance of each mode to the industry. In using the World Bank's database to assess the prospective effects of liberalization, we take a different approach. For cross-border trade, we focus solely on barriers to mode 1. However, for sizing up barriers to direct investment (see chapters 8 and 13), we focus on mode 3. Table 7A.1 summarizes the mode 1 and mode 3 data for China and the United States for five industries. According to the World Bank database, China has higher barriers against both modes for all five industries, with the exception of mode 1 (cross-border) trade in professional services.

Table 7A.1   World Bank STRI

	United States		China	
	Mode 1	Mode 3	Mode 1	Mode 3
Finance	19.39	25.00	71.77	31.46
Telecommunications	n.a.	0	n.a.	50.00
Retail	n.a.	0	n.a.	25.00
Transportation	12.50	16.67	37.50	22.22
Professional services	8.33	50.00	0	70.00
Average	13.41	18.33	36.42	39.74

n.a. = not applicable; STRI = Services Trade Restrictiveness Index

Source: World Bank STRI database, iresearch.worldbank.org (accessed on July 4, 2014).

Table 7A.2   OECD STRI

	United States	China
Accounting	15	41
Architecture	16	26
Engineering	20	29
Legal	14	52
Motion pictures	6	45
Broadcasting	30	78
Sound recording	5	31
Telecoms	12	53
Air transport	58	59
Maritime transport	38	39
Rail freight transport	12	42
Road freight transport	14	38
Courier	37	87
Distribution	7	36
Commercial banking	13	49
Insurance	22	50
Construction	16	29
Computer	15	29
Simple average	19	45

OECD = Organization for Economic Cooperation and Development; STRI = Services Trade Restrictiveness Index

Note: Closer to 100 indicates more restrictive.

Source: OECD STRI, www.oecd.org (accessed on July 4, 2014).

Services Trade Restrictiveness Index

The STRI was released in May 2014 by the Organization for Economic Cooperation and Development (OECD) after preparation for seven years. Table 7A.2 shows the scores from this index for the United States and China. The STRI uses binary scoring, where answers to most measures are either yes or no. The OECD notes that in some cases the measures constitute hierarchies in which a combination might close a market segment or a mode of supply, while in other cases, one restriction would render other measures irrelevant. The database measures over 14,000 trade-related rules, regulations, and laws using this binary score.

The index covers the 34 OECD members plus Brazil, China, India, Indonesia, Russia, and South Africa. The measures are organized under five categories: restrictions on foreign market entry, restrictions on the movement of people, other discriminatory measures, barriers to competition, and regulatory

Figure 7A.1 OECD and World Bank STRIs

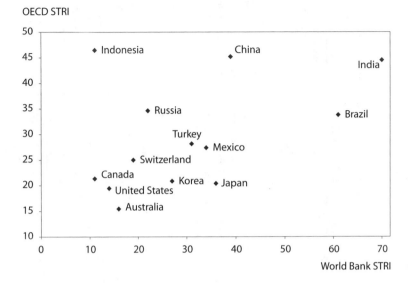

OECD STRI

World Bank STRI

OECD = Organization for Economic Cooperation and Development; STRI = Services Trade Restrictiveness Index

Note: Scores for the OECD STRI were calculated by taking a simple average of the countries' scores in the 18 sectors. The closer to 100, the more restrictive.

Sources: OECD STRI, oecd.org (accessed on July 4, 2014). World Bank STRI database, iresearch.worldbank.org (accessed on July 4, 2014).

transparency. The OECD says that the index provides policymakers with a powerful tool for assessing services trade restrictiveness and diagnosing options for reform. The scatterplot in figure 7A.1 compares the World Bank's STRI scores with the OECD's STRI scores. Except for Indonesia, the correlation seems reasonably high between World Bank and OECD index scores for the selected countries.

Estimating the Effect of Trade Barriers

While the STRI is useful to compare countries' levels of restrictiveness, it does not indicate the extent to which those barriers increase the costs of imports. Estimating the effect of nontariff barriers in marking up the cost of imported services requires the estimation of tariff equivalents. We summarize the results of several of these studies in table 7A.3. The resulting estimates differ substantially based on modelling methodology and data availability. A study by the Australian Productivity Commission (Warren 2000), not shown in table 7A.3, reported that US barriers against mode 1 trade in telecommunications amounted to a 0.2 percent tariff equivalent against foreigners, while Chinese barriers were estimated at a 495 percent tariff equivalent. Dihel and Shepherd (2007), using a similar methodology, estimated that Chinese barriers in the

Table 7A.3   Services barriers, estimated AVE tariff (percent)

	Modes of service trade	Service industry	China	United States	Short description
Walsh (2006)	All	**Overall**	**121.3**	**77.0**	Relies on a gravity model, reports overall estimates. Results strongly influenced by data availability.
Dihel and Shepherd (2007)	Mode 1	**Weighted average**	**71.3**		This study relies on price–cost margins, as in the Australian Productivity Commission study (Warren 2000). The average is weighted by Chinese import data from the Ministry of Commerce. Distribution services consist primarily of retail and wholesale trade.
		Banking	2.0		
		Insurance	130.3		
		Telecommunications, fixed	18.0		
		Telecommunications, mobile	13.4		
		Engineering	91.9		
		Distribution	13.7		
Hufbauer, Schott, and Wong (2010)	Mode 1 and mode 2	**Overall**	**67.9**	**6.0**	Based on a very simple gravity model. No industry detail.
Miroudot, Sauvage, and Shepherd (2010)	Mode 1 and mode 2	**Overall**	**183**	**144**	Gravity model includes natural barriers in the index value, e.g., language, adjacent borders, and other features not controlled by independent variables.

(continues on next page)

Table 7A.3   Services barriers, estimated AVE tariff (percent) *(continued)*

	Modes of service trade	Service industry	China	United States	Short description
Fontagné, Guillin, and Mitaritonna (2011)	Mode 1	**Weighted average**	**77.7**	**36.2**	Relies on a gravity model and reports sectoral estimates. US barriers are weighted by US imports, Chinese barriers weighted by US exports. (However, weighting by Chinese imports results in similar estimates.) Other includes education, health, defense, and public administration. Transportation refers to the movement of goods, rather than passengers. Trade services consist primarily of retail and wholesale trade.
		Communication	85.9	36.9	
		Construction	45.6	95.4	
		Finance	92.6	51.3	
		Insurance	40.7	43.7	
		Business	98.1	42.3	
		Other	59.6	8.8	
		Trade	32.9	61.5	
		Transport	52.8	17.5	

	Modes of service trade	Service industry	China	United States	Short description
Berden et al. (2009)	Mode 1	**Weighted average**		14.5	Estimates barriers faced by EU services exporters. "Other business services" is a heterogenous group, but primarily made up of professional consulting services.
		Finance		31.7	
		Information and communication technology services		3.9	
		Insurance		19.1	
		Construction		2.5	
		Communication		1.7	
		Other business services		3.9	

AVE = ad valorem equivalent

Figure 7A.2   Relationship between World Bank STRI and AVEs

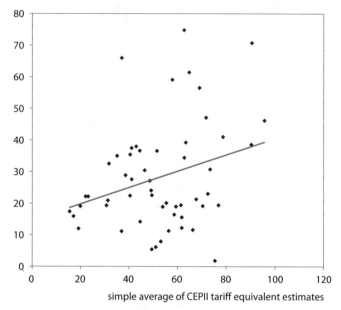

overall mode 1 World Bank STRI

simple average of CEPII tariff equivalent estimates

AVE = ad valorem equivalent; CEPII = Centre d' Etudes Prospectives et d' Informations Internationales; STRI = Services Trade Restrictiveness Index

Notes: Equivalent estimates are of 55 countries. Pearson correlation coefficient = 0.29.

Sources: World Bank STRI database, iresearch.worldbank.org (accessed on July 5, 2014) Fontagné, Guillin, and Mitaritonna (2011).

telecom sector are equivalent to a less than 20 percent tariff. Although the studies cover different time periods, it seems unlikely that Chinese barriers fell by such a large magnitude over the course of a few years.

Authors use several means to arrive at tariff equivalent estimates; we describe some of these methods briefly in chapter 7. The price-cost margin method, used in APC (Warren 2000) and Dihel and Shepherd (2007), identifies relevant trade barriers and estimates their effects based on price and cost data. They estimate Chinese tariff equivalent barriers for six sectors, with a weighted average of 71.3 percent for mode 1. Insurance is subject to the highest tariff equivalent barriers in their study, at 130 percent.

Other studies have sought to estimate trade barriers via a gravity approach. Walsh (2006) made an early contribution, but by the author's own admission, data availability led to questionable results. His study reported that Canada (81.7 percent) and New Zealand (82.8 percent) imposed barriers more than twice as restrictive as Argentina (39.2 percent). For the United States and China, the estimated tariff equivalents were 77.0 percent and 121.3 percent, respectively.

Figure 7A.3 OECD STRI and AVE tariff levels

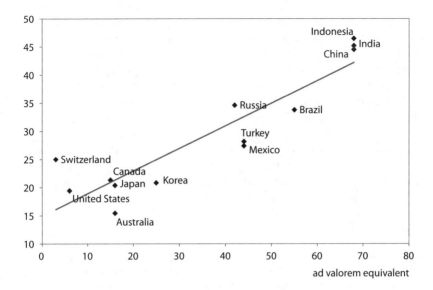

AVE = ad valorem equivalent; STRI = Services Trade Restrictiveness Index
Note: The closer to 100, the more restrictive. Scores for the OECD STRI were calculated by taking a simple average of the countries' scores in the 18 sectors. Pearson correlation coefficient for AVE = 0.91.
Sources: OECD STRI, oecd.org (accessed on July 4, 2014); Fontagné, Guillin, and Mitaritonna (2011).

Later studies refined the gravity method and used more data on control variables, generating more reliable estimates of services barriers. Miroudot, Sauvage, and Shepherd (2010) estimated that foreign service providers selling into the US market faced 144 percent tariff equivalent barriers, while those selling in the Chinese market faced 183 percent tariff equivalent barriers. However, since their estimates included natural barriers, the policy implications are limited.

Fontagné, Guillin, and Mitaritonna (2011) offer, at this writing, the best estimates of the costs policy barriers impose on foreign services providers. The results are broken into eight service sectors. Weighting US barriers by US imports and Chinese barriers by US exports, we find that US barriers amount to a 36.2 percent tariff equivalent and Chinese barriers amount to a 77.7 percent tariff equivalent. Weighting Chinese barriers by Chinese imports (from 2009) yields a similar result, a 79.1 percent average tariff equivalent estimate for China. Figure 7A.2 shows the relationship between these ad valorem equivalent (AVE) estimates and World Bank STRI values for 55 countries. The tariff estimates and values appear to be weakly linked with a Pearson correlation coefficient of 0.29. However, in figure 7A.3, which shows the relationship between AVE estimates and OECD simple average STRI index values for 13 countries, the Pearson's correlation coefficient is 0.91, considerably higher.

Koen G. Berden and colleagues (2009) look specifically at nontariff measures affecting US–EU trade and include the effects of nondiscriminatory regulatory divergences. The study develops an index of nontariff measures facing various industries based on business surveys and the relevant literature, covering seven services sectors as well as numerous goods sectors. This index is used as an independent variable in a gravity model and the coefficient is used in their regression to generate tariff equivalent estimates. Weighting these estimates by US imports, we find that EU services exporters face US barriers equivalent to a 14.5 percent tariff. Calculations cited in Hufbauer, Schott, and Wong (2010) give the US average tariff equivalent barrier for all services as 6 percent, while for China the figure is nearly 68 percent. The Chinese figure may be high as, for lack of data, it was assumed to be the same as the tariff equivalent estimate for Indonesia. For purposes of projecting trade gains, the modeling exercises in chapter 2 assume that Chinese liberalization will cut 40 percentage points off its tariff equivalent barriers on services imports.

References

Berden, Koen G., Joseph Francois, Martin Thelle, Paul Wymenga, and Saara Tamminen. 2009. *Non-Tariff Measures in EU-US Trade and Investment: An Economic Analysis*. Rotterdam: Ecorys.

Dihel, Nora, and Ben Shepherd. 2007. *Modal Estimates of Services Barriers*. OECD Trade Policy Papers 51. Paris: Organization for Economic Cooperation and Development.

Fontagné, Lionel, Amélie Guillin, and Cristina Mitaritonna. 2011. *Estimations of Tariff Equivalents for the Services Sector*. Paper 2011-24. Paris: Centre d'Etudes Prospectives et d'Informations Internationales.

Hufbauer, Gary Clyde, Jeffrey J. Schott, and Woan Foong Wong. 2010. *Figuring Out the Doha Round*. Policy Analyses in International Economics 91. Washington: Peterson Institute for International Economics.

Miroudot, Sébastien, Jehan Sauvage, and Ben Shepherd. 2010. *Measuring the Cost of International Trade in Services*. Working Paper (October 4). Paris: Groupe d'Economie Mondiale.

Walsh, Keith. 2006. *Trade in Services: Does Gravity Hold? A Gravity Model Approach to Estimating Barriers to Service Trade*. Discussion Paper 183. Dublin: Institute for International Integration Studies, Trinity College.

Warren, Tony. 2000. The Impact on Output of Impediments to Trade and Investment in Telecommunications Services. In *Impediments to Trade in Services: Measurement and Policy Implications*, ed. Christopher Findlay and Tony Warren. London: Routledge.

8

Financial Services

The US financial services sector—including insurance, banking, and securities[1]—was responsible for roughly $1.2 trillion of value added in 2012, about 8 percent of GDP.[2] On the international front, gross financial services exports from US firms totaled $88 billion, just 4 percent of the total value of US exports.[3] Although services tend to be underrepresented in exports, as discussed in chapter 7, it seems apparent that many of the natural barriers that inhibit trade in other services—say, the necessity of a face-to-face relationship between buyer and seller—do not apply with equal force to financial services. Recent advances in communications technology have greatly expanded the potential for cross-border trade in financial services. However, modern regulatory structures have not advanced quite so quickly and substantial artificial barriers remain in place.

World Trade Organization Rulebook

The financial services sector is covered under the General Agreement on Trade in Services (GATS), along with other services. Within the agreement, the Annex on Financial Services includes definitions and the prudential exception. The

---

1. Some sources, such as the Bureau of Economic Analysis (BEA), do not include insurance under financial services. When citing figures from such sources, we add insurance into financial services in order to maintain consistency.

2. BEA, gross domestic product (GDP) by industry data, 2014, value added by industry, www.bea.gov (accessed on July 9, 2014).

3. IMF, balance of payment statistics, 2014, exports of goods and services, www.imf.org (accessed on July 9, 2014).

Understanding of Commitments in Financial Services enumerates additional commitments specific to the sector that apply when a member schedules its obligations on the basis of the understanding. The annex ensures that members do not sacrifice autonomy in setting their prudential regulations, although prudential measures should not be used to avoid their commitments, and protects privacy. The annex allows, but does not require, members to grant mutual recognition to each other's regulatory structures.

World Trade Organization (WTO) members could not agree on a satisfactory level of liberalization during the Uruguay Round. Accordingly, financial services negotiations continued multilaterally until 1997. Further negotiations achieved greater transparency in the financial services policies of WTO members, but it did not deliver much new liberalization. By and large, the commitments codified the status quo, although a few countries made new commitments (Dobson and Jacquet 1998). China did not directly participate in the negotiations, as it was not then a WTO member, but the results influenced the financial services commitments subsequently required of China. China's commitments are stronger than those of some Association of Southeast Asian Nations (ASEAN) countries that joined the 1997 negotiations.

US Restrictions

US restrictions on foreign financial service providers are relatively few at the federal level. Foreign firms trying to establish their first foray into the United States are subject to extra scrutiny, but once a foreign firm has gained initial approval, it is usually subject to the same federal restrictions as its US financial counterpart. The remaining restrictions include nationality requirements for members of the board of a US chartered bank and restrictions on solicitations by foreign banks.[4] However, meaningful federal restrictions exist in the insurance sector; auto liability insurance, which is compulsory in nearly all states, cannot be supplied on a cross-border basis.

Remaining US restrictions on foreign financial firms are largely at the state level. The federal government has the power to override state restrictions under the Commerce Clause of the US Constitution, but is politically reluctant to exercise this power. Accordingly, state barriers tend to survive trade negotiations. Many states ban all government-owned or -controlled insurance firms from operating subsidiaries within the state. In the Korea–US Free Trade Agreement (KORUS), registration of foreign financial firms is considered a prudential measure (article 13(5)(3)). However, when registration requirements are burdensome, this requirement sharply limits cross-border supply in insurance products.

---

4. World Bank, Services Trade Restrictions Database, key restrictions, United States, data.worldbank.org (accessed on July 9, 2014).

Chinese Restrictions

Banking and Securities

Foreign banks were subject to heavy restrictions before China's accession to the WTO. China limited foreign banks mostly to foreign currency transactions and allowed them to practice only in specific cities. Foreign participation in the domestic currency business was limited to two cities, Beijing and Shanghai. China made somewhat more robust banking commitments in its WTO accession protocol, but in several aspects of finance, China's restrictions still cause concern. The data in table 8.1 show that foreign banks' market share has stayed around 2 percent since China's WTO accession.

The capital requirements required of foreign bank branches and headquarters are particularly demanding by international standards. A firm must first maintain a representative office in China for no less than two years and hold more than $10 billion in assets before establishing a branch in China. A foreign bank must operate for three years and have at least two years of consecutive profit before it may fully participate in the domestic currency business. Banks operating as branches face additional restrictions, particularly in offering domestic currency services. Foreign bank branches may accept deposits only larger than RMB1 million and may not make RMB loans to local individuals.[5] Furthermore, bank branches may not issue domestic currency credit or debit cards, or make loans to Chinese individuals, although they are permitted to make loans to Chinese firms. Incorporating as a subsidiary carries additional costs, since a subsidiary, as a separately incorporated firm, requires its own capital, supplied by the parent firm.

Also troublesome are banks jointly owned by Chinese and foreign firms. China committed to allow qualified foreign firms to establish joint ventures with Chinese firms without limiting the percentage stake held by the foreign firm. Nevertheless, China has yet to allow the foreign ownership share in an existing state-owned bank to exceed 25 percent (USTR 2012). Under Chinese regulations, generally a bank ceases to be categorized as Chinese when foreign ownership exceeds 25 percent. However, this test does not apply to publicly listed banks, which can have more than 25 percent foreign ownership and still be treated as domestic. In principle, therefore, a foreign bank could acquire more than 25 percent of the equity of a listed state bank, but in practice this has yet to happen. Offices of foreign securities firms may establish joint ventures with Chinese firms, with ownership up to 50 percent. The joint ventures may become members of all Chinese stock exchanges and in this capacity underwrite shares as well as government and corporate bonds.

The annual US–China Strategic and Economic Dialogue (S&ED) meetings, which began in 2009, have been somewhat successful in securing additional

---

5. GOV.cn, "Regulations of People's Republic of China on Administration of Foreign-Funded Banks," World Law Direct, May 2, 2007, www.worldlawdirect.com (accessed on May 30, 2014).

Table 8.1 Foreign bank assets in China, 1999–2012

		Foreign bank assets	
	Number of institutions	**Billions of renminbi**	**Market share** (percent)
1999	177	263	1.53
2000	191	285	1.70
2001	190	373	2.10
2002	180	324	1.50
2003	192	416	1.50
2004	188	582	1.84
2005	207	716	1.91
2006	224	928	2.11
2007	274	1,253	2.38
2008	311	1,345	2.16
2009	338	1,349	2.17
2010	360	1,742	1.85
2011	387	2,154	1.93
2012	412	2,380	1.82

Source: Bank of China (2012).

commitments from China. US financial firms saw increasing freedom in the interbank market following the 2010 S&ED and were allowed to sell mutual fund shares to Chinese investors following the 2011 S&ED.[6] At the 2012 S&ED, China committed to liberalize its restrictions on auto financing, particularly for foreign invested firms.[7] US auto manufacturers had pressed for this change, as nine out of ten car purchases were made in cash as recently as 2010.[8] At that same S&ED meeting, China agreed to allow foreign firms to hold up to 49 percent of equity in a joint securities firm, up from 33 percent.

6. US Department of the Treasury, "Third Meeting of the U.S.–China Strategic & Economic Dialogue Joint U.S.–China Economic Track Fact Sheet," May 10, 2011, www.treasury.gov (accessed on May 30, 2014).

7. US Department of the Treasury, "Joint U.S.–China Economic Track Fact Sheet—Fourth Meeting of the U.S.–China Strategic and Economic Dialogue (S&ED)," May 4, 2012, www.treasury.gov (accessed on May 30, 2014).

8. "Ford, GM Promote Financing in China as 90% of Drivers Pay in Cash for Cars," *Bloomberg*, April 28, 2010, www.bloomberg.com (accessed on May 30, 2014).

Chinese Interest Rate Controls

The People's Bank of China (PBOC), China's central bank, has intervened massively in the foreign exchange market in the past decade, purchasing more than $4 trillion of foreign exchange (mainly dollars) with domestic currency. Without additional action, intervention on this scale would have generated substantial inflation as the freshly printed renminbi flowed into the domestic economy. To forestall that outcome, the PBOC dramatically increased the reserve ratio that banks operating in China faced.[9] This effectively required banks to hold a large share of their assets in very low yield deposits at the PBOC, reducing the banks' profit margins. To maintain the profitability of the banking sector, the PBOC then imposed a floor on lending rates and a ceiling on deposit rates, ensuring that the banks remained both profitable and solvent. At the same time, these price controls essentially eliminated competition between banks.

In July 2013 the PBOC removed the floor on lending rates, but kept the ceiling on deposit rates, a step toward a more competitive financial system.[10] The growth of unregulated shadow banks has further pressured China's system of controlled interest rates, since these quasi-banks can pay higher rates on deposits and charge higher rates on loans (Borst 2013).

But foreign firms have only limited participation in the shadow banking market, permitted only in areas such as wealth management. And while the official banking rules apply to both foreign and domestic firms, they affect foreign banks' ability to gain market share in the Chinese financial sector. Following the relaxation of the lending floor, a bank with a superior ability to evaluate risk can offer better interest rates to low-risk borrowers. If done correctly, the smarter bank will have a smaller proportion of nonperforming loans than other banks, and therefore be more profitable. However, this bank will still have trouble expanding, as the ceiling on deposit rates limits its ability to attract more funds. Thus, even if foreign banks are better able to size up risks than their Chinese competitors, price controls still inhibit their ability to increase market share.

In the absence of price-based competition, Chinese banks tend to build large networks of branches to attract depositors. The Industrial and Commercial Bank of China (ICBC), the world's largest by profit and market capitalization, and the Bank of China maintain networks of roughly 17,000 and 11,000 branches, respectively (ICBC 2012; Bank of China 2012). Until online banking is widely accepted, it will be hard for any foreign firm to establish a network that can compete with existing Chinese networks.

---

9. Nicholas Lardy, "Increasing Market Access for US Financial Firms in China: Update on Progress of the SED," testimony before the House Committee on Financial Services, May 16, 2012.

10. Gordon G. Chang, "China's Interest-Rate Reform: Starting or Stalling?" *Forbes*, July 21, 2013, www.forbes.com (accessed on May 30, 2014).

China: Electronic Payment Services (DS413)[11]

In a 2011 case filed with the WTO's Dispute Settlement Body (DSB), the United States alleged that various measures China took were inconsistent with its GATS obligations. (A general description of WTO DSB procedure is spelled out in our chapter 18.) The United States argued that China had granted the Chinese company China UnionPay (CUP) a monopoly on handling several types of transactions, as well as mandating that all ATMs and merchant processing equipment be capable of accepting CUP payment cards, though not, as China pointed out, to the exclusion of other cards. The United States also objected to a requirement that all payment cards bear the Yin Lian/UnionPay logo and be able to operate on the Yin Lian/UnionPay network. A distinction was made between the company, referred to as CUP, and the network maintained by that company, referred to Yin Lian/UnionPay. Cards were required to bear the logo of the network, not the logo of the company.

The United States argued that electronic payment services (EPS) fell under paragraph 7.B(d) of China's GATS schedule, which includes "all payment and money transmission services." The WTO panel largely agreed, finding that China had national treatment and market access obligations for the supply of EPS through an affiliate and national treatment obligations for the cross-border supply of EPS, though no market access obligation. Accordingly, the panel then examined the specific US allegations to determine whether or not China's policies were inconsistent with its GATS obligations.

The panel rejected the broadest US claim, finding insufficient evidence to conclude that China had granted CUP a total monopoly on all electronic renminbi transactions. However, the panel ruled against China in most other areas, finding that several de facto and de jure requirements were in violation of GATS. On July 23, 2013, China claimed to have implemented changes conforming with the panel rulings. The United States expressed skepticism, noting that China's status report and its statement of compliance failed to mention certain measures that were supposed to be changed.[12]

Insurance

There has been some progress in the insurance sector in recent years, particularly in life insurance, although substantial barriers remain. China committed to allow foreign life insurers to operate with a 50 percent equity share in a joint venture, as well as allowing 51 percent foreign-owned partnerships and wholly foreign-owned subsidiaries to operate in several non–life insurance areas.

---

11. World Trade Organization, "China—Certain Measures Affecting Electronic Payment Services," www.wto.org (accessed on May 30, 2014).

12. WTO Dispute Settlement Board via Inside Trade, July 2013, Surveillance of Implementation of Recommendations Adopted by the DSB-China-Electronic Payment Services, insidetrade.com (accessed on July 9, 2014).

China also committed to reduce restrictions on the establishment of branches for non-life insurance firms, and announced that firms already established in China would not face the same hurdles that applied to new entrants. The China Insurance Regulatory Commission (CIRC) has implemented several measures to accommodate these reforms, but the US Trade Representative (USTR) reports that US insurers still face substantial difficulties.[13] CIRC has reportedly been quite slow in responding to branching applications from US firms. Firms report particular difficulty gaining timely approval of multiple applications that are submitted concurrently.

China allows the cross-border sale of insurance policies only for reinsurance, international marine, aviation, and transport, and large-scale commercial risks—limits that are similar to US regulations. However, a liberal stance on foreign direct investment (FDI) in insurance allows foreign companies to provide individual insurance to Chinese citizens, including health, group, and pension, as well as the full range of non-life insurance.

Bilateral Trade in Financial Services

US Exports

The United States maintains a surplus in the financial services trade with China, although the potential for huge growth is readily apparent. In 2011, US financial services exports to China totaled $2.2 billion, while US imports were $0.4 billion.[14] Although the US surplus is significant in dollar terms, the exports to China are not particularly large compared to total US services exports to China (8 percent). Financial services made up 14 percent of US services exports to all countries, so US financial firms play an even more limited role in trade with China than they do in general.[15] Furthermore, US firms have seen only limited penetration of the Chinese market. Before China's WTO accession, foreign banks held 1.5 percent of the total assets of the Chinese banking system. After accession, foreign banks saw their assets grow roughly at the pace of Chinese financial sector growth overall, but did not gain much ground in market share. The foreign share of bank assets was at its highest point in 2007 at 2.38 percent, but has since regressed to 1.9 percent (table 8.1).[16]

---

13. USTR, "China," 2013 national trade estimate report on foreign trade barriers, www.ustr.gov (accessed on May 30, 2014).

14. BEA, International Services Statistics, 2013, US trade in services; note that we combine the BEA's financial services and insurance numbers, as described earlier in this chapter.

15. World Bank, Insurance and Financial Services (percent of service exports, BoP), data.worldbank.org (accessed on May 30, 2014).

16. Lardy, "Increasing Market Access."

Insurance firms have not fared much better in the Chinese market. Foreign-invested life insurers expanded their market share to 8.9 percent in 2005, but this share fell to 4.8 percent in 2012. Foreign-invested property and casualty insurers held only 1.2 percent of the market (AmCham China 2013), below the share they held when China joined the WTO, even though China's automobile insurance market has grown rapidly over the past decade. If China's recent opening to financial services, signaled by the Shanghai Free Trade Zone, proves to be genuine, auto insurance could offer a major opportunity for US firms.

Chinese Exports

Chinese participation in the US financial sector is limited, but has grown in recent years. After receiving approval from the Federal Reserve in 2008,[17] ICBC has operated an uninsured state-licensed branch in New York City. ICBC bolstered its position in the United States in 2012 when the Fed approved it as a bank holding company, facilitating its purchase of a controlling stake in the US arm of the Bank of East Asia (BEA).[18] The Fed's decision to allow this purchase was motivated by the International Monetary Fund (IMF) 2011 financial system stability assessment (FSSA) of China. The IMF found that the Chinese financial sector was relatively well regulated by international standards, stating that "the laws, rules and guidance that CBRC [China Banking Regulatory Commission] operates under generally establish a benchmark of prudential standards that is of high quality and was drawn extensively from international standards and the [Basel Core Principles] themselves" (IMF 2011). Two other Chinese government-controlled entities, Central Huijin Investment and China Investment Corporation (CIC), were also approved as bank holding companies in the same Fed decision. Although the only acquisition at issue was the ICBC's purchase of equity in BEA, Huijin and CIC both had to gain approval due to their equity stakes in ICBC. CIC controls Huijin, which owns roughly one-third of ICBC.

Financial Services in US Free Trade Agreements

North American Free Trade Agreement

The United States has pursued financial services liberalization in previous free trade agreements (FTAs), notably the North American Free Trade Agreement (NAFTA), US–Singapore, and KORUS. Gaining access to Mexico's financial markets was an important goal for US negotiators in NAFTA. To that end,

---

17. Federal Reserve System, "Order Approving Establishment of a Branch," August 2008, www.federalreserve.gov (accessed on May 30, 2014).

18. Federal Reserve System, "Order Approving Acquisition of Shares in a Bank," May 9, 2012, www.federalreserve.gov (accessed on May 30, 2014).

NAFTA's chapter 14 on financial services contains relatively strong commitments. National treatment obligations for financial service firms are framed in de facto terms, not just de jure. This goes beyond the basic protection against outright discrimination, when firms from different countries are treated differently under the law. Paragraph 1405(7) of NAFTA notes that disparate outcomes in, say, market share or profitability are not sufficient to prove discrimination, but can be used as evidence to support a claim of discrimination.[19]

Initially, Mexico was scheduled to implement stricter requirements over several years, but it opted for much more rapid liberalization in the wake of the 1994 financial crisis (Hufbauer and Schott 2005). The crisis, precipitated by a rapid devaluation of the Mexican peso, resulted not only in Mexico opening its financial markets to US and Canadian firms ahead of schedule, but also extending financial liberalization to non-NAFTA members.

US–Singapore FTA

Chapter 10 of the US–Singapore FTA covers financial services. Singapore's law has some troubling restrictions, such as limiting foreign banks to a combined 25 branches and ATMs. Furthermore, Singapore had imposed a ban on new licenses for full-service and wholesale banks. Under the FTA, restrictions are eliminated on the number of locations that fully licensed US banks can operate.[20] Since 2007, US banks have been able to apply for access to Singapore's ATM network, although some banks have chosen to join an independent network of foreign banks. Insurance firms benefited under the FTA with the removal of all barriers pertaining to establishing subsidiaries, branches, and joint ventures. Singapore also lifted the ban on the cross-border supply of insurance services.[21]

Within the United States, chapter 10 did not require changes from state and local governments. Existing laws and regulations were grandfathered as nonconforming measures; however, states may not adopt new discriminatory measures. Consistent with the approach in the agreement's annex on financial services, public retirement plans and social security systems were excluded from coverage.[22]

---

19. North American Free Trade Agreement, chapter 14, www.worldtradelaw.net (accessed on May 30, 2014).

20. Dick K. Nanto, "The U.S.–Singapore Free Trade Agreement: Effects After Five Years," Congressional Research Service, March 26, 2010.

21. USTR, "Free Trade with Singapore: America's First Free Trade Agreement in Asia," December 2001, www.ustr.gov (accessed on May 30, 2014).

22. US House Ways and Means Committee, "U.S.–Singapore Free Trade Agreement—Impact on State and Local Governments," waysandmeans.house.gov (accessed on May 30, 2014).

KORUS

Chapter 13 of KORUS set out financial services commitments. The chapter included several notable commitments in both banking and insurance. Korea's insurance market, the second largest in Asia, was relatively open at the time, but there were some concerns for US firms. Some organizations, such as the state-owned Korea Post and a handful of Korean cooperatives, were not subject to the same outside regulations as private insurance firms. The agreement sought to level the playing field by increasing the regulatory powers of the Financial Supervisory Commission (FSC). Furthermore, Korea Post was forbidden from issuing new insurance products.

KORUS also made progress in freeing up the storage of consumer data. Before the agreement, Korea's strict privacy laws limited firms' ability to transfer financial information for data processing purposes. To ease these restrictions, Korea committed to alter its regulatory regime to allow firms to transfer information as ordinary business needs require.

Financial Services in Chinese FTAs

China's FTA with New Zealand (2008) is the most recent of China's FTAs and certainly the most robust. The FTA includes financial services commitments in its annex 8, dealing with specific commitments on services, although they are limited in nature. China's commitments were listed on a positive list basis: only the listed areas are liberalized and all others are unbound, that is, not subject to new commitments. Even horizontal commitments do not apply to the unlisted sectors, at least in this case. New Zealand's Ministry of Foreign Affairs and Trade (MFAT) noted that New Zealand would have preferred a negative list approach, in which only listed sectors are exempt.[23] Furthermore, the analysis stated that "China's upfront commitments in addition to its existing WTO commitments are limited" in the services sector overall.

Conclusions and Recommendations

In multilateral and bilateral trade negotiations, the United States has consistently played offense regarding financial services liberalization, especially when dealing with developing countries. Most US partners further liberalized their market in FTA negotiations, eliminating equity caps and limitations on licensing and permitting branching. The established pattern of Chinese reluctance and the apparent imperative of US negotiators in securing the liberalization of China's financial markets suggest that a good deal of ground would need to be covered in a China–US trade and investment agreement (CHUSTIA).

---

23. New Zealand Ministry for Foreign Affairs and Trade, "New Zealand–China FTA: National Interest Analysis," Wellington, www.chinafta.govt.nz/ (accessed on May 30, 2014).

There are signs that US negotiators could achieve more liberalization in the Chinese financial sector than skeptics might expect. China has made several concessions in recent S&ED talks, in some cases going beyond what its WTO accession protocol required, although full compliance remains elusive. More generally, China has been gradually liberalizing its domestic financial sector, partially responding to pressure from its trading partners. One vehicle is the permitted growth of unregulated shadow banking. Of greater interest to its trading partners, China's July 2013 creation of the new free trade zone in Shanghai would, in principle, host a very liberal financial sector.[24] While some senior officials may still consider strong control over financial markets an imperative, it seems that others are willing to experiment with liberalization. Targets of opportunity include renminbi deposits, home mortgages, ATMs, non–life insurance, mutual funds, and credit cards.

As significant restrictions remain in the financial services sector, several accomplishments are possible. Explicit barriers on foreign ownership and the activities of foreign-invested firms seem achievable targets. Greater application of the principle of national treatment, particularly with respect to branching in the insurance sector, might be attained. A CHUSTIA might crack China's mode 1 restrictions that limit cross-border electronic trade in financial services. As the United States, like China, is wary of cross-border electronic commerce in retail banking products and securities, additional negotiations about wholesale financial services might be fruitful. In the run-up to negotiations, China might come closer to full compliance with its WTO obligations as a show of readiness. These changes would add up to significant progress.

References

AmCham China (American Chamber of Commerce in the People's Republic of China). 2013. *American Business in China White Paper.* Beijing.

Bank of China. 2012. *2012 Annual Report.* Beijing.

Borst, Nicholas. 2013. *Shadow Deposits as a Source of Financial Instability: Lessons from the American Experience in China.* Policy Brief no. 13-14. Washington: Peterson Institute for International Economics.

Dobson, Wendy, and Pierre Jacquet. 1998. *Financial Services Liberalization in the WTO.* Washington: Peterson Institute for International Economics.

Hufbauer, Gary Clyde, and Jeffrey J. Schott. 2005. *NAFTA Revisited: Achievements and Challenges.* Washington: Peterson Institute for International Economics.

ICBC (Industrial and Commercial Bank of China). 2012. *2012 Annual Report.* Hong Kong.

IMF (International Monetary Fund). 2011. *People's Republic of China: Financial System Stability Assessment.* Country Report no. 11-321. Washington.

USTR (United States Trade Representative). 2012. *Report to Congress on China's WTO Compliance.* Washington.

---

24. David Barboza, "China to Test Free Trade Zone in Shanghai as Part of Economic Overhaul," *New York Times*, July 4, 2013.

9

Intellectual Property Rights

Intellectual property rights (IPRs) have been contentious between the United States and China for more than a decade. US firms claim that China's legal regime to protect IPRs has gaps and enforcement of IPRs is deeply deficient. In the 1990s the US software industry calculated that well over 90 percent of personal computer (PC) software used in China was pirated; while there has been some improvement, US sources claim that the figure today is still around 77 percent.[1] This chapter surveys outstanding IPR issues and draws on recent US free trade agreement (FTA) experience and Trans-Pacific Partnership (TPP) negotiations to outline salient issues in potential talks for a China–US trade and investment agreement (CHUSTIA). This chapter is written from a US perspective; we do not pretend to convey Chinese views on IPR issues. Trade secret theft through cyberespionage and other means has recently grabbed headlines on US-China relations; we handle that topic in chapter 16.

Intellectual property constitutes a huge part of US wealth. One way to size this up is to look at the difference between book value and market value of firms belonging to the Standard and Poor's (S&P) 500. Book value roughly measures the value of tangible assets: plant, equipment, and land. Market value reflects investors' collective view of the prospective discounted cash flows from the business, including its managerial know-how, trade secrets, patents, copyrights, and trademarks. In June 2014 the combined market value of the S&P 500 companies was nearly $17 trillion, or 2.74 times their book value.[2]

---

1. See Business Software Alliance (BSA), "2011 BSA Global Software Piracy Study," May 2012, portal.bsa.org (accessed on June 2, 2014).

2. Bloomberg L.P., *Market Capitalization and Book Value of S&P 500*, retrieved June 24, 2014, from Bloomberg Terminal.

Very roughly, it appears that almost 65 percent, or $11 trillion of market value, corresponded to intangible assets—including intellectual property.[3] A significant fraction of this value is at stake in IPR disputes between the United States and China.

Measuring the extent of IPR piracy is challenging. The International Chamber of Commerce estimated that in 2011 the total value of counterfeit and pirated goods in all markets was $1 trillion.[4] Earlier the Organization for Economic Cooperation and Development (OECD 2009) suggested that the value of counterfeit and pirated goods entering international trade might have been $250 billion in 2007. As one snapshot on domestic markets, the Business Software Alliance (BSA) put the world value of unlicensed software in 2011 at about $63 billion. While the BSA estimated the software piracy rate in China at 77 percent, other countries—notably Bangladesh, Zimbabwe, and Georgia—were estimated at or above 90 percent.[5] A 2011 study by the US International Trade Commission (USITC 2011) reported that overall IP infringement cost the US economy around $107 billion annually. Of course counterfeit and pirated goods are produced and sold everywhere, including the United States, but Chinese IPR violations are egregious and ongoing.

From the US point of view, the costs of China's weak IPR enforcement and legal gaps are huge. Smaller US companies doing business in China are particularly vulnerable. But China incurs costs as well. Just as the protection of property rights in tangible objects—agricultural land, apartment buildings, industrial plant and equipment—fosters investment and productivity, so the protection of intellectual property fosters invention and innovation. China cannot truly become a nation of indigenous innovation without stronger IPR protection. The US–China Business Council (USCBC) found that, because of weak IPR protection, 40 percent of US companies limited the types of products they were willing to comanufacture in China; a further 40 percent stated that research and development (R&D) spending in China was limited; and 36 percent curtailed the types of products they would manufacture in China.[6] Japanese and European firms probably react similarly. The implications for Chinese companies that contemplate substantial R&D outlays are worrisome.

We start by summarizing provisions of the World Trade Organization (WTO) Agreement on Trade-Related Aspects of Intellectual Property Rights (TRIPS), high-standard FTAs, and salient IPR issues in the current TPP talks.

---

3. Ocean Tomo, "Ocean Tomo 300 Patent Index," www.oceantomo.com (accessed on June 2, 2014). Intangible assets also include goodwill, usually acquired through mergers and acquisitions, but not usually considered intellectual property.

4. See International Chamber of Commerce, "Global Impacts Study," www.iccwbo.org (accessed on June 2, 2014).

5. See BSA, "Software Piracy Study."

6. USCBC, "Intellectual Property Rights Review and Recommendations," May 2013, uschina.org (accessed on June 2, 2014).

We then catalogue Chinese IPR deficiencies, as seen through US eyes. Finally we speculate on plausible US aspirations for a Chinese IPR regime that might be accomplished in a CHUSTIA.

WTO TRIPS

Part of the Uruguay Round package that created the WTO in 2005, TRIPS in essence accomplished four things. First, it required all WTO members to extend national treatment and most favored nation (MFN) treatment to virtually all aspects of IPR protection and enforcement. Second, it created minimum standards of protection, for all WTO members to legislate for their own jurisdictions, covering patents, copyrights, trademarks, and other forms of intellectual property. Third, it obligated all WTO members to provide enforcement procedures for IPRs so as to permit effective action against infringement, including "expeditious remedies to prevent infringements and remedies which constitute a deterrent to further infringements." Fourth, it applied the WTO's dispute settlement system to the agreement.[7] Least developed countries were given until July 1, 2013, to implement their obligations to the TRIPS agreement, a period since extended to July 1, 2021.[8] Of course China is not among least developed countries.

In 2007 the United States brought a WTO case against China alleging several violations of the TRIPS agreement.[9] The results were mixed. The United States prevailed on its assertion that China could not deny copyright protection in the period while creative works—movies, books, music—were under review by the Chinese censor, a practice that created wide opportunities for counterfeiting. Nor could Chinese authorities merely remove fraudulent trademarks from handbags, clothes, and other products and then put them back into commercial circulation. But on the big question of the adequacy of Chinese enforcement procedures and penalties, the WTO ruled that the United States had not provided sufficient evidence that China's practices violated China's WTO obligations.

High-Standard FTAs

Chapter 16 in the US–Singapore FTA and chapter 18 in the US–Korea FTA represent the gold standard for IPR coverage in US trade agreements, going well beyond commitments made in the TRIPS agreement. Text in the US–Singapore FTA runs for 22 pages, supplemented by an annex on protection of copyrights that have been wrongly appropriated on the internet. Text in the

---

7. WTO, "Overview: The TRIPS Agreement," www.wto.org (accessed on June 2, 2014).

8. WTO, "China—Measures Affecting the Protection and Enforcement of Intellectual Property Rights," www.wto.org (accessed on June 2, 2014).

9. WTO, "China—Intellectual Property Rights," www.wto.org (accessed on June 2, 2014).

US–Korea FTA runs for 34 pages, supplemented by four confirmation letters dealing with enforcement issues and patent linkage disputes. Both FTAs accomplish several goals in the IPR realm:

- They list numerous patent, copyright, trademark, domain name, and similar treaties and conventions to which both FTA parties must adhere;

- They specify minimum terms for patent and copyright protection, in line with US standards (e.g., life plus 70 years for copyrights);

- They allow for the free sale and licensing of intellectual property rights;

- Copyright holders are assured the right to protect and enforce their rights in digital copies of works (movies, books, etc.) distributed online and are protected from internet piracy and other forms of counterfeiting;

- Copyright holders are protected against circumvention of technological measures used to protect their works, which is of particular value for digital copies;

- Trademarks are protected from various forms of fraudulent use;

- Patent terms are extended to compensate for administrative delays in issuing patents;

- Test data and trade secrets submitted in connection with a patent application are shielded from disclosure (e.g., 5 years for pharmaceuticals, 10 years for agricultural chemicals);

- All central government agencies are required to use only licensed software;

- Parties commit to facilitate enforcement of rights, including through civil and administrative enforcement, and strong criminal and civil penalties are mandated to deter piracy and counterfeiting, both in the home market and in international commerce.

New Issues in the TPP

Patent Extensions

While it is still unknown exactly what new requirements for IPRs will be written into the TPP, indications point to some increases in the term of patent protection. An early draft IPR chapter, while heavily bracketed, gives some indication of the TPP landscape. The WTO TRIPS agreement requires patent protection for a minimum of 20 years from the date of filing, and for some countries this is the maximum.[10] However, it might take a government patent office months to approve or deny a patent application, and then the health authority years to approve its sale. Those delays shorten the useful life of the patent. Patent term extensions are designed to alleviate some of the problems US companies

---

10. WTO, "Obligations and Exceptions," fact sheet, TRIPS and pharmaceutical patents, www.wto .org (accessed on June 2, 2014).

(especially pharmaceutical companies) have with long delays. Term extensions compensate for the time required, for example, to approve the novelty of a new drug, and then to approve the drug for marketing (approving its safety and efficacy). The draft IP chapter for the TPP, which was leaked to the public in August 2013, gave considerable insight into what can be expected from the final agreement. Among other issues, the United States is pushing an extension of patent terms beyond the normal 20 years to compensate for the time a country's health agency takes to approve a drug for commercial marketing and sale.[11]

Data Exclusivity

Pharmaceutical companies are required to submit reams of expensive test data in their applications to market a new drug. The TRIPS agreement requires that WTO members protect the test data so that it will not be wrongly appropriated for "unfair commercial use." Data exclusivity provisions go beyond the unfair commercial use concept by granting the originator exclusive rights to the test data for a period of years, thereby prohibiting countries from allowing the sale of identical generic substitutes, once the patent expires, on the basis of test data the originating company already submitted.[12] In the TPP negotiations, the United States is promoting data exclusivity provisions similar to those found in its other FTAs.[13] Some TPP countries object, arguing that the patent term already provides a long enough period for the originator to recoup its costs and earn a profit. Possibly the issue will be settled by agreeing on a shorter data exclusivity period than the United States is seeking, say, 5 rather than 12 years.

Data exclusivity is especially important for biopharmaceuticals, usually called biologics, which are drugs or vaccines derived from living organisms. Biologics are seen as the future of cancer treatments, diabetes, arthritis, and a host of other illnesses. Developing these drugs and testing them is extremely costly and time consuming, resulting in large sunk costs for the originating firm. In some cases it might take longer than the standard patent term for the firm to recover its costs and earn a profit. In other cases a competing firm might produce a generic version of the biologic, called a biosimilar, which is sufficiently distinct not to infringe the original patent, but sufficiently similar that it could be approved on the basis of the originator's test data—if the data are publicly available. Data exclusivity provides extra protection for the originator in these circumstances.

11. Inside US Trade, "Wikileaks Posts Aug. 30 Negotiating Text for TPP IPR Chapter Indicating Country Positions," World Trade Online, November 13, 2013, insidetrade.com (accessed on June 2, 2014).

12. World Health Organization, "WTO and the TRIPS Agreement," www.who.int (accessed on June 2, 2014).

13. "Trans-Pacific Partnership Intellectual Property Rights Chapter," September 2011, infojustice .org (accessed on June 2, 2014).

Parallel Imports

The importation of a genuine product, legally produced but imported without the permission of the IP holder (patent, copyright, or trademark) constitutes a parallel import.[14] Sometimes national IP laws permit this; other times they do not. Whether it is permitted or not depends on the national rule with respect to exhaustion of IP rights. These rules differ between copyrighted and patented products.

The United States holds that an IP owner exhausts its rights with respect to transactions in patented and copyrighted goods and services after the first sale in the country of production. After that point, the buyer can then resell the product within the United States without restriction by the IP owner. However, until a very recent decision by the US Supreme Court, a US copyright owner could, by contract, prevent a buyer or licensee from reselling the copyrighted product into the United States from outside the foreign territory of its original sale (e.g., Thailand). This is known as a policy of domestic exhaustion. In *Kirtsaeng v. John Wiley & Sons* (133 S.Ct. 1351), decided in March 2013, the Supreme Court held that, under the US statute governing copyrights, the first-sale doctrine had worldwide application with respect to all copyrighted products (books, journals, films, music, software, etc.).

In IP circles, the Supreme Court's holding is known as a rule of international exhaustion, a rule that Australia, for example, has long followed. With respect to copyrighted products, Australian law holds that, after the first sale, the buyer—whether foreign or domestic—can resell the product within Australia, no matter what the contract with the copyright holder says. The European Union follows a regional exhaustion policy with respect to transactions within the Union, but not with respect to imports. Under the third amendment to its patent law, enacted in 2008, China permits parallel imports, though it follows a domestic exhaustion policy for goods produced in China.[15] To make matters more confusing, the domestic exhaustion rule still applies in the United States regarding patented products, such as mobile phones and pharmaceuticals. The *Kirtsaeng* decision, which permits imports into the United States of legally produced movies, books, and software—no matter what restrictions are built into the contract between licensee and licensor—was limited to the interpretation of the US copyright statute.

While exhaustion policies differ among countries and types of IPRs, developing countries generally adopt an international exhaustion policy for their imports, thereby permitting parallel imports of copyrighted and patented goods. Article 6 of the TRIPS agreement leaves the legal treatment of parallel imports up to each WTO member country. IP holders generally argue that parallel imports limit their ability to recoup costs and dull their incentive

---

14. This section draws heavily on Maskus (2012).

15. See "What Does the Third Amendment to China's Patent Law Mean to You?" Jones Day, January 2009, www.jonesday.com (accessed on June 2, 2014).

to develop local markets. But many countries see parallel imports as a way of encouraging price competition. Empirical evidence summarized by Keith E. Maskus (2012) suggests that outcomes are complicated. The practice of allowing parallel imports might or might not cause prices to converge, and price convergence, if it happens, might or might not improve economic welfare.

In the United States, the parallel import issue is particularly acute for pharmaceuticals. If a pharmaceutical company agrees to sell its products in a developing country at a cut-rate price, it does not want that product reexported to an advanced country, undercutting its prices in the advanced market. The same concern arises if the company sells its drugs to a monopolistic buyer such as Health Canada, at a low price, and the drugs are then resold in the United States. Consequently, the United States has sought to prohibit parallel imports, at least of pharmaceuticals, in its trade agreements. The same US push for domestic exhaustion policies is likely to characterize TPP negotiations.

IPR Deficiencies

Every year, the office of the US Trade Representative (USTR) devotes a few pages to Chinese IPR issues in its national trade estimate report on foreign trade barriers. In a special report, the USTR also annually identifies countries with deficient IPR practices on a priority watch list. China regularly appears on this list. In its trade barriers report the USTR states that "key concerns include unacceptable levels of retail and wholesale counterfeiting; persistently high levels of book and journal piracy; end-user piracy of business software; lack of effective trade secret protection and enforcement; and copyright piracy over the Internet."[16] US concerns cover a mix of legal text, enforcement practices, and customs barriers. When a Chinese joint venture partner wrongfully appropriates US trade secrets, legal remedies may be nonexistent, and even where they exist, enforcement action is often weak. Delays in customs clearance for legitimate books and movies spur counterfeit products. In the patent area, the United States objects to the Chinese practice of excluding postfiling supplementary test data that might bolster the original patent application.

IPR Enforcement

China's inadequate IPR enforcement has long been a matter of contention with the United States. While China has a relatively strong legal framework, enforcement has been seriously deficient. The US-China Business Council found in 2012 that the greatest IPR concerns of US firms doing business in China, in order of importance, were trade secrets, trademarks, patents, and copyrights. In that same survey over 95 percent of business firms polled said

---

16. USTR, "2013 National Trade Estimate Report on Foreign Trade Barriers," www.ustr.gov (accessed on June 24, 2014).

they were somewhat or very concerned about IPRs.[17] While the central government has made strides in protecting IPRs, the main obstacles to stronger enforcement are found at the provincial level.

Prosecuting IPR violations at the provincial level can be difficult. In the realm of patents, China has set up the State Intellectual Property Office (SIPO), with a national office to grant patents and local offices to enforce them. Filing a complaint at the local SIPO is the usual way to address a patent violation. However, there is little incentive for provincial leaders to curb IPR violations because enforcement could damage the prospects of local firms. Many provincial leaders are powerful in their own right and authorities in Beijing often have difficulty convincing them to step up enforcement efforts.

Another method for addressing IPR violations is through the civil court system. Chinese civil courts handled nearly 84,000 lawsuits for IPRs in 2012, a rise of 44 percent from 2011, indicating that courts are becoming increasingly important in the enforcement battle.[18] But again the provinces have significant sway over litigation and a civil court case decision may be appealed to the Provincial High People's Court, giving a second opportunity to tilt the decision in favor of local business firms.

Another issue is inadequately trained judges and prosecutors with limited ability to make correct calls in the IP realm. Effective training will take time, but will pay dividends in the long run through better IP protection throughout China. Procedural issues are also a barrier to effective enforcement, as red tape seriously obstructs firms that would like to prosecute IP violations. For end-user piracy actions, applications for pretrial court orders for the defendant to preserve evidence are often rejected by the courts because of unnecessarily high barriers, making it difficult or impossible to bring a case.[19] Reforms would go a long way to improving enforcement and complying with IPR agreements.

Penalties for IPR Infringement

Civil penalties for IPR violations are generally weak and thus serve as only a mild deterrent. The accounting method for assessing damages in copyright cases is badly flawed (see below), and internet infringement is not seriously penalized.[20] Moreover, China does not impose criminal penalties for copyright violations in circumstances where the infringer makes no revenue, as in piracy of software within a business or other organization. Firms that profit from copyright infringement are rarely punished in the criminal system as long as

17. USCBC, submission to USTR Special 301 Review, 2012, www.uschina.org (accessed on June 2, 2014).

18. "China's IPR Suits See Spike in 2012," *China Daily*, www.china.org.cn (accessed on June 2, 2014).

19. See International Intellectual Property Alliance (IIPA), "2013 Special 301 Report," February 8, 2013, www.iipa.com/ (accessed on June 2, 2014).

20. Ibid.

their activity is not on a "commercial scale" (the language of Article 61 of the TRIPS agreement). According to the WTO Appellate Body, "commercial scale" means "the magnitude or extent of typical or usual commercial activity with respect to a given product in a given market."[21] This definition allows considerable scope for flexible interpretation. One knowledgeable commentator has complained that China's criminal law with respect to IPR theft is much too lenient.[22] Statutory damages are too low to be a deterrent and punitive damages are not available even in cases of willful or repeated infringement.

A recent case against an online music provider in China that had been selling copyrighted music on its website provides a great example. According to the *Beijing News*, Tencent was found guilty of copyright infringement on its online music service in December 2012 and was fined about $2,400—a symbolic punishment, as Tencent had annual revenue of over $7 billion in 2012 (Tencent 2012). China's new IPR draft laws would increase the fines for sales of counterfeit and pirated goods. The draft copyright law states that fines can be of "one to five" times the amount of revenue of the illegal sales, as long as those sales are above 50,000 renminbi (approximately $8,100).[23] While this is a positive step, the draft law does not address the means to ensure stronger enforcement. And the new draft law fails to provide clear language that would compel the imposition of much higher fines.[24]

Malicious Registration of Trademarks

Brand protection in China is difficult, and the problem is exacerbated when firms or individuals preemptively register copyrights, trademarks, and patents hoping to cash in. In a move called squatting, these companies attempt to register trademarks and patents that the true owner of the trademark, or true owner of the invention, will later be forced to buy. China, like nearly all countries, follows the first-to-file practice, which means that the person or company that first lodges an application in a patent or trademark office has priority. There are exceptions to the first-to-file rule for well-known brands and bad-faith registrations, but these are very difficult to prove. The luxury brand Hermès had been using its trademark in China since 1977, but had registered

---

21. WTO, "China—Intellectual Property Rights."

22. In September 2012 Michael Schlesinger of the IIPA wrote a letter to the USTR stating that China was in violation of the WTO TRIPS agreement. One of his arguments was that criminal penalties need to be enforced more strongly, including against end-users of pirated software, as well as against hard disk loading piracy and circumvention of technological protection measures. He also argued that the threshold for criminal enforcement must be lowered for those that commit piracy. See WTO, "China—Intellectual Property Rights."

23. "IP Penalties Soar Significantly as Laws Revised IPR in China," Intellectual Property Protection in China, March 13, 2013, www.chinaipr.gov.cn (accessed on June 2, 2014).

24. Joe Simone, "Comments on the PRC Trademark Law Amendments," China IPR, January 27, 2013, chinaipr.com (accessed on June 2, 2014).

only the trademark in English. In 1995 a Chinese company registered a name very similar to the Hermès name in Chinese (Ai Ma Shi in phonetic Chinese). Hermès sued but lost the dispute due to "lack of evidence."[25]

Malcolm Moore, writing in April 2012 for the *Daily Telegraph*, described how extensive trademark squatting had become. His article claims that Chinese individuals have extensively registered UK brands, from clothing companies to technology firms.[26] Companies that have had their trademarks registered by squatters may have no choice but to pay up or start over in China with another name.

Sale of Counterfeit Goods

The US Customs and Border Protection report on seizure statistics for 2012 found that China and Hong Kong shipped 84 percent of the counterfeited goods US authorities seized. The market value of these counterfeit goods was estimated at $1.1 billion, a 10 percent increase over the previous year.[27] The larger problem is the sale of pirated software within China, costing US companies billions of lost revenue.[28] The US software industry has battled China over piracy issues for more than a decade, but the government, state-owned enterprises, and private companies alike still widely use pirated copies.

The World Health Organization (WHO 2010) estimates that counterfeit pharmaceuticals bring in $75 billion annually worldwide, and China is among the largest producers. The WHO states that 60 percent of all pharmaceuticals sold in developing countries are fakes and many do not contain the ingredients they claim.[29] These products sometimes contain hazardous chemicals, causing dangerous side effects. Fake drugs from China show up all over the world in different forms, from fake vitamins, fake contraceptives, and fake toothpaste to fake malaria pills. A new regulatory body, the China Food and Drug Administration, has already faced corruption allegations and charges of poor oversight of Chinese chemical and drug companies.

25. Sam Abrams, "China Trademark Squatters Have Not Been Ignoring the UK," China Hearsay, April 30, 2012, www.chinahearsay.com (accessed on June 2, 2014).

26. Malcolm Moore, "Asda in China? That'll Be Mr Liu in Shenzhen," *Telegraph*, April 30, 2012, www.telegraph.co.uk (accessed on June 2, 2014).

27. US Customs and Border Protection, Office of International Trade, "Intellectual Property Rights: Fiscal Year 2012 Seizure Statistics," Department of Homeland Security, www.cbp.gov (accessed on June 2, 2014).

28. See BSA, "Software Piracy Study."

29. WHO, "General Information on Counterfeit Medicines," www.who.int (accessed on June 2, 2014).

Utility Model Patent System

China's patent law took effect in 1985, allowing three types of patent protection: invention, design, and utility model patents (UMPs). The UMP system makes it easier for small companies and individuals to register a patent, as it is cheaper, faster, and goes unchecked by SIPO until another party questions its validity and an infringement action is launched. This proved to be a great catalyst for patent applications in China and the number of UMPs has skyrocketed.

Today, bad-faith registrations by those who are not the true inventor or patent owner, as well as patents filed to meet local quotas, have threatened the system.[30] One study notes that, from 2001 to 2012, applications for patent filings increased significantly in December of each year, and based on the renewal rate as well as the grant rate, it appears that many of these were of low quality, an indication of officials trying to meet quotas.[31] The World Intellectual Property Organization found that nearly 83 percent of all the UMPs filed in the world in 2011 were filed in China. This study also suggested that UMPs were more likely to be used aggressively against foreign companies.[32] The former senior intellectual property attaché at the US Embassy, writing in a report for the US Chamber of Commerce, stated that a consensus exists in the business community that "the current UMP system in China presents a potentially significant threat to the US and foreign companies seeking to innovate."[33]

Conclusions

Our analysis has already indicated IPR goals that the United States will seek in FTA talks. The United States would start with the high-standard provisions in recent FTAs—illustrated in the Singapore and Korea FTAs—and add improvements that might be accepted in the TPP negotiations.

At best, that is what a CHUSTIA could accomplish. But IPR problems in China have deeper roots than the shortcomings of legal texts and enforcement

---

30. In 2012 over 2 million patent applications were filed with SIPO in China and 1.2 million patents were granted, with a very high percentage of these from domestic applications for UMPs. This was an increase of over 26 percent in applications from the year before. Tian Lipu, director of SIPO, said that "compared with those steeple-crowned invention patents in developed countries, many of ours are patents for small improvements, utility models or design." See "Patent Applications Surge in China, Quality Low," *China Daily*, April 26, 2013, usa.chinadaily.com.cn (accessed on June 2, 2014).

31. Zhen Lei, "Autumnal Hook 2012 Update," China IPR, February 16, 2013, chinaipr.com (accessed on June 24, 2014).

32. Joff Wild, "Chinese Authorities Plan to Take Action on Bad Faith Utility Model and Design Patent Applications," *Intellectual Asset Management*, February 22, 2013, www.iam-magazine.com (accessed on June 2, 2014).

33. Mark Cohen, former senior intellectual property attaché, US Embassy, wrote a forward and commentary in Moga (2012).

efforts. It is not easy to rewrite a history of IPR violations going unpunished, or to alter wide social acceptance of counterfeit products. The central government can launch public campaigns and demand more from local officials, but cultural norms stand in the way of IPR protection. At the retail level, widespread official corruption, desperate pursuit of wealth, and obsession with luxury brands all erode IPR protection (Kapp 2012). At the wholesale level, China's dedicated search for advanced technology and its practice of pressuring foreign companies to reveal proprietary knowledge both weaken IPR protection. A strong IPR chapter in a China–US FTA can be a start, but only a start, in changing deep-rooted attitudes.

References

Kapp, Robert A. 2012. Intellectual Property in Larger Context: Challenges to US–China Relations. In *US-China Economic Relations in the Next Ten Years*. Hong Kong: China–US Exchange Foundation.

Maskus, Keith E. 2012. *Private Rights and Public Problems*. Washington: Peterson Institute for International Economics.

Moga, Thomas T. 2012. *China's Utility Model Patent System: Innovation Driver or Deterrent?* Washington: US Chamber of Commerce.

OECD (Organization for Economic Cooperation and Development). 2009. *Magnitude of Counterfeiting and Piracy of Tangible Products: An Update*. Paris.

Tencent. 2012. *2012 Annual Report*. Hong Kong.

USITC (US International Trade Commission). 2011. *China: Effects of Intellectual Property Infringement and Indigenous Innovation Policies on the U.S. Economy*. Investigation 332-519. Washington.

WHO (World Health Organization). 2010. Growing Threat from Counterfeit Medicines. *Bulletin of the World Health Organization* 88, no. 4 (April): 247–48.

10

Labor Policy

Since the dawn of the industrial revolution, low wages and poor working conditions have been recurring topics in Western politics. While concerns about domestic labor practices remain a factor, globalization has increasingly shifted the focus of the labor debate to developing countries that export to advanced nations. The United States and Europe are quick to encourage developing countries to adopt stronger labor laws, while developing countries are equally quick to question the altruistic motives of advanced nations, seeing in these US and European campaigns a thinly veiled attempt to reduce the competitiveness of developing-country industries and drive production back to the shores of advanced nations. These two perspectives will influence the conversation around a China–US trade and investment agreement (CHUSTIA).

Labor Standards

Although foreign critics of China's labor policies are numerous, they have few avenues to directly influence Chinese regulations. Multinational corporations (MNCs) that do business in China are generally seen as more pragmatic targets. In 2012, when the wages of Foxconn workers became national news in the West, several of Foxconn's clients faced public outrage. Apple was the favorite target, but Foxconn's clients also included Nokia, Sony, Dell, Google, and Toshiba. The issues raised with respect to Foxconn were not unique. Low wages, long hours, and questionable working conditions do not play well with Western audiences.

Safety regulations took center stage after the April 2013 collapse of a building in Bangladesh. Over 1,100 people were killed, making it the deadliest accidental structural failure in modern times.[1] The collapse gained particular notoriety not only because of its human toll, but also because of the prior gross negligence of the building owners and lead tenants. The building contained a bank and several shops on its lower floors, but these were closed on the day of the collapse because large cracks had been discovered the preceding day. Despite this finding, managers ordered their factory workers to report to work as usual.[2] In the aftermath of the accident, President Barack Obama suspended Bangladesh's trade preferences under the Generalized System of Preferences (GSP), citing the government's failure to fulfill the applicable labor rights requirements. While the decision was prompted by the collapse, the US Trade Representative (USTR) press release implied that Bangladesh had long been under investigation for its labor practices.[3]

The Bangladesh tragedy prompted a response beyond public disapproval: a fresh rallying cry for meaningful labor provisions in trade agreements. The USTR reaffirmed its commitment to "include stronger labor obligations that will further strengthen labor laws in conformity with international standards"[4] in the Trans-Pacific Partnership (TPP). Speaking at the Peterson Institute, Congressman Sander Levin (D-MI) asserted that "the events in Bangladesh represent an undeniable challenge"[5] to reliance on market forces to improve labor conditions in developing countries.

The World Trade Organization (WTO) makes no attempt to establish labor standards. Most developing countries adamantly oppose initiatives in this direction, fearing that advanced countries will use labor standards as a protectionist tool. They are right to be concerned: Labor unions and their political champions have urged a global minimum wage, enforced as necessary by countervailing duties.[6] But while the WTO has steered clear of labor rights, free trade agreements (FTAs) are another matter. Starting with the North American Free Trade Agreement (NAFTA), US free trade agreements have included a labor chapter, and successive editions have become more demanding in terms of both labor standards and enforcement measures.

---

1. "Bangladesh Building Collapse Death Toll Passes 500," *BBC*, May 3, 2013.

2. Farid Ahmed, "Bangladesh Building Collapse Kills At Least 123, Injures More Than 1,000," *CNN*, April 25, 2013, edition.cnn.com (accessed on June 3, 2014).

3. USTR, "U.S. Trade Representative Michael Froman Comments on President's Decision to Suspend GSP Benefits for Bangladesh," press release, June 2013, www.ustr.gov (accessed on June 3, 2014).

4. Ibid.

5. Ways and Means Committee Democrats, "Levin Remarks on Trade at Peterson Institute for International Economics," democrats.waysandmeans.house.gov (accessed on June 3, 2014).

6. See, e.g., "Support a Global Minimum Wage," globalminimumwage.org (accessed on June 3, 2014).

China's Labor Union

The only union allowed in China is the government-controlled All-China Federation of Trade Unions (ACFTU). It is the largest union in the world, boasting over 280 million members. It is also China's only legal labor union; it operates under the Trade Union Law of the People's Republic of China, in effect since 1992 and amended in 2001. Funding for the ACFTU comes from companies, which are required to pay 2 percent of the entire payroll to the union. As the ACFTU is supposed to defend workers' rights but is also a servant of the Communist Party, there is an inherent tension in its mandate if attempts to push for change conflict with party goals. When it comes to improving working conditions, the ACFTU's options are limited. The union has never called for a strike, and the plight of migrant workers is seldom heard, as they are not separately organized.

WTO Rulebook

For practical purposes, as mentioned above, the WTO has been silent on labor issues. Developed countries have tried to introduce labor standards as production process methods (PPMs) in the WTO, but their attempts have largely failed. At the 1996 Singapore Ministerial Conference, WTO members affirmed their commitment to "core labor standards," generally understood at the time to mean a prohibition of forced labor and child labor, consistent with Articles XX(b) and XX(e) in the General Agreement on Tariffs and Trade (GATT). Aside from that gesture, the International Labor Organization (ILO) was identified as the proper place for labor issues to be handled. The declaration issued at the Singapore Ministerial went so far as to note that the comparative advantage of developing countries in this area "must in no way be put into question."[7] The concluding remarks by Yeo Cheow Tong, chairman of the conference and Singapore's trade minister, went even further (WTO 1997):

> Fourth, it does not inscribe the relationship between trade and core labour standards on the WTO agenda. Fifth, there is no authorization in the text for any new work on this issue. Sixth, we note that the WTO and the ILO Secretariats will continue their existing collaboration, as with many other intergovernmental organizations. The collaboration respects fully the respective and separate mandates of the two Organizations. Some delegations had expressed the concern that this text may lead the WTO to acquire a competence to undertake further work in the relationship between trade and core labour standards. I want to assure these delegations that this text will not permit such a development.

---

7. WTO, "Singapore Ministerial Declaration," December 18, 1996, www.wto.org (accessed on June 3, 2014).

Labor standards were again raised in 1999 at the ill-fated ministerial conference in Seattle. In his address to the conference, President Bill Clinton remarked on the importance of adding labor and environmental issues to the WTO framework.[8] Both suggestions galvanized the opposition of developing countries in the conference halls while strident labor and environmental advocates protested on Seattle's streets. The ministerial conference was suspended without issuing the customary declaration (Schott 2000).

Developed countries made another push to tackle labor standards at the Doha Ministerial in 2001, hoping to include the issue in the Doha Round. Developing countries remained in opposition, standing behind the notion that increased trade would spur economic development that would lead to better labor standards in the natural course of economic progress.[9] The declaration following the ministerial reaffirmed the commitment to ILO core labor standards made in 1996, but no specific official discussion was held.

Labor in US FTAs

NAFTA

The famous NAFTA side letter on labor, at the insistence of President Clinton, established the North American Agreement on Labor Cooperation (NAALC) to address questions of labor abuse. The Commission on Labor Cooperation (CLC), based in Washington, oversees the operation of the NAALC. In substantive terms, the NAALC calls for each NAFTA member to enforce its own labor laws. Complaints about inadequate enforcement are submitted to the national administrative office (NAO) of the complaining party (e.g., for the United States, the AFL-CIO).[10] If consultations do not resolve the matter, it can be referred to a government-to-government dispute settlement mechanism, which in theory can lead to the creation of an arbitration panel and the imposition of a monetary fine. This murky mechanism—developed at the insistence of Canada and Mexico—was designed not to work and in fact no arbitration panel has been established in 20 years. US labor advocates were intensely dissatisfied with both the substantive standard ("enforce national laws") and the dispute procedure. The result is a more robust approach on both counts in the most recent batch of FTAs, explained in the discussion below on the Peru–US FTA (2011).

---

8. Text of Clinton's address at "Agendas Clash as Trade Talks Begin," *PBS NewsHour*, December 2, 1999, www.pbs.org (accessed on July 9, 2014).

9. WTO, "Trade and Labor Standards: A Difficult Issue for Many WTO Member Governments," Doha ministerial 2001 briefing notes, www.wto.org (accessed on June 3, 2014).

10. The American Federation of Labor and Congress of Industrial Organizations.

May 10th Agreement

US FTAs did not address labor issues for the first several years of the George W. Bush administration. However, a change in policy was needed to secure congressional approval for new FTAs following the midterm elections of 2006. To that end, the White House and congressional Democrats negotiated the May 10th Agreement in 2007. The agreement allowed sanctions or fines to be imposed if it was found that a country systematically failed to enforce its own labor laws, including the ILO Declaration on Fundamental Principles, in a manner that affected bilateral trade.

The Peru FTA, the first US FTA that was subject to the agreement, establishes substantive standards for labor rights that go well beyond the NAFTA prescription for each country to enforce its own laws. Article 17.2 of chapter 17 requires each party to adopt, in its own laws, the fundamental rights enunciated in the ILO Declaration and not to derogate from those rights:

1. Each Party shall adopt and maintain in its statutes and regulations, and practices thereunder, the following rights, as stated in the *ILO Declaration on Fundamental Principles and Rights at Work and its Follow-Up (1998)* (ILO Declaration):
(a) freedom of association;
(b) the effective recognition of the right to collective bargaining;
(c) the elimination of all forms of compulsory or forced labor;
(d) the effective abolition of child labor and, for purposes of this Agreement, a prohibition on the worst forms of child labor; and
(e) the elimination of discrimination in respect of employment and occupation.

2. Neither Party shall waive or otherwise derogate from, or offer to waive or otherwise derogate from, its statutes or regulations implementing paragraph 1 in a manner affecting trade or investment between the Parties, where the waiver or derogation would be inconsistent with a fundamental right set out in that paragraph.

Chapter 17 establishes a cabinet-level labor affairs council that oversees consultations when one party questions the labor practices of the other party. If consultations between the parties under council auspices fail to resolve the matter, the complaining party can seek another set of consultations under chapter 21 (Article 21.4), a meeting of the cabinet-level free trade commission (Article 21.5), and finally, arbitration under the provisions of chapter 21. Unlike NAFTA, which went no further than official consultations on labor matters, the Peru FTA opens the possibility of arbitration, just as for commercial disputes. If the arbitration decision goes against the respondent party, a monetary fine may be assessed. If the party fails to pay, the complaining party can institute a suspension of FTA benefits (Article 21.16).

Other US FTA agreements of the same vintage as the Peru FTA—those with Korea, Panama, and Colombia—contain highly similar if not identical labor standards and dispute settlement provisions, regarding both subject matter and procedure. This represents the current US model for labor practices, which the United States will urge on other countries in the TPP. But there are signs of resistance, and it seems likely that the US model will be modified in TPP talks, especially with respect to dispute settlement, in which many countries favor a solely consultative approach.

In the current climate, the May 10th Agreement seems to remain an acceptable compromise between labor activists and other interests. A letter to President Obama signed by 23 US senators urged a number of provisions in the TPP,[11] including "an enforceable obligation to protect fundamental labor rights."[12] This goal seems to fall squarely within the scope of the May 10th Agreement and the provisions in the Peru and Colombia FTAs.

Outside of the US government, organized labor groups can be expected to push for stronger provisions. Perhaps the AFL-CIO will have the loudest voice, arguing for labor provisions in the TPP that go beyond the May 10th Agreement. In a statement released on May 10, 2013, the AFL-CIO stated that "the USTR should fulfill the promise that the 'May 10' provisions will serve as a floor, not a ceiling, on labor rights. These provisions represented an important step forward for labor rights, but did not contain all of the essential elements of an effective labor chapter."[13] The AFL-CIO advocated that all labor rights violations be subject to dispute settlement in the trade agreement, not only violations that are recurring or sustained and pertain to international trade.

Labor Disputes in US FTAs

The NAALC has seen far more labor rights complaints than any other US agreement, with 23 complaints filed with the US national administrative office out of 38 total. Twenty of these have been directed at alleged abuses in Mexico.[14] Labor unions in all three NAFTA countries, as well as international workers' rights groups, are particularly active in filing complaints. Reflecting that fact,

---

11. The provisions urged included safeguards against currency manipulation, a chapter on state-owned enterprise disciplines of Buy America, and protections against offshoring of manufacturing and service jobs, in addition to enforceable labor rights.

12. See letter from 23 senators to President Obama, United States Senate, November 30, 2012, cwafiles.org (accessed on June 3, 2014).

13. AFL-CIO, "AFL-CIO Response to Request for Comments on the 'Trans-Atlantic Trade and Investment Partnership,'" federal register, April 1, 2013, docket number USTR-2013-0019, www.aflcio.org (accessed on June 3, 2014).

14. NAALC Public Communications and Results, 1994–2008, www.naalc.org (accessed on June 25, 2014).

24 of the 38 cases filed have pertained to freedom of association and 16 of those have also involved collective bargaining rights.[15]

Even though complaints under the NAALC have limited enforcement consequences, some cases have spurred action by national governments. A 2000 complaint filed by the Coalition for Justice in the Maquiladoras, plus more than a dozen other nongovernmental organizations (NGOs) and unions, alleged insufficient safety standards and inadequate compensation for injuries. After observation by NAO staff, the NAO requested ministerial consultations. The consultations resulted in the establishment of a working group on occupational safety and health.

In a 2003 case, the United Students Against Sweatshops (USAS) filed a complaint concerning conditions at a Mexican garment factory. After review, the US Secretary of Labor requested ministerial consultations, eventually leading to ministerial talks between all three NAFTA countries. The ministers issued a joint declaration pledging to resolve the issues raised in the complaint. Several other cases have resulted in outreach programs, intended to increase Mexican awareness of labor protection. Some of these campaigns have focused on protections for the rights of pregnant women and the freedom of association.

Although other agreements have stronger labor provisions, none have seen as many disputes as NAFTA. The Central American Free Trade Agreement–Dominican Republic (CAFTA–DR), which covers five Central American countries and the Dominican Republic, has seen three labor complaints in total. The remaining complaints were filed against Bahrain and Peru. Perhaps the most notable complaint, however, is the current Guatemalan case, which the AFL-CIO and several Guatemalan organizations filed in 2008. The complaint alleged that Guatemala was systematically failing to enforce its own laws, a claim substantiated by a 2009 Department of Labor report.[16] Based on the report, the United States requested consultations, under the labor chapter of CAFTA–DR, to resolve violations of Guatemala's commitments, but consultations failed to resolve the complaint.

The United States then moved to establish an arbitral panel to resolve the issue. The panel was formed, but quickly suspended by mutual agreement as the United States and Guatemala sought a diplomatic resolution. In April 2013 the two agreed on an enforcement plan calling on Guatemala to substantially improve its labor policy. Under the plan, Guatemala committed to strengthening labor inspections, expediting and streamlining the process of sanctioning employers and ordering remediation of labor violations, increasing labor law compliance by exporting companies, improving the monitoring and enforcement of labor court orders, publishing labor law enforcement information,

15. Statistics from the Department of Labor, Bureau of International Labor Affairs, www.dol.gov (accessed on June 25, 2014).

16. Department of Labor, Public Report of Review of Office of Trade and Labor Affairs US Submission 2008-01 (Guatemala), January 16, 2009, www.dol.gov (accessed on June 25, 2014).

and establishing mechanisms to ensure that workers are paid what they are owed when factories close.[17] If the plan is fully implemented, the arbitral panel will be terminated without additional proceedings.

Labor in Chinese FTAs

Unsurprisingly, labor issues have not been prominent in Chinese FTAs. Both the China–Chile and China–New Zealand agreements addressed labor issues through a memorandum of understanding rather than a full chapter or side agreements. The memoranda used in the two FTAs are largely identical. Parties reaffirm their commitments as ILO members, including the Declaration on Fundamental Principles, while respecting each nation's rights to set and enforce its own labor laws.

In the memoranda, the countries agree to carry out "mutually agreed cooperation activities"[18] in improving labor conditions, among other important areas. Both parties are supposed to "seek to secure funds required to support co-operation activities and shall undertake the co-ordination of the departments responsible for the implementation of this Memorandum," but no specific activities or schedules for establishing such activities are laid out. As a general rule, memoranda of understanding are not legally binding in the sense that they can provide the basis for dispute settlement proceedings.

Conclusions

For many members of the US House and Senate, strong labor chapters are a crucial part of all future US FTAs. Some groups, such as the AFL-CIO, view the May 10th Agreement as a first step and are likely to push for stronger provisions in future agreements.[19] Given this political landscape, a CHUSTIA will face potentially insurmountable opposition if a labor chapter is not part of the text. At the same time, China has no tolerance for a string of dispute settlement cases mounted by US labor unions and other NGOs. China is the quintessential beneficiary of comparative advantage stemming from low wages relative to productivity levels, and Chinese officials will adamantly resist attempts to erode that advantage.

It might be possible to square the circle by judiciously modifying the dispute settlement provisions found in recent US trade agreements, starting with the Peru–US FTA. If the inevitable TPP labor chapter can satisfy US labor

---

17. Department of Labor, Guatemala Submission under CAFTA-DR, "Mutually Agreed Enforcement Action Plan between the Government of the United States and the Government of Guatemala," www.dol.gov (accessed on June 25, 2014).

18. Memorandum of Understanding on Labour and Social Security Cooperation, www.sice.oas.org (accessed on June 3, 2014).

19. AFL-CIO, "AFL-CIO Response."

advocates, it might be a useful template as well. The key sticking points could be the extent of state-to-state consultations before a last-ditch resort to arbitration, and a cap on trade penalties.

References

Schott, Jeffrey J. 2000. *The WTO after Seattle*. Washington: Peterson Institute for International Economics.

WTO (World Trade Organization). 1997. Success in Singapore. *Focus* no. 15 (January): 1–40. Geneva.

11

Environmental Policy

Environmental damage, like the hardships of low-income workers, furnishes a ready target for globalization critics. Lax labor and environmental standards confer a financial benefit on manufacturing, mining, and forestry firms in some countries, as critics around the world are quick to point out. But countries on the receiving end of these criticisms are wary of such concerns, often suggesting that environmental complaints are a smokescreen for industrial protection. These could be a difficult topic for a possible China–US trade and investment agreement (CHUSTIA), given China's extensive air and water pollution. Beijing's leaders put a high priority on environmental improvement, but they may be wary of international obligations as the best way forward.

Climate Change

The overriding global environmental issue, for at least the next two generations, is very likely climate change. On the greenhouse gas front, China and the United States are the leading polluters. They are the world's first- and second-largest sources of CO_2 emissions, and together accounted for over 40 percent of global CO_2 emissions in 2010.[1] In the past, neither the World Trade Organization (WTO) nor bilateral trade agreements have tackled greenhouse gases.[2] Conceivably a CHUSTIA could mark a breakthrough. However, existing US free trade agreements (FTAs) essentially require partner countries

---

1. US Energy Information Administration, International Energy Statistics, www.eia.gov (accessed on June 4, 2014).

2. The United Nations Framework Convention on Climate Change has been the leading forum for promoting international cooperation, but with limited success. See UK House of Commons Energy and Climate Change Committee, "The Road to UNFCCC COP 18 and Beyond," second

to enforce their own environmental standards; the FTAs do not establish new and higher standards for environmental protection on CO_2 or anything else. As for the WTO, its imprint on environmental questions principally arises in the context of trade disputes, in which one party asserts an environmental justification for some sort of trade restriction. The cases litigated so far in the WTO have dealt with far smaller environmental issues than climate change.[3]

Several indicators of US and Chinese carbon emissions are summarized in table 11.1, covering the period 1990 to 2010. The United States had long been the largest source of carbon emissions, but China captured the top spot in 2006. The switch was due partly to a modest decline in US emissions, but mainly to rapid growth in Chinese emissions. Between 2002 and 2010, total US emissions fell by about 5 percent, while total Chinese emissions more than doubled. Over the past two decades, US emissions increased by an eighth while Chinese emissions more than tripled.

Energy consumption figures, shown in table 11.2, explain China's ascent to the position of top emitter. Between 1990 and 2010, US coal and petroleum consumption increased by 10 percent, while natural gas consumption increased by about 25 percent. Energy derived from natural gas emits half the carbon footprint as the same energy derived from coal; hence faster growth of US natural gas consumption was an environmental positive. The same thing happened in China, but the overall growth of Chinese energy consumption far outstripped that of the United States. Between 1990 and 2010, China's coal consumption increased by 250 percent, petroleum consumption by nearly 300 percent, and natural gas consumption by 600 percent.

WTO Environmental Cases

The WTO does not include specific rules, much less a code, pertaining to the environment. Under Articles XX(b) and XX(g), the General Agreement on Tariffs and Trade (GATT) permits members to adopt trade measures to protect the environment, but such measures are carefully scrutinized to test their consistency with the chapeau of Article XX, which reads:

> Subject to the requirement that such measures are not applied in a manner which would constitute a means of arbitrary or unjustifiable discrimination between countries where the same conditions prevail, or a disguised restriction on international trade, nothing in this Agreement shall be construed to prevent the adoption or enforcement by any contracting party of measures: ...

report of session 2012-13, July 17, 2012, www.publications.parliament.uk (accessed on June 4, 2014).

3. See, e.g., *United States—Import Prohibition of Certain Shrimp and Shrimp Products* case (DS58), complaint by India, Malaysia, Pakistan, and Thailand; also *Brazil—Measures Affecting Imports of Retreaded Tyres,* case (DS332), complaint by the European Communities.

Table 11.1   US and Chinese annual CO_2 emissions, 1990–2010

	China			United States		
	Billion metric tons	Metric tons per capita	Kilogram per dollar of GDP	Billion metric tons	Metric tons per capita	Kilogram per dollar of GDP
1990	2.5	2.1	2.0	4.8	18.8	0.6
1991	2.6	2.2	1.9	4.8	18.9	0.6
1992	2.7	2.3	1.7	4.9	19.1	0.6
1993	2.9	2.4	1.6	5.0	19.3	0.6
1994	3.1	2.5	1.5	5.1	19.4	0.6
1995	3.3	2.7	1.5	5.2	19.4	0.6
1996	3.5	2.8	1.4	5.3	19.6	0.6
1997	3.5	2.8	1.3	5.4	19.9	0.6
1998	3.3	2.7	1.2	5.5	19.8	0.5
1999	3.3	2.6	1.1	5.5	19.8	0.5
2000	3.4	2.7	1.0	5.7	20.2	0.5
2001	3.5	2.7	1.0	5.6	19.6	0.5
2002	3.7	2.9	0.9	5.7	19.6	0.5
2003	4.5	3.5	1.0	5.7	19.5	0.5
2004	5.3	4.1	1.1	5.8	19.7	0.5
2005	5.8	4.4	1.1	5.8	19.6	0.5
2006	6.4	4.9	1.1	5.7	19.2	0.4
2007	6.8	5.1	1.0	5.8	19.3	0.4
2008	7.0	5.3	0.9	5.7	18.5	0.4
2009	7.7	5.8	0.9	5.3	17.3	0.4
2010	8.3	6.2	0.9	5.4	17.5	0.4

Source: US Department of Energy, Carbon Dioxide Information Analysis Center, Environmental Sciences Division (2013), www.energy.gov.

The article then lists permissible measures. Several cases in which countries sought to defend their trade restrictions under article XX illustrate the workings of WTO jurisprudence.[4] We summarize six of these cases.

United States: Tuna-Dolphin (Disputes 4 and 5 and DS381)

The United States has repeatedly run afoul of GATT in its quest to save the dolphins. The first two complaints were filed under the old GATT system,

---

4. In these cases, a great deal of effort goes into determining whether the application of trade restrictions is arbitrary or unjustifiable. For a brief explanation of the WTO's Dispute Settlement Body (DSB), see chapter 18.

Table 11.2 US and Chinese energy consumption by source, 1990–2010
(quadrillion BTUs)

	China				United States			
	Petroleum	**Natural gas**	**Coal**	**Renewable**	**Petroleum**	**Natural gas**	**Coal**	**Renewable**
1990	4.9	0.6	19.3	1.3	33.6	19.6	19.2	3.9
1991	5.3	0.6	20.2	1.3	32.8	20.0	19.0	3.9
1992	5.6	0.6	20.9	1.3	33.5	20.7	19.2	3.6
1993	4.8	0.6	21.7	1.5	33.7	21.2	19.9	3.9
1994	6.6	0.7	23.4	1.7	34.6	21.7	20.0	3.7
1995	7.0	0.7	23.5	1.9	34.4	22.7	20.1	4.2
1996	7.5	0.8	24.7	1.9	35.7	23.1	21.0	4.7
1997	8.1	0.8	27.3	2.0	36.2	23.2	21.5	4.7
1998	8.5	0.8	28.0	2.1	36.8	22.8	21.7	4.3
1999	9.0	0.9	26.8	2.2	37.8	22.9	21.7	4.3
2000	9.9	0.9	27.7	2.3	38.3	23.8	22.6	3.9
2001	10.1	1.0	28.4	2.9	38.2	22.8	21.9	3.3
2002	10.6	1.1	32.4	2.9	38.2	23.5	22.0	4.0
2003	11.5	1.2	37.0	2.9	38.8	22.8	22.4	4.1
2004	13.2	1.4	40.9	3.5	40.3	22.9	22.6	3.7
2005	13.7	1.7	48.0	4.0	40.4	22.6	22.8	3.8
2006	14.9	2.1	52.5	4.3	40.0	22.2	22.5	4.0
2007	15.3	2.6	56.0	4.8	39.8	23.7	22.8	3.7
2008	15.8	2.9	59.3	5.9	37.3	23.8	22.4	4.0
2009	17.5	3.3	66.7	6.2	35.4	23.4	19.7	4.3
2010	19.1	4.0	69.7	7.5	36.0	24.6	20.8	4.4

BTU = British thermal unit

Source: US Energy Information Administration, International Energy Statistics (2013), www.eia.gov.

before the founding of the WTO. At the time, the United States placed an embargo on tuna and tuna products from any country that failed to show that its fishing laws protected dolphins sufficiently. An embargo also applied to countries that imported tuna from a country with subpar fishing practices, in an effort to prevent the indirect export of offending tuna.

Mexico and the European Union filed GATT disputes (4 and 5, respectively) in response to the US embargoes.[5] In both cases, the GATT panel found that the United States could not impose an embargo based on the way tuna

---

5. World Trade Organization (WTO), "Mexico Etc. Versus US: 'Tuna-Dolphin,'" www.wto.org (accessed on June 4, 2014); "EU Versus US: 'Son of Dolphin-Tuna,'" www.wto.org (accessed on June 4, 2014).

was caught if there was no discernible effect on quality. In other words, trade restrictions based on offensive production process methods (PPMs) of the exporting country were not permissible, according to the GATT panels. The GATT faded into history before the General Council adopted these panel findings, and today they have no legal effect. Post-1994 environmental cases, within the WTO framework, proved somewhat more sympathetic to environmental restrictions, though there are still limits. The US shrimp case (DS58), discussed in a moment, gives a more accurate picture of what is permissible today. As for the tuna-dolphin dispute, Mexico and the United States reached an agreement outside of GATT.

The more recent tuna-dolphin case filed by Mexico challenged the US dolphin-safe labeling scheme.[6] This US Department of Commerce label is awarded only to firms that give evidence that their fishing practices conform to US standards of dolphin protection. The measure is an effort to ban the practice of setting on dolphins, in which ships follow and encircle dolphins in an attempt to catch their tuna travelling companions. Even though US imports are not required to be dolphin-safe, the WTO's Appellate Body found that the labeling scheme modified the conditions of competition because the United States awarded it far more often to US tuna products than to Mexican tuna products. To defend its classification system, the United States attempted to demonstrate that dolphin-safe tuna would actually be less harmful to dolphins. However, the Appellate Body ruled that the requirements did not appropriately consider harm to dolphins stemming from other causes or the differing risks between regions. Accordingly the labeling system was held inconsistent with the Technical Barriers to Trade (TBT) Agreement. The US Trade Representative (USTR) recently informed the WTO that it has complied with the latest ruling,[7] but Mexico has expressed dissatisfaction with the new US measures.[8]

United States: Gasoline (DS4)

In 1996 Venezuela and Brazil brought a case to the WTO challenging new US environmental standards on gasoline imports.[9] The standards for imported gasoline were more stringent than for domestic gasoline. The WTO panel found, and the Appellate Body confirmed, that this violated the principle of

---

6. WTO, "United States—Measures Concerning the Importation, Marketing and Sale of Tuna and Tuna Products," www.wto.org (accessed on June 4, 2014).

7. USTR, "U.S. Announces Compliance in World Trade Organization 'Dolphin-Safe' Labeling Dispute," press release, July 12, 2013, www.ustr.gov (accessed on June 4, 2014).

8. Inside US Trade, "Mexico Will Challenge the New U.S. Dolphin-Safe Labeling Regulation before the WTO," *World Trade Online*, insidetrade.com (accessed on June 4, 2014).

9. WTO, "United States—Standards for Reformulated and Conventional Gasoline," www.wto.org (accessed on June 4, 2014).

national treatment.[10] The United States argued that domestic refineries needed time to conform to the new rules. The Appellate Body rejected this defense, noting that foreign refineries did not receive equal consideration. In this case the Appellate Body explicitly confirmed the right of a WTO member to impose environmental standards, but emphasized that they must be applied consistent with the national treatment obligation.

United States: Shrimp (DS58)

In a landmark case over PPMs, the US import ban on shrimp imports from several Asian countries was challenged in 2001.[11] Asian trawlers did not use nets designed to protect sea turtles, as US law required. The Appellate Body found that the US requirement constituted arbitrary and unjustifiable discrimination, largely due to the lack of flexibility. Under the US regulations, any country exporting shrimp to the United States would have to adopt the same technology as US trawlers, and this requirement was deemed unreasonable. This case established the proposition that environmentally motivated trade restrictions that prescribe a particular PPM will be carefully scrutinized.

Brazil: Retreaded Tires (DS332)

The European Union challenged Brazil's ban on the importation of retreaded tires in a 2007 case. Brazil argued that retreaded tires were likely to be discarded, providing a breeding ground for mosquitoes.[12] The Appellate Body upheld Brazil's claim that the measure was designed to protect human and plant health, but found that the ban on imports from Europe amounted to a disguised restriction on international trade because Brazil allowed imports of retreaded tires from its Mercosur partners.[13] The quantity of retread imports from Mercosur partners was small, but the Appellate Body held that the intent of the measure is determinative, rather than its quantitative effect.

10. WTO, "United States—Standards for Reformulated and Conventional Gasoline," Appellate Body and panel report, May 20, 1996, www.wto.org (accessed on June 4, 2014).

11. Summary available at WTO, "United States—Import Prohibition of Certain Shrimp and Shrimp Products," www.wto.org (accessed on May 20, 1996); see also WTO, "United States—Import Prohibition of Certain Shrimp and Shrimp Products," Appellate Body report, October 12, 1998, www.wto.org (accessed on June 4, 2014).

12. WTO, "Brazil—Measures Affecting Imports of Retreaded Tyres," www.wto.org (accessed on June 4, 2014).

13. WTO, "Brazil—Measures Affecting Imports of Retreaded Tyres," Appellate Body report, December 3, 2007, www.worldtradelaw.net (accessed on June 4, 2014).

China: Raw Materials (DS394)

In a 2009 case, the United States challenged Chinese export restrictions on several important raw materials,[14] including bauxite, coke, magnesium, silicon, and zinc.[15] When China acceded to the WTO in 2001 it committed to remove all export quotas and export duties, aside from those duties listed in annex 6 of its accession protocol.[16] The annex justified none of the contested duties, so China attempted to defend its restrictions under GATT Article XX, claiming that some of its export duties and quotas were needed to conserve an exhaustible natural resource. However, China failed to show that these restrictions were coupled with restrictions on domestic production or consumption. Similarly, it argued that some of the other restrictions were needed to preserve the health of the populace. Again China was unable to show that the restrictions would reduce pollution in the short or long term, as no such restrictions applied domestically. The panel noted that a sizable gap had developed between domestic and export prices for several goods, so the export restrictions gave domestic manufacturers a competitive advantage.

Moldova: Environmental Charge (DS421)

In a case brought in 2011 and currently under consideration, Ukraine is challenging Moldova's law[17] that imposes charges on imported products the use of which contaminates the environment, as well as charges on certain types of packaging. Ukraine alleges that no comparable fees exist on domestic products, and therefore the Moldovan law violates its national treatment obligation. Third parties include China, the European Union, and the United States. In June 2011 the DSB agreed to form a panel to examine the case, but a panel has not yet been composed. This is unusual for WTO disputes, as a party can force the composition of a panel 20 days after the panel is established. In July 2011 the DSB established a panel for a case brought by Moldova against the Ukraine regarding taxes on distilled spirits. The panel for the distilled spirits

---

14. Summary available at WTO, "China—Measures Related to the Exportation of Various Raw Materials," www.wto.org (accessed on June 4, 2014).

15. WTO, "China—Measures Related to the Exportation of Various Raw Materials," Appellate Body report, January 30, 2012, www.wto.org (accessed on June 4, 2014). In a subsequent case, DS431 (China—Rare Earths), the United States asks China to remove export restrictions on rare earths, tungsten, and molybdenum. This case was filed soon after the Appellate Body ruled on DS394 and the complaints are quite similar. The European Union and Japan have filed parallel cases, DS432 and DS433, respectively.

16. WTO, "Accession of the People's Republic of China," November 23, 2001, www.worldtradelaw. net (accessed on June 4, 2014).

17. Summary available at WTO, "Moldova—Measures Affecting the Importation and Internal Sale of Goods (Environmental Charge)," www.wto.org (accessed on June 4, 2014).

case, like the panel for the environmental charge case, is awaiting composition. It appears that Moldova and Ukraine are refraining from vigorous pursuit of their respective complaints.

WTO Lessons for the United States and China

The above cases offer examples of what sorts of trade-restrictive policies are permissible in the name of environmental protection. Clearly import or export restrictions must be accompanied by domestic consumption and production restrictions aimed at the same environmental goals. Moreover, trade restrictions cannot pick and choose among WTO members; they should apply with reasonable uniformity to all members. Trade restrictions designed to penalize environmentally unsound PPMs will be carefully scrutinized. However, hints can be found in the Appellate Body decision in the US shrimp case, and in speeches by Pascal Lamy, former WTO director-general, that trade restrictions in support of a multilateral environmental agreement would be viewed sympathetically in future WTO cases.[18] Within these broad guidelines, both China and the United States can impose trade restrictions to further environmental goals. That said, nothing in the WTO agreements or cases requires China, the United States, or any other member to raise its environmental standards.

Environment in US FTAs

North American Free Trade Agreement

The North American Free Trade Agreement (NAFTA) was the first FTA between two developed nations and one developing nation. As such, concerns about a race to the bottom in terms of environmental policy were particularly prominent during negotiations. Environmental groups worried that a member with less strict environmental policy might label the policies of a stricter nation as nontariff barriers and bring pressure to weaken those restrictions. The groups were also worried that polluting industries might migrate to the less strict country, thereby escaping environmental mandates, yet still sell their products throughout North America.

NAFTA's chapter 11 established an investor-state arbitration system to hear complaints by private firms that the host state had directly or indirectly expropriated its assets, by either physical seizure (rare) or laws or regulations that sharply eroded their economic value. Cases are decided by arbitrators operating under the rules of the International Center for the Settlement of Investment Disputes (ICSID), an agency housed in the World Bank. Some 15

---

18. See WTO, "Shrimp and Shrimp Products," Appellate Body report, paragraph 171, note 174, and Hufbauer, Charnovitz, and Kim (2009), 73–75 and 99–100.

investor-state cases have been decided since NAFTA entered into force.[19] The most controversial cases have been those where new environmental provisions arguably eroded enterprise value. In light of these controversies, subsequent US FTAs have modified the legal description of permitted causes of action to provide greater policy space for environmental provisions.[20]

To address the fear that Mexico, in particular, might fail to enforce its own environmental provisions as a means of attracting investment, the North American Agreement on Environmental Cooperation (NAAEC) was negotiated as a side agreement to NAFTA. This side agreement did not enumerate new environmental policy commitments, but it did attempt to ensure that the parties would enforce their own laws. The NAAEC contains a dispute resolution system under which a member can file a claim if it believes another member is consistently and systematically failing to enforce its own laws in trade-related sectors. Proceedings under part 5 of the NAAEC can be initiated only by a government, and violations can theoretically result in fines or sanctions. No such proceedings have yet been initiated.

The agreement also established a Council on Environmental Cooperation (CEC), which can make environmental policy proposals, but member countries are required only to give consideration to these proposals. Individuals and nongovernmental organizations (NGOs) can submit claims that a country is failing to enforce its environmental laws to the CEC, and these complaints will be entered into the factual record if justifiable. This process is distinct from cases brought under part 5 in two major practical ways. First, only governments can bring part 5 cases, but individuals and NGOs can lodge CEC complaints; and second, the CEC findings do not have a binding effect. Substantial procedural differences exist as well. Despite the absence of binding enforcement procedures, governments have responded to the proceedings in some cases. The Cozumel coral reef in Mexico was declared a national park following a submission to the CEC.

---

19. Mexico and Canada are not members of the ICSID, but ICSID hears cases involving those countries under its additional facility rules designed for nonmembers.

20. NAFTA Article 1110, paragraph (1) has this language: "No Party may directly or indirectly nationalize or expropriate an investment of an investor of another Party in its territory or take a measure tantamount to nationalization or expropriation of such an investment ("expropriation")." The paragraph then lists exceptions, but does not reference environmental measures. However, the Korea–US FTA, in annex 11-B, paragraph 3(b), contains the following exception:

> Except in rare circumstances, such as, for example, when an action or a series of actions is extremely severe or disproportionate in light of its purpose or effect, non-discriminatory regulatory actions by a Party that are designed and applied to protect legitimate public welfare objectives, such as public health, safety, the environment, and real estate price stabilization (through, for example, measures to improve the housing conditions for low-income households), do not constitute indirect expropriations.

May 10th Agreement

FTAs largely left environmental issues unaddressed for quite some time after NAFTA until the Agreement of May 10th, 2007. This agreement, struck between the George W. Bush administration and newly empowered congressional Democrats, covered a wide range of topics, notably the inclusion of multilateral environmental agreements (MEAs) in future FTAs.[21] Protections for endangered species, marine pollution, and ozone emissions, among others, would be enforceable in future US FTAs, pursuant to the May 10th Agreement. The use of trade sanctions, as opposed to fines, also became the standard response to environmental violations in US FTAs. The general theme of these rules is that countries are required to enforce their own environmental laws, including obligations resulting from international agreements to which they belong.

The US–Peru FTA, under negotiation at the time of the May 10th Agreement, was the first to reflect the new compact. In addition to the commitments above, the issue of illegal logging was given special attention. Annex 18.3.4 spells out commitments in this regard.[22] The FTA required Peru to provide increased resources in budget and manpower to its logging enforcement agencies, and to institute stiffer civil and criminal penalties for a wide range of illegal logging activities. Furthermore, Peruvian exports of mahogany to the United States require a government certification verifying that the wood was harvested in a legal and sustainable manner.[23] The number of permits is subject to a quota, as the Convention on International Trade in Endangered Species of Wild Fauna and Flora (CITES) requires. Many other requirements, mostly stemming from CITES, affect Peru's logging industry. In principle, the US government can initiate action, including sanctions, against Peru if the various requirements are not met. However, no action has yet been taken.

Environmental organizations will certainly express concerns related to the formation of a CHUSTIA. In response to the Trans-Pacific Partnership (TPP) negotiations, many groups have called for the inclusion of an environmental chapter, with different groups emphasizing varying elements with varying degrees of strength. A joint letter issued by eight major environmental groups, including the Sierra Club, Oceana, and the World Wildlife Fund, stated that the United States should insist on environmental provisions at least as strong as those in the May 10th Agreement, with a few augmentations.[24] A major

---

21. USTR, "Bipartisan Trade Deal," May 2007, www.ustr.gov (accessed on June 4, 2014).

22. USTR, US–Peru Trade Promotion Agreement, "Chapter Eighteen: Environment," www.ustr.org (accessed on June 4, 2014).

23. Enforcement of this provision was later questioned. See Pervaze A. Sheikh, "Illegal Logging: Background and Issues," Congressional Research Service, March 19, 2007.

24. See "Re: Environmental Chapter of the Trans-Pacific Partnership Agreement," letter from various environmental groups to Michael Froman, US trade representative, July 11, 2013, www.sierraclub.org (accessed on June 4, 2014).

issue for Oceana is the prevalence of fishing subsidies,[25] and the objective of reducing those subsidies is reflected in the joint letter.

The joint letter described above represents bottom-line environmental concerns with respect to the TPP. Several parties to the letter have made stronger requests on an individual basis. The Sierra Club is particularly concerned about the prospect of relaxing export controls on natural gas, fearing that increasing the price US producers receive will increase the occurrence of fracking and greenhouse gas emissions.[26] The Friends of the Earth and other groups strongly oppose the inclusion of an investor-state dispute resolution mechanism.[27] Many NGOs are concerned about any measure that carries the possibility of reducing federal or state regulatory autonomy regarding US environmental policy.

Environment in Chinese FTAs

As one might expect, environmental issues have been less prominent in Chinese FTAs. In the China–New Zealand FTA, parties reaffirmed commitments made in multilateral environmental agreements, but no dispute settlement mechanism was put in place. In China–Chile, environmental issues were given similar, limited treatment. In both cases, environmental issues were handled in memoranda of understanding.

Plurilateral Agreements on Environment

In January 2014, 14 members of the WTO, including the United States and China, launched negotiations to reduce or eliminate tariffs on green goods and services at meetings related to the World Economic Forum. US Trade Ambassador Michael Froman said "we believe that environmental agreements are absolutely critical to further efforts to liberalize trade." The announcement stems from the 2012 Asia-Pacific Economic Cooperation (APEC) meeting that looked to reduce tariffs on environmental goods. The agreement seeks to combat climate change while fostering environmental innovation and creating jobs. Froman noted that this deal is one of the key initiatives in President Obama's climate action plan and that the market in environmental goods amounts to nearly $1 trillion annually. Members of the new plurilateral pact cover 86 percent of environmental goods trade globally.[28]

25. Oceana, "The Trans-Pacific Partnership: Promoting Sustainable Trade in Seafood Products," handout, December 2011, oceana.org (accessed on June 4, 2014).

26. Sierra Club, "An Explosion of Fracking? One of the Dirtiest Secrets of the Trans-Pacific Partnership Free Trade Agreement," fact sheet, www.sierraclub.org (accessed on June 4, 2014).

27. Bill Waren, "Old Trade Deal Wine in New Bottle," Friends of the Earth, news release, May 4, 2012, www.foe.org (accessed on June 4, 2014).

28. "Environmental Goods Talks Underway," *Washington Trade Daily*, January 27, 2014.

Conclusions

A potential CHUSTIA is sure to face a high degree of scrutiny from many US groups, environmentalists among them. Past US FTAs have often drawn the ire of the environmental lobby, both during negotiations and after the fact. At the same time, China is unlikely to acquiesce to any program that entails cutting industrial output. But that does not mean that compromises are impossible.

Like the United States, China is a signatory to CITES, the Montreal Protocol to control ozone-depleting emissions, and other multilateral environmental agreements. Moreover, the United States and China have cooperated on several environmental issues in recent times. In 2008 they initiated a ten-year framework on energy and environment cooperation, resulting in the US–China EcoPartnerships Program, which facilitates and supports environmentally minded cooperation among private entities in both countries.[29] More recently, the United States and China agreed to work with other countries to reduce consumption and production of hydrofluorocarbons (HFCs), a potent class of greenhouse gases. This initiative could cut greenhouse gas emissions by up to 90 gigatons of CO_2 equivalent by 2050, roughly two years of global emissions at current rates.[30] The two countries reaffirmed their climate commitment at the contentious September 2013 Group of 20 (G-20) summit, which was otherwise dominated by Syria. In addition to the bilateral agreement between the United States and China, other G-20 members voiced their support for the initiative. The United States and China sought to deepen cooperation further in July 2013 with the establishment of a working group to develop cooperative action plans pursuant to five environmental initiatives, including reducing emissions from heavy-duty vehicles, improving viability and use of carbon capture technology, and increasing energy efficiency in industry and transportation.[31] These examples of cooperation, taken together, could form a basis for a strong environmental chapter in a CHUSTIA.

Conceivably a CHUSTIA could include provisions designed to encourage a sharp drop in US emissions and less rapid growth of Chinese emissions. Both countries might use their best efforts to reduce the greenhouse gas intensity of GDP, specifying indicative intensity figures at 10-year intervals (2020, 2030, 2040). Even though these commitments would not be legally binding, they would represent a dramatic advance over prior trade agreements and might help establish global norms. Environmental groups might champion such a

---

29. US Department of State, "The US–China EcoPartnerships Program," fact sheet, July 10, 2013, www.state.gov (accessed on June 4, 2014).

30. White House Office of the Press Secretary, "United States and China Agree to Work Together on Phase Down of HFCs," press release, June 8, 2013, www.whitehouse.gov (accessed on June 4, 2014).

31. US Department of State, "US–China Climate Change Working Group Fact Sheet," fact sheet, July 10, 2013, www.state.gov (accessed on June 4, 2014).

provision, while the Chinese government would maintain control over specific industrial policies. Likewise, in the spirit of NAFTA, a China–US FTA could include a fact-finding commission akin to the CEC that, when called upon, would conduct studies and issue reports. The reports would not lead to binding enforcement measures, but they would bring public pressure to bear on environmental problems.

References

Hufbauer, Gary Clyde, Steve Charnovitz, and Jisun Kim. 2009. *Global Warming and the World Trading System*. Washington: Peterson Institute for International Economics.

12

Export Controls

ASHA SUNDARAM

A central benefit of a possible China–US trade and investment agreement (CHUSTIA) is the opportunity for China and the United States to exploit gains from trade by orienting production toward sectors where they enjoy comparative advantages. For China this will include manufacturing sectors more intensive in labor, particularly less-skilled workers; for the United States, it will imply growth in high-tech manufactures, as well as agriculture and services. A portion of high-tech trade, however, is covered by US national security export controls that attempt to limit sales abroad of dual-use (civilian and military) products and technology that might be diverted to military purposes.

China has previously expressed concern about the restrictiveness of US export controls in high-tech sectors, while the United States has insisted that its licensing requirements aim not to curb overall exports in these sectors, but to discourage specific uses of technology embedded in the controlled products. The US Bureau of Industry and Security claims that a very small portion of total US exports to China actually require an export license.[1]

Trade negotiations under a CHUSTIA umbrella will very likely address the US export control regime, in response to China's demands. The goal of this chapter is to arrive at an estimate of how much the US export control regime affects exports to China, and to identify sectors the regime covers that are of most interest to China. This is done by establishing an alternative norm against which to measure US–China high-tech bilateral trade. To define the

Asha Sundaram is a senior lecturer at the School of Economics, University of Cape Town, South Africa. The author would like to thank J. David Richardson and Barry Naughton for their comments.

1. See Inside US Trade, "US Officials Downplay Chinese Complaints on Export Control Restraints," www.insidetrade.com, July 26, 2013 (accessed on June 25, 2014).

norm, we use an enhanced gravity model of international trade that, in its simplest form, posits that bilateral trade between two countries is associated positively with the product of their economic sizes, and negatively with greater bilateral distance between them. The exercise compares the United States as an exporter to other advanced exporters.

More specifically, the analysis looks at how high-tech exports to China would differ if the United States behaved like Germany, the United Kingdom, or Japan. These advanced countries are traditional export rivals; they have export controls on high-tech products, like the United States, but their controls are alleged to be less strict. The analysis is performed across six high-tech standard international trade classification (SITC) sectors. This allows the identification of sectors with the largest discrepancies, indicating that the bite of US export controls to China in these sectors is abnormal.

The counterfactual estimates indicate that US exports would rise by between $6.8 billion and $16.4 billion if the United States were to behave like Germany or the United Kingdom under their export control regimes. The next two sections of this chapter provide a brief background of export control regimes in both the United States and China, followed by a discussion of trends in high-tech exports by the United States to emerging economies as well as Chinese high-tech imports from the United States and its peers. The last two sections analyze the counterfactuals and conclude the chapter.

In the broader context of export controls, US partners in free trade agreements (FTAs) enjoy preferred access to US exports of liquefied natural gas (LNG). Thanks to shale gas and hydrofracturing technology (fracking), the United States has recently become one of the largest natural gas producers in the world. Under current law, the Department of Energy (DOE) must approve LNG exports, but this approval is automatic for US FTA partners under the mandate of the US Energy Policy Act of 1992, which calls for expedited review of natural gas exports to FTA partner countries (Hufbauer, Bagnall, and Muir 2013). The US–Canada FTA set the precedent for this in 1989, as it required both partners to observe the principle of national treatment when selling energy supplies to the other. Meanwhile, the DOE assesses LNG exports to non-FTA partners case by case, examining their effects on the public interest. Under a CHUSTIA, China would benefit from equal access to US natural gas supplies, making it possible for China to use long-term LNG supplies from the United States as a bargaining chip when it signs contracts with alternative suppliers, such as Australia, Qatar, and Russia.[2]

---

2. In CHUSTIA talks, China could also seek guarantees against future US export restrictions on agricultural products, such as soybeans, in times of global shortage. See chapter 6.

US Export Controls

Between the 1950s and the 1980s, US export controls were primarily targeted against the former Soviet Union. By the late 1980s, China was seen as a possible adversary to the Soviet Union, and this vision abetted some US sales of armaments to China. The relaxed policy was reversed after the Tiananmen Square protests in 1989, and US exports to China of military technology thereafter dwindled. About the same time, the Soviet empire crumbled, and US export controls reoriented away from countries formerly part of the Soviet Union and toward new emerging powers with capabilities in nuclear and biological weapons technologies, including China.

Since the mid-1990s, the US export control regime has classified China as a medium-threat country, meaning a security risk primarily due to its military capabilities in nuclear, chemical, and biological weapons, as well as missile technology. China's status as a risk continues today, reflecting US concerns about cybersecurity, China's military aggression toward its neighbors—including military deployment along the Indian border and near the Senkaku Islands—coupled with worries about China's own export control policies. These concerns prevent an easy reclassification of China as a nonthreat country. Currently two separate lists govern high-tech exports to China: the munitions list under the International Trade in Arms Regulation and a Department of Commerce control list under the Bureau of Industry and Security. Exports of items covered by these lists require export licenses and must adhere to reporting and tracking requirements.

There is no doubt that the US classification of China as a potential threat has left Beijing disgruntled. China views US export controls as thwarting its ability to import high-tech products from the United States that are seen as essential for China's growth. As a consequence, China sees itself pushed to seek sources in Europe and Japan, and answers demands from Washington to liberalize its trade and exchange rate regime with complaints about US controls in high-tech sectors.

In turn, Washington asserts that export controls are not meant to smother exports of advanced technology goods to China. Such a policy would not be credible, given China's close relations with traditional US peers such as Germany and Britain, which, even though they remain signatories to the multilateral Wassenaar Arrangement governing export controls on high-tech products, are known to enforce these controls with limited enthusiasm. In addition, China's prominence in global supply chains necessitates trade in high-tech products, especially in electronics and electrical machinery, where civilian and military end uses are hard to disentangle. The goal of export controls, according to Washington, is to deter exports of dual-use technologies that might be detrimental to US national security, but this goal clashes with China's pursuit of an integrated civilian and military industrial base (Cheng 2010).

Tensions notwithstanding, US reforms in the late 2000s have facilitated acquisition of export licenses for shipments to China. In 2007 the United States introduced a validated end-user program as part of the reform initiative. Under this program, US firms exporting to Chinese companies that fulfill certain requirements can obtain a general authorization and do not require multiple export licenses. Similarly US exporters can ship multiple exports under a special comprehensive license rather than having to apply for individual licenses.

Chinese Export Controls

As China has grown more conscious of its international standing, it has attempted to align its export control regime with international standards, taking several steps since the early 2000s. In 2003 the Ministry of Commerce and Chinese customs jointly issued directives outlining customs inspection procedure and requirements. The 2000s also saw the introduction of various control lists of missiles, weapons, and other dual-use technology products for which export licenses are now required. China constantly updates these lists to ensure that they are in line with control lists under various international multilateral export control agreements.

China's greatest challenge has been to establish an effective licensing regime and the legal processes and institutions necessary to ensure its smooth functioning. Concerns about effective Chinese enforcement have kept the United States and its European peers from encouraging Chinese membership in multilateral export control agreements, even though China has signaled an interest in these agreements. In 2004 China sought membership to the Missile Technology Control Regime (MTCR) but its application was rejected, causing consternation in Beijing. China currently remains outside the MTCR, the Australia Group, and the Wassenaar Arrangement.

Meanwhile Chinese capabilities for exporting missiles, dual-use chemicals, and nuclear technology continue to expand. Given this, it is encouraging that Beijing expressed an interest in arms and dual-use controls. However, some of China's export control procedures remain opaque, and as mentioned above, China faces challenges in enforcing its licensing regime. Moving toward increased Chinese participation in the multilateral export control regime and integrating China into the global effort toward arms control will require support from the United States and other peers, as well as Chinese efforts to ensure transparency in its export controls and consistent enforcement of its standards.

US High-Tech Exports to Emerging Economies

The US classification of China as a medium-threat importer of high-tech products, along with US reluctance to encourage Chinese membership in the multilateral export control regime, portend US export losses. But the

Figure 12.1 US high-technology exports to emerging economies, 1995–2010

billions of 2005 US dollars

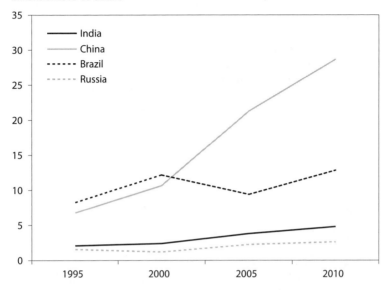

Source: UN Comtrade, comtrade.un.org (accessed on July 4, 2014).

situation is more complex than that. Figures 12.1 and 12.2 look at the US–China trade relationship in the high-tech sectors of metal products, industrial and office machinery, electrical machinery, transport equipment, scientific equipment, and weapons, and compare trade flows to other relevant relationships. Figure 12.1 plots US high-tech exports to selected emerging economies across six SITC sectors over five-year intervals, starting in 1995 and ending in 2010. Data are obtained from the UN Comtrade database. The emerging importers compared here are Brazil, Russia, India, and China. Like China, India and Russia are classified under the export control regime as medium-threat importers of high-tech products, while Brazil is classified as a neutral importer.

While Russia's imports from the United States in high-tech products have remained relatively tepid, US exports to India show a slight rise after 2000; they increase to Brazil after 2005. However, US exports to China grow most impressively, from over $7 billion in 2000 to about $29 billion in 2010, outstripping growth in exports to the three other emerging importers, regardless of their threat status.

Figure 12.2 plots high-tech exports to China from the United States and its traditional rival exporters, Germany, Japan, and the United Kingdom. As the figure shows, US exports to China pick up after 2000. UK exports to

Figure 12.2   US and peer high-technology exports to China, 1995–2010

billions of 2005 US dollars

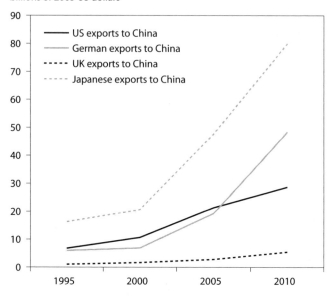

Source: UN Comtrade, comtrade.un.org (accessed on July 4, 2014).

China also increase after 2005. In absolute numbers, however, UK exports fall substantially short of US exports. In 2010, US exports were up to six times larger than UK exports. Japanese exports to China, however, are larger than US exports throughout, and mirror the spike in US exports after 2000. In 2010 Japan exported almost three times more high-tech goods to China than the United States. More striking in figure 12.2 is that the spectacular growth of German high-tech exports overshadowed the rise in US exports. While US exports to China exceeded Germany's by about $2 billion in 2005, by 2010 German exports exceeded US exports by about $19 billion. Counterfactual analysis shows that if the United States behaved like Germany as an exporter, it would experience export gains to China. It would also experience export gains if it behaved like Japan or the United Kingdom. The next section details this analysis.

Counterfactuals

Apart from determining the overall effect of the US export control regime on exports to China in high-tech sectors, we aim to identify sectors that appear crucial to Chinese interests. Toward this goal, table 12.1 provides counterfactual calculations for the year 2010. The differences are estimated after

Table 12.1 Counterfactuals based on exports of other advanced countries to China (millions of 2005 US dollars)

	Basic metals	Industrial/office machinery	Electrical machinery, telecommunications	Transport equipment	Scientific equipment	Weapons	Total
Actual measured level of US exports to China of dual-use products in 2010	737	10,200	9,840	3,990	3,920	1	28,688
Estimated difference in US exports to China in 2010 if the United States were Germany	1,242	353	556	3,072	1,654	6	6,884
Estimated difference in US exports to China in 2010 if the United States were the United Kingdom	367	–1,279	–1,404	18,181	603	4	16,471
Estimated difference in US exports to China in 2010 if the United States were Japan	184	972	2,012	1,758	4,255	10	9,190

Notes: Results based on regressions in Sundaram and Richardson (2013). Figures are based on estimated coefficients for Germany, the United Kingdom, and Japan, relative to the United States, on exports to China.

Sources: UN Comtrade, comtrade.un.org (accessed on July 4, 2014); authors' calculations.

accounting for normal factors that determine trade between two countries, such as economic size, income levels, and geographic distance.

Rows 1, 2, and 3 perform the counterfactual exercises, showing US exports to China if the United States were a high-tech exporter like Germany, the United Kingdom, or Japan, under the common export control regime that treats China as a medium threat. These estimates are obtained after accounting for several other drivers of trade that might be specific to exporter-importer pairs (e.g., cultural similarities, a common language or colonizer), to changes in comparative advantage or changing consumer preferences for imports, or in China's case, to its changing role in the global value chain. These changes are captured by fixed-effect terms in the gravity model equations.

The counterfactuals in row 1 show overall estimated US export gains to China if the United States behaved like Germany in imposing targeted controls on exports to China. The estimates indicate that US export gains would occur in all sectors, with especially large gains in transport equipment, followed by gains in scientific equipment. Overall US export gains would add up to $6.9 billion. This figure becomes larger if the United States behaved like Japan under its export control regime. Row 3 estimates show US export gains of $9.2 billion, with the largest gains in scientific equipment. US export gains would be largest if the United States behaved like the United Kingdom. Row 2 estimates indicate that US export gains could amount to $16.5 billion, with the largest gains in transport equipment, one of the United Kingdom's two biggest exports to China (the second being machinery).[3] In sum, table 12.1 suggests that under a CHUSTIA, with some relaxation of export controls, US export gains would most likely occur in transport and scientific equipment and Chinese import interests would probably center on these particular high-tech sectors.

Conclusions

Talks toward a CHUSTIA are very likely to include a dialogue on US national security–oriented export controls, at China's behest, given its strong interest in high-tech imports from the United States. China has expressed its chagrin at being a target of US high-tech export controls in the past, and its frustration at not being invited to join global multilateral export control arrangements. The analysis in this chapter shows US export gains of $6.9 billion if the United States were to behave like Germany, $9.2 billion if it were to behave like Japan, and $16.5 billion if it were to behave like the United Kingdom. Gains would be concentrated in particular high-tech sectors, specifically transport and scientific equipment. Potentially these will be sectors that draw attention if negotiations toward an FTA between China and the United States gather steam.

---

3. See Foreign and Commonwealth Office Economics Unit, "UK Exports to China: Now and in the Future," London, January 2013.

References

Cheng, Dean. 2010. *Export Controls and the Hard Case of China*. Backgrounder 2501 (December 13). Washington: Heritage Foundation.

Hufbauer, Gary Clyde, Allie E. Bagnall, and Julia Muir. 2013. *Liquefied Natural Gas Exports: An Opportunity for America*. Policy Brief 13-6. Washington: Peterson Institute for International Economics.

Sundaram, Asha, and J. David Richardson. 2013. *Peers and Tiers and US High-Tech Export Controls: A New Approach to Estimating Export Shortfalls*. Working Paper Series WP13-5. Washington: Peterson Institute for International Economics.

IV

THE INVESTMENT CLUSTER

13

Foreign Direct Investment

This chapter begins with a warning. Unlike in chapter 2, which offers forecasts showing the effects of liberalization on trade flows, we cannot predict with any confidence the trajectory of two-way foreign direct investment (FDI) following a major reduction of policy barriers, nor can we quantify the benefits to the United States and China from increased two-way FDI. For reasons spelled out below, we believe that two-way FDI would expand significantly under a China–US trade and investment agreement (CHUSTIA) or a variant arrangement, and the benefits for both countries would be substantial. But readers who are looking for quantitative projections will be disappointed. After a short survey of the available statistics, and some crystal ball gazing into 2020, we delve into the regulatory barriers that obstruct direct investment and that a CHUSTIA should address.

US Direct Investment in China

US direct investment in China remains abnormally small, despite the huge volume of bilateral trade in goods and services. A walk through the numbers establishes this core proposition. China publishes global figures on the stock of inward direct investment, shown in table 13.1. It does not publish a breakdown by country of origin, but the total inward stock was $2.16 trillion at the end of 2012. The US Bureau of Economic Analysis (BEA) publishes US figures on outward direct investment in China, also shown in table 13.1. At the end of 2012, the United States accounted for $51 billion of FDI in China, about 2 percent of the total. By any measure, this is pretty modest. For comparison, at the end of 2012, the EU-27 accounted for $159 billion of FDI stock in China (according to Eurostat)—not a huge amount, but at 5 percent of China's

Table 13.1 Chinese inward FDI stock, 2008–12

(billions of US dollars)

	Total	United States	European Union[a]
2008	916	54	74
2009	1,315	54	86
2010	1,570	59	109
2011	1,907	55	139
2012	2,160	51	159

FDI = foreign direct investment

a. Converted from euros at a rate of 1 euro = 1.35 US dollars.

Sources: US Bureau of Economic Analysis, "Direct Investment and Multinational Companies"; Eurostat, "EU Direct Investment Outward Stocks"; Chinese State Administration of Foreign Exchange.

total inward stock, about three times the US share. Table 13.2 further illustrates the deficiency by contrasting the US FDI picture between Latin America and China. China produces roughly twice the GDP of Latin America, while the United States has somewhat more two-way trade with Latin American (the main difference is on the US export side). But the US FDI stock in Latin America, at $284 billion at the end of 2012, was almost five times as large as the US FDI stock in China.

The paradox of inward Chinese FDI is that China is commonly reported to impose high barriers on foreign investment in many sectors, yet it ranked first for inward FDI flows in both 2012 and 2013.[1] Is China really that restrictive? And what are the trends? Is China becoming more restrictive? Unfortunately few metrics provide definitive answers.

The World Bank's *Doing Business* report measures business regulations and their enforcement for most of the world's economies using 10 indicators, combining them to measure the overall ease of doing business.[2] In 2014 China ranked 96th out of 189 economies, improved slightly from a rank of 99 in 2013, the first year the World Bank assigned China an overall grade. By comparison, the United States ranked 4th, behind only Singapore, Hong Kong, and New Zealand. Two of the categories for China that fell from 2013 to 2014 were starting a business (from 153rd to 158th) and protecting investors (from

---

1. According to China's State Administration of Foreign Exchange (SAFE), China's net FDI inflows in 2012 were $253 billion, while the United States had inflows of $166 billion, according to the BEA.

2. The World Bank's *Doing Business* report can be found at www.doingbusiness.org (accessed on June 25, 2014).

Table 13.2 Two-way FDI stock and trade flows between the United States and selected partners, 2012 (billions of US dollars)

		Latin America	China
United States	Outward FDI stock to	284.0	51.4
	Inward FDI stock from	25.7	5.1
	Exports to	466	142
	Imports from	480	439
	Population (millions)	573	1,351
	GDP	5,615	8,227

FDI = foreign direct investment

Notes: Latin America includes South and Central America. Trade data include goods and services.

Sources: Bureau of Economic Analysis, www.bea.gov (accessed on July 4, 2014); World Bank, World Development Indicators (2014), data.worldbank.org (accessed on July 4, 2014).

95th to 98th). China also scored low in dealing with construction permits and paying taxes.[3]

The US–China Business Council's (USCBC) report on China's business environment polls US firms operating in China. One of the top concerns for 2013 and the seven previous years was administrative licensing, referring to the wide range of licenses and government approvals required to do business in China. The top types of licensing problems were product approval delays, operation expansion delays, foreign investment delays, and business license delays. Firms listed uneven enforcement or implementation of Chinese laws and regulations and nondiscrimination and national treatment near the top of their concerns, signifying that foreign firms still feel that they are treated unfairly compared with domestic Chinese competitors. Further, the USCBC listed foreign investment restrictions as one of the main challenges to investing in China, noting that China's Foreign Investment Catalogue restricts foreign ownership in nearly 100 manufacturing and service sector categories.[4] All things considered, it appears that the huge size and rapid growth of the Chinese market explains the paradox of very large inward FDI flows in the face of Chinese investment restrictions.

---

3. China disputes the rankings and calls them biased. An independent panel hired by the World Bank found that the report can be misinterpreted and relies on a narrow base of information. The panel also found that the use of aggregate rankings was problematic, and suggested several areas where the report could be improved.

4. US–China Business Council, "China Business Environment," October 8, 2013, www.uschina.org (accessed on June 25, 2014).

Chinese Direct Investment in the United States

Chinese direct investment in the United States seems fairly normal, after correcting statistical confusion. The starting point in sorting out the confusion is that official figures from US and Chinese sources differ greatly (see table 13.3). According to official BEA data, Chinese FDI stock in the United States was a trivial $5 billion at the end of 2012. No one believes this number, and official Chinese figures are widely regarded as superior for counting Chinese outward FDI stock placed in the United States. According to the Chinese Ministry of Commerce (MOFCOM), the stock figure was $17 billion at the end of 2012.

While Chinese official figures are better than US figures, both sources suffer a common defect: Chinese direct investment in the United States is sometimes routed through third countries with tax and other advantages. Hong Kong is the favorite; Luxembourg and Mauritius are minor alternatives. But such investments are counted as if they came from the intermediate country. Private sources attempt to correct for this defect. Probably the best is the Rhodium Group,[5] which pegs the Chinese FDI stock in the United States at $36 billion at the end of 2013, reflecting major acquisitions during the year—foremost, the acquisition by Shuanghui International Holdings of Smithfield Foods for $7.1 billion (equity and assumed debt).

According to MOFCOM figures, China's global outward FDI at the end of 2012 was about $530 billion, but Rhodium's analysis of mirror data from partner countries, collected by the International Monetary Fund (IMF), suggests that the MOFCOM figure may understate the stock by $90 billion. If we add another $80 billion for outward flows in 2013, the global figure at the end of 2013 might have reached $700 billion. On this reckoning, using the Rhodium figure of $36 billion, Chinese FDI in the United States is 5 percent of the Chinese outward FDI stock.

How does the percentage compare with other emerging countries? Combining BEA data on US inward FDI with *World Investment Report* data on outward FDI, we calculate that major emerging countries, excluding China, have placed in the aggregate about 4 percent of their outward FDI stocks in the United States.[6] BEA data on inward FDI from these other emerging countries may share similar if not so extreme undercounting defects as BEA data on inward FDI from China. Even allowing for that possibility, it appears that inward FDI from China, following surges in the past few years, is not abnormally low. A report from April 2014 by the Rhodium Group and the US Chamber of Commerce shines light on data showing that Chinese FDI flows into the United States exceeded US FDI flows into China for 2012, with the

---

5. The Rhodium Group's China Investment Monitor is available at rhg.com (accessed on June 25, 2014).

6. The countries covered by this calculation are Brazil, India, Malaysia, Mexico, South Africa, Taiwan, and Venezuela.

Table 13.3 Chinese outward FDI stock in the United States, 2008–13

(billions of US dollars)

	Chinese Ministry of Commerce	US Bureau of Economic Analysis	Rhodium Group
2008	2.4	1.1	3.6
2009	3.3	1.6	5.3
2010	4.9	3.3	9.9
2011	9.0	3.7	14.8
2012	17.1	5.2	21.9
2013	n.a.	n.a.	35.9

FDI = foreign direct investment; n.a. = not available

Sources: Chinese Ministry of Commerce, Statistical Yearbook; US Bureau of Economic Analysis, "Foreign Direct Investment in the United States" (FDIUS); Rhodium Group, China Investment Monitor, rhg.com (accessed on July 15, 2014).

trend most likely continuing in 2013.[7] This is a huge change and reflects the importance of nourishing this behavior, ensuring a continuation of increasing bilateral FDI flow.

Industry Composition of FDI

US outward FDI stocks in China are concentrated in manufacturing: Some 61 percent of the $51 billion total represents manufacturing investment, and only 21 percent represents services. The composition of US FDI in China is very different from the overall composition of US outward FDI: Some 73 percent of FDI in the world is invested in services, and only 14 percent in manufactures. Of course China is renowned for its manufacturing prowess, but the difference reflects, in part, Chinese barriers to investment in key service sectors.

Chinese outward FDI stocks in the United States are concentrated in energy, manufacturing, and foodstuffs, reflecting both Chinese industrial strengths and its hunger for natural resources. Only 19 percent represents investment in services, counting Lenovo and other information technology as principally hardware (Hanemann, forthcoming). This is very different from the composition of most inward FDI in the United States: About 45 percent is invested in services.

---

7. Dan Rosen and Thilo Hanemann, "New Realities in the US–China Investment Relationship," Rhodium Group, April 2014, rhg.com (accessed on June 25, 2014).

Direct Investment Negotiating Goals

Improving pathways for two-way US–China FDI will be a leading rationale and key goal, both for the bilateral investment treaty (BIT) now being negotiated, and later, with enhancements, for a CHUSTIA. Expanded two-way direct investment will foster stronger economic ties between the United States and China. Global supply chains depend on direct investment to link their geographically dispersed sites. Likewise, to provide business services abroad, a firm must establish an operation abroad—a bank, a medical center, an engineering consultancy. Direct investment through mergers and acquisitions (M&As) enables the purchase of cutting-edge technology, whether in meat processing or computer software. Equally important, through direct investment multinational corporations can earn better returns by applying their costly proprietary knowledge in more markets around the world. This possibility serves as a spur to research and development (R&D) and global innovation.

Crystal Ball Gazing

There are good reasons why two-way FDI is not larger. Foremost are the geographic and cultural distances between the United States and China. To illustrate these effects, the Moran-Oldenski (2013) gravity model finds a logarithmic coefficient of –0.62 for the negative effect of distance on the size of sales associated with inward FDI in the United States. This means that sales by foreign firms from their US establishments decline by 6.2 percent for every 10 percent increase in distance between the FDI home country and the United States. The same calculations find a coefficient of 0.94 on a dummy variable (0 or 1) indicating whether or not the foreign country uses English as its official language. This finding implies that, all other things being equal, FDI-related sales from a country such as China, which does not use English, would be only 64 percent of the size of sales from a country such as Australia, which does use English.

Besides such relatively natural barriers, additional reasons for the limited two-way stock of FDI are intentional and unintentional policy barriers on the parts of both countries. Among the objectives of the BIT and CHUSTIA are to reduce if not eliminate these policy barriers. The potential is huge. Daniel H. Rosen and Thilo Hanemann (2011) foresee global Chinese outward FDI flow reaching $100 to $200 billion annually over the next ten years.[8] If Chinese FDI in the United States rises to 8 percent of a $150 billion global outflow figure, that would imply a flow of $12 billion annually to the United States and a cumulated stock of $122 billion by 2020, more than three times the Rhodium Group's estimate of the 2013 level ($36 billion).[9]

---

8. He and colleagues (2012, appendix 3) project a very large Chinese outward FDI stock in 2020 ($5 trillion), assuming full capital account liberalization by China. This seems unlikely.

9. See the Rhodium Group's China Investment Monitor.

Meanwhile, if Chinese inward FDI continues to expand at $250 billion annually, the total inward stock will reach nearly $4 trillion by 2020. If the US share of the FDI stock in China doubles to 4 percent, owing to more liberal conditions, US FDI could reach $160 billion, more than three times the present level. With these magnitudes at stake, it is worth putting a lot of effort into reducing policy barriers.

Services Trade Restrictiveness Index

The World Bank's Services Trade Restrictiveness Index (STRI) is one of the better quantitative guides to direct investment barriers—mode 3 trade, in the parlance of the General Agreement on Trade in Services (GATS). In May 2014, the Organization for Economic Cooperation and Development (OECD) published its own set of service barrier indexes, compiled over a period of seven years. Table 13.4 shows the values, by service industry, of the World Bank's STRI for the United States and China. Overall, the simple average index value for China is more than twice as high as the US index value (40 versus 18). Similarly the OECD's index showed that China had generally more restrictive investment barriers for many more sectors in the service industry than the 40 economies they analyzed. According to the World Bank's STRI values, China is particularly restrictive relative to the United States toward inward FDI in telecommunications and retail trade. With this quantitative overview, we turn now to qualitative descriptions of the most salient US and Chinese policy barriers.

US Policy Barriers

US policy barriers to inward FDI can be divided into two categories. In the first category, certain industries and sectors are either entirely off limits to foreign ownership, or reservations are preserved with respect to national treatment, most favored nation (MFN) treatment, local presence, performance requirements, or management. Such industries are scheduled in US free trade agreements (FTAs) with reference to the US federal or state statutes that act as barriers to inward FDI. US reservations in the US–Singapore FTA are set forth in annexes 8A and 8B and summarized in box 13.1; Singapore has similar reservations. Notable US reservations limit market access in transportation, radio communications, cable television, and natural resources. Several of the reserved sectors or industries may be of interest to European investors, and thus a subject of Transatlantic Trade and Investment Partnership (TTIP) negotiations. Others may be of interest to Chinese investors, such as Huawei or ZTE.

US policy barriers in the second category are more troublesome to Chinese commentators. These are the discretionary barriers that spring either from political objections—as perceived in Chinese eyes—to M&As aimed at US firms, or from objections raised by the Committee on Foreign Investment in the United

Table 13.4   STRI mode 3 values for the United States and China

	United States	China
Financial	25.00	31.46
Telecommunications	0	50.00
Retail	0	25.00
Transportation	16.67	22.22
Professional	50.00	70.00
Simple average	18.33	39.74

STRI = Services Trade Restrictiveness Index

Source: World Bank STRI database, iresearch.worldbank.org (accessed on July 4, 2014).

States (CFIUS). The concept of political objections can have various meanings, including regulatory objections, but even in the face of such objections investments can move forward. When Coca-Cola Co. attempted to acquire Huiyuan, there was lively opposition in the Chinese press, but Coca-Cola pursued acquisition anyway. Possibly influenced by the public uproar in China, MOFCOM finally rejected the bid.

In the United States, the only way a transaction can be blocked is by a CFIUS finding, affirmed by the president, that the transaction raises national security concerns. US experts are quick to note that the president has explicitly rejected only two proposed acquisitions following a CFIUS review. However, a substantial number of cases have been subject to investigation (129 out of 562 cases filed between 2008 and 2012) and a number of the proposed acquisitions have been withdrawn (86 out of the 562 cases; see CFIUS 2010 and 2012). In any event, the low number of explicit rejections does not comfort Chinese commentators, nor do they persuade Chinese officials that the US door is open to Chinese FDI. The reason is that several high-profile M&A attempts that Chinese firms launched, summarized in box 13.2, have run aground on congressional shoals or CFIUS reviews in the past decade. Knowledgeable Chinese commentators claim that this record amounts to discrimination against China, especially when compared to the investment welcome the United States extends to Europe or Canada. But this has not deterred Chinese firms too much, as the number of notices Chinese firms filed to CFIUS has risen. From 2007 to 2009, Chinese firms filed 13 notices. This number rose to 39 from 2010 to 2012, with 23 of those in 2012 alone. Comparatively, the United Kingdom filed 68 notices for the period 2010–12, the most of any country, followed by France with 31 and Canada with 28. A notice filed to CFIUS does not mean the committee will investigate the deal; in 2012 fewer than half of the filed notices went to investigation (CFIUS 2012).

Box 13.1   US restrictions on investment in the US-Singapore FTA

	Acquisition or merger can be blocked for national security reasons
Limitations on foreign ownership/market access	Transportation: - Voting interest in US air carriers limited to 25 percent - Control of the board of a US air carrier limited to one-third Communications: - Foreign governments may not hold radio broadcast licenses - Ownership of corporations with broadcast licences capped at 20 percent - Ownership of parent companies of said firms capped at 20 percent Natural resources and energy: - Entities that are controlled by foreign interests may not control nuclear facilities - Foreign involvement in nuclear production, utilization, or enrichment requires additional evaluation - Foreign direct ownership of US mineral deposits is forbidden - Foreigners can directly control a US firm that owns such deposits - Foreign direct ownership of deepwater drilling restricted
National treatment	Excludes the following sectors: - Atomic energy - Cross-border services of certain technology and software - Oil and gas pipelines - Certain mineral resources - Domestic air transport and specialty air services - Customs brokers - Radio communications
Local presence requirements	- Applications for a certificate of review require a domestic presence. - Applications for a license from the US Bureau of Industry and Security may be made only by a person in the United States

Source: United States–Singapore Free Trade Agreement, 2003, ustr.gov (accessed on July 6, 2014).

Nothing written in a BIT or FTA can foreclose congressional objections to future acquisitions by Chinese firms or any other foreign country. The US Congress consists of 435 representatives and 100 senators, and each one enjoys constitutional rights both to voice opposition to takeover attempts and to introduce blocking legislation. But blocking legislation is unlikely in many cases, including the Shuanghui takeover of Smithfield Foods, which CFIUS vetted favorably in 2013.[10] The US Senate held a hearing on the Smithfield takeover in July 2013 and, according to a trade press report, all of the committee members appeared dubious or worse about the takeover. Senator Mike Johanns (R-NB) remarked that, despite all of the objections, "there isn't really a

---

10. CFIUS cleared Shuanghui to purchase Smithfield in September 2013. See Shruti Singh and Bradley Olsen, "Smithfield Receives US Approval for Biggest Chinese Takeover," *Bloomberg*, September 6, 2013, www.bloomberg.com (accessed on June 6, 2014).

Box 13.2 Selected cases of failed foreign M&A bids in the United States, 1987–2012

Name	Date	Foreign country	Reason for rejection or modification	Outcome
Ralls Corporation acquisition of four wind farm project companies	2012	China	National security threat: concern regarding the proximity of the proposed windfarms to US naval weapons systems training facility airspace	Blocked by presidential executive order
Huawei Technologies Company acquisition of specific assets of 3Leaf Systems	2011	China	Ties to China's People's Liberation Army, potential leakage of sensitive cybertechnologies	Bid withdrawn
Tangshan Caofeidian Investment Corporation acquisition of Emcore	2010	China	National security threat: undisclosed regulatory concerns	Bid withdrawn
Angang Steel company acquisition of stake in Steel Development Company	2010	China	Political backlash based on national security concerns: ties to China's Asset Supervision Commission of the State Council, access to key US technologies and information on national security infrastructure projects	Bid withdrawn
Northwest Nonferrous International Investment Corporation acquisition of Firstgold	2009	China	National security threat: concern that Firstgold had properties near US military bases	Bid withdrawn
Check Point Software Technologies acquisition of Sourcefire	2006	Israel	National security concerns related to security software used by the US government	Bid withdrawn
Dubai Ports World acquisition of the Peninsular and Oriental Steam Navigation Company	2005	United Arab Emirates	National security concerns related to terrorist activity, government ownership, and the control of critical US infrastructure	Dubai Ports World agreed to sell its US port facilities
CNOOC acquisition of Unocal	2005	China	Concerns that Unocal's energy supplies could be diverted to meet Chinese needs	Bid withdrawn
Thomson acquisition of LTV Corporation's missile and aerospace divisions	1992	France	National security concerns related to the transfer of sensitive US defense technology	Bid withdrawn
China National Aero-Technology Import and Export Corporation acquisition of MAMCO Manufacturing	1990	China	National security threat: concerns that CATIC could gain access to technology that it would otherwise have to obtain under an export license	Presidential executive order to Chinese company to divest its new acquisition

(continues on next page)

legal mechanism in place that really reviews this much or that could likely stop it."[11] At least in principle, a BIT or FTA could modify the procedures CFIUS followed in its review of M&As by foreign firms. But this is highly unlikely, not least because, as a quid pro quo, China would have to put its own national security review procedures on the table for modification. With those realities in mind, it is worth delving briefly into the history of CFIUS.

CFIUS in Brief[12]

An interagency committee led by the Treasury, CFIUS was established by executive order in 1975 to vet foreign acquisitions of US companies.[13] Its creation was sparked by public fears that Middle East oil kingdoms would acquire vast US real estate assets following the first oil shock. Those fears were enormously exaggerated,[14] but CFIUS thereafter became a public watchdog, designed to bark if foreign acquisitions threatened US interests.

In 1988 Congress gave CFIUS a statutory basis and legal bite, prompted by the proposed sale of a US company, Fairchild Semiconductor, by Schlumberger

---

11. Daniel Ryntjes, "Shuanghui-Smithfield Deal: CEO Reassures Sceptical US Public," CCTV, July 11, 2013, english.cntv.cn (accessed on July 9, 2014). Senator Johanns stated that the only other way to stop the transaction, apart from an adverse CFIUS review on national security grounds, would be to pass legislation barring the takeover, but he saw no possibility of this happening.

12. This snapshot draws heavily on Moran (2009) and Moran and Oldenski (2013).

13. CFIUS procedures, executive orders, and regulations can be found at US Department of the Treasury, Resource Center, "The Committee on Foreign Investment in the United States (CFIUS)," www.treasury.gov (accessed on June 6, 2014).

14. Saudi Arabia and other Middle East oil kingdoms used their oil revenues to acquire treasury securities and other portfolio assets, but not much real estate and very few operating companies.

of France to Fujitsu of Japan in 1987. Two prominent cabinet secretaries opposed the sale on national security grounds.[15] At the time, President Ronald Reagan had no authority to block the sale, but Fujitsu withdrew its bid and Fairchild was acquired by National Semiconductor, an American firm. Shortly after, Congress passed the Exon-Florio Amendment to the Omnibus Trade Act of 1988, giving the president power to block acquisitions in the interests of national security. In turn, the president delegated investigatory authority to CFIUS.

The CFIUS process was subject to fresh congressional legislation in 2007 following the attempted takeover, in October 2005, by Dubai Ports World of the Peninsular and Oriental Steam Navigation Company (P&O), a British firm that owned ports in 14 countries including the United States. CFIUS rather quickly approved the takeover in November 2005, setting off a congressional storm. The House Appropriations Committee voted 62 to 2 against the takeover, and Dubai Ports World, controlled by the emir of Dubai, withdrew its bid in March 2006.

Over the next year, Congress debated changes in the Exon-Florio Amendment of 1988. The Foreign Investment and National Security Act (FINSA) of 2007 extended the definition of national security to include potential adverse effects resulting from acquisitions resulting in direct or indirect control by a foreign government, acquisitions leading to the leakage of military goods or equipment or technology to a foreign country, or acquisitions leading to foreign control of crucial infrastructure. The first situation identified in the FINSA has been interpreted to mean that CFIUS must review all acquisitions by a state-owned enterprise (SOE). Professor Theodore Moran, the leading academic analyst of the CFIUS process, has interpreted FINSA to distinguish the particular adverse effects, under these three headings, that should lead to outright rejection of an M&A attempt, or an appropriate mitigation agreement (Moran 2009). But CFIUS's focus remains on national security. Unlike foreign investment review statutes and practices in many other countries, FINSA did not insert an economic interest test into the CFIUS review process.

CFIUS regulations, issued in 2008 pursuant to the FINSA statute, require any acquisition by a foreign government–controlled entity to be reviewed, even if the entity operates purely in accordance with commercial considerations. While private foreign firms are not required to submit their intended acquisitions for CFIUS review, they generally do for good reasons: first, the CFIUS review somewhat insulates the M&A bid from congressional politics; second, in the absence of a review, the president can subsequently order divestment. Following its review, the CFIUS reports negative recommendations to the president within a short period (normally 30 days, but in controversial cases this can

---

15. Defense Secretary Casper Weinberger and Commerce Secretary Malcolm Baldridge, both prominent members of the Reagan cabinet.

stretch to 90 days or longer). In the final analysis, only the president can block a transaction or compel a mitigation agreement.

Blocked Transactions

Box 13.2 sketches prominent foreign M&A bids since 1987 blocked either by congressional opposition or by negative CFIUS reviews. In the 1980s and 1990s Japanese takeovers were the center of attention; in the 2000s Chinese takeovers gained prominence. In two leading cases cited by Chinese critics of US investment policy, political or legal obstacles deterred Chinese firms. In 2005 China National Offshore Oil Corporation (CNOOC), an oil giant and SOE, tried to buy Unocal, a medium-sized US oil firm. The proposed acquisition triggered a congressional uproar and CNOOC dropped out of the bidding well before the CFIUS review. In 2003 Huawei, a privately owned Chinese telecommunications firm with retired military officers in senior positions, formed a joint venture with the US firm 3Com (called H3C), which in turn was purchased by 3Com in 2006. In 2008 Huawei then tried to acquire 3Com from Bain & Company, but CFIUS blocked the merger. Similarly, in 2011 Huawei withdrew its purchase of 3Leaf systems following another negative CFIUS review. However, Chinese firms are increasingly undeterred by episodes of political opposition, as evidenced by the recent Smithfield transaction, Wanxiang's acquisition of A123 Systems, and BGI-Shenzhen's acquisition of California-based Genome. Even CNOOC secured CFIUS approval for the purchase of the Canadian firm Nexen, which had assets in the United States, after CNOOC gave up operating control of its oil rigs in the Gulf of Mexico.

Chinese Aspirations

Chinese critics of the CFIUS process would like a BIT or FTA to accomplish two things: first, ensure greater transparency so that Chinese firms, especially SOEs, better understand the decision criteria in a CFIUS review; and second, apply the same criteria to a Chinese takeover, even by an SOE, that would be applied to a British takeover—in other words, MFN treatment.

Regarding transparency, under present procedures, an experienced lawyer handling a CFIUS review will quickly come to know any objections the committee raises. These objections will often become apparent in the terms of a proposed mitigation agreement. As partial satisfaction to China, a BIT or FTA might call for CFIUS to furnish a written mitigation proposal to the acquiring Chinese firm within a certain number of days of the Chinese firm supplying all the information CFIUS requests. Moreover, with respect to infrastructure, M&As, or greenfield investment, CFIUS might issue its opinion before the Chinese firm satisfies all the local, state, and federal permitting requirements. But it is hard to envisage BIT or FTA language that would require Congress to narrow FINSA legislation with respect to the scope of a national security review.

Regarding MFN status, neither Congress nor CFIUS has treated all foreign countries equally. This was evident in 1987 when two cabinet secretaries objected to the sale of Fairchild, already owned by a French company, to a Japanese firm. The same element of discrimination surfaced in 2006 when Congress loudly objected to the takeover by Dubai World Ports of P&O, a British firm. Quite possibly CFIUS would have approved the proposed takeovers of 3Com and 3Leaf if the acquiring firm were British Telecom rather than Huawei. Most recently, in reviewing CNOOC's takeover of Nexen, a Canadian oil company with minor US operations, CFIUS has insisted that CNOOC have no control of drilling activity in the Gulf of Mexico (though CNOOC can receive the revenue stream). As everyone knows, British Petroleum (BP) has long carried out extensive drilling operations in the Gulf.

The discrimination these episodes illustrate—between British and Canadian companies on the one hand and Chinese companies on the other—underscores the absence of mutual trust, to use a phrase Chinese commentators often voice. But it is hard to envisage the MFN principle operating nearly to the same extent in the realm of national security as it does in the realm of commercial policy. For national security purposes, China and the United States both categorize foreign powers as allies, friends, adversaries, or enemies. Gradually since 1950, relations between the United States and China have become more cordial, but the two countries are not allies. Some of the US agencies involved in CFIUS are the same agencies concerned with cyber-enabled economic espionage and China's assertive military posture in the Asia-Pacific region.[16]

Realistically, what can be hoped is that CFIUS reviews sharply distinguish between genuine national security threats and exaggerated or imagined threats, following the template outlined in Moran (2009). Moran identifies three situations in which foreign M&As could genuinely threaten US national security. The first is the critical supply case: foreign acquisition of a US firm in a concentrated industry that could enable the denial of crucial products to the US economy. The second is the technology leakage case: foreign acquisition of a US firm that possesses key technology or management expertise, which could enable the foreign country to acquire the valuable know-how. The third is the infiltration, surveillance, or sabotage case: foreign acquisition of network systems (such as telecommunications or ports) that could enable a foreign government to spy on or sabotage the US economy. Even when foreign acquisition poses one or more of these threats, Moran outlines operating procedures that can protect US national security interests.[17] Perhaps helpful in the context of the CHUSTIA would be a CFIUS policy statement that, in broad terms, subscribes

---

16. Particular agencies include the State and Defense Departments, as well as the Central Intelligence Agency.

17. Examples would include an agreement that the entire management or certain positions be filled by Americans, or a "Chinese wall" that insulates certain operations from the foreign parent company.

to the Moran template and illustrates examples of unacceptable threats and threats that appropriate operating procedures can mitigate.

Chinese Investment in US Infrastructure

Enormous opportunities await Chinese firms in US infrastructure, according to the US Chamber of Commerce (2013).[18] The report estimates that over $8 trillion will need to be invested in US transportation, energy, and water infrastructure over the next 17 years. There are many avenues for foreign firms to participate, including equity and debt financing and supplying the goods or services. Equity investment can take the form of acquiring an existing US firm or building infrastructure from the ground up (greenfield). Debt finance can take the form of bank loans or corporate bonds. The sale of construction materials and the provision of construction management are additional avenues. However, until China signs the World Trade Organization (WTO) Government Procurement Agreement (GPA), Chinese participation in US infrastructure will be limited.[19]

For public infrastructure, a foreign firm can participate in project design, construction, operation, maintenance, or finance. Public agencies may also contract with private firms in public-private partnerships (PPPs), which can include anything from procurement and financing to completing all aspects of design and construction. PPPs are becoming more popular, although they usually require broad public approval as well as assent from the relevant federal or state agencies. Some 33 states have enacted legislation permitting PPP transportation projects and, as of September 2013, private firms were looking at approximately $34 billion of projects in energy, transport, and water.

Infrastructure investments offer relatively safe long-term returns. So far, most Chinese investments have been in the energy sector, acquiring stakes in US firms. China Investment Corporation (CIC), one of China's sovereign wealth funds, purchased 15 percent of the US power company AES, and China Huaneng Group invested $1.2 billion in US utility InterGen for a 50 percent stake. Energy might be the strongest magnet for Chinese future investments, with an estimated $4.6 trillion needed up to the year 2030. Another attractive area will be transportation projects, estimated to need $3.0 trillion over the same time frame.

But Chinese investors face real difficulties. Besides national security issues, Chinese firms may encounter adverse public reactions as well as legal hurdles. Apart from a CFIUS review, foreign firms that purchase more than a 10 percent stake in energy companies must get approval from the Federal Energy

---

18. Data cited in this section are from the US Chamber of Commerce report.

19. To be accepted as a signatory by other GPA members, China will need to schedule procurement by several SOEs, as well as provincial and central government agencies. Negotiations to this effect are ongoing. *Inside US Trade*, "New China GPA Offer Adds Provinces, Services; But Still Falls Short," January 10, 2014.

Regulatory Commission (FERC). An array of agencies covers the transportation field: the Federal Aviation Administration (FAA) for airports, the Surface Transportation Board (STB) and the Federal Railroad Administration (FRA) for railways and public transit, and the Federal Highway Administration (FHWA) for roadways. The Environmental Protection Agency (EPA) must approve water-related infrastructure investments. In addition, state agencies review most forms of infrastructure investment. As mentioned above, one improvement that might be agreed in a CHUSTIA is to put the CFIUS review ahead of the various federal and state permitting regimes.

Chinese Policy Barriers

Chinese policies toward inward FDI range from the warmest welcome to the coldest rejection. In the late 1980s and throughout the 1990s, the Chinese welcome mat was prominent: free land in industrial zones and zero or low corporate taxes. By 1993 China became the second-largest destination for FDI inflows after the United States. In the first half of 2012 China surpassed the United States as the largest recipient of FDI inflows.[20] Foreign investment in China has concentrated in the manufacturing sector, partly due to the more restrictive policies for FDI in services. Most investment has been in light and textile industries, furniture, electronics, chemicals, machinery, and transport equipment. This trend could be ending, as manufacturing currently accounts for around 40 percent of FDI inflows and services account for around half.[21] In the 2000s, China adopted selective policies, and today many firms regard China as a tough place to invest. Here we survey policies that will feature in bilateral negotiations, whether in current BIT talks or in future FTA talks.[22]

The umbrella for Chinese economic policies is China's current five-year plan, and the most recent was issued in 2011. Like its predecessor, the 12th five-year plan calls for foreign firms to bring advanced technology to China and to be mindful of the environment and energy efficiency. The plan encourages the development of domestic strategic emerging industries, which are, in theory, open to foreign investment.[23] However, in practice favorable tax

---

20. In terms of inward FDI stock, China ranks seventh in the world, after the United States, United Kingdom, Hong Kong, France, Belgium, and Germany. Statistics from the United Nations Conference on Trade and Development (UNCTAD) FDI database, unctad.org (accessed on July 9, 2014).

21. Statistics from MOFCOM's 2013 database on foreign investment, english.mofcom.gov.cn (accessed on July 9, 2014).

22. This description draws heavily on US Chamber of Commerce, "Doing Business in China: 2012 Country Commercial Guide for US Companies," chapter 6, export.gov (accessed on June 7, 2014).

23. China designated the following strategic emerging industries in its latest five-year plan: energy-efficient and environmental technology, next generation information technology, biotechnology, high-end equipment manufacturing, new energy, new materials, and new energy vehicles (USCBC

treatment and government financing as well as government procurement policies give domestic firms an advantage in these industries (see chapter 14).

Policy guidance immediately under the five-year plan comes in *China's Catalogue Guiding Foreign Investment in Industry*; the latest edition was issued in January 2012. The catalogue classifies sectors among those where foreign investment is encouraged, restricted, or prohibited. Restricted and prohibited are sectors with a national security flavor and sectors of low priority for China's national development.[24] In some restricted sectors, foreign investment is permitted, but with less than 50 percent ownership in a joint venture. In a sense, the catalogue is the Chinese counterpart to restrictions scheduled in US FTAs, but without the same precision. But there are very significant differences between the two approaches. In its FTAs, the United States schedules a negative list, in which foreign investments are precluded. In its catalogue, China's description of fields in which foreign investment is encouraged, restricted, or prohibited is rather loose, as Chinese regulators may block investments even on the encouraged list.

Mechanics of China's FDI Approval Process

China's FDI approval processes are complicated and the screening criteria reflect both national security and economic interest considerations (US-Chamber of Commerce 2012).[25] China is the polar opposite of the one-stop-shopping many emerging countries advertise. The flood of FDI into China, despite the bureaucratic hurdles, speaks to the profitability of doing business there.[26] Securing an approval provides remunerative work for knowledgeable lawyers and other facilitators.[27]

The FDI approval path differs somewhat for a joint venture, a wholly foreign-owned enterprise, and a strategic portfolio interest (at least 10 percent of shares) in a publicly traded Chinese company. There are also slightly different paths for service industries scheduled by China in the GATS, and for adding new branches to an existing service enterprise. The general approval process has seven steps; variants have about the same number. The key players

---

2012). USCBC, "China's Strategic Emerging Industries: Policy, Implementation, Challenges, and Recommendations," March 2013, uschina.org (accessed on June 25, 2014).

24. See Baker and McKenzie's "Security Review Industry Table," unofficial translation of several local commerce departments' security review industry tables, www.bmhk.com (accessed on June 7, 2014).

25. This section draws heavily on US Chamber of Commerce (2012).

26. According to a survey conducted by the US–China Business Council, in 2012 some 89 percent of US firms doing business in China reported that their operations were profitable and 75 percent said that operations in China were either the same as or more profitable than their overall operations. See USCBC (2012).

27. For those interested in details, we recommend the roadmap published by the US Chamber of Commerce (2013). Here we sketch the players and the process.

are the State Council, the National Development and Reform Commission (NDRC), and MOFCOM. In regulated services, such as legal services, banking, securities, and education, industry regulators are also key players.

The NDRC is the central agency charged with implementing the foreign investment catalogue, often in conjunction with provincial or local development and reform commissions (DRCs).[28] At the central level, the NDRC conducts an interagency review for both greenfield and M&A investments, with representation from the line ministries with industrial policy objectives. When it wishes, the State Council (China's cabinet) can override the NDRC or speed up an application. The State Council plays a decisive role when an M&A proposal raises national security issues;[29] however, in the normal course of events, the NDRC and the DRCs are where foreign investors face their first bureaucratic hurdles. Reflecting Chinese priorities, some projects are fast-tracked while others are sidetracked.

Once NDRC approval is granted, the investor then applies to MOFCOM to establish a company; at the same time an application is often made to the provincial or local department of commerce. At MOFCOM a second review takes place to ensure that the project does not infringe on the Anti-Monopoly Law (in the case of M&A transactions) or impair national security. The security review, conducted jointly by the NDRC and MOFCOM, considers not only national security as commonly understood but also national economic security and social order. A green light from MOFCOM enables the investor to obtain a business license from the State Administration for Industry and Commerce (SAIC) and register with tax and foreign exchange authorities.

As of December 2011 MOFCOM had reviewed 250 M&A transactions and had approved 97 percent of them unconditionally.[30] This seems like a high approval rate, only modestly lower than CFIUS's official record. However, the comparison is of apples to oranges, as MOFCOM's review is for antimonopoly purposes whereas CFIUS's review pertains to national security. The Chinese system may have rejected other transactions on national security grounds without entering the MOFCOM count. The opaque nature of the Chinese approval process makes it difficult to identify rejected M&A bids or greenfield investment projects. Indirect evidence suggests that a considerable amount of potential foreign investment is discouraged. For 2011 the USCBC (2012) found that 17 percent of US firms reduced or stopped their planned investments in China; for half of these firms the reason was market access restrictions.

---

28. Anecdotal and survey reports often comment on the difficulty of obtaining approvals from DRCs. See USCBC (2012).

29. National security screening is carried out pursuant to a State Council notice regarding the establishment of a security review mechanism for foreign investors acquiring domestic enterprises. The US Chamber of Commerce observes that the criteria and procedures for a review under this notice are unclear.

30. Bureau of Economic and Business Affairs, "2012 Investment Climate Statement—China," US Department of State, www.state.gov (accessed on June 8, 2014).

Moreover, 85 percent of firms had seen no improvement from China's pledge, made in 2011, to delink indigenous innovation requirements from government procurement decisions. China's pressure to transfer technology as the quid pro quo for investment access seems to be the most onerous performance requirement that foreign firms face.

Comments offered by the US Chamber of Commerce on the interim provisions of the MOFCOM security review of M&A transactions illuminates the difficulties foreign firms face when they try to acquire a Chinese firm (US Chamber of Commerce 2012). The timeline of the security review process is unknown. There are no defined start or end dates in cases where the file is forwarded to the State Council. Companies are in the dark whether they should navigate, within the MOFCOM bureaucracy, the Anti-Monopoly Law at the same time as the national security review, or in sequence. The practice of allowing third-party objections, especially after a MOFCOM decision, is another source of uncertainty and concern.

All countries are flexible in their definition of national security, but China is perhaps more so than the United States. For example, agriculture is both "related" to national security and "encouraged" for foreign investment. The security review process often lacks confidentiality, leading to public disclosure of the identity of applicants and commercially sensitive knowledge. This leads investors to be insecure about the application process, and thus less likely to invest. All of this is complicated by the fact that foreign investment in China is subject to a constantly changing political environment, where even industries subject to review are uncertain.

In 2006, the minister for the State-Owned Assets Supervision and Administration Commission (SASAC) listed seven industries where, in his opinion, the state should maintain "absolute control": aviation, coal, defense, electric power generation and transmission, oil and petrochemicals, shipping, and telecommunications.[31] The minister also listed industries where the state should keep "relative control": automotive, chemical, construction, exploration and design, electronic information, equipment manufacturing, iron and steel, nonferrous metals, and science and technology. The lists were said to be the minister's personal opinion, but in fact they almost certainly represent official policy. Taken at face value they exclude large swaths of economic activity from foreign investment.

A lot of discussion concerns the role of the provinces in processing applications for foreign investment. US business leaders are worried that the prospective devolution of authority to the provincial level will open the door to more discrimination against foreign investors. The United States does not require the states to subscribe to new liberalization in US bilateral investment treaties (BITs), but they are required to maintain their existing degrees of openness. If China follows a reciprocal policy, then both states and provinces will not be

---

31. Ren Fang and Liu Bing, "SASAC: The State Economy Must Maintain Absolute Control Power over Seven Sectors," Xinhua, December 18, 2006, www.gov.cn (accessed on June 8, 2014).

obligated to accept fresh liberalization for either greenfield or M&A investment. Possibly, in the context of BIT negotiations, the federal government might persuade five to ten large states to adhere to the treaty. That would open the way for China to reciprocate with key provinces.

Given the daunting array of bureaucratic review and the extensive schedule of off-limits investments, the United States would like to accomplish five major goals in a BIT or FTA. First, an agreement should spell out exactly which industries are open to foreign investment and which are not. A negative list would be a good way to accomplish this goal. China's foreign investment catalogue is not as precise as it should be. Second, the agreement should cut through the extensive bureaucratic review by enumerating preestablishment rights with respect to permitted investments. China accepted this proposition in principle in the July 2013 Strategic and Economic Dialogue (S&ED) meetings. Third, the agreement should bring China closer to a one-stop-shopping model by consolidating more review functions in the NDRC in an open and transparent fashion. Fourth, the agreement should address China's greater use of the Anti-Monopoly Law in its review process.[32] Finally, even if language in a BIT or FTA allows wide scope for each party to define essential security, the parties should discuss the asymmetry between China's national security review and the US review under the CFIUS process.

Lessons from the China–Japan–Korea Investment Pact

As a precursor to their impending FTA negotiations, China, Japan, and Korea (CJK) signed a trilateral investment agreement on May 13, 2012.[33] It has not yet entered into force. The agreement aims to set the groundwork for "greater transparency of investment regulations and laws, a more stable policy framework and more liberalized regimes for foreign investors"[34] to increase opportunities for intraregional FDI. China has become the largest FDI host country in the developing world and a major FDI destination for Japan and Korea; their outward FDI stocks in China were estimated at $83 billion and $54 billion, respectively, in 2011. By contrast, Chinese FDI in Japan and Korea remains very limited, as is Korean FDI in Japan, though China has expressed intentions to increase its FDI in the two countries.

Both Japan and Korea had negotiated basic BITs with China more than 20 years ago. The new trilateral agreement aligns the investment standards of the three countries, including provisions for performance requirements, transparency, and intellectual property rights. These advances are particularly

---

32. Grace Ng, "China Flexing Its Anti-Monopoly Law Muscle: Revenge or Self-Defense?" MedCity News, July 10, 2013, medcitynews.com (accessed on June 8, 2014).

33. This section is based on an unpublished summary prepared by Jeffrey J. Schott and Cathleen Cimino.

34. Japanese Ministry of Economy, Trade, and Industry, Joint Study Report for an FTA among China, Japan, and Korea, December 16, 2011, www.meti.go.jp (accessed on June 25, 2014).

important for Japan, as the 1988 Japan–China BIT had not included such provisions, while the 1992 Korea–China BIT was amended in 2007 to cover them. The CJK investment pact is a significant improvement over past regional accords. It establishes national treatment and MFN treatment as basic standards, limits expropriation and promises prompt and adequate compensation, prohibits performance requirements, and creates a functional investment dispute settlement mechanism.

However, the pact falls short in establishing protections as comprehensive as those sought by the United States. It does not create preestablishment rights, and excludes investor-state dispute settlement; disputes can be decided only by a "competent court of the disputing Contracting Party."[35] Transparency requirements are light, environmental obligations are weak, labor obligations are nonexistent, and intellectual property provisions are sparse.

Bilateral Investment Treaty

Probably the first step in creating a more cordial investment climate between the United States and China, and reducing some of the policy barriers, will be for each party to conclude and ratify the BIT. The tenth round of US and China BIT negotiations kicked off in late October 2013, when experts and lawyers spent a full week together hashing out details of the treaty.

On July 10 and 11, 2013, the United States and China held their annual S&ED in Washington, with renewed interest in the BIT talks headlining the meeting. The Treasury Department hailed several commitments from the Chinese side. For the first time, China was willing to negotiate using a negative list approach, rather than insisting on a positive list approach that would track its foreign investment catalogue. A negative list would open foreign investment to all sectors and industries that were not specifically excluded. The guiding principle for inward foreign investment would be national treatment and MFN treatment; any exceptions would need to be specifically listed for each sector and industry. Also announced at the S&ED was progress on another contentious issue: preestablishment rights, namely, ensuring national treatment at the most preliminary phase of an investment project.

Put simply, BITs are designed to ensure a calibrated degree of investment access for firms in one country to the markets of the other, and to establish reciprocal rules for the treatment of firms and protection of investments once established.[36] The United States currently has 41 BITs in force, of which 38

---

35. From the report "Agreement among the Government of Japan, the Government of Korea, and the Government of the People's Republic of China for the Promotion, Facilitation, and Protection of Investment," 2012, www.mofa.go.jp (accessed on June 25, 2014).

36. See, e.g., Shayerah Ilias Akhtar and Martin A. Weiss, "U.S. International Investment Agreements: Issues for Congress," Congressional Research Service, 2013, fas.org (accessed on June 25, 2014).

are with developing countries and 3 are with advanced countries (table 13.5).[37] China has 104 BITs in force, of which 78 are with developing countries and 26 are with advanced nations (table 13.6); 24 remain unratified.

BITs took off slowly; today the global number exceeds 2,800 (UNCTAD 2012). The United States and Russia signed a BIT in 1992, which the US Senate ratified the following year, but Russia's parliament has yet to ratify the treaty. But the approval of a China–US BIT on the US side is far from certain. As BITs are formal treaties, the Senate must approve them by a two-thirds vote. Intense scrutiny in the Senate is ensured, as evidenced by a bipartisan congressional letter to the Obama administration, dated July 9, 2013, complaining about China's regulatory process, "opaque and discriminatory" investment restrictions, currency misalignment, "indigenous innovation" policies, cyberespionage of trade secrets, and China's "woefully inadequate and incomplete" fulfillment of commitments made bilaterally and in the WTO.[38] The letter was signed by Senate Finance Committee chairman Max Baucus (D-MT) and ranking member Orrin Hatch (R-UT), along with Ways and Means chairman Dave Camp (R-MI) and ranking member Sander Levin (D-MI). Their laundry list of complaints goes well beyond the subject matter of a BIT, but the question is whether collateral issues might delay ratification of a China–US BIT for a very considerable period.

During the July 2013 S&ED talks, China addressed some but not all of the congressional concerns by stating that it will move more rapidly toward a market-determined exchange rate and speed up financial and banking sector reforms. The United States and China jointly issued a statement recognizing the importance of trade secret protection and promising vigorous enforcement. China also affirmed its commitment to establish a Shanghai Free Trade Zone (FTZ) as a pilot program. The Shanghai FTZ has since been launched, and the US business community hopes that, in implementation, the FTZ will ensure equal access for foreign enterprises.

US Aspirations

Though all 2,800-plus BITs are identified by a common acronym, they are not cookie-cutter treaties. Their content has evolved over time; moreover, the United States starts with a very different model than most countries, including China. According to the US Trade Representative, the US BIT is designed to provide US investors with six core benefits.[39] First, investors and covered investments are afforded both national treatment ("treated as favorably as the host party treats its own investors and their investments") and MFN treatment ("treated

---

37. The United States has signed an additional six BITs, all with developing countries, that have yet to be ratified.

38. "Will a Treaty Increase US Investment in China?" *Washington Trade Report*, July 15, 2013.

39. Core benefits of US BITs are drawn from Office of the United States Trade Representative (USTR), "Bilateral Investment Treaties," www.ustr.gov (accessed on June 8, 2014).

Table 13.5   US bilateral investment treaties as of June 2013

Partner	Date of signature	Date of entry into force
Belarus	January 15, 1994	—
El Salvador	March 10, 1999	—
Haiti	December 13, 1983	—
Nicaragua	July 1, 1995	—
Russia	June 17, 1992	—
Uzbekistan	December 16, 1994	—
Rwanda	February 19, 2008	January 1, 2012
Uruguay	November 4, 2005	November 1, 2006
Mozambique	December 1, 1998	March 3, 2005
Czech Republic	December 10, 2003	August 10, 2004
Jordan	July 2, 1997	June 12, 2003
Lithuania	January 14, 1998	November 22, 2001
Azerbaijan	August 1, 1997	August 2, 2001
Honduras	July 1, 1995	July 11, 2001
Croatia	July 13, 1996	June 20, 2001
Bolivia	April 17, 1998	June 6, 2001
Bahrain	September 29, 1999	May 30, 2001
Georgia	March 7, 1994	August 10, 1999
Albania	January 11, 1995	January 4, 1998
Ecuador	August 27, 1993	May 11, 1997
Jamaica	February 4, 1994	March 1, 1997
Estonia	April 18, 1994	February 16, 1997
Mongolia	October 6, 1994	January 4, 1997
Trinidad and Tobago	September 26, 1994	December 29, 1996
Latvia	January 13, 1995	December 26, 1996
Ukraine	March 4, 1994	November 16, 1996
Armenia	September 23, 1992	March 29, 1996
Moldova	April 21, 1993	November 26, 1994
Argentina	November 14, 1991	October 20, 1994
Congo	February 12, 1990	August 13, 1994
Poland	March 21, 1990	August 6, 1994
Bulgaria	September 23, 1992	June 2, 1994
Romania	May 28, 1992	January 15, 1994
Kazakhstan	May 19, 1992	January 12, 1994

(continues on next page)

Table 13.5   US bilateral investment treaties as of June 2013 *(continued)*

Partner	Date of signature	Date of entry into force
Kyrgyzstan	January 19, 1993	January 11, 1994
Sri Lanka	September 20, 1991	May 1, 1993
Tunisia	May 15, 1990	February 7, 1993
Slovakia	October 22, 1991	December 19, 1992
Egypt	March 11, 1986	June 27, 1992
Panama	October 27, 1982	May 30, 1991
Morocco	July 22, 1985	May 29, 1991
Senegal	December 6, 1983	October 25, 1990
Turkey	December 3, 1985	May 18, 1990
Democratic Republic of the Congo	August 3, 1984	July 28, 1989
Cameroon	February 26, 1986	April 6, 1989
Grenada	May 2, 1986	March 3, 1989
Bangladesh	July 25, 1985	March 12, 1986

— = not applicable

Sources: United Nations Conference on Trade and Development, unctad.org; US Department of Commerce, Trade Compliance Center (2013), tcc.export.gov (accessed on July 4, 2014).

as favorably as investors and investments from any third country"). National treatment and MFN treatment are afforded for all phases of investment. This is crucial, as phases of investment cover the "full life-cycle of investment," including establishment or acquisition, management, operation, expansion, and disposition. Second, limits are established on justifiable reasons for expropriation and "prompt, adequate, and effective compensation" must be paid when expropriation occurs. Third, the ability to transfer investment-related funds across borders is ensured "without delay and using a market rate of exchange." Fourth, restrictions are set forth on performance requirements, such as local content requirements. Fifth, the right to employ top managerial personnel, regardless of nationality, is guaranteed. Finally, the right to international arbitration for an investment dispute with the host country government is ensured, with no requirement to use domestic courts.

All of the above may sound reasonable to US ears, but BITs come in different flavors, and the current US model BIT is probably the most demanding in contemporary usage. The US model, updated in 2012 after three years of interagency review, calls for tougher standards than the already demanding 2004 model did (Johnson 2012). Only Uruguay and Rwanda accepted the 2004 model, and negotiations with India, Pakistan, and China using the 2012 model have moved slowly. For aspiring partners, four features of the latest

Table 13.6 Chinese bilateral investment treaties as of June 2013

Partner	Date of signature	Date of entry into force
Botswana	June 12, 2000	—
Brunei Darussalam	November 17, 2000	—
Côte d'Ivoire	September 23, 2002	—
Algeria	October 17, 1996	—
Bahamas	September 4, 2009	—
Benin	February 18, 2004	—
Chad	April 26, 2010	—
Congo	March 20, 2000	—
Democratic Republic of the Congo	August 11, 2011	—
Costa Rica	October 24, 2007	—
Dijbouti	August 18, 2003	—
Equatorial Guinea	October 20, 2005	—
Guinea	November 18, 2005	—
Jordan	November 15, 2001	—
Kenya	July 16, 2001	—
Libya	August 4, 2010	—
Namibia	November 17, 2005	—
Nigeria	August 27, 2001	—
Seychelles	February 10, 2007	—
Sierra Leone	May 16, 2001	—
Tunisia	June 21, 2004	—
Uganda	May 27, 2004	—
Vanuatu	April 7, 2006	—
Zambia	June 21, 1996	—
Canada	September 9, 2012	—
Colombia	November 22, 2008	July 2, 2012
Uzbekistan	April 19, 2011	September 1, 2011
France	November 26, 2007	August 20, 2010
Switzerland	January 27, 2009	April 13, 2010
Belgium and Luxembourg	June 6, 2005	December 1, 2009
Romania	April 16, 2007	September 1, 2009
Mali	February 12, 2009	July 16, 2009
Mexico	July 11, 2008	June 6, 2009

(continues on next page)

Table 13.6 Chinese bilateral investment treaties as of June 2013 (continued)

Partner	Date of signature	Date of entry into force
Russia	November 9, 2006	May 1, 2009
Malta	February 22, 2009	April 1, 2009
Gabon	May 9, 1997	February 16, 2009
Israel	April 10, 1995	January 13, 2009
Cuba	April 20, 2007	December 1, 2008
Portugal	December 9, 2005	July 26, 2008
Spain	November 14, 2005	July 1, 2008
Korea	September 7, 2007	December 1, 2007
Bulgaria	June 26, 2007	November 10, 2007
India	November 21, 2006	August 1, 2007
Madagascar	November 21, 2005	June 1, 2007
Slovakia	December 7, 2005	May 25, 2007
Finland	November 15, 2004	November 15, 2006
Czech Republic	December 8, 2005	September 1, 2006
Latvia	April 15, 2004	February 1, 2006
Germany	December 1, 2003	November 11, 2005
Democratic People's Republic of Korea (North Korea)	March 22, 2005	October 1, 2005
Iran	July 22, 2000	July 1, 2005
Bosnia and Herzegovina	June 26, 2002	January 1, 2005
Guyana	March 27, 2003	October 26, 2004
Sweden	September 27, 2004	September 27, 2004
Netherlands	November 26, 2001	August 1, 2004
Trinidad and Tobago	July 22, 2002	May 24, 2004
Myanmar	December 12, 2001	May 21, 2002
Cyprus	January 17, 2001	April 29, 2002
Yemen	February 16, 1998	April 10, 2002
Mozambique	July 10, 2001	February 26, 2002
Syria	December 9, 1996	November 1, 2001
Cape Verde	April 21, 1998	January 1, 2001
Ethiopia	May 11, 1998	May 1, 2000
Bahrain	June 17, 1999	April 27, 2000

(continues on next page)

Table 13.6 Chinese bilateral investment treaties as of June 2013 *(continued)*

Partner	Date of signature	Date of entry into force
Qatar	April 9, 1999	April 1, 2000
Cambodia	July 19, 1996	February 1, 2000
Morocco	March 27, 1995	November 27, 1999
Barbados	July 20, 1998	October 1, 1999
Sudan	May 30, 1997	July 1, 1998
South Africa	December 30, 1997	April 1, 1998
Zimbabwe	May 21, 1996	March 1, 1998
Uruguay	December 2, 1993	December 1, 1997
Macedonia	June 9, 1997	November 1, 1997
Lebanon	June 13, 1996	July 10, 1997
Ecuador	March 21, 1994	July 1, 1997
Mauritius	May 4, 1996	June 8, 1997
Saudi Arabia	February 29, 1996	May 1, 1997
Bangladesh	September 12, 1996	March 25, 1997
Iceland	March 31, 1994	March 1, 1997
Serbia	December 18, 1995	September 13, 1996
Bolivia	May 8, 1992	September 1, 1996
Egypt	April 21, 1994	April 1, 1996
Jamaica	October 26, 1994	April 1, 1996
Kyrgyzstan	May 14, 1992	September 8, 1995
Philippines	July 20, 1992	September 8, 1995
Albania	February 13, 1993	September 1, 1995
Chile	March 23, 1994	August 1, 1995
Oman	March 18, 1995	August 1, 1995
Azerbaijan	March 8, 1994	April 1, 1995
Indonesia	November 18, 1994	April 1, 1995
Armenia	July 4, 1992	March 18, 1995
Georgia	June 3, 1993	March 1, 1995
Moldova	November 6, 1992	March 1, 1995
Peru	June 9, 1994	February 1, 1995
Belarus	January 11, 1993	January 14, 1995
Slovenia	September 13, 1993	January 1, 1995
United Arab Emirates	July 1, 1993	September 28, 1994

(continues on next page)

Table 13.6 Chinese bilateral investment treaties as of June 2013 (continued)

Partner	Date of signature	Date of entry into force
Turkey	November 13, 1990	August 20, 1994
Kazakhstan	August 10, 1992	August 13, 1994
Argentina	November 5, 1992	August 1, 1994
Croatia	June 7, 1993	July 1, 1994
Turkmenistan	November 21, 1992	June 4, 1994
Estonia	September 2, 1993	June 1, 1994
Lithuania	November 8, 1993	June 1, 1994
Tajikistan	March 9, 1993	January 20, 1994
Greece	June 25, 1992	December 21, 1993
Mongolia	August 25, 1991	November 1, 1993
Vietnam	December 2, 1992	September 1, 1993
Laos	January 31, 1993	June 1, 1993
Ukraine	October 31, 1992	May 29, 1993
Hungary	May 29, 1991	April 1, 1993
Papua New Guinea	April 12, 1991	February 12, 1993
Ghana	October 12, 1989	November 22, 1991
Pakistan	February 12, 1989	September 30, 1990
Malaysia	November 21, 1988	March 31, 1990
Japan	August 27, 1988	May 14, 1989
New Zealand	November 22, 1988	March 25, 1989
Poland	June 7, 1988	January 8, 1989
Australia	July 11, 1988	July 11, 1988
Italy	January 28, 1985	August 28, 1987
Sri Lanka	March 13, 1986	March 25, 1987
Kuwait	November 23, 1985	December 24, 1986
Austria	September 12, 1985	October 11, 1986
United Kingdom	May 15, 1986	May 15, 1986
Singapore	November 21, 1985	February 7, 1986
Thailand	March 12, 1985	December 13, 1985
Norway	November 21, 1984	July 10, 1985
Denmark	April 29, 1985	April 29, 1985

— = not applicable

Source: United Nations Conference on Trade and Development, unctad.org (accessed on July 4, 2014).

US model have proven most difficult: first, strong transparency obligations on matters affecting investment, applied not only to government agencies but also to SOEs; second, advance publication of proposed laws and regulations and an opportunity to comment; third, a commitment not to require the use of technologies that give preference to domestic companies, and commitment to allow foreign firms a voice in setting technical standards; and fourth, commitments not to waive or derogate from the operation of domestic laws that protect labor or the environment, to enforce domestic laws in these areas, and to recognize International Labor Organization (ILO) declarations and multilateral environmental agreements, such as the Montreal Protocol or Convention on International Trade of Endangered Species (CITES).

The US 2012 model amends nonderogable labor rights to include all four core labor rights under the ILO 1998 Declaration,[40] in addition to the right to acceptable conditions of work.[41] Expanded labor obligations within the BIT framework could be a challenge for China. China is an ILO member and has ratified four of the eight fundamental ILO conventions covering equal remuneration, nondiscrimination, minimum age, and the worst forms of child labor. However, China continues to restrict the rights of workers to organize by failing to ratify ILO conventions 87 (freedom of association and protection of the right to organize) and 98 (right to organize and collective bargaining). Moreover, China has not ratified two conventions on the use of forced labor (29 and 105).

As mentioned, China has entered into 128 BITs, of which 24 remain to be ratified. Taking the China–Canada BIT (yet to be ratified) as the current template, several features are evident in the Chinese model. There is language fostering cooperation and encouraging foreign investment. The definition of investment is broad, including not only bricks and mortar but also intellectual property rights and certain financial assets. Returns on investment are entitled to the same protection as the original investment (e.g., repatriation rights). With extensive exceptions, the BITs provide for national treatment and MFN treatment.[42] The BITs also promise "prompt, adequate and effective" compensation—or words of similar effect—in the event of expropriation. Finally, in

---

40. The core labor rights as established by the ILO Declaration on Fundamental Principles and Rights of Work include freedom of association and the effective recognition of the right to collective bargaining; elimination of all forms of forced or compulsory labor; effective abolition of child labor; and elimination of discrimination in respect of employment and occupation.

41. However, Prislan and Zandvliet (2013) also note that while the commitments to labor standards are more demanding in the US 2012 model, the BIT still "lacks clear obligation to adopt and maintain ILO standards as a minimum, and does not allow [labor] disputes to be submitted to arbitration."

42. The right of establishment does not appear in the Canada-China investment agreement. Article 6 (national treatment) does not provide national treatment for establishment, but rather for "the expansion, management, conduct, operation and sale or other disposition of investments." This allows both parties to block new investments (Woods and Walsh 2012). Moreover, the concept of "expansion" applies only to "sectors not subject to a prior approval process ... and may be subject to prescribed formalities and other information requirements" (Canada-

the event of investment disputes, the BITs generally provide for arbitration of state-to-state and investor-state disputes.[43]

A functioning arbitration system for resolving bilateral investment disputes is an important feature for expanding FDI in China. The more recent Chinese BITs provide for investor-state arbitration predominantly through the International Center for Settlement of Investment Disputes (ICSID). China is a signatory to the New York Convention on the Recognition and Enforcement of Foreign Arbitration Awards and has acceded to the ICSID Convention. However, investor-state arbitration is used predominantly as a last resort and very few cases have gone through international arbitration. Dispute settlement done through domestic institutions, such as the China International Economic and Trade Arbitration Commission, are confidential and claims brought to domestic courts are often not reported. However, Chinese arbitration institutions are reported to be independent and impartial (Trakman 2012).

Finally, a CHUSTIA might prohibit all forms of pressure for technology transfer as a condition of investment access. In the view of many US firms, technology transfer requirements are the most objectionable performance requirements that Chinese authorities currently impose.[44]

Sticking Points in BIT Negotiations

BIT talks were launched in 2008 during the presidencies of George W. Bush and Hu Jintao. After President Obama was elected in 2008, talks were put on hold while responsible US officials debated and drafted the new US 2012 model BIT.[45] The 13th negotiating round was held in Beijing in June 2014. From these extensive talks, 6 related sticking points have emerged with respect

---

China FIPA, Article 6(1)). MFN treatment, however, does apply to both pre- and post-establishment investments.

43. For investor-state disputes, BITs typically give investors the option of arbitration through an ad hoc tribunal under United Nations Commission on International Trade Law (UNCITRAL) rules or through an institutional tribunal such as the ICSID. China's first-generation BITs limited dispute settlement to compensation for expropriation only and did not provide open-ended arbitration through ICSID or any other tribunal. Rather, investors had to first submit the dispute to a local Chinese court, which had to acknowledge that there was expropriation; after that the case could be submitted to the ICSID. China's second-generation BITs, starting in the 1990s, include more comprehensive dispute settlement provisions and provide arbitration for disputes not related to expropriation, thereby giving investors the option of arbitration through ad hoc panels and ICSID (Hong 2009).

44. Article 8, paragraph 1(f) in the US model BIT states that neither party may require a foreign investor "to transfer a particular technology, a production process, or other proprietary knowledge to a person in its territory."

45. In drafting the model BIT, and in subsequent negotiations with China, the USTR and State Department play the leading roles, while Treasury and Commerce play supporting roles.

to Chinese concessions:[46] preestablishment rights for US firms,[47] much greater transparency of the approval process, market disciplines applied to Chinese SOEs and state-supported enterprises (SSEs), limits on subsidization of SOEs and SSEs, effective investor-state dispute settlement and guarantees against retaliation, and reforms of forced technology-transfer policies and intellectual property localization.

Little has been disclosed regarding what concessions China has asked of the United States. The press has not reported a list of Chinese industries for which the United States is aggressively seeking market access. Nor has the press reported whether Chinese negotiators are demanding investment access to sectors typically reserved in US BITs and FTAs, or whether they are seeking disciplines on CFIUS procedures. We think the United States should refrain from adding an economic interest test in future legislative reviews of CFIUS. The BIT should also limit the scope of CFIUS reviews, and reviews by Chinese authorities, to national security concerns. Not all SOEs act of behalf of the Chinese government (i.e., are equivalent to "public bodies" in WTO terminology). Many operate as private concerns. Only investments by those SOEs that also act as "public bodies" should be automatically reviewed by CFIUS to determine whether they create security concerns.

Preestablishment Rights

As mentioned earlier, the US 2012 model BIT calls for national treatment and MFN treatment in all phases of the investment process, with a limited number of exceptions for central, state, and local investment measures. Among other things, this means that US firms should be permitted to seek investment rights (greenfield or M&A) in any industry or sector in which Chinese or third-country firms are allowed to invest. China has never conceded preestablishment right in its 128 BITs. From the Chinese perspective, permission for a foreign firm to invest in any industry or sector can be granted only on a case-by-case basis, consistent with guidelines spelled out in China's most recent foreign investment catalogue.[48]

---

46. See Inside US Trade, "AmCham Shanghai Sees China BIT as Way to Lift Investment Curbs," September 19, 2013; "US, China Still Discussing A-V Compliance, New Regulation under Review," January 24, 2013; "Treasury Official Touts New Chinese Investment Commitments at S&ED," July 11, 2013.

47. Preestablishment rights ensure that a potential foreign investor can obtain visas for its personnel to enter the host country, establish a temporary office for scouting purposes, receive equal treatment from government agencies on par with domestic or third-country investors, and not be subjected to performance requirements as a condition of investment. Without these rights, the potential foreign investor might face numerous bureaucratic obstacles getting to first base, or onerous surprise conditions to obtain the necessary investment permits.

48. The latest catalogue stresses investment opportunities in central and western China. Consistent with this theme, in June 2012 the Fortune 500 Forum held its meeting in Chengdu.

SOE/SSE Disciplines

The large (if declining) prominence of SOEs and SSEs in the Chinese economy gives rise to many US concerns, and these are surfacing in the BIT negotiations. Chapter 14 in this volume examines the SOE and SSE question in detail. Here we flag the leading and overlapping concerns: transparency of SOE-SSE financial statements; disclosure when the Chinese government delegates regulatory authority to an SOE or SSE and when such an enterprise receives preferences; disclosure of both subsidies received by SOEs or SSEs and offsetting costs incurred by them in providing public services; enforcement of competition rules against SOEs and SSEs; and transparency and justification when SOEs or SSEs voice their industrial policy objectives in competition reviews (under the Anti-Monopoly Law) of inward investment.

Investor-State Dispute Settlement

Perhaps Chinese negotiators have already accepted the investor-state dispute settlement (ISDS) provisions normally found in US FTAs and the US model BIT. In any event, from the perspective of US firms, BIT obligations are not effective without ISDS mechanisms. This view is colored by the business perception that obligations undertaken when China joined the WTO are often ignored but not called out because the WTO dispute settlement system is costly, cumbersome, and often politicized. A big problem is apprehension that companies seeking remedies through dispute settlement will be subject to threats of retaliation, or actual retaliation, whether a case is brought in the WTO or a future CHUSTIA. Imagination is needed to design effective safeguards against the retaliatory threat.

Beyond the BIT: Progress in the FTA

Assuming the United States and China ratify a quality BIT, what issues would remain in the investment realm for subsequent FTA talks? Three related subjects seem the most likely candidates for upgrading in CHUSTIA.

First, in the BIT, both countries will very likely inscribe negative lists. In July 2013 China agreed to this approach, which liberalizes investments in all sectors and measures unless specified in a list of nonconforming measures, including exceptions to national treatment, MFN, performance requirements, and senior management and board of directors. In an FTA, these prohibitions and limitations might be defined more narrowly. Some aspects of telecommunications or civil aviation might be opened to foreign ownership, and joint venture limitations in the range of 10 to 40 percent might be raised to less than 50 percent.

Second, many Chinese investment restrictions will inevitably relate to SOE-dominated sectors. A CHUSTIA would put greater disciplines on SOEs and to some extent open affected sectors to foreign firms. In Chapter 14 we discuss SOE disciplines, including transparency, subsidies, and competition law. Additionally, a CHUSTIA might call for gradual privatization of some SOEs and an end to their regulatory prerogatives that serve to exclude foreign firms.

References

CFIUS (Committee on Foreign Investment in the United States). 2010. *CFIUS Annual Report to Congress*. Washington.

CFIUS (Committee on Foreign Investment in the United States). 2012. *CFIUS Annual Report to Congress*. Washington.

Hanemann, Thilo. 2014 (forthcoming). Following the Money: Alternative Approaches to Tracking Chinese Outward FDI. Conference paper presented at 21st Century China Program, University of California, San Diego.

He, Dong, Lillian Cheung, Wenlang Zhang, and Tommy Wu. 2012. *How Would Capital Account Liberalisation Affect China's Capital Flows and the Renminbi Real Exchange Rates?* Hong Kong: Hong Kong Institute for Monetary Research.

Hong, Guang. 2009. Scope of Arbitration in Chinese BITs: Policies and Implications. University of Miami School of Law. Photocopy.

Johnson, Lise. 2012. The 2012 US Model BIT and What the Changes (or Lack Thereof) Suggest about Future Investment Treaties. *Political Risk Insurance Newsletter* 8, no. 2 (November): 1–5.

Moran, Theodore H. 2009. *Three Threats: An Analytical Framework for the CFIUS Process*. Policy Analyses in International Economics 89. Washington: Peterson Institute for International Economics.

Moran, Theodore H., and Lindsay Oldenski. 2013. *Foreign Direct Investment in the United States: Benefits, Suspicions, and Risks*. Policy Analyses in International Economics 100. Washington: Peterson Institute for International Economics.

Prislin, Vid, and Ruben Zandvliet. 2013. *Normal-Trade Relations (Most Favored Nation) Policy of the United States*. CRS Report to Congress RL31558 (December 15). Washington: Congressional Research Service.

Rosen, Daniel H., and Thilo Hanemann. 2011. *An American Open Door? Maximizing the Benefits of Chinese Foreign Direct Investment*. New York: Asia Society.

Trakman, Leon. 2012. *China and Investor-State Arbitration*. UNSW Law Research Paper 2012-48. Kensington: University of New South Wales.

UNCTAD (United Nations Conference on Trade and Development). 2012. *World Investment Report 2012*. Geneva.

USCBC (US-China Business Council). 2012. *USCBC 2012 China Business Environment Survey Results: Continued Growth and Profitability; Tempered Optimism Due to Rising Costs, Competition, and Market Barriers*. Washington.

US Chamber of Commerce. 2012. *China's Approval Process for Inbound Foreign Direct Investment*. Washington.

US Chamber of Commerce. 2013. *From International to Interstates: Assessing the Opportunity for Chinese Participation in U.S. Infrastructure*. Washington.

Woods, Michael G., and Catherine Walsh. 2012. *The Canada-China Foreign Investment Protection and Promotion Agreement: A Comparative Analysis to Canada's Model FIPA*. Ottawa: Heenan Blaikie.

14

State-Owned Enterprises

Private firms based in the United States and other market economies are troubled by the huge, though shrinking, role of Chinese state-owned enterprises (SOEs), state-supported enterprises (SSEs), and state-controlled enterprises (SCEs; for convenience, we refer to SOEs, SSEs, and SCEs collectively as SOEs).[1] The complaint is often heard that, when they compete abroad, SOEs enjoy the advantages of opaque subsidies and protected home markets, allowing them to grab market share from private firms in the rest of the world. Multinational corporations (MNCs) attempting to enter or expand in certain sectors of the Chinese economy sometimes find themselves facing "no trespassing" signs posted by the government to shelter the domain of SOEs. More often they find that their SOE rivals face fewer regulatory constraints, less burdensome enforcement of the Anti-Monopoly Law (AML), and easier access to credit from state-owned banks, among other favors granted by the Communist Party apparatus. Finally, some governments—notably but not only the US and Canadian governments—are wary of SOE takeovers of natural resource and high-tech firms, illustrated by rebuffs to the China National Offshore Oil Company (CNOOC) and Huawei.

Private sector complaints from abroad demand a level playing field. Within China, as Lardy (2014) and other scholars have urged, there are good reasons

---

1. In this chapter we do not address sovereign wealth funds (SWFs). For detailed examinations of SOEs, see Gang and Hope (2013) and Lardy (2014).

to continue diminishing the role of SOEs.[2] But neither US nor other private firms seek to dismantle or privatize Chinese SOEs. What they seek are new rules in trade and investment agreements that foster market-oriented behavior in SOEs.

While historically important in China's economic development, the role of SOEs entered a long decline after Deng Xiaoping inaugurated a market economy in 1979. Table 14.1 classifies the different types of enterprises in China, including asset ownership and the laws that governs them. Figure 14.1 portrays the long view, showing a steady secular fall in the proportion of production by SOEs relative to privately owned enterprises (POEs). Nevertheless SOEs remain an important feature of the Chinese economic landscape. In 2011 they accounted for 42 percent of industrial assets, 26 percent of industrial production, 25 percent of employment, and 13 percent of exports (National Bureau of Statistics of China 2012). In key sectors—telecommunications, oil and gas, and finance—SOEs retain almost exclusive control. Table 14.2, supplied by the Organization for Economic Cooperation and Development (OECD), lists the leading Chinese SOEs and enumerates their salient characteristics. For China, as measured by the OECD, the country SOE share (CSS) of economic activity by top firms is 96 percent. This figure is exaggerated because the OECD excludes a large number of less-than-giant and medium-sized private companies.[3] Nevertheless, using the same metric, the contrast with the United States is startling: The CSS for the United States in 2011 was less than 1 percent, and this was entirely attributed to General Motors, which has since returned to majority private ownership.

The performances of many Chinese SOEs have lagged, and they seem to rely heavily on debt rather than equity capital. Many loans are extended on favorable terms, and since state-owned banks provide nearly all debt finance, the lending preferences reflect public policy. Figure 14.2 shows the loans outstanding in 2011 for state-owned, state-controlled, collective-controlled, privately controlled, and a few other types of firms. In that year, some 49 percent of loans outstanding were extended to SOEs or SCEs and 10 percent to collective-controlled enterprises, while private firms had just 33 percent of the loans outstanding. The figures for new loans to SOEs are trending down, however. In 2010 only 36 percent of new loans went to SOEs and in 2011 only 28 percent. The opposite was true for collective-controlled and private firms, as their loan

---

2. Hu Jintao slowed and even reversed the dismantling process during his presidency (2002–12), but at the Third Plenum in November 2013, President Xi Jinping renewed the call for a smaller SOE role in the Chinese economy.

3. The OECD measures CSS as an equally weighted average of SOE shares of sales, assets, and market values among a country's top ten companies, and ranges from 0 percent (no state ownership) to 100 percent (SOEs account for all sales, assets, and market value of a country's largest companies). In many industries in China, most of the top ten companies are SOEs.

Table 14.1 Enterprise classification system

Enterprise type	Asset ownership	Law
State-owned enterprise (国有企业)	Owned by state	Law of the PRC of Industrial Enterprises Owned by the Whole People (1988); Law of the People's Republic of China on the State-Owned Assets of Enterprises (2009)
Collective enterprise (集体企业)	Ownership shared by employees and other economic entities	Provisional Regulations of the People's Republic of China on Urban and Township Collective Enterprises (1991)
Share cooperative enterprise (股份合作企业)	Shareholders are employees of enterprise, initial startup using some public funds	Provisional Regulations of the People's Republic of China on Urban and Township Collective Enterprises (1992)
Joint enterprise (联营企业)	Jointly invested by two or more enterprises or institutions as legal person or from different ownership	Provisional Regulations of the People's Republic of China on Urban and Township Collective Enterprises (1992)
Limited liability corporation (有限责任公司)	Ownership based on capital contributions	Company Law (1994; revised 2006)
Shareholding limited corporation (股份有限公司)	Ownership based on shareholdings	Company Law (1994; revised 2006)
Private enterprise (私营企业)	Enterprise established by a natural person or majority owned by a natural person	Provisional Regulations of the People's Republic of China on Private Enterprises (1988); Sole Proprietorship Enterprise Law (2000); Partnership Law (1997; revised 2007); Company Law (1994; revised 2006)

Source: National Bureau of Statistics of China (2012).

Figure 14.1 China's gross industrial output by ownership, 1999–2011 (percent)

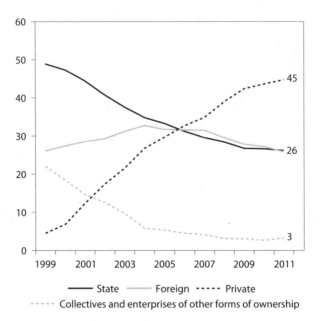

Source: National Bureau of Statistics of China (2012), China Statistical Yearbook, www.stats.gov.cn.

shares trended upward. The profits of central SOEs under the control of the State-owned Assets Supervision and Administration Commission (SASAC)—namely the largest state-owned firms—rose from 1.9 percent of GDP in 2002 to 3.8 percent in 2007, but dropped to 2.5 percent in 2012. These are all fairly modest results, considering the large size of central SOEs, and reflect low average productivity.[4]

Not surprisingly, the conduct of SOEs will loom large in any US trade or investment agreement with China. There are good reasons why SOEs will raise hot-button issues in talks with China, far more so than in talks with other countries. First are the sheer size, striking success, and financial strength of certain Chinese SOEs, both at home and abroad. Second, the Communist Party picks the leaders of the top SOEs and coordinates key decisions through encrypted red-phone links to Party headquarters. Because there are zero degrees of separation between the Party and the top SOEs, some SOEs may respond as much to political guidance as to market forces. The rotation of top

---

4. Data from Lardy (2014).

Figure 14.2   Loans outstanding for China's enterprises, 2011

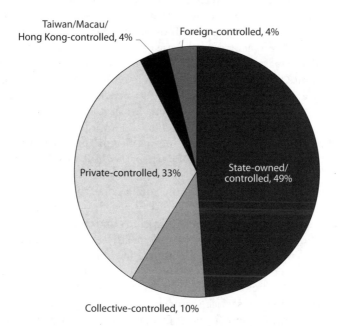

Sources: China Banking Society (2011, 322; 2012, 369).

executives among top SOEs, coupled with Party coordination of these firms, creates an atmosphere of cooperating oligopolies, conducive to price fixing, market sharing, and cross-subsidization—all features that are not supposed to characterize a competitive market economy.

New understandings and rules in trade and investment agreements will be phrased to apply symmetrically to both partners, but in practice the greatest effect will be on Chinese SOEs. In the parlance of trade negotiators, US interests are offensive and Chinese interests are defensive. But understandings about SOE conduct will not be written on a blank slate. The World Trade Organization (WTO) inherited an SOE rulebook of sorts from the General Agreement on Tariffs and Trade (GATT), and these rules were augmented by China's protocol of accession to the WTO in 2001. The United States has added to the WTO/protocol rulebook in its bilateral free trade agreements (FTAs), notably the US–Singapore FTA. Further additions are likely in the Trans-Pacific Partnership (TPP) agreement. In the discussion that follows, we walk through the existing rules as they already apply or might apply to China.

WTO Rulebook

In 1994 the newly minted WTO reenacted the GATT-1947 as the GATT-1994 and adopted several new agreements, including the General Agreement on Trade in Services (GATS), the Agreement on Subsidies and Countervailing Measures (ASCM), and the agreement on Trade-Related Investment Measures (TRIMS). Selected provisions in all these texts affect the conduct of SOEs.

The WTO creates a commercial rulebook for a world economy dominated by private firms. In this rulebook, market systems are the norm; state-run systems are the exception. But China's ascendance as an economic power has significantly enlarged the exception. Most rules in the WTO texts do not distinguish between POEs and SOEs, and antidumping duties, countervailing duties, safeguard measures, and intellectual property remedies apply with equal force to POEs and SOEs when they sell merchandise or invest abroad.

But when it comes to services, the core architecture of the GATS allows for distinctions between the obligations imposed on POEs and SOEs. The reason is that members must meet obligations under the GATS on a positive list basis—the service in question must be positively scheduled before foreign firms are guaranteed the right to compete in domestic markets. Table 14.3 summarizes China's commitments scheduled under the GATS in those service sectors where SOEs hold more than 50 percent of fixed asset investment. As a generalization, in those service sectors, China requires foreign firms to form joint ventures with Chinese firms, or China retains discretionary control (e.g., capital requirements) on the local establishment of foreign firms.

An unsettled question is whether Chinese SOEs are public bodies, for purposes of the ASCM, when they confer a subsidy on another Chinese firm, whether a POE or SOE. At one time, the US Department of Commerce took the view that all Chinese SOEs are public bodies, but the WTO Appellate Body rejected this view in 2011.[5] Instead, it adopted a case-by-case approach, to determine whether the SOE in question is carrying out a government mission (Ding 2014). State ownership is one factor, but not the decisive factor, in deciding whether subsidies an SOE gives to another firm are the actions of a public body that can be attributed to the WTO member.[6]

Article XVII of the GATT places special obligations on state trading enterprises (STEs). This article addressed apprehensions after World War II when it was feared that some government-sanctioned monopolies might play fast

---

5. United States—Definitive Anti-Dumping and Countervailing Duties on Certain Products from China, WT/DS379/AB/R11, adopted March 11, 2011.

6. Other factors might include the active participation of senior public officials in key meetings of the SOE. See, e.g., WTO, "European Communities—Countervailing Measures on Dynamic Random Access Memory Chips from Korea (WT/DS299)," 75ff, docs.wto.org (accessed on June 9, 2014).

Table 14.2   China's GATS schedule of commitments in service sectors where SOEs account for over 50 percent of total fixed asset investment (FAI)

Service sector[1]	Corresponding GATS sector	Scheduled commitment	Restrictions
Transportation, storage, and postal services	2. Communication	Postal services are excluded	n.a.
	11. Transport	yes, except subsectors 11D (space transportation), 11G (pipeline transportation), and 11I (other)	■ Air transport services: Chinese side must hold controlling share in joint venture, and licenses are subject to economic needs test. ■ Minimum capital requirements for establishing a corporate entity. ■ Maritime agency services: foreign equity share in joint ventures may not exceed 49 percent. ■ Freight forwarding services: capital requirements and restrictions on the number of and timeframe under which foreign investor may establish joint ventures.
Education	5. Education	yes	■ Foreign suppliers must be invited or employed by Chinese schools. ■ Excludes national compulsory primary and secondary education.
Management of water conservancy, environment, and public facilities	6. Environmental services	yes	■ Foreign suppliers are permitted to provide services only in the form of joint ventures. Majority ownership permitted.

(continues on next page)

Table 14.2   China's GATS schedule of commitments in service sectors where SOEs account for over 50 percent of total fixed asset investment (FAI) *(continued)*

Service sector[1]	Corresponding GATS sector	Scheduled commitment	Restrictions
Information transmission, computer services, and software	1. Business	yes, except 1C (research and development services)	■ Computer services: permitted only in the form of joint ventures. Foreign majority ownership permitted.
	2. Communication	yes, except subsectors 2A (postal services) and 2E (other services)	■ Information transmission: foreign investment shall not exceed 50 percent.
			■ Telecommunications: all international service providers shall go through gateways established with the approval of Chinese telecommunication authorities, which act as a regulator.
			■ Telecommunication and audiovisual services: foreign investment restricted to 49 percent.
			■ Importation rights for audiovisual home entertainment products limited to wholly owned state enterprises.[3]
Health, social security, and social welfare	8. Health and related social services	no	n.a.

(continues on next page)

Table 14.2   China's GATS schedule of commitments in service sectors where SOEs account for over 50 percent of total fixed asset investment (FAI) *(continued)*

Service sector[1]	Corresponding GATS sector	Scheduled commitment	Restrictions
Financial intermediation	7. Financial services	yes, except 7C (other)	▪ Banking: capital requirements for the establishment of foreign bank subsidiaries and branches, and Chinese-foreign joint banks or Chinese-foreign joint finance companies.
			▪ Banking: economic needs test for foreign financial institutions to engage in local currency business.
			▪ Insurance: capital requirements to establish a foreign insurance company.
			▪ Insurance: foreign insurance providers may not participate in the statutory insurance business.

n.a. = not available

1. Service sectors are defined by China's National Bureau of Statistics.
2. GATS categorizes services sectors using the services sectoral classification list (w/120) and the United Nations' Central Product Classification (CPC) for service subsectors.
3. The United States brought a case against China for restricting imports and distribution of audiovisual and other software products to Chinese SOEs. In 2009 the WTO ruled in favor of the United States, finding that China's system of importing and distributing material was in violation of GATS Articles XVI (market access) and XVII (national treatment).

Sources: WTO Services Database, 2013, http://wto.org; National Bureau of Statistics of China (2012), www.stats.gov.cn/english/.

and loose by manipulating markets. In subsequent decades, STEs have distorted world trade in important and not-so-important commodities: oil—the Organization of the Petroleum Exporting Countries (OPEC) cartel and its daughters at the national level—as well as rice, cocoa, coffee, tin, and a few other commodities. However, Article XVII has rarely been invoked in GATT or WTO disputes. One reason is that the language of Article XVII, in the absence of an expansive judicial interpretation, appears to deprive the article of an effective bite against abusive trading practices. Article XVII(1)(a) calls on governments to ensure that an STE "shall, in its purchases or sales involving either imports or exports, act in a manner consistent with the general principles of non-discriminatory treatment." Article XVII(1)(b) goes on to announce that STEs shall

> make any such purchases or sales solely in accordance with commercial considerations,[7] including price, quality, availability, marketability, transportation and other conditions of purchase or sale, and shall afford the enterprises of the other contracting parties adequate opportunity, in accordance with customary business practice, to compete for participation in such purchases or sales.

Practically the only Appellate Body case centering on Article XVII was DS276 in 2004, regarding Canada and imports of grains.[8] The United States asserted that the Canadian Wheat Board did not conduct transactions in accordance with "commercial considerations." The panel rejected the US allegations for lack of sufficient evidence. One commentator (Smith 2006) observed that the term *commercial considerations* is rather fuzzy, making it hard to bring a successful case in the WTO. Footnote 7, explaining the meaning of "commercial considerations," allows ample latitude for STEs to practice price discrimination as they wish.

In 1999, before the decision regarding Canada's Wheat Board, the WTO Working Party on State Trading Enterprises adopted its Illustrative List of Relationships between Governments and State Trading Enterprises and the Kinds of Activities Engaged in by these Enterprises (G/STR/4). The list is specific as to which sorts of firms WTO members had notified as STEs. While the list does not bind a future Appellate Body interpretation of Article XVII, the examples clearly cover those SOEs that enjoy "exclusive or special rights or privileges" with the result that the SOE influences the "level or direction of imports or direction of imports or exports." However, the "commercial considerations" language cited above probably allows nearly all SOEs that might be defined as STEs ample wiggle room to escape discipline under Article XVII. These are among the background factors that commend stronger language on SOE practices in FTAs.

---

7. The note to the paragraph reads: "The charging by a state enterprise of different prices for its sales of a product in different markets is not precluded by the provisions of this article, provided that such different prices are charged for commercial reasons, to meet conditions of supply and demand in export markets."

8. See WTO, "Canada—Measures Relating to Exports of Wheat and Treatment of Imported Grain," www.wto.org (accessed on June 9, 2014).

Article VIII of the GATS may provide an avenue to attack abusive practices of SOEs in service industries, such as banking and telecommunications. Article VIII(1) requires "monopoly suppliers" to observe the most favored nation (MFN) principle in their dealings with other WTO members, and Article VIII(2) prohibits the "abuse of [a supplier's] monopoly position" when it competes outside the scope of its monopoly rights, but only if the member country has committed specifically to fair dealing. Article VIII(5) applies the foregoing provisions to "exclusive service suppliers" when the member country has established a small number of noncompetitive suppliers to do business in its territory. As GATS Article VIII has not yet been tested in a case before the Appellate Body, it is hard to know whether the provisions would significantly curb abusive SOE practices.

China's Accession Protocol to the WTO

China subscribed to detailed conditions to join the WTO in 2002. These took the form of a working party report, agreed between China and the existing WTO members, after 13 years of bilateral negotiations with the largest WTO members. Paragraph 46 of the report, which applies to both SOEs and SSEs, essentially repeated the language of GATT Article XVII(1)(b), quoted above, but went on to add this sentence:

> In addition, the Government of China would not influence, directly or indirectly, commercial decisions on the part of state-owned or state-invested enterprises, including on the quantity, value or country of origin of any goods purchased or sold, except in a manner consistent with the WTO Agreement.

The additional sentence, if Chinese authorities respect it, would go some distance to ensure that SOEs and SSEs act "in accordance with commercial considerations." But in practice it will always be difficult for outsiders to know whether Chinese authorities meddle in the commercial decisions of SOEs or SSEs.

China's accession protocol called for liberalization in certain sectors that Chinese SOEs dominated in 2001. The banking sector was opened in a limited fashion to foreign firms. Rights to import and export (trading rights) were no longer limited to SOEs and other privileged firms. Subsidies to money-losing SOEs were phased out over time, export subsidies were immediately phased out, and subsidies given by one SOE to other SOEs were defined as specific for the purposes of applying the ASCM.[9] These commitments were far-reaching,

---

9. A finding of specificity is one of the requirements for bringing a case against domestic subsidies (subsidies that are not targeted on exports).

but left room for informal and hidden government guidance to SOEs and murky financial arrangements between the Chinese government, SOEs, and the private sector. The absence of transparent and detailed accounting by SOEs of their purchases, sales, and sundry receipts and payments to private firms and the Chinese government makes it almost impossible to assess whether mischief is afoot.

Bilateral and Regional FTAs

Competition chapters, including disciplines on SOEs, are now standard fare in US FTAs. These chapters have evolved in the 20 years since the signing of the North American Free Trade Agreement (NAFTA).

North American Free Trade Agreement

Among its FTAs, the United States first addressed the SOE question in NAFTA, signed in 1993. In chapter 15, dealing with competition, monopolies, and state enterprises, Articles 1502 and 1503 announced limited disciplines in situations where the state authorizes a monopoly or operates a commercial enterprise.[10] Designated monopolies are supposed to act in accordance with commercial considerations except when their mandate says otherwise (e.g., provide cheap gasoline to the public). SOEs are given more leeway: They are simply admonished not to abuse NAFTA obligations when they use delegated governmental powers, such as the power to grant licenses, approve commercial transactions, or impose quotas or fees. The giant Mexican oil monopoly Pemex was subject to these disciplines, and beginning in 2003, Pemex was required to open its procurement to Canadian and US firms. This history could serve as an example for the giant Chinese oil firms Sinopec and CNOOC.

Whatever punch chapter 15 of NAFTA may have, however, is eroded by limiting dispute settlement to state-to-state consultations. In practice, this means that an aggrieved POE can ask its government to seek consultations with other NAFTA partners, but such consultations have no time limit and are unlikely to resolve difficult questions.[11] A China–US trade and investment

---

10. See OECD, "Session I: Competition Provisions in Regional Trade Agreements: Note by the United States," prepared for the Latin American Competition Forum, August 19, 2008, www.ftc.gov (accessed on June 9, 2014).

11. In the context of the ICSID arbitration case against Canada in 2007, alleging breach of Canada's obligations under NAFTA with respect to Canada Post, the US government declined to bring a state-to-state case. See International Center for Settlement of Investment Disputes, "Certificate: United Parcel Service of America v. Government of Canada," Washington, June 11, 2007, www.naftaclaims.com (accessed on June 9, 2014).

agreement (CHUSTIA) should seriously consider a POE-SOE dispute settlement system, akin to the investor-state dispute settlement system.

US–Singapore FTA

Language similar to NAFTA was a staple of US FTAs with Australia, Chile, Korea, and Peru. The US–Singapore FTA, signed in 2003, contained more detailed and stronger terms, and in its day was the most advanced agreement on SOEs, reflecting their importance in the Singapore economy. That agreement calls for enhanced transparency, requires SOEs to act in accordance with commercial considerations and not abuse their monopoly or regulatory powers, and prohibits direct government influence on SOEs. Box 14.1 presents operative language from chapter 12 of the FTA; presumably the United States and Singapore are using this language as a point of departure in the TPP.

The US–Singapore SOE provisions are subject to meaningful dispute settlement. However, the FTA has important omissions. The FTA does not mandate that SOEs publish their financial accounts in accordance with generally accepted accounting principles (GAAP) or international financial reporting standards (IFRS), requirements that would hold SOEs to the same accounting standards as private enterprises and ensure that SOEs provide relevant information to outside observers. The US–Singapore FTA defines a monopoly as an entity that has been designated as the sole provider or purchaser of a good or service; this definition does not encompass government-controlled oligopolies, which are prominent in China. Finally the FTA does not address the financing and taxation of SOEs to guard against public subsidies.

Investment Guidelines

In recent decades, most countries have laid out the welcome mat for inward foreign direct investment (FDI), sometimes providing generous financial incentives. Even so, many countries are wary when a foreign SOE seeks to buy an iconic domestic firm or acquire significant natural resources, or when a domestic firm competes in its home territory with a foreign SOE. To illuminate the concerns surrounding SOEs, we cite the current US model bilateral investment treaty (BIT), the recent Canadian guidelines issued under the Investment Canada Act, and the US approach under the revised regulations for the Committee on Foreign Investment in the United States (CFIUS). These provisions arise in diverse contexts and address other questions besides SOE concerns.

**Box 14.1   Excerpts from chapter 12 of the US–Singapore
Free Trade Agreement, on anticompetitive business
conduct, designated monopolies, and government
enterprises, signed in May 2003**

2. Government Enterprises

(a) Nothing in this Agreement shall be construed to prevent a Party from establishing or maintaining a government enterprise.

(b) Each Party shall ensure that any government enterprise that it establishes or maintains acts in a manner that is not inconsistent with the Party's obligations under this Agreement wherever such enterprise exercises any regulatory, administrative, or other governmental authority that the Party has delegated to it, such as the power to expropriate, grant licenses, approve commercial transactions, or impose quotas, fees, or other charges.

(c) The United States shall ensure that any government enterprise that it establishes or maintains accords non-discriminatory treatment in the sale of its goods or services to covered investments.

(d) Singapore shall ensure that any government enterprise:

(i) acts solely in accordance with commercial considerations in its purchase or sale of goods or services, such as with regard to price, quality, availability, marketability, transportation, and other terms and conditions of purchase or sale, and provides non-discriminatory treatment to covered investments, to goods of the United States, and to service suppliers of the United States, including with respect to its purchases or sales; and

(ii) does not, either directly or indirectly, including through its dealings with its parent, subsidiaries, or other enterprises with common ownership:

(A) enter into agreements among competitors that restrain competition on price or output or allocate customers for which there is no plausible efficiency justification, or

(B) engage in exclusionary practices that substantially lessen competition in a market in Singapore to the detriment of consumers.

(e) Singapore shall take no action or attempt in any way, directly or indirectly, to influence or direct decisions of its government enterprises, including through the exercise of any rights or interests conferring effective influence over such enterprises, except in a manner consistent with this Agreement. However, Singapore may exercise its voting rights in government enterprises in a manner that is not inconsistent with this Agreement.

(f) Singapore shall continue reducing, with a goal of substantially eliminating, its aggregate ownership and other interests that confer effective influence in entities organized under the laws of Singapore, taking into account, in the timing of individual divestments, the state of relevant capital markets.

(continues on next page)

Box 14.1 Excerpts from chapter 12 of the US–Singapore Free Trade Agreement, on anticompetitive business conduct, designated monopolies, and government enterprises, signed in May 2003 *(continued)*

(g) Singapore shall:

(i) at least annually, make public a consolidated report that details for each covered entity:

(A) the percentage of shares and the percentage of voting rights that Singapore and its government enterprises cumulatively own; the Parties recognize that shareholders do not oversee the day-to-day operations of enterprises. Nothing in this provision is intended to require or encourage action that would be inconsistent with applicable U.S. or Singapore law.

(B) a description of any special shares or special voting or other rights that Singapore or its government enterprises hold, to the extent different from the rights attached to the general common shares of such entity;

(C) the name and government title(s) of any government official serving as an officer or member of the board of directors; and

(D) its annual revenue or total assets, or both, depending on the basis on which the enterprise qualifies as a covered entity.

(ii) on receipt from the United States of a request regarding a specific enterprise, provide to the United States the information listed in clause (i), for any enterprise that is not a covered entity or an enterprise excluded under Article 12.8.1(d) and 12.8.1(e), with the understanding that the information may be made public.

3. The charging of different prices in different markets, or within the same market, where such differences are based on normal commercial considerations, such as taking account of supply and demand conditions, is not in itself inconsistent with this Article.

4. This Article does not apply to government procurement.

Source: US Trade Representative, US–Singapore FTA, www.ustr.gov (accessed on July 6, 2014).

US Model Bilateral Investment Treaty (2012)

The US model BIT contains three provisions that address potential SOE practices, even though they cover practices unrelated to SOEs.[12] In delegating government authority, Article 2 clarifies circumstances in which a party has delegated government authority to an SOE or another entity, to ensure that BIT obligations fully cover SOE actions. Delegated government authority includes a legislative grant, government order, directive, or other action transferring government authority to the SOE. Regarding domestic technology requirements, Article 8 on performance requirements contains disciplines to prevent parties from imposing domestic technology requirements (e.g., requiring the purchase and use of, or accord a preference to, domestically development technology) that would advantage a party's own investors, investments, or technology. Finally, in participation in standard setting, Article 11 on transparency requires parties to allow investors of the other party to participate in the development of standards and technical regulations on nondiscriminatory terms. Nongovernmental standard-setting bodies are required to follow this guideline.

As part of the 2008 US–China Strategic and Economic Dialogue (S&ED), the United States and China agreed to negotiate a BIT. BIT negotiations with China aim to secure a number of rights for US companies.[13] In the 2013 S&ED, the headline result was a renewed push to conclude the treaty coupled with China's concession to a negative list approach and preestablishment rights.[14] The US government will table supplementary text on SOEs in the BIT negotiations, and the new language might address investment-related challenges associated with SOEs.

Canadian Foreign Investment Guidelines

Canada recently reviewed its rules on inward FDI in response to BHP Billiton's attempted (and rejected) takeover of Potash Company of Saskatchewan and CNOOC's successful takeover of Nexen. These cases, and others on the horizon, led to a new set of guidelines, issued in 2013, interpreting the Investment Canada Act. In the guidelines, Canada adopted a net-benefit test regarding SOE acquisitions, with the burden of proof assigned to the acquiring firm:[15]

---

12. For the text of the US Model BIT, see US Department of State, "Bilateral Investment Treaties and Related Agreements," www.state.gov (accessed on June 9, 2014).

13. Office of the United States Trade Representative, "United States Launches Negotiations of an Investment Treaty with China," fact sheet, June 2008, www.ustr.gov (accessed on June 8, 2014).

14. Chapter 13 examines these issues and other items on the BIT agenda with China.

15. The guidelines (equivalent to regulations in US parlance) under the Investment Canada Act can be found at Industry Canada, "Investment Canada Act," www.ic.gc.ca (accessed on June 8, 2014). How the United States deals with investment screening in the context of a BIT will be a

It is the policy of the Government of Canada to ensure that the governance and commercial orientation of SOEs are considered in determining whether reviewable acquisitions of control in Canada by the SOE are of net benefit to Canada. In doing so, investors will be expected to address in their plans and undertakings, the inherent characteristics of SOEs, specifically that they are susceptible to state influence. Investors will also need to demonstrate their strong commitment to transparent and commercial operations.

The Minister will apply the principles already embedded in the Act to determine whether a reviewable acquisition of control by a non-Canadian who is an SOE is of net benefit to Canada. Under the Act, the burden of proof is on foreign investors to demonstrate to the satisfaction of the Minister that proposed investments are likely to be of net benefit to Canada.

US Foreign Investment Regulations

CFIUS, an interagency committee led by the Treasury, was established in 1975 to vet foreign acquisitions of US companies (see chapter 13).[16] Today it focuses on acquisitions that might endanger national security. After congressional debate in 2007, there is still no economic interest test in CFIUS reviews. The committee reports to the president within a short period—normally 30 days, but in controversial cases this can stretch to 90 days or longer—and only the president can block a transaction.

In two prominent cases, Chinese firms have faced obstacles in attempting to acquire US firms. In one case, CNOOC, an oil giant and SOE, tried to buy Unocal, a medium-sized US oil firm, in 2005. The attempted acquisition sparked a Congressional uproar and CNOOC withdrew well before a review by the CFIUS committee. In another case, Huawei, a privately owned but state-supported telecommunications firm (an SSE), formed a joint venture with 3Com in 2003 (called H3C), which was purchased by 3Com in 2006. In 2008, Huawei tried to acquire 3Com from Bain & Company, but CFIUS blocked the merger. Similarly, Huawei withdrew its purchase of 3Leaf systems in 2010, following a review by the CFIUS. The current CFIUS regulations issued in 2008, pursuant to the statute, require the committee to review any acquisition by a foreign government–controlled entity, even if the entity operates purely in accordance with commercial considerations.

---

sensitive issue. The United States will be pressing Canada, in the TPP negotiations, to schedule a nonconforming measure for its net benefit test that is as narrow as possible.

16. CFIUS procedures, executive orders, and regulations can be found at US Department of the Treasury, "The Committee on Foreign Investment in the United States," www.treasury.gov (accessed on June 9, 2014).

China's SASAC

One cannot mention China's SOEs without discussing SASAC. Considered to be the world's largest controlling shareholder, SASAC controls over 100 of the largest SOEs in China. Li-Wen Lin and Curtis J. Milhaupt (2013, 35) detail the power and complex nature of the group,[17] asserting that SASAC "directly or indirectly controls a majority stake in virtually every leading firm in every critical industry in China." Established in 2003 under the control of the State Council, SASAC's purpose is to enhance the value of state-owned assets, appoint and remove top executives at SOEs, and draft regulations on the management of SOE assets. In 2008 China enacted the SOE Asset Law, establishing the priority of the state-owned economy, designating SASAC as a shareholder of these SOEs, and giving it more power than traditional shareholders.

The powers of SASAC as a controlling shareholder stem from different sources. Part of SASAC acts as a large human resources department, controlling the hiring and firing of SOE executives and setting their compensation. However, the Communist Party retains the power to appoint the top three executives of the 53 largest state firms (McGregor 2012, 72), and the Party may override SASAC decisions in other cases. As Lin and Milhaupt note, before SASAC was created, various Party organs held appointment powers over certain SOEs and some of these powers have been ceded to SASAC. In any event, "political qualities," such as Communist Party membership, are among the selection criteria. Midlevel managers in SOEs are usually trained in the Party School to advance their chances for promotion. Boards of directors have no say in selecting managers; fewer than half of the 117 national business groups even have a board of directors. Where boards exist, the Communist Party has little interest in letting them exercise the power to appoint senior executives. The Party and SASAC sometimes rotate the most senior executives among SOEs (McGregor 2012, 72), perhaps to foster "close cooperation" and perhaps to keep individuals from gaining too much power.

SASAC must approve the transfer of assets and shares among SOEs, a power that Chinese courts have upheld under the SOE Asset Law. But the separation of control rights from cash flow rights creates a problem for SASAC. This can manifest itself in various ways, such as the improper use of SOE cash for political influence and corruption. SOE dividends are paid to the state, but only a portion goes to SASAC; that portion is used for acquiring assets, restructurings, and supporting failing enterprises. Lin and Milhaupt (2013, 49) claim that because of this feature, "SASAC does not fully internalize the financial consequences of its control rights over the national-champion groups and it cross-subsidizes the firms under its supervision with the cash flow rights that it does hold."

---

17. This section draws heavily from that study.

The above features make SASAC weak in some areas and strong in others. The commission can be viewed as part of the larger network of connections that control SOEs and the Communist Party. Because of the opaque nature of these networks, many observers fear the worst, meaning that the government may use SOEs to monopolize certain business sectors, stifle competition from private firms, and exert political influence. Some SOEs or sovereign wealth funds based elsewhere, such as Singapore's Temasek, have more transparent structures and fewer ties to the government. Temasek's board does not have government officials, only businesspeople. US officials are more comfortable with this kind of structure.

How can rules be written that discipline SOEs dominated by government influence? One suggestion is to examine, on a case-by-case basis, the relationships between SOEs and their governments, thereby creating a list of, say, green, amber, and red SOEs: Under this approach, green SOEs would be treated like private firms, amber SOEs would face some disciplines, and red SOEs would face the full range of disciplines.

SOEs in the Third Plenum

China's Third Plenum of the 18th Party Congress was a big moment for President Xi Jinping and his reform agenda. SOEs featured prominently and several notable directives were aimed at them. The Plenum declared that China needed to shape its SOEs into modern enterprises. Groundbreaking statements previewed private ownership of some SOEs. Equally important, the government could reduce its role as SOE manager, possibly bringing in professional business leaders. Additional statements suggested that the government would reduce the number of monopolies. If implemented, these various proposals would steer SOEs in the right direction and possibly alleviate private firms' concerns.

Issues for a CHUSTIA

While SOEs are subject to the same trade remedies—antidumping duties, countervailing duties, safeguard actions—as POEs, a core issue is disclosure. POEs are presumed to act with a view to making profits, meaning that, in the ordinary course of business, they buy from the cheapest source and sell at the best possible price. SOEs, on the other hand, sometimes answer to different public goals: perhaps increasing employment well beyond the needs of the enterprise, perhaps favoring domestic suppliers and buyers in their pricing arrangements, and perhaps fulfilling foreign policy goals.

The dividing line between POEs and SOEs is not as clear-cut as the acronyms seem to imply. Some POEs may have substantial government ownership—more than 30 percent—and some SOEs may operate at arm's length from their government shareholders. Hence the definition of SOEs covered in an FTA is crucial. Should the FTA cover only SOEs engaged in commercial activities? Should it cover only SOEs controlled by the central government? Should it exclude SOEs with passive government ownership?

All the above issues may be part of US proposals in the TPP talks. However, in a CHUSTIA the United States should seek additional coverage. Beyond SOEs, the language should cover SSEs and SCEs, whether sponsored by central or provincial governments. It also should contain a meaningful definition of acting "in accordance with commercial considerations." Language along the following lines could be useful: "in accordance with commercial considerations" could mean "free from government influence and consistent with normal business practices of privately held enterprises in the relevant business or industry."

In addition, language similar to the Singapore–US FTA Article 12.3(1)(c)(iv), on the abusive use of a monopoly position, but extended to oligopolies, is needed.[18] So is a section on national treatment for firms of both countries, to ensure that SOEs treat imports the same as domestically produced goods, services, and intellectual property. To further clarify the provisions, an illustrative list of common violations could be written into the agreement, clarifying gray areas. All these provisions would need to be symmetrical, meaning they would affect the conduct of US public enterprises—but that is a reason for, not against, including them in a CHUSTIA. As well as substantive obligations, the CHUSTIA would need to spell out the nature and coverage of its dispute settlement provisions (see chapter 18).[19]

Bearing in mind the distinction between POEs and SOEs, the leading issues reflect the need for greater transparency in the governance and activities of SOEs. Several topics under this broad heading can be identified and some of them are likely to be included in the TPP:

- An impartial regulator and impartial regulation are paramount.
- Parties should submit their SOEs to the jurisdiction of other parties when they engage in commercial activities in the other party's jurisdiction (in other words, no claims of "foreign sovereign immunity" by SOEs).
- Covered SOEs should not be allowed to combine different lines of business to a greater extent than any private company with which they compete would be allowed under domestic competition law.

---

18. Article 12.3(1)(c)(iv) obligates a monopoly entity to "not use its monopoly position to engage, either directly or indirectly, including through its dealings with its parent, subsidiaries, or other enterprises with common ownership, in anticompetitive practices in a non-monopolized market in its territory that adversely affect covered investments."

19. The draft TPP text attempts to address any lack of transparency by establishing a prima facie case against the SOE if there is a pattern of noncompliance or refusal to provide requested information.

- Timely publication of financial accounts should be required, according to IFRS.

- Nondiscriminatory procurement should be practiced in accordance with China's WTO commitments (Article 46 of the Working Paper Report), along with periodic summary disclosure of purchases from domestic and foreign suppliers.

- Leading officers and all directors, and their past and present connections to government office, should be disclosed.

- Policy directives or suggestions received from government officials should be disclosed. An exemption for any SOE from any measure, regulation, or law should be published and made available on request to any party or interested person within such a party.

- Loan terms from state-owned banks and all transactions with other state-owned companies should be disclosed.

- Tax payments and preferences, along with any incentives or subsidies received from the central, state, or provincial governments, should be disclosed.[20]

- There should be agreement as to which SOEs will be considered public bodies for determining whether payments or concessions they make to other Chinese firms qualify as subsidies under the WTO ASCM.

- SOEs should be subject fully to the obligations of the agreement with respect to laws relating to the protection of intellectual property, anti-bribery, and anticorruption, in accordance with international standards.

In addition to provisions along the above lines, TPP negotiators will need to wrestle with novel issues. We identify four. First, should TPP rules be written to allow sovereign wealth funds (SWFs), like Temasek in Singapore, to hold controlling interests in operating companies (such as Chesapeake Energy) without subjecting the SWFs to full coverage under the SOE chapter? Often SWFs claim that their controlled companies are completely independent of the parent SWF. Can a limited definitional carve-out be crafted that does not throw the barn door wide open? Or should such SOEs controlled by SWFs be evaluated case by case?

Second, some commentators suggest that China's SWFs may not play within the same parameters as the more transparent SWFs sponsored by countries like Norway (Government Pension Fund) and Singapore (Temasek), as well as the state of California (Calpers). Because Chinese SWFs do not have the

---

20. The Canada–EU FTA (CETA) has draft provisions that limit preferential financing for SOEs. Similar provisions could be an issue in a CHUSTIA. In any event, with proper disclosure, competing foreign companies that lose sales will be better positioned to bring trade remedy cases (antidumping and countervailing duty).

same disclosure requirements at home, should they be subject to more intrusive disclosure requirements when they purchase noncontrolling stakes in US companies?

Third, rules may need to be written to cover a situation that arises when a foreign SOE launches a commercial subsidiary in the United States (or another TPP member). Should that subsidiary be subject to the higher transparency and disclosure requirements set forth in the TPP chapter, or only to the host country's normal transparency and disclosure laws? If the higher requirements are the norm, then the parent SOE can rightly complain about stigmatization and denial of national treatment. But in the United States, if the normal laws apply—which are very forgiving for privately held companies, such as Cargill and Koch—then many noncommercial practices could be carried out without disclosure or remedy. As legal scholars know, the Robinson-Patman and Clayton Act provisions against predatory behavior have been dead letters for decades, and antidumping and countervailing duty laws do not apply for sales within the United States, or within other countries.

Fourth and finally, there is the issue of distinguishing between federal and subfederal SOEs. As a political matter, the US Trade Representative strongly argues that it cannot write rules that bind the states. But if the SOE chapter in the TPP is limited to federal governments, will that create an escape hatch for other countries?

As mentioned above, at China's Third Plenum of the 18th Party Congress, held in November 2013, President Xi Jinping prominently pushed for reforms. The communiqué declared that SOEs should become more focused on profits, like private companies, and pay larger dividends to SASAC. Protected SOE haven industries, such as energy and finance, should open up and allow greater room for private firms. Another decree promised modest changes in SOE ownership structures, allowing employee stock ownership plans. But the largest reform could come from market-based pricing for energy products and interest rates, which currently act as huge subsidies for SOEs.[21] Time will tell whether true reforms take place; for the moment, most foreign observers remain skeptical.

References

China Banking Society. 2011. *Almanac of China's Finance and Banking 2011*. Beijing: China Financial Publishing House.

China Banking Society. 2012. *Almanac of China's Finance and Banking 2012*. Beijing: China Financial Publishing House.

Ding, Ru. 2014. "Public Body" or Not: Chinese State-Owned Enterprise. *Journal of World Trade* 48, no. 1 (February): 167–89.

---

21. Simon Rabinovitch, "China Reforms Chip Away at Privileges of State-Owned Companies," *Financial Times*, November 19, 2013.

Gang, Fan, and Nicholas C. Hope. 2013. The Role of State-Owned Enterprises in the Chinese Economy. In *US–China Relations in the Next Ten Years: Towards Deeper Engagement and Mutual Benefit.* Hong Kong: China–United States Exchange Foundation.

Lardy, Nicholas R. 2014. *Markets Over Mao: The Rise of Private Business in China.* Washington: Peterson Institute for International Economics.

Lin, Li-Wen, and Curtis J. Milhaupt. 2013. We Are the (National) Champions: Understanding the Mechanisms of State Capitalism in China. *Stanford Law Review* 65, no. 4 (April): 697–759.

McGregor, James. 2012. *No Ancient Wisdom, No Followers: The Challenges of Chinese Authoritarian Capitalism.* Westport, CT: Prospecta Press.

National Bureau of Statistics of China. 2012. *National Statistics Yearbook 2012.* Beijing.

Smith, Vincent. H. 2006. *Regulating State Trading Enterprises in the GATT: An Urgent Need for Change? Evidence from the 2003–2004 US–Canada Grain Dispute.* Agricultural Marketing Policy Paper 12 (February). Bozeman, MT: Montana State University.

15

Competition Policy

Competition is the cornerstone of a market economy. There are two core justifications for this exalted position: competitive firms deliver lower prices to consumers than monopolies and competitive industries innovate more rapidly than cartels. The framework for world trade created by the General Agreement on Tariffs and Trade (GATT) and the World Trade Organization (WTO) implicitly assumes a global economy built on competitive precepts, but GATT and WTO rules do not rule out national monopolies and state-owned enterprises (SOEs). Competition policy attempts to make the implicit assumption as to the framework of a global economy more explicit. The general goal is to discipline monopolistic and collusive practices, predatory behavior, and government regulations that tilt the playing field in favor of national champions. As China does not yet have a true market economy but a mixed economy with extensive direction from the state, the role of competition policy and its relationship to trade and investment take on added significance.

Yet attempts to add an explicit competition code to the WTO have proved unattainable. Competition policy was initially introduced at the Singapore Ministerial in December 1996, and a working group on the interaction between trade and competition policy (WGTCP) was established.[1] Negotiations continued into the Doha Development Round, launched in 2001: paragraphs 23 through 25 of the ministerial declaration there recognized the case for a multilateral framework to enhance the contribution of competition policy to international trade and development. The declaration also recognized the

---

1. Competition, investment, government procurement, and trade facilitation are the four topics referred to as the Singapore issues, named after the ministerial meeting at which they were first raised.

needs of developing countries for technical assistance and capacity building, and stated that the WGTCP would focus on the core principles of transparency, nondiscrimination, and procedural fairness; in addition, it would discipline hardcore cartels, create modalities for voluntary cooperation, and ensure support for competition institutions.

No progress was made at the Cancún Ministerial in December 2003, the fifth ministerial after the conclusion of the Uruguay Round in 1994. Trade talks at Cancún failed on almost all levels, with advanced countries pushing hard for new rules on competition and giving little on issues of interest to developing countries, such as cutting agricultural subsidies. At the sixth ministerial conference, held in Hong Kong in December 2005, developing countries continued to voice their objections to international standards for competition policy, while the antitrust agencies of the United States and Europe were keen advocates. With little progress since then in the WTO, bilateral and regional free trade agreements (FTAs) have increasingly become the site for competition chapters in trade agreements.

Evolving Notions of Competition Policy

Global competition laws have become increasingly similar. David J. Gerber (2010) used the term *convergence* to describe this greater similarity in the characteristics that competition law regimes share. Virtually all laws address collusion, dominance, single-firm conduct, horizontal and vertical restraints, and merger review. Two forces are driving countries toward convergence in their competition laws. One force is the practice of reviewing and revising outdated laws; in this process, countries learn from each other. A stronger force is the prospect of better economic performance through lower prices and increased efficiency. However, while laws on the books have converged, enforcement policy varies quite considerably. Convergence remains elusive as the economic theories used to analyze alleged violations can often stray from a consumer welfare orientation and toward support for competitors and promotion of industrial policy.

Trade-Related Antitrust Measures

One proposal to further convergence, put forward by Edward M. Graham and J. David Richardson (1997), is a WTO competition agreement patterned on the Agreement on Trade-Related Aspects of Intellectual Property Rights (TRIPS). The authors wrote their volume before China was admitted to the WTO in 2001, and long before SOEs and state-supported enterprises (SSEs) became a priority issue on the international agenda. Their concept of trade-related antitrust measures (TRAMs) is a multilateral code for market access restrictions, designed to establish a framework for safeguards to assist declining industries and deal with other aspects of competition policy.

To lay the groundwork for TRAMs, Graham and Richardson first spell out how the WTO deals with government measures that impede market access, including voluntary export restraints, orderly marketing arrangements, and antidumping duties. They then explain how the WTO is less capable of handling private measures that are anticompetitive.[2] What they say about private measures applies with force to SOEs and SSEs. Graham and Richardson explore three alternative ways of handling such private measures, and rule out both unilateral action (the status quo) and supranational mechanisms.[3] That leaves "cooperative unilateralism" as the most promising route. Cooperative unilateralism is the idea that competition authorities in a nation or region could review and possibly remedy, in a coordinated fashion, private anticompetitive measures within their jurisdictions that have international effects. These situations would include anticompetitive behavior by incumbent firms and mergers with effects that cross borders.

Two ways to attain cooperation, Graham and Richardson suggest, would be positive comity and extending the WTO consultations and dispute settlement procedures under a multilateral TRAM agreement. Positive comity involves one nation's appeal to authorities in another nation to investigate and possibly take action. A step beyond positive comity is to create a WTO consultative mechanism to review implementation of law and policy at the national level. This would require expanding the interpretation of GATT Article XXIII to allow countries to bring competition policy cases as a type of "nullification and impairment."[4]

This is where Graham and Richardson suggest TRAMs fit in. TRAMs would be a new agreement in the WTO that would allow certain aspects of competition policy to be argued in the consultative mechanisms in the WTO, notably GATT Article XXII. Graham and Richardson (1997) argue that this should include national treatment for local affiliates of foreign firms, international control of cartels and cartel-like behavior, enlargement of WTO consultative procedures, mergers and acquisitions (M&A) notifications, and TRAMs-plus—a new way to handle antidumping complaints by allowing declining industries to qualify for escape-clause relief (GATT Article XIX).

---

2. Graham and Richardson examined the adoption of a working group recommendation by WTO members in 1960. The working group asserted that GATT Article XXIII(1)(c) ("nullification and impairment") should not be the basis for bringing complaints about closed markets owing to anticompetitive behavior by private companies.

3. Graham and Richardson discussed supranational mechanisms in the context of the EU Court of Justice (ECJ). In creating the ECJ, member states gave up some sovereignty, allowing the court to act as final arbiter in competition policy disputes. Even though this has been successful in the European Union, Graham and Richardson thought it was unlikely that other countries would be willing to cede equivalent sovereign power to a supranational agency.

4. A "nullification and impairment" case under Article XXIII arises from damage to a country's rightful benefits, based on its reasonable expectation of gains from WTO membership. The damage usually results from changes in another country's trade regime, whether or not the changes are consistent with the other country's WTO obligations. Graham and Richardson's suggestion, if adopted, would overturn the 1960 GATT working party recommendation and allow an Article XXIII case against private measures that impair reasonable expectations.

Graham and Richardson see TRAMs as a modest step forward. While both the United States and China would be very reluctant to surrender jurisdiction over competition policy to an external authority, in the conclusion to this chapter we suggest that Graham and Richardson's ideas deserve to be explored.

Prohibition of Antidumping Duties

While the prohibition of antidumping actions in a China–US trade and investment agreement (CHUSTIA) seems very unlikely, it is useful to observe that the elimination of antidumping actions in other trade agreements reflected a high degree of cooperation to lay the groundwork. A key aspect is that prior convergence of competition laws in the partner countries had created either alternative remedies for addressing predatory dumping practices or a common understanding that, in a market economy, the consumer benefits from low prices are generally more important than the harm to competing firms. However, in the China context, competition cases that arise from predatory pricing may give pause. The economic analysis associated with any predatory pricing practices involving an SOE—as either plaintiff or defendant—is complicated, as the Chinese enforcement authority may have difficulty placing an economic value on any favored relationship between the SOE and its government.

The elimination of antidumping and countervailing duties within the European Union, dating back to the Treaty of Paris of 1951, was exceptional and reflected European leaders' postwar ambitions to create an integrated economy much like that of the United States.[5] However, the Australia–New Zealand Closer Economic Relations Trade Agreement of 1983 was perhaps the first instance where antidumping actions were abolished in an FTA. Harmonization of competition rules in the two countries made this possible. This began in 1986, when New Zealand adopted many provisions from Australia's Trade Practices Act of 1974. Then, in 1990, both countries passed new trade laws giving each country's competition statutes extraterritorial application. Among other results, any dominant firm is now subject to the competition statutes of both countries. At the same time, the antidumping laws were abolished, partly because of their redundancy with the competition rules and partly because of the declining number of antidumping rulings (Farha 2013).

Other FTAs have prohibited antidumping actions, even though the partners' competition rules were not harmonized to the same extent as those of Australia and New Zealand. However, a report by Sweden's National Board of Trade found that 90 percent of regional trade agreements still allow the use of antidumping measures between the FTA members, while just 11 regional trade agreements had eliminated the use of antidumping measures. Some of

---

5. Sweden's National Board of Trade found that the abolition of antidumping measures in the European Union did not cause injury to industries in terms of price undercutting or market share. See Kommerskollegium (2013a).

these 11 agreements also eliminated countervailing duties (CVDs) for subsidized imports and safeguard measures for imports that cause serious harm (Kommerskollegium 2013b). In all these cases, the pre-FTA incidence of antidumping and other trade remedy actions between the partners was quite low—a very different picture from trade remedy actions between the United States and China.

In 2004 China eliminated antidumping actions in its Closer Economic Partnership Agreements (CEPAs) with Hong Kong and Macau. This is due not to the harmonization of competition laws but to the extraordinary relationship between the economies. Neither of these agreements has provisions that deal with competition, and none of the jurisdictions has used its competition laws against the other.[6]

Competition Policy in US FTAs

Korea–US FTA Provisions

The Korea–US FTA (KORUS) deals with competition policy mainly in its chapter 16 on competition-related matters. The US International Trade Commission (USITC 2007) states that the chapter can provide greater certainty to US firms and answer a common complaint about lax enforcement of competition laws in Korea. The chapter obligates the United States and Korea to maintain and enforce their competition laws, and to provide transparent and nondiscriminatory ways to solve disputes. One important development in KORUS was the emphasis on due process provisions to ensure that competition enforcement is done in a manner that enables the party under investigation to understand the case brought against it and to prepare an adequate defense. A core provision is the right to cross-examine witnesses. FTA provisions that guarantee procedural fairness in applying competition statutes are important to US companies. Companies fear that many foreign competition authorities might otherwise operate as black boxes, with the result that the economic analysis underpinning decisions can be highly suspect. A guarantee of procedural fairness affords a company facing questionable economic theories an ability to challenge them and present counterfactual evidence. Finally, the FTA provides an institutionalized channel for bilateral consultation and cooperation on competition-related matters.

Articles 16.2 and 16.3 in KORUS state that "designated monopolies" and SOEs must adhere to the obligations set forth in the FTA, especially when these enterprises exercise any regulatory, administrative, or other governmental authority delegated to them, such as the power to expropriate property, grant licenses, approve commercial transactions, or impose quotas, fees,

---

6. See Ministry of Commerce (MOFCOM), People's Republic of China, "Statistics," english. mofcom.gov.cn (accessed on June 10, 2014).

or other charges.[7] The articles also state that designated monopolies and SOEs must provide nondiscriminatory treatment in the sale of goods and services to foreign investments covered in the FTA. Additionally, designated monopolies must act solely in accordance with commercial considerations.

The Korea Fair Trade Commission (KFTC) has the authority to conduct investigations, impose penalties, shape restructuring plans, and curb the abuse of patent rights. As one payoff, KORUS has enabled the KFTC to be more active in enforcing competition law, advocating regulatory reform, and restructuring distressed corporations.

Enforcing Competition Law in KORUS

In KORUS, the parties confirm the broad authority of their national agencies responsible for competition policy. In the United States, the relevant agencies are the antitrust division of the Justice Department and the Federal Trade Commission. In Korea, the responsible agency is the Korea Fair Trade Commission. But KORUS goes on to stipulate that SOEs must treat US and Korean firms equally with respect to the goods and services the SOEs sell. SOEs must also provide government-type services equally, including import licenses and fees charged. This is an important provision when SOEs operate infrastructure, particularly for ports.

Moreover, KORUS provides meaningful dispute settlement over selected competition issues, covered in Articles 16.2 through 16.5: designated monopolies, state enterprises, differences in pricing, and transparency. If an issue arises and 60 days pass without resolution since a party requested consultations, then the matter is sent to a three-member panel. Once the panel is established, the parties can present their arguments in a public hearing. The panel delivers its initial report within 180 days, including findings and determinations. Then the parties have 14 days to submit written requests to the panel. The panel delivers its final report within 45 days of the initial report. If, within 45 days of receiving the final report, a party at fault has not implemented the recommendations, the complaining party has several options. One option is that the panel will determine an amount of FTA benefits that the complaining party may suspend against the responding party. Or the responding party may decide to pay a monetary sum, in an amount the panel decides.

Competition Policy in the TPP

Building on the momentum from KORUS, the United States is trying to install tougher language for competition policy in the TPP. Perhaps the most significant advances related to the competition enforcement expected in the TPP call

---

7. Designated monopolies are not specifically named, but the term is defined in chapter 16 of KORUS to cover measures that "establish, designate, or authorize a monopoly or ... expand the scope of a monopoly to cover an additional good or service."

for more detailed provisions designed to support procedural fairness and due process. However, these provisions, while likely written as binding obligations, are not expected to be subject to dispute settlement proceedings. US policy-makers want to ensure that the partners in the TPP cooperate in enforcing competition laws both by exchanging information and through consulta-tions. As in KORUS, designated monopolies and SOEs will have to operate within the framework of the TPP agreement. The US business community has made clear its desire to create a competitive business environment, especially covering SOEs (see chapter 14). Signaling that a discriminatory state-capitalist system is contrary to an open business environment, the US business commu-nity stated:[8]

> Several TPP negotiating parties have economies characterized by high degrees of state capitalism. While each country is entitled to pursue its own economic strategy, the state capitalist approach is increasingly resulting in discrimi-nation against U.S. goods and services and is putting our companies at a competitive disadvantage in those and third markets. It is critical, therefore, that the ultimate TPP agreement addresses these issues directly to create a fair competitive environment for U.S. companies and workers. Failure to address this issue concretely not only undermines the benefits of the TPP, it also runs a high risk of signaling to other countries that the United States will tolerate a discriminatory state-capitalism system.

Competition Law in China

The Chinese context for domestic competition law reflects a strong state role in the economy, with an emphasis on community benefits rather than economic freedom. Chairman Mao insisted that government must serve the masses and keep prices under control. This philosophy is still an aspiration in modern China, but it conceals friction between strong provincial officials and central government leaders. Provinces have their own goals, which may conflict with low prices for the masses, and they often resist directives from Beijing. Moreover, Chinese officials at all levels face tremendous pressure to maintain rapid economic growth. In analyzing China's competition policy, it is useful to keep these aspects in mind. Competition law in China attempts to strike a balance between provincial leaders' pursuit of champion companies and ensuring fair business practices.

China's competition law developed under different circumstances than comparable laws in the West. The prospect of heading down a path where competition between firms drives the economy to a greater extent than the

---

8. See letter to then-Deputy Assistant to the President and Deputy National Security Advisor Michael Froman, from the Coalition of Service Industries (CSI), the Emergency Committee for American Trade (ECAT), the National Association of Manufacturers (NAM), the National Foreign Trade Council (NFTC), the United States Council for International Business (USCIB), and the US Chamber of Commerce, April 15, 2011, www.nftc.org (accessed on June 10, 2014) in support of US engagement in the TPP talks.

central government is not a welcome vision for the Communist Party. Hence drafting the Anti-Monopoly Law (AML) was a highly contentious undertaking. Powerful SOEs strongly opposed it, perceiving threats to their prerogatives. Eventually a consensus emerged within the leadership that more competition would promote faster economic growth. Moreover, since the Communist Party advocated policies for spreading wealth, competition law could not be ignored. Stronger economic ties to the outside world added foreign voices favoring competition. Finally, China's entry into the WTO in 2001 hastened the AML's enactment. While WTO membership does not mandate a domestic competition law, China wished to show the world its readiness to operate under market principles. The AML seemed like one way to signal a new direction.

The AML was enacted in August 2007 and took effect on August 1, 2008. It is written in a manner largely consistent with international norms for competition law, perhaps being most similar to the EU law, particularly regarding questions related to dominance and conduct, while adding a few unique Chinese characteristics—chief among them flexibility for SOEs. The AML prohibits administrative monopolies and the use of governmental power to maintain a private firm's monopoly positions. However, like many Western statutes, including the landmark Sherman Anti-Trust Act of 1890, the AML is relatively general, leaving much to subsequent interpretation. This is where China's historical experience will play out.

Three different institutions are entrusted with enforcement. The Ministry of Commerce (MOFCOM) is in charge of mergers, the State Administration for Industry and Commerce (SAIC) deals with abuse of dominance, and the National Development and Reform Commission (NDRC) handles other anticompetitive acts. A council of high-ranking officials helps coordinate the three institutions' decisions.[9]

While foreign experience influenced China's competition law, it was adapted to meet domestic political and economic needs. One example is the role that courts play in applying the law. The independence of some courts in China has been suspect, and Chinese judges are not always regarded as qualified to deal with economic matters. Consequently the role of courts is noticeably reduced compared to courts in the United States, where perhaps 90 percent of enforcement comes through private litigation.

The near-exemption of SOEs managed by the State-owned Assets Supervision and Administration Commission of the State Council (SASAC) from AML review has been questioned. Article 7 of the AML requires the state to "protect the lawful business activities" of SOEs in areas in which there are legal monopolies.[10] SASAC is a government body that essentially controls around one-fifth of China's SOEs, including some of the world's largest companies by revenue (Lardy 2014). The Chinese Communist Party tightly manages these

---

9. This section on the history of China's AML draws heavily from Gerber (2010).

10. See competition policy chapter in AmCham China (2011).

companies, appointing the top three executives at each of the operating firms (see chapter 14).

Application of the AML

During its first few years, the application of the AML was largely limited to merger reviews. During this time MOFCOM developed a reputation for two things: being very slow to clear mergers (typically the last jurisdiction to clear large global transactions); and ultimately clearing most mergers but only after placing unusual conditions on the transactions. These conditions led global practitioners and foreign governments to question AML's economic theories and speculate on the true industrial policy motives behind the remedies imposed.[11]

Recently many more cases are being brought. In January 2013 the NDRC imposed penalties of around $57 million on Korean and Taiwanese makers of liquid-crystal display (LCD) panels, citing horizontal price collusion. This was the first instance where the NDRC punished international companies. In February 2013 the NDRC imposed a record fine of $73 million on two state-owned liquor companies for setting a minimum resale price for their distributors.[12] In July 2013 the NDRC initiated investigations of five foreign firms for their pricing of infant formula. Some of the firms immediately made plans to lower prices,[13] but in August 2013 the NDRC fined six infant milk powder companies $109 million for anticompetitive behavior and price fixing—the largest fine China has yet issued for violations of the AML. The targets were Abbott Laboratories of the United States; Biostime International of Hong Kong; Dumex Baby Food, a subsidiary of Danone of France; Fonterra Cooperative Group of New Zealand; Mead Johnson Nutrition of the United States; and Royal FrieslandCampina of the Netherlands. Also in July 2013, 60 pharmaceutical companies came under NDRC scrutiny for controlling input costs and setting drug prices.[14] The same week, SAIC launched an investigation for abuse of dominance by Tetra Pak, a Swedish food packaging giant, the first large case for SAIC. Xinhua's news agency opined in the same month that

---

11. Notably, Coca-Cola's acquisition by of Huiyuan was blocked. The explanation given was related to a questionable "conglomerate effects" theory that falls well outside international norms.

12. David A. Livdahl, Jenny Sheng, Karen Song, and Jora Guo, "NDRC's Recent Enforcement of the PRC Anti-Monopoly Law: A More Aggressive and Transparent Direction," *Lexology*, April 25, 2013, www.lexology.com (accessed on June 10, 2014).

13. Stephanie Wong, "Danone, Nestle Will Cut China Prices Amid State Probe," *Bloomberg*, July 3, 2013, www.bloomberg.com (accessed on June 10, 2014).

14. Andrew Jack, "China Drug Audit Gives Pharmaceutical Groups the Chills," *Financial Times*, July 4, 2013.

foreign automakers are making "exorbitant" profits on luxury car imports and that they should face antitrust investigations.[15]

Moreover, the US Trade Representative's national trade estimate report (USTR 2014) mentions that US firms are facing pressure from Chinese government officials reflecting China's pursuit of national technical standards, even when international standards have been vetted. The report also claims that US firms are asked to license their technology and intellectual property on unfavorable terms. China's plans to implement domestic technical standards and its demands for concessional technology license both create significant obstacles for multinational corporations.

Many see the flurry of activity as the natural course of the AML, and not a targeted campaign against foreign companies, but the international business community is watching with a skeptical eye. Concerns are growing about basic issues regarding transparency and due process, the ability to understand the alleged violations, the opportunity to engage with the AML authorities to challenge the evidence and underlying economic theories, and the opportunity to present exculpatory evidence. Other commentators have begun to see disturbing trends in China's application of the AML. Mario Mariniello (2013) suggests that MOFCOM has asymmetrically targeted foreign companies with respect to M&A activity compared with Chinese companies, although this does not seem to be the case for the other antitrust authorities, SAIC and NDRC, which appear more focused on protecting consumers. Table 15.1 lists mergers involving foreign companies that MOFCOM has blocked or conditionally approved under the AML. One cannot help noticing that MOFCOM seems to be imposing conditions as a means of asserting its bureaucratic power, while giving future M&A applicants notice that conditions are to be expected.

Additionally, Mariniello points to fundamental differences in the way MOFCOM implements its decisions, making use of "behavioral" remedies such as price caps and other provisions that are seemingly aimed at preserving the status quo in the competitive environment. These remedies require continued monitoring, putting additional pressure on firms and authorities. Behavioral remedies contrast with "structural" remedies, such as divestitures, which European and American authorities favor, and may actually enhance the competitive environment. Mariniello suggests two reasons for the Chinese preference: the public "marketing value" of behavioral remedies and the possibility that these remedies create more room for industrial policy objectives. Protecting the welfare of the Chinese consumer and increasing competition are MOFCOM's nominal goals, but its actions in some instances harm consumers and stifle competition. Putting price caps on products of merged firms, as in Henkel Hong Kong and Tiande, and prohibiting merged companies from entering into specific lines of business, as happened with the merger of Inbev and Anheuser-Busch, as well as the merger of Niu Hao and Walmart, very likely

---

15. Samuel Shen and Jonathan Standing, "China Should Probe Foreign Luxury Carmakers over Prices: Xinhua," *Reuters*, July 29, 2013.

Table 15.1 Mergers involving foreign companies blocked or conditionally approved by MOFCOM's AML, 2009–13

Date	Acquirer	Target	Condition
April 23, 2013	Marubeni	Gavilon	Agriculture: MOFCOM requires Marubeni and Gavilon to set up two independent legal entities for exporting and selling soybeans in the Chinese market.
April 16, 2013	Glencore	Xstrata	Mining: MOFCOM requires Glencore to divest all its equity in Las Bambas copper mine, and provide specific contract offers of copper, zinc, and lead concentrate products to Chinese customers.
December 16, 2012	ARM, Giesecke and Devrient, Gemalto	none	Secured services for connected devices: MOFCOM requires ARM to abide by nondiscrimination rules and release codes and other information for its TEE (trusted execution environments) technology.
August 14, 2012	Walmart	Xstrata	Online retailing: MOFCOM requires that the acquisition be limited to direct sales segments of Yihaodian, and places restriction on network platform and structure use.
June 15, 2012	United Technologies	Goodrich	Aircraft: MOFCOM requires Goodrich to divest its power systems business.
May 19, 2012	Google	Motorola Mobility	Telecommunications: MOFCOM requires Google to license Android free of charge and in open source, to treat all original equipment manufacturers in a nondiscriminatory manner, and to continue to comply with obligations on patents and license them in a "fair, reasonable, and nondiscriminatory" way.
March 2, 2012	Western Digital	Viviti (Hitachi GST)	Hard disk drive: MOFCOM requires Western Digital to divest the 3.5 inch HDD business under Viviti, and maintain Viviti as an independent competitor.
February 10, 2012	Henkel	Tiande Chemical	Chemical: MOFCOM requires Tiande to supply products to all downstream customers in a "fair, reasonable, and nondiscriminatory" manner.
December 12, 2011	Seagate	Samsung	Hard disk drive: MOFCOM requires Samsung hard disk drive to remain an independent competitor.
November 10, 2011	GE China	CSCLC (Shenhua)	Coal to liquid fuel: MOFCOM prohibits the JV from forcing use of its technology through restricting supply of raw coal or raising the cost of other technologies.

(continues on next page)

Table 15.1 Mergers involving foreign companies blocked or conditionally approved by MOFCOM's AML, 2009–13 *(continued)*

Date	Acquirer	Target	Condition
October 31, 2011	Alpha V	Savio	Textile machinery: MOFCOM requires Alpha V to divest its shares in Uster.
June 2, 2011	Uralkali	Silvinit	Potash: MOFCOM requires the JV to maintain current sales and operations procedures when supplying potassium chloride to customers in China.
August 13, 2010	Novartis	Alcon	Pharmaceutical: MOFCOM requires Novartis to cease sales of Infectoflam in China and terminate contracts with Shanghai Shikang and Haichang.
October 30, 2009	Panasonic	SANYO	Electronics: MOFCOM requires SANYO to divest all its rechargeable coin-shaped lithium battery operations and nickel-metal hydride battery operations in Japan, and Panasonic to divest its nickel-metal hydride battery operations and to reduce ownership in PEVE, an offshore JV.
September 29, 2009	Pfizer	Wyeth	Pharmaceutical: MOFCOM requires Pfizer to divest Respisure and Respisure One brand businesses in China.
September 28, 2009	GM	Delphi	Automotive: MOFCOM requires GM not to seek commercial information on Chinese companies from Delphi, to continue supplying Chinese customers in a nondiscriminatory way and complying with multisourcing and nondiscrimination principles in purchasing.
April 24, 2009	Mitsubishi Rayon	Lucite	Chemical: MOFCOM requires Lucite International (China) Chemical Industry Co., Ltd. to divest upfront 50 percent of its annual methyl methacrylate production.
March 18, 2009	Coca-Cola	Huiyuan	Beverage: MOFCOM blocks the proposed acquisition, citing adverse effects on competition in China's beverage sector as the reason.
November 18, 2008	Inbev	Anheuser-Busch	Brewing: MOFCOM requires Anheuser-Busch to not increase its existing 27 percent stake in Tsingtao Brewery, Inbev to not increase its existing 28.56 percent stake in Zhujiang Brewery, and the merged company not to hold any stake in China Resource Snow Brewery or Beijing Yanjing Brewery.

AML = Anti-Monopoly Law; JV = joint venture; MOFCOM = Ministry of Commerce

Source: MOFCOM, fldj.mofcom.gov.cn (accessed on June 26, 2013).

slow competition. Moreover, such remedies tend to favor domestic firms rather than benefiting consumers or promoting competition.

A comparison of MOFCOM's and the European Union's handling of domestic merger applications tells the story. Between 2008 and 2013, MOFCOM cleared all domestic mergers without conditions, while the European Union placed conditions on 60 percent of the domestic mergers. The difference hints at a soft touch by MOFCOM when reviewing domestic mergers. Surely, given the size of many domestic mergers in China, there should have been some cause for concern among authorities. Often domestic merger partners do not report to MOFCOM as they should. Nonreporting may avoid the evaluation process but, as far as is known, there have been no punishments for failure to report. Additionally, SOEs do not seem to fall under the umbrella of merger control. The merger of SOE telecom giants China Unicom and China Netcom did not go through the MOFCOM evaluation process. The largest 110 SOEs conducted over 900 M&A deals in 2012, and of the 20 merger deals evaluated and cleared that year, the only one involving an SOE was the acquisition of an SOE by a foreign buyer.

Mariniello concludes that Chinese institutions are more or less in line with their Western counterparts, except for industrial policy considerations, in the application of competition policy. In this respect, merger control authorities appear to favor the protection of competitors rather than competition.

China's FTAs

Since the AML had not then been enacted, there was no competition chapter in China's early FTAs. Even in the detailed FTA with New Zealand (2008), there is no competition chapter, as China had only recently passed the AML. The newer FTA with Costa Rica (2011) covers competition policy. Australia and China have been holding talks since 2005, and if an FTA is concluded it should also have a competition policy chapter.[16]

China–Costa Rica FTA

The inclusion of a clause on competition in China's FTA with Costa Rica marks a significant moment. However short, Article 126 in Chapter 11 states that the two countries will cooperate in areas of competition. This covers, among other subjects, cooperation to promote the implementation of enforcement mechanisms, including notification, consultation, and exchange of information between the authorities in charge of competition. The parties will cooperate to proscribe anticompetitive practices or economic concentration that discourages competition. The FTA also promotes the exchange of experience,

---

16. China is also a member of the Asia-Pacific Economic Cooperation (APEC) Competition Policy and Law Group (CPLG), which meets annually to discuss the implementation of competition policy.

technical assistance, and training of human resources to strengthen and effectively enforce competition laws in areas such as mergers, subsidies, intellectual property, market access, and jurisprudence.

By signing the FTA with Costa Rica, China has indicated a willingness to embrace competition policy. While Article 126 is short and general, it could be a platform for competition policy chapters in China's future FTAs. Whether the article will open new opportunities for Costa Rican companies in China remains to be seen, but US negotiators can be encouraged by Article 126. Further, the United States and China in 2011 signed a memorandum of understanding (MOU) between their competition authorities to further cooperation and guide collaborative enforcement with regard to merger review and international cartels. This MOU could be another starting point for a competition chapter in a CHUSTIA.

Competition Policy in a CHUSTIA

The contemporary global approach to competition policy calls for the energetic application of national competition laws. The most important cases and the greatest number arise regarding M&As. Reviews are intended to avert significant unfavorable effects on consumers and substantial harm to other business firms. Table 15.2 lists the merger control regimes in Group of 20 (G-20) countries.

Investments between China and the United States are growing rapidly, and China's share of global outbound foreign direct investment (FDI) has expanded from 1 percent to around 5 percent in recent years. As Chinese firms reach for horizontal and vertical integration abroad, foreign concerns about Chinese control are bound to escalate. The main concern today is the role of the Communist Party when it comes to Chinese firms, both SOEs and privately owned enterprises (POEs). Special attention has focused on Chinese SOEs and their M&A activity abroad. As most SOEs are subject to Communist Party control, and as many of the top executives are members of top Party organizations, the question naturally arises: How much influence does the Party have? One event gives an example. In 2011 MOFCOM and SASAC signed a memorandum of collaboration to establish coordination between SOEs when they make acquisitions abroad. This memo stated that it wanted to "prevent unhealthy competition,"[17] in order to keep one SOE from bidding against another. This seems to suggest state-mandated collusion, and political influence may extend to POEs as well. Vast networks of associations, large firms, and firms in strategic areas, observers argue, may fall within the sphere of Communist Party control. The 2010 restrictions on rare earth exports illustrate this concern. The murky nature of political influence leads outsiders to

---

17. See MOFCOM and SASAC Signed Cooperation Memorandum to Regulate State-owned Enterprises Going-out, Xinhua News Agency, August 23, 2011, news.xinhuanet.com (accessed on June 26, 2014).

Table 15.2   Merger control regimes in G-20 countries

Country	Name of law	Year	Agency	Substantive text	Notification test
Argentina	Argentinean Competition Act 25, 156	1999	Argentinean National Commission for the Defense of Competition	Restrict or reduce competition	Turnover
Australia	Trade Practices Act	1974	Australian Competition and Consumer Commission Foreign Investment Review Board; Australian Competition Tribunal	Substantial lessening of competition	Market share
Brazil	Brazilian Antitrust Law	1994	Administrative Council for Economic Defense Secretariat of Economic Monitoring; Ministry of Finance Secretariat of Economic Law; Ministry of Justice	Either creates or strengthens a dominant position, or results in a substantial lessening or restriction of competition	Turnover, market share
Canada	Federal Competition Act	1984	Commissioner of Competition; Canadian Competition Bureau; Competition Tribunal	Substantial prevention or lessening of competition	Turnover
China	Anti-Monopoly Law	2008	Ministry of Commerce; State Administration of Industry and Commerce; National Development and Reform Commission	Effect of eliminating or restricting competition	Turnover
European Union	EC Merger Regulation	2004	Directorate-General for Competition of the European Commission	Significantly impedes effective competition (SIEC), in particular as a result of the creation or strengthening of a dominant position (SIEC test)	Turnover

(continues on next page)

Table 15.2   Merger control regimes in G-20 countries (continued)

Country	Name of law	Year	Agency	Substantive text	Notification test
France	French Commercial Code, Law on the Modernization of the Economy	2009	Competition Authority General Directorate of Competition, Consumer Affairs and Fraud Control (Ministry of Economics)	Significantly lessens competition, especially by creating or strengthening an individual or dominant position	Turnover
Germany	Act Against Restraints of Competition 1958	1973	Federal Cartel Office	Creates or strengthens a dominant position	Turnover
India	Companies Act	1953	Regional high courts; Securities and Exchange Board of India; Competition Commission of India	Contrary to public interest or is patently unfair to any group of shareholders	Turnover
Indonesia	Competition Law	1999	Commission for the Supervision of Business Competition	Monopolistic practices or unfair competition	Turnover, market share
Italy	Law No. 287 of October 10, 1990	1990	Italian Antitrust Authority	Creates or strengthens a dominant position	Turnover
Japan	Act Concerning Prohibition of Private Monopolization and Maintenance of Fair Trade	1947	Japan Fair Trade Commission	Substantially restrains competition	Turnover
Mexico	Federal Law on Economic Competition	1993	Federal Competition Commission	Reduces, impairs, or prevents competition	Turnover, control

(continues on next page)

Table 15.2　Merger control regimes in G-20 countries *(continued)*

Country	Name of law	Year	Agency	Substantive text	Notification test
Russia	Federal Law no. 135	2006	Federal Antimonopoly Service; Central Bank of the Russian Federation	Creates or strengthens a dominant position	Turnover, market share
Saudi Arabia	Competition Law	2004	Council for Competition Protection	Restricts the trade of or violation of competition among firms; misuses dominant position	Market share
South Africa	Competition Act	1998	South African Competition Commission; South African Competition Tribunal	Substantially prevents or lessens competition	Turnover
South Korea	Monopoly Regulation and Fair Trade Act	1980	Korea Fair Trade Commission	Anticompetitive effects	Turnover
Turkey	Act no. 4054 on the Protection of Competition of 1994	1994	Turkish Competition Authority	Creates or strengthens a dominant position, or significantly impedes effective competition	Turnover, market share
United Kingdom	Enterprise Act 2002	2003	Office of Fair Trading; Competition Commission; Department of Business, Enterprise, and Regulatory Reform	Substantial lessening of competition	Turnover, market share
United States	Clayton Act	1914	Federal Trade Commission; Antitrust Division of the Department of Justice	Substantial lessening of competition, or creation of a monopoly	Turnover, size of transaction
	Sherman Act	1980			
	Federal Trade Commission Act	1914			
	Hart-Scott-Rodino Antitrust Improvements Act	1976			

Sources: Peterson Institute for International Economics, International Merger Law Database, mergercontrol.net (accessed on July 4, 2014); national government sources.

assume that the Party is pulling the strings, even when the actors are all private firms.

Article 7 of the AML states that lawful business operations in SOE-controlled industries that concern national security are protected by the state, which seemingly exempts many SOEs from competition law. By design, China's AML allows decisions to reflect considerations well outside the domain of competition law as practiced in the United States. The three institutions that preside over AML enforcement are also heavily involved in China's industrial policy agenda, allowing ample room for protective arguments based on national champions and indigenous innovation. The AML also enables the authorities to block M&A deals not only for defense-related interests but also for economic and social interests, obscuring the process further.

China has certainly come a long way in its commitment to competition policy. As of March 31, 2013, MOFCOM had reviewed 579 cases for AML merger review and approved 562 of them. Some 16 cases were conditionally approved and 1 was blocked outright (table 15.1 gives more detail).[18] In the cases reviewed to date, patterns that raise concern may be forming. While the overwhelming majority of mergers are cleared, it appears that mergers involving foreign firms uniquely attract conditions for merger approval. Furthermore, looking at these conditions, the merging parties are seemingly required to accept remedies that are not entirely consistent with the goal of enhancing consumer welfare. Instead some of the remedies—limiting future transactions or entering into contractual obligations with domestic firms—seem designed to protect competitors. MOFCOM explanations that accompany the imposed remedies offer little insight into the rationale or decision-making process. Finally, it is unknown how many M&A deals never got off the ground because of a preliminary negative indication from MOFCOM or another agency.

Daniel H. Rosen and Thilo Hanemann (2013) find that the behavior of Chinese firms abroad, both SOEs and POEs, focuses on market considerations and profit maximization, not government mandates. But the authors also conclude that concerns about political influence were warranted, and that an evaluation of worst-case scenarios made sense. The large role of SOE investment abroad obviously creates a challenge for the United States, especially for M&A deals. Moreover, US firms see higher hurdles obstructing their own investments in China. Several industries seem to be off-limits. Accordingly, knowledgeable US observers are calling for symmetry in market access.[19]

---

18. See MOFCOM, "MOFCOM Spokesman Yao Jian Answered Questions from the Media Regarding the Anti-Monopoly Review of Concentration of Undertakings," transcript, May 27, 2013, english.mofcom.gov.cn (accessed on June 10, 2014).

19. See Robert Herzstein, "Smithfield Foods Purchase Exposes Need for Broader Oversight," *Washington Post*, May 31, 2013, www.washingtonpost.com (accessed on June 10, 2014). Herzstein argues that US companies have a hard time investing in similar industries in China, even though Chinese companies are free to acquire US firms.

The danger is that without more comprehensive international rules on competition policy—rules that ensure transparency and guarantee due process in competition enforcement proceedings—nations will retreat to self-help that excludes certain foreign firms. Canada has stiffened its screening of SOEs that might enjoy nonmarket advantages, such as access to cheap capital, and the European Commission is calling for reciprocity in market access. These initiatives are inspired in part by fears, justified or not, of China's outward investment profile. The latent threat to an open regime for global investment, arising from quarters in the United States, cannot be ignored. But for now, the United States is pushing for new rules on SOEs in TPP talks rather than new restrictions on inward FDI.

Conclusions

The challenges facing implementation of a competition policy chapter in a CHUSTIA are immense. China has 113 SOEs that are administered by SASAC, with net revenue of over $1.80 trillion in the first half of 2013.[20] Given that SOEs and SSEs span multiple industries, US firms perceive asymmetry and unfairness in areas where Chinese SOEs conduct business.

The newfound assertiveness of Chinese agencies in charge of implementing the AML requires greater transparency and balance toward SOEs and SSEs. Recent NDRC actions seem to have disproportionately targeted foreign firms, while Chinese SOEs seem to have an almost free pass. The US–Singapore FTA offers the most extensive architectural framework so far designed to ensure fair competition between POEs and SOEs. However, even that FTA does not call on competition authorities to ensure a level playing field between SOEs and POEs. How would a framework ensure that NDRC regulates collusion of all companies equally? How could it ensure that SAIC challenges abuse of dominance by a Chinese firm just as it would a foreign firm? How could it prompt MOFCOM to allow a US company to acquire a Chinese SOE when there is no legitimate national security issue?

Some of the above concerns might be addressed if the dispute settlement framework in a CHUSTIA enabled consultations culminating, in exceptional cases, in a panel process that could call for reconsideration of an NDRC or MOFCOM decision. For symmetry the panel process should also have the power to call for reconsideration of a decision by the Justice Department or the Federal Trade Commission. Further complicating matters is that competition cases arising from private rights of action—which, in the United States, represent the overwhelming majority of competition enforcement activity—involve the courts, not government enforcement authorities. The dispute settlement framework would very likely need to cover such cases. While conferring power on a panel process to call for reconsideration of a court decision might seem

---

20. "Central SOEs Profits up 18.2 pct in H1," China Weekly, July 29, 2013, news.xinhuanet.com (accessed on June 10, 2014).

like a far reach, such an agreement would signal a new day in competition policy between the United States and China. Of course CFIUS or SAIC decisions based on national security considerations would be excluded from panel review, but decisions based on normal competition policy concerns, such as price fixing, excessive concentration resulting from an M&A deal, or abuse of a dominant position, would be fair game for the dispute mechanism.

Before invoking a panel mechanism, extensive consultations would have to be held between the competition policy agencies when one of them initiated the complaint or challenged the action of the other party. However, when the complaint or challenge was solely between some mix of POEs and SOEs, the dispute panel would essentially act as an appellate body with the power to remand decisions to the relevant national court.

We do not envisage that the panel mechanism would be used often, but its presence in a CHUSTIA would ensure a higher degree of transparency and consistency in national competition policy decisions. For a mechanism along these lines to work, the CHUSTIA should have detailed rules on the standards for evaluating competition enforcement decisions to determine when such decisions might fall well outside generally accepted theories of economic harm. Likewise, explicit limits might be placed on the directives that the government can provide to commercial firms, whether SOEs or POEs. A strong requirement could be written to disclose financial and nonfinancial benefits that the government provides to SOEs and POEs.

Of course, China can go a long way toward easing the concerns of US business and government if the agencies charged with enforcing the AML are seen to operate as their Western counterparts do. It will also help if SOEs doing business abroad publish their accounts in a manner similar to Western multinational corporations, so that they are clearly seen to maximize profits rather than pursue other objectives.

References

AmCham China (American Chamber of Commerce in the People's Republic of China). 2011. *American Business in China*. Beijing.

Farha, Ryan. 2013. A Right Unexercised Is a Right Lost? Abolishing Antidumping in Regional Trade Agreements. *Georgetown Journal of International Law* 44, no. 1: 211–48.

Gerber, David J. 2010. *Global Competition: Law, Markets and Globalization*. New York: Oxford University Press.

Graham, Edward M., and J. David Richardson. 1997. *Competition Policies for the Global Economy*. Policy Analyses in International Economics 51. Washington: Peterson Institute for International Economics.

Kommerskollegium (National Board of Trade, Sweden). 2013a. *Effects on Trade and Competition of Abolishing Anti-Dumping Measures: The European Union Experience*. Stockholm.

Kommerskollegium (National Board of Trade, Sweden). 2013b. *Eliminating Anti-Dumping Measures in Regional Trade Agreements: The European Union Example*. Stockholm.

Lardy, Nicholas R. 2014. *Markets over Mao: The Rise of Private Business in China*. Washington: Peterson Institute for International Economics.

Mariniello, Mario. 2013. *The Dragon Awakes: Is Chinese Competition Policy a Cause for Concern?* Bruegel Policy Contribution (October). Brussels: Bruegel.

Rosen, Daniel H., and Thilo Hanemann. 2013. *China's Rise as Global Direct Investor: Policy Implications.* Washington: Peterson Institute for International Economics.

USITC (US International Trade Commission). 2007. *US–Korea Free Trade Agreement: Potential Economy-Wide and Selected Sectoral Effects.* Investigation TA-2104-24. Washington.

USTR (US Trade Representative). 2014. *2014 National Trade Estimate Report on Foreign Trade Barriers.* Washington.

V

PARALLEL ISSUES

16

Cyberespionage

The practice of espionage dates, in recorded history, to at least 1300 BCE. More recently, in 1942, German intelligence was tapping the telephone calls of foreign leaders (Kern 2003). In World War II, US Army Signals Intelligence deciphered Japan's Purple encryption code and Alan Turing, the British genius of Bletchley Park, broke Germany's Enigma code. Only two interrelated features are arguably new about the cyberespionage debate between China and the United States: the use of internet networks to access private companies' commercial secrets, and on a grand scale. However, traditional geopolitical espionage still remains a prominent issue, as Edward Snowden's revelations about clandestine data collection by the National Security Agency (NSA) show. In 2013 Tom Donilon, then national security advisor to President Obama, remarked in a speech at Asia Society that cybersecurity "has become a growing challenge to our economic relationship." Donilon argued that China and the United States should engage in "constructive direct dialogue to establish acceptable norms of behavior in cyberspace."[1]

Within the past year, several excellent reports,[2] authored or led by persons with extensive experience in intelligence, have examined the cyberespionage question. Drawing on these reports, we first sketch the magnitude of losses and the extent of legal protection against cyberespionage. We then examine relevant World Trade Organization (WTO) and free trade agreement (FTA)

---

1. Tom Donilon, Speech at Asia Society in New York, March 11, 2013, asiasociety.org (accessed on July 11, 2014).

2. See Commission on the Theft of American Intellectual Property (2013), Lewis (2013), and Negroponte, McLarty Associates, and Palmisano (2013).

rules, suggesting the limited contribution that might be made in a China–US trade and investment agreement (CHUSTIA).

Magnitude of Losses

The magnitude of cyberespionage is large, but even rough dimensions are elusive. General Keith Alexander, head of the NSA, calls it "the greatest wealth transfer in history" and estimates that US companies annually lose $250 billion through intellectual property theft.[3] The Commission on the Theft of American Intellectual Property (2013) summarizes other estimates. The International Data Corporation (IDC 2013, 3–4) claims that the "potential losses from data breaches could reach nearly $350 billion" in 2013, including indirect as well as direct costs, such as the cost of cleaning out viruses and installing defensive mechanisms after a cybercrime. A report from McAfee and the Center for Strategic and International Studies (2014) estimated global losses from cybercrime at more than $400 billion. Coupling these losses with studies of how employment is connected to export growth, the report estimated that cybercrime could translate into losses of as many as 200,000 US jobs and 150,000 European jobs.

The foregoing rough guesses were made by organizations with a vested interest in drawing attention to the cyberespionage problem and could be biased on the upside. More conservatively and focusing on China, the US International Trade Commission (USITC) offered a central estimate to the effect that, in 2009, the value of US intellectual property Chinese firms purloined was around $48 billion, a figure that includes both lost sales (about 76 percent of the total) and lost royalties and license fees (24 percent).[4]

China clearly looms large in the world of cyberespionage. In February 2013 the US computer security firm Mandiant released a report that traced a large volume of cyberespionage to a single 12-story building in Shanghai that serves as the headquarters for People's Liberation Army (PLA) Unit 61398.[5] A similar report from security company CrowdStrike (2014) detailed further cyberintrusions by a unit from the PLA. The report described a group CrowdStrike called Putter Panda because of its tendency to go after company executives who liked to golf. The group, likely the PLA's 3rd Department 12th Bureau Unit 61486, conducted intelligence gathering of numerous defense contractors, government agencies, and research and development (R&D) centers in the United States, specifically targeting space, aerospace, and communications.

---

3. Josh Rogin, "NSA Chief: Cybercrime Constitutes the Greatest Transfer of Wealth in History," *Foreign Policy*, July 9, 2012, thecable.foreignpolicy.com (accessed on June 11, 2014).

4. See USITC (2011, 3–37). The upper bound of the USITC range of losses to the US economy was $90.5 billion and the lower bound was $14.2 billion.

5. See Mandiant (2013). The Mandiant report was publicized in the *New York Times* on February 18, 2013.

Whatever the role of the PLA, whatever the total losses, and whatever their division between lost sales, lost royalties and fees, and cleanup costs, a significant share of US economic activity is at risk from cyberespionage. The Economics and Statistics Administration and US Patent and Trademark Office (2012) estimated that IP-intensive industries contributed around 35 percent of the US economy in 2010—a value added of $5 trillion—and directly supported 27 million jobs.

In May 2014 the US Justice Department filed criminal charges against five Chinese military officers, alleging they hacked US corporate computer systems, trade associations, law firms, and unions. The Justice Department alleges the hackers stole business plans, email communications, pricing and marketing schemes, and product designs, giving the material to Chinese state-owned enterprises (SOEs) to use for commercial advantage. The companies and entities the hackers are accused of hacking into are Westinghouse, US Steel, Alcoa, Allegheny Technology, SolarWorld, and the United Steelworkers union. China fired back with a series of op-eds and a report by the China Internet Media Research Center claiming that China was the main target of US surveillance. China called the United States a hypocritical cyberbully, conducting surveillance around the world through the NSA and other means.

Reactions in China

Revelations from Edward Snowden have shown that concerns over spying are not one-sided. The NSA targeted China's Tsinghua University, which hosts the country's oldest internet hub, as recently as January 2009. Tsinghua currently routes data for tens of millions of Chinese users.[6] Snowden also alleged that the NSA had been intercepting millions of text messages from Chinese mobile subscribers, although it is not clear if any leaks directly support this claim.[7]

The US Congress passed a law in March 2013 that could restrict purchases of information technology (IT) equipment from China; obviously the law could spark repercussions on the Chinese side,[8] especially since at the same time, the NSA was creating back doors into Huawei, China's telecom giant. Snowden's documents show the NSA had found its way into the servers of

---

6. Lana Lam, "NSA Targeted China's Tsinghua University in Extensive Hacking Attacks, Says Snowden," *South China Morning Post*, June 22, 2013, www.scmp.com (accessed on June 11, 2014).

7. Eleni Himaras, "Snowden NSA-China Hacking Claims Complicate Extradition," *Bloomberg*, June 21, 2013, www.bloomberg.com (accessed on June 11, 2014).

8. HR 933 is a spending law with a provision requiring certain agencies to consult law enforcement authorities when considering the purchase of IT systems. The most obvious targets of this legislation are Huawei and ZTE, two giant Chinese telecom firms. In retaliation, China might restrict telecom equipment and software purchases from such companies as Lucent, Verizon, and Google.

Huawei's network in Shenzhen.[9] In the wake of this episode, China decried US hypocrisy.

The revelations about PRISM—the code name for NSA's collection program—have inspired the official media in China to call for a de-Cisco campaign. The state-backed *China Economic Weekly* published an article stating that eight large US IT firms had penetrated the Chinese market, calling them "guardian warriors." Cisco was the largest target, as it has gained a market share of more than 50 percent in information infrastructure in key sectors such as banking, defense, and government. Qualcomm, Intel, and Apple were included in the list of US firms and a significant share of their global revenue comes from China. The status quo is likely to start changing, as Chinese and US authorities ramp up protection in IT and other areas.[10]

National Self-Help

Patent laws grant the holder an exclusive right to use, license, or sell an invention for a limited period, often 20 years. To obtain patents, inventors must publicly disclose the nature and scope of their inventions. Disclosure, of course, gives competing companies full knowledge of the invention and guidelines for making a copy. Patent protection in many countries is poor, and for this reason alone, companies often choose to protect their intellectual property as trade secrets rather than through the patent system. In addition there is the benefit of no time limit on the legal protection of trade secrets (versus 20 years for a patent), but the company bears the responsibility for preserving business confidentiality.[11] Even so, many companies are retreating to the age-old method of protecting useful ideas—that is, business confidentiality—rather than relying on national patent offices and courts. This is where cyberespionage enters the picture: Theft of trade secrets across the internet is far more efficient than planting spies or bribing employees. What protection does the legal system offer against this new assault?

Modern trade secret law began with an English court decision in 1817 (*Newbery v. James*), followed by a US decision in 1837 (*Vickery v. Welch*).[12] State courts and legislatures gradually expanded the statutory and common law of trade secrets and, in 1974, the US Supreme Court held that the congressional power to issue patents did not preempt the state power to enact trade secret

---

9. David Sanger and Nicole Perlroth, "N.S.A. Breached Chinese Servers Seen as Security Threat," *New York Times*, March 22, 2014.

10. For more see Daniel H. Rosen and Beibei Bao, "Eight Guardian Warriors: PRISM and Its Implications for US Businesses in China," Rhodium Group, July 18, 2013, rhg.com (accessed on June 11, 2013).

11. The formulas for Coca-Cola and Chartreuse are often cited as trade secrets maintained over very long periods of time.

12. See the exposition in First (2011).

statutes (*Kewanee Oil Co. v. Bicron Corp.*). Today state laws are largely codified under the Uniform Trade Secrets Act (UTSA), which 46 states have adopted. In principle, injunctive relief and damages for trade secret theft by any means can be pursued in state courts, but in practice it is difficult to obtain jurisdiction over a foreign defendant and to prove cyberespionage. Moreover, trade secret laws vary greatly across US states, making it costly for companies to set up enforcement and compliance programs. Multistate trade secret enforcement is also burdensome, as many states do not provide for national service of process, instead requiring plaintiffs to obtain letters rogatory or initiate several proceedings in different states. Finally, some state laws provide only limited remedies that do not include ex parte seizures and mandatory royalties, which can be important for plaintiffs.

Federal legal protection of trade secrets is fairly recent and has focused on the theft itself. In 1996 the United States enacted the Economic Espionage Act (EEA), which criminalized two distinct acts: stealing trade secrets with the intent of benefiting a foreign government or agency, and stealing trade secrets with the intent of converting their use to the economic benefit of anyone but the owner. Because the EEA is a criminal statute, conviction requires proof beyond a reasonable doubt, and the defendant must come within the jurisdiction of the United States.[13] Any ambiguities in criminal statutes are also generally interpreted in favor of the defendant. Proving intent to benefit a foreign government adds another burden on the prosecutor, so nearly all EEA cases have broadly alleged the intent to benefit anyone else but the owner of the trade secret. Moreover, the enforcement of criminal statutes is at government discretion, and resource constraints often cause only the most egregious crimes to be prosecuted. Around 125 EEA cases have been brought since the statute was enacted, averaging perhaps 8 a year.[14] Criminal penalties punish the miscreants but have practically no deterrent effect on cyberespionage launched from abroad. Finally, criminal statutes do not compensate private parties for the harm suffered. For these reasons, Congress has explored the creation of a civil cause of action, either as part of the EEA or outside the criminal code, a suggestion recommended in this chapter's conclusion.

In April 2014 two US senators introduced legislation, the Defend Trade Secrets Act, to help combat theft of trade secrets. This act seeks to protect US companies from having their trade secrets stolen by any means, including cybertheft. The act would provide greater legal protection to victims of trade secret theft, giving trade secrets the same protection as intellectual property. The measures include harmonizing US criminal and civil law by building on the EEA, providing for injunctions and damages, preserving evidence, preventing

---

13. The original EEA specified the theft of trade secrets in "products." The Second Circuit Court of Appeals, reading the statute narrowly, reversed a conviction for the theft of 500,000 lines of financial code, declaring software was not a product. The Trade Secrets Clarification Act, enacted in 2012, extended the EEA to cover services.

14. "Can You Keep a Secret?" *Economist*, March 6, 2013.

disclosure, and accounting for economic harm to firms that have had trade secrets stolen.

What other avenues of self-help are available? Section 337 of the Tariff Act allows the USITC to exclude imports derived from "unfair methods of competition" or "unfair acts" from the US market.[15] Such exclusions will be granted in the case of infringements of federally protected intellectual property rights (IPRs), such as patents, copyrights, and trademarks, even without showing injury. An amendment to Section 337 of the 1930 Tariff Act could eliminate the need to show injury in import exclusion actions based on trade secret misappropriation, which would lower the burden for bringing such claims and place Section 337 actions based on trade secret misappropriation on similar footing to actions based on infringements of other IPRs.

As another form of self-help, the Department of Treasury's Office of Foreign Assets Control (OFAC) might be granted greater authority to sanction individuals and entities involved in trade secret theft, as it does in other instances of trafficking or criminal activity. Although Title III of the Patriot Act already contains a wide array of measures, a further broadening of OFAC's authority could be considered as part of general efforts to strengthen protection of trade secrets.

A third self-help defense against cyberespionage, mentioned in the reports cited, is authorizing private corporations to hack back—in other words, corporations could contaminate or incapacitate the digital networks of entities that are attempting to invade their own networks. But it seems doubtful that the US government will authorize the computerized equivalent of stand-your-ground gun laws found in many states. The problems are legion: sufficient evidence of the original intrusion; harm to innocent bystanders; and proportionality of the hacking back response.[16] For the moment, defensive mechanisms are centered on firewalls erected at private expense, together with limited assistance from the NSA to alert US companies that they have been targeted.[17] However, as the Commission on the Theft of American Intellectual Property (2013, 79–80) summarizes the problem:

> vulnerability-mitigation measures have proved largely ineffective in defending against targeted hackers, who are hired specifically to pursue American corporations' intellectual property.... Effective security concepts against targeted attacks must be based on the reality that a perfect defense against intrusion is impossible.

Fourth and finally, an annual cybertheft, economic espionage, and online trade secrets protection report could be published by the US Trade

---

15. Section 337, Tariff Act of 1930, Investigations of Unfair Practices in Import Trade, www.usitc.gov (accessed on June 20, 2014).

16. See Commission on the Theft of American Intellectual Property (2013, 81).

17. Ibid., 79.

Representative (USTR) or the Department of Homeland Security (DHS), in coordination with other agencies. The report could not only name and shame governments or private parties engaged in or condoning various forms of cybertheft and trade secrets misappropriation, but could make specific recommendations to improve national laws protecting trade secrets and guarding against cybertheft and other forms of commercial espionage.

WTO Rulebook

The WTO Agreement on Trade-Related Aspects of Intellectual Property Rights (TRIPS), which all members signed in 1994 and China accepted in 2001, creates an obligation on WTO members to prohibit, among other forms of IPR theft, cyberespionage directed against foreign commercial firms.[18] Part II, section 7, of TRIPS deals with protection of undisclosed information; in that section, Article 29, paragraph 2, reads:

> Natural and legal persons shall have the possibility of preventing information lawfully within their control from being disclosed to, acquired by, or used by others without their consent in a manner contrary to honest commercial practices[19] so long as such information [the text then enumerates steps a business firm must take to preserve its trade secrets]. ...

Moreover, the TRIPS Agreement requires members to enact laws and procedures that permit "effective action" against any act of infringement, obviously including cyberespionage. Part III of TRIPS on enforcement, in section 1, article 41, dealing with general obligations, reads:

> Members shall ensure that enforcement procedures as specified in this Part are available under their law so as to permit effective action against any act of infringement of intellectual property rights covered by this Agreement, including expeditious remedies to prevent infringements and remedies which constitute a deterrent to further infringements. These procedures shall be applied in such a manner as to avoid the creation of barriers to legitimate trade and to provide for safeguards against their abuse.

Article 61 in part III requires criminal penalties for "willful trademark counterfeiting or copyright piracy on a commercial scale," but criminal penalties for cyberespionage are not required. Article 73 in part VII makes exceptions for states that claim a national security exemption. But how far should

---

18. For the TRIPS Agreement text, see WTO, "Agreement on Trade-Related Aspects of Intellectual Property," www.wto.org (accessed on June 11, 2014).

19. The note to the paragraph reads: "For the purpose of this provision, 'a manner contrary to honest commercial practices' shall mean at least practices such as breach of contract, breach of confidence and inducement to breach, and includes the acquisition of undisclosed information by third parties who knew, or were grossly negligent in failing to know, that such practices were involved in the acquisition."

the exemption extend into the information and communications technology realm?

James A. Lewis (2013) recommends that the United States bring a WTO case against China for sponsoring, or at least failing to control, cyberespionage directed against private US firms. While Lewis is not specific on the legal route, he seems to have two paths in mind, and they are not mutually exclusive. One path would rely on General Agreement on Tariffs and Trade (GATT) Article XXI on security exceptions. The argument is that cyberespionage requires a bold response, such as punitive tariffs contrary to other GATT obligations, because cyberespionage creates, in the language of Article XXI(b)(iii), an "emergency in international relations." The second path would rely on GATT Article XXII and General Agreement on Trade in Services (GATS) Article XXIII. These articles invoke the concept of "nullification or impairment," meaning that, on account of massive cyberespionage, the complaining party is not receiving the benefits it rightly expects under the TRIPS Agreement, even if there is no formal violation of WTO rules. However, a nonviolation nullification or impairment claim is not currently available under TRIPS, as such claims have been subject to a long-standing moratorium that has been extended multiple times. The current moratorium was extended during the recent WTO ministerial in Bali, though pressure is beginning to build not to extend the moratorium any further. The US government in particular appears to favor letting the TRIPS moratorium lapse.

A few observations can be made about Lewis's proposal. First, asking the WTO to deal with cyberespionage recalls the attempt, launched in 2004, by the Fair Currency Alliance—a coalition of trade associations, including the National Association of Manufacturers—to prompt the USTR to bring a WTO case directed at Chinese currency manipulation (Hufbauer, Wong, and Sheth 2006). In that long-running episode, the US Treasury, under both presidents George W. Bush and Barack Obama, flatly excluded the WTO from dealing with currency questions.[20] One wonders whether the NSA or the Pentagon would want the WTO to engage in the cyberespionage file, especially as a solid case might require disclosure of classified sources and methods. If, despite these concerns, the United States brought a WTO case under GATT Article XXII or GATS Article XXIII, legal victory is possible but far from assured. The respondent might put up a good defense claiming three points: the respondent was doing everything possible to stop cyberespionage, the respondent is just as much a victim as the complainant, and the hackers' origin has not been proved.

Unilateral action from the United States citing Article XXI on security exceptions, without the benefit of an affirmative finding from the WTO Appellate Body, could invite retaliatory action by a member country. A foreign country might choose to impose punitive measures on US exports or investment in

---

20. In 2012 Brazil attempted to raise the issue of currency manipulation in the WTO, but was rebuffed by the United States and China, among others.

response to NSA methods of gathering data on foreign governments, firms, and individuals.

FTA Provisions

Article 1711 in the North American Free Trade Agreement (NAFTA) specifically addresses trade secrets. This article preceded the TRIPS Agreement, and the initial paragraph provided the model for TRIPS:

> Each Party shall provide the legal means for any person to prevent trade secrets from being disclosed to, acquired by, or used by others without the consent of the person lawfully in control of the information in a manner contrary to honest commercial practices, in so far as: [the text then enumerates steps a business firm must take to preserve its trade secrets]. ...

After NAFTA, the United States apparently decided to rely on the TRIPS text because a trade secrets article has not become standard fare in subsequent FTAs. To the extent addressed in recent FTAs, cyberespionage of trade secrets falls under the general IPR chapter. As chapter 9 of this volume explains, IPR chapters in US FTAs have considerably greater detail than the TRIPS Agreement, spelling out the rights of copyright, trademark, and patent holders. However, regarding trade secrets, obligations must be inferred from the general text, or in the margins of texts dealing with other subjects. The Korea–US FTA has a side letter on internet copyright piracy, and some provisions might be broadly construed to require legal action against cyberespionage of trade secrets. The relevant passage of the side letter reads:[21]

> Korea also agrees on the objective of shutting down Internet sites that permit the unauthorized downloading (and other forms of piracy) of copyright works, including so-called webhard services, and providing for more effective enforcement of intellectual property rights on the Internet, including in particular with regard to peer-to-peer (P2P) services. To this end, Korea will strengthen enforcement of intellectual property rights in Korea, and work to prevent, investigate, and prosecute Internet piracy. As part of this effort, Korea will work with the private sector and with the United States and other foreign authorities.

> In furtherance thereof, Korea agrees to issue as soon as possible, but no later than six months after the date the Agreement enters into force, a policy directive establishing clear jurisdiction for a division or joint investigation team to engage in effective enforcement against online piracy. This team will investigate and initiate criminal actions to address online piracy, including with respect to U.S. and other foreign works, whether *ex officio* or at the request of a right holder.

---

21. See the side letter, from Hyun Chong Kim to Ambassador Susan C. Schwab, US trade representative, June 30, 2007, www.ustr.gov (accessed on June 11, 2014).

Conclusions

Business firms seem unable to withstand state-sponsored cyberattackers that can invest billions of dollars and spend decades uncovering the vulnerabilities in information systems. The principal defenses against cyberespionage, now and in the foreseeable future, will rely on national self-help measures. These measures will entail better network security and stronger firewalls, as well as timely alerts from the NSA and other national agencies to private companies. In 2013 the US government informed US internet providers of addresses linked to suspected Chinese hackers.[22] In addition, the US Congress is seriously considering a civil counterpart to the EEA, namely the Defend Trade Secrets Act. The new law should enable a private US firm to bring a case in federal court against the cybertheft of trade secrets and to win an award by a preponderance of the evidence—a much lower threshold than proving a case beyond a reasonable doubt. As discussed above, additional self-help could result from revisions to the 1930 Tariff Act and from an amendment to the Patriot Act conferring more authority on the OFAC. An annual surveillance report jointly authored by the USTR and DHS also seems like a useful idea. Self-help by hacking back seems a doubtful mechanism for redressing harm.

In addition to the three defenses above, the Commission on the Theft of American Intellectual Property (2013) recommends harsh trade sanctions against China: a tariff sufficiently high to generate revenue equal to 150 percent of all IP losses, as estimated by the Secretary of Commerce. Based on the USITC's central estimate of $48 billion IP losses in 2009, the recommended tariff revenue would need to be $72 billion, implying an ad valorem tariff rate of nearly 20 percent. Based on General Keith Alexander's much higher estimate of $250 billion, the tariff rate could be so high that very little trade would take place—and, of course, no revenue would be raised. Readers of the commission's report will understand the frustration that prompted these strong recommendations. Yet an across-the-board US tariff of even 20 percent on Chinese exports might inspire drastic retaliation from China, smashing both trade and investment, leading to a commercial cold war between the two countries and possibly a global recession. Less draconian and better-tailored approaches might entail sector-specific penalty tariffs, with the proceeds paid over to injured US firms.

It is clear that concrete and clear rules need to be set. According to the US–China Economic and Security Review Commission *Annual Report to Congress* (2013), China agreed in a UN report that international law extends to cyberspace. This is important because international law, which includes the law of armed conflict, enunciates principles such as distinction between military and civilian targets, proportionality, military necessity, and limitation.

---

22. See Danny Yadron and Siobhan Gorman, "US Firms Draw Bead on Chinese Cyberspies," *Wall Street Journal*, July 12, 2013. While this had a very short-term effect, it is seen as a step in the right direction.

Additionally, international law declares that its precepts are essential to maintaining peace and stability and promoting an open, secure, and accessible economic environment, including in the area of information and communication technology. Additional and more specific rules should be the subject of future multilateral agreements. Coordination by groups like the Organization for Economic Cooperation and Development or the Group of Seven would be a good start, possibly leading to a code in the WTO. Concrete rules might also be written in the Trans-Pacific Partnership and the Transatlantic Trade and Investment Partnership.

US requests in this area will likely be complicated by the leaks exposing the NSA's data collection abroad. While one can draw a line between geopolitical and commercial espionage, it is optimistic to believe that the geopolitical dimension would not spill over into commercial negotiations. The potential fallout from bulk data collection by governments has already spurred action, with several US tech giants banding together to lobby for legal restraints on international spy programs.[23]

We do not harbor a romantic view of what might be achieved through the cyberespionage file in a China–US FTA, but we think limited progress is possible. Building on the TRIPS Agreement, the IP chapter of a CHUSTIA could require each partner to enact criminal and civil counterparts to the EEA. Whether based in China or the United States, commercial firms, including state-owned enterprises, should have standing to bring civil cases against trade secret theft in the courts of both countries. The CHUSTIA could take a further step and enable monetary damages awarded by the courts of one partner to be enforced by the courts of the other partner. This could be an alternative to the sector-specific penalty tariffs just mentioned.

Much more will need to be done in the long run. As long as one country's gains from cybertheft outweigh losses to the other country, the incentives to stop are weakened. The task ahead is to create an incentive structure that motivates states and firms to play fairly.

References

Commission on the Theft of American Intellectual Property. 2013. *The IP Commission Report*. Washington: National Bureau of Asian Research.

CrowdStrike. 2014. *Global Threat Report: 2013 Year in Review*. Irvine, California.

Economics and Statistics Administration and US Patent and Trademark Office. 2012. *Intellectual Property and the US Economy: Industries in Focus*. Washington: US Department of Commerce.

Falliere, Nicolas, Liam Ó Murchú, and Eric Chien. 2011. *W32.Stuxnet Dossier*. Cupertino, CA: Symantec.

---

23. *Economist*, "The Empire Strikes Back," Dec. 9, 2013, www.economist.com/blogs/schumpeter/2013/12/online-surveillance?fsrc=scn%2Ftw%2Fte%2Fbl%2Ftheempirestrikesback (accessed on July 5, 2014).

First, Harry. 2011. *Trade Secrets and Antitrust Law*. Law and Economics Working Paper 255. New York: New York University.

Hufbauer, Gary Clyde, Yee Wong, and Ketki Sheth. 2006. *US–China Trade Disputes: Rising Tide, Rising Stakes*. Policy Analyses in International Economics 78. Washington: Peterson Institute for International Economics.

IDC (International Data Corporation). 2013. *The Dangerous World of Counterfeit and Pirated Software*. White Paper (March). Framingham, MA.

Kern, Gary. 2003. How "Uncle Joe" Bugged FDR. *Studies in Intelligence* 47, no. 1.

Lewis, James A. 2013. *Conflict and Negotiation in Cyberspace*. Washington: Center for Strategic and International Studies.

Mandiant. 2013. *APT1: Exposing One of China's Cyber Espionage Units*. Alexandria, VA.

McAfee and Center for Strategic and International Studies. 2014. *Net Losses: Estimating the Global Cost of Cybercrime. Economic Impact of Cybercrime II*. Santa Clara, CA.

Negroponte, John D., McLarty Associates, and Samuel J. Palmisano. 2013. *Defending an Open, Global, Secure, and Resilient Internet*. New York: Council on Foreign Relations.

US-China Economic and Security Review Commission. 2013. *Annual Report to Congress*. Washington.

USITC (US International Trade Commission). 2011. *China: Effects of Intellectual Property Infringement and Indigenous Innovation Policies on the U.S. Economy*. Publication 4226 (May). Washington.

17

Trade and Currency

Exchange rates have a major effect on trade flows and trade balances. A persistently undervalued exchange rate distorts the distribution of production and employment in an economy in favor of tradable goods and services. It thus leads to an excessive concentration of output and jobs in that sector. A persistently overvalued exchange rate will favor nontradables and lead a country to underexport and overimport.

Research by William R. Cline at the Peterson Institute for International Economics, following a lengthy tradition, demonstrates that a 1 percent weakening (strengthening) of the trade-weighted inflation-adjusted exchange rate of the dollar, the real effective exchange rate (REER), will lead to a reduction (increase) of about $35 billion in the US global current account deficit after a lag of two to three years (Cline 2013a). In dollar terms, since the higher price and lower volume of imports roughly cancel each other out, the trade effect is fully realized through an increase in exports, so total US trade expands considerably. In real terms, the net effect is divided roughly half-and-half between a rise (decline) in exports and a reduction (increase) in imports. Cline's research similarly shows that a 1 percent strengthening (weakening) of the REER of the renminbi (RMB) leads to a lagged reduction (increase) of China's global current account surplus by about $20 billion.

Exchange rates between major currencies, such as the dollar and RMB, fluctuate by several percentage points in a normal year. The rate between the dollar and the euro has moved between €1 = $0.80 and €1 = $1.60 over the life of the European currency since 1999. The rate between the dollar and the yen fluctuated between 80 to 1 and 150 to 1 within just three years from 1995 to 1998 and more recently moved from 75 to 1 to more than 100 to 1 in only three months in late 2012 and early 2013. Exchange rate changes of these magnitudes can have a major effect on trade flows. Paul Volcker has observed that "trade is more affected by the movement of exchange rates in 10 minutes than by tariff changes that are negotiated over 10 years." It seems logical to include currency issues in trade agreements.

A second consideration is official policy actions that affect the foreign exchange markets. A number of countries either maintain fixed exchange rates or, like China, manage the levels at which their currencies fluctuate and hence intervene in those markets regularly. The international monetary system permits such exchange rate systems, along with free floating, as embodied in the International Monetary Fund (IMF) articles of agreement and implementing guidelines.

The levels at which rates are maintained under managed regimes can, however, result in sustained undervaluations and thus charges of competitive depreciation, through which countries deliberately weaken their currencies' value to improve their international competitive positions. Such practices played an important role in deepening the Great Depression in the 1930s and are explicitly barred by the IMF articles. Competitive nonappreciation, through which countries block or limit the rise in value of their currencies that would result from the interplay of market forces, has the same effect.

Policy interventions that alter exchange rate levels for a sustained period can distort trade flows and trade balances in a manner similar to trade policy actions themselves. Direct intervention in the foreign exchange markets to weaken a currency can be viewed as the equivalent of a simultaneous export subsidy and import barrier because it lowers the price of exports (or raises export profits) and raises the price of imports (or the profits of import substitutes). Currency actions can violate the objective of maintaining a level playing field between trading partners as much as, if not more than, the traditional trade policy mechanisms of tariffs and quotas.

Concerns about Chinese currency policy have prompted a series of responses from the United States and other countries over the past decade. Successive administrations, and especially treasury secretaries, have repeatedly criticized China's heavy intervention to limit renminbi appreciation and frequently discussed currency issues with their Chinese counterparts. The United States and others have unsuccessfully sought IMF action on the issue, although the Fund reportedly came very close to labeling the Chinese currency as "fundamentally misaligned" and launching a special consultation on the issue in 2008 (Blustein 2013). Congress, frustrated both with the executive branch's inability to deliver stronger results and with China and the IMF, has frequently threatened to enact action-forcing legislation. The House of Representatives passed such a bill in 2010 and the Senate did so in 2011, but no consensus legislation has emerged. Brazil has initiated discussion in the World Trade Organization (WTO).

Meanwhile, the RMB exchange rate has appreciated by 30 to 40 percent, and the Chinese global current account surplus declined significantly, since 2005. There is considerably less anxiety over the issue now than in 2007 and

2008, when Chinese intervention was averaging $2 billion per working day, its surplus peaked at 10 percent of GDP, and the US global deficit peaked at 6 percent of its economy. But there is still substantial concern about renminbi undervaluation and the continued high level and possible renewed rise in Chinese surpluses. The latest estimates of fundamental equilibrium exchange rates at the Peterson Institute show that the renminbi would have to appreciate by 18 percent to fully eliminate China's global current account surplus (Cline 2013b). In addition, China's buildup of foreign exchange reserves returned to a record level of about $500 billion in 2013 and continued into early 2014.

China is by far the largest currency manipulator but at least 20 countries have pursued such policies, with major economic effects, in recent years (Bergsten and Gagnon 2012, updated in Gagnon 2013).[1] For these reasons, coupled with the failure of the IMF and traditional international monetary channels to resolve the problem, an unusual bipartisan majority of both houses of Congress now insists that all future US trade agreements must address the currency issue. Sixty members of the Senate and 230 members of the House of Representatives, concerned especially by the weakening of the Japanese yen in late 2012, sent letters to President Obama and other top administration officials in September and June 2013, respectively, calling for inclusion of "strong and enforceable foreign currency manipulation disciplines"[2] in the Trans-Pacific Partnership (TPP) that is now under negotiation "and all future free trade agreements." Inclusion of such a chapter in the TPP, or in the Transatlantic Trade and Investment Partnership (TTIP) that the United States is simultaneously negotiating with the European Union, would represent an important precedent for addressing the issue in any new trade agreement with China. Some observers have suggested that US insistence on including a currency chapter in the TPP would kill the agreement, but this ignores the fact that only one or two of the participating countries at most—Singapore and possibly Malaysia—would be subjected to the new discipline (Gagnon 2014). Such a chapter's main purpose would be to deter future manipulation by Japan and others that have engaged in the practice in the past but are not doing so now, and prospectively by additional members that might join in the future, such as Korea and China.

Countries can also affect the level of their currencies indirectly through changes in monetary policy and other macroeconomic instruments. China has expressed concern about upward pressure on its currency that can emanate from the quantitative easing (QE) monetary policies of the Federal Reserve in the United States and the Bank of Japan. These measures are aimed primarily at the domestic economy and are implemented through domestic instruments

---

1. Also updated in Fred Bergsten, "Our Chance to Slash the High Costs of Currency Manipulation," *Financial Times*, December 16, 2013.

2. See letter to Secretary Jack Lew and Ambassador Michael Froman, September 23, 2013, US Senate, www.collins.senate.gov (accessed on July 15, 2014).

such as government securities, however, and are widely regarded as acceptable. Moreover, IMF studies show that other countries benefit from the export spill-over, and thus growth, effects that QE policies transmit to their economies. A Group of Seven (G-7) statement of February 2013 emphasized the distinction between unacceptable direct intervention in the currency markets and the acceptable effects on exchange rates of QE and other primarily domestic policies.[3]

The exchange rate is, of course, only part of the balance of payments adjustment, or rebalancing, process. As discussed in chapter 2, China has committed itself since 2004 to rebalance its economy away from the trade surpluses and high levels of investment that have characterized its development model since the start of the last decade. That model has produced high growth rates, but also excess capacity in many sectors and unacceptable levels of pollution. It has proven to be relatively inefficient in creating the millions of jobs that China's burgeoning population needs, and has constrained the liberalization of the financial system—including the exchange rate—that is an essential component of modernizing the Chinese economy. It has also relied heavily on large trade surpluses, which grew dramatically until 2007–08, that occasioned sharp pushback from the United States and a number of its other trading partners.

China's rebalancing strategy seeks to emphasize consumption instead of savings and investment, services instead of industry, and domestic demand instead of the trade surplus. All these steps would reduce the country's external surplus and thus moderate concerns over any continuation of its currency manipulation. Implementation has been quite modest to date, however. The sizable decline in the surplus has been due primarily to the sharp slowdown in China's main markets, especially Europe and the United States, and the lagged effects of the substantial renminbi appreciation that has taken place over the past decade.

As noted in chapter 2, further strengthening of the exchange rate is essential if the posited rebalancing is to occur. Such a change in relative prices will have three effects. It will reduce the cost of imports and thus encourage domestic consumption. It will also raise the cost of exports and thus shift production from heavy industry to services. Finally, it will release monetary policy to pursue its domestic objectives by freeing it from holding down the exchange rate by selling large amounts of renminbi that expand the money supply and create inflationary pressures (Lardy 2012). Hence the exchange rate will remain a central focus of the China–United States economic relationship and a key determinant of trade flows and policy between them.

---

3. Charles Clover, Robin Harding, and Alice Ross, "G20 Agrees to Avoid Currency Wars," *Financial Times*, February 12, 2013.

The Historical Context

Previous trade agreements have not addressed currency issues, at the bilateral, regional, or global levels.[4] In the North American Free Trade Agreement (NAFTA), a substantial price was paid for ignoring them. Mexico experienced its peso crisis and devalued immediately after NAFTA's entry into force in late 1994, altering the pattern of the Mexican economy on which the negotiation had been based and producing a sharp improvement in Mexico's trade balance with the United States. This development has been blamed on NAFTA, and used as an argument against future free trade agreements (FTAs), ever since (Hufbauer, Cimino, and Moran 2014).

There are two basic reasons for the historical pattern of disassociating currency issues and trade agreements, one substantive and one institutional. The main conceptual consideration is that exchange rates have generally been viewed as affecting trade balances rather than the level of trade flows. In turn, trade balances are seen as mainly a macroeconomic issue, reflecting saving-investment differences and broader fundamentals of the economy. The level and composition of trade is seen as microeconomic, reflecting the resource endowments and comparative productive advantage of national economies. Hence trade balances, and the exchange rates that play such an important role in determining them, have been viewed as best addressed through monetary, fiscal, and other macroeconomic policies, while tariffs, quotas, and other instruments of trade policy are properly addressed to the level and composition of trade flows. Timing has also played a major role in this traditional differentiation. Trade imbalances, and the currency misalignments that often produce them, have usually been viewed as transitory developments that will self-correct (in markets) or be corrected (through governmental policies) within relatively short periods of time. Trade agreements, by contrast, are intended to alter economic relations between participating nations permanently.

A problem can arise, however, when trade imbalances persist for extended periods of time. The United States has run sizable current account deficits for most of the past thirty years. China has run sizable surpluses since the early 2000s. The IMF guidelines for managed floating inveigh against "protracted" intervention because it can prolong imbalances beyond their normal short-run horizons.[5] One objective of maintaining the distinction between trade and currency issues has been to discourage the use of protectionist trade policy devices to try to reduce trade deficits. Following the same logic, trade

---

4. NAFTA Section 1410 says that "nothing in this part (which addresses financial services) applies to exchange rate policies."

5. Protracted trade imbalances violate the assumption of balanced trade that informs most trade models in the same way that prolonged periods of unemployment violate most models' assumption of full employment. These are among the reasons that economic models do not always accurately reflect the real world, as noted in chapter 1. See Irwin (2011).

agreements (both multilateral and bilateral) have been premised on the principle of reciprocity; they have not aimed at adjusting trade imbalances.

The second and institutional issue is that different authorities in national governments and different international organizations manage currency policy and trade policy. Finance ministries and central banks, which add another complication because of their independence from governments in many countries, are usually responsible for exchange rates, while trade or commerce or foreign ministries handle trade policy. At the international level, the IMF is responsible for exchange rates while the WTO addresses trade. The management principle of functional specificity has frequently been invoked to justify this bifurcation at both national and international levels.

In the United States, occasional efforts have been made over the years to coordinate trade and monetary policy. Such coordination has generally required intervention at the highest levels of government, as when President Richard Nixon instituted an import surcharge to help negotiate the devaluation of the dollar in 1971. Congress has also forced coordination. In 1971 its threat of protectionist trade action helped induce the Nixon administration to act on the exchange rate. In 1985 House passage of protectionist bills prompted the second Reagan administration to initiate the Plaza Agreement to sharply reduce the value of the dollar. Congress initiated a similar effort in 2005 when Chinese surpluses and intervention became a major concern, and continues to the present in the broader context of the TPP noted above. Institutional complications exist in Congress as well, as different committees have primary jurisdiction over trade matters (House Ways and Means, Senate Finance) and financial issues (House Financial Services, Senate Banking); their inability to get together, especially in the Senate, has limited the progress of currency legislation on some occasions.

More routine coordination between US trade and monetary officials has occurred on the few occasions when financial issues have become part of trade agreements, as with the Financial Services Agreement in the new WTO that followed the Uruguay Round in the late 1990s and the provisions banning capital controls in some US FTAs. In these cases, the Treasury Department largely handled the substantive negotiations, with the US Trade Representative (USTR) trying to ensure that those talks were consistent with the broader trade policy context.

For their part, officials at the IMF and WTO have frequently discussed better coordination and have occasionally set up mechanisms to promote it. In practice, the currency-related clauses of the WTO charter, which would require advice from the IMF to be activated, have never been tested. The IMF staff vetoed including currency considerations in China's protocol of accession to the WTO on the grounds that such a provision was within the jurisdiction of the IMF rather than that of the trade organization (IMF Independent Evaluation Office 2009).

There are thus arguments both for and against including currency clauses in trade agreements, including in an FTA between China and the United

States. It would be highly desirable to pursue the issue multilaterally and in the IMF rather than in a bilateral or even multilateral trade agreement. Those preferable alternatives, however, have failed to make sufficient progress on the issue despite its prevalence for many years. Even if continued renminbi appreciation and other policy steps over the next few years were to fully eliminate China's present surpluses and the United States' chronic deficits, memories of the prolonged period of sizable imbalances, heavy intervention, and resulting economic damage would call for serious efforts to erect new mechanisms to prevent future replication of such developments. Failing a new burst of vitality in the IMF and other monetary channels, there is a strong likelihood that currency will have to be considered in any China–US trade and investment agreement (CHUSTIA), especially if a precedent for doing so has already been set in the TPP or TTIP. We turn now to an appraisal of what a currency chapter of a trade agreement might comprise.

A Currency Chapter

Most FTAs, including all those the United States has negotiated, have a series of chapters on specific topics to be covered by the agreement. The TPP has 29 chapters and the United States hopes that it will become the template for future agreements. The TPP is, in turn, based largely on the Korea–United States FTA (KORUS), which is the model agreement at this point. As currency questions have not been included in these previous agreements, they would represent an additional chapter. China's trade agreements have generally been less extensive in their coverage, and less detailed in their requirements, than those of the United States. They too have not covered currency questions, and would require an additional component if those topics were to be addressed.

A currency chapter could have three components: a statement of objectives, criteria for defining and pursuing those objectives, and a set of policy measures to foster their implementation. It would be desirable to conform those elements as closely as possible to existing international agreements to which both countries are already parties, especially the IMF Articles of Agreement. Both countries are already committed to those rules and procedures, which should ease the process of incorporating them into any new bilateral or broader agreements. New language will be necessary if additional obligations, particularly with regard to implementation, are to be adopted.

The objectives of the currency chapter could be drawn from the IMF articles. The basic IMF commitment is to "avoid manipulating the exchange rate or the international monetary system in order to prevent effective balance of payments adjustment or to gain unfair competitive advantage over other members" (Article IV, Section iii). The principles of IMF surveillance over exchange rate policies call for it to consider, as among those developments that might indicate the need for discussions with a member, "protracted large-scale intervention in one direction in the exchange markets." The articles also call on member countries to "take into account in their intervention policies the interests of other members, including those of the countries in whose currencies they intervene." These precepts could provide the foundation for specifying the goals of a currency component of a CHUSTIA and could even be incorporated by reference.

The G-7 has also adopted a nonbinding commitment to consult within the group before undertaking intervention activities and the members have largely adhered to that agreement. Group of 20 (G-20) communiqués have pledged that its members "will not target our exchange rates for competitive purposes,"[6] though some of them have obviously ignored that stricture. Such pledges could be incorporated in trade agreements, especially if binding commitments cannot be agreed, but would fall far short of what is needed.

The method for pursuing the agreed objectives should start with commitments to provide data on the relevant variables, as agreed IMF conventions require in most cases. These should particularly cover reserve levels, including those outside official monetary reserves (notably sovereign wealth funds), intervention in the exchange markets, and the currency composition of official reserves. Data reconciliation committees could be set up to compare and try to resolve differences in the national data series on such key issues as trade and current account balances, as the United States and Canada did under their original FTA.

It has been traditional in efforts of this type to try to determine the existence and extent of currency misalignment as a trigger for remedial action. The exchange rate itself could be defined in either or both of two ways: the REER, the trade-weighted (thus global) and real exchange rate of the two currencies; or the bilateral nominal dollar-renminbi rate. The REER is preferred for most analytical and policy purposes as it relates directly to countries' global current accounts and trade positions. For a bilateral FTA, however, it can be argued that the bilateral rate is more appropriate; it could be included in either nominal or real terms, but the nominal rate is more available on a real-time basis and is more familiar to the public and most officials. It might thus be desirable for an FTA to encompass both the REER and the nominal bilateral rate. In practical terms, changes in exchange rates are usually the focus of attention; hence degrees of misalignment and time periods would become germane.

It has proven enormously difficult, however, to reach agreement on any of the key variables. There are numerous conceptual approaches to defining and measuring currency misalignments. The IMF itself uses three different measures that often produce very different results. Most official discussions, and even many academic efforts, have foundered at this initial level.

Hence it would be more fruitful to ignore the determination of disequilibrium and misalignment in favor of more straightforward and objective indicators (Gagnon 2013). The goal of the exercise is rather simple: to prevent a country from running large and persistent external surpluses, at least partly

6. Clover, Harding, and Ross, "G20 Agrees to Avoid Currency Wars."

because it overtly depresses the role of its exchange rate in currency markets. Both criteria—a large and persistent external surplus and significant direct intervention—would have to be met for a country to be in violation of its obligations. This approach requires only three variables: current account surpluses; levels of reserves, to determine if they are excessive; and amounts of intervention, or changes in reserve levels as a proxy if actual intervention numbers are not available on a timely basis.

Intervention is, of course, a key concept. Direct purchases of foreign exchange with local currency are straightforward, and substantial amounts thereof should be a central criterion for triggering the currency provision in an FTA. The member countries should fully disclose their intervention activities promptly and transparently. Such reporting could initially remain confidential if necessary in a transition period.

The more complex questions surround oral and indirect intervention, and whether they can be defined with sufficient precision to be included. Oral intervention can be obvious or subtle, but should be encompassed because of its potentially powerful effects, at least in the short run. If the new rules covering overt intervention were credible, however, oral intervention would lose much of its effectiveness as authorities could not back up the statements with subsequent direct intervention.

Indirect intervention could include a wide range of policies that affect exchange rates, intentionally or not, such as capital controls on inflows or outflows and macroprudential financial regulations. It would be extremely difficult to define such measures with sufficient precision to include them, however, because most of them are usually adopted for much broader purposes. They will probably have to be left for ad hoc consideration if and when they appear to have important exchange rate effects.

Macroeconomic policies, including monetary policies such as QE, should not be included for the reasons noted above. They of course affect exchange rates and trade flows but do so only as a byproduct of their primary domestic focus. Including them would distract and indeed distort the whole process.

Particularly in the case of measures that indirectly affect exchange rates, whether macroeconomic or microeconomic, intent becomes a major consideration. Were the steps undertaken to influence exchange rates, or were such influences solely a byproduct of their primary domestic purpose? The requirement to demonstrate intent to competitively devalue under current IMF doctrine has been a major obstacle to effectively implementing its rules. This problem strongly reinforces the desirability of relying on reserve increases, direct intervention, and current account surpluses as triggers for action.

The definition of *reserves* is thus important, especially as changes in them could be included as a proxy for intervention. The amount of foreign exchange holdings already reported would be the baseline number, though the timeliness of those reports should be improved. However, China holds foreign exchange in other governmental or quasi-governmental entities. Its sovereign wealth funds are particularly important because of their magnitude; their foreign assets must be included. The foreign assets of the banking system could also be considered, especially as China's authorities control the banks to a significant extent.

Agreement would have to be reached on several dimensions of the above key variables. First, what constitutes an excessive level of reserves, beyond which a country should avoid further increases? The traditional rule of thumb is an amount equal to the value of three months' worth of imports, but most countries, especially since the Asian crisis in 1997–98, have sought much higher reserve levels than in the past as a form of self-insurance against future disturbances. A limit of six months' equivalent could be accepted to provide participating countries with considerably more latitude. A more recently suggested criterion is the level of a country's short-term—that is, less than one year—external financial liabilities denominated in foreign currencies (Greenspan-Guidotti rule; IMF 2011). A currency chapter could include either or both of these variables. China's reserves of about $4 trillion exceed both thresholds by considerable amounts. US reserves are far below both thresholds, but the United States is obviously a special case because of its ability to borrow by issuing new dollar liabilities.

Second, what constitutes an excessive level of intervention? In principle, all intervention should be banned for a country that is already beyond the agreed threshold for reserve levels. Some de minimis exceptions could be granted, particularly for brief time periods, but there is no rationale for adding further to reserves that are already fully, or much more than fully, adequate. Doing so cannot be justified as financial self-insurance and can only be interpreted as aimed at preventing appreciation to strengthen the country's price competitiveness.

Third, what constitutes an excessive current account surplus? Again, any prolonged surplus that coincides with substantial intervention seems inappropriate when reserves have already reached an agreed threshold level. Again, some de minimis exceptions could be permitted with respect to amounts or time periods; a modest surplus that was clearly due to cyclical factors would normally be acceptable, and would not be a reason for action anyway unless inappropriate intervention were also taking place.

There are several more controversial questions. Would there be automatic triggers for consideration of currency issues, or would a party to the CHUSTIA have to raise the matter explicitly with the other? Automatic triggers for such purposes have been discussed over the years, dating back at least to the Committee of 20 in the IMF, which sought to write new rules for the international monetary system after the breakdown of fixed exchange rates in 1971. More recently, Korea, the United States, and initially China made such proposals for the G-20 summit in 2010. Such triggers could be based on reserve increases or current account surpluses above the agreed threshold levels. The 4 percent of GDP level reportedly suggested in the G-20 discussions in 2010, and even more so the EU Commission's 6 percent of GDP threshold for surplus countries within the euro area, are far too high, however, to exercise meaningful discipline in this area.[7]

A central issue will be the decision-making process through which these and other CHUSTIA issues will be decided. As chapter 18 discusses in more detail, there are fairly clear guideposts both from traditional practices in the WTO and in other FTAs. First, the aggrieved country requests consultation with the alleged violator of the rules—unless an automatic trigger has been agreed—and a major effort is made to reach a mutually satisfactory voluntary agreement. If the consultations fail to produce agreement, a panel of experts is chosen from a contingent list to recommend a solution within a fairly tight time limit, usually 90 days. If a country is found to have violated the rules and fails to accept the recommended solution within another tight time limit—again, usually 90 days—the case moves to the penalty phase, in which a separate compliance panel authorizes compensation or countermeasures.

The final question is what enforcement mechanisms could be included to make the agreement work and ensure its credibility, as the absence of such mechanisms has been a cardinal flaw of the IMF system throughout its existence. Five types of measures are possible: withdrawal of concessions made in the FTA itself, imposition of countervailing duties, import surcharges, monetary penalties such as fines, and countervailing currency intervention (CCI). Each type of measure allows gradation, with modest penalties adopted in a first phase and more extensive responses if the violation is more serious or persists for a prolonged period of time.

The usual technique for withdrawing concessions in an FTA is the snapback clause, under which tariffs are returned to pre-FTA levels—usually the most favored nation (MFN) rate—for breach of the agreement. Snapbacks are typically applied on a product-specific basis to counter violations in a particular sector, but would presumably be installed across the board for currency obligations, as such violations cover all trade simultaneously. It would also be possible to apply the snapback concept to concessions other than tariffs, as in the current WTO case in which Brazil has been authorized to withdraw some of its commitments regarding intellectual property rights if the United States continues to violate the Dispute Settlement Body's ruling on its cotton subsidies. The original concessions would be restored when termination of the inappropriate intervention or elimination of the excessive current account surplus corrects the problem.

More extensive retaliation can be envisaged. Countervailing duties could be authorized on the grounds that deliberate currency undervaluation is a

---

7. In their periodic calculation of "fundamental equilibrium exchange rates" over the years, economists at the Peterson Institute for International Economics have typically posited normative ceilings of 3 percent of GDP for current account deficits and surpluses (see Cline 2013b for the latest example). However, Cline (2013a) also analyzes an "aggressive rebalancing scenario" in which current account targets are set at zero for China and the United States, and the Institute's in-depth analyses of China (especially Goldstein and Lardy 2008) espoused a similar goal.

countervailable subsidy like any other.[8] Given the modest level of most MFN tariffs, in both the United States and China, import surcharges could be authorized as well to provide adequate recompense for significant manipulation. Monetary penalties could be added to the arsenal of potential measures, such as NAFTA provides for violation of its labor and environmental disciplines, or those through which the United States initially compensated Brazil for the US violation of WTO agreements in the cotton sector.

The problem with each of the options cited in the previous paragraph, however, is that they require a calculation of the amount of the currency undervaluation generated by the proscribed intervention to provide a basis for determining the magnitude of the permitted retaliation. As indicated above, such calculations are fraught with both intellectual uncertainty and great political sensitivity. Hence they should be avoided in fashioning a workable currency provision in trade agreements.[9] The snapback approach avoids that difficulty, and is a familiar remedy for violations of a country's obligations under an FTA; as such, it should be used as the trade policy response to manipulation under a CHUSTIA.

It would also be useful to add a monetary rather than trade policy tool for possible retaliation. An aggrieved country could be authorized to employ CCI for this purpose—that is, purchases of the currency of the manipulating country to offset the effect of that country's own intervention in the foreign exchange markets. If China buys $10 billion of dollars to push or keep the dollar up and hold the renminbi down, the United States could buy $10 billion of renminbi to neutralize the effect on the renminbi-dollar rate. A clear US indication that it was prepared to act on such authorizations should deter future manipulation efforts. The Treasury and the Fed could carry out CCIs under current legislative authorities. The idea was also included, as "remedial currency intervention," in the currency bill passed by the Senate in 2011.[10]

Until recently, it has been widely thought that the United States—or any other country—could not fully implement CCI against extensive Chinese intervention because there might not be enough renminbi available in the markets to permit totally offsetting purchases. It now appears, however, that the offshore renminbi markets in Hong Kong and perhaps Singapore could accommodate at least a substantial portion of the prescribed purchases. Even a partial US CCI would send powerful policy and market signals, however, and would presumably trigger sympathetic movements of private capital—such as

---

8. This is the preferred strategy of many of the Brazilian economists who call for action against currency manipulation. See, for example, de Lima-Campos and Gaviria (2012).

9. I have suggested inclusion of these remedies in some of my own earlier writings, including most recently Bergsten (2014).

10. Senate bill S. 1619 (112th): Currency Exchange Rate Oversight Reform Act of 2011 that passed the Senate but not the House.

leads and lags in payments for trade transactions—that would reinforce the US action and augment its effectiveness in achieving the needed realignment.

Negotiating Alternatives

It might prove impossible in a CHUSTIA to forge an agreement on binding and comprehensive rules, subject to an effective dispute settlement mechanism and consequent sanctions. Compromises thus may have to be made at one or more stages of the process: the ambition of the rules, the degree to which they become legal commitments, the vigor of the dispute settlement mechanism, or the severity of the sanctions against offenders.

In considering such compromises, however, it must be remembered why the issue has remained unresolved for so long and why Congress is insisting on addressing it in trade agreements. The IMF articles contain objectives that are largely adequate and legally binding on its member countries, but no enforcement tools and a dispute settlement mechanism that has proven to be enormously difficult to navigate (Blustein 2013). The WTO charter encompasses such vague obligations that they have failed to trigger its relatively efficient dispute settlement mechanism and powerful sanctions. Any effective currency chapter in a trade agreement would have to be sufficiently ambitious on all counts to provide for a credible response, and thus an effective deterrent, to currency manipulation.

It would be a serious mistake to weaken either the firm obligations to avoid manipulation or the potency of the available remedies, both of which are already enshrined in long-standing global agreements. The most plausible wiggle room lies in the ambitiousness of the criteria that would trigger action. The term *excessive*, as applied to levels of reserves and intervention as well as current account surpluses, could be set high enough that only the most egregious violators would be caught.[11] This should be acceptable, as the objective of the exercise is to discipline extreme behavior rather than every minor violation. Another possible avenue of compromise relates to the interaction the trade agreement provides between the degree to which the obligations bind the participants and the method through which they are to be implemented. A country wishing to limit its risk of exposure will want to trade off soft obligations against hard dispute settlement provisions, or vice versa. The indicators of violations of the agreed currency obligations could become presumptions or even illustrations, rather than legally binding commitments. The adjudicatory panels could be limited to making recommendations to a politically constructed final arbiter rather than issuing binding protocols, as the GATT in fact provided before the creation of the WTO. It is perfectly plausible to set

---

11. The European Commission obviously tried to appease Germany by setting a very high trigger of 6 percent of GDP for including surplus countries in its new balance of payments surveillance mechanism. Germany has exceeded that threshold over the last three years, however, so it is now being addressed.

up a separate dispute mechanism for the currency chapter, to fine-tune such considerations to the overall negotiation of the issue.[12]

As noted above, it would be preferable to address currency issues in a multilateral and monetary forum, most naturally the IMF. Perhaps those mechanisms will become more effective once it is realized that their failures will inevitably lead to other remedies, and even to other institutions being created to carry out what should be the IMF's mandates. In any event, it would ultimately be desirable to embed any new enforcement instruments in global rules and institutions, primarily by amending the IMF's Articles of Agreement and possibly the WTO charter. The process may have to start by including currency clauses in trade agreements, however—perhaps the TPP, as the US Congress is calling for, and subsequently in a CHUSTIA.

Finally, transition issues could affect a CHUSTIA in the currency area. The proposals outlined in this book assume that the external balances and exchange rates of the two countries are in approximate equilibrium when the agreement goes into effect; the currency chapter would seek to provide rules and procedures for addressing subsequent changes that create new imbalances. If, to the contrary, significant misalignments exist when the agreement is scheduled to enter into effect, there might have to be a side negotiation to provide for an agreed starting point that will not disrupt the arrangement at its outset. In light of the large and persistent imbalances China and the United States have run over the past decade, such a side agreement, which could focus on the overall rebalancing issue rather than the exchange rate per se, might well be necessary in a CHUSTIA, just as the United States has insisted on side agreements with Japan, to address the seemingly intractable issues of Japanese barriers to agricultural and automobile imports, as a condition for its acceptance into the TPP negotiations.

Conclusion

Including currency issues in a bilateral FTA is complex and likely to be contentious. This is partly because it is unprecedented; such a linkage has never been attempted in the past, let alone implemented. It is partly because the issue is fraught with intellectual difficulties, especially how to determine the existence and magnitude of currency misalignments—although this could be largely overcome by the methods suggested here. Finally, it is also because of the high degree of political sensitivity involved. The United States and China have been debating the matter for a decade and neither is satisfied with the results to date.

The problems are formidable. However, they underline the basic rationale for launching a new negotiation between China and the United States that attempts to forge an FTA or at least a series of stand-alone compacts that

---

12. NAFTA has six different dispute settlement mechanisms for different parts of the agreement, though that is not widely regarded as one of its finer features.

could, over time, be amalgamated into a single agreement. The creation of agreed rules and procedures to address future currency disputes would be a milestone in the relationship between the two countries and—particularly if joined by similar accords on other high-profile issues, such as cybersecurity and industrial policies—could preempt future disputes that could otherwise be highly destructive in both economic and political terms.

There is also a largely unrecognized potential for reciprocity regarding currency. The United States has been the demandeur for the past decade. But China could seek to broaden the negotiation to embrace reserve management issues and the role of the dollar in the international monetary system, both of which are clearly linked to exchange rates and reserve levels. Such bilateral talks could even provide a foundation for broader conversations, eventually bringing in other key countries on the future of the global financial architecture and how a rising China could cooperate with the United States as the incumbent leader—and key currency country—in pursuit of international monetary stability.

A fundamental purpose of an FTA negotiation would be to provide a mechanism through which China and the United States could, for the first time, conduct in-depth and continuing discussions on the central issues that confront them as the two largest players in the world economy. Whether or not the negotiations ever produce a full-blown FTA, or anything approaching it, such a conversation could be of immense value in deepening each country's awareness and understanding of the other's keenest interests and sensitivities, both defensive and offensive, and in countering the mistrust that is now so pervasive on virtually all issues. Despite the obvious difficulties and pitfalls, there is a strong case, ranging far beyond the immediate congressional pressures in the United States, for attempting to include a currency chapter in this discussion.

References

Bergsten, C. Fred. 2014. *Addressing Currency Manipulation through Trade Agreements*. Policy Brief 14-2. Washington: Peterson Institute for International Economics.

Bergsten, C. Fred, and Joseph E. Gagnon. 2012. *Currency Manipulation, the US Economy, and the Global Economic Order*. Policy Brief 12-25. Washington: Peterson Institute for International Economics.

Blustein, Paul. 2013. *Off Balance: The Travails of Institutions that Govern the Global Financial System*. Waterloo: Centre for International Governance Innovation.

Cline, William R. 2013a. *Estimates of Fundamental Equilibrium Exchange Rates, May 2013*. Policy Brief 13-15. Washington: Peterson Institute for International Economics.

Cline, William R. 2013b. *Estimates of Fundamental Equilibrium Exchange Rates, November 2013*. Policy Brief 13-29. Washington: Peterson Institute for International Economics.

de Lima-Campos, Aluisio, and Juan Antonio Guiviria. 2012. A Case for Misaligned Currencies as Countervailable Subsidies. *Journal of World Trade* 46, no. 5: 1017–44.

Gagnon, Joseph E. 2013. *Stabilizing Properties of Flexible Exchange Rates: Evidence from the Global Financial Crisis*. Policy Brief 13-28. Washington: Peterson Institute for International Economics.

Gagnon, Joseph E. 2014. *Alternatives to Currency Manipulation: What Switzerland, Singapore, and Hong Kong Can Do*. Policy Brief no. 14-17. Washington: Peterson Institute for International Economics.

Goldstein, Morris, and Nicholas Lardy. 2008. *The Future of China's Exchange Rate Policy*. Policy Analyses in International Economics 87. Washington: Peterson Institute for International Economics.

Hufbauer, Gary Clyde, Cathleen Cimino, and Tyler Moran. 2014. *NAFTA at 20: Misleading Charges and Positive Achievements*. Policy Brief 14-13. Washington: Peterson Institute for International Economics.

IMF (International Monetary Fund). 2011. *Assessing Reserve Adequacy*. Washington.

IMF Independent Evaluation Office. 2009. *IMF Involvement in International Trade Policy Issues*. Washington: International Monetary Fund.

Irwin, Douglas. 2011. Esprit de Currency. *Finance and Development* 48, no. 2 (June): 30–33.

Lardy, Nicholas R. 2012. *Sustaining China's Economic Growth after the Global Financial Crisis*. Washington: Peterson Institute for International Economics.

VI

WRAPPING UP

18

Dispute Settlement

Before World War II, trade agreements rarely contained dispute settlement chapters. Tariff reductions were the core of those agreements, and there was little ambiguity about the rates specified (though tariff classification issues might arise). In any event, diplomatic consultation was the normal way of handling disputes. This approach carried into the General Agreement on Tariffs and Trade (GATT) in 1947, but with a slightly sharper edge. Consultations between trade officials were regarded as the main mechanism for settling disputes, but the agreement also created a voluntary system of panel arbitration, increasingly used in successive decades. The GATT-1947 system could be characterized as voluntary because the respondent member—the country accused of violating its obligations—could obstruct the system both at the start, by not agreeing to panelists, and at the end, by voting against adoption of an adverse panel report, as the agreement required unanimity in the General Council to adopt a report.

All the above changed with the creation of the World Trade Organization (WTO) in 1994. The WTO Dispute Settlement Body (DSB) is composed of expert panels and an Appellate Body. The WTO director-general appoints panels if parties to the complaint cannot agree, and reports of the panels and Appellate Body are automatically accepted unless a consensus of WTO members rejects them. The Dispute Settlement Understanding (DSU) establishes procedures for handling disputes, permitting third-party participation, and setting timetables.

Since the WTO's creation, more than 300 bilateral and regional free trade agreements (FTAs) have been notified to its secretariat. Some of them have their own dispute settlement systems but with important differences from the DSU. It would be a novel and good idea if FTA partners approached the WTO,

Table 18.1 WTO disputes directly involving the United States or China, 2002–13

	United States	China
Complainant (total)	39	12
Respondent (total)	64	32
Complainant (bilateral)	15	9

Source: WTO, "Dispute Settlement," www.wto.org (accessed on July 4, 2014).

asking the DSB to settle disputes that arise between the FTA parties. This would require the assent of the entire WTO membership, financial support from the FTAs, and additional personnel in the WTO Rules Division, but it would have several advantages. First, if the FTA parties so wished, the DSB could simultaneously adjudicate claims arising under the FTA and claims arising under WTO agreements. Second, the arrangement would spare the FTA parties the need to create their own dispute settlement mechanisms, and it would give the parties the benefit of a proven and expeditious system. Finally, resolution of FTA disputes in Geneva would reinforce the centrality of the WTO in the realm of trade and investment disputes between member states.

The WTO System

Table 18.1 shows the record of US and Chinese participation in WTO disputes between 2002—the year after China acceded to the WTO—and 2013. During this decade, the United States was a complainant in 39 cases and a respondent in 64 cases. Out of this total, the United States launched 15 cases against China and defended 9 cases brought by China. During the same period, China was a complainant in 12 cases and a respondent in 32 cases. As mentioned, China launched 9 cases against the United States and defended 15 cases brought by the United States. The total number of US-China cases came to 24, and of these, 9 concerned various kinds of penalty duties, mainly antidumping and countervailing duties.

Table 18.2 summarizes the win-loss record in the US-China cases that were resolved by the end of 2013. Thus far, 10 cases in which the United States was the complainant have been resolved, with 7 cases receiving a ruling in favor of the United States and 3 settled through consultations, also in the United States' favor. Conversely, China has won 4 of the cases it brought and lost one. Table 18.2 gives average figures for the number of days between the date consultations were initiated in US-China cases and the date a final report was delivered (by either a panel or the Appellate Body). For cases the United States brought, the average case lasted 672 days, while for China the average case took 700 days to resolve. The resolution process requires two years on average.

Table 18.2   Resolved WTO disputes between the United States and China, 2002–13

	United States	China
Successful cases brought	7	4
Unsuccessful cases brought[a]	0	1
Cases resolved without ruling	3	0
Average time to resolution (days)	672	700

a. From the US standpoint, the fact of zero unsuccessful cases means that all cases brought were successful.

Source: WTO, "Dispute Settlement," www.wto.org (accessed on July 4, 2014).

Officials in the United States, China, and other major powers are satisfied with the DSB; it is widely regarded as the most successful component of the WTO, far more successful than the struggling Doha Development Round. Private firms nevertheless voice four complaints about the system generally. First, only member governments can bring cases in the DSB. Often it is difficult for a private firm—particularly a smaller firm—to persuade its own government to espouse a case. This happens because the government does not want to overload the DSB, because the government only wants to bring cases that have a high probability of success, because the government prefers to handle the issue through diplomatic channels, or simply because the firm does not have enough political clout. Second, while the number of days between the start of consultations and the delivery of a final report is not particularly long by the standards of civil litigation in many countries, the duration is not as speedy as the advertised timetables in the DSU: a normal period of one year when a panel report is appealed to the Appellate Body. Delays mainly arise from difficulties in composing an agreed panel, and then coordinating the schedules of panelists, usually professionals based outside Geneva. Third, once a decision is rendered, the losing party may stall coming into compliance. It will then take additional time for a compliance panel to determine appropriate countermeasures. These delays entail no penalty. Finally, the DSU has no provision for retroactive relief or monetary awards to private firms. Satisfaction to the winning party is strictly limited to future compliance.

China lost an important WTO case in March 2014 concerning its control of rare earth exports. The United States, Japan, the European Union, and a dozen other third parties charged China with using export duties and export quotas on rare earths and some precious metals to artificially drive up international prices. The panel decided against China, finding that the duties and quotas were inconsistent with China's WTO accession protocols and its GATT commitments. Moreover, the panel held that China had failed to justify its restrictions as legitimate environmental measures under the terms of GATT Article XX.[1]

WTO Dispute Settlement Procedures

The WTO establishes a clear framework for settling disputes.[2] First the complaining member requests consultation with the respondent member. If consultations fail, then the complainant and respondent jointly choose a panel of experts to hear the dispute (the WTO director-general chooses panelists if the parties cannot agree). After the panel report is delivered, one or both parties may appeal, and the Appellate Body is tasked to issue a decision within 90 days. If violations are found, the member concerned is supposed to bring its measures into conformity with the decision within a reasonable period of time. If that does not happen, a compliance panel may be established—usually the experts on the original panel—and that panel can authorize the complaining member to take countermeasures, normally an imposition of penalty duties on imports from the respondent.

Dispute Settlement in US FTAs

Among FTAs and customs unions, the European Union stands apart for having the strongest system of settling commercial disputes among its member countries. In commercial matters covered by multiple EU treaties, the European Court of Justice has all the powers of a supreme court. This reflects the historic nation-building dimension of the European enterprise. Other FTAs do not have that aspiration and, as one consequence, their dispute settlement systems, if they exist at all, have far more limited powers.

North American Free Trade Agreement (2004)

The North American Free Trade Agreement (NAFTA) established a high-water mark of dispute settlement in US FTAs,[3] with six distinct dispute settlement mechanisms, each dealing with different provisions in the agreement.[4] Chapter 11, perhaps the most controversial, established an investor-state arbitration system to hear complaints by private firms that the host state had directly or indirectly expropriated the firms' assets (see chapter 13 of this volume). Chapter

---

1. See WTO "China—Measures Related to the Exportation of Rare Earths, Tungsten and Molybdenum," www.wto.org (accessed on June 16, 2014). China has 60 days to adopt the panel report or appeal; as of this writing a decision had not been made.

2. Professor John Jackson of Georgetown University was the principal architect of the WTO dispute settlement system.

3. The NAFTA text and related documents are available at US Trade Representative (USTR), "North American Free Trade Agreement (NAFTA)," www.ustr.gov (accessed on June 16, 2014).

4. For an appraisal and much greater detail, see chapters 2, 3, and 4 in Hufbauer and Schott (2005).

14 established a panel arbitration system and a financial services committee to hear complaints about financial market access or investor-state disputes involving financial firms. The chapter gives ample scope for financial regulators to exclude foreign financial firms on prudential grounds; in any event all three NAFTA countries have significantly opened their financial markets to foreign firms. Investment disputes are rare. Accordingly, no financial sector cases have been brought and these provisions have not made an appearance in subsequent US FTAs.

Chapter 19 established a panel arbitration system to hear complaints from private firms concerning improper national administration of antidumping and countervailing duty laws. Arbitrators are instructed to determine whether national trade agency decisions are consistent with the substantive law of the country itself—not the law of another NAFTA member or WTO rules.[5] Over the life of NAFTA, more than 150 chapter 19 cases have been brought, but in recent years NAFTA members have increasingly resorted to the WTO system to settle trade remedy disputes.[6] One reason is that WTO panelists decide trade remedy determinations against GATT standards, not simply national standards. Another reason is that the WTO dispute system proved its utility after NAFTA was ratified. Chapter 19 was somewhat controversial in the United States and became the subject of a constitutional challenge, which the Federal Circuit Court of Appeals rejected. In any event, subsequent US FTAs have not adopted the chapter 19 style of review.

Chapter 20 lays out a soft consultative mechanism designed to handle disputes not covered in chapters 11, 14, and 19, such as interpretation of NAFTA itself, or domestic measures that might be inconsistent with NAFTA or nullify or impair expected benefits from the agreement. It also provides for the review of safeguard measures.[7] Chapter 20 has no panel arbitration mechanism and instead creates a free trade commission of senior officials who can, if they wish, establish an advisory panel of independent experts. While this commission does not report its consultative work, it has been invoked probably fewer than 20 times. Subsequent FTAs have followed the spirit but not the letter of chapter 20. The Peru–US FTA (2011), discussed below, like many others, establishes a free trade commission with oversight and consultative responsibilities,

---

5. Chapter 18 contains an extraordinary challenge committee procedure to hear claims that panel arbitrators were biased or exceeded their authority.

6. As of December 2009, there had been 137 cases brought under Chapter 19: 22 against Canada, 97 against the United States, and 18 against Mexico. Of these, 62 were terminated before the panel rendered a decision, 47 concerning the United States, 7 concerning Mexico, and 8 concerning Canada. See Donald McRae and John Siwiec, "NAFTA Dispute Settlement: Success or Failure?" biblio.juridicas.unam.mx (accessed on July 11, 2014).

7. Safeguard measures are emergency actions taken to reduce imports when a domestic industry is seriously injured, even though the imports are perfectly "fair" from the standpoint of antidumping and countervailing duty provisions, and intellectual property rights. The concepts of "nullification" and "impairment" are based on GATT Article XXIII.

plus the power to establish genuine arbitration panels (unlike NAFTA chapter 20). The famous side letters to NAFTA created an unworkable dispute settlement mechanism for labor rights (see chapter 10 of this volume) and a more active commission to deal with environmental issues (see chapter 11 of this volume). Subsequent FTAs contain somewhat more muscular provisions (see below).

Peru–US FTA (2011)

Like NAFTA, the Peru–US FTA creates arbitration panels for investor-state disputes (chapter 10), but allows policy space for regulations designed to protect human, animal, or plant life, conserve natural resources, or protect the environment (Articles 10.9(3)(c) and 10.11).[8] Unlike NAFTA, the Peru–US FTA contains no provisions for reviewing the bilateral application of remedies against trade practices perceived as unfair, such as antidumping and countervailing duties. Also unlike NAFTA, the Peru–US FTA spells out the right of the complaining party to seek relief in an alternative forum—usually the WTO—if it wishes.[9]

For disputes heard under the FTA, dispute resolution starts with consultations under the auspices of a senior free trade commission (chapter 20). If consultations do not succeed, the commission can appoint an arbitration panel that operates under standard procedures (chapter 21). If the panel's recommendation to correct nonconforming measures is not implemented, a compliance panel can authorize appropriate compensation or countermeasures, such as partial suspension of FTA benefits.

The Peru FTA establishes substantive standards for labor rights that go well beyond the NAFTA prescription for each country to enforce its own laws (see this volume's chapter 10). For environmental matters, the Peru–US FTA adheres to the NAFTA prescription of each country enforcing its own laws. Chapter 18 establishes a senior environmental affairs council that, in the first instance, oversees consultations when one party questions the vigor of the other party's enforcement. As with labor matters, if consultations under council auspices fail to resolve the environmental matter, the complaining party can resort to chapter 21 and eventually seek arbitration of the respondent party's alleged failure to enforce its own environmental laws. And as with labor matters, the environmental dispute settlement provisions go much further than their NAFTA counterparts do.[10]

---

8. For the text of the Peru–US FTA, see US Trade Representative, Peru Trade Promotion Agreement, "Final Text," www.ustr.gov (accessed on June 16, 2014).

9. As mentioned, in practice many antidumping and countervailing duty cases between NAFTA parties ended up in the WTO, rather than NAFTA chapter 19.

10. A report by Public Citizen states that an investigation by the US Labor Department found multiple violations of the labor agreement, with child and forced labor continuing to be practiced.

As mentioned in earlier chapters, other US FTAs of the same vintage as the Peru FTA—the Korea, Panama, and Colombia FTAs—contain highly similar, often identical, dispute settlement provisions, both as to subject matter coverage and procedure. The United States is urging this model on other countries in the Trans-Pacific Partnership (TPP), but signs indicate resistance from other parties. It seems likely that the model will be modified in TPP talks, especially with respect to labor and environmental disputes, where many countries favor a consultative approach.

Dispute Settlement in Chinese FTAs

We examine the Chile–China FTA and the New Zealand–China FTA to understand the flavor of Chinese dispute settlement provisions with Western countries.[11] In many respects the provisions are similar to those found in US FTAs, but broadly speaking the subject matter coverage is less ambitious.

Chile–China FTA (2005)

The Chile–China agreement focuses on merchandise trade and has no chapters on services, investment, labor, or the environment. Accordingly there is no need for dispute settlement mechanisms for those subjects. Many, perhaps most, potential disputes over merchandise trade—such as the application of antidumping and countervailing duties—are referred to the WTO Dispute Settlement Body. Chapter X deals with disputes that arise under the FTA, but allows the complaining party to choose an alternative forum if one exists (usually the WTO). A joint senior commission first holds consultations; if consultations do not resolve the matter, the commission can establish an arbitration panel that operates under standard procedures with well-defined time deadlines. The arbitration panel can issue a recommendation to bring nonconforming practices into compliance, but cannot authorize countermeasures.

If the country at fault does not bring its practices into compliance, the commission can authorize a second arbitration panel on the question of compliance, and this panel can authorize equivalent compensation or suspension of equivalent FTA benefits. Because the joint commission must decide affirmatively to establish both the original panel and the compliance panel, the Chile–China dispute settlement process lacks the automaticity of the WTO DSB.

See Public Citizen, "A Year after Implementation of Peru Free Trade Agreement, US and Peru Left with Broken Promises and No New Trade Model," www.citizen.org (accessed on July 11, 2014).

11. See Organization of American States, "China–Chile Free Trade Agreement," www.sice.oas.org (accessed on July 11, 2014); New Zealand–China Free Trade Agreement, www.chinafta.govt.nz (accessed on July 11, 2014).

New Zealand–China FTA (2008)

Like the Chile-China FTA, the New Zealand-China FTA focuses on merchandise, and the first eight chapters are devoted to multiple aspects of goods trade. Evidently lawyers in both countries got to work because the New Zealand FTA text is considerably more detailed than the Chile text. Unlike the Chile FTA, the New Zealand FTA has extensive service and investment provisions. Chapter 9 liberalizes a range of business services, and chapter 10 permits, in innovative ways, the movement of natural persons. Chapter 11 deals with investment, containing many provisions that are found in standard bilateral investment treaties (BITs), including investor-state dispute settlement, with ICSID arbitration.[12] The New Zealand FTA does not have labor or environmental chapters.

Chapter 16 in the New Zealand FTA deals with dispute settlement for all chapters of the FTA.[13] As in most FTAs, the complaining party can pursue its case under either the FTA or another agreement—most likely the WTO. A senior FTA joint commission (chapter 15) oversees the entire FTA, but the dispute settlement provisions in chapter 16 of the New Zealand FTA seem fairly automatic compared with the rules in chapter X of the Chile FTA. In particular, after the usual round of consultations, a complaining party can require the establishment of an arbitration panel, without the say-so of the FTA joint commission. The panel can recommend the correction of nonconforming measures. If the measures are not corrected, a second compliance panel can authorize equivalent compensation or countermeasures.

Enforcing Currency Provisions

Currency provisions would be novel in an FTA, but if they are agreed, considering the huge effects that exchange rate changes have on trade, methods for enforcing currency provisions need to be considered. As explained in chapter 17 of this volume, one possibility is to impose monetary penalties, determined by the dispute settlement process, with the money paid to injured private parties. Another possibility is for the aggrieved party to directly retaliate by imposing countervailing duties across the board, equal to the rate of currency undervaluation during the period under investigation. The most popular enforcement method is to withdraw concessions made in the FTA itself, resulting in an across-the-board snapback of tariffs to pre-FTA levels. This may be a better option, as it avoids a calculation of damages, and is a familiar remedy for violations of an FTA. An agreement with one or more of these enforcement

---

12. Article 153 also permits arbitration under the rules of the United Nations Commission on International Trade Law (UNCITRAL), but in practice the great majority of investor-state disputes are handled by ICSID.

13. There are exceptions for certain matters in the relevant chapters. Disputes over antidumping and countervailing duties are referred to the WTO, and the exceptions enumerated in GATT Articles XX and XXI are also exceptions in the New Zealand FTA.

mechanisms would be a milestone, and might lead to future dispute settlement agreements on currency questions.

Conclusions

Dispute settlement systems in US and Chinese FTAs have several points in common that are auspicious for a China–US trade and investment agreement (CHUSTIA). Major commonalities can be listed:

- Allowing the complaining party to bring a dispute under the FTA or an alternative forum, usually the WTO.
- Special provisions for investor-state dispute settlement, with similar policy space for environmental and health regulations.
- Consigning disputes over unfair trade remedies, such as antidumping and countervailing duties, to the WTO.
- Consigning all disputes that might arise under the FTA to a single dispute settlement chapter, other than investor-state and trade remedy disputes.
- Similar procedures and timelines as the WTO for holding consultations, selecting arbitrators, and issuing panel reports.
- Enabling a compliance panel to authorize compensation or countermeasures.

The most important difference between US and Chinese FTAs is subject matter coverage regarding labor and environmental questions. Put starkly, Chinese FTAs deliberately exclude these questions and US FTAs deliberately—and insistently—include them. Moreover, in its latest FTAs, the United States makes arbitration a feasible mode of dispute settlement for both labor and environmental questions. It would be difficult, perhaps politically impossible, for the United States to revert to the NAFTA-era approach of each country enforcing its own laws in the realm of labor affairs, but the United States still follows that approach for environmental questions. The United States might accept a greater role for consultation on both labor and environmental issues in the TPP and a CHUSTIA.

As in the WTO, neither Chinese nor US FTAs do much to enlarge the power of a private firm to launch a complaint. Apart from investor-state disputes, private firms in nearly all cases must first persuade their own officials as to the merits of their claim, and then overcome assorted official objections, before the dispute settlement machinery can be put into motion. Again as in the WTO, FTA relief is prospective, not retroactive, and there are no provisions for compensating private parties for damages incurred. The FTA dispute settlement machinery has been so little used, apart from NAFTA in trade remedy cases, that it is hard to predict whether FTAs will resolve disputes more or less expeditiously than the WTO, with its average resolution times of almost two years. However, a close reading of all the steps required in FTA dispute settlement—consultation, formation of panels, issuing reports, and evaluating compliance—suggests that FTA machinery is not likely to prove more expeditious than the WTO.

References

Hufbauer, Gary Clyde, and Jeffrey J. Schott. 2005. *NAFTA Revisited: Achievements and Challenges.* Washington: Peterson Institute for International Economics.

19

Conclusions and Recommendations

Both China and the United States are pursuing very active trade policy agendas. China is negotiating its largest bilateral free trade agreements (FTAs) ever, with Korea and Australia. It is contemplating a tripartite pact in Northeast Asia with Japan and Korea. It has begun talks with 15 neighboring countries to forge a Regional Comprehensive Economic Partnership (RCEP) that would create a free trade zone comprising most of East and South Asia, ranging from Japan through Australia to India. It has proposed in APEC an early feasibility study of a comprehensive Free Trade Area of the Asia-Pacific (FTAAP). For its part, the United States is engaged in two megaregional negotiations. The Trans-Pacific Partnership (TPP), with eleven Asian and Western Hemisphere partners, is well advanced. Talks toward a Transatlantic Trade and Investment Partnership (TTIP) with the European Union, which could become the largest such agreement in history, began in 2013.

China and the United States are also negotiating a bilateral investment treaty (BIT) with each other. They are involved in several plurilateral negotiations at or around the WTO. Both are participating in the effort to expand the International Technology Agreement (ITA2). They have been trying for some time to bring China into the Government Procurement Agreement (GPA). China asked in 2013 to join the negotiations for the Trade in Services Agreement (TiSA) and in early 2014 joined the new effort to eliminate tariffs on trade in a wide range of environmental products. Both countries' interests in freer trade, with each other and with other partners, can be taken as a positive sign pointing toward the possibility a comprehensive China–US trade and investment agreement (CHUSTIA).

Thus heavily engaged on the trade front, China and the United States are unlikely to initiate major additions to their agendas in the near future, despite China's interest in the TPP beginning in 2013 and initial feelers for a free trade negotiation between China and the European Union. The success or lack thereof of current negotiations will be a very important determinant of the mindset in each country regarding future trade initiatives, especially with each other. The alleged failures of the North American Free Trade Agreement (NAFTA) have poisoned US trade politics for twenty years, most clearly in that agreement's de facto extension to Central America a decade later and subsequently other Latin American countries. The perceived effect of the TPP on the US economy, and on US relations with much of Asia, will likewise have a major effect on the US appetite for an additional pact with China. That said, the current negotiations are likely to be concluded relatively soon, and these talks will have dynamic effects on other countries, including China and the United States themselves, that may spawn important new policy initiatives. Successful conclusion of both the TPP and TTIP will generate substantial new trade diversion losses for China. It is not too soon for the two countries to be thinking beyond their current agendas to ask what comes next.

China and the United States face a series of economically serious, politically charged, and growing trade disputes. Traditional debates over dumping, subsidies, safeguard measures, and export restrictions continue to nourish bilateral tensions and spawn WTO cases. The decade-long disagreement over exchange rates and China's policies in that area, despite substantial renminbi appreciation and the reduction of both China's current account surplus and the US external deficit, remain a central concern. China continues to believe that the United States discriminates against it in applying US export controls, especially of high-technology products. Perhaps most important, several major new issues have come onto the bilateral agenda and threaten a significant escalation of tensions. China wants to become a major investor around the world, especially in the United States, but feels stymied by allegedly restrictive and discriminatory US implementation of its inward investment rules. The United States sees China renewing its focus on promoting national champions, mainly state-owned and state-supported enterprises (SOEs and SSEs), through a variety of industrial policies that discriminate against foreign firms. The United States continues to believe that inadequate protection of intellectual property rights (IPRs) in China costs it tens of billions, perhaps hundreds of billions, of dollars annually.

The newest flashpoint is cybersecurity. China and the United States acknowledge that they spy on each other for national security reasons. But it has now become clear that China's hacking, in addition, seeks to penetrate commercial secrets and may amount to the greatest economic provocation of all. The United States initiated legal action in May 2014, sharply escalating that conflict. At the same time, the revelations of widespread National Security Agency (NSA) surveillance of foreigners have raised similar questions in China regarding US clandestine activities.

The two countries are also at loggerheads in plurilateral talks. The United States has led the opposition to China's position on ITA2 and has successfully proposed suspension of the negotiations on two occasions as a result. It has led the resistance to China's application to join the TiSA effort by referencing its stance on ITA2. It has for some time regarded China's proposals to join the GPA as insufficient. It accepted China into the new negotiation on green goods only when China gave up its initial opposition to the initiative's terms of reference and agreed to accept the mandate agreed by the other participants.

The strategic question for China and the United States is whether they should continue responding to the rapidly expanding and contentious agenda between them issue by issue, focusing attention only when problems come to a head and without any overarching framework of agreed principles and institutional arrangements. Their trade relationship is anchored in the increasingly outmoded rules of the WTO, which are largely irrelevant to many of the key issues under dispute. Virtually all other pairs of large countries with substantial trade between them have adopted bilateral or regional agreements to create a framework for their relationships: France, Germany, and the United Kingdom in the European Union; the United States and Canada bilaterally and then with NAFTA; Brazil and Argentina with the Southern Common Market (Mercosur); Australia and New Zealand in their bilateral pact; Russia and its nearest trading partners in their Eurasian Customs Union; and now the United States with its main Asian counterparts, including Korea and Japan, bilaterally or via the TPP.

The world has entered a second major wave of bilateral and regional trade agreements. The first wave brought together geographical neighbors and included a few linkages of large and small countries that were some distance apart. The second wave is pairing the world's largest economies across different continents. The United States has made or is making agreements with the European Union, Korea, Japan, and other Asian countries. The European Union is making agreements with Korea, India, and possibly Mercosur. India has made an agreement with Japan and is possibly making more with China and others. The absence of any such arrangement between China and the United States, or even any serious discussion of it, stands out as a major anomaly in the global trade, finance, and political architecture.[1] Continuation of this vacuum could create major risks in terms of future escalation of economic conflict, and hence deterioration of overall relations, between the two superpowers.

The risk of escalation is heightened by the mutual increasing trade discrimination between China and the United States resulting from the preferential trade agreements that each country will probably conclude shortly with most of its other trading partners. As chapter 2 shows, the TPP alone could eventually cost China about $100 billion in exports and national income per year. Europe and the United States are China's leading export markets and estimates by the Ifo Institute, a leading German research center, suggest that

---

1. The largest other anomaly is the absence of an agreement between the United States and India. See Bergsten and Subramanian (forthcoming).

China could lose one-third of its exports to the United States—another $100 billion or so—and perhaps half that amount to the European Union under a TTIP (Ifo Institut 2013). The United States will suffer losses from China's growing array of trade pacts, though these are likely to be of much smaller magnitude in light of the lesser degree of liberalization in those agreements.

The traditional dynamic of competitive liberalization, through which one group of countries' adoption of significant preferential agreements places considerable pressure on nonmembers to join the group or develop counterpart compacts of their own, suggests that China should seek to counter the TPP and TTIP costs by getting together with the United States, perhaps by joining TPP through a CHUSTIA. This would enable each to overcome the discrimination against it that is inherent in the other country's current and pending FTAs. The alternative is a new and probably growing source of friction that will add to the difficulties of the relationship.

Meanwhile, each country is working to strengthen its own economy, and to implement a new model of sustainable growth for the foreseeable future. The United States needs to move toward higher saving and investment, less consumption, and more exports. China has clearly stated its intention to promote domestic consumption, sharply expand the role of services in its economy, and deemphasize heavy investment and exports. Inauguration of the Shanghai Pilot Free Trade Zone is a potentially important step in carrying out some of these concepts. Successfully fulfilling these strategies is key to reducing their internal misalignments as well as their international imbalances, which have been the chief target of global rebalancing strategies for the past six years.

Chapter 2 shows that trade liberalization between China and the United States would support most of the countries' economic goals and could play a leading role in promoting them. An FTA between them would generate cheaper and more diversified imports, which would enhance consumer welfare in China. China would gain substantially from the liberalization of its services sector, as would the United States from greater exports to that sector. There are indications that the plans of the Xi Jinping government to accelerate economic reform in China have already led to a significant increase in the country's interest in considering new trade initiatives, whether plurilateral (the TiSA), regional (the TPP or FTAAP), or bilateral (a new BIT with the United States and even an FTA with the European Union or a CHUSTIA).

Economic Effects

Both countries would derive substantial aggregate gains from a comprehensive CHUSTIA. The analysis in chapter 2 suggests that such an agreement would produce increases in exports of about $400 billion to $500 billion per year for both. US exports to China would almost double. This would create almost 9 million export-related jobs in China and almost 2 million in the United States. (The job number is much larger in China because the level of productivity in the United States is much higher.) It would translate into income and GDP gains of $300 billion to $400 billion per year (about 2 percent) for China and about $130 billion per year (about 0.6 percent) for the United States, without incorporating estimates of the effects of investment liberalization and possible higher degrees of services liberalization.

China would enjoy larger GDP gains because it would start the process with considerably higher trade barriers. It would thus liberalize considerably more than the United States, leading to a large expansion of imports and new investment that would cut user prices and boost Chinese productivity. The United States would see the corresponding export gains; its global exports would grow faster in percentage terms (13 percent) than China's (10 percent) as a result of the agreement, though China's would grow more in absolute terms because they start from a higher base.

Both countries would enjoy substantial increases in their productivity levels from a CHUSTIA: 0.8 percent for the United States and 1.9 percent for China. This would be an especially welcome improvement for the United States, as the risk of declining productivity growth is a widespread concern regarding the future prospects for the US economy. This higher productivity is an important source of the income gains for both countries.

It is difficult to identify the payoff from any discrete trade agreement because so many other things are happening at the same time. We assume that the TPP and RCEP will conclude before any CHUSTIA and then estimate the effects of all three together. The three agreements taken together provide income gains for both China and the United States that are about 50 percent higher than for a CHUSTIA alone. Our analyses suggest that a CHUSTIA would be more important than the TPP for the United States and more important than the RCEP for China. Both countries' rebalancing strategies also will help set the macroeconomic context and must be assessed alongside the trade agreements.

In addition to a CHUSTIA's explicit benefits, a major advantage for both countries is that it should reduce the risks of future trade conflict between them and the costs of whatever conflicts might still arise. One of a CHUSTIA's major objectives would be to address future disputes within an agreed policy framework. The WTO's dispute settlement mechanism (DSM) has helped depoliticize and resolve trade disputes between China and the United States; the more far-ranging DSM of a CHUSTIA should be able to broaden that effect considerably, as NAFTA's DSM has for the United States and Canada. Moderation of economic disagreements should strengthen the overall relationship between the two countries. It will not resolve their security and broader political problems but, over time, it could help establish greater understanding and trust between the two countries and significantly strengthen their ties.

By limiting the risks of economic conflict between the world's two largest traders, and contributing importantly to the needed rebalancing of the two countries, a CHUSTIA would also enhance the strength and stability of the international economy. It would thus provide a global public good of considerable value. It would be an extremely important exercise of constructive world leadership that would provide tangible evidence of the ability of the incumbent hegemon and the rising power to come together to promote wider interests along with their own.

Many US partners in previous trade negotiations have used those initiatives to generate constructive adjustment pressures on their own economies. Mexico did so through NAFTA and its economy is much stronger today, twenty years later, partly as a result. China did so to win entry to the WTO, and permanent normal trade relations (PNTR) status from the United States, and aggressively used the newly embraced rules to augment and accelerate domestic reforms in the late 1990s and the early 2000s. Korea used the negotiations that produced its FTA with the United States (KORUS), along with a number of other FTAs, to reform its agricultural sector.

High-income countries have used the strategy as well. Prime Minister Shinzo Abe of Japan characterized his country's decision to join the TPP in 2013 as driven by that agreement's impetus to needed structural changes in Japan, portraying the TPP as the "third arrow" of his economic revitalization program.[2] The European Union used the external pressure from multilateral trade negotiations in the General Agreement on Tariffs and Trade (GATT) to win political support for a succession of needed reforms in its common agricultural policy. US administrations have used external pressure to carry out policy changes for which they had previously been unable to win congressional support, such as decontrol of energy prices in the late 1970s and some of the tax reform legislation of 1986.

The global trade imbalances of the partner countries, a large Chinese surplus and larger US deficit, could be substantially reduced or even eliminated (see chapter 2) if the macroeconomic rebalancing process that has been under way for several years precedes or continues alongside the new trade agreement. Trade agreements are not normally expected to alter trade balances in partner countries over the long run, or produce changes in aggregate employment, but a comprehensive CHUSTIA would make it easier to implement the needed rebalancing. US resources would move into exporting industries and the investments that support them. Chinese resources would move into domestic consumption, dampening the high saving rate that underlies the country's large external surplus. One result would be further renminbi appreciation.

There are several ways that the adjustments could come about. A CHUSTIA that ensured substantial liberalization of China's services sector would enable the United States to increase its exports of services to China, and the investment income of its services firms there, by more than $200 billion per year (see chapters 2 and 7). The United States could gain as much as $100 billion annually from China's effective implementation of its existing intellectual property laws—and even more if its commercial cyberespionage practices could

---

2. "Japan Is Back: A Conversation with Shinzo Abe," interview, *Foreign Affairs*, August 2013.

be brought even partially under control. As mentioned, China would be eliminating its remaining tariff protection from a considerably higher level than the United States. During a period of high unemployment in the United States and sizable current account imbalances in both countries, a CHUSTIA could contribute to meaningful adjustment during a rather long transition period.

In addition to its effects on the two countries' trade balances, a CHUSTIA would affect the distribution of economic activity in both. As always, trade liberalization permits countries to do more of what they do best and tap other countries for goods and services for which they do not possess comparative productive advantage. This is the source of the very large gains to the partner countries from the agreement, especially given China's high tariff and nontariff barriers. China would experience a modest further increase from baseline projections in its manufacturing sector (which accounts for about 20 percent of its total employment). It would see modest declines in employment from baseline projections in some services and agriculture subsectors, though its continued rapid overall economic growth would produce output gains from present levels in those sectors as well. The United States would experience the opposite pattern, with significant increases in services—which make up over 80 percent of its labor force—and agriculture. Services exports, which already run a substantial (almost 3:1) surplus with China, would grow twice as fast as services imports. Most US manufacturing sectors would see some falloff in their employment totals from baseline projections, which are already declining modestly due to continued productivity growth, although almost all of them too would enjoy substantially higher output levels than at present.

In this study, we use three different approaches to assess the US employment impact of a CHUSTIA. The first and most frequently used approach assumes that, over the medium term, an agreement that liberalizes trade does not change the aggregate level of employment. In other words, the unemployment rate neither rises nor falls as a consequence of the trade agreement. The rationale behind this assumption is that, following a policy change that temporarily increases or decreases employment, labor markets will, over the medium term, return to an equilibrium level in which everyone who truly wants a job finds a job—either by moving to a different locale or by accepting a slightly lower wage. Full employment prevails, and the only unemployment observed when labor markets are in equilibrium is frictional unemployment, reflecting search time as workers move between jobs. In the United States, frictional unemployment is commonly regarded as a rate of 4 to 5 percent of the labor force.

Under this standard assumption, involuntary separations occur in industries that face more intense competition from imports, while the same number of new jobs spring up in other industries that enjoy growing exports. In chapter 2, Peter Petri, Michael Plummer, and Fan Zhai adopt the standard assumption in carrying out their computable general equilibrium (CGE) calculations illustrating the effect of a CHUSTIA. While total employment is not affected, the authors can assess the number of involuntary separations in import-competing sectors and the corresponding number of jobs added in export sectors. As a CHUSTIA is phased in over 10 years, Petri and his colleagues estimate that, on average, 170,000 jobs will be lost annually in import-competing sectors, and the same number of jobs will be created annually in the export-related sectors of the US economy. Individual workers will seldom move directly from import-competing positions to export-related positions. Instead workers will move among many sectors of the economy. In the overall scheme of the US labor force, with 155 million jobs and 20 million involuntary separations annually, these CHUSTIA effects are small, yet clearly important to affected workers. For the nation as a whole, the payoff from CHUSTIA is higher national income, which results from improved productivity.

In a second approach, not so standard, Petri and his colleagues posit that, alongside a CHUSTIA, both China and the United States will undertake companion measures to reduce their trade imbalances. Under this scenario, China will reduce its annual global trade surplus by $286 billion by 2020. To balance their CGE model in a convenient manner, Petri and his colleagues assume that the United States will reduce its annual global trade deficit by the same amount. This scenario (if not the precise details) is inspired by the reality that, in mid-2014, the US labor market is some distance from equilibrium, since the unemployment rate is 6.1 percent, compared with a full employment norm of 4 to 5 percent. Equally serious, the labor force participation rate as a share of the working-age population dropped sharply following the onset of the Great Recession, from 66.0 percent in 2007 to 63.1 percent in early 2014, as many potential workers gave up the search for a satisfactory job. Moreover, a great many workers who want full-time jobs can only find part-time work.[3] In June 2014 over 7.5 million Americans were working part-time for economic reasons, compared with 4.3 million in June 2006.[4] Given these facts, even partially closing the large US trade gap could put Americans who have been pushed out of the labor force back to work full-time. The exact size of this effect is outside the scope of the modeling in chapter 2, but even a more modest fall in the US trade deficit could provide jobs for some 1 million discouraged US workers over the next 10 years.[5]

In chapter 3, Robert Lawrence presents a third approach to the jobs question. The Lawrence methodology is bottom-up, contrasted with the top-down CGE approaches Petri and his colleagues use. Lawrence uses input-output

---

3. M. Zuckerman, "The Full-Time Scandal of Part-Time America," *Wall Street Journal*, July 13, 2014.

4. Federal Reserve Bank of St. Louis, "Employment Situation," research.stlouisfed.org (accessed on July 17, 2014).

5. Scaling the results from the accelerated rebalancing scenario in chapter 2 to a reduction of $150 billion annually in the US trade deficit, about one half the posited reduction in China's global surplus, we would expect a $56 billion decline in imports and a $94 billion increase in exports. Using the figures cited in the *Payoff from the World Trade Agenda*—5,500 jobs per $1 billion (2010 USD) in exports and some 7,500 jobs needed to replace $1 billion of imports—we might expect nearly 1 million jobs to be created over the 10-year implementation period in this scenario.

coefficients to calculate the number of direct and indirect US jobs corresponding to a billion dollars of additional imports from China. The figure was roughly 7,500 jobs in 2012. Adjusted for aggregate demand effects and the distinction between voluntary quits and involuntary separations, the estimated increment in Chinese imports under a CHUSTIA over the period 2015 to 2025 suggests that 1.04 million involuntary separations will occur, after accounting for productivity increases. Involuntary separations by this arithmetic will amount to about 104,000 a year. Lawrence does not calculate jobs gained in exporting sectors.

Although a CHUSTIA is expected to create income gains for US workers overall, many workers displaced by import competition will probably see lower wages as they reenter the workforce. Chapter 3 estimates that a worker displaced in a mass layoff could face income losses of up to $100,000 over the course of his lifetime.[6] While these losses are substantial, the expected gains to the US economy are an order of magnitude greater: $1.25 million for each job loss and social benefits that are twelve times as great as these income losses. Furthermore, the adjustment costs are incurred only once while the income gains are earned every year after full implementation in perpetuity.

Nevertheless, obtaining political support for a CHUSTIA in the United States will require adequate policy support for the adjustments. Part of this can be achieved by phasing in the liberalization of sectors that could experience significant job loss over lengthy periods of time, ranging up to 20 years in the most sensitive cases.

In addition, three types of domestic support measures will be needed. Taken in combination with the TPP and TTIP, a CHUSTIA will first require the United States to strengthen its international competitiveness in a variety of ways. Continued fiscal correction is essential over the medium term, including to keep interest rates low. A new wave of infrastructure investment is badly needed, especially while interest rates remain low. Tax reform, with lower corporate rates, will help maintain the attractiveness of the United States as a home for multinational corporations. Continued emphasis on technological innovation, especially by the private sector but with necessary government support, will be central to future productivity growth. New trade agreements will magnify the benefits that accrue to the United States from refocusing on such policies, but those policies are also necessary to mitigate the potentially adverse effects of the trade agreements on output and employment.

Second, additional steps may be needed to respond to the adverse effects of further trade and investment liberalization on income distribution in the United States. The traditional, and still most straightforward, remedy is to add to the graduation of the income tax system to redistribute after-tax income

---

6. Using a different approach, Autor et al. (2013) examined the effect of competition from Chinese imports on US wages from 1992 to 2007. They found that the average manufacturing worker saw annual earnings fall by about 3 percent of base year wages. Thus the total decline over 15 years might cumulate to about 45 percent of the base year 1992 wage.

from the 1 percent to the 99 percent—especially its lower 20 to 40 percent. A redirection of government expenditures from their current overemphasis on the elderly, most of whom are relatively well off, to younger and especially low-income people would help as well.

Third, there will also be a need for measures that directly help trade-affected workers. Obamacare will contribute by providing health insurance that displaced workers can carry with them regardless of employment, which has been one of the leading sources of anxiety over job displacement. Unemployment insurance needs to be expanded as well to provide higher levels of benefits to more laid-off workers for longer periods of time. We also recommend that trade adjustment assistance (TAA) be tripled, from its current level of about $1 billion per year to at least $3 billion, and streamlined to provide much more rapid help for workers dislocated by expanded trade with China. There could be a dedicated China TAA program much as NAFTA had its own TAA program when it was first implemented. A mere 2 percent of the projected gains from a CHUSTIA for the overall economy would suffice to finance such a TAA program.

An alternative to expanded TAA, as President Obama has proposed and chapter 3 explains, is to consolidate and strengthen all of the current US worker assistance programs. In the US economy it is difficult to distinguish the causes of dislocation for individual workers—one key reason why TAA has not always reached its full target population. Modest changes in current tax policies could easily finance such a consolidated program, again drawing very marginally on the far larger gains to the economy from a CHUSTIA. All this comes on top of the essential macroeconomic rebalancing that we discuss elsewhere and that indicates that the United States, at least as much as China, will have to implement a series of complementary policies to make a CHUSTIA work.

Three major conclusions emerge from our analysis of the prospects for an FTA between China and the United States. First, both countries could obtain very sizable economic benefits. China could use a CHUSTIA to sharply accelerate the rebalancing of its internal economy in directions that the leadership has been espousing for a decade and that the Xi Jinping government is seemingly prioritizing.

Second, the very large benefits for the two economies are of very different natures. For the United States, they are in the traditional mercantilist mode: large expansions of exports and the creation of jobs that would go with them. For China, the most valuable gains accrue in the classic economic sense: cheaper and more diversified imports, bringing sizable welfare and income gains and spurring productivity growth as a result. In that classical sense, the United States has reaped much of the gains from increased trade with China over the past three decades and borrowed from China to finance them. China can now catch up at a time when it is seeking precisely such benefits. Moreover, these asymmetrical benefits fuse neatly together at the present time. Both countries need to rebalance their economies, both internally and externally—in the directions of greater consumption and domestic demand in China and more exports and investment in the United States. By spurring such adjustment, through a variety of channels, a CHUSTIA could make a major contribution to the essential global adjustment as well as the needed structural reorientation of the two economies themselves.

Third, the asymmetry in the nature of the benefits to the two countries will affect their approaches to the basic questions of whether to attempt a CHUSTIA and, if so, how to go about it. The United States will have many more requests in the traditional mercantilist trade-negotiating sense: for its services exports, protection of its intellectual property rights, remaining investment barriers in China, achievement and maintenance of an equilibrium exchange rate, and more access for its exports of agricultural and manufactured products. In familiar negotiating terms, the United States will be focusing primarily on its offensive rather than its defensive trade interests.

China's requests are likely to be more limited. They would focus primarily on US export controls in agriculture, energy resources, and especially high-technology products, and the US regime on inward direct investment. The key issue, especially for China, will be to conceptualize the issue broadly and in classical economic terms: to recall that the bulk of the income gains from trade derive from imports and inward foreign direct investment (FDI) and from the importance of such expansion in promoting fundamental economic progress, as China has demonstrated again and again historically and recently in its entry to the WTO.

The above points constitute the grand bargain that would have to underlie a successful CHUSTIA. Each country could use the agreement to pursue some of its fundamental, and most important, economic and social objectives. It would be a fitting foundation for a truly historic compact between the world's leading economies. There is a strong case for China and the United States to begin thinking about an FTA, even as they continue their current negotiations with others. Successfully concluding the present talks would add to the case for a CHUSTIA and, presumably, to the two countries' confidence in proceeding with each other in a further agreement. Those agreements might also resolve, or at least begin to provide relevant templates for, some of the issues that a CHUSTIA would have to address.

China and the United States could even begin informal discussions now, perhaps within the structure of their bilateral Strategic and Economic Dialogue or the regional context of the Asia-Pacific Economic Cooperation (APEC) forum, on how to make sure their current negotiations were conducted and concluded in ways that did not hinder or preclude a follow-on CHUSTIA. Such discussions in and of themselves, even if they did not eventuate in a new CHUSTIA any time soon, would enhance the relationship between the countries and help to overcome the mistrust that now characterizes so much of it. Another possible interim step, building on the precedents of many of the trade agreements negotiated in Asia in recent years, would be for the two governments to officially commission further studies of the CHUSTIA idea by some combination of think tanks, private companies, and government officials in the two countries.

With or without interim steps, China and the United States should plan to begin negotiations to achieve freer trade between them shortly after the conclusions of their current megaregional talks for the TPP and, if it progresses on a reasonably parallel timetable, for the RCEP. This could be done in any of several ways: a traditional bilateral FTA between the two countries, China's accession to the TPP, a merger between the TPP and RCEP into a full Free Trade Area of the Asia Pacific (FTAAP) or a separate FTAAP. We address these alternatives after reviewing the possible content of a CHUSTIA.

The Content of a CHUSTIA

The pursuit of a comprehensive agreement between China and the United States should be carried out with the greatest flexibility possible. We could envisage the negotiation of a comprehensive, single compact that covered the entire range of topics together, or a step-by-step process in which individual issues were tackled sequentially (see chapter 1). The latter approach would rest on the idea that, in addition to the merits of dealing with each issue discretely, the agreements could become building blocks and confidence-building measures for an overall arrangement that would come together over an extended period of time. All previous US FTAs have been of the single, comprehensive type, while most of China's agreements have been at least partially sequential, often addressing some or all goods trade first and then adding services, and perhaps investment and other issues, at a later stage. China seems to have pursued this latter approach in its current negotiations with Australia.

In either case, we believe that the substantive agenda would be quite similar, though it might be addressed differently under the two scenarios. The stepping-stone approach would presumably prioritize sectors that offer an opportunity for self-balancing concessions, where each partner has interests that could be traded off within that sector itself. That approach could also count some of the plurilateral negotiations in which China and the United States are both participating, potentially including the TiSA and GPA, as components of the bilateral accord, as they would help pursue the goal of freer trade between the two countries. The step-by-step approach might also benefit from addressing some of the less difficult issues first. The BIT talks now under way could be viewed as a first installment on this strategy, which has been launched with far less fanfare than a full FTA initiative. The plurilateral accords could come next or proceed in parallel with the BIT, as some of them are now doing. On the other hand, the sequential approach would probably call for multiple congressional approvals, starting with ratification of the BIT—which, like any treaty, requires a two-thirds vote of the Senate rather than a simple majority of both houses of Congress, and might thus face a higher US political hurdle than an FTA would.

By contrast, the all-in approach would require including sectors in which one partner clearly had the preponderance of requests that would require tradeoffs against another sector for the entire agreement to achieve reciprocity. Prioritization might then be very different, as each country would put all of its requests on the table at once, each emphasizing those that promised the largest payoffs for itself. This variant would presumably result in much greater public attention and involvement, including from Congress in the United States, at both the launch and approval stages.

A few issues may be better handled through parallel agreements than in a CHUSTIA itself. Renewed efforts to address cyberespionage and exchange rates may work better through existing (currency) or new (cyber) rules and institutional arrangements that are specific to each issue and that range well beyond normal trade policy considerations. At the same time, it is essential that these issues be handled much more effectively than at present, and there are strong pressures, at least in the United States, to include them in future trade agreements as a result. This could be done if other alternatives cannot be achieved (see below).

We begin our discussion of possible components of a CHUSTIA with the issues for which intrasectoral reciprocity, and thus stand-alone agreements, might be possible. We then turn to those that would probably need to be part of a broader compact and, finally, to those that may also need to be included if preferable parallel arrangements cannot be fashioned outside the domain of trade policy.

Potential Stand-Alone Agreements

Tariffs, especially on manufactured products, form the centerpiece of most trade agreements and are still the main element of many Asia-only agreements, including those involving China. This is partly because tariffs are still fairly high in the region, and previous compacts have excluded some products, especially in agriculture. There has also been reluctance to tackle nontariff barriers and other less familiar and perhaps more sensitive issues.

A zero-for-zero agreement on tariffs could play a valuable role in a CHUSTIA. China's average bound tariff (9.5 percent) is more than double the US average (4 percent), although weighted averages show that applied rates amount to only 5.5 percent for US exports to China and 2.7 percent for Chinese products entering the United States. Multinational enterprises nevertheless continue to highly prioritize tariff elimination to remove impediments to their supply chains, many of which include direct trade between China and the United States.

A stand-alone agreement on tariffs might be desirable to follow up the BIT and begin the initial process of liberalization. This is partly due to its simplicity and familiarity to the negotiators of both countries. It would also take advantage of the small difference between applied rates, the economic effect of which is narrowed further because China's higher rates apply to a considerably lower level of current trade, while the lower US tariffs affect the much higher volume of Chinese exports.

A second candidate for a stand-alone agreement is one dealing with *agriculture*. Chapter 2 shows that US exports of farm products to China could increase by enough to expand the entire US farm sector by 5 percent if China's extensive barriers, including tariffs averaging more than 15 percent—with much higher rates on sensitive products and extensive nontariff impediments—were eliminated. As with most of its other trade agreements, this would normally cast the United States as *demandeur* in this sector. However, China is keen on ensuring its access to US agricultural exports for reasons of food security; this is one reason why China is eager for the United States to adopt strict limitations on its use of export controls. If severe drought affects China in the next decade or so, Beijing might be even more willing to negotiate a stand-alone agricultural agreement. China could also expect a significant expansion of its own specialty farm exports to the United States, albeit at a much lower level of trade.

China has indicated a willingness to liberalize its agricultural barriers substantially over time in earlier FTAs with Chile and New Zealand. Though Chile and New Zealand are small countries, they are large agricultural exporters, and China's agreements with them would surely be viewed as benchmarks for any deal with the United States. China is also now negotiating an FTA with Australia, which will surely insist on substantial market access for its much larger agricultural sales.

The key issue is whether China is willing to continue its liberalization of agricultural imports, as the old policy of food self-sufficiency is now largely limited to rice and wheat. There have been intermittent signs that it was prepared to do so but some indications to the contrary as well. If China decided to rely more fully on international trade in this sector too, as it has already in manufacturing and some services, a free trade deal with the United States that enabled it to bring in food and feed crops without the costs of higher tariffs might be quite attractive. In the event of a further change in China's attitude toward food security, it would be possible to envisage an intrasectoral arrangement on agriculture. China would significantly liberalize US access to its market for food products by phasing out its tariffs and nontariff barriers, perhaps over 5 to 10 years, as in its agreements with Chile and New Zealand, perhaps with an exception for rice as already granted to Korea under KORUS. The United States would assure China of access to its food supplies by strictly limiting its future recourse to export controls. Such a bargain would be immensely popular with the US agricultural community, as it would benefit from both sides of the deal. The countries could also set up a committee on sanitary and phytosanitary measures (SPS), modeled on similar committees created under the US–Australia and KORUS agreements—with dispute settlement perhaps still handled in the WTO—to address contentious issues under that heading.

Another important issue relating to export controls and primary products is the US legal restriction on *crude oil* and especially *liquefied natural gas*

(LNG) sales to other countries (Hufbauer, Bagnall, and Muir 2013). The relevant legislation mandates automatic approval of LNG exports to FTA partner countries, which could be of considerable interest to China in light of the growing supplies and much lower prices in the United States. China could also use the availability of US gas as a bargaining chip in its negotiations with alternative suppliers, such as Australia, Qatar, and Russia. This would be an important benefit to China of engaging in a CHUSTIA, especially if some of its competitors in Asia join the TPP and thus receive preferential treatment from the United States before China can do so.

Government procurement accounts for a considerable share of the world economy, perhaps about 15 percent, or about $10 trillion. It is estimated to exceed $1 trillion in both China and the United States, amounting to 11 to 12 percent of the total economy in the United States and 20 percent in China. A significant majority—almost 70 percent in the United States and about 90 percent in China—comes from noncentral authorities. Both countries plan to make sizable infrastructure investments in the coming years that are of considerable interest to potential suppliers in the other. National security procurement would presumably remain largely limited to domestic producers, but represents a minority of government purchases in both countries.

Exports of both countries to each other's governmental entities are very modest, and liberalization even more so, due to domestic political pressures for governments to buy from local sources. Countervailing pressures are also present, however, to economize on government spending and maximize the cost-effectiveness of procurement policies. An international agreement would presumably have the additional advantage for the central government of China of increasing its authority over the procurement practices, and thus some of the policies, of the provinces. As both China and the United States could gain substantially from expanding procurement from each other, there would be potential for a considerable amount of intrasectoral reciprocity and the possibility of a stand-alone agreement.

A China–US procurement agreement, whether alone or part of a broader CHUSTIA, would need three components. First, the countries would have to agree whether to proceed on the basis of positive or negative lists. A negative list approach, under which all governmental entities would be covered unless they were explicitly excluded, would be far preferable to a positive list technique, which would include only those entities that are explicitly listed. China has recently agreed to a negative list approach for the renewed BIT negotiations. However, the United States and all other members of the GPA have pursued a positive list approach.

Second, it would be very important to include subfederal entities, notably provincial governments in China and state governments in the United States, to the maximum extent possible. Their engagement would multiply the potential economic value of the agreement. It would also be highly desirable to include SOEs and SSEs in both countries, especially in China, in light of their continued importance there. US coverage of state agencies in both the GPA and previous FTAs—with the partial exception of NAFTA because of the appeal of doing business in Canada and Mexico—has been rather sparse, and the US Trade Representative (USTR) has taken the position that it cannot compel the states to comply, even though the Constitution seems to suggest that it has the power to do so.

Third, China and the United States would have to decide how to reconcile the preferential treatment they would presumably give each other with the plurilateral GPA in the WTO. The United States was a charter member of the GPA and has been spearheading an effort for several years to expand both its entity coverage and its country membership, especially to include China. China agreed to join the GPA "as soon as possible"[7] when it joined the WTO in 2001, and regretted being outside the agreement when it could not compete for US stimulus projects in 2008–09. However, its successive offers to join have been uniformly disappointing, and the current GPA participants have essentially rejected it. Its most recent offer still excluded SOE purchases and included fewer than half of its provinces, autonomous regions, and municipalities.

The United States could redouble its efforts to persuade China to join the WTO agreement and, if its offer were sufficiently attractive, agree to count China's doing so as a contribution to a CHUSTIA. Conversely, if China were prepared to liberalize ambitiously with the United States but not in the broader plurilateral context, the United States could drop the GPA effort for a while and concentrate on striking a bilateral deal that offered it maximum access to the Chinese procurement market. Such a GPA-plus deal could ideally be rolled into the plurilateral agreement later, to avoid the GPA's permanent abandonment.

Components of a Broader Compact

The *services sector* should be the highest US priority in any effort to liberalize and reform its trade relationship with China. The opportunities for expanding US exports and thus creating US jobs are clearest and most extensive in this sector, for four reasons. First, the overall Chinese economy is obviously very large. Second, it is growing very rapidly and will probably continue to do so for at least another decade or two. These factors are a stimulus for all US exports, not only services. But, third, the share of services in the large and rapidly growing Chinese economy is likely to rise substantially from its abnormally low current level of about 45 percent, which has hardly increased over the past decade due to China's policy distortions—repressed interest rates, suppressed energy prices, an undervalued exchange rate—that favor manufacturing. China's services sector is likely to grow to at least the average of more than 60 percent of GDP for upper-middle-income countries, if not the 75 percent average among Organization for Economic Cooperation and Development

---

7. WTO, *Report of the Working Party on the Accession of China*, November 10, 2001, WT/MIN(01)3.

(OECD) countries. Fourth, Chinese barriers to services imports, mainly of the nontariff variety, are very high.

The second and fourth of these factors are present in most emerging-market and developing economies. The United States should aggressively seek liberalization of their services sectors as well, mainly through the recently initiated TiSA. However, China is the only member of the BRICS—the other four are Brazil, India, Russia, and South Africa—to indicate interest in participating in the TiSA talks. Previous multilateral efforts, including the WTO's Uruguay and Doha rounds, have largely failed to liberalize services trade, despite the creation of the General Agreement on Trade in Services (GATS). In any event, none of the emerging markets offers nearly as large a market for services as China does, or is as likely to grow as fast as China is, in the foreseeable future. None of them is likely to expand the services share in its economy nearly as much as China is. China uniquely offers the prospect of rapidly growing services in a rapidly growing and very large economy currently festooned with pervasive barriers to external participation, setting up a unique quadruple play. Our calculations suggest that the United States could gain more than half as much expansion in its services exports from an ambitious bilateral CHUSTIA as from an ambitious plurilateral TiSA.

Taken together, the above factors suggest that the potential for expanding US services exports offers a powerful rationale all by itself for the United States to seek an FTA with China. This is particularly the case because the United States has an established record of international competitiveness across a wide range of services sectors. Despite all the foreign barriers, which are widespread in high-income countries as well, the United States runs annual global surpluses of $200 billion in this sector, as opposed to an annual global deficit of about $700 billion in manufacturing.

In addition to their exports, an important part of the international earnings of US services firms comes from their investments in foreign countries. These earnings are included in the investment income component of the US current account whether or not they are repatriated to the United States (they are offset by direct investment outflows in the capital account to the extent they are reinvested abroad rather than repatriated). These US gains are in addition to the almost $200 billion surplus in services trade as conventionally defined and the potentially large increases cited throughout this study. They would add to the benefits to the US economy from liberalization of the Chinese services sector.

It has long been thought that opportunities for substantially expanding US services exports were limited because many service products, exemplified by haircuts, are not tradable. J. Bradford Jensen (2011), however, shows that the great majority of US business services output is tradable and that US services firms have only begun to scratch the surface of foreign markets. Hence the highly elastic US supply side of this particular equation meshes very nicely with the vast possibilities on the demand side.

The following table, repeated from chapter 7, estimates the potential exports increases in individual US services sectors under an ambitious CHUSTIA. These numbers are highly uncertain: They posit a very substantial reduction of Chinese barriers, which would be difficult for China and would at best be phased in over a number of years, and they rely on educated guesses as to the effect on trade of present Chinese barriers measured in tariff-equivalent terms. Even if the precise findings are off by a factor of two, however, the results are striking and affirm our conclusion that this sector alone strongly supports a US effort to negotiate significant trade liberalization with China. Total US exports of services almost triple. The exports of many individual US services more than triple. Six subsectors wind up exporting more than $30 billion annually to the Chinese market when the liberalization is fully implemented (see table 19.1).

There are close linkages between impediments to the expansion of US services activities in China and several other components of any wide-ranging CHUSTIA, particularly its chapters on investment and SOEs. Much of the delivery of US services to China, such as financial services (see chapter 8), takes place through direct investment, in which the supplying firm establishes a subsidiary or branch in the host country. The inward investment regime of that country thus is key in determining the potential scope of activity for the foreign-based company. Likewise, Chinese protection of its SOEs can virtually preclude foreign competitors' participation. These considerations add to the desirability of embedding the services issue in a reasonably comprehensive agreement with China.

In pursuing a services chapter in a CHUSTIA, the United States should again urge China to base the negotiations on a negative rather than a positive list approach. China has recently accepted such a model for its BIT negotiations with the United States, where the central topic of investment has important links to the services sector. The new Shanghai Free Trade Zone also employs a negative list approach. The plurilateral group negotiating the TiSA in the WTO, in an important breakthrough, has agreed to use negative lists for that agreement's national treatment provisions. So one might reasonably expect agreement on such an approach for services talks.

The main complication in a CHUSTIA will be that the United States is, again, clearly the *demandeur* in this component of the negotiation. China's import barriers in the services sector, measured in tariff-equivalent terms, are several times as high as those of the United States. Its service trade restrictions index (STRI) is more than double that of the United States. Its services commitments in previous FTAs are only about one-third as great as those the United States has made in its agreements to date. However, as noted above, China would also gain enormously from substantial liberalization of the services sector. A central element in the Chinese rebalancing strategy, as it attempts to replace its past export-led development model with a consumption-led model, is a sharp enlargement of the services sector. Trade and investment expansion could both benefit from that structural change and promote its acceleration.

Table 19.1   Projected gains in US services exports to China (billions of dollars)

	Baseline (2025)	Projected increase from CHUSTIA	Projected total (2025)
Total	126.0	218.0	344.0
Banking	10.4	27.5	37.9
Insurance	0.4	5.7	6.1
Transportation	11.5	29.6	41.1
Communications	0.5	4.7	5.2
Computer/infomation services	1.8	4.8	6.6
Royalties/licenses	20.2	44.9	65.1
Professional business services	5.4	49.9	55.4
Education	24.0	8.4	32.5
Travel	51.8	42.4	94.2

CHUSTIA = China–US trade and investment agreement

Source: Authors' calculations.

Inward FDI in the services sector has already been one of the main drivers increasing Chinese productivity. A large portion of the income gains to China from a CHUSTIA would emerge from precisely this phenomenon.

China wants to strengthen its own services firms as it contemplates sharp expansion of that component of its economy. But the potential magnitude of that sector, in light of the sheer size of the Chinese economy and the growing share of services in it, suggests that there should be plenty of room for both domestic and external participants; chapter 2 in this volume shows such an outcome. Foreign and domestic firms should reinforce each other in promoting productivity and other benefits that China would seek from its internal reforms and a CHUSTIA. Thus there should be strong mutual interest between China and the United States in placing services trade liberalization at the center of any CHUSTIA. This could conceivably provide the basis for a stand-alone services-only agreement. One way to achieve a somewhat similar outcome, at least as a first step, would be for China to join the TiSA if it was willing to make a contribution that was sufficiently ambitious for the United States to count it.

If more traditional mercantilist—that is, export-based—considerations were to prevail, the likely net gains for the United States suggest that a far-reaching agreement on services would have to be part of a broader overall CHUSTIA. Even on that basis, however, some subsectors of services would be appropriate for self-balancing deals. In tourism the United States might offer visa-free access to Chinese tourists, as it now does for Japanese and Korean tourists. This is estimated to increase the number of such travelers by

50 percent within a year or so; visitors from Korea, a much smaller country, rose by about that amount within 18 months of Korea's admission into the visa waiver program in 2008. The number could double by 2022 (Zhang 2012, appendix B). The United States could make this offer in return for China's liberalizing its foreign exchange controls, which are anachronistic anyway in light of the country's holding almost $4 trillion of foreign exchange reserves, to permit Chinese travelers to spend more abroad. Other possibilities might lie in the realm of business and professional services, such as accounting and legal, where the STRI scores for the two countries are not too different.

The United States has an enormous national interest in pursuing *IPR protection* with China. As chapter 9 summarizes, the International Trade Commission has estimated that the US economy probably loses about $100 billion annually from Chinese IPR violations. Estimates of global IPR piracy, of which China constitutes a very substantial share—50 to 80 percent according to the Commission on the Theft of American Intellectual Property (2013)—range from $250 billion for all goods as early as 2007 to $1 trillion in 2011; sectoral losses of $75 billion for pharmaceuticals and $63 billion for software in 2011; and $25 billion for copyright infringements for movies, music, software, and video games in 2005. These numbers are all very rough and predate more recent revelations about cyberespionage, except for one by the office of the National Counterintelligence Executive (2011) suggesting that global US economic espionage losses could range as high as $400 billion per year.

Traditionally there have been two basic concerns about IPR protection or the lack thereof: the laws of the countries in which piracy prevails and local enforcement of those laws. Most observers, including aggrieved companies and the US government, conclude that while China's legal framework has gaps, it is largely adequate to deal with traditional IP violations. The problem lies primarily with enforcement, which broadens the issue to provincial and local authorities as much as, or even more than, the central authorities in Beijing. The problem is tangled in institutional and even cultural terms. Chinese authorities appear to tolerate, if not promote, IP violations. The inclusion of cyberespionage under IPR concerns further complicates and intensifies the issue, raising the question of how a trade agreement could effectively cover it.

The WTO's rules have not been very helpful regarding IPR protection, even apart from cyberespionage. The United States took China to the WTO's DSB in 2007, but the DSB ruled that there was insufficient evidence to prove that China's enforcement practices were deficient or that they had caused economic damage to US firms. By contrast, US FTAs with several countries have mandated strong criminal and civil penalties to deter piracy and counterfeiting; thus they offer better prospects, though certainly no assurances, of better enforcement by offending countries. The United States could seek to include the suggestion of the Commission on the Theft of American Intellectual Property (2013) that violators be subjected to tough penalties, including banking sanctions and import bans, in a CHUSTIA.

The obvious questions are why China would agree to a significant tightening of its IPR regime and, even if it wanted to do so, whether it could in practice. China has not been idle in addressing the issue in recent years. Chinese civil courts handled nearly 84,000 IPR lawsuits in 2012, up 40 percent from the previous year. China has created a State Intellectual Property Office (SIPO), which grants patents and local offices that enforce them. It has drafted new IPR laws that would increase fines for sales of counterfeit and pirated goods. The number of patents sought in China has skyrocketed and 83 percent of all utility model patents in the world in 2011 were filed in China, though many of these may have been intended to preempt foreign registrations rather than protect truly new products. These partial steps suggest that China, like most developing countries, is ambivalent about IPRs. On the one hand, it has a national strategy of acquiring foreign technologies by whatever means possible, including theft, to speed its own growth and evolve to higher value-added production. On the other hand, China realizes that it will never become a nation of indigenous innovation without much stronger protection for its own IPRs. A recent survey by the US–China Business Council (USCBC 2012) found that, because of weak IPR protection, 40 percent of all US companies limit the types of products they manufacture in China and their research and development (R&D) spending there.

The possibility of Chinese acceptance of a strong IPR chapter in a CHUSTIA, including effective means of enforcement against norm violations, especially at the provincial level, thus relates directly to the view of its top authorities of how IPR protection would fit into its economic reform strategy. If the authorities recognize the importance of IPR protection for China's own development, they might be willing. Chinese leaders might even seek to use such a chapter to help promulgate new rules, enforcement mechanisms, and even cultural mindsets, as their predecessors used WTO membership over a decade ago to promote needed market-oriented reforms in that period. The United States will have to work with Chinese reformers who share its basic goals for IPRs (see chapter 9) if the huge potential of such agreements is to be realized in a CHUSTIA. Otherwise, the issue constitutes another major US request that, if achievable at all, would have to be gained through large US concessions in other parts of a comprehensive agreement.

An important Chinese request in CHUSTIA negotiation would be substantial relaxation in *US controls of high-technology exports to China*. China argues consistently and vocally that the United States discriminates against it in the application of those controls.

Chapter 12 shows that US high-tech exports to China are quite substantial and growing rapidly, from $7 billion in 2000 to almost $30 billion in 2010, especially after the United States reformed its control system in the late 2000s. Our analysis also suggests that China is treated less restrictively under the US export control regime than other major emerging market economies—especially Russia, which is included in the same medium-threat category as China.

Chapter 12 also shows that US high-tech exports to China would be considerably higher, perhaps by 25 to 50 percent, if its export control regime functioned like those of Germany or the United Kingdom.[8] Most of the difference appears to lie in the treatment of transport equipment and scientific equipment. The bottom line of our analysis is that the US controls do retain a significant bite and are therefore a legitimate topic for inclusion in a CHUSTIA negotiation.

The other key point from our analysis is that China is currently outside all international export control arrangements, despite maintaining its own export controls and applying to join at least one of them, the Missile Technology Control Regime. The others are the Australia Group and the Wassenaar Arrangement. If it were possible to include China in these groups, they would offer another plurilateral approach to addressing China's concerns about discrimination by the United States and other countries.

The Investment Cluster

Investment is central to any FTA, as a major motive of any country participating in such an agreement is to stimulate additional investment, domestic but especially foreign, to take advantage of the expanded market opportunities and improved economic climate that result. This motivation is especially conducive to pursuing FTAs because there are very few global rules and institutional arrangements regarding FDI; despite many proposals over many years, there is no GATT for investment, nor is there likely to be one for the foreseeable future.

Investment issues loom particularly large for China and the United States. They are the world's two largest host countries to FDI inflows, and, with Japan, they are now two of the three largest origin countries for FDI outflows. Chapter 13 suggests that FDI in both directions could triple by 2020. China and the United States thus have great needs for predictable and conducive environments for FDI, to defend their own companies abroad and maintain their appeal for foreign companies to keep coming to their shores. These interests are particularly keen at present, as both countries are planning to undertake sizable infrastructure investment programs that will be of considerable interest to foreign participants. Both seek to improve their respective investment climates.

Economists cannot calculate gains from investment with the same precision as gains from trade, but one of the main reasons that model-based estimates of FTAs usually turn out to be too conservative is their inability to capture the investment dynamic. The potential for unexploited gains may thus be even higher for investment than in the trade areas previously discussed.

---

8. The absolute amounts involved—$7 billion to $15 billion annually—would help reduce US and Chinese global and bilateral trade imbalances. They would not go very far to do so, however, despite frequent Chinese assertions to the contrary.

Chapter 2 suggests that significant investment liberalization could add 25 percent to the payoff from a CHUSTIA.

The potential gains are of several types. For the United States, new research confirms that both outward FDI (Hufbauer, Moran, and Oldenski 2013) and inward FDI (Moran and Oldenski 2013) strongly support increases in US output and job creation. For US outward FDI, this will be especially true for investment in China, the world's second-largest and most rapidly growing market. For China, inward FDI has been a key driver of growth and development from the early days of economic reform. It could again be central to promoting the rebalancing and reorientation of the economy that the Xi government is pursuing.

There are political economy as well as purely economic gains. The United States would benefit from "taking hostages" by letting Chinese firms, which would then have a vested interest in avoiding China–US economic conflict, invest in the United States, just as China has so wisely "taken hostages" by letting numerous US firms, that now defend its interests—quite effectively—in policy debates in Washington, invest in China. Japan made the huge mistake of failing to take many such "hostages" throughout its period of economic ascendance, and thus subjected itself to three decades of bashing with very few economic allies in the United States.

The potential for new investment benefits is substantial partly because the policies of the two countries deter current flows. The uncertainties and opaqueness surrounding US attitudes—formally in the Committee on Foreign Investment in the United States (CFIUS) and informally in periodic outbursts of congressional or public opinion—clearly discourage some Chinese FDI in the United States. Substantial US investment in China is clearly deterred by China's FDI regime, which the OECD ranks as the most restrictive in the world,[9] at three times the average level of restrictiveness of non-OECD countries and one-third greater than that of India, which is not very investment-friendly.

It is a paradox that the world's second-largest host country maintains so many barriers, still requiring case-by-case approval of all applications for mergers and acquisitions (M&As) and imposing performance requirements on many firms. Mutual suspicions run high. Some observers worry that China over the past few years has been reverting back to its earlier models of state capitalism. Many US firms believe that Chinese authorities discriminate against them and in favor of their own SOEs, including through the use of competition policy. Many Chinese firms believe that US practices and policies, including those of CFIUS, discriminate against them. Both countries seek greater transparency in the investment policies of the other and want nondiscriminatory treatment in practice as well as in principle. Agreement in these areas would go far to start building greater trust in the relationship.

---

9. OECD FDI regulatory restrictiveness index, 2013, www.oecd.org (accessed on July 17, 2014).

The two governments have begun to recognize the problems and accordingly renewed their negotiations for a BIT that would address some of these investment-related issues. The governments implicitly view the BIT as a self-balancing agreement of the type we are suggesting for tariffs, agriculture, government procurement, and possibly services. In the case of FDI, the United States has incumbent investment to protect and opportunities that are now deterred, while China has a strong desire for enhanced market access. The BIT would seek to ensure a calibrated degree of investment access for firms in one country to the markets of the other, and to establish reciprocal rules for the treatment of firms and protection of investments once established.

BIT negotiations are far from complete so it is unclear how far they will go in resolving the problems. The latest round got off to an encouraging start, with President Xi personally informing President Obama at their Sunnylands summit in June 2013 that China was prepared to cover all sectors and stages of investment. This includes the critically important preestablishment stage, when initial decisions are being made while actual investment has yet to take place. China has never covered this in any of its previous 128 BITs. As mentioned above, China also agreed to proceed on the basis of a negative list rather than a positive list. China had already agreed to a series of significant, though still inadequate, reforms of its policies in its investment pact with Korea and Japan in 2012, which has not yet entered into force.

China's change of heart presumably reflects the high value that the leadership places on incoming FDI for its own reform program as well as its desire for a far-reaching agreement that will enhance the access of Chinese FDI to the United States. Some reform-minded Chinese refer to the BIT talks with the United States as "a second WTO negotiation." The length of the Chinese negative list remains to be seen as of this writing (mid-2014) but the conceptual shift is potentially very important. It is doubtful that the BIT will cover some of China's main concerns about US attitudes toward incoming FDI, including the CFIUS process and the occasional political outbursts against such investment, however, so this issue will probably remain a major Chinese request in a CHUSTIA even after the BIT's successful completion.

The BIT negotiations are also unlikely to fully satisfy the United States. The US model treaty, developed in 2012 after three years of internal review, includes a series of ambitious objectives that no partner country has yet to agree to. It includes a number of features regarding labor and the environment, but also regarding dispute settlement and intellectual property rights, that China has not included in any of its 128 BITs to date.

Hence the BIT negotiation can be viewed as a first step down a path that could eventually lead to a comprehensive FTA, through either a series of additional stand-alone agreements like the BIT or a single all-in effort. It is doubly significant that both governments perceive investment as sufficiently important to proceed to the head of the line.

At least two other major topics—SOEs and competition policy—are part of the investment cluster of issues that will remain to be addressed after conclusion of even the most ambitious possible BIT. Foreign-invested firms often compete with SOEs, and are thus particularly susceptible to any favoritism that SOEs receive from the Chinese government. Competition policy is normally the best instrument for maintaining a level playing field, though it is also another tool that the government can use to discriminate against foreigners, as some US firms have recently charged. We believe this cluster of issues should be conceptualized together in determining the goals and procedures for substantially improving the investment climates in both China and the United States. Our proposals seek to embody fundamental principles that would apply equally to both countries:

- Transparency in both the setting and implementation of laws and policies;

- Advance publication of proposed changes in laws and policies so that foreigners can understand and comment on them;

- National treatment of firms from the other party, i.e., no discrimination against them in favor of domestic firms;

- Most favored nation treatment of firms from the other party, i.e., no discrimination against them in favor of nationals of other countries;

- Open and objective dispute settlement mechanisms, including bilateral consultation and eventual resort to binding arbitration when necessary, and with provisions for investor-state cases and assurances against retaliation against plaintiffs;

- Market disciplines, e.g., behavior based on commercial conditions and strict limits on subsidies; and

- Full adoption of these principles by subfederal entities (e.g., states and provinces) as well as central governments.

In addition to these overarching principles, we suggest several items for priority in the three interrelated investment chapters of any CHUSTIA.

Regarding FDI, in either the BIT or more likely the follow-on FTA, the United States should agree to apply the transparency and level playing field criteria to its CFIUS process along the lines Theodore H. Moran (2009) proposes: limiting the application of the national security principle to the only three cases where it can be justified, that is, actual denial of supplies, technology linkage, and infiltration or sabotage. China should eliminate all performance requirements, especially those regarding technology transfer, from all sectors except those included on its negative list, and it should reduce the sectors included on that list. Both countries should make maximum efforts to include their subfederal entities, the US states and the Chinese provinces, where much of the actual decision making on FDI takes place.

Regarding SOEs, the United States should repeal its CFIUS requirement from 2008 that all acquisitions by a foreign government-controlled entity have to be reviewed. China should abolish all preferential government procurement from SOEs and confirm its recent commitment to avoid requiring such treatment for procurement by private companies. Both should waive any right to invoke the sovereign immunity doctrine when their SOEs become involved in legal disputes in the partner country, forcing them to respond like other commercial entities. The agreement itself should define the key criteria where SOEs should act "in accordance with commercial considerations"[10] as chapter 14 suggests. It should cover oligopolies as well as monopolies. It should require timely publication of financial accounts according to international standards. Most important, it should require disclosure of all policy directives or suggestions from government officials, loan terms from state-owned banks and all transactions with other state-owned companies, and tax payments, preferences, or any other incentives or subsidies received from central or noncentral government bodies.

On competition policy, as elaborated in chapter 15, both countries should clearly enunciate the goal of protecting consumers rather than competitors. They should pledge to avoid any discriminatory treatment of foreign firms, especially in M&A activity. The agreement should require both countries to implement their own competition policies faithfully, provide for extensive exchanges of information and consultation on their respective activities, subject the decisions of each to the dispute settlement mechanism of the CHUSTIA, and authorize substantive remedies in cases of violations—perhaps loss of CHUSTIA benefits or monetary fines, as in KORUS. China included competition issues in its FTA with Costa Rica in 2011, and they have been a staple of all recent US FTAs, so it seems natural to include them in a CHUSTIA.

Parallel Issues

Traditional trade agreements have not included a few exceedingly important issues in the China–US trade and investment relationship. Their salience, crucially to Congress, suggests that they will have to be addressed effectively for a CHUSTIA to succeed. Conceptual and institutional considerations may counsel handling them through parallel mechanisms rather than in the trade agreement itself, however. Moreover, it is quite possible that their urgency may result in their being resolved before a CHUSTIA could be pursued anyway.

The two issues where parallel treatment seems most appropriate are cyberespionage and exchange rates. Both are quintessentially multilateral issues in which the interplay among a number of countries determines outcomes, calling for effective international cooperation. Even more important, both issues range well beyond trade and investment: cyberespionage enters into the domain of national security and currency relates to international capital flows, monetary policy, and domestic macroeconomic considerations. Virtually all governments handle both issues very differently from trade policy: trade officials, like the USTR, bear very little responsibility for either issue and would have to draw other governmental agencies into negotiations for a trade agreement.

---

10. Article XVII of the GATT, www.wto.org (accessed on July 17, 2014).

In the United States, this would also involve different congressional committees in authorizing, overseeing, and approving them.

China and the United States are clearly the most important players in both topics and cannot evade them. The operational question is whether parallel arrangements could satisfy the substance of these issues and the domestic political interest that they command, at least in the United States, rather than integrating them into a CHUSTIA. Some guidance in answering this question can be derived from the recent history of the other two issues where parallel treatment might also be considered: labor and the environment. In those cases, the United States pursued meaningful stand-alone multilateral accords for many years, with very modest results. Realizing that successive administrations' efforts for labor and the environment were less than enthusiastic, the concerned constituencies eventually forced their inclusion, usually through Congress, in all major US FTAs, starting with NAFTA in the early 1990s, and they have become a standard (if still often disputed) feature of those agreements in recent years. Environmental concerns are also increasingly included in trade agreements that do not involve the United States, including some concluded by China, and they are slowly becoming a staple of the global trade regime.

There are two significant differences between the history of labor and environment issues in the past and the prospects for improvements in cybersecurity and currency management now. First, the United States failed for many years to inject those issues directly into multilateral trade agreements—the only type that was then being negotiated—and so far has only succeeded with respect to environment. Second, and closely related, the FTA partners that the United States acquired in subsequent years would never have been influential enough to sway broader multilateral processes even if they had fully joined the United States in trying to do so; Canada and Mexico, or later Australia and Korea, could not have helped convince the WTO to adopt rules to sanction countries that banned collective bargaining or persuade the world to adopt an effective convention to limit global warming.

China and the United States together, however, might be able to do so. Chinese–US agreement to curb cyberespionage for commercial purposes might well attract concurrence from the small number of other countries that are capable of such practices. Chinese-US agreement to provide effective International Monetary Fund (IMF) enforcement of its prohibition of competitive currency undervaluation might likewise enlist widespread support, particularly as much of the world's currency manipulation is conducted by countries defending themselves against China's own practices.

Hence, in the two key issue areas of cyberespionage and exchange rates, China and the United States should launch major efforts to forge effective multilateral responses as soon as possible. In the case of cyberespionage, rules need to be conceptualized and agreed. China must join the United States if there is to be any hope of doing so, making this one of the first arenas where the ascending and incumbent superpowers could work together to create a wholly new global regime. It is encouraging that the two countries have created a working group on the issue and they should use it to move in these directions promptly and forcefully, perhaps with added impetus stemming from the US legal action of May 2014 against PLA hackers, despite China's initial negative reaction.

In the case of currency manipulation, we have elsewhere proposed specific blueprints for reform of the rules and especially the enforcement machinery of the IMF and WTO, which would provide them with effective tools to carry out in practice one of their central mandates (Bergsten and Gagnon 2012; Hufbauer and Schott 2012). The political salience of the issue escalated sharply in the United States in 2013 with the transmission of letters to the president from unique bipartisan majorities in both houses of Congress (60 senators, 230 representatives) insisting on the inclusion of "strong and enforceable foreign currency manipulation disciplines"[11] in the TPP and all future US free trade agreements. Much of the increased congressional interest was motivated by developments in Japan since 2012 with the advent of the Abe government, but China has been central to the currency debate and similar attitudes would undoubtedly be expressed at least as vocally concerning a CHUSTIA.

It is possible that congressional pressure will lead to the inclusion of a currency chapter in the TPP. If so, that would set a strong precedent for any future China–US arrangement. The current pressure could also lead to unilateral US action, such as the institution of countervailing duties against exports subsidized by currency manipulation, countervailing currency intervention by the US Treasury, or even congressional legislation that would, for better or worse, preempt the need to address the issue in trade agreements. Another possibility would be a stand-alone China–US agreement on currency, negotiated separately and presumably by different authorities on both sides of the CHUSTIA.

As described in chapter 17, exchange rates are only part of the broader issue of balance of payments adjustment or, in the current parlance, rebalancing. It might be possible to handle currency in that broader context if China could agree on firm metrics for progress, such as a low ceiling for its global current account surplus or its intervention in foreign exchange markets. The acceptability of such an arrangement in Congress, however, is uncertain. In any event, the two countries should use the next few years to consider and hopefully reach agreement on currency and broader rebalancing issues before they pursue a CHUSTIA. Such agreements could defuse important elements of potential opposition to a CHUSTIA as well as deal substantively with some of the thorniest issues that could otherwise plague the relationship. They could clear the decks for a trade negotiation and might even be viewed as preconditions for launching bilateral negotiations.

---

11. See website of Senator Debbie Stabenow, "Bipartisan Senate Manufacturing Caucus Co-Chairs Debbie Stabenow and Lindsey Graham Continue to Press Administration to Address Currency Manipulation in TPP," January 8, 2014, www.stabenow.senate.gov (accessed on July 17, 2014).

Failing a broader approach—or perhaps in addition to it—China and the United States could seek to include these two topics in a CHUSTIA. Cyberespionage could be embedded in an IPR chapter, as noted above, and as it is presently covered under prior FTAs, or treated separately at some point in the text. As with IPRs, a cyberespionage chapter would have to include two major obligations for each country: domestic laws that prohibit the practice and enforcement mechanisms to make those prohibitions effective. The United States would need to adopt new legislation to do so, as described in chapter 16, including a civil counterpart to the Economic Espionage Act of 1996 and amendments to the 1970 Tariff Act and the authorities of the Office of Foreign Assets Control in the Treasury Department. A CHUSTIA would also need to provide for sanctions against a failure by either party to effectively implement such obligations. Such sanctions could include monetary penalties and new trade barriers, keyed either to the violating country's gains from the trade agreement or to the aggrieved party's full estimated economic loss. The DSB of the CHUSTIA would presumably arbitrate such cases.

The exchange rate issue would be slightly easier to incorporate into a CHUSTIA because, in the IMF Articles of Agreement, the practice to be prohibited—in this case, currency manipulation to maintain undervaluation—is articulated more clearly and precisely than the relatively recent problem of cyberespionage is addressed in the WTO Agreement on Trade-Related Aspects of Intellectual Property Rights (TRIPS). Enforcement mechanisms would then have to be added and decision-making machinery set up to activate the agreement. A currency chapter of a CHUSTIA, or a similar side agreement if that proved impossible to negotiate, could thus include several elements:

- Renewed agreement on the nature of the problem, incorporated from the IMF articles: a prohibition of competitive undervaluation and of "large, protracted and one-way" (IMF 1977) intervention to maintain such an exchange rate;

- Agreement that a country could be accused of currency manipulation if it possessed excessive foreign exchange reserves and significantly increased those reserves while running excessive current account surpluses;

- An obligation to provide full and timely data on reserve levels, intervention magnitudes, the currency composition of reserves, and current account positions so that the agreement could be faithfully implemented;

- An obligation, as called for by the IMF articles and agreed in the G-7, to consult before intervening (especially in the partner country's currency); this obligation should encompass indirect and oral as well as direct market intervention;

- Agreement that effective sanctions, applied on a graduated basis and including both countervailing currency intervention and snapbacks of trade concessions extended through the CHUSTIA itself, could be levied against violations of the agreed norms; and

- Use of the CHUSTIA's own DSM, including through the creation of independent expert panels, to decide on the validity of complaints under the chapter.

The other two issues that should in principle be handled through parallel agreements are labor and the environment. They could best be addressed, respectively, through the conventions and practices of the International Labor Organization (ILO) and the growing number of multilateral environmental agreements (MEAs). However, US trade policy has moved beyond the point where that preferred outcome is politically feasible. Both issues have been incorporated, initially as side agreements and more recently as integral components, in all US trade agreements since NAFTA. In light of deep US concerns over labor and environmental conditions in China, there would surely be insistence on covering these issues as part of a comprehensive CHUSTIA. Since China is moving rapidly toward addressing its huge environmental problems, it probably would not strongly resist the substance of new environmental obligations—though it might resist accepting new international commitments to carry them out.

The main substantive issue regarding both labor and the environment is whether a CHUSTIA would only require the two countries to effectively implement existing laws or commit them to conform their domestic laws to more far-reaching norms, notably the ILO Declaration on Fundamental Principles and Rights at Work. All recent US FTAs, starting with Peru in 2007, reflect the agreement of May 10, 2007, between the George W. Bush administration and congressional Democrats to insist that US partners adopt, in their own laws, the key components of the ILO Declaration: freedom of association, collective bargaining, elimination of compulsory or forced labor, elimination of child labor, and elimination of discrimination in respect of employment and occupation. These FTAs also include dispute settlement procedures that range from consultations over perceived abuses to arbitration, just as for commercial disputes, that can lead to the imposition of fines or trade sanctions.

China has addressed labor issues in its recent FTAs with Chile and New Zealand, but only through memoranda of understanding, which are legally nonbinding and even weaker than the NAFTA side letters. The memoranda simply reaffirm each country's commitments as ILO members while explicitly recognizing the right of each to set and enforce its own labor laws. Meanwhile, in the TPP negotiations, there is already significant pushback to US proposals on labor standards. Hence the revised template that emerges from these talks may be more agreeable to China. This will undoubtedly be a difficult issue for a CHUSTIA, however, and the United States will have to work through its internal processes to decide how much priority to attach to it and how to trade it off against the numerous other US interests.

The focus of environmental issues in trade agreements has been defensive from a trade policy standpoint: to avoid a country's trying to justify protectionist measures on environmental grounds and enhancing its competitive position through weak environmental policies—perhaps triggering a race to the bottom in environmental standards. Since NAFTA, US FTAs have insisted that partner countries fully implement their domestic environmental laws. Since the May 2007 agreement, this includes adherence to MEAs to which they belong. Trade sanctions, rather than fines as in the original NAFTA approach, have become the authorized response mechanism, though none has ever been implemented. China's FTAs with Chile and New Zealand reaffirmed the participants' commitments to MEAs through nonbinding memoranda of understanding, but eschewed any DSM. No trade agreements to date, whether bilateral, regional, or in the WTO, have obligated countries to increase their environmental standards.

Climate change is by far the most pressing environmental issue at present. China and the United States, along with the rest of the world, have been unable to work out a binding international convention to limit carbon emissions. The two countries, however, reached several agreements on specific goals and policy measures that move significantly in that direction. The most recent, announced at the G-20 summit in Russia in September 2013, was to use the Montreal Protocol on protection of the ozone layer to reduce their future use of hydrofluorocarbons (HFCs), which are a major source of emissions. They are thus exercising an important degree of joint leadership of the effort to combat global warming.

China and the United States could use CHUSTIA negotiations to further their environmental leadership. They could try to work out national commitments, at least on a best-efforts basis, to reduce their carbon emissions from projected baselines by substantial amounts—geared to global carbon dioxide targets—over the coming years and decades. Since China and the United States are the world's two largest polluters, such targets could become the basis for widespread international agreement. The two countries should also adopt specific new policies through which they could meet their targets. In addition, they should set up a consultative mechanism to review progress toward reaching targets and implementing policies. An agreement of this type would stamp a CHUSTIA as the most forward-looking trade agreement of all time, from an environmental perspective, and represent another historical milestone.

For more traditional environmental issues, a CHUSTIA should replicate the now standard requirement for each country to enforce its own standards and use the DSM to handle complaints from either party that the other is failing to do so. A CHUSTIA could also create a fact-finding commission, like the Council on Environmental Cooperation (CEC) under NAFTA, that would conduct studies and make proposals that would not be binding but could help point the way toward further constructive environmental initiatives in the partner countries.

Conclusions

China and the United States have a strong mutual interest in continuing and completing their pursuit of free trade and investment. Both would achieve substantial economic benefits through an agreement, or series of agreements, between them. Both would gain greatly from reducing the risk of future economic and perhaps broader conflict. The compact itself and the increased exchanges that would be necessary to create it would increase mutual understanding and begin to counter the mistrust that now poisons much of the overall relationship. Both countries would gain enormously from creating a stable economic architecture in the dynamic but volatile Asia-Pacific region, checking the escalation of growing trade diversion from the competing liberalization tracks there and providing a foundation for pan-Pacific arrangements that could eventually unite the entire area.

The even larger benefits for both countries, however, would derive from the major contribution that an ambitious FTA would make to their strategic economic goals. The United States is seeking to rebalance and restructure its economy in the direction of higher investment and more exports. China is seeking to rebalance and restructure its economy in the direction of greater domestic consumption and services. Trade liberalization could affect both these efforts positively and substantially. This, in turn, would reinforce the effects of the macroeconomic rebalancing steps that are already under way. The interests of the two mesh so positively that both would benefit from the same features of the agreement; the usual search for tradeoffs, in the mercantilist tradition of trade negotiations that exclusively emphasize increased export opportunities rather than the benefits of import expansion, becomes unnecessary.

It would be highly desirable if a CHUSTIA adopted the most ambitious possible standards for each of the issues that it covered. This would provide maximum economic benefits for both countries, including the strongest impetus for their respective reform efforts. In recognition of the less developed state and much lower income level of the Chinese economy, this might require US acceptance of longer transition periods to implement some of the commitments that China undertook in the agreement.

Both countries will bring specific requests to the table that will need to be satisfied if a comprehensive agreement is to be struck. China will have to greatly open its services sector; achieve accelerated rebalancing of its economy, including through further currency appreciation, rather than just talk about it; buttress its IPR enforcement; and avoid discriminatory favoritism of its SOEs and other national champions through competition policy, government procurement, and investment policies. The United States will have to respect China's desire for increased investment opportunities in the United States by increasing the transparency and predictability of the CFIUS process and avoiding other impediments to Chinese firms. The United States also will need to limit its future recourse to export controls, especially of agricultural products to allay Chinese anxieties about food security, but also of energy resources and of high-technology products wherever compatible with national security concerns.[12]

Several major issues for which China and the United States have mutual interests in new approaches might best be handled through parallel arrangements to an FTA. The three of greatest importance are cyberespionage, exchange rates, and climate change. The two countries have been engaged in extensive discussion of each of these topics for several years and should bring them to closure, perhaps along with a few other countries and the use or creation of broader international forums.

China and the United States will have to resolve two central and closely related strategic questions in deciding how to pursue free trade between them if they decide to seek that goal. One is whether to seek a comprehensive agreement all at once, or to launch a sequence of stand-alone negotiations on individual topics to build confidence as the process evolves in the direction of eventual coverage of most or all key issues. The step-by-step approach could start with the current BIT. It could turn next to potentially self-balancing sectors such as tariffs and government procurement and possibly even agriculture and services. An important innovation would be to link the China–US bilateral process to plurilateral agreements already in place but being expanded (e.g., the GPA and ITA2) or now being negotiated (e.g., the TiSA and the new effort to eliminate tariffs on environmental goods). The two countries could agree to count those broader arrangements as part of their own evolving relationship and progress toward freer trade without a high-profile bilateral initiative.

There would be important timing advantages to the strategy of sequential negotiation. It could more easily proceed in parallel with the rest of the ambitious trade agendas both countries are pursuing, rather than having to await a new window of opportunity after completion of the present initiatives. There might also be important domestic advantages in both countries. The step-by-step approach would attract fewer headlines, and probably stir up less political pushback, than the launch of a high-profile comprehensive negotiation. It would also obviate the need for each country to work out a complex negotiating position at the outset of the talks, with tradeoffs across politically disparate sectors.

An even larger strategic question is whether the two countries should proceed bilaterally toward a conventional FTA or embed free trade between them in a regional context. This could be achieved either through Chinese

---

12. China has also periodically asked the United States to immediately grant it market economy status (MES), which would eliminate the somewhat arbitrary methods now used to apply antidumping and countervailing duties against it and other nonmarket economies. Under the terms of China's accession to the WTO, the United States has already agreed to provide MES in 2016. This is considerably earlier than any conceivable agreement on a CHUSTIA, or even on significant progress toward one, so the issue would be moot by the time such talks were under way.

accession to the TPP, a comprehensive FTAAP, or a fusion between the TPP and RCEP, if the latter Asia-only construct seemed likely to eventuate on a timetable in reasonable proximity to the former Pacific-track deal now headed for conclusion in 2014—and if the original TPP members, including the United States, were willing to accept India, Cambodia, Laos, and Myanmar, the non-APEC members of the RCEP.

The bilateral approach would be superior in enhancing ties between the two countries, deepening their relationship and presumably helping to relax tensions and mistrust. In their seminal report on distrust between China and the United States, Kenneth Lieberthal and Wang Jisi (2012, 38 and 40) conclude that China wants the relationship to be clearly defined before it will engage and cooperate, and that "both sides need to think in terms of initiatives that can alter current narratives that enhance strategic distrust." Negotiating and implementing a CHUSTIA would meet those criteria. It might also be harder for China to sign onto an agreement that a number of other countries have negotiated than to be an original participant in a new bilateral compact.

On the other hand, the regional approach has several advantages. It might be less contentious in the domestic politics of the two countries, especially in the United States, if the surprisingly widespread acceptance so far of Japanese membership in the TPP is any guide. It would probably reduce the risk that trade talks would be politicized by the broader foreign policy and security problems that are likely to arise in China–US relations from time to time. It would presumably reduce the cost of failure of the negotiations, which could be much more serious for the overall China–US relationship if it befell a bilateral effort. It would accommodate important partner countries, many of which would suffer considerable trade diversion from a bilateral CHUSTIA—especially if no RCEP had been agreed beforehand—and would therefore encourage both China and the United States to conclude a successful negotiation.

With joint Chinese and US leadership, the regional approach might also be more likely to lead the world back to global liberalization at the WTO. The Asia-Pacific and transatlantic megaregional agreements would otherwise create substantial differences between two major components of international trade and investment, and both would have major incentives to align their provisions. We deliberately subtitle this study "Toward Free Trade and Investment between China and the United States" rather than "Toward a China–United States Free Trade and Investment Agreement" to encompass these different possible routes. It is similar to the formulation of APEC's original Bogor Goals, to achieve "free and open trade and investment in the Asia-Pacific region" rather than "an Asia-Pacific free trade and investment agreement."

China's chairmanship of APEC in 2014 might be an opportune time for it to express interest in a TPP-related approach if China decided to pursue that alternative. As with Japan, the United States and some other member countries might insist on addressing issues with China that range beyond those encompassed in the TPP—such as rebalancing—through one or more parallel side agreements. The ultimate substantive agenda for the TPP option might therefore not differ very much from what we have outlined here for a bilateral CHUSTIA, even if the TPP turns out to be not quite as comprehensive or deep, and it might still be possible to pursue at least some of those issues sequentially, even though the TPP is likely to present a fairly comprehensive set of conditions to which new members would have to adhere.

The central purposes of this study are to comprehensively analyze the possible elements involved in achieving freer trade between China and the United States, and to present a suite of alternative approaches for pursuing and eventually attaining that goal. Our preference is to embed China–US freer trade across the widest possible spectrum of issues with the highest possible standards in the broadest possible Asia-Pacific regional context. Such an approach would require both countries to complete their current rebalancing agendas and adopt an ambitious set of complementary domestic policies to deal with the agreement's adjustment implications. Our overriding conclusion, however, is that freer trade is of such enormous importance to the two countries, and the world as a whole, in political and security as well as economic terms, that they should choose whatever path toward its realization is most likely to command support from their respective bodies politic.

China and the United States are the world's two largest economies, its two largest trading nations, its two largest energy users, and its two largest polluters. They are, respectively, the largest holder of reserves and the largest deficit country. They are, respectively, the rising global power and the incumbent hegemon. They are very different countries. One is rich and the other is still developing. One operates a market economy and the other still has large pockets of central planning and SOEs. Their political systems are quite distinct. Their histories and cultures are notably dissimilar. But they possess notable similarities as well. Their firms are highly entrepreneurial. They are probably the only two countries that now view world affairs through a globally strategic lens. They have shared great international enterprises together in the past, in World War II and in resistance to the Soviet Union.

It would be an enormous achievement, in terms of both payoffs and overcoming hurdles, for China and the United States to achieve anything close to free trade between them in the foreseeable future. But a fortuitous constellation of economic, political, and regional developments appears to be aligning to convert an idea that was unthinkable only a few years ago into a plausible possibility, perhaps along the lines described in chapter 1 that converted the equally implausible idea of a free trade agreement between Korea and the United States into reality over the past decade. It will undoubtedly take years of hard work, good will, and most of all far-sighted statesmanship in both countries to realize this prospect. We hope this study can contribute to that process.

References

Autor, David, David Dorn, Gordon H. Hanson, and Jae Song. 2013. *Trade Adjustment: Worker Level Evidence*. Working Paper no. 19226. Cambridge, MA: National Bureau of Economic Research.

Bergsten, C. Fred, and Joseph E. Gagnon. 2012. *Currency Manipulation, the US Economy, and the Global Economic Order*. Policy Brief 12-25. Washington: Peterson Institute for International Economics.

Bergsten, C. Fred, and Arvind Subramanian. (Forthcoming.) *From Wariness to Partnership: Integrating the Economies of India and the United States*. Washington: Peterson Institute for International Economics.

Commission on the Theft of American Intellectual Property. 2013. *The IP Commission Report*. Washington: National Bureau of Asian Research.

Hufbauer, Gary Clyde, Allie Bagnall, and Julia Muir. 2013. *Liquefied Natural Gas Exports: An Opportunity for America*. Policy Brief 13-6. Washington: Peterson Institute for International Economics.

Hufbauer, Gary Clyde, Theodore H. Moran, and Lindsay Oldenski. 2013. *Outward Foreign Direct Investment, US Exports, US Jobs, and US R&D: Implications for US Policy*. Policy Analyses in International Economics 101. Washington: Peterson Institute for International Economics.

Hufbauer, Gary Clyde, and Jeffrey J. Schott. 2012. *Will the World Trade Organization Enjoy a Bright Future?* Policy Brief 12-11. Washington: Peterson Institute for International Economics.

Ifo Institut. 2013. *Dimensionen und Auswirkungen eines Freihandelsabkommens zwischen der EU und den USA*. Munich.

IMF (International Monetary Fund). 1977. Surveillance over Exchange Rate Policies. Washington (April 29).

Jensen, J. Bradford. 2011. *Global Trade in Services: Fear, Facts, and Offshoring*. Washington: Peterson Institute for International Economics.

Lieberthal, Kenneth, and Wang Jisi. 2012. *Addressing US–China Strategic Distrust*. Washington: Brookings Institution.

Moran, Theodore H. 2009. *Three Threats: An Analytical Framework for the CFIUS Process*. Policy Analyses in International Economics 89. Washington: Peterson Institute for International Economics.

Moran, Theodore H., and Lindsay Oldenski. 2013. *Foreign Direct Investment in the United States: Benefits, Suspicions, and Risks with Special Attention to FDI from China*. Policy Analyses in International Economics 100. Washington: Peterson Institute for International Economics.

National Counterintelligence Executive. 2011. *Foreign Spies Stealing US Economic Secrets in Cyberspace*. Washington: Office of the National Counterintelligence Executive.

USCBC (US–China Business Council). 2012. *USCBC 2012 China Business Environment Survey Results: Continued Growth and Profitability; Tempered Optimism Due to Rising Costs, Competition, and Market Barriers*. Washington.

Zhang, Yangsheng. 2012. US–China Cooperation in Tourism. In *US–China 2022: US–China Economic Relations in the Next Ten Years*. Hong Kong: China–United States Exchange Foundation.

Index

economic reform
  China, 8, 16–17, 20, 196–97, 302, 319, 322, 392, 420
  rebalancing (*See* macroeconomic rebalancing)
  US, 16–17, 21, 392, 420
Economics and Statistics Administration, 351
economic shocks, 67*n*, 101
economic systems, comparison of, 16–17, 121
education services, 187
Eisenhower, Dwight D., 154
electronic payment services (EPS), 212
emerging economies. *See also specific country*
  foreign direct investment, 270–71
  high-technology exports to, 258–60, 259*f*–260*f*
  services liberalization, 405
employment. *See also* labor
  assistance programs (*See* trade adjustment assistance)
  composition of, 4, 10, 13–14, 52–64, 81
    China, 58*t*–59*t*
    export-based, 62–63, 63*t*, 71, 98–99
    US, 57, 60*t*–61*t*, 62, 71, 81, 86
  displaced workers (*See* worker displacement)
  effects of Chinese imports on, 88–94, 91*t*, 395–96
  input-output tables, 90–92, 91*t*, 98
  job gains, 98–100
  in manufacturing (*See* manufacturing)
  in services, 4, 57, 60*t*–61*t*, 71, 81, 169
  simulations, 37, 395–96
  unemployment benefits, 87–88, 100, 102, 104, 398
  US hires and separations, 89, 89*f*, 92–94, 95*t*
  wage effects, 87–88, 94–96, 99, 197, 232, 397
  wage-loss insurance, 104–105
energy consumption, 242, 244*t*
energy supplies, 23, 148, 256, 281
entertainment industry, 170
environment, 241–53
  climate change, 241–42, 419
  in free trade agreements, 248–51, 384–86, 415, 419
  in investment treaties, 295, 412
  parallel agreement on, 6, 415, 418–19, 421
  plurilateral agreements on, 251, 252
  WTO cases, 242–48
    environmental charge (Moldova), 247
    gasoline, 245–46
    lessons from, 248

  raw materials (China), 247
  retreaded tires (Brazil), 246
  shrimp, 245, 246
  tuna-dolphin, 243–45
Environmental Goods Agreement (EGA), tariffs on, 5, 8, 123, 251
Environmental Protection Agency (EPA), 282
equity ceilings, 187
espionage. *See* cyberespionage
European Union
  Asia-Pacific agreement and, 12
  Chinese agreement with, 7
  competition policy, 337, 343
  currency issues, 370–71, 373*n*
  currency provisions, 363
  dispute settlement, 382
  economic reforms, 394
  EU Court of Justice (ECJ), 327
  exhaustion policy, 224
  as FTA precedent, 25
  investment in China, 267, 268*t*
  Japanese negotiations with, 31
  penalty provisions, 120, 328
  services barriers, 206
  tire case, 246
  tuna-dolphin case, 244–45
  US partnership with (*See* Transatlantic Trade and Investment Partnership)
exceptionally high tariffs, 126, 128*t*–137*t*, 139
exchange rates. *See* currency
exclusions, services trade, 181, 183–84
exhaustion policies, 224–25
Exon-Florio Amendment, 278
export controls, 255–63
  Chinese, 258
  counterfactuals, 260–62, 261*t*
  high-technology, 258–60, 259*f*–260*f*, 409–10
  as priority issue, 11, 23
  US, 257–58
export gains
  benefits from, 10
  employment effects, 62–63, 63*t*, 71, 81, 96–98
  estimates of, 3–4, 46, 47*t*
  financial services, 213–14
  high-tech exports, 262, 409–10
  regional agreements compared, 74, 78*t*–79*t*, 80
  services, 172, 173*t*, 195, 406, 407*t*
  summary of, 81, 392–93
  US promotion of, 21
Express Delivery Service (EDS), 191
extraordinary challenge committee procedure, 383*n*

Mercosur, 246
mergers and acquisitions (M&As)
    Chinese approval process, 284–85, 411
    competition policy, 327, 334–37, 335t–336t
    G-20 control regimes, 338, 339t–341t
    negotiating goals, 272, 414
    state-owned enterprises, 337
    US approval process, 274–77, 276b–277b
Mexico
    economic reform, 394
    environmental policy, 249
    financial services, 215
    labor standards, 237
    peso crisis, 365
    tuna-dolphin case, 244–45
    US import tariffs and, 125n, 139
MFN. See most favored nation status
Middle East oil kingdoms, 277
Ministry of Agriculture (MOA), 162
Ministry of Foreign Commerce (MOFCOM),
    258, 270, 284–85, 332–34, 337, 338,
    342–44
Ministry of Industry and Information Tech-
    nology (MIIT), 147, 187
minority affairs, 183
Missile Technology Control Regime (MTCR),
    258, 410
mistrust, 18–19, 280, 411, 422
mixed tariffs, 122
Moldova, 247–48
monetary policy, 21, 64, 88n, 362–66, 369
monopoly, 313, 320, 329–31, 330n
Montreal Protocol, 252, 295, 419
moral hazard, 104
most favored nation (MFN) status
    agriculture, 157
    government procurement, 144
    intellectual property rights, 221
    investment, 273, 279–80, 287, 288, 290, 297
    services barriers, 175, 181, 183–85
    state-owned enterprises, 311, 413
    tariff rates, 92, 124–26, 138–39, 142, 160,
        163
multilateral approach. See plurilateral ap-
    proach
multilateral environmental agreements
    (MEAs), 250, 252, 418–19
Multi-Level Protection Scheme (MLPS), 188,
    191
multinational corporations (MNCs), 231, 301
munitions lists, 257–58
music industry, 227

NAFTA. See North American Free Trade Agree-
    ment
National Aeronautics and Space Administra-
    tion (NASA), 185n, 191
National Association of Manufacturers, 356
National Development and Reform Commis-
    sion (NDRC), 162, 284, 332, 333, 343
National Foreign Trade Council (NFTC),
    190–91
national security
    CHUSTIA and, 9, 12, 390
    competition policy, 344, 413
    definition of, 278, 285
    export controls, 257–63
    government procurement, 403
    investment barriers, 274, 278–80, 284n, 285
    services barriers, 182–83
National Security Agency (NSA), 18, 188, 349,
    351–52, 359, 390
National Semiconductor, 278
national treatment
    competition policy, 327, 413
    energy supplies, 256
    financial services, 212, 217
    gasoline case, 246
    government procurement exclusion, 143
    intellectual property rights, 221
    investment, 273, 287, 288, 290, 297
    services barriers, 175, 181, 193
natural gas, 256, 402–403
negative lists
    financial services, 216
    government procurement, 403
    investment, 283, 286, 298, 406, 412
    services, 178, 181, 185, 193–94, 195
negotiations (CHUSTIA)
    approaches to, 5, 21–25, 399–401, 421–23
    background to, 6–10
    hurdles in, 13–19
    interim steps, 25–27, 421
    priority issues for, 5–6, 11, 23, 420–21
    timing issues, 26
New Balance, 141n
Newbery v. James, 352
New York Convention on the Recognition
    and Enforcement of Foreign Arbitration
    Awards, 296
New York Metropolitan Transport Authority,
    146n
New Zealand
    Australia, Closer Economic Relations Trade
        agreement, 120, 328
    China FTA, 161–62, 216, 251, 337, 386, 402,
        418–19

Other Publications from the
Peterson Institute for International Economics

WORKING PAPERS

22 Targets and Indicators: A Blueprint for the International Coordination of Economic Policy   John Williamson and Marcus Miller
September 1987   ISBN 0-88132-051-X
23 Capital Flight: The Problem and Policy Responses*   Donald R. Lessard and John Williamson
December 1987   ISBN 0-88132-059-5
24 United States-Canada Free Trade: An Evaluation of the Agreement*
Jeffrey J. Schott
April 1988   ISBN 0-88132-072-2
25 Voluntary Approaches to Debt Relief*
John Williamson
Sept. 1988, rev. May 1989
ISBN 0-88132-098-6
26 American Trade Adjustment: The Global Impact*   William R. Cline
March 1989   ISBN 0-88132-095-1
27 More Free Trade Areas?*   Jeffrey J. Schott
May 1989   ISBN 0-88132-085-4
28 The Progress of Policy Reform in Latin America*   John Williamson
January 1990   ISBN 0-88132-100-1
29 The Global Trade Negotiations: What Can Be Achieved?*   Jeffrey J. Schott
September 1990   ISBN 0-88132-137-0
30 Economic Policy Coordination: Requiem for Prologue?*   Wendy Dobson
April 1991   ISBN 0-88132-102-8
31 The Economic Opening of Eastern Europe*
John Williamson
May 1991   ISBN 0-88132-186-9
32 Eastern Europe and the Soviet Union in the World Economy*   Susan Collins and Dani Rodrik
May 1991   ISBN 0-88132-157-5
33 African Economic Reform: The External Dimension*   Carol Lancaster
June 1991   ISBN 0-88132-096-X
34 Has the Adjustment Process Worked?*
Paul R. Krugman
October 1991   ISBN 0-88132-116-8
35 From Soviet DisUnion to Eastern Economic Community?*   Oleh Havrylyshyn and John Williamson
October 1991   ISBN 0-88132-192-3
36 Global Warming: The Economic Stakes*
William R. Cline
May 1992   ISBN 0-88132-172-9
37 Trade and Payments after Soviet Disintegration*   John Williamson
June 1992   ISBN 0-88132-173-7
38 Trade and Migration: NAFTA and Agriculture*   Philip L. Martin
October 1993   ISBN 0-88132-201-6
39 The Exchange Rate System and the IMF: A Modest Agenda   Morris Goldstein
June 1995   ISBN 0-88132-219-9
40 What Role for Currency Boards?
John Williamson
September 1995   ISBN 0-88132-222-9
41 Predicting External Imbalances for the United States and Japan*   William R. Cline
September 1995   ISBN 0-88132-220-2

42 Standards and APEC: An Action Agenda*
John S. Wilson
October 1995   ISBN 0-88132-223-7
43 Fundamental Tax Reform and Border Tax Adjustments*   Gary Clyde Hufbauer
January 1996   ISBN 0-88132-225-3
44 Global Telecom Talks: A Trillion Dollar Deal*   Ben A. Petrazzini
June 1996   ISBN 0-88132-230-X
45 WTO 2000: Setting the Course for World Trade   Jeffrey J. Schott
September 1996   ISBN 0-88132-234-2
46 The National Economic Council: A Work in Progress*   I. M. Destler
November 1996   ISBN 0-88132-239-3
47 The Case for an International Banking Standard   Morris Goldstein
April 1997   ISBN 0-88132-244-X
48 Transatlantic Trade: A Strategic Agenda*
Ellen L. Frost
May 1997   ISBN 0-88132-228-8
49 Cooperating with Europe's Monetary Union   C. Randall Henning
May 1997   ISBN 0-88132-245-8
50 Renewing Fast Track Legislation*
I. M. Destler
September 1997   ISBN 0-88132-252-0
51 Competition Policies for the Global Economy   Edward M. Graham and J. David Richardson
November 1997   ISBN 0-88132-249-0
52 Improving Trade Policy Reviews in the World Trade Organization   Donald Keesing
April 1998   ISBN 0-88132-251-2
53 Agricultural Trade Policy: Completing the Reform   Timothy Josling
April 1998   ISBN 0-88132-256-3
54 Real Exchange Rates for the Year 2000
Simon Wren Lewis and Rebecca Driver
April 1998   ISBN 0-88132-253-9
55 The Asian Financial Crisis: Causes, Cures, and Systemic Implications
Morris Goldstein
June 1998   ISBN 0-88132-261-X
56 Global Economic Effects of the Asian Currency Devaluations   Marcus Noland, LiGang Liu, Sherman Robinson, and Zhi Wang
July 1998   ISBN 0-88132-260-1
57 The Exchange Stabilization Fund: Slush Money or War Chest?   C. Randall Henning
May 1999   ISBN 0-88132-271-7
58 The New Politics of American Trade: Trade, Labor, and the Environment   I. M. Destler and Peter J. Balint
October 1999   ISBN 0-88132-269-5
59 Congressional Trade Votes: From NAFTA Approval to Fast Track Defeat
Robert E. Baldwin and Christopher S. Magee
February 2000   ISBN 0-88132-267-9
60 Exchange Rate Regimes for Emerging Markets: Reviving the Intermediate Option
John Williamson
September 2000   ISBN 0-88132-293-8

US Taxation of International Income:
Blueprint for Reform　Gary Clyde Hufbauer,
assisted by Joanna M. van Rooij
October 1992　ISBN 0-88132-134-6

Who's Bashing Whom? Trade Conflict in High-Technology Industries　Laura D'Andrea Tyson
November 1992　ISBN 0-88132-106-0

Korea in the World Economy*　Il SaKong
January 1993　ISBN 0-88132-183-4

Pacific Dynamism and the International Economic System*　C. Fred Bergsten and
Marcus Noland, eds.
May 1993　ISBN 0-88132-196-6

Economic Consequences of Soviet Disintegration*　John Williamson, ed.
May 1993　ISBN 0-88132-190-7

Reconcilable Differences? United States-Japan Economic Conflict*　C. Fred Bergsten and
Marcus Noland
June 1993　ISBN 0-88132-129-X

Does Foreign Exchange Intervention Work?
Kathryn M. Dominguez and Jeffrey A. Frankel
September 1993　ISBN 0-88132-104-4

Sizing Up U.S. Export Disincentives*
J. David Richardson
September 1993　ISBN 0-88132-107-9

NAFTA: An Assessment　Gary Clyde Hufbauer
and Jeffrey J. Schott, *rev. ed.*
October 1993　ISBN 0-88132-199-0

Adjusting to Volatile Energy Prices
Philip K. Verleger, Jr.
November 1993　ISBN 0-88132-069-2

The Political Economy of Policy Reform
John Williamson, ed.
January 1994　ISBN 0-88132-195-8

Measuring the Costs of Protection in the United States　Gary Clyde Hufbauer and
Kimberly Ann Elliott
January 1994　ISBN 0-88132-108-7

The Dynamics of Korean Economic Development*　Cho Soon
March 1994　ISBN 0-88132-162-1

Reviving the European Union*
C. Randall Henning, Eduard Hochreiter, and
Gary Clyde Hufbauer, eds.
April 1994　ISBN 0-88132-208-3

China in the World Economy　Nicholas R. Lardy
April 1994　ISBN 0-88132-200-8

Greening the GATT: Trade, Environment, and the Future　Daniel C. Esty
July 1994　ISBN 0-88132-205-9

Western Hemisphere Economic Integration*
Gary Clyde Hufbauer and Jeffrey J. Schott
July 1994　ISBN 0-88132-159-1

Currencies and Politics in the United States, Germany, and Japan　C. Randall Henning
September 1994　ISBN 0-88132-127-3

Estimating Equilibrium Exchange Rates
John Williamson, ed.
September 1994　ISBN 0-88132-076-5

Managing the World Economy: Fifty Years after Bretton Woods　Peter B. Kenen, ed.
September 1994　ISBN 0-88132-212-1

Reciprocity and Retaliation in U.S. Trade Policy
Thomas O. Bayard and Kimberly Ann Elliott
September 1994　ISBN 0-88132-084-6

The Uruguay Round: An Assessment*　Jeffrey J.
Schott, assisted by Johanna Buurman
November 1994　ISBN 0-88132-206-7

Measuring the Costs of Protection in Japan*
Yoko Sazanami, Shujiro Urata, and Hiroki Kawai
January 1995　ISBN 0-88132-211-3

Foreign Direct Investment in the United States, 3d ed.　Edward M. Graham and Paul R. Krugman
January 1995　ISBN 0-88132-204-0

The Political Economy of Korea-United States Cooperation*　C. Fred Bergsten and
Il SaKong, eds.
February 1995　ISBN 0-88132-213-X

International Debt Reexamined*
William R. Cline
February 1995　ISBN 0-88132-083-8

American Trade Politics, 3d ed.　I. M. Destler
April 1995　ISBN 0-88132-215-6

Managing Official Export Credits: The Quest for a Global Regime*　John E. Ray
July 1995　ISBN 0-88132-207-5

Asia Pacific Fusion: Japan's Role in APEC*
Yoichi Funabashi
October 1995　ISBN 0-88132-224-5

Korea-United States Cooperation in the New World Order*　C. Fred Bergsten and
Il SaKong, eds.
February 1996　ISBN 0-88132-226-1

Why Exports Really Matter!*
ISBN 0-88132-221-0

Why Exports Matter More!*　ISBN 0-88132-229-6
J. David Richardson and Karin Rindal
July 1995; February 1996

Global Corporations and National Governments
Edward M. Graham
May 1996　ISBN 0-88132-111-7

Global Economic Leadership and the Group of Seven　C. Fred Bergsten and C. Randall Henning
May 1996　ISBN 0-88132-218-0

The Trading System after the Uruguay Round*
John Whalley and Colleen Hamilton
July 1996　ISBN 0-88132-131-1

Private Capital Flows to Emerging Markets after the Mexican Crisis*　Guillermo A. Calvo, Morris
Goldstein, and Eduard Hochreiter
September 1996　ISBN 0-88132-232-6

The Crawling Band as an Exchange Rate Regime: Lessons from Chile, Colombia, and Israel　John Williamson
September 1996　ISBN 0-88132-231-8

Flying High: Liberalizing Civil Aviation in the Asia Pacific*　Gary Clyde Hufbauer and
Christopher Findlay
November 1996　ISBN 0-88132-227-X

Measuring the Costs of Visible Protection in Korea*　Namdoo Kim
November 1996　ISBN 0-88132-236-9

The World Trading System: Challenges Ahead
Jeffrey J. Schott
December 1996　ISBN 0-88132-235-0

Has Globalization Gone Too Far?　Dani Rodrik
March 1997　ISBN paper 0-88132-241-5

Korea-United States Economic Relationship*
C. Fred Bergsten and Il SaKong, eds.
March 1997　ISBN 0-88132-240-7

Reintegrating India with the World Economy
T. N. Srinivasan and Suresh D. Tendulkar
March 2003 ISBN 0-88132-280-6

After the Washington Consensus: Restarting Growth and Reform in Latin America Pedro-Pablo Kuczynski and John Williamson, eds.
March 2003 ISBN 0-88132-347-0

The Decline of US Labor Unions and the Role of Trade Robert E. Baldwin
June 2003 ISBN 0-88132-341-1

Can Labor Standards Improve under Globalization? Kimberly Ann Elliott and Richard B. Freeman
June 2003 ISBN 0-88132-332-2

Crimes and Punishments? Retaliation under the WTO Robert Z. Lawrence
October 2003 ISBN 0-88132-359-4

Inflation Targeting in the World Economy
Edwin M. Truman
October 2003 ISBN 0-88132-345-4

Foreign Direct Investment and Tax Competition
John H. Mutti
November 2003 ISBN 0-88132-352-7

Has Globalization Gone Far Enough? The Costs of Fragmented Markets Scott C. Bradford and Robert Z. Lawrence
February 2004 ISBN 0-88132-349-7

Food Regulation and Trade: Toward a Safe and Open Global System Tim Josling, Donna Roberts, and David Orden
March 2004 ISBN 0-88132-346-2

Controlling Currency Mismatches in Emerging Markets Morris Goldstein and Philip Turner
April 2004 ISBN 0-88132-360-8

Free Trade Agreements: US Strategies and Priorities Jeffrey J. Schott, ed.
April 2004 ISBN 0-88132-361-6

Trade Policy and Global Poverty
William R. Cline
June 2004 ISBN 0-88132-365-9

Bailouts or Bail-ins? Responding to Financial Crises in Emerging Economies Nouriel Roubini and Brad Setser
August 2004 ISBN 0-88132-371-3

Transforming the European Economy Martin Neil Baily and Jacob Funk Kirkegaard
September 2004 ISBN 0-88132-343-8

Chasing Dirty Money: The Fight Against Money Laundering Peter Reuter and Edwin M. Truman
November 2004 ISBN 0-88132-370-5

The United States and the World Economy: Foreign Economic Policy for the Next Decade
C. Fred Bergsten
January 2005 ISBN 0-88132-380-2

Does Foreign Direct Investment Promote Development? Theodore H. Moran, Edward M. Graham, and Magnus Blomström, eds.
April 2005 ISBN 0-88132-381-0

American Trade Politics, 4th ed. I. M. Destler
June 2005 ISBN 0-88132-382-9

Why Does Immigration Divide America? Public Finance and Political Opposition to Open Borders Gordon H. Hanson
August 2005 ISBN 0-88132-400-0

Reforming the US Corporate Tax Gary Clyde Hufbauer and Paul L. E. Grieco
September 2005 ISBN 0-88132-384-5

The United States as a Debtor Nation
William R. Cline
September 2005 ISBN 0-88132-399-3

NAFTA Revisited: Achievements and Challenges Gary Clyde Hufbauer and Jeffrey J. Schott, assisted by Paul L. E. Grieco and Yee Wong
October 2005 ISBN 0-88132-334-9

US National Security and Foreign Direct Investment Edward M. Graham and David M. Marchick
May 2006 ISBN 978-0-88132-391-7

Accelerating the Globalization of America: The Role for Information Technology Catherine L. Mann, assisted by Jacob Funk Kirkegaard
June 2006 ISBN 978-0-88132-390-0

Delivering on Doha: Farm Trade and the Poor
Kimberly Ann Elliott
July 2006 ISBN 978-0-88132-392-4

Case Studies in US Trade Negotiation, Vol. 1: Making the Rules Charan Devereaux, Robert Z. Lawrence, and Michael Watkins
September 2006 ISBN 978-0-88132-362-7

Case Studies in US Trade Negotiation, Vol. 2: Resolving Disputes Charan Devereaux, Robert Z. Lawrence, and Michael Watkins
September 2006 ISBN 978-0-88132-363-2

C. Fred Bergsten and the World Economy
Michael Mussa, ed.
December 2006 ISBN 978-0-88132-397-9

Working Papers, Volume I Peterson Institute
December 2006 ISBN 978-0-88132-388-7

The Arab Economies in a Changing World
Marcus Noland and Howard Pack
April 2007 ISBN 978-0-88132-393-1

Working Papers, Volume II Peterson Institute
April 2007 ISBN 978-0-88132-404-4

Global Warming and Agriculture: Impact Estimates by Country William R. Cline
July 2007 ISBN 978-0-88132-403-7

US Taxation of Foreign Income Gary Clyde Hufbauer and Ariel Assa
October 2007 ISBN 978-0-88132-405-1

Russia's Capitalist Revolution: Why Market Reform Succeeded and Democracy Failed
Anders Åslund
October 2007 ISBN 978-0-88132-409-9

Economic Sanctions Reconsidered, 3d ed.
Gary Clyde Hufbauer, Jeffrey J. Schott, Kimberly Ann Elliott, and Barbara Oegg
November 2007
ISBN hardcover 978-0-88132-407-5
ISBN hardcover/CD-ROM 978-0-88132-408-2

Debating China's Exchange Rate Policy
Morris Goldstein and Nicholas R. Lardy, eds.
April 2008 ISBN 978-0-88132-415-0

Leveling the Carbon Playing Field: International Competition and US Climate Policy Design
Trevor Houser, Rob Bradley, Britt Childs, Jacob Werksman, and Robert Heilmayr
May 2008 ISBN 978-0-88132-420-4

SPECIAL REPORTS

WORKS IN PROGRESS

DISTRIBUTORS OUTSIDE THE UNITED STATES

Australia, New Zealand,
and Papua New Guinea
Co Info Pty Ltd
648 Whitehorse Road Mitcham VIC 3132
Australia
Tel: +61 3 9210 77567
Fax: +61 3 9210 7788
Email: babadilla@coinfo.com.au
www.coinfo.com.au

India, Bangladesh, Nepal, and Sri Lanka
Viva Books Private Limited
Mr. Vinod Vasishtha
4737/23 Ansari Road
Daryaganj, New Delhi 110002
India
Tel: 91-11-4224-2200
Fax: 91-11-4224-2240
Email: viva@vivagroupindia.net
www.vivagroupindia.com

Mexico, Central America, South America,
and Puerto Rico
US PubRep, Inc.
311 Dean Drive
Rockville, MD 20851
Tel: 301-838-9276
Fax: 301-838-9278
Email: c.falk@ieee.org

Asia (*Brunei, Burma, Cambodia, China,*
Hong Kong, Indonesia, Korea, Laos, Malaysia,
Philippines, Singapore, Taiwan, Thailand,
and Vietnam)
East-West Export Books (EWEB)
University of Hawaii Press
2840 Kolowalu Street
Honolulu, Hawaii 96822-1888
Tel: 808-956-8830
Fax: 808-988-6052
Email: eweb@hawaii.edu

Canada
Renouf Bookstore
5369 Canotek Road, Unit 1
Ottawa, Ontario KlJ 9J3, Canada
Tel: 613-745-2665
Fax: 613-745-7660
www.renoufbooks.com

Japan
United Publishers Services Ltd.
1-32-5, Higashi-shinagawa
Shinagawa-ku, Tokyo 140-0002
Japan
Tel: 81-3-5479-7251
Fax: 81-3-5479-7307
Email: purchasing@ups.co.jp
For trade accounts only. Individuals will find
Institute books in leading Tokyo bookstores.

Middle East
MERIC
2 Bahgat Ali Street, El Masry Towers
Tower D, Apt. 24
Zamalek, Cairo
Egypt
Tel. 20-2-7633824
Fax: 20-2-7369355
Email: mahmoud_fouda@mericonline.com
www.mericonline.com

United Kingdom, Europe
(*including Russia and Turkey*)**, Africa,**
and Israel
The Eurospan Group
c/o Turpin Distribution
Pegasus Drive
Stratton Business Park
Biggleswade, Bedfordshire
SG18 8TQ
United Kingdom
Tel: 44 (0) 1767-604972
Fax: 44 (0) 1767-601640
Email: eurospan@turpin-distribution.com
www.eurospangroup.com/bookstore

Visit our website at:
www.piie.com
E-mail orders to:
petersonmail@presswarehouse.com